AUSTIN-HEALEY SPRITE MK. 1 and MK. 2

MG MIDGET MK. 1

MECHANICAL AND BODY SERVICE PARTS LIST

PUBLICATION NO.
AKD 3566 ISSUE 6 AND AKD 3567 ISSUE 3

British Leyland Motor Corporation Limited
BMC Service division
COWLEY · OXFORD · ENGLAND
Telephone - - - - - - - - - - - - Oxford 78941
Telegrams - - - - - - - - - BMCSERV. Telex. Oxford
Telex - - - - - - - - - - BMCSERV. Oxford 83145/6/7
Cables - - - - - - - - - BMCSERV. Telex. Oxford. England
Codes - - - - - - Bentley's, Bentley's Second Phrase, A.B.C. (5th and 6th Editions), Western Union and Private

Identification Data

AUSTIN-HEALEY

Model		Commencing	Finishing
Sprite (Mark I) (H-AN5)	Engine No.	9C/U/H101	9C/U/H49201
	Car No.	H-AN5-501	H-AN5-50116
Sprite (Mark II)	Engine No.	9CG/ {Da/H, Da/L} 101	9CG/ {Da/H, Da/L} 36711
		10CG/ {Da/H, Da/L} 101	10CG/ {Da/H, Da/L} 21048
	Car No.	H-AN6-101	H-AN6-24731
		H-AN7-24732	H-AN7-38828

M.G.

Model		Commencing	Finishing
Midget (Mark I)	Engine No.	9CG/ {Da/H, Da/L} 101	9CG/ {Da/H, Da/L} 36711
		10CG/ {Da/H, Da/L} 101	10CG/ {Da/H, Da/L} 21048
	Car No.	G-AN1-101	G-AN1-16183
		G-AN2-16184	G-AN2-25787

CONTENTS

	Section	Page
Identification Data		2
Explanatory and Abbreviations		5
Vehicle Identification Serial Number Prefix Code		7
Power Unit Identification Serial Number Prefix Code		7
Location of Number Units		8
MECHANICAL SERVICE PARTS LIST - AKD 3566		
Alphabetical Index		10
Part Number Index		13
Engine 950cc 9C/U/H	MA	25
Engine 950cc 9CG/Da/H	MA	51
Engine 1098cc 10CG/Da/H	MA	75
Ignition Equipment	MB	106
Radiator and Fittings	MC	120
Fuel System	MD	122
Clutch and Controls	ME	130
Gearbox	MF	136
Propeller Shaft	MG	164
Rear Axle and Rear Suspension	MH	166
Steering	MJ	175
Front Suspension	MK	180
Shock Absorbers	ML	190
Brake Controls	MM	192
Electrical Equipment	MN	200
Instruments	MO	260
Road Wheels	MP	268
Tools	MR	270
Special Tuning	MT	273
S.U. CARBURETTER SERVICE PARTS LIST - Extract from AKD 5036		
Carburetters - Type H1 - AUC 863 Twin Installation	SA	292
Carburetters - Type HS2 - AUC 990 Twin Installation	SH	300
Carburetters - Type HS2 - AUC 73 Twin Installation	SH	306
BODY SERVICE PARTS LIST - AKD 3567		
Key to Body Exterior and Main Trim Colour		314
Alphabetical Index		319
Part Number Index		320
Body Shell	BA	325
Bonnet and Control Details	BB	338
Wings	BC	344
Boot Lid and Fittings	BD	346
Doors and Fittings	BF	350
Side Curtains and Sidescreens	BG	352
Windscreen, Windscreen Washer and Mirrors	BH	358
Radiator Grille	BJ	366
Bumpers and Number-Plates	BK	368
Hood, Tonneau Cover and Hard Top	BL	374
Fascia Details	BM	382
Trimming Details	BN	384
Seats and Fittings	BO	417
Heating and Ventilating Equipment	BP	427
Paints	BQ	434

The Austin-Healey Sprite (Mark I) (H-AN5)

The Austin-Healey Sprite (Mark II)

The M.G. Midget (Mark I)

●EXPLANATORY

- The range of parts in this List covers all serviceable components on model/models to the standard specification. Where the part is confined to one specification this is clearly defined in the Description or Remarks column, and where the part listed is not serviced, this is indicated by the letters NSP in the Part No. column.
- This List is provided with a Group Index on the title-page, and also more detailed indexes at the beginning of each separate Section. Additionally, a Part Number Index is also provided in the preface pages.
- The Part Number Index will be issued twice yearly.
- Items comprising an assembly (or sub-assembly) are inset for easy reference. This principle is followed in all Parts Lists, typical examples being given below.

Examples:

Crankshaft assembly .... AMK 2254
  Plug .... AMK 97

Panel assembly—rear lower .... CZA 418
  Angle—attachment—rear bumper .... CZA 147
  Bracket—rear bumper support .... CZA 164

- The word 'Quantity' as shown in the heading of all text pages is intended to convey that all figures appearing in that column are quantities used on a particular application and not quantities used per vehicle.
- The assemblies and components in the plate illustrations are identified by numbers which correspond with the illustration references appearing on the facing text page in the column immediately following the Part Number. Note the use of squares, rectangles, and circles on the Illustration Plates. The square rectangle indicates an assembly which comprises all component parts shown enclosed. The components can, in turn, be supplied separately providing Illustration Numbers are shown against them. A circle embracing certain components is used to give a magnified view of the items which are too small to show up in detail if illustrated on the same scale as the other parts on the plate.
- It is essential first to identify the part against the illustration in the appropriate Section of the List, and then make use of the illustration reference number to locate the correct Part Number and official description on the adjacent page, taking into account Engine, Car, and Commission Numbers, etc.

EXPLANATORY—*continued*

- ABBREVIATIONS: Standard abbreviations are employed. The complete range of abbreviations covering all lists is given below.

A	Ambulance	ID	Inside diameter	(RA)	Rear axle number
A/R	As required	I.P.T.O.	Independent Power Take-off	RH	Right-hand
B	Basic	J	Convertible	RHD	Right-hand drive
(B)	Body number	K	Truck	RHT	Right-hand thread
(BP)	Belt pulley number	KPH	Kilometres per hour	(RP)	Rear pulley number
B.R.S.	British Road Services	L	Hire Car	S	4-door Saloon
C	Chassis number	LC	Low compression	(S)	Super de-luxe
(C)	Car number	LH	Left-hand	ST	Soft Top
(CB)	Cab number	LHD	Left-hand drive	STD	Standard
(CN)	Commission number	LHT	Left-hand thread	SWB	Short Wheelbase
CP	Chrome-plated	LWB	Long wheelbase	2S	2-door Saloon
D	Coupé or GT	M	Limousine	T	4-seater Tourer
(D)	De-luxe	MB	Minibus/Omnicoach	T.I.B.	Technical Information Bulletin
DC	Double-coil	MPH	Miles per hour	U	Pick-up
D/E	Double-ended	N	2-seater Tourer	UK	Gt. Britain and Northern Ireland
dia	Diameter	No.	Number	U/S	Undersize
E	G.P.O. Engineering	NSP	Non-serviceable part	V	Van
(E)	Engine number	OD	Outside diameter	W	Dual-purpose (wood framing)
EP	G.P.O. Planning	(OD)	Overdrive number	WB	Wheelbase
EXP	Export	O/S	Oversize	Ws	Dual-purpose (all-metal)
(FA)	Front axle number	P	Hard Top	W.S.E.	When Stock Exhausted
G	G.P.O. Postal	pr	Pair	X	Taxi
(G)	Gearbox number	psi	Pounds/square inch		
GP	General Purpose Carrier	PSV	Public Service Vehicle		
H	Hearse	P.T.O.	Power Take-off		
HC	High compression	Q	Chassis and Cab		
(HU)	Hydraulic unit number	R	Chassis and Scuttle		

- Amendments to this List will be effected by means of revised pages. Should it be necessary to add an additional page or pages to interrupt the existing sequence of page numbers, the added pages will be numbered as in the following examples, which illustrate what would happen if it became necessary (A) to extend the information on a text page beyond the limits of that page or (B) to add an illustration page between existing illustration pages. Use of the decimal notation avoids the necessity of re-numbering and reprinting all pages in any section after the newly introduced page.

  Example (A)

  Existing text pages ... ... MA 5, MA 6, MA 7, etc.
  Added text pages ... ... MA 5·1, MA 5·2, MA 5·3
  Page sequence will then read ... ... MA 5, MA 5·1, MA 5·2, MA 5·3, MA 6, etc.

  Example (B)

  Existing plates ... ... A 5, A 6, A 7, etc.
  Added plates ... ... A 5·1, A 5·2, A 5·3
  Plate sequence will then read ... ... A 5, A 5·1, A 5·2, A 5·3, A 6, etc.

- Each circulation of revised pages will be issued under a cover page. This cover page will always appear as the first page and will, in addition to indicating the circulation number, show all part numbers with their page reference that are new and additional to this List.

- Where information on a page has been revised this is shown by the inclusion of a dagger †, indicating what has been revised at that time.

- As revised pages are issued a complete index showing all the pages/plates, with their latest issue, now comprising this Service Parts List will be added to the List and reprinted with each circulation of revised pages.

Claims under Warranty

Claims for the replacement of material or parts under Warranty must always be submitted to the supplying Distributor or Dealer, or when this is not possible, to the nearest Distributor or Dealer, informing them of the vendor's name and address.

Vehicle Identification
Serial Number Prefix Letter Code

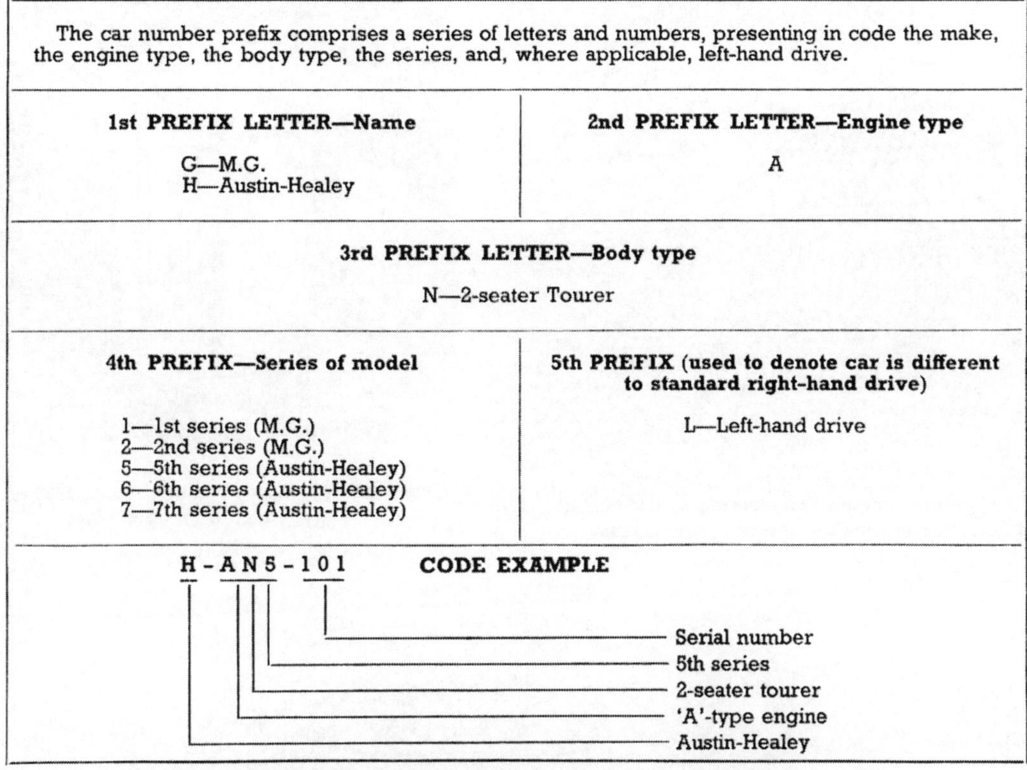

The car number prefix comprises a series of letters and numbers, presenting in code the make, the engine type, the body type, the series, and, where applicable, left-hand drive.

1st PREFIX LETTER—Name	**2nd PREFIX LETTER—Engine type**
G—M.G. H—Austin-Healey	A

3rd PREFIX LETTER—Body type

N—2-seater Tourer

4th PREFIX—Series of model	**5th PREFIX (used to denote car is different to standard right-hand drive)**
1—1st series (M.G.) 2—2nd series (M.G.) 5—5th series (Austin-Healey) 6—6th series (Austin-Healey) 7—7th series (Austin-Healey)	L—Left-hand drive

H - A N 5 - 1 0 1 **CODE EXAMPLE**

Serial number
5th series
2-seater tourer
'A'-type engine
Austin-Healey

Always quote these prefixes with Car Serial Numbers

Power Unit Identification
Serial Number Prefix Letter Code

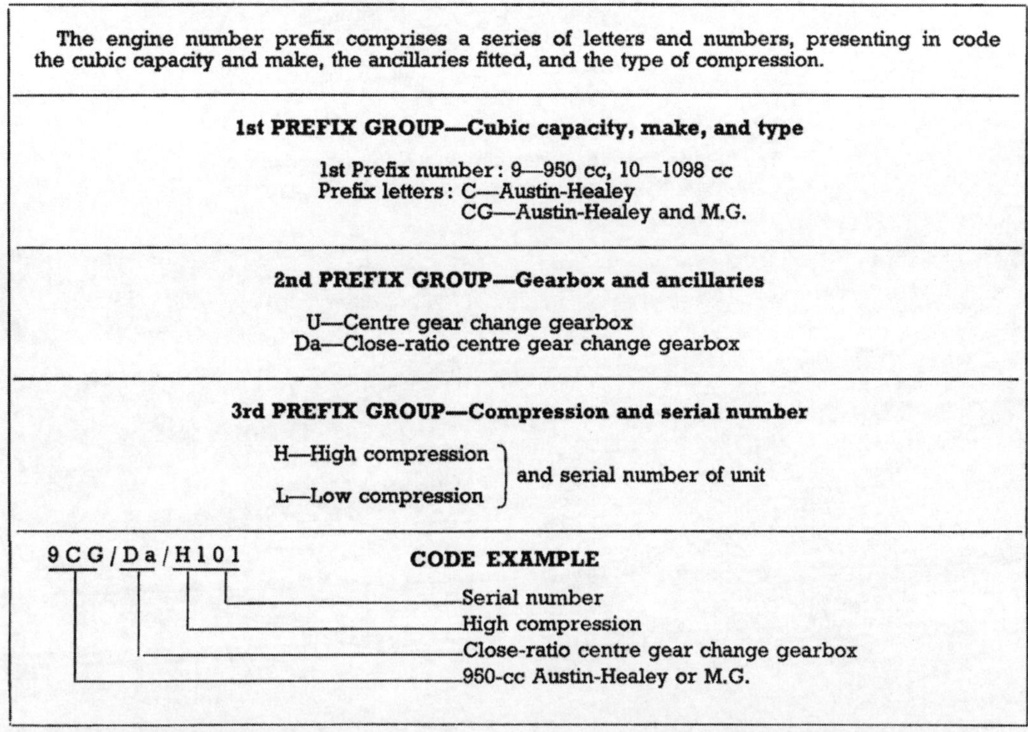

The engine number prefix comprises a series of letters and numbers, presenting in code the cubic capacity and make, the ancillaries fitted, and the type of compression.

1st PREFIX GROUP—Cubic capacity, make, and type

1st Prefix number: 9—950 cc, 10—1098 cc
Prefix letters: C—Austin-Healey
CG—Austin-Healey and M.G.

2nd PREFIX GROUP—Gearbox and ancillaries

U—Centre gear change gearbox
Da—Close-ratio centre gear change gearbox

3rd PREFIX GROUP—Compression and serial number

H—High compression } and serial number of unit
L—Low compression }

9 C G / D a / H 1 0 1 **CODE EXAMPLE**

Serial number
High compression
Close-ratio centre gear change gearbox
950-cc Austin-Healey or M.G.

Always quote these prefixes with Engine Serial Numbers

Location of Unit Numbers

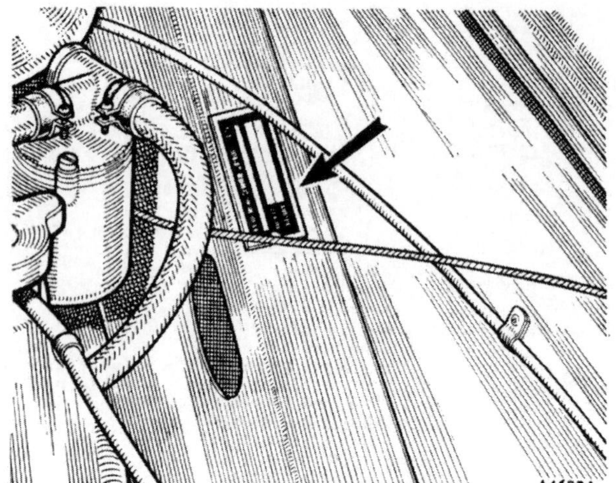

The **Car Number** is stamped on a plate secured to the left-hand inner wheel arch valance under the bonnet

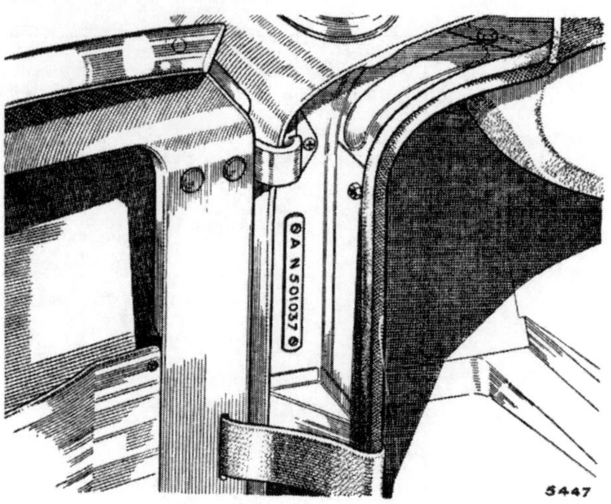

The **Body Number** is stamped on a plate secured to the left-hand front door pillar

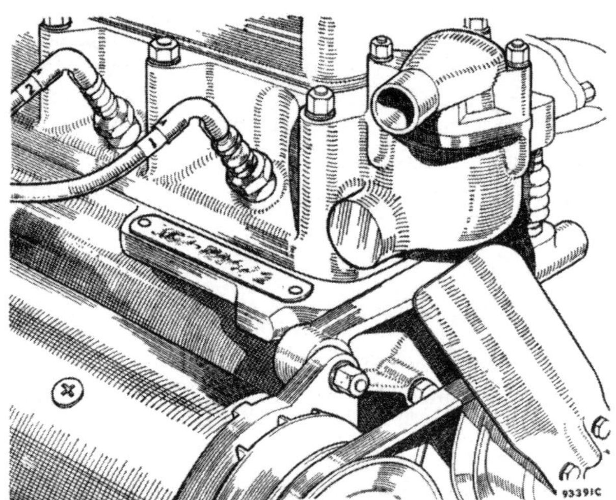

The **Engine Number** is stamped on a plate secured to the right-hand side of the cylinder block above the dynamo

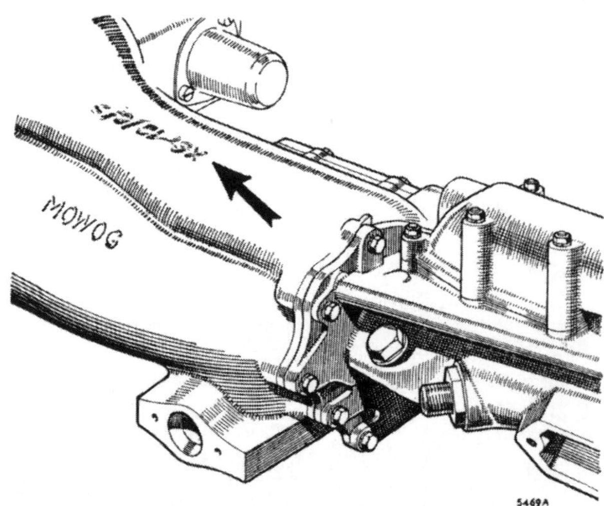

The **Gearbox Number** is stamped on the top of the gearbox casting

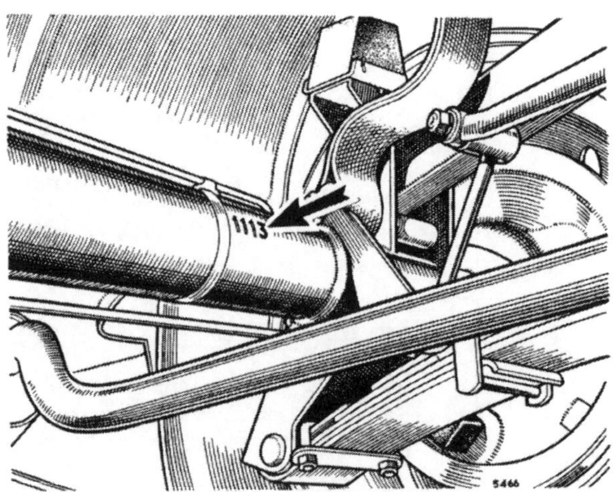

The **Rear Axle Number** is stamped on the front of the left-hand rear axle tube adjacent to the spring anchorage

AUSTIN-HEALEY SPRITE MK. 1 and MK. 2 MG MIDGET MK. 1 MECHANICAL SERVICE PARTS LIST AKD 3566

CONTENTS

	Section	Page
Alphabetical Index		10
Part Number Index		13
Engine 950cc 9C/U/H	MA	25
Engine 950cc 9CG/Da/H	MA	51
Engine 1098cc 10CG/Da/H	MA	75
Ignition Equipment	MB	106
Radiator and Fittings	MC	120
Fuel System	MD	122
Clutch and Controls	ME	130
Gearbox	MF	136
Propeller Shaft	MG	164
Rear Axle and Rear Suspension	MH	166
Steering	MJ	175
Front Suspension	MK	180
Shock Absorbers	ML	190
Brake Controls	MM	192
Electrical Equipment	MN	200
Instruments	MO	260
Road Wheels	MP	268
Tools	MR	270
Special Tuning	MT	273

British Leyland Motor Corporation Limited
BMC Service division
COWLEY · OXFORD · ENGLAND
Telephone - - - - - - - - - - Oxford 78941
Telegrams - - - - - - - BMCSERV. Telex. Oxford
Telex - - - - - - - - BMCSERV. Oxford 83145/6/7
Cables - - - - - - - BMCSERV. Telex. Oxford. England
Codes - - - - - - Bentley's, Bentley's Second Phrase, A.B.C. (5th and 6th Editions), Western Union and Private

Alphabetical Index

A *Page*

Absorber—shock—front .. MK 5
Absorber—shock—rear .. .. ML 2
Adaptor—oil filter MA 13, MA 27, MA 41
Adjuster—front brake-shoe .. MK 4
Adjuster—rear brake-shoe .. MH 4
Air cleaner .. .. .. MD 5
Arm—distributor rotor .. MB 3, MB 4
Arm—windscreen wiper MN 20, MN21
Armature—dynamo .. .. MN 3
Armature—starter .. .. MN 4
Axle—rear .. .. .. MH 2
Axle shaft—rear .. .. MH 3
Axle—swivel .. .. .. MK 2

B

Ball socket—steering tie-rod .. MJ 2
Barrel lock—lighting and ignition switch .. .. MN 5
Battery .. .. MN 2
Bearing—clutch release ME 3, ME 5, ME 7
Bearing—connecting rod MA 5, MA 21, MA 35
Bearing—crankshaft main MA 5, MA 21, MA 35
Bearing—differential .. .. MH 2
Bearing—front hub .. .. MK 3
Bearing—gearbox MF 4, MF 10, MF 15, MF 16
Bearing—needle—propeller shaft MG 1
Bearing—rear axle .. MH 2, MH 3
Bearing—rear hub .. .. MH 3
Bearing—steering pinion .. MJ 2
Belt—fan MA 15, MA 29, MA 43
Blade—fan MA 15, MA 29, MA 43
Blade—windscreen wiper MN 20, MN 21
Block—cylinder .. MA 3, MA 19, MA 33
Body—oil pump MA 12, MA 26, MA 40
Body—water pump MA 14, MA 28, MA 42
Boot—master cylinder .. .. MM 3
Boot—rear wheel cylinder .. MH 4
Boot—steering ball socket .. MJ 2
Box—control .. .. MN 5, MN 6
Box—fuse .. .. MN 5, MN 6
Box—pedal .. .. .. MM 2
Bracket—coil to dynamo .. MB 5
Bracket—dynamo MA 15, MA 29, MA 43
Bracket—engine mounting .. MA 46
Bracket—exhaust .. .. MA 47
Bracket—hand brake .. .. MM 6
Bracket—mixture control to carburetter .. .. MA 49
Bracket—radiator to wheel arch MC 2
Bracket—rear suspension mounting .. .. ML 2
Bracket—steering-column mounting .. .. MJ 3
Bracket—steering-rack mounting .. .. MJ 2
Brake—front .. .. .. MK 4
Brake—rear .. .. .. MH 5
Brake-plate—front .. .. MK 4
Brake-plate—rear .. .. MH 4
Brushes—dynamo .. .. MN 3
Brushes—starter.. .. .. MN 4
Buffer—front suspension and rebound .. .. MK 5
Bulb—instrument .. .. MN 24
Bulb—lamp .. MN 7—MN 24
Bulb holder—instrument .. MN 24
Bumper—rear axle .. .. MH 2
Bush—clutch withdrawal lever MF 3, MF 9
Bush—rear spring .. .. MH 6
Bush—shock absorber .. .. ML 2
Bush—speedometer pinion MF 6, MF 12, MF 17
Bushes—gearbox .. MF 3—MF 17

C *Page*

Cable—accelerator control .. MA 48
Cable—choke control .. .. MA 49
Cable—hand brake .. .. MM 6
Cable—harness .. MN 22, MN 24
Cable—H.T. .. MB 5, MB 8, MB 11
Cable—speedometer .. MO 2, MO 5
Cable—starter control .. .. MN 5
Cable—tachometer .. MO 3, MO 5
Cables and connections MN 22, MN 24
Cage—differential .. .. MH 2
Calliper unit—disc brake .. MK 4
Camshaft .. .. MA 5, MA 21, MA 35
Cap—distributor.. MB 3, MB 4, MB 7, MB 10
Cap—fuel filler .. .. .. MD 2
Cap—main bearing MA 3, MA 19, MA 33
Cap—master cylinder filler .. MM 3
Cap—oil filler .. MA 9, MA 24, MA 38
Cap—radiator .. .. .. MC 2
Cap—wheel .. .. .. MP 2
Carbon and spring—distributor MB 3, MB 4, MB 7, MB 10
Carrier—differential .. .. MH 2
Case—axle .. .. .. MH 2
Case—gearbox .. MF 3, MF 9, MF 14
Casing—gearbox remote control MF 6, MF 12, MF 17
Clamp—battery .. .. .. MN 2
Clamp—exhaust manifold .. MA 47
Clamp—spare wheel .. .. MP 2
Cleaner—air .. .. .. MD 5
Clip—spring leaf .. .. MH 6
Clutch .. .. ME 3, ME 5, ME 7
Coil—ignition .. MB 5, MB 8, MB 11
Collar—fuel tank filler .. .. MD 2
Column—steering .. .. MJ 3
Condenser—distributor .. MB 3, MB 4, MB 7, MB 10
Connecting rod .. MA 5, MA 21, MA 35
Connections—brake and clutch pipe .. .. .. MM 4, MM 5
Contact set—distributor MB 3, MB 4, MB 7, MB 10
Control—starter switch .. MN 5
Controls—brake .. .. MM 2
Cooling system .. .. .. MC 2
Core—radiator .. .. .. MC 2
Cotter—valve .. MA 7, MA 23, MA 37
Cover—clutch .. ME 3, ME 5, ME 7
Cover—dust—clutch bell housing MF 3, MF 9, MF 15
Cover—dust—clutch withdrawal lever .. .. MF 3, MF 9, MF 15
Cover—engine front MA 10, MA 25, MA 39
Cover—engine side MA 10, MA 25, MA 39
Cover—gearbox front and side MF 3, MF 9, MF 14
Cover—gearbox remote control MF 6, MF 12, MF 17
Cover—horn .. .. .. MN 18
Cover—oil pump body MA 12, MA 26, MA 40
Cover—starter pinion .. MF 3, MF 9, MF 14
Cover—valve rocker .. MA 9, MA 24, MA 38
Crankshaft .. MA 5, MA 21, MA 35
Cross-head and rack—windscreen wiper .. .. .. MN 20, MN 21
Cross-rod—hand brake .. .. MM 6
Crown wheel and pinion .. MH 3
Cylinder block .. MA 3, MA 19, MA 33
Cylinder—clutch slave .. .. ME 8
Cylinder head .. MA 7, MA 23, MA 37
Cylinder—master .. .. MM 3
Cylinder—rear wheel .. .. MH 4

D

Diaphragm—fuel pump.. .. MD 4
Differential assembly .. .. MH 2

Page

Disc—brake .. .. .. MK 4
Disc—wheel .. .. .. MP 2
Distributor MB 3, MB 4, MB 7, MB 10
Dog—distributor driving MB 3, MB 4, MB 7, MB 10
Drum—front brake .. .. MK 4
Drum—rear brake .. .. MH 5
Dynamo .. .. MN 3

E

Elbow—water outlet MA 9, MA 24, MA 38
Electrical equipment MN 2–MN 26
Element—oil filter MA 13, MA 27, MA 41
Engine .. .. MA 3, MA 19, MA 39
Excluder—draught—pedal box MM 2
Exhaust manifold MA 17, MA 31, MA 45
Exhaust system .. .. .. MA 47
Extension—gearbox .. MF 6, MF 12, MF 17
Extension—silencer tail pipe .. MA 47

F

Fan—dynamo MA 15, MA 29, MA 43
Filter—oil MA 13, MA 27, MA 41
Flange—propeller shaft yoke .. MG 1
Flange—universal joint—rear axle .. .. MH 3
Flasher unit .. .. .. MN 16
Flywheel .. .. MA 6, MA 22, MA 36
Forks—gear striking .. MF 3, MF 9, MF 14
Front axle and suspension MK 2–MK 5
Fuel pump .. .. .. MD 4
Fuse .. .. .. MN 5, MN 6
Fusebox .. .. .. MN 5, MN 6

G

Gauge—fuel .. .. MO 2, MO 4
Gauge—oil pressure and radiator thermometer .. .. MO 2, MO 4
Gauge unit—fuel tank .. .. MD 2
Gear—camshaft .. MA 5, MA 21, MA 35
Gear—crankshaft MA 5, MA 21, MA 35
Gear—differential .. .. MH 2
Gear—2nd speed MF 5, MF 11, MF 17
Gear—3rd speed MF 5, MF 11, MF 17
Gearbox .. .. MF 3, MF 9, MF 14
Grommet—gear lever .. MF 7, MF 12, MF 17
Gudgeon pin .. MA 4, MA 20, MA 34
Guide—valve .. MA 7, MA 23, MA 37

H

Hand brake .. .. MM 6, MM 7
Harness—wiring MN 22, MN 24
Head—cylinder .. MA 7, MA 23, MA 37
Headlamp .. MN 7–MN 15
Head—oil filter MA 13, MA 27, MA 41
Heat shield .. .. .. MD 5
Horn .. .. MN 18, MN 19
Horn-push .. MN 18, MN 19
Hose—air cleaner to rocker cover MD 5
Hose—brake .. .. .. MM 4
Hose—radiator .. .. .. MC 2
Housing—distributor .. MA 6, MA 22, MA 36
Housing—steering and tie-rod ball .. .. MJ 2
Housing—steering-rack and damper pad .. .. .. MJ 2
Hub—front .. .. .. MK 3
Hub—rear .. .. .. MH 3
Hub—water pump pulley MA 14, MA 28, MA 42

Alphabetical Index—*continued*

Page

I

Ignition coil .. MB 5, MB 8, MB 11
Ignition equipment MB 3, MB 7, MB 10
Inlet manifold MA 17, MA 31, MA 45
Instruments .. MO 2–MO 5

J

Joint—crankcase rear cover .. MA 3, MA 19, MA 33
Joint—cylinder head .. MA 8, MA 23, MA 37
Joint—differential carrier to axle case .. .. MH 2
Joint—engine front cover MA 10, MA 25, MA 39
Joint—engine side cover MA 10, MA 25, MA 39
Joint—front engine mounting plate .. MA 5, MA 21, MA 35
Joint—fuel pump .. .. MD 4
Joint—gearbox extension .. MF 7, MF 12, MF 17
Joint—gearbox front cover .. MF 3, MF 9, MF 14
Joint—gearbox side cover MF 3, MF 9, MF 14
Joint—inlet and exhaust manifold .. MA 17, MA 31, MA 45
Joint—oil filter MA 13, MA 27, MA 41
Joint—oil pump to block .. MA 12, MA 26, MA 40
Joint—rear engine mounting plate .. MA 10, MA 25, MA 39
Joint—rocker cover MA 9, MA 24, MA 38
Joint—set—engine decarbonizing .. MA 16, MA 30, MA 44
Joint set—engine supplementary MA 16, MA 30, MA 44
Journal and needle kit set .. MG 1

K

Key—camshaft gear .. MA 5, MA 21, MA 35
Key—crankshaft gear .. MA 5, MA 21, MA 35
Key—ignition .. .. MN 5, MN 6
Key—steering-column .. .. MJ 3
Kit—calliper unit repair .. MK 4
Kit—clutch cylinder repair .. ME 8
Kit—engine service MA 16, MA 30, MA 44
Kit—front wheel cylinder repair MK 4
Kit—fuel pump repair .. .. MD 4
Kit—master cylinder repair .. MM 3
Kit—rear wheel cylinder repair MH 5
Kit—swivel pin and bush repair MK 3
Kit—tool .. .. MR 2
Kit—water pump repair .. MA 14, MA 28, MA 42
Knob—change speed lever .. MF 7, MF 12, MF 17
Knob—horn-push MN 18, MN 19

L

Lamp—fog .. .. .. MN 17
Lamp—number-plate MN 10, MN 17
Lamp—side and flasher.. MN 8, MN 16
Lamp—stop/tail/flasher and reflex .. .. MN 10, MN 17
Lamp—warning .. MN 22, MN 24
Lamps—road .. MN 7–MN 17
Laygear .. MF 4, MF 10, MF 15
Layshaft .. MF 4, MF 10, MF 15
Leaves—road spring .. .. MH 6
Lever—accelerator pedal .. MA 48
Lever—brake balance .. .. MM 7
Lever—change speed .. MF 7, MF 12, MF 17
Lever—clutch withdrawal MF 3, MF 9
Lever—gearbox control.. MF 6, MF 12, MF 17
Lever—gearbox front and rear selector .. MF 6, MF 12, MF 17
Lever—hand brake—wheel cylinder .. .. .. MH 5
Lever—steering .. .. .. MK 2
Liner—cylinder .. .. .. MA 3
Lining—clutch .. ME 3, ME 5, ME 7
Lining—front brake .. .. MK 4
Lining—rear brake .. .. MH 4
Link—accelerator pedal .. MA 48
Link—dynamo adjusting .. MA 15, MA 29, MA 43
Link—hand brake balance .. MM 6
Link—lower—front suspension MK 2
Link—rear shock absorber .. ML 2
Link—top—rear shock absorber ML 2
Literature, see Publication No. AKD 858
Lock—ignition switch .. MN 5, MN 6
Lock—steering—column .. MJ 3

M

Manifold—exhaust .. .. MA 17, MA 31, MA 45
Manifold—inlet MA 17, MA 31, MA 45
Mask—front brake-shoe adjuster MK 4
Mask—rear brake-shoe adjuster MH 4
Motor—windscreen wiper MN 20, MN 21
Mounting—dynamo .. .. MA 15, MA 29, MA 43
Mounting—engine .. .. MA 46
Mounting—exhaust pipe .. MA 47

N

Nut—wheel stud .. MH 3, MK 3

O

Oil filter .. MA 13, MA 27, MA 41
Oil pump .. MA 12, MA 26, MA 40
Oil seal—front hub .. .. MK 3
Oil seal—gearbox extension .. MF 6, MF 12, MF 17
Oil seal—rear axle pinion .. MH 3
Oil seal—rear hub .. .. MH 3
Oil seal—valve .. .. .. MA 7
Oil thrower—crankshaft MA 5, MA 21

P

Packing—crankshaft .. MA 5, MA 21, MA 35
Pad—brake pedal .. .. MM 2
Pad—calliper unit—disc brake MK 4
Pad—clutch pedal .. .. ME 8
Pad—steering-rack damper .. MJ 2
Pawl—hand brake .. .. MM 6
Pedal—accelerator .. .. MA 48
Pedal—brake .. .. .. MM 2
Pedal—clutch .. .. .. ME 8
Pillar—dynamo adjusting link MA 15, MA 29, MA 43
Pin—differential .. .. MH 2
Pin—gudgeon MA 4, MA 20, MA 34
Pin—rear spring .. .. MH 6
Pin—steering swivel .. .. MK 2
Pinion and barrel—starter .. MN 4
Pinion—differential .. .. MH 2
Pinion—speedometer .. MF 6, MF 12, MF 17
Pinion—steering .. .. MJ 2
Pipe—air cleaner to rocker cover MD 5
Pipe—carburetter feed .. .. MD 3
Pipe—crankcase vent .. .. MA 10, MA 25, MA 39
Pipe—exhaust .. .. .. MA 47
Pipe—fuel pump to carburetter MD 3
Pipe—oil filter to crankcase .. MA 13, MA 27, MA 41
Pipe—oil gauge .. .. MO 2, MO 4
Pipe—vacuum ignition control MB 5, MB 8, MB 11
Pipe with oil strainer bracket—suction .. MA 12, MA 26, MA 40
Pipes—brake and clutch .. MM 4
Pipes—fuel tank and pump .. MD 3
Piston—clutch slave cylinder .. ME 8
Piston—engine MA 4, MA 20, MA 34
Piston—master cylinder .. MM 3
Plate—clutch driven ME 3, ME 5, ME 7
Plate—clutch pressure .. .. ME 3, ME 5, ME 7
Plate—engine rear mounting support .. .. MA 46
Plate—front brake .. .. MK 4
Plate—front engine mounting .. MA 5, MA 21, MA 35
Plate—heater tap hole cover .. MA 9, MA 24, MA 37
Plate—rear brake .. .. MH 4
Plate—rear engine mounting .. MA 10, MA 25, MA 39
Plinth—number-plate lamp .. MN 17
Plug—fuel tank drain .. .. MD 2
Plug—sparking MA 9, MA 24, MA 38
Plug—sump drain MA 11, MA 26, MA 40
Plugs—axle drain and filler .. MH 2
Plugs—gearbox drain and filler MF 3, MF 9, MF 14
Propeller shaft .. .. MG 1
Pulley—crankshaft MA 5, MA 21, MA 35
Pulley—dynamo MA 15, MA 29, MA 43
Pulley—fan and water pump .. MA 14, MA 28, MA 42
Pump—fuel .. .. .. MD 4
Pump—oil MA 12, MA 26, MA 40
Pump—water MA 14, MA 28, MA 42
Push-rod—clutch slave cylinder ME 8
Push-rod—master cylinder .. MM 2
Push-rod—tappet MA 6, MA 22, MA 36

R

Rack—steering .. .. .. MJ 2
Radiator .. .. MC 2
Ratio box—tachometer MO 3, MO 5
Rear axle and suspension .. MH 2
Ring—piston MA 4, MA 20, MA 34
Ring—starter MA 6, MA 22, MA 36
Rocker—valve MA 9, MA 24, MA 38
Rod—battery fixing .. .. MN 2
Rod—brake cross .. .. MM 6
Rod—connecting MA 5, MA 21, MA 35
Rod—dipper MA 11, MA 26, MA 40
Rods—change speed mechanism MF 3, MF 9, MF 14
Rotor—oil pump MA 12, MA 26, MA 40
Rotor arm—distributor MB 3, MB 4, MB 7, MB 10
Rubber—engine mounting .. MA 46

S

Seal—front hub oil .. .. MK 3
Seal—gearbox extension oil .. MF 6, MF 12, MF 17
Seal—oil—engine front cover .. MA 10, MA 25, MA 39
Seal—oil filter MA 13, MA 27, MA 41
Seal—rear axle oil .. .. MH 3
Seal—rear hub oil .. .. MH 3
Seal—speedometer pinion oil .. MF 6, MF 12, MF 17
Seal—steering-column .. .. MJ 3

Alphabetical Index—*continued*

Page

Seal—steering-rack .. .. MJ 2
Seal—water pump MA 14, MA 28, MA 42
Seat—coil spring .. .. .. MK 5
Service kit—engine .. .. MA 16, MA 30, MA 44
Service tools .. .. .. MR 2
Shaft—distributor drive .. MB 3, MB 7, MB 10
Shaft—gearbox 1st motion .. MF 4, MF 10. MF 15
Shaft—gearbox 3rd motion .. MF 4, MF 10, MF 15
Shaft—gearbox remote control MF 6, MF 12, MF 17
Shaft—gearbox reverse .. MF 5, MF 11, MF 16
Shaft—oil pump MA 12, MA 26, MA 40
Shaft—propeller .. .. MG 1
Shaft—rear axle .. .. MH 3
Shaft—valve rocker .. .. MA 8, MA 23, MA 37
Shield—heat .. .. .. MD 5
Shock absorbers—front .. MK 5
Shock absorbers—rear .. .. ML 2
Shoe—front brake .. .. MK 4
Shoe—rear brake .. .. MH 4
Shroud—valve guide .. .. MA 47
Silencer—exhaust .. .. MA 47
Sleeve—universal joint .. .. MG 1
Socket—steering ball .. .. MJ 2
Solenoid—starter .. .. MN 6
Sparking plug MA 9, MA 24, MA 38
Speedometer .. MO 2, MO 5
Spindle—distributor driving .. MA 6, MA 22, MA 36
Spindle—water pump .. .. MA 14, MA 28, MA 42
Spindle and gear—windscreen wiper .. .. MN 20, MN 21

Page

Spring—accelerator pedal return MA 49
Spring—brake pedal return .. MM 2
Spring—brake-shoe front .. MK 4
Spring—brake-shoe rear .. MH 4
Spring—clutch pedal return .. ME 3, ME 5, ME 7
Spring—clutch thrust .. .. ME 3, ME 5, ME 7
Spring—coil .. .. .. MK 5
Spring—piston return—master cylinder .. .. .. MM 3
Spring—road .. .. .. MH 5
Spring—starter—main .. .. MN 4
Spring—valve MA 9, MA 23, MA 37
Starter .. .. MN 4
Steering .. .. MJ 2
Strainer—oil MA 12, MA 26, MA 40
Strap—axle check .. .. ML 2
Strap—stowage—spare wheel .. MP 2
Stud—front wheel .. .. MK 3
Stud—rear wheel .. .. MH 3
Sump—engine MA 11, MA 26, MA 40
Sump—oil filter MA 13, MA 27, MA 41
Suppressor—sparking plug MB 5, MB 8
Suspension—front .. .. MK 2
Switch—stop light .. .. MM 5
Switches—electrical .. MN 5, MN 6
Swivel pin—steering .. .. MK 2
Synchronizer—2nd speed MF 11, MF 16
Synchronizer—3rd and 4th speed MF 4, MF 10, MF 15

T

Tachometer .. .. MO 3, MO 5
Tank—fuel .. .. .. MD 2
Tap—cylinder drain .. .. MA 10, MA 25, MA 39
Tap—radiator drain .. .. MC 2

Page

Tappet—valve MA 6, MA 22, MA 36
Thermostat MA 9, MA 24, MA 38
Thrower—oil—crankshaft MA 5, MA 21
Tie-rod—steering .. .. MJ 2
Tools .. .. MR 2
Transmission .. .. .. MG 1
Tray—battery .. .. .. MN 2
Tube—steering-column .. .. MJ 3

U

Unit—fuel tank gauge .. .. MD 2

V

Vacuum ignition control .. MB 5, MB 8, MB 11
Vacuum unit—distributor .. MB 3, MB 5, MB 7
Valve—inlet and exhaust .. MA 7, MA 23, MA 37
Valve—master cylinder .. MM 3
Valve—oil release MA 11, MA 26, MA 40
Vane—water pump .. .. MA 14, MA 28, MA 42

W

Washer—carburetter insulating MD 5
Water pump MA 14, MA 28, MA 42
Wheel—1st speed—gearbox .. MF 5, MF 11, MF 16
Wheel—reverse—gearbox .. MF 5, MF 11, MF 16
Wheel—steering .. .. .. MJ 3
Wheelbox—windscreen wiper .. MN 20, MN 21
Wheels—road .. .. .. MP 2
Wiper—windscreen MN 20, MN 21

Part Number Index

The following is a complete index of parts in this List, giving the page reference of each part number

Part Number	Page	Part Number	Page	Part Number	Page	Part Number	Page	Part Number	Page
1A 1559	MA 5	2A 85	MA 35	2A 404	MD 2	2A 721	MB 3	C–2A 955 20	MT 2
1A 1559	MA 21	2A 98	MA 11	2A 494	MA 12	2A 755	MA 4	C–2A 955 30	MT 2
1A 1559	MA 35	2A 102	MA 17	2A 494	MA 26	2A 0755 10	MA 4	C–2A 955 40	MT 2
1A 1716	MA 5	2A 106	MA 16	2A 504	MD 2	2A 0755 20	MA 4	2A 956	MA 9
1A 1716	MA 21	2A 106	MA 17	2A 515	MA 8	2A 0755 30	MA 4	2A 957	MA 12
1A 1716 03	MA 5	2A 110	MA 17	2A 515	MA 23	2A 0755 40	MA 4	2A 957	MA 26
1A 1716 03	MA 21	2A 110	MA 31	2A 515	MA 37	2A 758	MA 15	2A 962	MA 12
1A 1717	MA 5	2A 110	MA 45	2A 516	MA 6	2A 758	MA 29	2A 962	MA 26
1A 1717	MA 21	2A 113	MA 16	2A 522	MA 12	2A 759	MA 5	2A 962	MA 40
1A 1717 03	MA 5	2A 113	MA 30	2A 522	MA 26	2A 759	MA 21	2A 964	MA 8
1A 1717 03	MA 21	2A 113	MA 44	2A 522	MA 40	2A 759	MA 35	2A 964	MA 37
1A 1964	MA 3	2A 113	MD 4	2A 533	MA 8	2A 770	MA 10	2A 971	MA 8
1A 1964	MA 19	2A 118	MA 10	2A 533	MA 23	2A 774	MA 14	2A 971	MA 16
1A 1964	MA 33	2A 118	MA 25	2A 533	MA 37	2A 774	MA 28	2A 1015	MA 5
1A 2093	MA 10	2A 118	MA 39	2A 535	MA 8	2A 775	MA 14	2A 1015	MA 21
1A 2093	MA 25	2A 123	MA 10	2A 535	MA 23	2A 777	MA 14	2A 1015	MA 39
1A 2093	MA 39	2A 123	MA 25	2A 535	MA 37	2A 777	MA 28	2A 2069	MD 2
1A 2149	MA 9	2A 125	MA 5	2A 536	MB 5	2A 777	MA 42	2A 2070	MD 2
1A 2156	MA 9	2A 125	MA 21	2A 544	MA 7	2A 778	MA 14	2A 2071	MD 2
1A 2156	MA 24	2A 125	MA 35	2A 545	MA 7	2A 778	MA 28	2A 2077	MA 48
1A 2156	MA 38	2A 126	MA 5	2A 550	MA 5	2A 778	MA 42	2A 2079	MA 48
1A 2199	MA 10	2A 126	MA 21	2A 552	MA 10	2A 784	MA 3	2A 2082	MC 2
1A 2203	MA 10	2A 127	MA 3	2A 571	MA 5	2A 787	MA 13	2A 2083	MC 2
1A 2206	MA 12	2A 127	MA 16	2A 601	MA 14	2A 803	MA 14	2A 2084	MC 2
1A 2206	MA 26	2A 127	MA 19	2A 601	MA 28	2A 803	MA 28	2A 2085	MN 5
1A 2206	MA 40	2A 127	MA 30	2A 601	MA 42	2A 803	MA 42	2A 2085	MN 6
1A 4744	MK 2	2A 127	MA 33	2A 608 10	MA 7	2A 805	MA 9	2A 2086	MA 49
		2A 128	MA 15	2A 0608 10	MA 7	2A 813	MA 12	2A 2088	MD 2
2A 6	MA 7	2A 128	MA 29	2A 612	MA 6	2A 816	MA 3	2A 2089	MA 47
2A 9	MA 7	2A 139	MA 6	2A 612	MA 22	2A 817	MA 3	2A 2091	MA 47
2A 9	MA 16	2A 139	MA 22	2A 612	MA 36	2A 819	MA 12	2A 2092	MA 47
2A 10	MA 7	2A 139	MA 36	2A 639	MA 7	2A 819	MA 26	2A 2181	MM 4
2A 11	MA 7	2A 150	MA 9	2A 639	MA 23	2A 835	MD 5	2A 3006	ME 7
2A 11	MA 23	2A 150	MA 24	2A 640	MA 7	2A 836	MD 5	2A 3006	MF 3
2A 11	MA 37	2A 150	MA 38	2A 640	MA 37	2A 837	MA 4	2A 3006	MF 9
2A 12	MA 7	2A 179	MA 44	2A 654	MA 5	2A 837	MA 20	2A 3007	MF 3
2A 12	MA 23	2A 180	MA 7	2A 654	MA 21	2A 0837 02	MA 4	2A 3007	MF 9
2A 12	MA 37	2A 180	MA 23	2A 656	MA 5	2A 0837 02	MA 20	2A 3019	MF 3
2A 13	MA 6	2A 180	MA 37	2A 656	MA 21	2A 0837 04	MA 4	2A 3019	MF 9
2A 13	MA 8	2A 237	MA 47	2A 659	MA 5	2A 0837 04	MA 20	2A 3021	MF 3
2A 13	MA 22	2A 242	MA 9	2A 659	MA 21	2A 0837 06	MA 4	2A 3021	MF 9
2A 13	MA 36	2A 242	MA 24	2A 660	MA 5	2A 0837 06	MA 20	2A 3023	MF 4
2A 0013 10	MA 6	2A 242	MA 38	2A 660	MA 21	2A 847	MA 6	2A 3023	MF 10
2A 0013 10	MA 22	2A 243	MA 9	2A 660	MA 23	2A 847	MA 22	2A 3023	MF 15
2A 0013 10	MA 36	2A 243	MA 14	2A 660	MA 35	2A 847	MA 36	2A 3024	MF 4
2A 0013 20	MA 6	2A 243	MA 24	2A 664	MA 14	2A 848	MD 5	2A 3024	MF 10
2A 0013 20	MA 22	2A 243	MA 28	2A 664	MA 28	2A 849	MD 5	2A 3024	MF 15
2A 0013	MA 36	2A 243	MA 38	2A 664	MA 42	2A 850	MA 49	2A 3025	MF 4
2A 14	MA 6	2A 243	MA 42	2A 665	MA 14	2A 877	MA 7	2A 3025	MF 10
2A 14	MA 22	2A 253	MA 3	2A 665	MA 28	2A 879	MA 7	2A 3025	MF 15
2A 14	MA 36	2A 258	MA 8	2A 667	MA 16	2A 879	MA 16	2A 3026	MF 4
2A 15	MA 23	2A 258	MA 23	2A 667	MA 30	2A 879	MA 23	2A 3026	MF 10
2A 16	MA 8	2A 258	MA 37	2A 668	MA 12	2A 879	MA 30	2A 3026	MF 15
2A 16	MA 23	2A 269	MA 12	2A 668	MA 26	2A 879	MA 37	2A 3027	MF 4
2A 16	MA 37	2A 269	MA 26	2A 668	MA 40	2A 879	MA 44	2A 3027	MF 10
2A 18	MA 23	2A 269	MA 40	2A 672	MA 12	2A 880	MA 7	2A 3027	MF 15
2A 18	MA 37	2A 280	MA 11	2A 677	MA 44	2A 935	MA 8	2A 3028	MF 3
2A 21	MA 8	2A 280	MA 16	2A 686	MA 4	2A 937	MA 10	2A 3028	MF 9
2A 21	MA 23	2A 280	MA 26	2A 0686 10	MA 4	2A 937	MA 25	2A 3028	MF 14
2A 21	MA 37	2A 280	MA 30	2A 0686 20	MA 4	2A 937	MA 39	2A 3034	MF 4
2A 22	MA 8	2A 280	MA 40	2A 0686 30	MA 4	2A 939	MA 10	2A 3035	MF 4
2A 22	MA 23	2A 280	MA 44	2A 0686 40	MA 4	2A 939	MA 25	2A 3035	MF 5
2A 23	MA 8	2A 280	MT 3	2A 687	MA 4	2A 939	MA 39	2A 3035	MF 10
2A 23	MA 23	2A 294	MA 11	2A 0687 10	MA 4	2A 940	MA 5	2A 3035	MF 11
2A 31	MA 30	2A 294	MA 26	2A 0687 20	MA 4	2A 940	MA 21	2A 3035	MF 15
2A 31	MA 44	2A 297	MA 5	2A 0687 30	MA 4	2A 940	MA 35	2A 3035	MF 16
2A 52	MA 3	2A 299	MA 5	2A 0687 40	MA 4	C–2A 946	MT 2	2A 3035	MT 4
2A 53	MA 3	2A 299	MA 21	2A 689	MA 8	C–2A 946 10	MT 2	2A 3042	MF 5
2A 53	MA 19	2A 299	MA 35	2A 700	MA 13	C–2A 946 20	MT 2	2A 3045	MF 5
2A 53	MA 33	2A 299	MT 2	2A 700	MA 27	C–2A 946 30	MT 2	2A 3057	MF 5
2A 54	MA 3	2A 305	MA 46	2A 700	MA 41	C–2A 946 40	MT 2	2A 3057	MF 11
2A 54	MA 19	2A 329	MA 38	2A 703	MA 13	C–2A 950	MT 2	2A 3061	MF 6
2A 54	MA 33	2A 339	MA 12	2A 704	MA 11	C–2A 954	MT 2	2A 3061	MF 12
2A 77	MA 5	2A 339	MA 26	2A 704	MA 26	C–2A 954 10	MT 2	2A 3061	MF 17
2A 84	MA 5	2A 339	MA 40	2A 711	MA 11	C–2A 954 20	MT 2	2A 3076	MF 3
2A 84	MA 21	2A 341	MA 12	2A 715	MA 13	C–2A 954 30	MT 2	2A 3076	MF 9
2A 84	MA 35	2A 375	MA 9	2A 715	MA 27	C–2A 954 40	MT 2	2A 3084	MF 3
2A 85	MA 5	2A 375	MA 24	2A 715	MA 41	C–2A 955	MT 2	2A 3085	MF 5
2A 85	MA 21	2A 378	MA 6	2A 719	MA 17	C–2A 955 10	MT 2	2A 3085	MF 11

Part Number Index—*continued*

Part Number	Page	Part Number	Page	Part Number	Page	Part Number	Page	Part Number	Page
2A 3087	MF 8	2A 3344	MF 6	2A 4082	MK 5	2A 6161	MN 19	12A 22	MA 39
2A 3087	MF 9	2A 3344	MF 12	2A 4129	MK 2	2A 6162	MN 18	12A 22	MA 44
2A 3108	MF 3	2A 3344	MF 17	2A 4137	MK 3	2A 6162	MN 19	12A 24	MA 10
2A 3108	MF 9	2A 3344	MT 4	2A 4147	MK 3	2A 7015	MH 2	12A 24	MA 25
2A 3108	MF 14	2A 3345	MF 6	2A 4148	MK 3	2A 7016	MH 2	12A 24	MA 30
2A 3110	MF 8	2A 3345	MF 12	2A 4168	MK 2	2A 7027	MH 2	12A 24	MA 39
2A 3110	MF 9	2A 3345	MF 17	2A 4169	MK 3	2A 7057	MM 7	12A 29	MA 24
2A 3110	MF 14	2A 3345	MT 4	2A 4172	MK 5	2A 7058	MM 7	12A 32	MA 16
2A 3141	MF 3	2A 3347	MF 3	2A 4174	MK 5	2A 7062	MH 2	12A 32	MA 30
2A 3141	MF 9	2A 3347	MF 9	2A 4176	MK 2	2A 7085	MH 3	12A 66	MA 4
2A 3141	MF 14	2A 3352	MF 6	2A 4205	MK 2	2A 7087	MH 3	12A 66	MA 20
2A 3142	MF 4	2A 3352	MF 12	2A 4206	MK 2	2A 7089	MH 3	12A 0066 10	MA 4
2A 3142	MF 5	2A 3352	MF 17	2A 4212	MK 3	2A 7091	MH 3	12A 0066 10	MA 20
2A 3142	MF 10	2A 3354	MF 7	2A 4213	MK 3	2A 7108	MH 2	12A 0066 20	MA 4
2A 3142	MF 11	2A 3357	MF 3	2A 4214	MK 5	2A 7142	MH 2	12A 0066 20	MA 20
2A 3145	MF 1	2A 3358	MF 4	2A 4272	MK 5	2A 7168	MH 5	12A 0066 30	MA 4
2A 3145	MF 10	2A 3359	MF 4	2A 4299	MK 3	2A 7168	MK 4	12A 0066 30	MA 20
2A 3147	MF 4	2A 3361	MF 5	2A 4304	MK 2	2A 7213	MH 3	12A 0066 40	MA 4
2A 3147	MF 5	2A 3363	MF 5	2A 4348	MK 3	2A 7226	MH 2	12A 0066 40	MA 20
2A 3147	MF 10	2A 3366	MF 4	2A 5379	MR 2	2A 7228	MH 5	12A 67	MA 4
2A 3147	MF 11	2A 3366	MF 10	2A 5412	MR 2	2A 7228	MK 4	12A 67	MA 20
2A 3160	MF 4	2A 3366	MF 15	2A 5419	MR 2	2A 7230	MT 4	12A 0067 10	MA 4
2A 3160	MF 11	2A 3367	MF 6	2A 5420	MA 46	2A 7242	MH 3	12A 0067 10	MA 20
2A 3161	MF 4	2A 3367	MF 12	2A 5422	MA 46	2A 7250	MH 2	12A 0067 20	MA 4
2A 3161	MF 11	2A 3371	MF 5	2A 5472	MR 2	2A 7271	MH 2	12A 0067 20	MA 20
2A 3168	MF 4	2A 3371	MF 11	2A 5538	MM 2	2A 7272	MG 2	12A 0067 30	MA 4
2A 3168	MF 10	2A 3371	MF 16	2A 5549	MM 2	2A 7278	ML 2	12A 0067 30	MA 20
2A 3168	MF 15	2A 3372	MF 6	2A 5552	MA 46	2A 7279	MH 6	12A 0067 40	MA 4
2A 3217	MF 4	2A 3375	MF 6	2A 5559	MM 2	2A 7279	ML 2	12A 0067 40	MA 20
2A 3218	MF 4	2A 3375	MF 12	2A 5564	ME 8	2A 7290	MM 6	12A 68	MA 4
2A 3219	MF 4	2A 3375	MF 17	2A 5564	MM 2	2A 7291	MM 6	12A 68	MA 20
2A 3220	MF 4	2A 3377	MF 6	2A 5565	MM 2	2A 7298	ML 2	12A 0068 10	MA 4
2A 3224	MF 4	2A 3378	MF 6	2A 5566	ME 8	2A 7299	ML 2	12A 0068 10	MA 20
2A 3226	MF 4	2A 3378	MF 12	2A 5568	MM 2	2A 7303	ML 2	12A 0068 20	MA 4
2A 3245	MF 5	2A 3378	MF 17	2A 5570	MA 46	2A 7306	ML 2	12A 0068 20	MA 20
2A 3245	MF 10	2A 3379	MF 7	2A 5571	MA 46	2A 7308	MM 6	12A 0068 30	MA 4
2A 3245	MF 11	2A 3379	MF 12	2A 5572	MM 2	2A 7309	MH 6	12A 0068 30	MA 20
2A 3245	MF 15	2A 3379	MF 17	2A 5573	ME 8	2A 7310	ML 2	12A 0068 40	MA 4
2A 3253	MF 3	2A 3383	MF 7	2A 5573	MM 2	2A 7314	ML 2	12A 0068 40	MA 20
2A 3253	MF 9	2A 3384	MF 6	2A 5574	ME 8	2A 7315	ML 2	12A 106	MA 16
2A 3253	MF 14	2A 3384	MF 12	2A 5574	MM 2	2A 8055	MP 2	12A 107	MA 12
2A 3254	MF 6	2A 3385	MF 6	2A 5575	MM 2	2A 8060	MP 2	12A 107	MA 26
2A 3255	MF 6	2A 3385	MF 12	2A 5576	MM 2	2A 9013	MN 10	12A 121	MA 4
2A 3256	MF 6	2A 3385	MF 17	2A 5587	MM 2	2A 9039	MO 2	12A 0121 10	MA 4
2A 3278	MF 6	2A 3388	MF 6	2A 5588	MM 2	2A 9040	MN 10	12A 0121 20	MA 4
2A 3282	MF 5	2A 3388	MF 12	2A 5589	MM 2	2A 9067	MO 2	12A 0121 30	MA 4
2A 3282	MF 11	2A 3388	MF 17	2A 5591	MC 2	2A 9068	MO 3	12A 0121 40	MA 4
2A 3282	MF 16	2A 3389	MF 7	2A 5592	MC 2	2A 9069	MO 2	12A 143	MA 41
2A 3282	MT 4	2A 3390	MF 7	2A 5605	MM 4	2A 9070	MO 2	12A 0145 03	MA 4
2A 3284	MF 3	2A 3390	MF 12	2A 5607	MM 4	2A 9071	MN 22	12A 0145 06	MA 4
2A 3284	MF 9	2A 3390	MF 17	2A 5609	MM 4	2A 9072	MN 22	12A 0145 13	MA 4
2A 3284	MF 14	2A 3401	MF 5	2A 5611	MM 4	2A 9073	MN 22	12A 0145 16	MA 4
2A 3286	MF 3	2A 3406	MF 3	2A 5615	ME 8	2A 9074	MN 5	12A 0145 23	MA 4
2A 3286	MF 9	2A 3406	MF 9	2A 5617	ME 8	2A 9074	MN 6	12A 0145 26	MA 4
2A 3286	MF 14	2A 3413	MF 3	2A 5619	MM 4	2A 9075	MN 2	12A 0145 33	MA 4
2A 3286	MT 4	2A 3416	MF 7	2A 5626	MR 2	2A 9075	MN5	12A 0145 36	MA 4
2A 3289	ME 7	2A 3416	MF 12	2A 5627	MR 2	2A 9076	MN 22	12A 0145 43	MA 4
2A 3289	MF 3	2A 3420	MF 6	2A 5635	MO 2	2A 9076	MO 25	12A 0145 46	MA 4
2A 3289	MF 9	2A 3420	MF 12	2A 5635	MO 4	2A 9077	MO 2	12A 165	MB 4
2A 3290	MF 5	2A 3420	MF 17	2A 5637	MO 2	2A 9097	MN 24	12A 183	MA 6
2A 3295	MF 7	2A 3467	MF 7	2A 5637	MO 4	2A 9102	MN 5	12A 183	MA 22
2A 3295	MF 12	2A 3467	MF 12	2A 5638	MD 3	2A 9104	MO 3	12A 184	MA 23
2A 3298	MF 5	2A 3467	MF 17	2A 5640	MO 2	2A 9104	MO 5	12A 186	MA 23
2A 3305	MF 3	2A 3468	MF 6	2A 5640	MO 4	2A 9105	MO 3	12A 186	MA 37
2A 3305	MF 9	2A 3468	MF 12	2A 6128	MJ 2	2A 9105	MO 5	12A 0186 10	MA 37
2A 3325	MF 6	2A 3468	MF 17	2A 6129	MJ 2	2A 9108	MO 3	12A 0187 03	MA 20
2A 3325	MF 12	2A 3664	MF 6	2A 6130	MJ 2	2A 9108	MO 5	12A 0187 06	MA 20
2A 3325	MF 17	2A 4003	MK 3	2A 6131	MJ 2	2A 9156	MN 16	12A 0187 13	MA 20
2A 3330	MF 5	2A 4005	MK 2	2A 6132	MJ 3			12A 0187 16	MA 20
2A 3333	MF 5	2A 4006	MK 2	2A 6133	MJ 3	12A 1	MD 4	12A 0187 23	MA 20
2A 3335	MF 6	2A 4007	MK 2	2A 6136	MJ 3	12A 14	MA 9	12A 0187 26	MA 20
2A 3335	MF 12	2A 4008	MK 2	2A 6140	MJ 3	12A 14	MA 16	12A 0187 33	MA 20
2A 3335	MF 17	2A 4009	MK 2	2A 6141	MJ 3	12A 14	MA 24	12A 0187 36	MA 20
2A 3339	MF 7	2A 4010	MK 2	2A 6142	MJ 3	12A 14	MA 30	12A 0187 43	MA 20
2A 3339	MF 12	2A 4011	MK 2	2A 6144	MJ 3	12A 14	MA 38	12A 0187 46	MA 20
2A 3339	MF 17	2A 4020	MK 3	2A 6145	MJ 2	12A 14	MA 44	12A 189	MA 22
2A 3340	MF 7	2A 4021	MK 5	2A 6146	MJ 2	12A 19	MA 11	12A 190	MA 23
2A 3340	MF 12	2A 4024	MK 5	2A 6156	MJ 3	12A 19	MA 26	12A 190	MA 37
2A 3340	MF 17	2A 4028	MK 5	2A 6157	MN 18	12A 20	MA 11	12A 191	MA 31
2A 3341	MF 7	2A 4029	MK 5	2A 6157	MN 19	12A 20	MA 26	12A 191	MA 45
2A 3341	MF 12	2A 4031	MK 5	2A 6158	MN 18	12A 22	MA 10	12A 192	MA 16
2A 3341	MF 17	2A 4066	MK 3	2A 6158	MN 19	12A 22	MA 16	12A 192	MA 17
2A 3341	MT 4	2A 4067	MK 3	2A 6161	MN 18	12A 22	MA 30	12A 192	MA 31

Part Number Index—*continued*

Part Number	Page	Part Number	Page	Part Number	Page	Part Number	Page	Part Number	Page
12A 192	MA 45	12A 1332	MA 28	22A 480	MF 17	ACA 6015	MJ 2	AEA 342	MD 3
12A 198	MA 12	12A 1332	MA 42	22A 481	MF 17	ACA 6017	MJ 2	AEA 346	MB 5
12A 198	MA 26	12A 1358	MA 9	22A 495	MF 4	ACA 6018	MJ 2	AEA 355	ME 3
12A 210	MA 23	12A 1358	MA 24	22A 495	MF 11	ACA 6019	MJ 2	AEA 355	ME 5
12A 210	MA 37	12A 1358	MA 38	22A 495	MF 16	ACA 6020	MJ 2	AEA 358	MA 7
12A 211	MA 23	12A 1389	MA 14	22A 517	MF 15	ACA 6026	MJ 2	AEA 393	MD 3
12A 211	MA 37	12A 1389	MA 28	22A 517	MF 16	ACA 6027	MJ 2	AEA 395	MD 5
12A 250	MA 6	12A 1389	MA 42	22A 525	MF 4	ACA 6028	MJ 2	AEA 400	MA 7
12A 250	MA 22	12A 1419	MA 10	22A 526	MF 4	ACA 6029	MJ 2	AEA 400	MA 23
12A 250	MA 36	12A 1419	MA 25	22A 527	MF 4	ACA 6030	MJ 2	AEA 400	MA 37
12A 0280 03	MA 20	12A 1419	MA 39	22A 528	MF 4	ACA 6031	MJ 2	AEA 401	MA 23
12A 0280 06	MA 20	12A 1591	MA 13	22A 536	MF 4	ACA 8014	MD 5	AEA 401	MA 37
12A 0280 13	MA 20	12A 1591	MA 27	22A 537	MF 4	ACA 9932	MR 2	AEA 401	MT 2
12A 0280 16	MA 20	12A 1591	MA 41	22A 538	MF 4			AEA 402	MA 23
12A 0280 23	MA 20			22A 550	MF 4	ACB 9162	MM 4	AEA 402	MA 37
12A 0280 26	MA 20	14A 4615	MN 10			ACB 9425	MJ 3	AEA 402	MT 2
12A 0280 33	MA 20	14A 4743	MN 10	24A 1032	MP 2	ACB 9427	MJ 3	AEA 403	MA 23
12A 0280 36	MA 20	14A 4801	MN 20			ACB 9428	MJ 3	AEA 403	MA 37
12A 0280 43	MA 20	14A 4801	MN 21	AAA 81	ME 8			C–AEA 411	MT 3
12A 0280 46	MA 20	14A 4802	MN 20	AAA 421	MH 4	ACC 5062	MA 48	C–AEA 432	MT 2
12A 293	MA 37	14A 4802	MN 21	AAA 421	MK 4	ACC 5062	MD 5	AEA 434	MA 7
12A 303	MA 12	14A 6511	MP 2	AAA 423	MH 4			AEA 434	MA 23
12A 303	MA 40			AAA 649	MA 49	ACG 5179	MN 17	AEA 443	MD 3
12A 394	MA 41	21A 137	MK 5	AAA 1534	MN 6	ACG 5180	MN 17	AEA 447	MB 5
12A 394	MA 44	21A 153	MK 3	AAA 1768	MA 48	ACG 6009	MJ 2	C–AEA 485	MT 6
12A 402	MA 9	21A 168	MD 2	AAA 4692	MH 4	ACG 6010	MJ 2	AEA 493	MT 2
12A 402	MA 24	22A 71	MF 12	AAA 4692	MK 4			AEA 494	MT 2
12A 402	MA 38	22A 71	MF 17	AAA 4714	MH 4	ACH 5854	MD 3	C–AEA 511	MT 3
12A 403	MA 9	22A 75	MF 3	AAA 4756	MM 3	ACH 6170	MJ 2	C–AEA 524	MT 9
12A 403	MA 24	22A 75	MF 7	AAA 4757	MM 3	ACH 6173	MJ 2	AEA 538	MA 21
12A 403	MA 38	22A 75	MF 9	AAA 4758	MM 3	ACH 8393	MA 49	AEA 538	MA 35
12A 413	MA 35	22A 75	MF 12	AAA 4775	MH 5	ACH 8529	MO 3	C–AEA 539	MT 2
12A 419	MB 4	22A 75	MF 14	AAA 4776	MK 4	ACH 8529	MO 5	AEA 574	MA 23
12A 451	MA 40	22A 75	MF 17	AAA 4777	MH 4	ACH 8977	MT 6	AEA 576	MA 31
12A 501	MA 9	22A 84	MF 7	AAA 4778	MH 4	ACH 8979	MA 49	AEA 579	MB 8
12A 501	MA 24	22A 84	MF 12	AAA 5981	MB 5	ACH 9009	MB 5	AEA 579	MB 11
12A 501	MA 38	22A 84	MF 17	AAA 5981	MB 8	ACH 9009	MB 8	AEA 581	MB 8
12A 526	MA 15	22A 85	MF 7	AAA 5981	MB 11	ACH 9009	MB 11	AEA 581	MB 11
12A 526	MA 29	22A 85	MF 12			ACH 9041	MB 8	AEA 582	MD 3
12A 526	MA 43	22A 85	MF 17	ACA 4000	MK 3	ACH 9041	MB 11	AEA 586	MD 5
12A 666	MA 10	22A 138	MF 4	ACA 5071	MD 5	ACH 9042	MA 49	AEA 588	MD 3
12A 666	MA 39	22A 138	MF 5	ACA 5118	MJ 2			AEA 589	MD 3
12A 723	MA 10	22A 138	MF 10	ACA 5128	MD 3	ADB 826	MN 20	AEA 592	MD 5
12A 723	MA 39	22A 138	MF 11	ACA 5129	MD 3	ADB 826	MN 21	AEA 596	MA 6
12A 747	MA 6	22A 139	MF 5	ACA 5208	MF 7			AEA 596	MA 22
12A 747	MA 22	22A 140	MF 5	ACA 5208	MF 12	ADC 560	MN 20	AEA 597	MA 48
12A 747	MA 36	22A 141	MF 4	ACA 5208	MF 17	ADC 560	MN 21	AEA 597	MD 5
12A 956	MA 10	22A 198	MF 3	ACA 5216	MR 2			AEA 601	MA 24
12A 956	MA 16	22A 198	MF 9	ACA 5244	MJ 2	ADG 1517	MN 18	AEA 602	MA 49
12A 956	MA 25	22A 200	MF 5	ACA 5245	MJ 2			AEA 602	MD 5
12A 956	MA 30	22A 203	MF 4	ACA 5246	MJ 2	ADH 785	MN 17	AEA 606	MA 48
12A 956	MA 39	22A 204	MF 5	ACA 5247	MJ 2			AEA 606	MD 5
12A 956	MA 44	22A 204	MF 11	ACA 5248	MJ 2	ADP 210	MA 23	AEA 630	MA 21
12A 1093	MA 9	22A 204	MT 4	ACA 5249	MJ 2	ADP 210	MA 37	AEA 630	MA 35
12A 1093	MA 24	22A 207	MF 10	ACA 5257	MJ 2	ADP 210	MA 38	AEA 633	MA 31
12A 1136	MA 6	22A 207	MT 4	ACA 5258	MJ 2	ADP 210	MA 45	AEA 633	MA 45
12A 1136	MA 22	22A 213	MF 4	ACA 5259	MJ 2			AEA 635	MA 31
12A 1136	MA 36	22A 218	ME 5	ACA 5260	MJ 2	AEA 19	MA 17	AEA 635	MA 45
12A 1139	MA 16	22A 219	MF 9	ACA 5261	MJ 2	AEA 90	MA 23	AEA 643	MA 43
12A 1139	MA 30	22A 224	MF 9	ACA 5275	MJ 2	AEA 90	MA 37	C–AEA 647	MT 3
12A 1139	MA 44	C–22A 226	MT 4	ACA 5283	MJ 2	AEA 301	MA 15	C–AEA 648	MT 4
12A 1148	MA 5	C–22A 227	MT 4	ACA 5284	MJ 2	AEA 301	MA 29	C–AEA 653	MT 2
12A 1148	MA 21	C–22A 228	MT 4	ACA 5285	MJ 2	AEA 301	MA 43	AEA 657	MA 13
12A 1148	MA 39	22A 233	ME 8	ACA 5286	MJ 2	AEA 303	MA 17	AEA 657	MA 27
12A 1170	MA 10	22A 287	MF 4	ACA 5290	MD 5	AEA 305	MA 13	AEA 657	MA 41
12A 1170	MA 25	22A 332	MF 5	ACA 5297	MJ 3	AEA 305	MA 27	AEA 658	MA 13
12A 1170	MA 39	22A 332	MF 11	ACA 5301	MJ 2	AEA 306	MA 9	AEA 658	MA 27
12A 1175	MA 10	22A 332	MT 4	ACA 5302	MJ 2	AEA 306	MA 24	AEA 658	MA 41
12A 1175	MA 25	22A 367	MF 15	ACA 5303	MJ 2	AEA 309	MN 3	AEA 663	MB 8
12A 1175	MA 39	22A 367	MF 16	ACA 5304	MJ 2	AEA 311	MA 7	AEA 663	MB 11
12A 1176	MA 10	22A 426	MT 4	ACA 5307	MJ 2	AEA 311	MA 23	AEA 678	MA 27
12A 1176	MA 25	22A 453	MF 16	ACA 5320	MJ 2	AEA 311	MA 37	AEA 678	MA 41
12A 1176	MA 39	22A 463	MF 16	ACA 5322	MA 48	AEA 312	MA 5	AEA 679	MA 43
12A 1177	MA 10	22A 465	MF 16	ACA 5375	MM 4	AEA 312	MA 21	C–AEA 692	MT 2
12A 1177	MA 25	22A 466	MF 16	ACA 5398	MJ 3	AEA 312	MA 35	C–AEA 731	MT 4
12A 1177	MA 39	22A 468	MF 14	ACA 5420	MO 2	AEA 313	MA 13	AEA 762	MA 7
12A 1215	MA 8	22A 469	MF 14	ACA 5420	MO 4	AEA 313	MA 27	AEA 762	MA 23
12A 1215	MA 23	22A 470	MF 14	ACA 5421	MO 2	AEA 325	MA 15	AEA 763	MA 7
12A 1215	MA 37	22A 471	MF 14	ACA 5421	MO 4	AEA 325	MA 29	AEA 763	MA 23
12A 1328	MA 14	22A 472	MF 14	ACA 5422	MO 2	AEA 327	MA 7	AEA 763	MA 37
12A 1328	MA 28	22A 474	MF 17	ACA 5422	MO 4	AEA 330	MA 9	AEA 767	MT 2
12A 1328	MA 42	22A 475	MF 17	ACA 5432	MR 2	AEA 338	MD 3	AEA 768	MT 2
12A 1332	MA 14	22A 476	MF 17	ACA 5453	MA 49	AEA 339	MD 5	AEA 849	MA 15

Part Number Index—*continued*

Part Number	Page
AEA 849	MA 29
AEA 3021	MF 9
AEA 3022	MF 10
AEA 3023	MF 11
AEA 3024	MF 11
AEA 3025	MF 11
AEA 3030	MF 5
AEA 3031	MF 9
AEA 3032	MF 10
AEA 3033	MF 11
AEA 3034	MF 11
AEA 3188	MF 7
AEA 3188	MF 12
AEA 3196	MF 10
AEA 3199	MF 11
AEA 3200	MF 11
AEA 3201	MF 11
AEA 3204	MF 11
AEA 3207	MF 11
AEC 82	MA 29
AEC 985	MD 3
AEC 895	MD 5
AEC 992	MD 3
AEC 997	MA 23
AEC 997	MA 37
AEC 2003	MD 3
AED 172	MA 13
AED 172	MA 27
AED 172	MA 41
AEG 181	MA 16
AEG 181	MA 30
AEG 181	MA 44
C–AEG 392	MT 2
AEG 399	MT 2
AEG 425	MT 2
C–AEG 579	MT 2
AEG 3122	MF 7
AEG 3122	MF 12
AEG 3122	MF 17
AEG 3123	MF 7
AEG 3123	MF 12
AEG 3123	MF 17
AEG 3124	MF 7
C–AEG 3138	MT 4
C–AEG 3139	MT 4
C–AEG 3140	MT 4
AEH 550	MD 3
AEH 551	MT 6
AEJ 48	MB 7
AEJ 49	MN 3
AEJ 63	MA 29
AEJ 63	MA 43
AEJ 78	MB 7
AHA 5217	MP 2
AHA 5218	MP 2
AHA 5221	MH 6
AHA 5222	MH 6
AHA 5224	ML 2
AHA 5235	MN 5
AHA 5238	MA 47
AHA 5239	MA 47
AHA 5272	MJ 3
AHA 5305	ML 2
AHA 5306	ML 2
AHA 5311	ML 2
AHA 5312	ML 2
AHA 5313	ML 2
AHA 5326	ME 8
AHA 5326	MM 2
AHA 5331	MH 6
AHA 5332	MH 6
AHA 5346	MH 6
AHA 5347	MH 6
AHA 5348	MH 6
AHA 5349	MH 6
AHA 5350	MH 6
AHA 5351	MH 6

Part Number	Page
AHA 5352	MH 6
AHA 5353	MH 6
AHA 5354	MA 47
AHA 5360	MA 47
AHA 5361	MA 47
AHA 5391	MJ 2
AHA 5392	MJ 2
AHA 5431	ME 8
AHA 5435	MJ 3
AHA 5445	MD 2
AHA 5447	MN 18
C–AHA 5448	MT 3
C–AHA 5449	MT 3
AHA 5454	MA 49
AHA 5457	MN 18
AHA 5458	MN 18
AHA 5468	MH 6
AHA 5469	MD 3
AHA 5470	MN 22
AHA 5471	MP 2
AHA 5484	MA 46
AHA 5496	MJ 2
AHA 5497	MN 22
AHA 5506	MR 2
AHA 5507	MM 4
AHA 5508	ME 8
AHA 5516	MN 6
AHA 5535	MD 3
AHA 5536	MD 3
AHA 5539	MP 2
AHA 5655	MN 24
AHA 5656	MN 24
AHA 5660	MP 2
AHA 5661	MN 19
AHA 5662	MD 2
AHA 5663	MD 2
AHA 5676	MA 49
AHA 5682	MJ 3
AHA 5688	MA 47
AHA 5689	MA 47
AHA 5690	MA 47
AHA 5692	MN 24
AHA 5703	MN 19
AHA 5704	MN 19
AHA 5746	MA 48
AHA 5805	MN 17
AHA 5806	MN 17
AHA 5809	MN 17
AHA 5845	MN 24
AHA 5873	MD 5
AHA 5874	MD 4
AHA 5893	MJ 3
AHA 5930	MD 5
AHA 5967	MJ 3
AHA 6166	MJ 3
AHA 6172	MA 47
AHA 6173	MA 47
AHA 6202	MN 6
AHA 6203	MA 49
AHA 6255	MA 48
AHA 6256	MA 48
AHA 6269	MN 6
AHA 6280	MN 25
AHA 6305	MN 2
AHA 6324	MN 25
AHA 6331	MO 4
AHA 6361	MN 17
AHA 6366	MM 2
AHA 6367	MA 49
AHA 6368	MN 17
AHA 6370	MH 6
AHA 6371	MN 19
AHA 6372	MJ3
AHA 6377	MP 2
AHA 6378	MK 5
AHA 6392	MO 4
AHA 6396	MN 24
AHA 6406	MM 6
AHA 6407	MM 2
AHA 6408	ME 8
AHA 6409	MM 2
AHA 6418	MH 6
C–AHA 6451	MT 11

Part Number	Page
C–AHA 6452	MT 11
C–AHA 6453	MT 11
C–AHA 6454	MT 11
AHA 6455	MP 2
AHA 6481	MN 18
AHA 6481	MN 19
AHA 6482	MM 4
AHA 6657	MN 19
AHA 6658	MN 19
AHA 6664	MP 2
AHA 6930	MN 24
AHA 6934	MN 2
AHA 6935	MN 2
AHA 7011	MT 11
AHA 7012	MT 11
AHA 7013	MT 11
AHA 7028	MT 11
C/AHA 7565	MD 2
C/AHA 7566	MD 2
C/AHA 7571	MD 2
C/AHA 7572	MD 2
C–AHA 7573	MT 12
AHA 7769	MN 2
C–AHA 7906	MT 11
C–AHA 7907	MT 11
AHA 7911	MC 2
AHA 7928	MG 2
AHA 7981	MC 2
AHA 7983	MC 2
AHA 7984	MC 2
C–AHA 8272	MT 11
C–AHA 8277	MT 11
C–AHA 8278	MT 11
AHA 8781	MM 4
AHA 8925	MM 4
AHB 9059	MT 6
AHH 5081	ML 2
AHH 5171	MA 47
AHH 5414	MN 20
AHH 5414	MN 21
AHH 5459	MP 2
C–AHH 5517	MT 12
C–AHH 5518	MT 12
C–AHH 5519	MT 12
AHH 5634	MM 5
AHH 5713	MT 6
AHH 5839	MR 2
AHH 5980	MN 10
AHH 5981	MN 10
AHH 6162	MT 3
AHH 6541	MT 11
AHH 6546	MT 11
AHH 7108	MN 25
AHH 7315	MP 2
AHH 7316	MP 2
AHH 7317	MP 2
AHH 7318	MP 2
AHH 8008	MP 2
AHH 8009	MP 2
C–AHT 1	MT 6
C–AHT 10	MT 6
C–AHT 11	MT 3
C–AHT 12	MT 3
C–AHT 14	MT 3
C–AHT 16	MT 12
C–AHT 56	MT 11
C–AHT 57	MT 12
AJA 5002	MH 5
AJA 5008	MH 5
AJA 5069	MN 10
AJA 5071	MN 10
AJA 5072	MN 10
AJA 5073	MN 10
AJA 5081	MN 7
AJA 5081	MN 7·1
AJA 5081	MN 7·2
AJA 5081	MN 8
AJA 5081	MN 8·1
AJA 5081	MN 9

Part Number	Page
AJA 5081	MN 9·1
AJA 5081	MN 11
AJA 5081	MN 12
AJA 5081	MN 13
AJA 5081	MN 13·1
AJA 5081	MN 14
AJA 5081	MN 15
AJA 5085	MK 4
AJA 5086	MH 4
AJD 1042	MT 6
AJD 1042	MT 7
AJD 1042	MT 9
AJD 1245 C	MN 16
AJD 1703 N	MN 5
AJD 1703 N	MN 6
AJD 3202 Z	MN 20
AJD 3202 Z	MN 21
AJD 3204 Z	MA 12
AJD 3204 Z	MA 26
AJD 3204 Z	MA 40
AJD 4205 Z	MA 12
AJD 4205 Z	MA 40
AJD 6155 Z	MJ 2
AJD 7032	MA 48
AJD 7032	MM 7
AJD 8012 Z	MT 6
AJD 8012 Z	MT 9
AJD 8014 Z	MT 6
AJD 8206 Z	MT 7
AJD 8206 Z	MT 9
AJG 5006	MM 3
AJG 5016	MM 3
AJH 5057	MN 17
AJH 5079	MN 20
AJH 5079	MN 21
AJH 5083	MM 3
AJH 5085	MM 3
AJH 5086	MM 3
AJH 5100	MN 10
AJH 5128	MM 3
AJH 5176	MO 2
AJH 5176	MO 3
AJH 5176	MO 5
AJH 5178	MO 2
AJH 5178	MO 2
AJH 5178	MO 5
AJH 5185	MO 4
AJH 5186	MO 4
C–AJJ 3304	MT 6
C–AJJ 3314	MT 11
C–AJJ 3319	MT 4
C–AJJ 3322	MT 11
C–AJJ 3324	MT 3
C–AJJ 3325	MT 2
C–AJJ 3333	MT 12
C–AJJ 3356	MT 11
C–AKD 1021 A	MT 12
C–AKD 4021 A	MT 12
C–AKD 5061	MT 12
C–AKD 5093	MT 12
C–AKD 5097	MT 12
C–AKD 5100	MT 12
AKF 1439	MD 2
ALH 2459	MD 2
AMK 777	MH 3
ANK 3458	MN 20
ANK 3458	MN 21
ANK 3459	MN 20
ANK 3459	MN 21
ANK 4646	MN 5
ANK 4646	MN 6
ANZ 103	MT 11

Part Number	Page
ARA 73	MC 2
ARA 77	MD 2
ARA 92	MC 2
ARA 114	MD 2
ARA 116	MA 47
ARA 134	MA 47
C–ARA 135	MT 3
ARA 241	MC 2
ARA 949	MD 2
ARA 967	MD 2
ARG 923	MD 2
ARH 672	MD 2
ARH 673	MD 2
ARH 1039	MC 2
ARH 1542	MC 2
ARH 1662	MC 2
ATA 4130	MK 3
ATA 4131	MK 3
ATA 4132	MK 3
ATA 7032	MH 2
ATA 7032	MT 4
ATA 7036	MH 2
ATA 7037	MH 2
ATA 7039	MH 2
ATA 7040	MT 4
ATA 7043	MH 3
ATA 7044	MH 3
ATA 7056	MH 3
ATA 7073	MT 4
ATA 7076	MH 4
ATA 7077	MH 4
ATA 7093	MT 4
ATA 7123	MH 3
ATA 7124	MH 3
ATA 7125	MH 3
ATA 7126	MH 3
ATA 7127	MH 3
ATA 7128	MH 3
ATA 7129	MH 3
ATA 7130	MH 3
ATA 7166	MH 3
ATA 7167	MT 4
ATA 7187	MM 7
ATA 7219	MH 3
ATA 7225	MH 3
ATA 7232	MH 3
ATA 7239	MT 4
ATA 7240	MT 4
ATA 7266	MH 3
ATA 7266	MT 4
ATA 7269	MH 2
ATA 7296	MH 2
ATA 7297	MH 2
ATA 7320	MM 7
ATA 7326	MH 2
ATA 7326	MT 4
ATA 7328	MH 3
ATA 7329	MH 2
ATA 7353	MT 4
C–ATA 7354	MT 4
ATA 7458	MM 6
ATA 7459	MM 6
ATA 7618	MH 2
ATC 4246	MK 2
AUC 1025	MT 6
AUC 1123	MT 7
AUC 1123	MT 9
AUC 1147	MT 8
AUC 1147	MT 10
AUC 1151	MT 7
AUC 1151	MT 9
AUC 1152	MT 8
AUC 1152	MT 10
AUC 1158	MT 7
AUC 1158	MT 9
AUC 1249	MT 7
AUC 1249	MT 9
AUC 1250	MT 7

Part Number Index—*continued*

Part Number	Page	Part Number	Page	Part Number	Page	Part Number	Page	Part Number	Page
AUC 1250	MT 9	AUC 4667	MT 7	BFS 355	MN 9	C-BHA 4448	MT 4	BTA 744	MK 2
AUC 1289	MT 7	AUC 4667	MT 9	BFS 355	MN 13	C-BHA 4449	MT 4	BTA 745	MK 2
AUC 1358	MT 7	AUC 4719	MT 7	BFS 355	MN 13·1	BHA 4514	MN 19	BTA 789	MK 4·1
AUC 1358	MT 5	AUC 4719	MT 9	BFS 370	MN 7·1	BHA 4548	MM 4	BTA 792	MK 2
AUC 1358	MT 7	AUC 4900	MT 7	BFS 380	MN 10			BTA 793	MK 2
AUC 1358	MT 9	AUC 4900	MT 9	BFS 380	MN 16	BLA 768	MF 7	C-BTA 816	MT 4
AUC 1384	MT 7	AUC 5004	MT 7	BFS 382	MN 10	BLA 768	MF 12	C-BTA 881	MT 4
AUC 1384	MT 9	AUC 5004	MT 9	BFS 382	MN 16	BLA 768	MF 17	C-BTA 940	MT 4
AUC 1387	MT 7	AUC 5009	MT 7	BFS 410	MN 7·2				
AUC 1388	MT 7	AUC 5009	MT 9	BFS 410	MN 14	BLS 107	MF 4	BTB 440	MH 3
AUC 1388	MT 9	AUC 5047	MT 6	BFS 411	MN 8	BLS 107	MF 5		
AUC 1389	MT 7	AUC 5058	MT 6	BFS 411	MN 8·1	BLS 107	MF 10	BTC 114	MK 4·1
AUC 1389	MT 9	AUC 8182	MT 7	BFS 411	MN 15	BLS 107	MF 11		
AUC 1534	MT 7	AUC 8182	MT 9	BFS 414	MN 7	BLS 107	MF 15	C4 110	MT 4
AUC 1534	MT 9	AUC 8209	MT 7	BFS 415	MN 9	BLS 107	MF 16		
AUC 1557	MT 8	AUC 8209	MT 9	BFS 415	MN 13	BLS 107	MT 4	CCN 210	MA 34
AUC 1557	MT 10	AUC 8396	MT 7	BFS 415	MN 13·1	BLS 110	MF 3	CCN 214	ME 8
AUC 1832	MT 8	AUC 8396	MT 9	BFS 987	MN 22	BLS 110	MF 7		
AUC 1867	MT 8	C-AUC 9353	MT 7	BFS 987	MN 24	BLS 110	MF 9	CHR 0307	MM 4
AUC 1867	MT 10	C-AUC 9354	MT 9	BFS 989	MN 10	BLS 110	MF 12	CHR 0405	MN 23
AUC 1928	MT 8			BFS 989	MN 17	BLS 110	MF 14	CHR 0405	MN 25
AUC 1928	MT 10	C-AUD 194	MT 6			BLS 110	MF 17		
AUC 2057	MT 7	AUD 1005	MT 7	BHA 4086	MO 3	BLS 112	MA 13	CHS 0415	MA 17
AUC 2057	MT 9	AUD 1005	MT 9	BHA 4086	MO 5			CHS 0522	MA 7
AUC 2106	MT 7	AUD 2283	MT 8	BHA 4092	MN 7·2	BMK 356	MB 8	CHS 2515	MA 37
AUC 2106	MT 9	AUD 2284	MT 10	BHA 4093	MN 8	BMK 403	MN 22	CHS 2620	MA 31
AUC 2114	MT 7	AUD 2285	MT 8	BHA 4130	MN 23	BMK 449	MN 24	CHS 2620	MA 45
AUC 2114	MT 9	AUD 2285	MT 10	BHA 4148	MN 10				
AUC 2117	MT 7	AUD 9024	MT 9	BHA 4151	MN 20	BNN 105	MA 17	CLZ 0314	MM 6
AUC 2117	MT 9	AUD 9047	MT 7	BHA 4151	MN 21	BNN 105	MA 31	CLZ 0514	MM 6
AUC 2118	MT 7	AUD 9096	MT 8	BHA 4153	MN 10	BNN 105	MA 45	CLZ 0515	MM 6
AUC 2118	MT 9	AUD 9096	MT 10	BHA 4153	MN 17	BNN 105	MA 47	CLZ 0517	ME 8
AUC 2119	MT 7	AUD 9500	MT 7	BHA 4163	MP 2				
AUC 2119	MT 9	AUD 9500	MT 9	BHA 4164	MP 2	BRT 2413	MD 3	CMZ 0210	MT 11
AUC 2120	MT 7			BHA 4175	MN 16			CMZ 0318	MN 6
AUC 2120	MT 9	AWZ 104	MM 6	BHA 4176	MN 16	BTA 108	MH 3	CMZ 0407	MK 4
AUC 2121	MT 7			BHA 4186	MN 18	BTA 339	MK 3	CMZ 0410	MH 3
AUC 2121	MT 9	1B 2121	MB 5	BHA 4186	MN 19	BTA 370	MK 4	CMZ 0410	MH 5
AUC 2122	MT 7	1B 2697	MA 49	BHA 4204	MN 16	BTA 372	MK 4·1		
AUC 2122	MT 9	1B 2802	MN 22	BHA 4208	MO 5	BTA 373	MK 4·1	CPS 0204	MT 7
AUC 2139	MT 8	1B 2802	MN 25	BHA 4209	MO 5	BTA 382	MK 2	CPS 0204	MT 9
AUC 2139	MT 10	1B 2925	MA 9	BHA 4210	MO 5	BTA 383	MK 4		
AUC 2141	MT 8	1B 2925	MA 24	BHA 4211	MO 5	BTA 384	MK 3	8D 5768	MN 20
AUC 2141	MT 10	1B 2925	MA 38	BHA 4212	MO 5	BTA 442	MK 2	8D 5678	MN 21
AUC 2144	MT 7	1B 3346	MF 3	BHA 4213	MO 5	BTA 443	MK 2		
AUC 2144	MT 9	1B 3346	MF 9	BHA 4214	MO 4	BTA 444	MK 4·1	11D 5264	MM 4
AUC 2175	MT 7	1B 3346	MF 14	BHA 4215	MO 4	BTA 466	MH 4		
AUC 2175	MT 9	1B 3498	MM 2	BHA 4216	MO 4	BTA 467	MH 4	17D 11	MA 43
AUC 2199	MT 7	1B 3664	MA 23	BHA 4217	MO 4	BTA 469	MK 4		
AUC 2199	MT 9	1B 3664	MA 37	BHA 4232	MN 25	BTA 470	MK 3	21D 69	MM 4
AUC 2381	MT 7	1B 3664	MA 35	BHA 4233	MN 25	BTA 471	MK 3		
AUC 2381	MT 9	1B 4316	MK 3	BHA 4234	MN 6	BTA 472	MK 4	FHS 2513	MA 7
AUC 2402	MT 6	1B 5329	MM 7	BHA 4235	MN 7·2	BTA 473	MK 4		
AUC 2451	MT 7	1B 7356	MT 11	BHA 4235	MN 8	BTA 488	MH 3	FLS 2513	MA 7
AUC 2451	MT 9	1B 7364	MM 6	BHA 4235	MN 9	BTA 489	MH 3		
AUC 2521	MT 7	1B 8077	MP 2	BHA 4235	MN 9·1	BTA 490	MH 3	FNN 104	MA 23
AUC 2521	MT 9	1B 8078	MP 2	BHA 4235	MN 11	BTA 491	MH 3	FNN 104	MA 37
AUC 2669	MT 6	1B 8806	MA 43	BHA 4235	MN 12	BTA 492	MH 3	FNN 105	MA 8
AUC 2698	MT 8	1B 8995	MR 2	BHA 4235	MN 13	BTA 493	MH 5	FNN 105	MA 23
AUC 2698	MT 10	1B 9007	MN 18	BHA 4235	MN 14	BTA 494	MM 6	FNN 105	MA 37
AUC 3116	MT 7	1B 9008	MN 18	BHA 4235	MN 15	BTA 495	MM 6	FNN 107	MH 2
AUC 3116	MT 9	1B 9100	MN 10	BHA 4237	MN 6	BTA 497	MM 6	FNN 207	MN 3
AUC 3212	MT 7	1B 9132	MO 3	BHA 4242	MN 16	BTA 498	MM 6	FNN 504	MF 9
AUC 3200	MT 8	1B 9132	MO 5	BHA 4247	MN 11	BTA 501	MH 3	FNN 504	MF 14
AUC 3200	MT 10			BHA 4249	MO 4	BTA 532	MH 3	FNN 612	MH 3
AUC 3230	MT 7	4B 2502	MJ 3	BHA 4250	MO 4	BTA 535	MT 4		
AUC 3230	MT 9			BHA 4253	MO 2	BTA 539	MH 3	FNZ 103	MD 2
AUC 3231	MT 7	11B 542	MA 49	BHA 4254	MP 2	BTA 549	MH 2	FNZ 103	MK 2
AUC 3231	MT 9	11B 542	MT 6	BHA 4257	MN 25	BTA 550	MH 2	FNZ 103	MN 6
AUC 3232	MT 7	11B 543	MA 49	BHA 4258	MP 2	BTA 566	MH 4	FNZ 103	MN 9·1
AUC 3232	MT 9	11B 543	MT 6	BHA 4259	MP 2	BTA 567	MH 4	FNZ 103	MN 18
AUC 3233	MT 7	11B 2037	MO 2	BHA 4265	MN 6	BTA 568	MH 2	FNZ 103	MN 23
AUC 3233	MT 9	11B 2037	MO 4	BHA 4311	MM 4	BTA 569	MH 2	FNZ 103	MT 11
AUC 3495	MT 9			BHA 4365	MM 3	BTA 600	MK 2	FNZ 104	MA 7
AUC 3496	MT 7	14B 5588	MN 20	BHA 4368	MR 2	BTA 601	MK 2	FNZ 104	MA 47
AUC 3513	MT 9			BHA 4372	MO 5	BTA 606	MK 2	FNZ 104	MA 48
AUC 4045	MT 7	BCA 4031	MM 4	BHA 4373	MO 5	BTA 607	MK 2	FNZ 104	MB 5
AUC 4045	MT 9	BCA 4163	MP 2	BHA 4380	MO 5	BTA 613	MK 2	FNZ 104	MB 8
AUC 4334	MT 6	BCA 4294	MN 6	BHA 4381	MO 4	BTA 648	MK 2	FNZ 104	MB 11
AUC 4454	MT 6	BCA 4308	MN 6	BHA 4382	MO 4	BTA 649	MK 2	FNZ 104	MC 2
AUC 4587	MT 7			BHA 4383	MO 4	BTA 652	MK 4·1	FNZ 104	MD 3
AUC 4587	MT 9	BFS 222	MN 16	BHA 4444	MN 19	BTA 653	MK 4·1	FNZ 104	MD 5
AUC 4612	MT 6	BFS 323	MN 17	BHA 4445	MN 19	C-BTA 696	MT 4	FNZ 104	MF 3

Part Number Index—*continued*

Part Number	Page	Part Number	Page	Part Number	Page	Part Number	Page	Part Number	Page
FNZ 104	MF 9	1G 2716	MA 15	8G 0745 20	MA 34	8G 8446	ME 8	12G 296	MA 37
FNZ 104	MF 14	1G 2984	MA 6	8G 2198	MA 5	8G 8452	MJ 2	12G 297	MA 45
FNZ 104	MM 5	1G 2984	MA 22	8G 2198	MA 21	8G 8646	MH 4	12G 300	MA 17
FNZ 104	MN 2	1G 2984	MA 36	8G 2198	MA 35	8G 8647	MH 4	12G 300	MA 30
FNZ 104	MN 18	1G 3584	MH 2	8G 2198 10	MA 5	8G 8667	MK 4·1	12G 300	MA 31
FNZ 104	MN 19	1G 3530	MF 16	8G 2198 10	MA 21	8G 8668	MK 4·1	12G 300	MA 44
FNZ 104	MO 3	1G 3667	MF 3	8G 2198 10	MA 35	8G 8670	MK 4	12G 300	MA 45
FNZ 104	MO 5	1G 3667	MF 9	8G 2198 20	MA 5	8G 8671	MH 4	12G 301	MA 45
FNZ 105	MA 9	1G 3707	MF 6	8G 2198 20	MA 21	8G 8672	MH 4	12G 0303 03	MA 34
FNZ 105	MA 24	1G 3707	MF 12	8G 2198 20	MA 35	8G 8672	MK 4	12G 0303 06	MA 34
FNZ 105	MA 38	1G 3707	MF 17	8G 2198 30	MA 5	8G 8741	MH 5	12G 0303 13	MA 34
FNZ 105	MA 39	1G 3709	MF 6	8G 2198 30	MA 21	8G 8762	MH 4	12G 0303 16	MA 34
FNZ 105	MA 46	1G 3863	MF 6	8G 2198 30	MA 35	8G 8763	MH 4	12G 0303 23	MA 34
FNZ 105	MA 47	1G 3863	MF 12	8G 2198 40	MA 5	8G 8766	MM 3	12G 0303 26	MA 34
FNZ 105	MD 2	1G 3863	MF 17	8G 2198 40	MA 21	8G 8813	MK 4·1	12G 0306 03	MA 34
FNZ 105	ME 7	1G 7439	MH 3	8G 2198 40	MA 35	8G 8979	MG 2	12G 0306 06	MA 34
FNZ 105	MF 3	1G 9198	MM 4	8G 2200	MA 16			12G 0306 13	MA 34
FNZ 105	MF 7			8G 2205	MD 4	11G 145	MA 38	12G 0306 16	MA 34
FNZ 105	MF 9	4G 6680	MN 2	8G 2206	MD 4	11G 214	MA 38	12G 0306 23	MA 34
FNZ 105	MF 12			8G 2222	MA 5	11G 221	MB 5	12G 0306 26	MA 34
FNZ 105	MF 17	8G 10	MA 3	8G 2222	MA 21	11G 291	MA 9	12G 312	MA 35
FNZ 105	MH 2	8G 16	MA 19	8G 2222 10	MA 5	11G 292	MA 38	12G 314	MA 43
FNZ 105	MH 4	8G 17	MA 19	8G 2222 10	MA 21	11G 2007	MN 5	12G 330	MA 9
FNZ 105	MH 6	8G 124	MA 33	8G 2222 20	MA 5	11G 2034	MA 48	12G 330	MA 16
FNZ 105	MK 2	8G 125	MA 33	8G 2222 20	MA 21	11G 9093	MN 5	12G 330	MA 24
FNZ 105	MM 2	8G 135	MA 33	8G 2222 30	MA 5			12G 330	MA 30
FNZ 105	MM 7	8G 136	MA 33	8G 2222 30	MA 21	12G 14	MA 38	12G 330	MA 38
FNZ 105	MN 6	8G 505	MD 2	8G 2222 40	MA 5	12G 50	MA 12	12G 330	MA 44
FNZ 105	MN 18	8G 531	MD 5	8G 2222 40	MA 21	12G 50	MA 26	12G 335	MB 10
FNZ 105	MT 11	8G 548	MN 5	8G 2232	MA 16	12G 50	MA 40	12G 337	MB 10
FNZ 106	MA 15	8G 549	MA 5	8G 2232	MA 30	12G 55	MA 34	12G 346	MB 11
FNZ 106	MA 29	8G 548	MN 6	8G 2232	MA 44	12G 0055 10	MA 34	12G 347	MB 11
FNZ 106	MA 43	8G 549	MA 21	8G 2268	MA 16	12G 0055 20	MA 34	12G 348	MB 11
FNZ 106	MA 46	8G 549	MA 35	8G 2312	MA 14	12G 56	MA 34	12G 349	MB 11
FNZ 106	ML 2	8G 550	MC 2	8G 2318	MA 16	12G 0056 10	MA 34	12G 350	MB 11
FNZ 106	MM 3	8G 576	MB 11	8G 2320	MA 30	12G 0056 20	MA 34	12G 377	MA 30
FNZ 106	MM 4	8G 589	MK 3	8G 2332	MA 35	12G 57	MA 34	12G 378	MA 30
FNZ 106	MM 6	8G 612	MA 9	8G 2332 10	MA 35	12G 0057	MA 34	12G 422	MA 39
FNZ 106	MN 4	8G 612	MA 24	8G 2332 20	MA 35	12G 0057 20	MA 34	12G 437	MB 10
FNZ 107	MH 6	8G 616	MB 5	8G 2332 30	MA 35	12G 69	MA 12	12G 583	MA 45
FNZ 107	ML 2	8G 621	MK 5	8G 2332 40	MA 35	12G 69	MA 16	12G 619	MA 5
FNZ 204	MA 48	8G 654	MD 2	8G 2361	MA 14	12G 69	MA 26	12G 619	MA 16
FNZ 204	ME 8	8G 664	MF 4	8G 2361	MA 28	12G 69	MA 30	12G 619	MA 21
FNZ 204	MM 2	8G 664	MF 10	8G 2361	MA 42	12G 69	MA 40	12G 619	MA 30
FNZ 205	MH 6	8G 664	MF 15	8G 2402	MA 30	12G 69	MA 44	12G 619	MA 44
FNZ 205	MM 2	8G 684	MA 13	8G 2402	MA 44	12G 93	MA 35	12G 695	MB 10
FNZ 206	MA 49	8G 684	MA 27	8G 2422	MA 35	12G 107	MA 40	12G 721	MA 37
FNZ 206	MD 5	8G 684	MA 41	8G 2422 03	MA 35	12G 114	MA 38	12G 791	MA 10
FNZ 206	MN 5	8G 0687 03	MA 4	8G 2422 30	MA 35	12G 120	MA 14	12G 791	MA 25
FNZ 206	MN 6	8G 0687 06	MA 4	8G 2423	MA 35	12G 120	MA 28	12G 791	MA 39
FNZ 210	MJ 2	8G 0687 13	MA 4	8G 2423 03	MA 35	12G 120	MA 42	12G 793	MA 12
FNZ 306	MK 5	8G 0687 16	MA 4	8G 2423 30	MA 35	12G 123	MA 35	12G 793	MA 26
FNZ 307	MK 2	8G 0687 23	MA 4	8G 2441 03	MA 34	12G 126	MA 35	12G 793	MA 40
FNZ 407	MJ 2	8G 0687 26	MA 4	8G 2441 06	MA 34	12G 148	MA 16	12G 793	MT 3
FNZ 506	MH 5	8G 0687 33	MA 4	8G 2441 13	MA 34	12G 148	MA 30	12G 1109	MA 8
		8G 0687 36	MA 4	8G 2441 16	MA 34	12G 148	MA 41	12G 1109	MA 23
1G 752	MA 10	8G 0687 43	MA 4	8G 2441 23	MA 34	12G 152	MA 39	12G 1109	MA 37
1G 752	MA 25	8G 0687 46	MA 4	8G 2441 26	MA 34	12G 163	MA 33	12G 1110	MA 8
1G 752	MA 39	8G 697	MA 14	8G 2443 03	MA 34	12G 165	MA 35	12G 1110	MA 23
1G 752	MF 3	8G 697	MA 28	8G 2443 06	MA 34	12G 173	MA 11	12G 1110	MA 37
1G 752	MF 9	8G 698	MA 14	8G 2443 13	MA 34	12G 173	MA 26	12G 1284	MA 14
1G 752	MF 14	8G 698	MA 28	8G 2443 16	MA 34	12G 173	MA 40	12G 1284	MA 28
1G 1167	MA 5	8G 712	MA 5	8G 2443 23	MA 34	12G 175	MA 40	12G 1284	MA 42
1G 1167	MA 21	8G 716	MA 11	8G 2443 26	MA 34	12G 180	MA 36	12G 1925	MT 2
1G 1167	MA 35	8G 716	MA 26	8G 2565	MB 5	12G 200	ME 7	12G 1926	MT 2
1G 1319	MA 5	8G 722	MA 11	8G 2565	MB 8	12G 209	MA 37	12G 1927	MT 2
1G 1319	MA 21	8G 722	MA 26	8G 2565	MB 11	12G 233	MB 10		
1G 1319	MA 35	8G 725	MA 5	8G 2570	MA 14	12G 243	MA 38	14G 3722	MN 20
1G 1365	MA 16	8G 725	MA 21	8G 2570	MA 28	12G 267	MA 37	14G 3722	MN 21
1G 1452	MA 12	8G 726	MB 10	8G 2570	MA 42	12G 270	MA 34	14G 5508	MN 2
1G 1452	MA 26	8G 731	MA 11	8G 3000	MG 2	12G 0270 10	MA 34	14G 7532	MN 2
1G 1452	MA 40	8G 731	MA 26	8G 4177	MK 2	12G 0270 20	MA 34	18G 8328	MH 4
1G 1783	MA 15	8G 731	MA 30	8G 4195	MK 2	12G 275	MA 39	18G 8329	MH 4
1G 1783	MA 26	8G 731	MA 40	8G 4208	MK 2	12G 276	MA 39	18G 8581	MA 47
1G 2062	MA 6	8G 731	MA 44	8G 7129	MT 4	12G 278	MA 39		
1G 2062	MA 22	8G 731	MT 3	8G 8146	ME 8	12G 289	MA 43	21G 5077	MA 48
1G 2062	MA 36	8G 733	MA 14	8G 8224	MM 3	12G 290	MA 36	21G 5078	MA 48
1G 2613	MN 5	8G 733	MA 28	8G 8243	MH 5	12G 293	MA 8	21G 9057	MN 7
1G 2624	MA 16	8G 733	MA 42	8G 8245	MK 4	12G 293	MA 16	21G 9057	MN 7·1
1G 2624	MA 30	8G 743	MF 15	8G 8255	MH 5	12G 293	MA 23	21G 9057	MN 7·2
1G 2624	MA 44	8G 743	MF 16	8G 8345	ME 3	12G 293	MA 30	21G 9057	MN 8
1G 2624	MD 5	8G 745	MA 34	8G 8345	ME 5	12G 293	MA 37	21G 9057	MN 8·1
1G 2673	MB 5	8G 0745 10	MA 34	8G 8347	ME 7	12G 293	MA 44	21G 9057	MN 9

Part Number Index—*continued*

Part Number	Page	Part Number	Page	Part Number	Page	Part Number	Page	Part Number	Page
21G 9057	MN 9·1	38G 316	MF 14	1H 3101	MF 6	3H 2138	MB 3	7H 1761	MA 41
21G 9057	MN 11	38G 319	MA 35	1H 3101	MF 7	3H 2138	MB 4	7H 1764	MA 13
21G 9057	MN 12	38G 336	MA 33	1H 3101	MF 12	3H 2138	MB 7	7H 1764	MA 27
21G 9057	MN 13	38G 337	MA 33	1H 3101	MF 17	3H 2138	MB 10	7H 1764	MA 41
21G 9057	MN 13·1			1H 3364	MH 2	3H 2138	MT 5	7H 1765	MA 13
21G 9057	MN 14	88G 202	MA 35	1H 9047	MO 2	3H 2192	MM 7	7H 1765	MA 27
21G 9057	MN 15	88G 203	MB 5	1H 9047	MO 5	3H 2274	MR 2	7H 1765	MA 41
21G 9057	MN 16	88G 205	MA 27	1H 9049	MO 2	3H 2287	MM 4	7H 1840	MA 13
		88G 208	MF 6	1H 9049	MO 5	3H 2287	MM 5	7H 1840	MA 27
22G 64	MF 15	88G 214	MF 3			3H 2424	MM 5	7H 1840	MA 41
22G 64	MF 16	88G 214	MF 9	2H 400	MM 4	3H 2428	ME 3	7H 3004	ME 3
22G 76	MF 15	88G 214	MF 14	2H 964	MA 23	3H 2428	MK 4	7H 3004	ME 5
22G 110	MF 7	88G 215	MA 14	2H 1082	MD 2	3H 2428	MM 5	7H 3008	ME 7
22G 110	MF 12	88G 215	MA 16	2H 1683	MR 2	3H 2518	MN 7	7H 3009	ME 7
22G 110	MF 17	88G 215	MA 28	2H 2617	MN 22	3H 2520	MN 7·1	7H 3025	ME 3
22G 118	MF 14	88G 215	MA 30	2H 2617	MN 24	3H 2521	MN 8	7H 3025	ME 5
22G 146	MF 15	88G 215	MA 42	2H 2649	MR 2	3H 2648	MR 2	7H 3028	ME 3
22G 147	MF 16	88G 215	MA 44	2H 2704	MN 22	3H 2686	MD 5	7H 3028	ME 5
22G 148	MF 16	88G 216	MF 5	2H 2704	MN 24	3H 2687	MA 16	7H 3029	ME 3
22G 149	MF 16	88G 216	MF 11	2H 3406	MN 22	3H 2687	MD 5	7H 3029	ME 5
22G 150	MF 15	88G 216	MF 16	2H 3406	MN 24	3H 2695	MB 5	7H 3031	ME 3
22G 152	MF 17	88G 217	MF 6	2H 4185	MN 5	3H 2695	MB 8	7H 3031	ME 5
22G 154	MF 16	88G 217	MF 12	2H 4185	MN 6	3H 2695	MB 11	7H 3036	ME 3
22G 155	MF 16	88G 218	MF 6	2H 4243	MB 5	3H 2696	MB 5	7H 3036	ME 5
22G 156	MF 16	88G 218	MF 12	2H 4243	MB 8	3H 2696	MB 11	7H 3043	ME 7
22G 157	MF 16	88G 219	MT 2	2H 4243	MB 11	3H 2962	MN 7	7H 3057	ME 7
22G 161	MF 16	88G 221	MA 7	2H 4244	MB 5	3H 2962	MN 7·1	7H 3060	ME 7
22G 165	MF 14	88G 221	MA 16	2H 4244	MB 8	3H 2962	MN 7·2	7H 3061	ME 7
22G 165	MT 4	88G 221	MA 23	2H 4244	MB 11	3H 2962	MN 8	7H 3078	ME 7
22G 168	ME 7	88G 221	MA 30	2H 4245	MB 5	3H 2962	MN 9	7H 3166	ME 3
22G 172	MF 15	88G 221	MA 37	2H 4245	MB 8	3H 2962	MN 13	7H 3166	ME 5
22G 173	MF 17	88G 221	MA 44	2H 4245	MB 11	3H 2962	MN 14	7H 3181	ME 3
22G 199	MF 14	88G 225	MA 5	2H 4246	MB 5	3H 2962	MN 15	7H 3181	ME 5
22G 240	MT 4	88G 225	MA 21	2H 4246	MB 8	3H 2963	MA 9	7H 3185	ME 3
22G 242	MF 5	88G 226	MA 10	2H 4246	MB 11	3H 2963	MA 24	7H 3185	ME 5
22G 257	MF 16	88G 226	MA 25	2H 4614	MR 2	3H 2963	MA 38	7H 3207	ME 7
22G 277	MF 4	88G 227	MA 6	2H 4927	ME 7	3H 2963	MJ 2	7H 3209	ME 7
22G 277	MF 10	88G 227	MA 22	2H 4992	MN 22	3H 3076	MA 47	7H 3221	ME 3
22G 277	MF 15	88G 229	MT 2			3H 3095	MN 5	7H 3221	ME 5
22G 278	MF 4	88G 257	MA 11	3H 550	MM 4	3H 3100	MN 5	7H 3222	ME 3
22G 278	MF 10	88G 257	MA 26	3H 550	MM 5	3H 3100	MN 6	7H 3222	ME 5
22G 278	MF 15	88G 257	MA 40	3H 576	MA 3			7H 3565	MJ 2
C-22G 304	MT 4	88G 274	MK 5	3H 576	MA 19	7H 25	MA 13	7H 3762	MJ 2
C-22G 305	MT 4	88G 278	MH 6	3H 576	MA 33	7H 25	MA 27	7H 3763	MJ 2
C-22G 306	MT 4	88G 291	MC 2	3H 688	MO 4	7H 25	MA 41	7H 3858	MG 2
22G 317	MF 15	88G 292	MA 47	3H 822	MO 3	7H 28	MA 13	7H 3874	MG 2
22G 317	MF 16	88G 294	MN 2	3H 822	MO 5	7H 28	MA 27	7H 3877	MG 2
22G 317	MT 4	88G 295	MM 6	3H 914	MN 22	7H 28	MA 41	7H 5028	MN 3
22G 318	MF 15	88G 308	MO 3	3H 949	MN 5	7H 147	MA 13	7H 5031	MN 3
22G 326	MT 4	88G 308	MO 4	3H 949	MN 6	7H 147	MA 27	7H 5034	MN 3
22G 328	MF 17	88G 320	MH 3	3H 950	MN 5	7H 147	MA 41	7H 5038	MN 4
22G 374	MF 5	88G 321	MK 3	3H 950	MN 6	7H 813	MD 4	7H 5039	MN 4
22G 673	MT 4	88G 322	MH 3	3H 952	MN 4	7H 816	MD 4	7H 5040	MN 4
		88G 322	MK 3	3H 1031	MN 7	7H 1379	MD 4	7H 5041	MN 4
24G 1345	MN 5	88G 329	MR 2	3H 1031	MN 7·1	7H 1381	MD 4	7H 5042	MN 4
24G 1345	MN 6	88G 349	MA 48	3H 1031	MN 7·2	7H 1382	MD 4	7H 5043	MN 4
		88G 396	MF 4	3H 1031	MN 8	7H 1384	MD 4	7H 5045	MN 4
28G 84	MA 3	88G 396	MF 10	3H 1031	MN 9	7H 1386	MD 4	7H 5046	MN 4
28G 85	MA 3	88G 396	MF 15	3H 1031	MN 13	7H 1387	MD 4	7H 5047	MN 4
28G 87	MF 3	88G 402	MA 13	3H 1031	MN 14	7H 1388	MD 4	7H 5048	MN 4
28G 87	MF 9	88G 402	MA 16	3H 1031	MN 15	7H 1389	MD 4	7H 5049	MN 4
28G 95	MA 5	88G 402	MA 27	3H 1422	MB 5	7H 1390	MD 4	7H 5050	MN 4
28G 95	MA 21	88G 402	MA 30	3H 1422	MB 8	7H 1391	MD 4	7H 5051	MN 4
28G 111	MF 3	88G 402	MA 41	3H 1557	MN 5	7H 1392	MD 4	7H 5062	MN 8
28G 130	MA 19	88G 402	MA 44	3H 1558	MN 5	7H 1393	MD 4	7H 5066	MN 5
28G 131	MA 19	88G 409	MF 10	3H 1655	MB 5	7H 1483	MD 4	7H 5066	MN 6
28G 133	MA 19	88G 409	MF 15	3H 1656	MB 5	7H 1561	MD 4	7H 5067	MN 5
28G 133	MA 33	88G 411	MA 12	3H 1657	MB 5	7H 1666	MD 4	7H 5067	MN 6
28G 134	MF 10	88G 411	MA 16	3H 1658	MB 5	7H 1667	MD 4	7H 5071	MN 8
28G 137	MA 3	88G 411	MA 26	3H 1813	MN 10	7H 1670	MD 4	7H 5086	MB 3
28G 138	MA 3	88G 411	MA 30	3H 1835	MN 5	7H 1679	MD 4	7H 5086	MB 4
28G 139	MA 19	88G 411	MA 40	3H 1894	MM 5	7H 1709	MP 2	7H 5086	MB 7
28G 140	MA 19	88G 411	MA 44	3H 2006	MA 9	7H 1756	MA 13	7H 5086	MB 10
28G 152	MF 9	88G 414	MJ 2	3H 2006	MA 24	7H 1756	MA 27	7H 5086	MT 5
28G 161	MA 7	88G 446	MA 14	3H 2006	MA 38	7H 1756	MA 41	7H 5111	MN 10
28G 191	MA 37	88G 446	MA 28	3H 2098	MA 15	7H 1758	MA 13	7H 5121	MN 10
28G 222	MA 37	88G 446	MA 42	3H 2098	MA 29	7H 1758	MA 27	7H 5122	MN 10
				3H 2110	MF 6	7H 1758	MA 41	7H 5123	MN 10
38G 306	MA 33	1H 529	MD 5	3H 2110	MF 12	7H 1759	MA 13	7H 5123	MN 17
38G 307	MA 33	1H 998	MA 15	3H 2118	MH 3	7H 1759	MA 27	7H 5128	MN 5
38G 310	MA 33	1H 998	MA 29	3H 2127	MA 5	7H 1759	MA 41	7H 5128	MN 6
38G 311	MA 33	1H 998	MA 43	3H 2127	MA 21	7H 1761	MA 13	7H 5130	MN 20
38G 313	MF 14	1H 2181	MD 3	3H 2127	MA 35	7H 1761	MA 27	7H 5130	MN 21

Part Number Index—*continued*

Part Number	Page	Part Number	Page	Part Number	Page	Part Number	Page	Part Number	Page
7H 5156	MN 4	12H 941	MA 10	13H 2526	MA 24	17H 1496	MO 5	17H 5146	MN 8
7H 5164	MN 10	12H 941	MA 25	13H 2782	MN 18	17H 1497	MO 3	17H 5147	MN 7
7H 5164	MN 17	12H 941	MA 39	13H 2792	MA 6	17H 1497	MO 5	17H 5147	MN 7·1
7H 5182	MN 10	12H 948	MA 10	13H 2792	MA 22	17H 1498	MO 3	17H 5147	MN 7·2
7H 5185	MN 10	12H 948	MA 25	13H 2792	MA 36	17H 1498	MO 5	17H 5147	MN 8
7H 5185	MN 17	12H 948	MA 39	13H 2972	MJ 3	17H 1499	MO 3	17H 5147	MN 8·1
7H 5202	MN 10	12H 1001	MD 3	13H 2584	MA 9	17H 1499	MO 5	17H 5147	MN 9
7H 5376	MN 3	12H 1734	MA 3	13H 3249	MA 13	17H 1642	MO 2	17H 5147	MN 9·1
7H 5388	MN 3	12H 1734	MA 19	13H 3249	MA 27	17H 1642	MO 4	17H 5147	MN 11
7H 5390	MN 3	12H 1734	MA 33	13H 3249	MA 41	17H 1650	MA 12	17H 5147	MN 13
7H 5483	MN 7			13H 3584	MA 24	17H 1658	MO 5	17H 5147	MN 14
7H 5485	MN 7·1	13H 21	ME 8	13H 3584	MA 38	17H 1669	MO 2	17H 5147	MN 15
7H 5486	MN 8	13H 23	MN 10	13H 3585	MA 9	17H 1669	MO 5	17H 5205	MN 7
7H 5522	MN 5	13H 50	MR 2	13H 3585	MA 24	17H 1678	MO 3	17H 5205	MN 7·1
7H 5522	MN 6	13H 66	MN 20	13H 3585	MA 38	17H 1678	MO 5	17H 5205	MN 7·2
7H 5527	MN 3	13H 66	MN 21	13H 3586	MA 9	17H 1679	MO 3	17H 5205	MN 8
7H 5529	MN 4	13H 68	MN 20	13H 3586	MA 24	17H 1679	MO 5	17H 5205	MN 9
7H 5536	MN 16	13H 68	MN 21	13H 3586	MA 38	17H 1822	MO 2	17H 5205	MN 13
7H 5944	MM 6	13H 69	MN 18	13H 3727	MA 9	17H 1963	MA 12	17H 5205	MN 13·1
7H 5945	MM 6	13H 72	MA 48	13H 3727	MA 24	17H 1963	MA 40	17H 5205	MN 14
7H 5946	MM 6	13H 80	ME 8	13H 3727	MA 38	17H 1964	MA 12	17H 5205	MN 15
7H 5947	MM 6	13H 83	MM 4	13H 3741	ME 7	17H 1964	MA 26	17H 5214	MN 12
7H 5948	MM 6	13H 110	MN 6	13H 4061	MA 10	17H 1964	MA 40	17H 5216	MN 16
7H 5949	MM 6	13H 135	ME 8	13H 4061	MA 25	17H 1965	MA 12	17H 5217	MN 3
7H 5950	MM 6	13H 142	MN 6	13H 4061	MA 39	17H 1965	MA 26	17H 5230	MN 9·1
7H 5951	MM 6	13H 153	MN 18	13H 4070	MA 9	17H 1965	MA 40	17H 5230	MN 12
7H 6807	MA 12	13H 176	MN 6	13H 4070	MA 24	17H 1964	MA 12	17H 5231	MN 7
7H 6807	MA 26	13H 184	MB 5	13H 4070	MA 38	17H 1964	MA 26	17H 5231	MN 7·1
7H 6808	MA 12	13H 184	MB 8	13H 4180	MJ 3	17H 1965	MA 12	17H 5231	MN 7·2
7H 6808	MA 26	13H 219	MN 3			17H 1965	MA 26	17H 5231	MN 8
7H 6810	MA 12	13H 252	MN 6	17H 4	MA 13	17H 2091	MM 6	17H 5231	MN 9
7H 6810	MA 26	13H 346	MN 9·1	17H 4	MA 27	17H 2093	MM 6	17H 5231	MN 9·1
7H 6813	MA 12	13H 412	MP 2	17H 4	MA 41	17H 2095	MM 6	17H 5231	MN 12
7H 6813	MA 26	13H 428	MN 16	17H 98	MD 4	17H 2460	MK 4·1	17H 5231	MN 13
7H 6838	MN 7	13H 429	MN 16	17H 689	MO 2	17H 2461	MK 4·1	17H 5231	MN 13·1
7H 6838	MN 7·1	13H 472	MN 19	17H 690	MO 2	17H 2639	MB 4	17H 5231	MN 14
7H 6838	MN 13·1	13H 473	MN 19	17H 843	MO 2	17H 2707	MN 20	17H 5231	MN 15
7H 6887	MN 4	13H 496	MN 11	17H 843	MO 5	17H 2721	ME 7	17H 5255	MN 20
7H 6894	MB 11	13H 559	MN 4	17H 844	MO 2	17H 2805	MJ 3	17H 5255	MN 21
7H 6915	MN 8	13H 565	MN 7	17H 844	MO 5	17H 2807	MJ 3	17H 5273	MN 9·1
7H 6993	MH 5	13H 565	MN 7·2	17H 856	MD 4	17H 2824	MH 5	17H 5273	MN 12
7H 7022	MM 3	13H 565	MN 8·1	17H 860	MD 4	17H 2825	MH 5	17H 5277	MN 9·1
7H 7368	MK 4	13H 565	MN 9·1	17H 861	MD 4	17H 2826	MH 5	17H 5277	MN 12
7H 7398	MH 4	13H 565	MN 11	17H 932	MO 2	17H 2827	MH 5	17H 5306	MN 7
7H 7398	MK 4	13H 565	MN 13	17H 932	MO 4	17H 2877	MA 13	17H 5306	MN 7·1
7H 7484	MM 3	13H 565	MN 14	17H 942	MA 13	17H 2877	MA 27	17H 5306	MN 9
7H 7487	MM 3	13H 565	MN 15	17H 942	MA 27	17H 3613	MP 2	17H 5306	MN 13
7H 7488	MM 3	13H 568	MJ 3	17H 942	MA 41	17H 3687	MM 3	17H 5306	MN 13·1
7H 7520	MK 4	13H 569	MJ 3	17H 943	MA 13	17H 3719	ME 7	17H 5361	MN 20
7H 7553	MA 27	13H 579	MN 11	17H 943	MA 27	17H 3721	MM 3	17H 5375	MN 9
7H 7847	MM 5	13H 591	MA 14	17H 943	MA 41	17H 3723	MM 3	17H 5375	MN 13
7H 7923	ME 8	13H 591	MA 28	17H 944	MA 13	17H 3744	MO 5	17H 5375	MN 13·1
7H 7923	MH 5	13H 630	MA 38	17H 945	MA 13	17H 3745	MO 5	17H 5385	MN 10
7H 7925	MM 3	13H 632	MO 3	17H 945	MA 27	17H 3818	MG 2	17H 5388	MN 20
7H 7928	MH 5	13H 632	MO 5	17H 945	MA 41	17H 3819	MG 2	17H 5394	MN 7
7H 7938	MK 4	13H 709	MJ 3	17H 1148	MA 13	17H 3828	MG 2	17H 5394	MN 7·1
7H 7939	MH 5	13H 772	MA 14	17H 1148	MA 27	17H 3894	MG 2	17H 5394	MN 7·2
7H 7939	MK 4	13H 772	MA 28	17H 1148	MA 41	17H 3984	MP 2	17H 5394	MN 8
7H 7940	MH 5	13H 772	MA 42	17H 1150	MA 13	17H 5064	MB 3	17H 5394	MN 8·2
7H 7941	MK 4	13H 783	ME 7	17H 1152	MA 13	17H 5065	MB 3	17H 5394	MN 9
7H 7942	MH 5	13H 784	MO 5	17H 1167	MA 13	17H 5065	MB 4	17H 5394	MN 13
7H 7949	MK 4	13H 815	ME 7	17H 1168	MA 13	17H 5065	MB 7	17H 5394	MN 13·1
7H 7950	MK 4	13H 826	MN 3	17H 1169	MA 13	17H 5065	MB 10	17H 5394	MN 14
7H 8338	MN 8	13H 923	MA 15	17H 1169	MA 27	17H 5065	MT 5	17H 5394	MN 15
7H 8355	MM 3	13H 956	MA 38	17H 1169	MA 41	17H 5066	MB 3	17H 5395	MN 7
7H 9830	MN 5	13H 957	MA 24	17H 1170	MA 13	17H 5069	MB 3	17H 5395	MN 7·1
7H 9830	MN 6	13H 957	MA 38	17H 1172	MA 13	17H 5071	MB 3	17H 5395	MN 7·2
		13H 988	ME 7	17H 1172	MA 27	17H 5095	MB 3	17H 5395	MN 8
11H 127	MD 3	13H 989	ME 7	17H 1172	MA 41	17H 5106	MB 3	17H 5395	MN 9
11H 169	MR 2	13H 998	MA 13	17H 1173	MA 13	17H 5106	MB 4	17H 5395	MN 13
11H 1051	MR 2	13H 998	MA 27	17H 1173	MA 27	17H 5106	MB 7	17H 5395	MN 13·1
		13H 998	MA 41	17H 1173	MA 41	17H 5106	MB 10	17H 5395	MN 14
12H 152	MA 10	13H 1329	MA 43	17H 1174	MA 13	17H 5106	MT 5	17H 5395	MN 15
12H 152	MA 25	13H 1412	MA 9	17H 1304	MO 2	17H 5118	MB 3	17H 5396	MN 20
12H 152	MA 39	13H 1452	MA 38	17H 1304	MO 3	17H 5143	MN 11	17H 5396	MN 21
12H 155	MA 10	13H 1731	MM 5	17H 1304	MO 5	17H 5143	MN 12	17H 5400	MN 17
12H 155	MA 25	13H 1924	MN 24	17H 1341	MO 3	17H 5143	MN 13	17H 5401	MN 17
12H 862	MA 16	13H 1927	MN 24	17H 1341	MO 5	17H 5143	MN 13·1	17H 5421	MB 3
12H 862	MA 30	13H 2316	MA 9	17H 1344	MO 3	17H 5143	MN 14	17H 5422	MB 3
12H 862	MA 44	13H 2316	MA 24	17H 1344	MO 5	17H 5143	MN 15	17H 5422	MB 4
12H 865	MA 12	13H 2317	MA 9	17H 1476	MA 13	17H 5145	MN 7	17H 5422	MB 7
12H 865	MA 26	13H 2317	MA 24	17H 1480	MO 2	17H 5145	MN 7·1	17H 5423	MB 3
12H 865	MA 40	13H 2526	MA 9	17H 1496	MO 2	17H 5145	MN 13·1	17H 5423	MB 4

Part Number Index—*continued*

Part Number	Page	Part Number	Page	Part Number	Page	Part Number	Page	Part Number	Page
17H 5423	MB 7	17H 8100	MB 8	27H 5354	MN 7·2	27H 8215	MO 5	47H 5012	MN 20
17H 5423	MB 10	17H 8100	MB 11	27H 5354	MN 8	27H 8495	MN 7	47H 5023	MN 20
17H 5423	MT 5	17H 8152	MH 5	27H 5354	MN 8·1	27H 9162	MN 20	47H 5100	MN 4
17H 5425	MN 16	17H 8250	MK 4·1	27H 5354	MN 9	27H 9162	MN 21	47H 5124	MN 7·2
17H 5427	MN 10	17H 8399	MH 5	27H 5354	MN 9·1	27H 9391	MJ 3	47H 5124	MN 8
17H 5431	MN 20	17H 8659	MJ 3	27H 5354	MN 11	27H 9394	MJ3	47H 5124	MN 14
17H 5431	MN 21	17H 9171	MB 5	27H 5354	MN 12			47H 5124	MN 15
17H 5433	MN 3	17H 9416	MB 10	27H 5354	MN 13			47H 5125	MN 7·2
17H 5441	MN 20	17H 9438	MK 4·1	27H 5354	MN 13·1	37H 436	MA 13	47H 5125	MN 8
17H 5441	MN 21	17H 9439	MK 4·1	27H 5354	MN 14	37H 436	MA 27	47H 5125	MN 8·1
17H 5442	MN 20	17H 9463	MA 27	27H 5354	MN 15	37H 436	MA 41	47H 5125	MN 14
17H 5443	MN 20	17H 9472	MN 9·1	27H 5374	MN 21	37H 613	MO 2	47H 5125	MN 15
17H 5444	MN 4	17H 9472	MN 11	27H 5420	MN 3	37H 613	MO 5	47H 5126	MN 7·2
17H 5469	MB 3	17H 9472	MN 12	27H 5512	MN 20	37H 632	MA 16	47H 5126	MN 8
17H 5469	MB 4	17H 9525	MD 3	27H 5519	MB 3	37H 640	MO 5	47H 5126	MN 8·1
17H 5469	MB 7	17H 9528	MN 23	27H 5545	MN 10	37H 678	MO 4	47H 5126	MN 9
17H 5469	MB 10	17H 9603	MD 3	27H 5554	MN 20	37H 689	MA 27	47H 5126	MN 9·1
17H 5469	MT 5			27H 5562	MN 22	37H 689	MA 41	47H 5126	MN 11
17H 5512	MN 20	27H 387	MO 2	27H 5564	MN 22	37H 732	MD 5	47H 5126	MN 12
17H 5512	MN 21	27H 387	MO 4	27H 5564	MN 24	37H 859	MA 13	47H 5126	MN 13
17H 5531	MB 3	27H 972	MO 4	27H 5565	MN 22	37H 860	MA 13	47H 5126	MN 14
17H 5531	MB 4	27H 1170	MD 4	27H 5565	MN 24	37H 861	MA 12	47H 5126	MN 15
17H 5531	MB 7	27H 1983	MA 13	27H 5566	MN 22	37H 861	MA 40	47H 5164	MB 4
17H 5531	MB 10	27H 1983	MA 27	27H 5572	MN 18	37H 863	MA 12	47H 5164	MB 7
17H 5531	MT 5	27H 1983	MA 41	27H 5572	MN 19	37H 863	MA 40	47H 5164	MB 10
17H 5532	MB 3	27H 2333	MN 7	27H 5581	MN 18	37H 864	MA 12	47H 5164	MT 5
17H 5532	MB 4	27H 2333	MN 7·1	27H 5582	MN 18	37H 864	MA 40	47H 5166	MN 22
17H 5543	MN 9	27H 2333	MN 13·1	27H 5583	MN 18	37H 1255	MD 4	47H 5212	MN 6
17H 5546	MN 9	27H 2421	MH 6	27H 5596	MN 22	37H 1368	MN 8·1	47H 5249	MB 4
17H 5546	MN 13	27H 2573	MA 13	27H 5596	MN 24	37H 1368	MN 15	47H 5249	MB 7
17H 6427	MA 12	27H 3101	ME 3	27H 5597	MN 22	37H 1528	MA 41	47H 5249	MB 10
17H 6427	MA 26	27H 3101	ME 5	27H 5597	MN 24	37H 1821	MD 4	47H 5249	MT 5
17H 6427	MA 40	27H 3102	ME 3	C-27H 5982	MT 2	C-37H 2147	MT 2	47H 5250	MB 3
17H 6540	MJ 3	27H 3177	ME 3	27H 6236	MJ 3	C-37H 2148	MT 2	47H 5250	MB 4
17H 6541	MJ 3	27H 3177	ME 5	27H 6237	MJ 3	C-37H 2149	MT 2	47H 5250	MB 7
17H 6552	MJ 3	27H 3231	ME 3	27H 6238	MJ 3	37H 2496	MM 3	47H 5250	MB 10
17H 6626	MB 10	27H 3231	ME 5	27H 6245	MJ 3	37H 2883	MB 5	47H 5250	MT 5
17H 6656	MB 10	27H 3275	ME 5	27H 6482	MN 7	37H 2883	MB 8	47H 5315	MN 20
17H 6657	MB 10	27H 3276	ME 5	27H 6482	MN 7·2	37H 2883	MB 11	47H 5315	MN 21
17H 6821	MN 3	27H 3338	MN 7	27H 6482	MN 8·1	37H 3800	MA 47	47H 5316	MN 20
17H 6822	MN 3	27H 3338	MN 7·1	27H 6482	MN 9	37H 5169	MN 20	47H 5316	MN 21
17H 6823	MN 3	27H 3338	MN 7·2	27H 6482	MN 9·1	37H 5169	MN 21	47H 5339	MN 4
17H 6861	MM 3	27H 3338	MN 8·1	27H 6482	MN 11	37H 5181	MN 22	47H 5340	MN 4
17H 7108	MM 5	27H 3338	MN 9	27H 6482	MN 12	37H 5181	MN 24	47H 5341	MN 4
17H 7123	MM 3	27H 3338	MN 9·1	27H 6482	MN 13	37H 5190	MN 7	47H 5342	MN 4
17H 7203	MH 5	27H 3338	MN 11	27H 6482	MN 13·1	37H 5190	MN 7·1	47H 5346	MN 4
17H 7268	ME 8	27H 3338	MN 12	27H 6482	MN 14	37H 5190	MN 7·2	47H 5365	MN 7
17H 7408	MM 3	27H 3338	MN 13	27H 6482	MN 15	37H 5190	MN 8	47H 5388	MN 3
17H 7480	MM 3	27H 3338	MN 13·1	27H 6503	MA 41	37H 5190	MN 8·1	47H 5389	MN 3
17H 7511	MH 5	27H 3338	MN 14	27H 6542	MD 4	37H 5190	MN 9	47H 5391	MN 3
17H 7515	MH 5	27H 3338	MN 15	27H 6713	MN 7	37H 5190	MN 9·1	47H 5394	MN 3
17H 7531	MM 3	27H 3363	MA 49	27H 6713	MN 7·1	37H 5190	MN 11	47H 5395	MN 3
17H 7539	ME 8	27H 3364	MA 49	27H 6713	MN 7·2	37H 5190	MN 12	47H 5419	MN 23
17H 7540	ME 8	27H 3496	MA 41	27H 6713	MN 8	37H 5190	MN 13	47H 5419	MN 24
17H 7541	ME 8	27H 3542	MN 21	27H 6713	MN 8·1	37H 5190	MN 13·1	47H 5496	MN 22
17H 7543	MK 4	27H 3573	MD 2	27H 6713	MN 9	37H 5190	MN 14	47H 5496	MN 24
17H 7544	MK 4	27H 3574	MN 3	27H 6713	MN 9·1	37H 5190	MN 15	47H 5499	MN 24
17H 7554	MM 3	27H 3755	MN 4	27H 6713	MN 10	37H 5192	MN 8	47H 5520	MB 3
17H 7571	MM 3	27H 4146	MN 7·2	27H 6713	MN 11	37H 5207	MN 3	47H 5520	MB 4
17H 7576	MK 4	27H 4146	MN 8	27H 6713	MN 12	37H 5288	MN 20	47H 5520	MB 7
17H 7580	ME 8	27H 4146	MN 8·1	27H 6713	MN 13	37H 5294	MN 16	47H 5522	MN 22
17H 7612	MH 5	27H 4146	MN 14	27H 6713	MN 13·1	37H 5409	MB 3	47H 5554	MN 12
17H 7613	MH 5	27H 4146	MN 15	27H 6713	MN 14	37H 5409	MB 4	47H 5555	MT 5
17H 7618	MH 4	27H 4149	MN 2	27H 6713	MN 15	37H 5410	MN 10	47H 5564	MN 9·1
17H 7619	MH 4	27H 4228	MG 2	27H 7395	MH 5	37H 5432	MN 16	47H 5589	MN 5
17H 7621	MH 4	27H 4230	MG 2	C-27H 7766	MT 5	37H 5438	MB 8	47H 5589	MN 6
17H 7622	MH 5	27H 4463	MN 21	27H 7824	MN 7·1	37H 5439	MB 3		
17H 7623	MH 5	27H 4464	MN 21	27H 7877	MO 2	37H 5440	MB 3	57H 5004	MN 9·1
17H 7626	MH 5	27H 4568	MD 4	27H 7877	MO 4	37H 5445	MB 4	57H 5009	MN 12
17H 7679	MK 4·1	27H 5253	MN 7	27H 7971	MN 7·1	37H 5445	MT 5	57H 5049	MB 4
17H 7707	MH 5	27H 5253	MN 7·1	C-27H 8022	MT 5	37H 5445	MB 7	57H 5049	MB 7
17H 7766	MH 5	27H 5253	MN 7·2	27H 8203	MN 11	37H 5445	MB 10	57H 5050	MB 4
17H 7841	ME 8	27H 5253	MN 8	27H 8204	MN 7·2	37H 5452	MN 16	57H 5050	MB 7
17H 7861	MH 5	27H 5253	MN 9	27H 8204	MN 14	37H 5459	MN 16	57H 5050	MT 5
17H 7868	ME 8	27H 5253	MN 13	27H 8206	MN 9	37H 5519	MN 10	57H 5084	MN 3
17H 7886	MM 3	27H 5253	MN 13·1	27H 8206	MN 13	37H 5520	MN 10	57H 5085	MN 3
17H 7917	MK 4·1	27H 5253	MN 14	27H 8206	MN 13·1	37H 5525	MN 16	57H 5128	MN 10
17H 7947	MH 4	27H 5253	MN 15	27H 8207	MN 9·1	37H 5527	MN 10	57H 5128	MN 17
17H 7948	MH 4	27H 5278	MN 5	27H 8207	MN 11	37H 5528	MN 10	57H 5133	MT 5
17H 7960	MK 4·1	27H 5309	MN 20	27H 8207	MN 12	37H 5531	MN 10	57H 5155	MN 16
17H 7963	MK 4·1	27H 5309	MN 21	27H 8209	MN 7	37H 5588	MN 7	57H 5156	MN 16
17H 7981	MM 3	27H 5354	MN 7	27H 8213	MO 5	37H 5588	MN 7·1	57H 5157	MN 16
17H 7984	MM 3	27H 5354	MN 7·1	27H 8214	MO 5	37H 5588	MN 13·1	57H 5158	MN 16

Part Number Index—*continued*

Part Number	Page	Part Number	Page	Part Number	Page	Part Number	Page	Part Number	Page
57H 5159	MN 16	67H 5025	MN 13·1	HNS 0404	MA 12	HZS 0510	MA 28	2K 5377	MK 3
57H 5184	MB 4	67H 5025	MN 14	HNS 0404	MA 26	HZS 0510	MA 29	2K 5806	MA 47
57H 5185	MB 4	67H 5025	MN 15	HNS 0404	MA 40	HZS 0510	MA 42	2K 5813	ME 7
57H 5206	MN 24	67H 5026	MN 7	HNS 0405	MA 17	HZS 0510	MA 43	2K 5813	MF 3
57H 5292	MN 11	67H 5026	MN 7·1	HNS 0406	MA 5	HZS 0514	MA 29	2K 5813	MF 9
57H 5292	MN 12	67H 5026	MN 7·2	HNS 0406	MA 21	HZS 0515	MA 14	2K 5820	MM 7
57H 5293	MN 21	67H 5026	MN 8·1	HNS 0406	MA 35	HZS 0515	MA 28	2K 5830	MF 3
57H 5294	MN 21	67H 5026	MN 9	HNS 0505	MK 4	HZS 0515	MA 42	2K 5830	MF 9
57H 5306	MN 16	67H 5026	MN 9·1			HZS 0518	MA 47	2K 5830	MF 14
57H 5307	MN 16	67H 5026	MN 11	HZS 0403	MA 10	HZS 0605	MN 22	2K 5943	MH 2
57H 5308	MN 16	67H 5026	MN 12	HZS 0403	MA 25	HZS 0605	MN 25	2K 6124	MA 14
57H 5309	MN 19	67H 5026	MN 13	HZS 0403	MA 39	HZS 0609	ML 2	2K 6124	MA 28
57H 5310	MN 18	67H 5026	MN 13·1	HZS 0404	MA 48	HZS 0610	ML 2	2K 6124	MA 42
57H 5310	MN 19	67H 5026	MN 14	HZS 0404	MB 4			2K 6167	MN 22
57H 5336	MN 17	67H 5026	MN 15	HZS 0404	MB 7	1K 52	MA 10	2K 6167	MN 25
57H 5338	MN 8	67H 5028	MN 7·2	HZS 0404	MB 10	1K 52	MA 25	2K 6677	MF 4
57H 5339	MN 8	67H 5028	MN 8	HZS 0404	MD 3	1K 1977	MO 3	2K 6677	MF 5
57H 5340	MN 8	67H 5028	MN 9	HZS 0404	MF 7	1K 1977	MO 5	2K 6677	MF 10
57H 5341	MN 8	67H 5028	MN 13	HZS 0404	MF 12			2K 6677	MF 11
57H 5344	MN 24	67H 5028	MN 14	HZS 0404	MF 17	2K 1345	MA 3	2K 6677	MF 15
57H 5346	MB 7	67H 5028	MN 15	HZS 0405	MA 14	2K 1345	MA 7	2K 6677	MF 16
57H 5353	MN 7·1	67H 5029	MN 9·1	HZS 0405	MA 26	2K 1345	MA 19	2K 6804	MT 3
57H 5353	MN 8·1	67H 5029	MN 12	HZS 0405	MB 5	2K 1345	MA 23	2K 6930	MM 6
57H 5353	MN 9			HZS 0405	MB 8	2K 1345	MA 33	2K 7140	MA 10
57H 5353	MN 11	97H 222	ML 2	HZS 0405	MB 11	2K 1345	MA 37	2K 7140	MA 30
57H 5354	MN 16	97H 626	MN 3	HZS 0405	MC 2	2K 1369	MO 3	2K 7140	MA 44
57H 5355	MN 16	97H 1585	MT 12	HZS 0405	MF 7	2K 1369	MO 5	2K 7440	MA 10
57H 5356	MN 16	97H 2071	MN 5	HZS 0405	MF 12	2K 4608	MA 3	2K 7440	MA 25
57H 5357	MN 16	97H 2071	MN 6	HZS 0405	MF 17	2K 4608	MA 8	2K 7440	MA 39
57H 5358	MN 16	97H 2072	MN 5	HZS 0405	MM 2	2K 4608	MA 23	2K 7778	MH 2
57H 5359	MN 16	97H 2072	MN 6	HZS 0405	MN 18	2K 4608	MA 37	2K 7779	MH 2
57H 5362	MB 7	97H 2073	MN 5	HZS 0406	MA 6	2K 4608	MT 2	2K 7816	MA 6
57H 5363	MB 7	97H 2073	MN 6	HZS 0406	MA 12	2K 4909	MF 3	2K 7816	MA 22
57H 5368	MN 10	97H 2074	MA 49	HZS 0406	MA 14	2K 4909	MF 7	2K 7816	MA 36
57H 5368	MN 17	97H 2075	MA 49	HZS 0406	MA 22	2K 4954	MA 3	2K 8158	MF 6
57H 5382	MN 11	97H 2076	MA 49	HZS 0406	MA 28	2K 4954	MA 10	2K 8158	MF 12
57H 5411	MN 19	97H 2724	MR 2	HZS 0406	MA 36	2K 4954	MA 16	2K 8158	MF 17
57H 5420	MB 4	97H 2797	MJ 3	HZS 0406	MA 42	2K 4954	MA 30	2K 8159	MA 17
57H 5420	MB 7			HZS 0406	MB 5	2K 4954	MA 44	2K 8159	MA 31
57H 5420	MB 10	HBN 0411	MA 12	HZS 0406	MC 2	2K 4956	MA 12	2K 8160	MH 3
57H 5420	MT 5	HBN 0411	MA 26	HZS 0407	MA 47	2K 4956	MA 26	2K 8169	MA 3
57H 5423	MN 18	HBN 0414	MA 12	HZS 0407	MA 48	2K 4956	MA 40	2K 8169	MA 19
57H 5423	MN 19	HBN 0414	MA 26	HZS 0407	MF 7	2K 4956	MF 3	2K 8169	MA 33
57H 5445	MN 24	HBN 0414	MA 40	HZS 0407	MF 12	2K 4956	MF 9	2K 8568	MA 9
57H 5456	MN 11			HZS 0407	MF 17	2K 4956	MF 14	2K 8568	MA 38
57H 5456	MN 12	HBZ 0405	MA 12	HZS 0408	ME 8	2K 4958	MA 10	2K 8623	MA 3
57H 5456	MN 13	HBZ 0408	MJ 3	HZS 0408	MM 2	2K 4958	MA 25	2K 8623	MA 19
57H 5456	MN 13·1	HBZ 0408	MM 5	HZS 0408	MO 3	2K 4958	MA 39	2K 8623	MA 33
57H 5456	MN 14	HBZ 0409	MM 5	HZS 0503	MK 4	2K 4960	MN 19	2K 8645	MN2
57H 5456	MN 15	HBZ 0414	MT 3	HZS 0504	MN 22	2K 4961	MD 4	2K 8737	MF 4
57H 5457	MN 13	HBZ 0510	MG 2	HZS 0504	MN 25	2K 4974	MA 14	2K 8737	MF 5
57H 5457	MN 13·1	HBZ 0513	MA 15	HZS 0505	MA 5	2K 4974	MA 28	2K 8737	MF 10
57H 5457	MN 14	HBZ 0513	MA 29	HZS 0505	MA 10	2K 4974	MA 42	2K 8737	MF 11
57H 5457	MN 15	HBZ 0513	MA 43	HZS 0505	MA 21	2K 4975	MA 3	2K 8737	MF 15
57H 5477	MB 3	HBZ 0515	MA 10	HZS 0505	MA 25	2K 4975	MA 16	2K 8737	MF 16
57H 5477	MB 4	HBZ 0515	MA 25	HZS 0505	MA 35	2K 4975	MA 19	2K 8738	MF 4
57H 5477	MB 7	HBZ 0515	MA 39	HZS 0505	MA 39	2K 4975	MA 30	2K 8738	MF 5
57H 5477	MB 10	HBZ 0515	MA 43	HZS 0505	MA 46	2K 4975	MA 33	2K 8738	MF 10
57H 5477	MT 5	HBZ 0612	ML 2	HZS 0505	MA 47	2K 4975	MA 44	2K 8738	MF 11
57H 5478	MB 10	HBZ 0613	MN 4	HZS 0505	MM 6	2K 4982	MA 12	2K 8738	MF 15
57H 5478	MT 5	HBZ 0618	ML 2	HZS 0505	MN 18	2K 4982	MA 26	2K 8738	MF 16
57H 5555	MN 21	HBZ 0624	MH 6	HZS 0505	MT 11	2K 4982	MA 40	2K 8739	MF 4
57H 5556	MN 18	HBZ 0624	MM 3	HZS 0506	MA 46	2K 4993	MA 3	2K 8739	MF 5
57H 5559	MN 21	HBZ 0626	MA 46	HZS 0506	MA 47	2K 4993	MA 19	2K 8739	MF 10
57H 5589	MN 21	HBZ 0626	MH 6	HZS 0506	MD 5	2K 4993	MA 33	2K 8739	MF 11
57H 5591	MN 6	HBZ 0626	MM 3	HZS 0506	ME 3	2K 4994	MA 12	2K 8739	MF 15
		HBZ 0630	ML 2	HZS 0506	ME 7	2K 4994	MA 26	2K 8739	MF 16
67H 5008	MN 4	HBZ 0732	ML 2	HZS 0506	MH 4	2K 4994	MA 40		
67H 5010	MN 4			HZS 0506	MJ 2	2K 5197	MA 10	6K 35	MD 3
67H 5012	MN 4	HCS 114	MD 2	HZS 0506	MM 7	2K 5197	MA 11	6K 35	MM 4
67H 5013	MN 4	HCS 0507	MD 5	HZS 0506	MT 11	2K 5197	MA 25	6K 431	MA 12
67H 5014	MN 4	HCS 1622	MD 2	HZS 0507	MA 15	2K 5197	MA 26	6K 431	MA 26
67H 5024	MN 11	HCS 0913	MC 2	HZS 0507	MA 29	2K 5197	MA 39	6K 431	MA 40
67H 5024	MN 12	HCS 2228	MD 2	HZS 0507	MA 43	2K 5197	MA 40	6K 464	MA 12
67H 5025	MN 7			HZS 0507	MA 47	2K 5211	MA 9	6K 464	MA 16
67H 5025	MN 7·1	HCZ 0304	MD 3	HZS 0508	MA 47	2K 5211	MA 24	6K 464	MA 30
67H 5025	MN 7·2	HCZ 0512	MJ 2	HZS 0508	MJ 2	2K 5211	MA 38	6K 464	MA 40
67H 5025	MN 8·1	HCZ 0536	MD 5	HZS 0509	MA 15	2K 5291	MM 7	6K 464	MA 44
67H 5025	MN 9	HCZ 0628	MA 13	HZS 0509	MA 29	2K 5319	MA 15	6K 490	MN 23
67H 5025	MN 9·1	HCZ 0628	MA 27	HZS 0509	MA 43	2K 5319	MA 29	6K 499	MH 2
67H 5025	MN 11	HCZ 0630	MA 13	HZS 0509	MF 7	2K 5319	MA 46	6K 555	MA 8
67H 5025	MN 12	HCZ 0630	MA 27	HZS 0509	MF 12	2K 5319	ME 3	6K 555	MA 23
67H 5025	MN 13	HCZ 0630	MA 41	HZS 0510	MA 14	2K 5319	ME 5	6K 555	MA 37

Part Number Index—*continued*

Part Number	Page	Part Number	Page	Part Number	Page	Part Number	Page	Part Number	Page
6K 556	MA 8	51K 255	MA 33	5L 286	MN 22	LWN 404	MF 9	LWZ 305	MA 25
6K 556	MA 23	51K 256	MA 3	5L 286	MN 24	LWN 404	MF 14	LWZ 305	MA 29
6K 556	MA 37	51K 256	MA 19	5L 287	MN 24	LWN 405	MD 2	LWZ 305	MA 35
6K 558	MF 5	51K 256	MA 33	5L 289	MN 22	LWN 405	MK 5	LWZ 305	MA 39
6K 558	MF 10	51K 328	MK 3	5L 289	MN 24	LWN 406	MM 4	LWZ 305	MA 43
6K 558	MF 11	51K 371	MA 8	5L 321	MN 10	LWN 504	MT 3	LWZ 305	MA 46
6K 558	MF 15	51K 371	MA 23	5L 321	MN 17	LWN 509	MJ 3	LWZ 305	MD 5
6K 558	MF 16	51K 371	MA 37					LWZ 305	ME 8
6K 559	MF 4	51K 448	MA 17	LNZ 104	MJ 3	LWZ 202	MN 5	LWZ 305	MF 7
6K 559	MF 5	51K 554	MA 7	LNZ 105	MA 47	LWZ 202	MN 6	LWZ 305	MF 12
6K 559	MF 10	51K 885	MA 7	LNZ 105	MG 2	LWZ 203	MD 2	LWZ 305	MF 17
6K 559	MF 11	51K 885	MA 23	LNZ 106	ML 2	LWZ 203	MK 2	LWZ 305	MG 2
6K 559	MF 15	51K 885	MA 37	LNZ 108	MH 6	LWZ 203	MM 4	LWZ 305	MH 4
6K 559	MF 16	51K 886	MH 2	LNZ 204	MN 17	LWZ 203	MN 5	LWZ 305	MK 2
6K 628	MA 5	51K 1368	MK 4	LNZ 205	MA 15	LWZ 203	MN 6	LWZ 305	MM 7
6K 628	MA 21	51K 1382	MA 5	LNZ 205	MA 29	LWZ 203	MN 10	LWZ 305	MN 22
6K 628	MA 35	51K 1382	MA 21	LNZ 205	MA 43	LWZ 203	MN 18	LWZ 305	MN 25
6K 629	MA 5	51K 1473	MA 7	LNZ 205	MA 47	LWZ 203	MN 23	LWZ 306	MA 15
6K 629	MA 21	51K 1473	MA 23	LNZ 205	MD 5	LWZ 203	MN 25	LWZ 306	MA 29
6K 629	MA 35	51K 1473	MA 37	LNZ 205	MG 2	LWZ 203	MO 3	LWZ 306	MA 43
6K 630	MA 6	51K 1671	MF 3	LNZ 205	MK 5	LWZ 203	MO 4	LWZ 306	MA 46
6K 630	MA 22	51K 1769	MK 2	LNZ 205	MT 11	LWZ 203	MT 11	LWZ 306	MH 6
6K 630	MA 36	51K 2036	ME 3	LNZ 206	MA 15	LWZ 204	MA 14	LWZ 306	MK 5
6K 631	MH 2	51K 2036	ME 5	LNZ 206	MA 29	LWZ 204	MA 42	LWZ 306	ML 2
6K 638	MA 3	51K 2036	ME 7	LNZ 206	MA 43	LWZ 204	MA 45	LWZ 306	MN 4
6K 638	MA 11	51K 2751	MK 3	LNZ 206	MK 5	LWZ 204	MA 47	LWZ 306	MN 22
6K 638	MA 16	51K 2824	MO 2	LNZ 206	ML 2	LWZ 204	MA 48	LWZ 306	MN 25
6K 638	MA 19	51K 2824	MO 4			LWZ 204	MB 5	LWZ 307	MH 6
6K 638	MA 26	51K 3424	MK 3	LWN 204	MA 10	LWZ 204	MB 8	LWZ 307	MK 4·1
6K 638	MA 30			LWN 204	MA 12	LWZ 204	MB 11	LWZ 307	ML 2
6K 638	MA 33	53K 152	ME 8	LWN 204	MA 25	LWZ 204	MC 2	LWZ 402	MO 5
6K 638	MA 40	53K 165	MD 2	LWN 204	MA 28	LWZ 204	MD 3	LWZ 404	MB 4
6K 638	MA 44	53K 371	MA 8	LWN 204	MA 39	LWZ 204	MD 5	LWZ 404	MB 7
6K 639	MA 11	53K 402	MA 7	LWN 204	MF 3	LWZ 204	MF 6	LWZ 404	MB 10
6K 639	MA 26	53K 402	MA 23	LWN 204	MF 7	LWZ 204	MF 7	LWZ 404	MM 3
6K 639	MA 40	53K 402	MA 37	LWN 204	MF 9	LWZ 204	MF 12	LWZ 405	MK 4
6K 639	MB 4	53K 463	MF 3	LWN 204	MF 14	LWZ 204	MF 17	LWZ 405	MT 11
6K 639	MB 7	53K 463	MF 9	LWN 204	MK 4	LWZ 204	MJ 2	LWZ 505	MK 4
6K 639	MB 10	53K 463	MF 14	LWN 205	MA 8	LWZ 204	MJ 3		
6K 643	MF 3	53K 486	MA 7	LWN 205	MA 23	LWZ 204	MM 5	MPS 4304	MM 6
6K 643	MF 9	53K 487	MA 7	LWN 205	MA 37	LWZ 204	MN 2		
6K 643	MF 14	53K 487	MA 23	LWN 205	MD 4	LWZ 204	MN 5	NCS 0608	MA 13
6K 648	MD 3	53K 487	MA 37	LWN 206	MA 13	LWZ 204	MN 6	NCS 0608	MA 27
6K 653	MK 2	53K 524	MA 33	LWN 206	MA 27	LWZ 204	MN 18	NCS 0608	MA 41
6K 654	MA 8	53K 525	MA 3	LWN 303	MD 4	LWZ 204	MN 19		
6K 654	MA 23	53K 525	MA 19	LWN 304	MA 7	LWZ 204	MO 5	PCR 0207	MO 3
6K 654	MA 37	53K 525	MA 33	LWN 304	MA 12	LWZ 205	MA 10	PCR 0207	MO 4
6K 685	MD 3	53K 528	MF 6	LWN 304	MA 27	LWZ 205	MA 24	PCR 0307	MO 3
6K 689	MM 6	53K 528	MF 12	LWN 304	MA 37	LWZ 205	MA 25	PCR 0307	MO 4
6K 690	MM 7	53K 528	MF 17	LWN 304	MB 5	LWZ 205	MA 46	PCR 0311	MM 4
6K 808	MA 7	53K 530	MA 7	LWN 304	MF 3	LWZ 205	MA 47	PCR 0407	MN 23
6K 808	MA 23	53K 530	MA 23	LWN 304	MF 9	LWZ 205	MD 5	PCR 0409	MD 3
6K 808	MA 37	53K 535	MF 6	LWN 304	MF 12	LWZ 205	MF 6	PCR 0409	MN 23
6K 831	MA 5	53K 535	MF 12	LWN 304	MF 14	LWZ 205	MF 12	PCR 0411	MD 3
6K 831	MA 21	53K 538	MF 17	LWN 304	MF 17	LWZ 205	MF 17	PCR 0607	MN 23
6K 831	MA 35	53K 1013	MJ 3	LWN 305	MA 5	LWZ 205	MH 2	PCR 0607	MN 25
6K 836	MA 5	53K 1023	MA 49	LWN 305	MA 14	LWZ 205	MJ 2	PCR 0609	MN 23
6K 836	MA 21	53K 1028	MA 3	LWN 305	MA 15	LWZ 205	MM 2	PCR 0709	MO 3
6K 836	MA 35	53K 1028	MA 19	LWN 305	MA 21	LWZ 205	MM 6	PCR 0709	MO 5
6K 853	MA 12	53K 1028	MA 33	LWN 305	MA 28	LWZ 205	MN 6	PCR 1007	MN 23
6K 853	MA 26	53K 1045	MA 3	LWN 305	MA 29	LWZ 205	MN 18	PCR 1009	MN 25
6K 853	MA 40	53K 1364	MK 5	LWN 305	MA 42	LWZ 205	MT 11		
6K 870	MM 6	53K 1368	MK 5	LWN 305	MA 43	LWZ 206	MA 13	PFS 326	MN 10
6K 871	MT 3	53K 1369	MT 11	LWN 305	MA 46	LWZ 206	MA 27	PFS 510	MN 10
6K 878	MA 8	53K 1370	MK 3	LWN 305	ME 3	LWZ 206	MA 41		
6K 878	MA 23	53K 1389	MK 5	LWN 305	ME 7	LWZ 206	MA 46	PJZ 602	MN 7
6K 878	MA 37	53K 1392	MA 49	LWN 305	MF 3	LWZ 206	ML 2	PJZ 602	MN 7·1
6K 878	MT 2	53K 1392	MT 6	LWN 305	MF 7	LWZ 206	MM 3	PJZ 602	MN 7·2
6K 927	MA 3	53K 1433	MA 14	LWN 305	MF 9	LWZ 207	MN 3	PJZ 602	MN 8
6K 927	MA 19	53K 1433	MA 28	LWN 305	MF 12	LWZ 212	MH 3	PJZ 602	MN 8·1
6K 927	MA 33	53K 1433	MA 42	LWN 305	MF 17	LWZ 302	MO 2	PJZ 602	MN 9
6K 9388	MN 18	53K 1435	MF 3	LWN 305	MK 4	LWZ 302	MO 4	PJZ 602	MN 9·1
6K 9388	MN 19	53K 1435	MF 9	LWN 307	MH 2	LWZ 303	MT 6	PJZ 602	MN 11
		53K 1435	MF 14	LWN 404	MA 5	LWZ 304	MC 2	PJZ 602	MN 12
11K 399	MA 9	53K 1722	MF 7	LWN 404	MA 6	LWZ 304	MF 7	PJZ 602	MN 13
11K 399	MA 24	53K 2016	MA 5	LWN 404	MA 12	LWZ 304	MF 9	PJZ 602	MN 13·1
11K 9101	MN 5	53K 2016	MA 21	LWN 404	MA 21	LWZ 304	MF 12	PJZ 602	MN 14
		53K 2016	MA 35	LWN 404	MA 22	LWZ 304	MF 17	PJZ 602	MN 15
51K 254	MA 3	53K 2599	MJ 3	LWN 404	MA 26	LWZ 304	MM 2	PJZ 1006	MN 10
51K 254	MA 19	53K 3503	MA 47	LWN 404	MA 35	LWZ 305	MA 5		
51K 254	MA 33			LWN 404	MA 36	LWZ 305	MA 10	PMZ 0205	MN 18
51K 255	MA 3	5L 64	MN 25	LWN 404	MA 40	LWZ 305	MA 15	PMZ 0205	MN 19
51K 255	MA 19	5L 285	MN 24	LWN 404	MF 3	LWZ 305	MA 21	PMZ 0206	MN 18

Part Number Index—*continued*

Part Number	Page	Part Number	Page	Part Number	Page	Part Number	Page	Part Number	Page
PMZ 0305	MM 4	PWZ 205	MN 10						
PMZ 0306	MN 23	PWZ 205	MN 18						
PMZ 0306	MO 3	PWZ 206	ML 2						
PMZ 0306	MO 4	PWZ 305	MA 15						
PMZ 0307	MN 5	PWZ 305	MA 29						
PMZ 0307	MN 23	PWZ 305	MA 43						
PMZ 0307	MT 11								
PMZ 0308	MD 2	RFN 110	MN 25						
PMZ 0308	MN 6	RFN 303	MA 49						
PMZ 0308	MN 10	RFN 303	MN 5						
PMZ 0308	MN 18	RFN 303	MN 6						
PMZ 0308	MN 25	RFN 303	MN 23						
PMZ 0308	MO 4	RFN 303	MN 25						
PMZ 0310	MN 5	RFN 305	MN 23						
PMZ 0310	MN 6	RFN 305	MN 25						
PMZ 0310	MN 23	RFN 305	MO 3						
PMZ 0312	MN 9·1	RFN 305	MO 5						
PMZ 0320	MN 5								
PMZ 0320	MN 6	RFR 110	MN 25						
PMZ 0406	MN 5								
PMZ 0408	MN 5	RMP 0308	MN 16						
PMZ 0408	MN 6								
PMZ 0410	MN 19	RRS 0405	MH 6						
PTZ 603	MN 23	TCN 206	MA 13						
PTZ 603	MN 25	TCN 206	MA 27						
PTZ 604	MN 10								
PTZ 803	MF 7	TRS 0710	MF 7						
PTZ 803	MF 12	TRS 0710	MF 12						
PTZ 803	MF 17	TRS 0710	MF 17						
PWN 105	MA 17	UHH 305	MJ 2						
PWN 105	MA 31								
PWN 106	MA 8	UHN 105	MM 6						
PWN 106	MA 13	UHN 305	MJ 2						
PWN 106	MA 15	UHN 400	MK 3						
PWN 106	MA 23	UHN 440	MK 2						
PWN 106	MA 29	UHN 445	MK 2						
PWN 106	MA 37	UHN 490	MK 2						
PWN 106	MA 41	UHN 490	MM 7						
PWN 107	MH 2								
PWN 204	MB 5	WKN 404	MF 6						
		WKN 404	MF 12						
PWZ 104	MA 39	WKN 404	MF 17						
PWZ 104	MA 45	WKN 404	MN 3						
PWZ 104	MA 48	WKN 505	MA 5						
PWZ 104	MC 2	WKN 505	MA 21						
PWZ 104	MD 3	WKN 505	MA 35						
PWZ 104	MD 5								
PWZ 104	MJ 3	WNZ 103	MB 10						
PWZ 104	MM 7								
PWZ 105	MA 9	ZCS 0404	MA 45						
PWZ 105	MA 39	ZCS 0404	MD 3						
PWZ 105	MA 45	ZCS 0505	MA 15						
PWZ 105	MA 46	ZCS 0505	MA 29						
PWZ 105	MA 47	ZCS 0505	MA 43						
PWZ 105	MD 2	ZCS 0506	MA 46						
PWZ 105	MD 5								
PWZ 105	ME 8	ZPS 0524	MK 4·1						
PWZ 105	MJ 2								
PWZ 105	MM 7	39731	MM 3						
PWZ 106	MA 46	68640	MK 4						
PWZ 106	MA 49								
PWZ 106	MD 5								
PWZ 106	MK 5								
PWZ 106	ML 2								
PWZ 106	MN 5								
PWZ 106	MN 6								
PWZ 107	MJ 2								
PWZ 107	ML 2								
PWZ 108	MH 6								
PWZ 203	MA 48								
PWZ 203	MD 2								
PWZ 203	MN 9·1								
PWZ 203	MN 10								
PWZ 204	MB 5								
PWZ 204	MB 8								
PWZ 204	MB 11								
PWZ 204	MC 2								
PWZ 205	MA 46								
PWZ 205	MA 47								
PWZ 205	MD 5								
PWZ 205	MN 6								

ENGINE MA

		Pages
950-cc	9C/U/H	MA 1 to MA 17

950-cc 9C ENGINE

	Page	Plate
CAMSHAFT	MA 5	A 2
CONNECTING RODS	MA 5	A 2
CONTROLS—ENGINE	MA 48, MA 49	A 30
COVER—VALVE ROCKER	MA 9	A 4
COVERS—CYLINDER	MA 10	A 5
CRANKSHAFT	MA 5	A 2
CYLINDER HEAD	MA 7	A 3
DISTRIBUTOR HOUSING—SPINDLE	MA 6	A 2
ELBOW—WATER OUTLET—THERMOSTAT	MA 9	A 4
ENGINE UNIT	MA 3	A 1
EXHAUST SYSTEM	MA 47	A 29
FAN—FAN BELT	MA 15	A 8
FILTER—OIL	MA 13	A 7
FLYWHEEL	MA 6	A 2
MANIFOLDS	MA 17	A 9
MOUNTINGS—DYNAMO	MA 15	A 8
MOUNTINGS—ENGINE	MA 46	A 28
PISTONS—ASSEMBLY—RINGS	MA 4	A 1
PLATE—ENGINE MOUNTING—FRONT	MA 5	A 2
PLATE—ENGINE MOUNTING—REAR	MA 10	A 5
PLUGS—SPARKING	MA 9	A 4
PUMP—OIL—STRAINER	MA 12	A 6
PUMP—WATER—FAN PULLEY	MA 14	A 8
SERVICE KITS—ENGINE	MA 16	
SHAFT—VALVE ROCKER	MA 8	A 3
SUMP OIL—DIPPER ROD	MA 11	A 6
TAP—CYLINDER DRAIN	MA 10	A 5
TAPPETS	MA 6	A 2

1
2
3
4
5
6
7
8
9
10
11
12
13
14
15
16
17
18
19
20
21
22
23
24
25
26
27
28
29
B7588

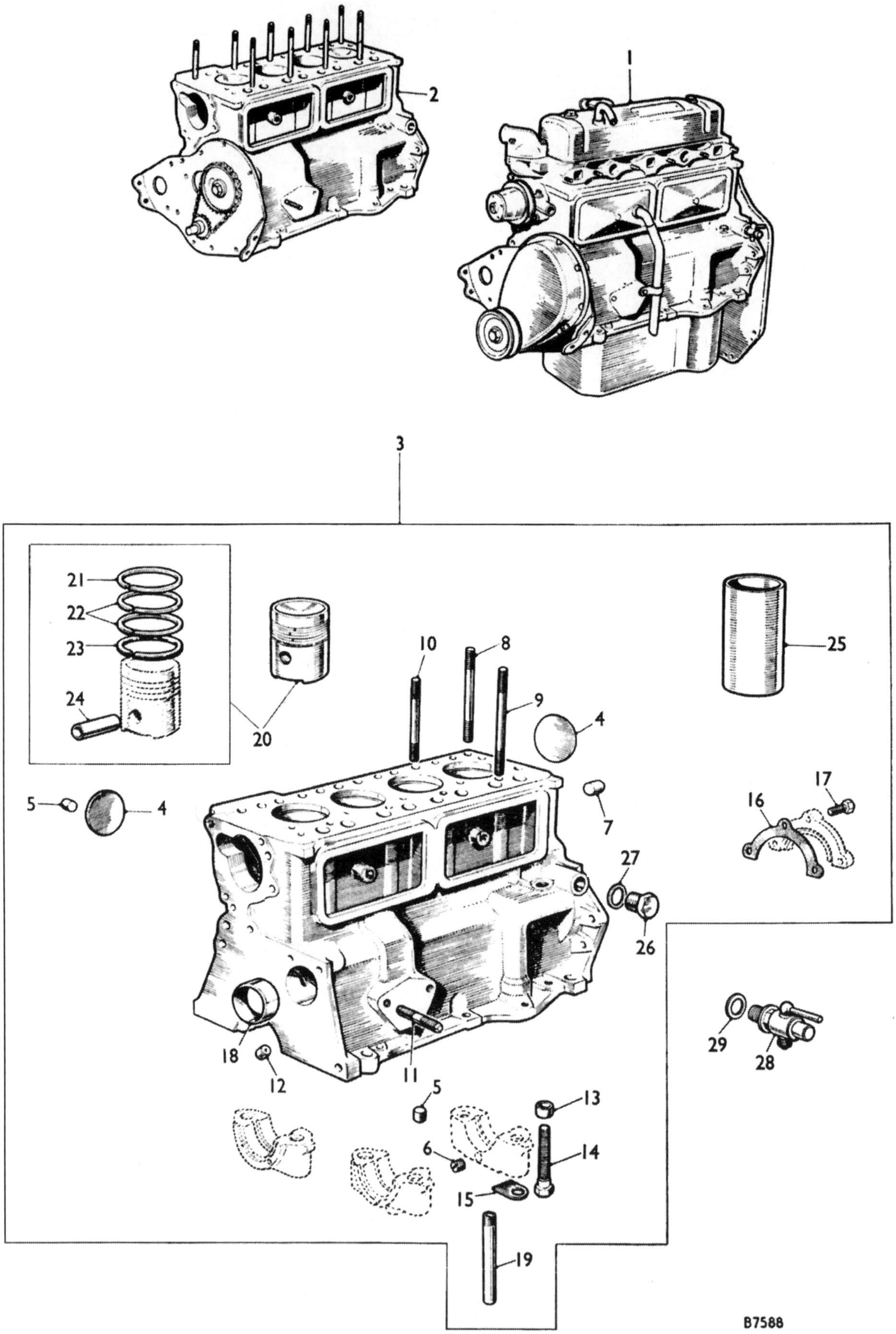

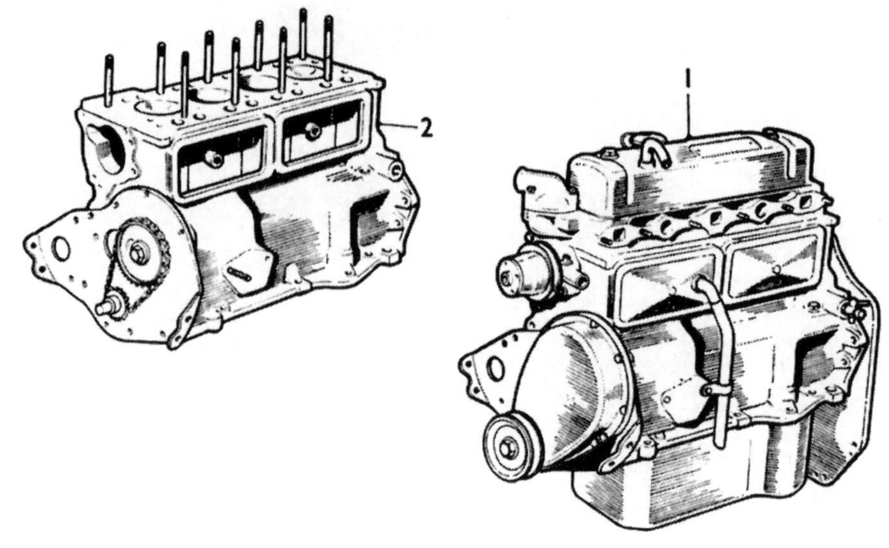

DESCRIPTION	Part No.	Illus. No.	Quantity	Change Point	REMARKS
ENGINE					
9C ENGINE UNIT					
Engine unit—stripped	8G 10	1	1		
Engine unit—half	†28G 85	2	1		W.S.E. use 28G 137
Engine unit—half	28G 137	2	1		
Block assembly—cylinder	†28G 84	3	1		W.S.E. use 28G 85
Block assembly—cylinder	†28G 138	3	1		W.S.E. use 28G 137
Plug					
Welch	2K 8169	4	4		
Oil release valve passage	2K 1345	5	2		
Rear main bearing cap—screwed	2K 4608	6	1	(E) 9C/U/H101 to H1168	
Oil gallery	2K 8623	7	2		W.S.E. use 12H 1734
Oil gallery	12H 1734	7	2		
Stud					
Cylinder head	51K 254	8	1		Use 51K 256 for this application
Cylinder head—long	51K 255	9	4		
Cylinder head—short	51K 256	10	4/5		Quantity increased at ▼
Fuel pump	53K 525	11	2		
Cap—main bearing					
Front	NSP		1		
Centre	NSP		1		
Rear	NSP		1		
Restrictor—camshaft bearing—oil feed	1A 1964	12	1		
Dowel—main bearing cap	2A 54	13	6		
Screw—main bearing cap	2A 53	14	6		
Washer—lock	6K 927	15	6		
Cover—crankcase—rear	NSP		1		
Gasket—cover—rear	2A 127	16	1		
Screw—cover—rear	53K 1045	17	3		Use 53K 1028 for this application
Screw—cover—rear	53K 1028	17	3		
Liner—camshaft—front	2A 42	18	1		
Pipe—drain—rear main bearing cap	2A 253	19	1		
Liner—cylinder block	2A 784	25	4		For Service purposes only
Plug—drain	2K 4993	26	1		
Washer	6K 638	27	1		
Tap—drain	2A 816	28	1	(E) 9C/U/H101 to H6358	W.S.E. use 37H 576 — For Service purposes only
	2A 817	28	1	(E) 9C/U/H101 to H6358	W.S.E. use 37H 576 — For Service purposes only
	3H 576	28	1	(E) 9C/U/H6359 on	For Service purposes only
Washer	†2K 4954	29	1	(E) 9C/U/H101 to H6358	Alternatives — For Service purposes only
Washer	†2K 4975	29	1	(E) 9C/U/H6359 on	Alternatives — For Service purposes only

▼ Change point not available

† Revised Information.

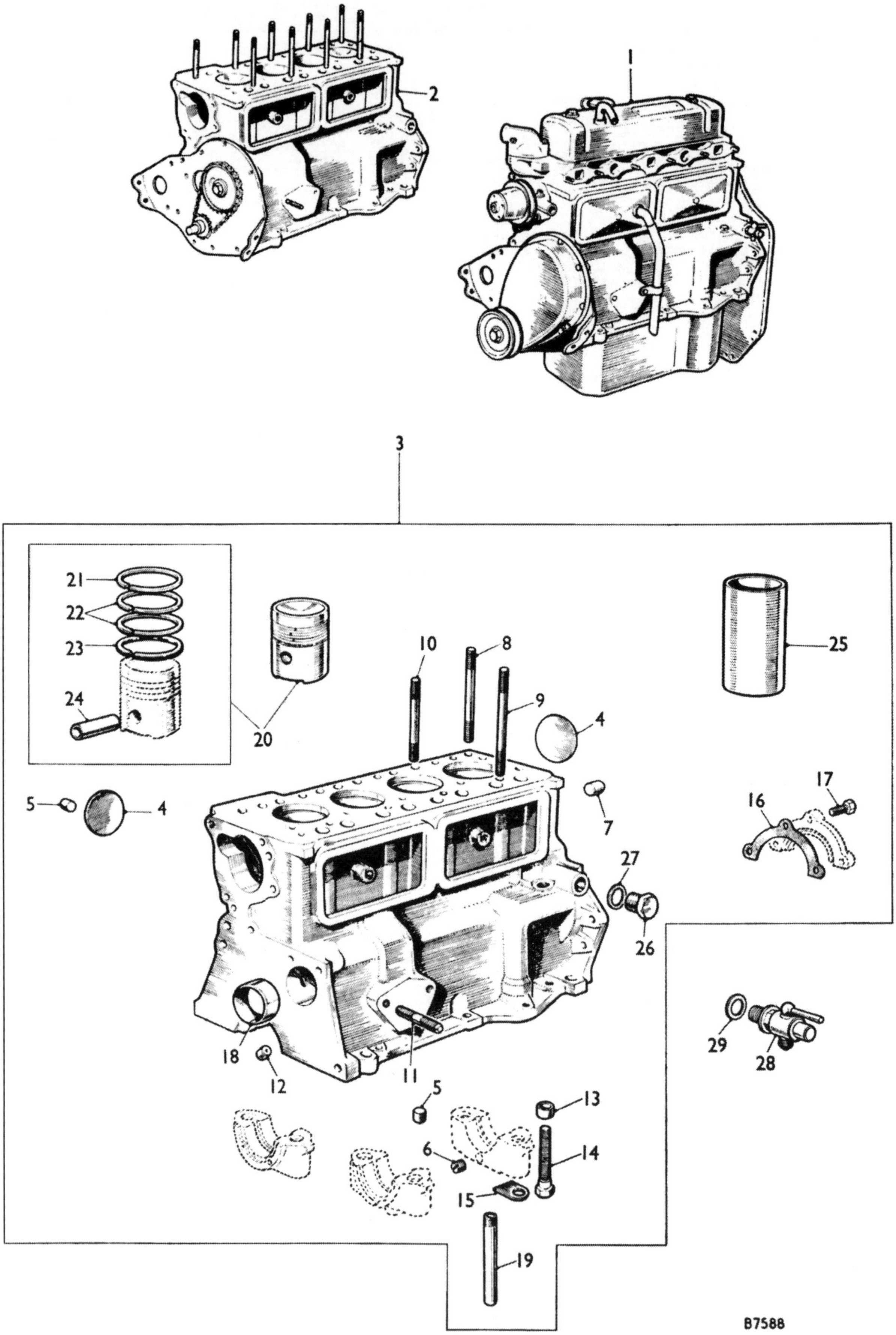

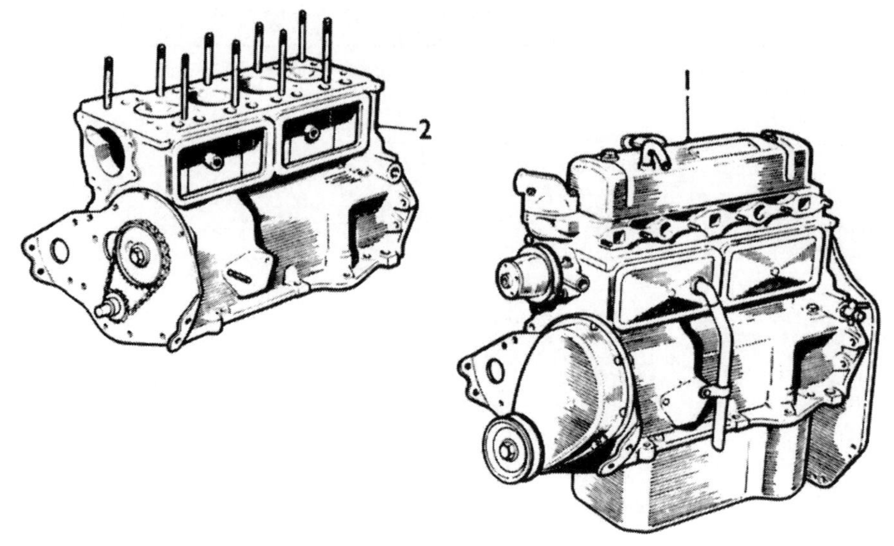
1
2
3
21
22
23
24
20
10
8
9
25
4
5
4
7
17
16
27
26
29
28
18
12
11
5
13
6
14
15
19
B7588

9C Engine—*continued*

DESCRIPTION	Part No.	Illus. No.	Quantity	Change Point	REMARKS
Piston assembly—Grade 3					
Standard	8G 0687 03	20	4		
·010" (·254 mm) O/S	8G 0687 13	20	4		
·020" (·508 mm) O/S	†8G 0687 23	20	4		W.S.E. use 12A 0145 23
·030" (·762 mm) O/S	†8G 0687 33	20	4		W.S.E. use 12A 0145 33
·040" (1·016 mm) O/S	†8G 0687 43	20	4		W.S.E. use 12A 0145 43
Piston assembly—Grade 6					
Standard	8G 0687 06	20	4		
·010" (·254 mm) O/S	†8G 0687 16	20	4		W.S.E. use 12A 0145 16
·020" (·508 mm) O/S	8G 0687 26	20	4		
·030" (·762 mm) O/S	8G 0687 36	20	4		
·040" (1·016 mm) O/S	8G 0687 46	20	4		
Ring—piston—top					
Standard	2A 755	21	4		
·010" (·254 mm) O/S	2A 0755 10	21	4		
·020" (·508 mm) O/S	2A 0755 20	21	4		
·030" (·762 mm) O/S	2A 0755 30	21	4		
·040" (1·016 mm) O/S	2A 0755 40	21	4	(E) 9C/U/H101 to ▼	
Ring—piston—2nd and 3rd					
Standard	2A 686	22	8		
·010" (·254 mm) O/S	2A 0686 10	22	8		
·020" (·508 mm) O/S	2A 0686 20	22	8		
·030" (·762 mm) O/S	2A 0686 30	22	8		
·040" (1·016 mm) O/S	2A 0686 40	22	8		
Ring—piston—scraper					
Standard	†2A 687	23	4		
·010" (·254 mm) O/S	†2A 0687 10	23	4		
·020" (·508 mm) O/S	†2A 0687 20	23	4		
·030" (·762 mm) O/S	†2A 0687 30	23	4		W.S.E. use 12A 121 and
·040" (1·016 mm) O/S	†2A 0687 40	23	4		oversizes
Ring—piston—scraper					
Standard	†12A 121	23	4		
·010" (·254 mm) O/S	†12A 0121 10	23	4		
·020" (5·08 mm) O/S	†12A 0121 20	23	4		
·030" (·762 mm) O/S	†12A 0121 30	23	4		
·040" (1·016 mm) O/S	†12A 0121 40	23	4		
Pin—gudgeon					
Standard	2A 837	24	4		
·002" (·0508 mm) O/S	2A 0837 02	24	4		
·004" (·1016 mm) O/S	2A 0837 04	24	4		
·006" (·1524 mm) O/S	2A 0837 06	24	4		
Piston assembly—Grade 3					
Standard	12A 0145 03	20	4		
·010" (·254 mm) O/S	12A 0145 13	20	4		
·020" (·508 mm) O/S	12A 0145 23	20	4		
·030" (·762 mm) O/S	12A 0145 33	20	4		
·040" (1·016 mm) O/S	12A 0145 43	20	4		
Piston assembly—Grade 6					
Standard	12A 0145 06	20	4		
·010" (·254 mm) O/S	12A 0145 16	20	4		
·020" (·508 mm) O/S	12A 0145 26	20	4		
·030" (·762 mm) O/S	12A 0145 36	20	4		
·040" (1·016 mm) O/S	12A 0145 46	20	4		
Ring—piston—top					
Standard	12A 66	21	4		
·010" (·254 mm) O/S	12A 0066 10	21	4	(E) 9C/U/ ▼ on	
·020" (·508 mm) O/S	12A 0066 20	21	4		
·030" (·762 mm) O/S	12A 0066 30	21	4		
·040" (1·016 mm) O/S	12A 0066 40	21	4		
Ring—piston—2nd and 3rd					
Standard	12A 67	22	8		
·010" (·254 mm) O/S	12A 0067 10	22	8		
·020" (·508 mm) O/S	12A 0067 20	22	8		
·030" (·762 mm) O/S	12A 0067 30	22	8		
·040" (1·016 mm) O/S	12A 0067 40	22	8		
Ring—piston—scraper					
Standard	12A 68	23	4		
·010" (·254 mm) O/S	12A 0068 10	23	4		
·020" (·508 mm) O/S	12A 0068 20	23	4		
·030" (·762 mm) O/S	12A 0068 30	23	4		
·040" (1·016 mm) O/S	12A 0068 40	23	4		
Pin—gudgeon					
Standard	2A 837	24	4		
·002" (·0508 mm) O/S	2A 0837 02	24	4		
·004" (·1016 mm) O/S	2A 0837 04	24	4		
·006" (·1524 mm) O/S	2A 0837 06	24	4		

▼ Change point not available

† Revised Information.

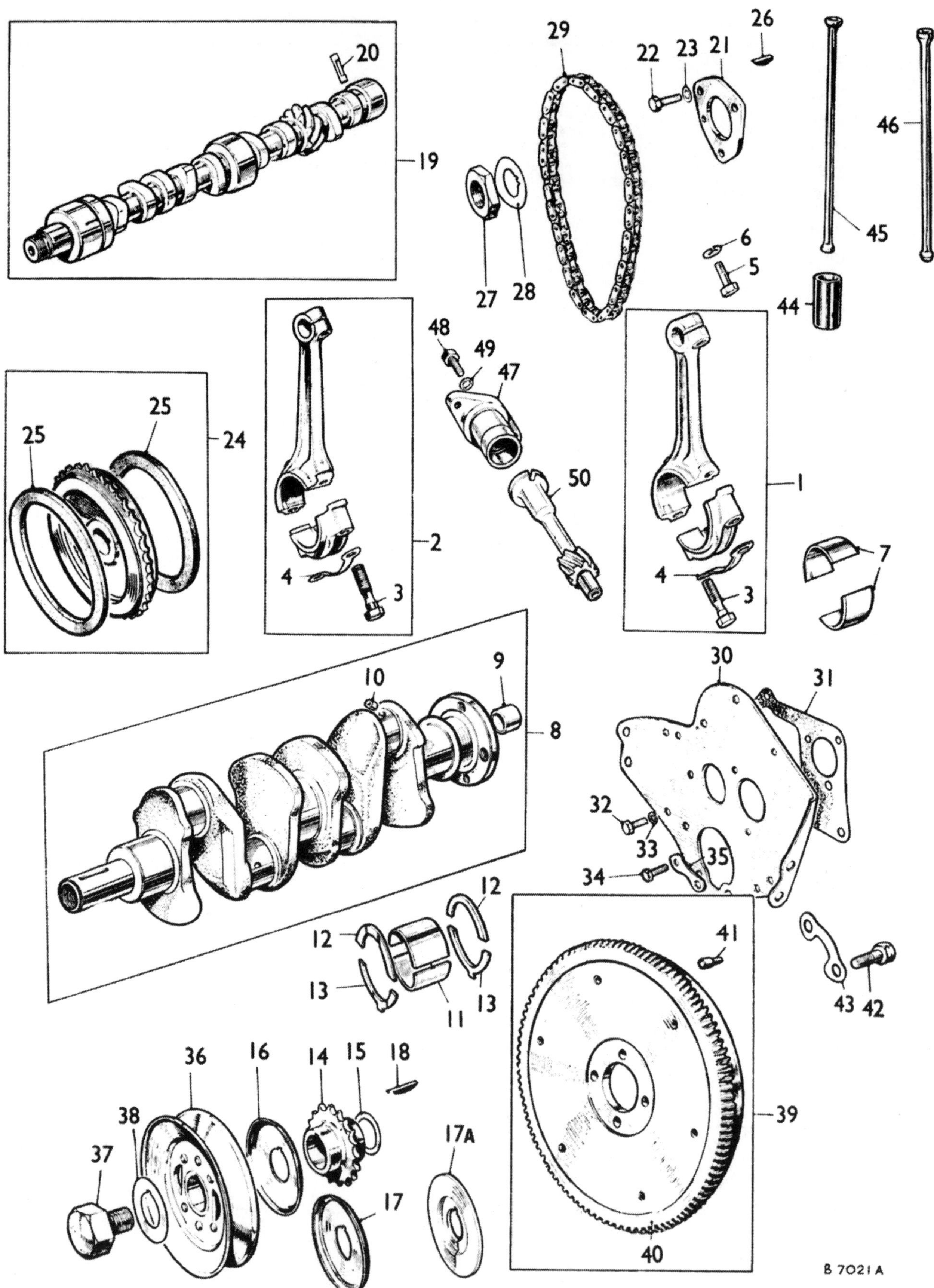

1
2
3
4
5
6
7
8
9
10
11
12
13
14
15
16
17
17A
18
19
20
21
22
23
24
25
26
27
28
29
30
31
32
33
34
35
36
37
38
39
40
41
42
43
44
45
46
47
48
49
50
B 7021 A

DESCRIPTION	Part No.	Illus. No.	Quantity	Change Point	REMARKS
9C Engine—*continued*					
Rod assembly—connecting cylinders Nos. 1 and 3	2A 656	1	2		
Rod assembly—connecting cylinders Nos. 2 and 4	2A 654	2	2		
Screw—connecting rod cap	2A 659	3	8		
Washer—lock	2A 660	4	4		
Screw—clamping	51K 1382	5	4		
Washer—spring	LWN 305	6	4		
Bearing—connecting rod					
Standard	8G 2198	7	1 set		
·010″ (·254 mm) U/S	8G 2198 10	7	1 set		
·020″ (·508 mm) U/S	8G 2198 20	7	1 set		
·030″ (·762 mm) U/S	8G 2198 30	7	1 set		
·040″ (1·016 mm) U/S	8G 2198 40	7	1 set		
CRANKSHAFT AND GEAR					
Crankshaft assembly	88G 225	8	1		Part No. change; was 2A 828 and 2A 830
Crankshaft (with bearings)	28G 95		1		UK market Exchange Unit Scheme only
Bush—1st motion shaft	1A 1559	9	1		
Restrictor—oil	1G 1167	10	4		
Bearing—main					
Standard	8G 2222	11	1 set		
·010″ (·254 mm) U/S	8G 2222 10	11	1 set		
·020″ (·508 mm) U/S	8G 2222 20	11	1 set		
·030″ (·762 mm) U/S	8G 2222 30	11	1 set		
·040″ (1·016 mm) U/S	8G 2222 40	11	1 set		
Washer—thrust					
Upper—standard	1A 1716	12	2		
Upper—·003″ (·076 mm) O/S	1A 1716 03	12	2		
Lower—standard	1A 1717	13	2		
Lower—·003″	1A 1717 03	13	2		
Gear—crankshaft	8G 725	14	1		
Washer—packing	6K 628	15	1		
Thrower—oil—front	2A 77	16	1	(E) 9C/U/H101 to H37646	
	2A 1015	17	1	(E) 9C/U/H37647 on	For service with front covers 2A 987 and 12A 723
	12A 1148	17A	1		For service with front cover 12G 791
Key—gear and crankshaft	6K 836	18	1		
CAMSHAFT					
Camshaft (with driving pin—oil pump)	2A 297	19	1		Alternatives; use 8G 712 for this application
	2A 571	19	1		
	8G 712	19	1		
Pin—driving—oil pump	2A 299	20	1		
Plate—locating	2A 84	21	1		
Screw	HNS 0406	22	3		
Washer—shakeproof	LWN 404	23	3		
Gear assembly—camshaft	2A 85	24	1		
Ring—tensioner	8G 549	25	2		
Key—gear	WKN 505	26	1		
Nut—gear	6K 629	27	1		
Washer—lock	2A 759	28	1		
Chain—camshaft drive	3H 2127	29	1		
FRONT MOUNTING PLATE					
Plate—engine mounting—front	2A 125	30	1		
Gasket—mounting plate	2A 126	31	1		W.S.E. use 12G 619
Gasket—mounting plate	12G 619	31	1		
Screw	HZS 0505	32	2		
Washer—spring	LWZ 305	33	2		
Screw—mounting plate to bearing cap	53K 2016	34	2		
Plate—locking	6K 831	35	1		
CRANKSHAFT PULLEY					
Pulley—crankshaft	2A 550	36	1		W.S.E. use 2A 940
Pulley—crankshaft	2A 940	36	1		
Bolt—crankshaft pulley	AEA 312	27	1		
Washer—lock	1G 1319	38	1		

† Revised Information.

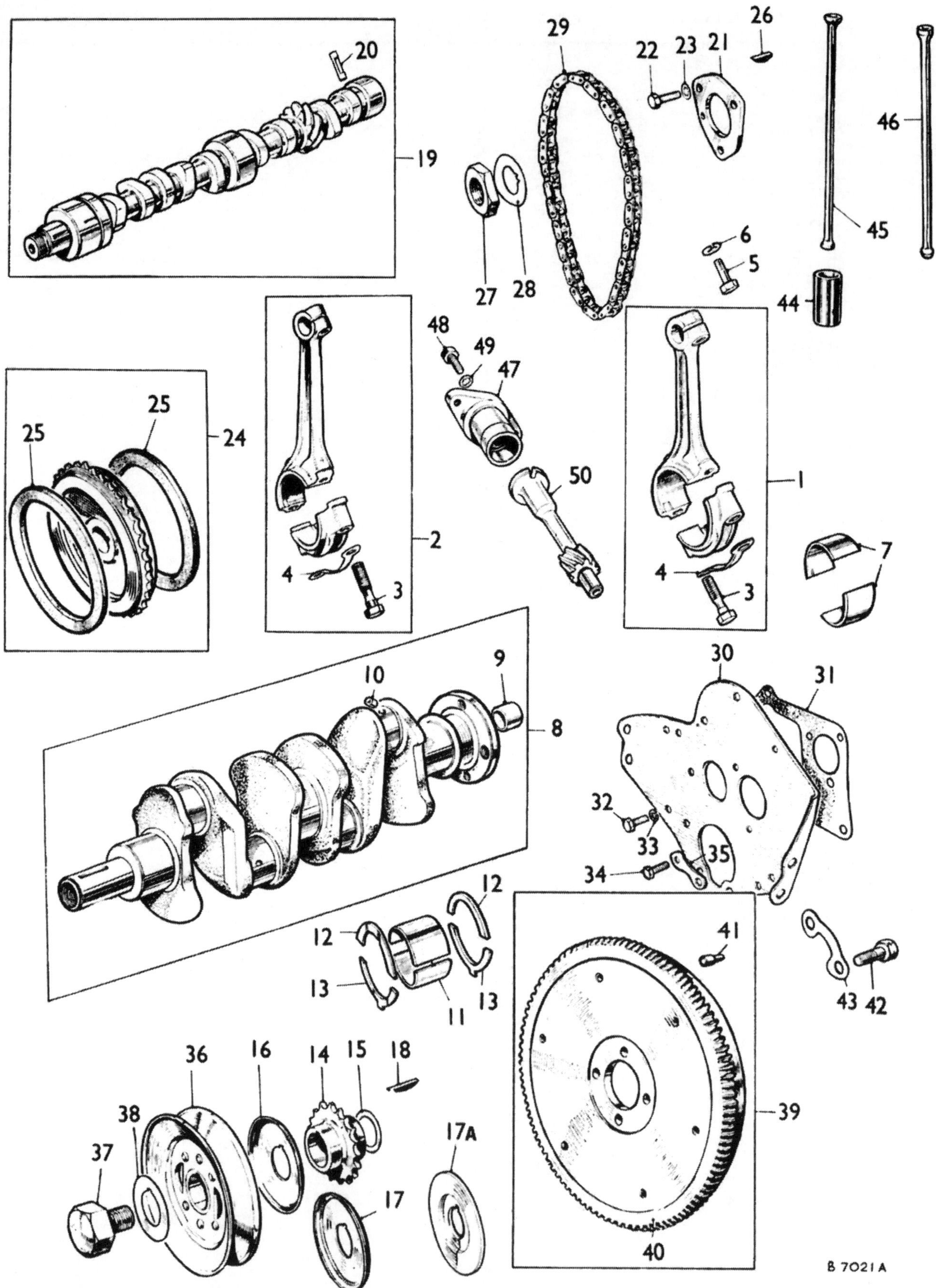
1
2
3
4
5
6
7
8
9
10
11
12
13
14
15
16
17
17A
18
19
20
21
22
23
24
25
26
27
28
29
30
31
32
33
34
35
36
37
38
39
40
41
42
43
44
45
46
47
48
49
50
B 7021 A

DESCRIPTION	Part No.	Illus. No.	Quantity	Change Point	REMARKS
9C Engine—*continued*					
FLYWHEEL					
Flywheel assembly	†2A 516	39	1	(E) 9C/U/H101 to H4833	W.S.E. use 88G 227
Gear—ring—starter	†2A 378	40	1		W.S.E. use AEA 596
Dowel—clutch to flywheel	1G 2984	41	2		
Flywheel assembly	88G 227	39	1	(E) 9C/U/H4834 on	Part No. change; was 12A 182 or AEA 594
Gear—ring—starter	†12A 183	40	1		W.S.E. use AEA 596
Gear—ring—starter	†AEA 596	40	1		
Dowel—clutch to flywheel	1G 2984	41	2		
Screw—flywheel to crankshaft	6K 630	42	4		
Washer—lock	2K 7816	43	2		
TAPPETS AND PUSH-RODS					
Tappet					
Standard	2A 13	44	8		
·010″ (·254 mm) O/S	2A 0013 10	44	8		
·020″ (·508 mm) O/S	2A 0013 20	44	8		
Push-rod	2A 14	45	8		Alternative in sets
	12A 250	45	8		
	†12A 747	45	8		
DISTRIBUTOR HOUSING AND SPINDLE					
Housing—distributor	†2A 612	47	1		W.S.E. use 12A 1136 together with 13H 2792 'O' ring
Housing—distributor	12A 1136	47	1		
'O' ring—seal	13H 2792		1		
Screw	HZS 0406	48	1		
Washer—shakeproof	LWN 404	49	1		
Spindle—distributor driving	†2A 139	50	1		Alternatives. W.S.E. use 1G 2062
	†2A 847	50	1		
	1G 2062	50	1		

† Revised Information.

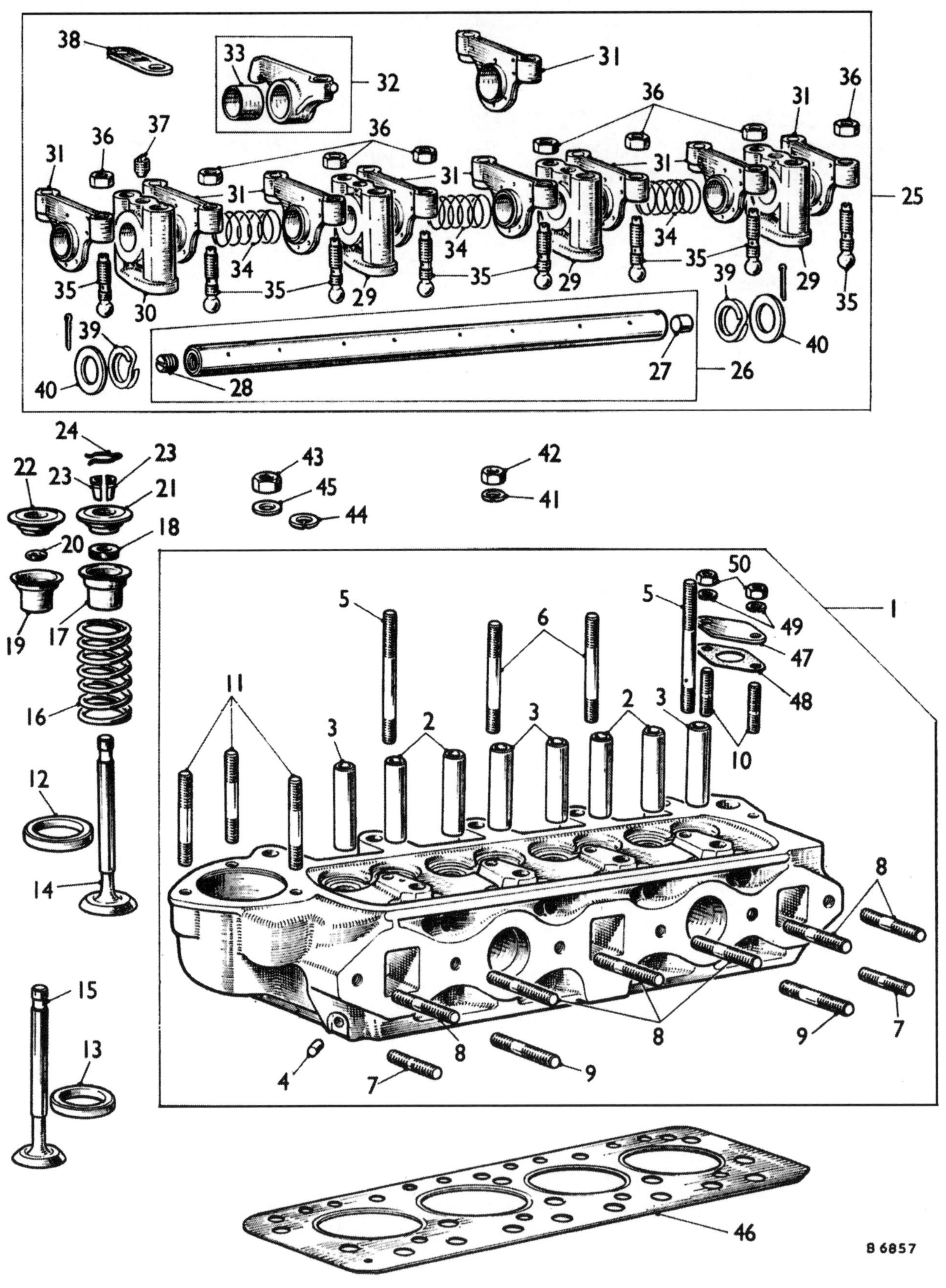
38
33
32
31
36
31
36
37
36
31
36
31
31
31
31
31
25
34
34
34
35
35
35
35
35
35
29
29
29
30
39
40
28
27
26
39
40
24
23
22
23
21
18
20
19
17
16
12
14
15
13
43
45
44
42
41
50
5
5
6
49
47
48
11
3
2
3
2
3
10
8
4
7
8
9
8
9
7
1
46
B 6857

9C Engine—*continued*

DESCRIPTION	Part No.	Illus. No.	Quantity	Change Point	REMARKS
CYLINDER HEAD DETAILS					
Head assembly—cylinder	NSP		1		Was 28G 86
Head—cylinder (with guides, plugs, and studs)	28G 161	1	1		
Guide—valve					
Inlet—standard	2A 608	2	4		
Inlet—·010″ (·254 mm) O/S	†2A 0608 10	2	4		
Exhaust—standard	2A 608	3	4		
Exhaust—·010″ (·254 mm) O/S	†2A 0608 10	3	4		
Plug—oil hole	†6K 808	4	1		W.S.E. use 2K 1345
Plug—oil hole	†2K 1345	4	1		
Stud					
Rocker bracket—long	51K 885	5	2		
Rocker bracket—short	51K 554	6	2	(E) 9C/U/H101 to H39894	
Rocker bracket—short	CHS 0522	6	2	(E) 9C/U/H39895 to H41829	
Rocker bracket—short	51K 1478	6	2	(E) 9C/U/H41830 on	
Exhaust manifold—long	†FLS 2513	9	2	(E) 9C/U/H101 to H39894	W.S.E. use FHS 2513
Exhaust manifold—long	†FHS 2513	9	2		Use 6 off 53K 487 for this application
Exhaust manifold—medium	†53K 487	8	2		
Exhaust manifold—short	†53K 486	7	2		
Exhaust manifold—medium	†53K 487	8	6	(E) 9C/U/H39895 on	
Cover plate	53K 402	10	2		
Water outlet elbow	53K 530	11	3		
Plate—cover—heater tap facing	2A 180	47	1		
Gasket—plate	†88G 221	48	1		Part No. change; was 2A 179 and 12A 32
Washer—spring	LWN 304	49	2		
Nut	FNZ 104	50	2		
Insert—valve seat					
Inlet—standard	2A 639	12	4		Alternatives. Inserts must be all standard or all oversize, not mixed (For service purposes only)
Inlet—$\frac{1}{16}$″ (1·58 mm) O/S	AEA 762	12	4		
Exhaust—standard	2A 640	13	4		Alternatives. Inserts must be all standard or all oversize, not mixed (For service purposes only)
Exhaust—$\frac{1}{16}$″ (1·58 mm) O/S	AEA 763	13	4		
Valve					
Inlet	2A 6	14	4	(E) 9C/U/H101 to H1396	
Exhaust	AEA 327	15	4		
Inlet	2A 877	14	4	(E) 9C/U/H1397 on	
Exhaust	†AEA 358	15	4	(E) 9C/U/H1397 to H36899	W.S.E. use AEA 400
Exhaust	AEA 434	15	4	(E) 9C/U/H36900 on	Use AEA 400 for this application
Exhaust	AEA 400	15	4		
Spring—valve	AEA 311	16	8		
Shroud—valve guide	2A 544	17	8	(E) 9C/U/H101 to H1396	
Seal—oil valve	2A 9	18	8		
Shroud—valve guide	2A 545	19	8	(E) 9C/U/H1397 on	
Ring—valve packing (rubber)	2A 879	20	8		
Cup—valve spring	2A 10	21	8	(E) 9C/U/H101 to H1396	
Cup—valve spring	2A 880	22	8	(E) 9C/U/H1397 on	
Cotter—valve	2A 11	23	16		
Circlip—valve cotter	2A 12	24	8		

† Revised Information.

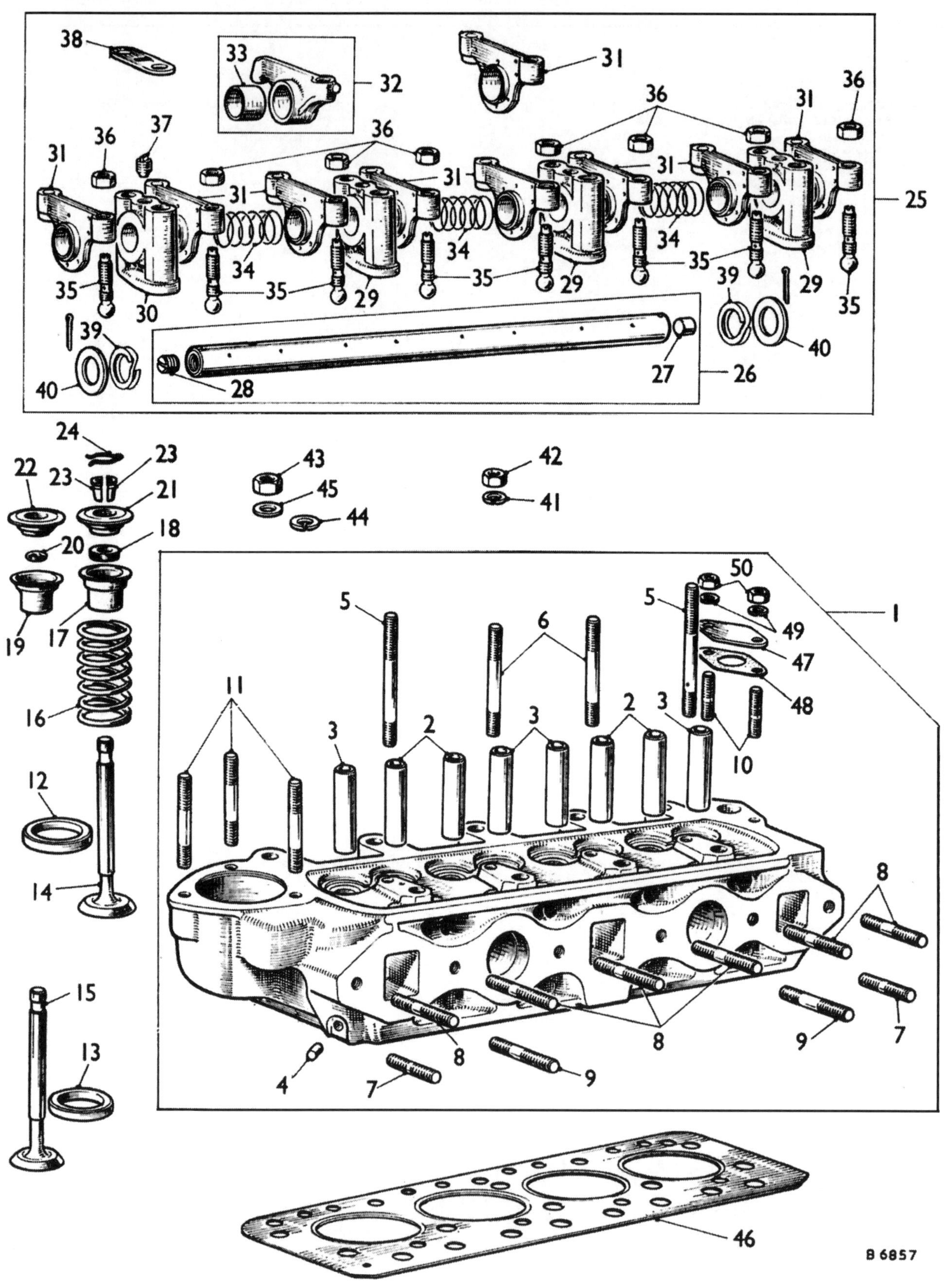
B 6857

DESCRIPTION	Part No.	Illus. No.	Quantity	Change Point	REMARKS
9C Engine—*continued*					
Shaft assembly—valve rocker	†NSP	25	1		Was 2A 15
Shaft—valve rocker—plugged	2A 16	26	1		
Plug	6K 878	27	1		
Plug	2K 4608	28	1		
Bracket—rocker shaft					
Plain	†2A 23	29	3		W.S.E. use 12G 1110
Plain	†12G 1110	29	3		
Tapped	†2A 22	30	1		W.S.E. use 12G 1109
Tapped	†12G 1109	30	1		
Rocker—valve—bushed	2A 964	31	8		Alternatives; interchangeable in sets only
Rocker valve—bushed	2A 533	32	8		
Bush—valve rocker	2A 21	33	8		
Rivet	5C 2436		8		
Spring—rocker spacing	6K 556	34	3		
Screw—tappet adjusting	†2A 535	35	8		W.S.E. use 12A 1115
Screw—tappet adjusting	12A 1215	35	8		
Locknut	6K 654	36	8		
Screw—rocker shaft—locating	2A 258	37	1		
Plate—rocker shaft bracket	2A 515	38	4		
Washer—spring	2A 13	39	2		
Washer	6K 555	40	2		
Washer—spring	LWN 205	41	4		
Nut	FNN 105	42	4		
	†53K 371	43	9		W.S.E. use 51K 371
	51K 371	43	9		
Washer—spring	LWN 205	44	4		
Washer—plain	PWN 106	45	5		
Gasket—cylinder head	†2A 689	46	1	(E) 9C/U/H101 to H1167	W.S.E. use 12G 293
	†2A 935	46	1	(E) 9C/U/H1168 to H6732	
	†2A 971	46	1	(E) 9C/U/H6733 on	
	†12G 293	46	1		

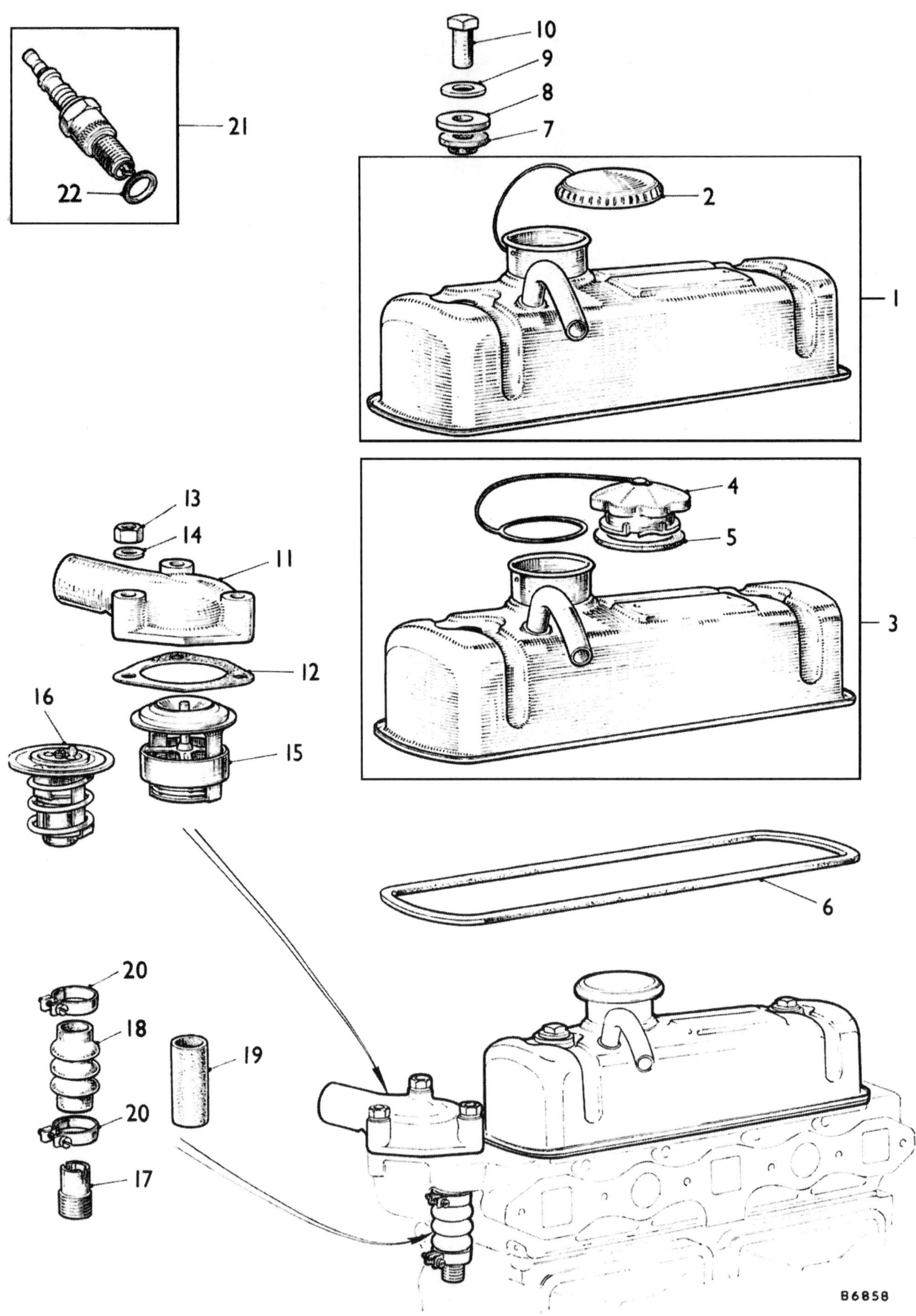
10
9
8
7
21
22
2
1
13
14
11
4
5
3
12
16
15
6
20
18
19
20
17
B6858

DESCRIPTION	Part No.	Illus. No.	Quantity	Change Point	REMARKS
9C Engine—*continued*					
VALVE ROCKER COVER AND OIL FILLER					
Cover—valve rocker (with cap)	AEA 330	1	1		Use **12A 501** for this application
Cap—oil filler	8G 612	2	1		Use **12A 402** for this application
Cover—valve rocker (with cap)	12A 501	3	1		
Cap—oil filler	12A 402	4	1		
Washer—oil filler cap	12A 403	5	1		
Gasket—valve rocker cover	†2A 805	6	1		W.S.E. use **12A 14**
	†2A 956	6	1		W.S.E. use **12A 14**
	12A 14	6	1		
Bush—rocker cover (rubber)	†2K 8568	7	2		W.S.E. use **12A 1358**
Bush—rocker cover (rubber)	†12A 1358	7	2		
Piece—distance—rocker cover nut	1B 2925	8	2		
Washer—rocker cover nut	1A 2156	9	2		
Nut—valve rocker cover	2A 150	10	2		
WATER OUTLET ELBOW AND THERMOSTAT					
Elbow—water outlet	AEA 306	11	1		
Gasket—water outlet elbow	1A 2149	12	1		Use **12G 330** for this application
Gasket—water outlet elbow	12G 330	12	1		
Nut	FNZ 105	13	3		
Washer—plain	PWZ 105	14	3		
Thermostat					
Bellows-type—73° C (163° F)	†11G 291	15	1		W.S.E. use **13H 3727** — Hot climates
Bellows-type—73° C (163° F)	†11K 399	15	1		W.S.E. use **13H 3727** — Hot climates
Wax-type—74° C (165° F)	†13H 1412	16	1		W.S.E. use **13H 3727** — Hot climates
Wax-type—74° C (165° F)	†13H 2526	16	1		W.S.E. use **13H 3727** — Hot climates
Wax-type—74° C (165° F)	†13H 3584	16	1		W.S.E. use **13H 3727** — Hot climates
Wax-type—74° C (165° F)	†13H 3727	16	1		Hot climates
Wax-type—82° C (180° F)	†13H 2317	16	1		W.S.E. use **13H 4070** — Temperate climates
Wax-type—82° C (180° F)	†13H 3585	16	1		W.S.E. use **13H 4070** — Temperate climates
Wax-type—82° C (180° F)	†13H 4070	16	1		Temperate climates
Wax-type—88° C (190° F)	†13H 2316	16	1		W.S.E. use **13H 3586** — Cold climates
Wax-type—88° C (190° F)	†13H 3586	16	1		Cold climates
Adaptor—by-pass	2A 243	17	1		
Connection—by-pass (rubber)	2A 242	18	1		Use **12A 1093** for this application
Connection—by-pass (rubber)	12A 1093	19	1		
Clip—connection	3H 2963	20	2		
SPARKING PLUGS					
Plug—sparking (N5)	3H 2006	21	4		
Plug—sparking (XN8)	2A 375	21	4		For use when short-wave radio is fitted
Gasket	2K 5211	22	4		

† Revised Information.

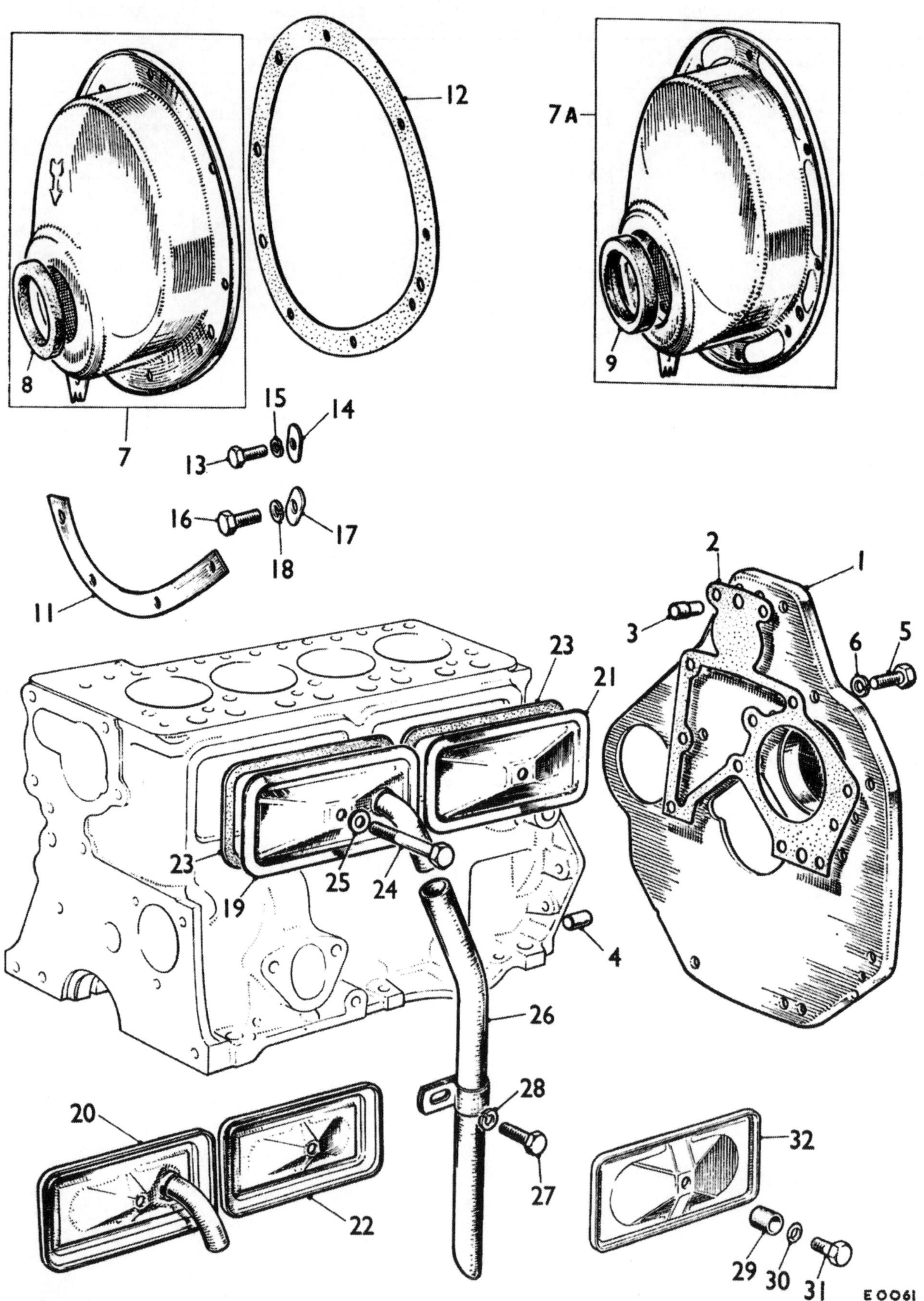
12
7A
8
9
7
15
14
13
16
17
18
11
2
1
3
6
5
23
21
23
25
24
19
4
26
28
20
32
22
27
29
30
31
E0061

9C Engine—*continued*

DESCRIPTION	Part No.	Illus. No.	Quantity	Change Point	REMARKS
REAR MOUNTING PLATE					
Plate—engine mounting—rear	88G 226	1	1		Part No. change; was 2A 800 and 2A 569
Gasket	2A 123	2	1		Use 12A 22 for this application
Gasket	12A 22	2	1		
Dowel—top	1K 52	3	1		
Dowel—bottom	1G 752	4	1		
Screw	HZS 0505	5	7		
Washer—spring	LWZ 305	6	7		
CYLINDER FRONT AND SIDE COVERS					
Cover—front	†2A 552	7	1	(E) 9C/U/H101 to H37646	W.S.E. use 12G 791 together with oil thrower 12A 1148 on page MA 5
	†2A 937	7	1	(E) 9C/U/H37647 on	(as above)
(With stiffener)	†12A 723	7	1		(as above)
(With timing pointer)	†12G 791	7A	1		W.S.E. use 12A 1419
	†12A 1419	7A	1		
Ring (felt)	2K 7140	8	1		For use with 2A 552
Seal—oil	†2A 939	9	1		W.S.E. use 13H 4061; For use with covers 2A 937, 12A 723 and 12G 791
Seal—oil	†13H 4061	9	1		For use with covers 2A 937, 12A 723 and 12G 791
Stiffener—front cover	12A 666	11	1		For use with 2A 552, 2A 937
Gasket	1A 2093	12	1		Use 12A 956 for this application
Gasket	12A 956	12	1		
Screw	HZS 0403	13	6		
Washer—plain	2K 5197	14	6/3		
Washer—spring	LWN 204	15	6		
Screw	HZS 0505	16	4		
Washer—plain	2K 7440	17	6/3		
Washer—spring	LWZ 305	18	4		
Cover—cylinder side					
Front (with elbow)	1A 2199	19	1		Use 12H 948 for this application
Front (with elbow)	12H 155	19	1		(as above)
Front (with elbow)	12H 948	20	1		
Rear	†2A 770	21	1		W.S.E. use 12A 1170 together with 1 off each joint 12A 1175, bush 12A 1176, cup 12A 1177, and screw HZS 0509
Rear	†13H 152	21	1		(as above)
Rear	†12H 941	22	1		(as above)
Rear	12A 1170	32	1		
Gasket	†1A 2208	23	2		W.S.E. use 12A 1139
	†12A 24	23	2		(as above)
	12A 1139	23	2		For service with side covers 1A 2199, 12H 155, 2A 770, 12H 948, 12H 152, and 12H 941
Screw—cover to crankcase	HBZ 0515	24	2		(as above)
Washer (fibre)	2K 4958	25	2		(as above)
Gasket	12A 1175	28	1		For service with side cover 12A 1170
Bush (rubber)	12A 1176	29	1		(as above)
Washer—cup	12A 1177	30	1		(as above)
Screw—cover to crankcase	HZS 0509	31	1		(as above)
Pipe—vent—lower (with clip)	2A 118	26	1		
Screw	HZS 0505	27	1		
Washer—spring	LWZ 205	28	1		

† Revised Information.

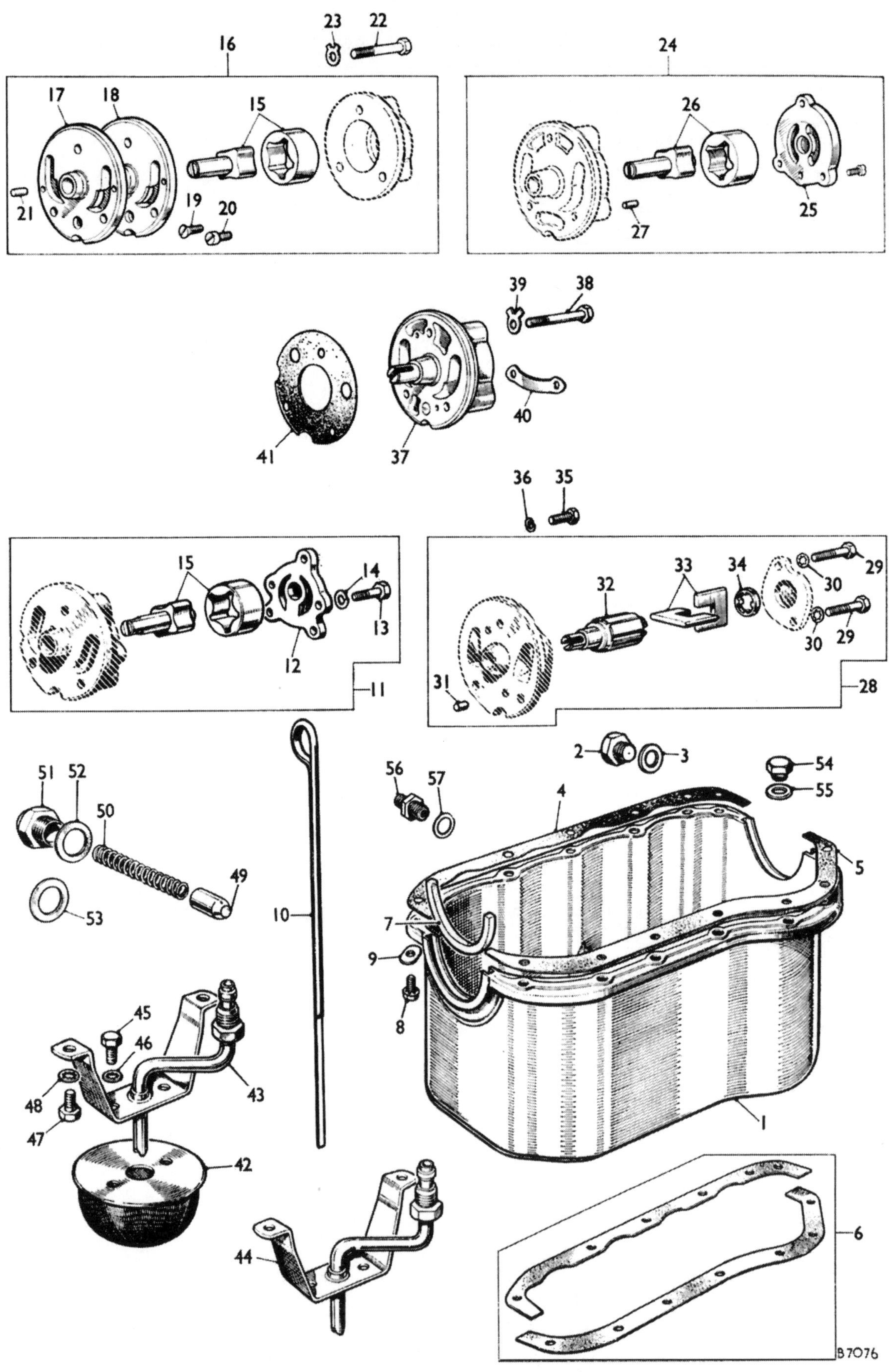
16
23
22
24
17
18
15
26
21
19
20
25
27
39
38
41
37
40
36
35
15
14
13
12
11
33
34
32
29
30
31
28
2
3
54
55
51
52
50
49
53
10
56
57
4
5
7
9
8
45
46
43
48
47
42
1
44
6
B7076

DESCRIPTION	Part No.	Illus. No.	Quantity	Change Point	REMARKS
9C Engine—*continued*					
SUMP AND DIPPER ROD					
Sump—oil	†2A 704	1	1		W.S.E. use 12G 173
Sump—oil	12G 173	1	1		
Plug—drain	88G 257	2	1		Part No. change; was 2F 4249 and 2A 380
Washer	6K 638	3	1		
Gasket—sump to crankcase Right-hand	†2A 711	4	1		W.S.E. use 8G 731
Right-hand	†12A 20	4	1		W.S.E. use 8G 731
Left-hand	†2A 98	5	1		W.S.E. use 8G 731
Left-hand	†12A 19	5	1		W.S.E. use 8G 731
	†8G 716	6	1 set		W.S.E. use 8G 731
	†8G 722	6	1 set		W.S.E. use 8G 731
	†8G 731	6	1 set		
Seal—oil—main bearing cap	2A 280	7	2		
Screw—sump to crankcase (with washer)	6K 639	8	14		
Washer—plain	2K 5197	9	14		
Rod—oil dipper	2A 294	10	1		
OIL PUMP—PIPE—STRAINER—RELEASE VALVE—PRESSURE UNION					
Pump—oil (Hobourn)	†2A 341	11	1		W.S.E. use 12A 303
Body	NSP		1		
Cover	†7H 1650	12	1		Correction; was 17H 1650
Screw—cover to body	HZS 0406	13	2		
Washer—spring	LWN 204	14	2		
Shaft—driving (with rotors)	17H 1965	15	1		
Pump—oil (Hobourn)	†2A 962	16	1		Alternative to 12G 793
Body	NSP		1		
Cover (countersunk holes)	17H 1963	17	1		
Cover (plain hole)	17H 6427	18	1		
Shaft driving (with rotors)	17H 1965	15	1		
Screw—countersunk	AJD 4205 Z	19	1		
Screw—cheese-head	AJD 3204 Z	20	1		
Dowel	17H 1964	21	2		
Screw	HBN 0414	22	3		
Washer—lock	2A 339	23	1		
Pump—oil (Hobourn)	12A 303	24	1		Alternative to 12G 50. W.S.E. use 2A 962
Body	NSP		1		
Cover	37H 863	25	1		
Shaft—driving (with rotor)	37H 861	21	1		
Dowel	37H 864	27	1		
Screw	AJD 3204 Z	18	1		
Pump—oil (Burman)	†2A 819		1		W.S.E. use 12A 303 or 12G 50
Body and cover	NSP		1		
Screw	HBN 0411	29	2		
Washer—shakeproof	LWN 404	30	2		
Dowel	7H 6813	31	2		
Rotor	7H 6810	32	1		
Vane—rotor	7H 6807	33	2		
Sleeve—rotor	7H 6808	34	1		
Screw	HBZ 0405	35	3		
Washer—spring	LWN 304	36	1		
Pump—oil (Concentric)	†2A 813	37	1		W.S.E. use 12G 793
	†12A 107	37	1		W.S.E. use 12G 793
	†12A 198	37	1		W.S.E. use 12G 793
	†12G 50	37	1		W.S.E. use 12G 793
	†12G 793	37	1		Alternative to 2A 962
Screw	HBN 0414	38	3		
Washer—lock	2A 339	39	1		
Plate—lock—mounting screw	2A 522	40	1		
Gasket—pump to crankcase	†2A 494	41	1		W.S.E. use 12G 69
Gasket	†12G 69	41	1		W.S.E. use 88G 411
	†88G 411	41	1		
Strainer—oil	2A 668	42	1		
Pipe—suction (with oil strainer bracket)	†2A 672	43	1	(E) 9C/U/H101 to H272	W.S.E. use 2A 957
Pipe—suction (with oil strainer bracket)	2A 957	44	1	(E) 9C/U/H273 on	
Screw	HNS 0404	45	2		
Washer—shakeproof	LWN 404	46	2		
Screw	HNS 0404	47	2		
Washer—shakeproof	LWN 404	48	2		
Valve—oil release	†1G 1452	49	1		W.S.E. use 12H 865
Valve—oil release	12H 865	49	1		
Spring—valve	6K 853	50	1		
Nut—cap—valve	1A 2206	51	1		
Washer (fibre)	2K 4982	52	1		Use 6K 431 for this application
Washer (copper)	6K 431	53	1		
Plug—oil priming	2K 4994	54	1		
Washer (copper)	6K 464	55	1		
Union—oil pressure	2A 269	56	1		
Washer (fibre)	2K 4956	57	1		

† Revised Information.

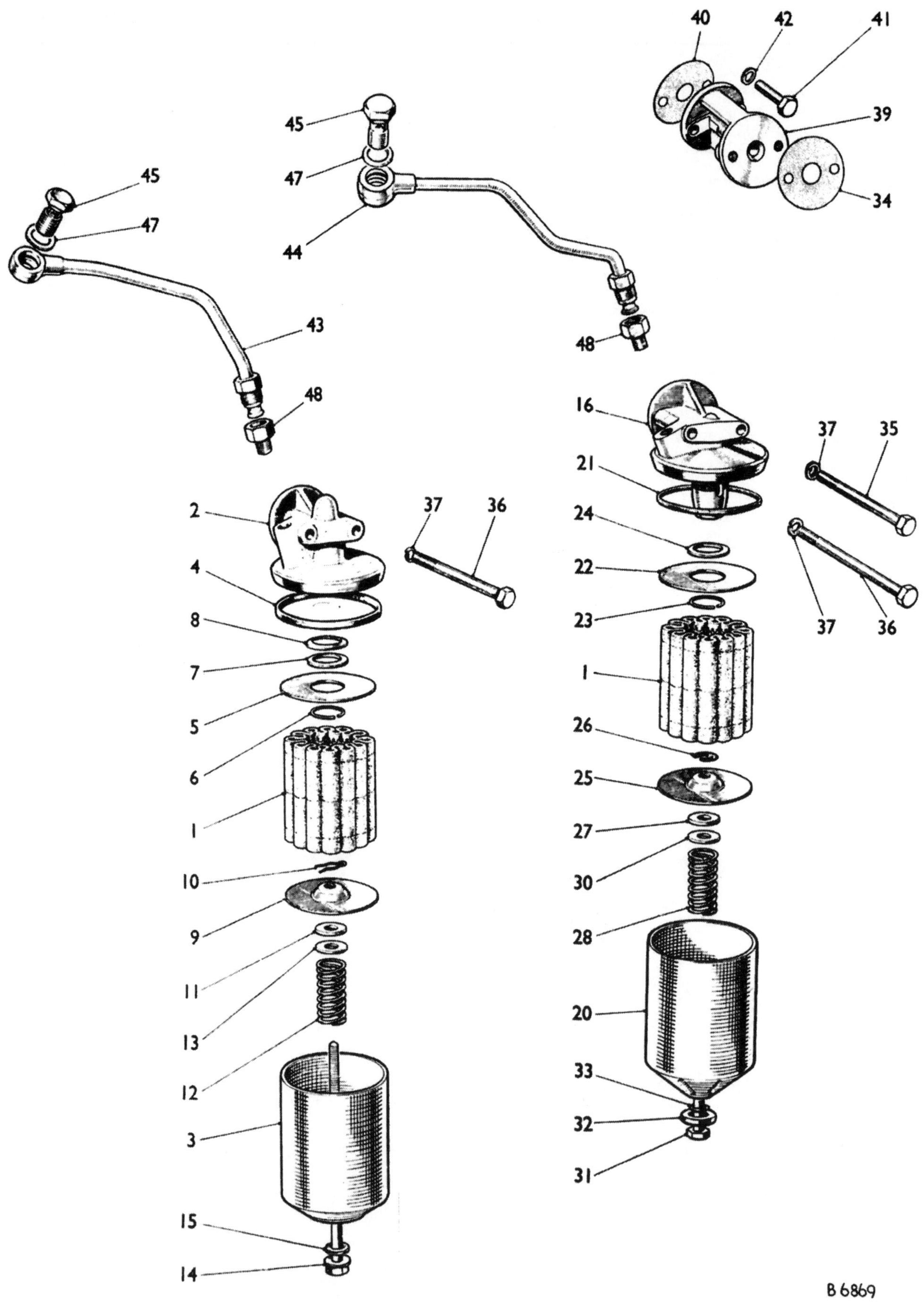
40
42
41
39
34
45
47
44
45
47
43
48
48
16
21
37
35
2
37
36
24
4
22
8
23
37
36
7
1
5
6
26
25
1
27
10
30
9
28
11
13
20
12
33
3
32
31
15
14
B 6869

DESCRIPTION	Part No.	Illus. No.	Quantity	Change Point	REMARKS
9C Engine—*continued*					
Filter—oil (Tecalemit)	†NSP		1		Alternative to Purolator filter
Element	8G 684	1	1		
Head	17H 945	2	1		
Sump	†17H 944	3	1		W.S.E. use 37H 436
Sump	37H 436	3	1		
Seal—sump to head	†17H 4	4	1		W.S.E. use 13H 998
Seal—sump to head	†13H 998	4	1		
Plate—element clamp	7H 147	5	1		
Circlip—plate to head	2A 700	6	1		
Washer—clamp plate (felt)	7H 1756	7	1		
Washer—dished—clamp plate	7H 1761	8	1		
Plate—pressure	17H 942	9	1		
Circlip—plate to centre bolt	7H 1840	10	1		W.S.E. use 17H 2877
Circlip—plate to centre bolt	17H 2877	10	1		
Washer—pressure plate (felt)	7H 1758	11	1		
Spring—pressure plate	7H 1764	12	1		
Washer—spring	7H 1765	13	1		
Bolt—centre	17H 943	14	1		
Seal—bolt to sump	7H 1759	15	1		
Filter—oil (Purolator)	†NSP		1		Alternative to Tecalemit filter
Element	8G 684	1	1		
Head assembly	17H 1170	16	1		
Ball	BLS 112	17	1		
Spring—ball	†37H 859	18	1		W.S.E. use 17H 1170
Seat—ball	†37H 860	19	1		
Sump	17H 1169	20	1		
Seal—sump to head	†17H 1168	21	1		W.S.E. use 12A 1591
	†27H 1983	21	1		
	†13H 3249	21	1		
	†12A 1591	21	1		
Plate—clamping	17H 1150	22	1		
Circlip—clamp plate to head	17H 1167	23	1		
Gasket—clamp plate to head	17H 1152	24	1		
Plate—pressure	17H 1148	25	1		
Circlip—plate to centre bolt	†17H 1476	26	1		W.S.E. use 27H 2573
Circlip—plate to centre bolt	27H 2573	26	1		
Seal—pressure plate	7H 28	27	1		
Spring—pressure plate	7H 25	28	1		
Washer—spring	†7H 7553	29	1		W.S.E. use PWN 106
Washer—spring	PWN 106	30	1		
Bolt—centre	17H 1174	31	1		
Collar—centre bolt	17H 1172	32	1		
Seal—'O' section collar to sump	17H 1173	33	1		
Gasket—oil filter to adaptor	†2A 703	34	1		W.S.E. use 88G 402
Gasket—oil filter to adaptor	88G 402	34	1		Part No. change; was 12G 148
Bolt	HCZ 0628	35	2		For use with AEA 305
Bolt	HCZ 0630	36	2		For use with AEA 657
Washer—spring	LWZ 206	37	2		
Adaptor—oil filter	†AEA 305	38	1		W.S.E. use AEA 657 together with 2 off bolt HCZ 0630 and 1 off pipe AEA 658
Adaptor—oil filter	AEA 657	39	1		
Gasket—adaptor to crankcase	†2A 703	40	1		W.S.E. use 88G 402
Gasket—adaptor to crankcase	88G 402	40	1		Part No. change; was 12G 148
Screw—adaptor to crankcase	†NCS 0608	41	2		
Washer—spring	LWN 206	42	2		
Pipe—oil filter to crankcase	†AEA 313	43	1		W.S.E. use AEA 658 together with 1 off adaptor AEA 657 and 2 off bolt HCZ 0630
Pipe—oil filter to crankcase	AEA 658	44	1		
Screw—banjo union	2A 715	45	1		
Washer (copper)	†2A 787	46	2		W.S.E. use AED 172
Washer (copper)	AED 172	47	2		
Connection	†TCN 206	48	1		Use AEA 678 for this application
Connection	†AEA 678	48	1		

† Revised Information.

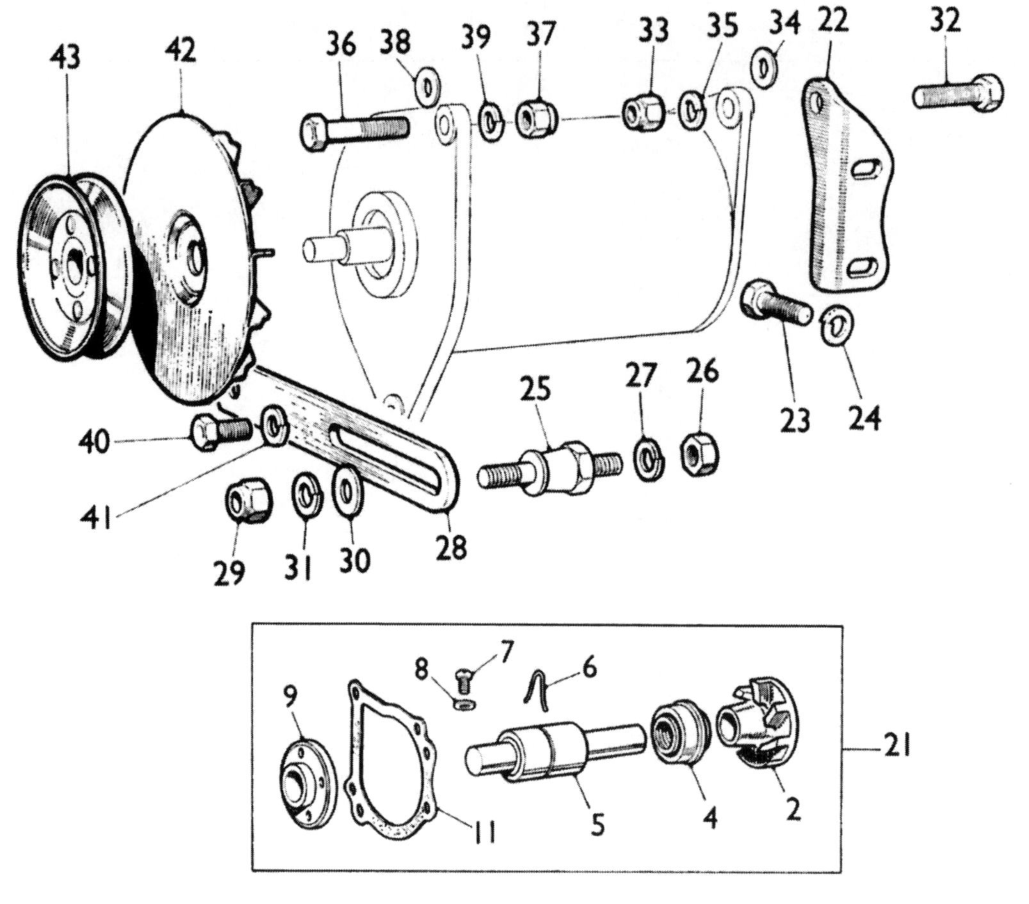
43
42
36
38
39
37
33
35
34
22
32
23
24
25
27
26
40
41
28
29
31
30
9
8
7
6
11
5
4
2
21

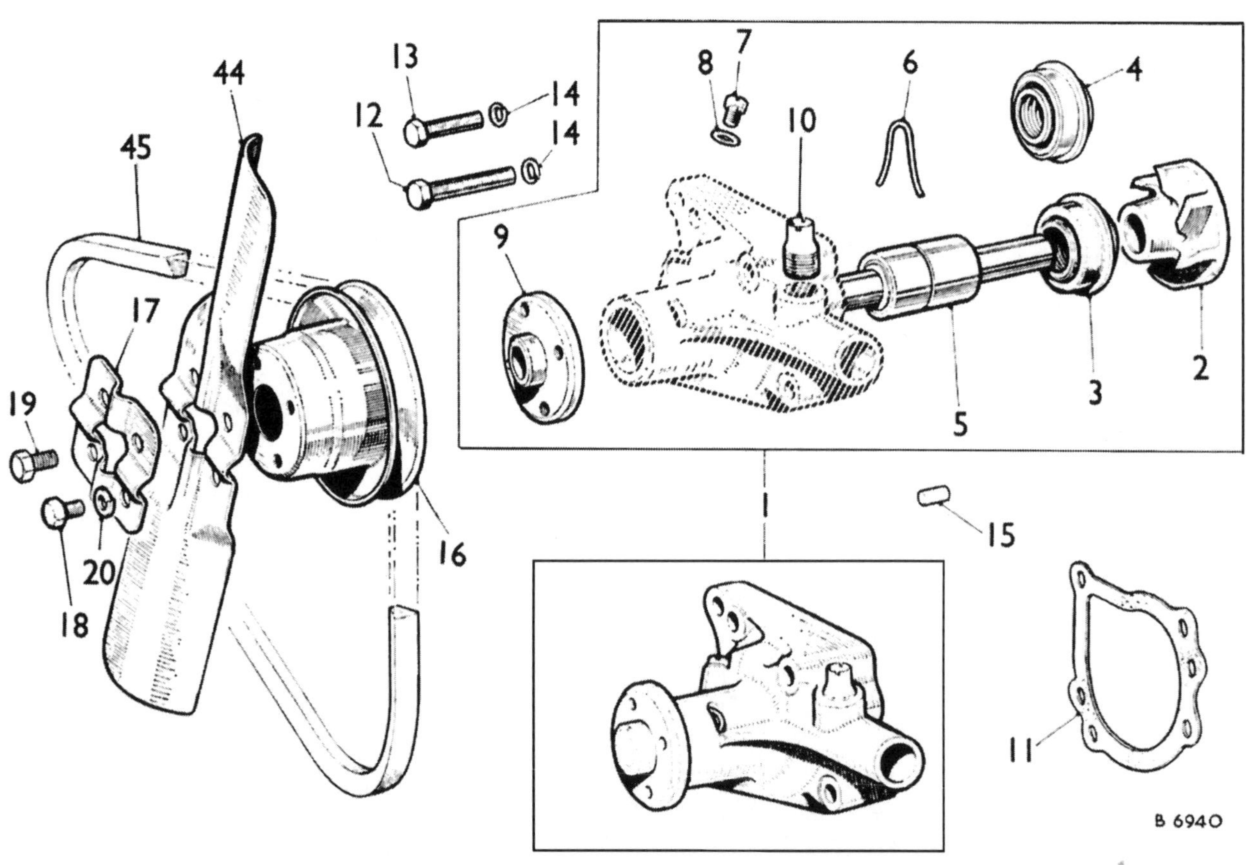
44
13
12
14
14
45
17
19
18
20
16
8
7
6
4
10
9
5
3
2
1
15
11
B 6940

9C Engine—*continued*

DESCRIPTION	Part No.	Illus. No.	Quantity	Change Point	REMARKS
WATER PUMP AND FAN PULLEY					
Pump assembly—water					
	†2A 775	1	1		W.S.E. use 12A 1332
	†2A 774	1	1		W.S.E. use 12A 1332
	†12G 120	1	1		W.S.E. use 12A 1332
	†12A 1332	1	1		W.S.E. use 12G 1284
	†12G 1284	1	1		
Body	NSP		1		
Vane	2A 664	2	1		
Seal	†8G 697	3	1		W.S.E. use 13H 591
	†8G 698	3	1		W.S.E. use 13H 591
	13H 591	3	1		For use with 2A 775 and 2A 774
	†13H 772	4	1		For use with 12G 120. W.S.E. use 88G 446.
	88G 446	4	1		
Bearing (with spindle)	†2A 777	5	1		W.S.E. use 12A 1328
	†12A 1328	5	1		W.S.E. use 12A 1389
	†12A 1389	1	1		
Wire—bearing locating	2A 778	6	1		For use with water pumps 2A 774, 2A 775, 12G 120, and 12A 1332
Screw—lubricating point	53K 1433	7	1		For use with water pumps 2A 774, 2A 775, 12G 120, and 12A 1332
Washer (fibre)	2K 4974	8	1		
Hub—pulley	2A 665	9	1		Use 8G 733 for this application
Hub—pulley	8G 733	9	1		
Adaptor—by-pass	2A 243	10	1		
Gasket—pump to crankcase	88G 215	11	1		Part No. change; was 2A 667 or 12A 31
Screw	HZS 0515	12	2		
Screw	HZS 0510	13	2		
Washer—spring	LWN 305	14	4		
Dowel—water pump	2K 6124	15	2		
Pulley—fan and water pump	2A 601	16	1		
Stiffener—fan blade	2A 803	17	1		
Screw	HZS 0405	18	4	(E) 9C/U/H101 to H358	
Screw	HZS 0406	19	4	(E) 9C/U/H359 on	
Washer—spring	LWZ 204	20	4		
Kit—water pump repair	†8G 2312	21	1		W.S.E. use 8G 2361
	†8G 2361	21	1		W.S.E. use 8G 2570
	†8G 2570	21	1		
Gasket	88G 215	11	1		
Vane	2A 664	2	1		
Seal	88G 446	4	1		
Bearing (with spindle)	12A 1328	5	1		
Wire—bearing locating	2A 778	6	1		
Screw—lubricating point	53K 1433	7	1		
Washer (fibre)	2K 4974	8	1		
Hub—pulley	8G 733	9	1		

† Revised Information.

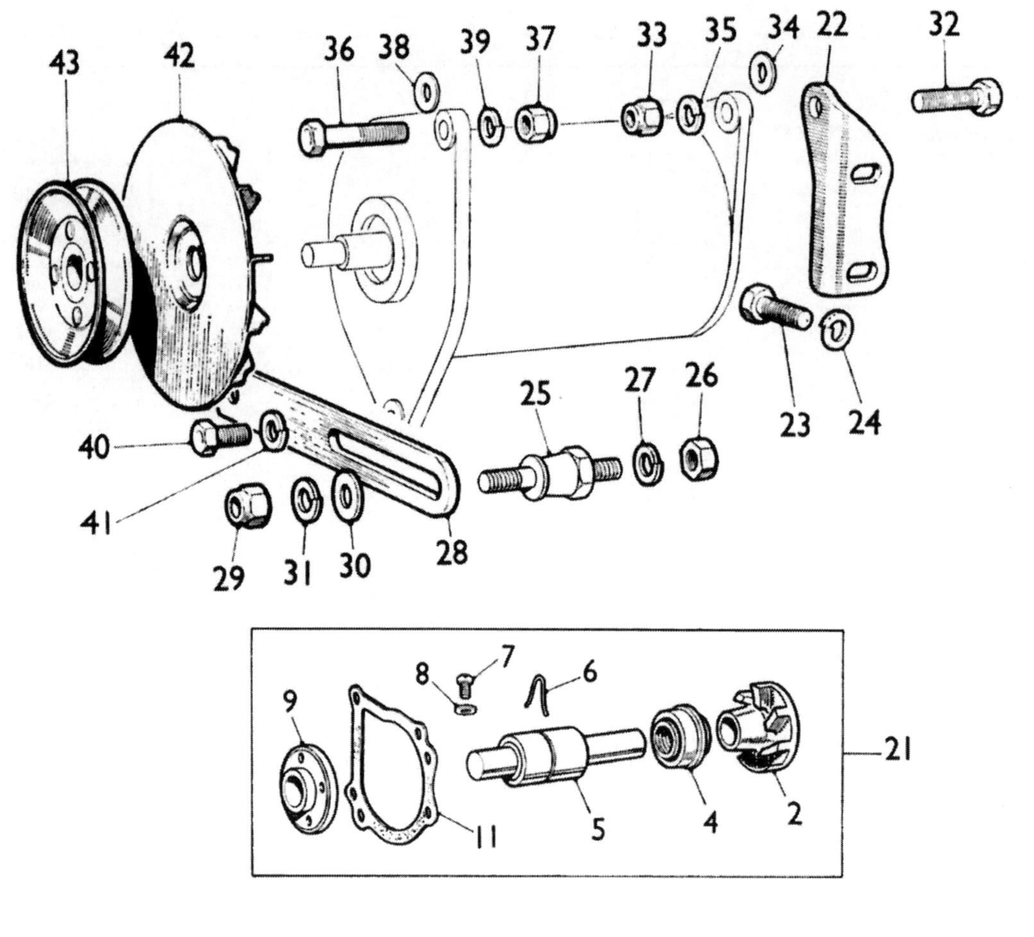
43
42
36
38
39
37
33
35
34
22
32
23
24
25
27
26
40
41
29
31
30
28
8
7
6
9
21
11
5
4
2

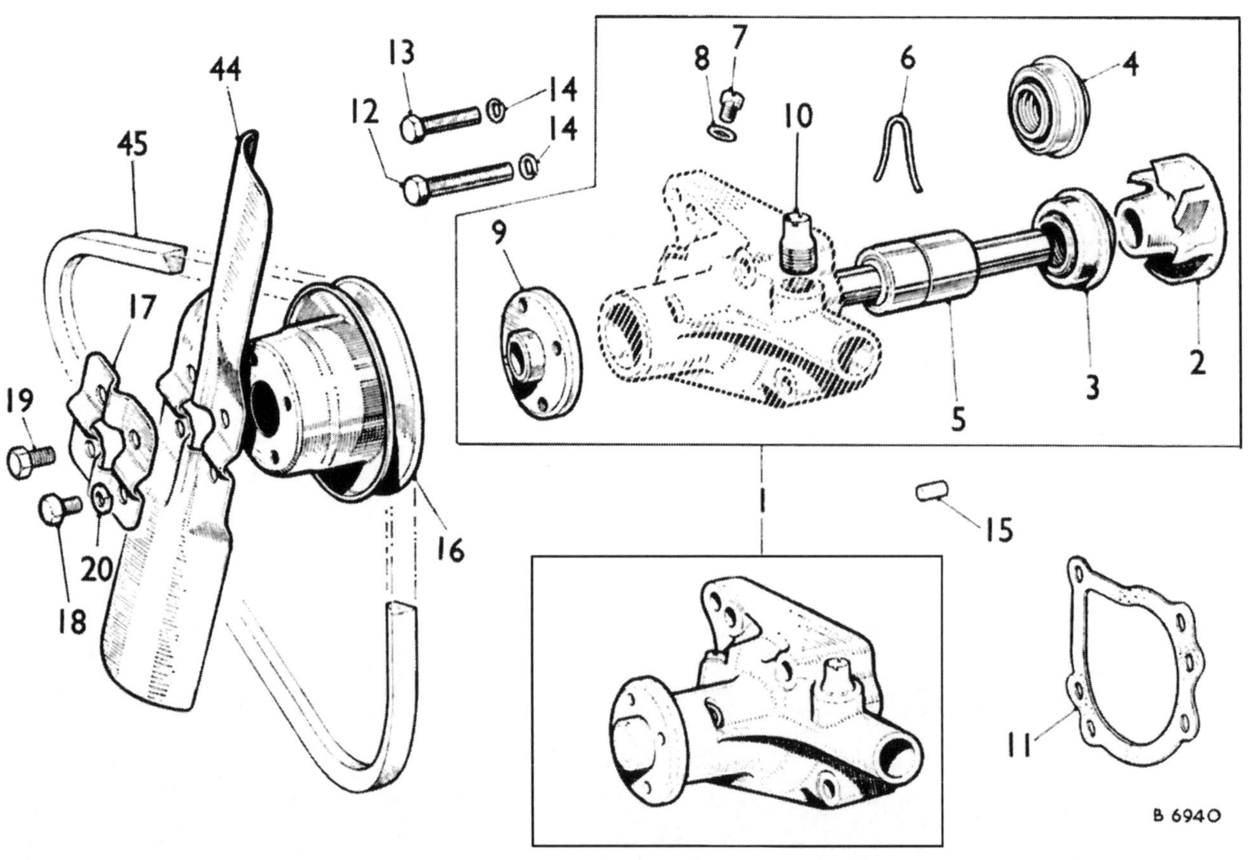
44
45
13
12
14
14
8
7
10
6
4
9
17
19
20
18
16
5
3
2
1
15
11
B 6940

DESCRIPTION	Part No.	Illus. No.	Quantity	Change Point	REMARKS
9C Engine—*continued*					
DYNAMO MOUNTING					
Bracket—dynamo—rear	†2A 758	22	1		W.S.E. use 12A 526
Bracket—dynamo—rear	12A 526	22	1		
Screw	HZS 0507	23	2		
Washer—spring	LWZ 305	24	2		
Pillar—dynamo adjusting link	2A 128	25	1		
Nut	FNZ 106	26	1		
Washer—spring	LWZ 306	27	1		
Link—dynamo adjusting	AEA 325	28	1		
Nut	LNZ 206	29	1		
Washer—plain	PWN 106	30	1		
Washer—spring	LWZ 306	31	1		
Bolt	HZS 0509	32	1		
Nut	LNZ 205	33	1		
Washer—plain	PWZ 305	34	1		
Washer—spring	†2K 5319	35	1		W.S.E. use LWN 305
Washer—spring	LWN 305	35	1		
Bolt	HBZ 0513	36	1		
Nut	LNZ 205	37	1		
Washer—plain	PWZ 305	38	1		
Washer—spring	LWZ 305	39	1		
Screw—adjusting link to dynamo	†3H 2098	40	1		W.S.E. use ZCS 0505
Screw—adjusting link to dynamo	†ZCS 0505	40	1		
Washer—spring	LWZ 305	41	1		
Fan—dynamo	1G 1783	42	1		
Pulley	1H 998	43	1		
FAN AND FAN BELT					
Blade—fan	AEA 301	44	1/2		Quantity increased at (E) 9C/H359
Belt—fan—wedge-type	†1G 2716	45	1		W.S.E. use 13H 923
	†AEA 849	45	1		W.S.E. use 13H 923
	13H 923	45	1		
9C Engine—*continued*					
ENGINE SERVICE KITS					
Set—gasket—engine decarbonizing	8G 2200		1		W.S.E. use 8G 2318
	8G 2268		1		W.S.E. use 8G 2318
	8G 2318		1		
Gasket					
Cylinder head	†12G 293		1		
Manifold	†AEG 181		1		
Water outlet elbow	12G 330		1		
Rocker cover	12A 14		1		
Cover plate	†88G 221		1		
Thermostat	1G 1365		1		
Carburetter	3H 2687		6		
Carburetter backing	†87H 632		2		Not required for this application
Carburetter hot spot	†2A 106		1		Not required for this application
Carburetter	1G 2624		6		
Air cleaner	†12H 862		2		Not required for this application
Set—gasket—supplementary	8G 2232				Use with 8G 2318 for complete engine overhaul
Gasket					
Front mounting plate	†12G 619		1		
Cylinder front cover	12A 956		1		
Cylinder side cover	†12A 1139		2		
Oil pump	†88G 411		1		
Sump	8G 731		1		
Water pump	†88G 215		1		
Petrol pump	2A 113		1		
Rear mounting plate	12A 22		1		
Crankcase rear cover	2A 127		1		
Oil filter to adaptor and adaptor to crankcase	†88G 402		2		
Seal—oil—main bearing cap	2A 280		2		
Washer					
Oil priming plug	6K 464		1		
Sump drain plug	6K 638		1		
Drain tap	2K 4954		1		Alternatives
Drain tap	†2K 4975		1		Alternatives

† Revised Information.

DESCRIPTION	Part No.	Illus. No.	Quantity	Change Point	REMARKS
9C Engine—*continued*					
INLET AND EXHAUST MANIFOLD					
Manifold—inlet (with plugs and studs)	AEA 19	1	1		
Plug	2K 8159	2	2		
Stud	51K 448	3	4	(E) 9C/U/H101 to H46891	
Stud	CHS 0415	3	4	(E) 9C/U/H46892 on	
Manifold—exhaust	2A 102	4	1		
Plate—exhaust manifold—blanking	AEA 308	5	1		
Gasket—blanking plate	2A 106	6	1		
Screw	HNS 0405	7	4		
Gasket—inlet and exhaust manifold to head	†2A 719	8	1		W.S.E. use 12G 300
	†12A 192	8	1		W.S.E. use 12G 300
	12G 300	8	1		
Nut	BNN 105	9	2		
Washer	PWN 105	10	2		
Nut	BNN 105	11	4		
Washer—inlet and exhaust manifold stud	2A 110	12	4		

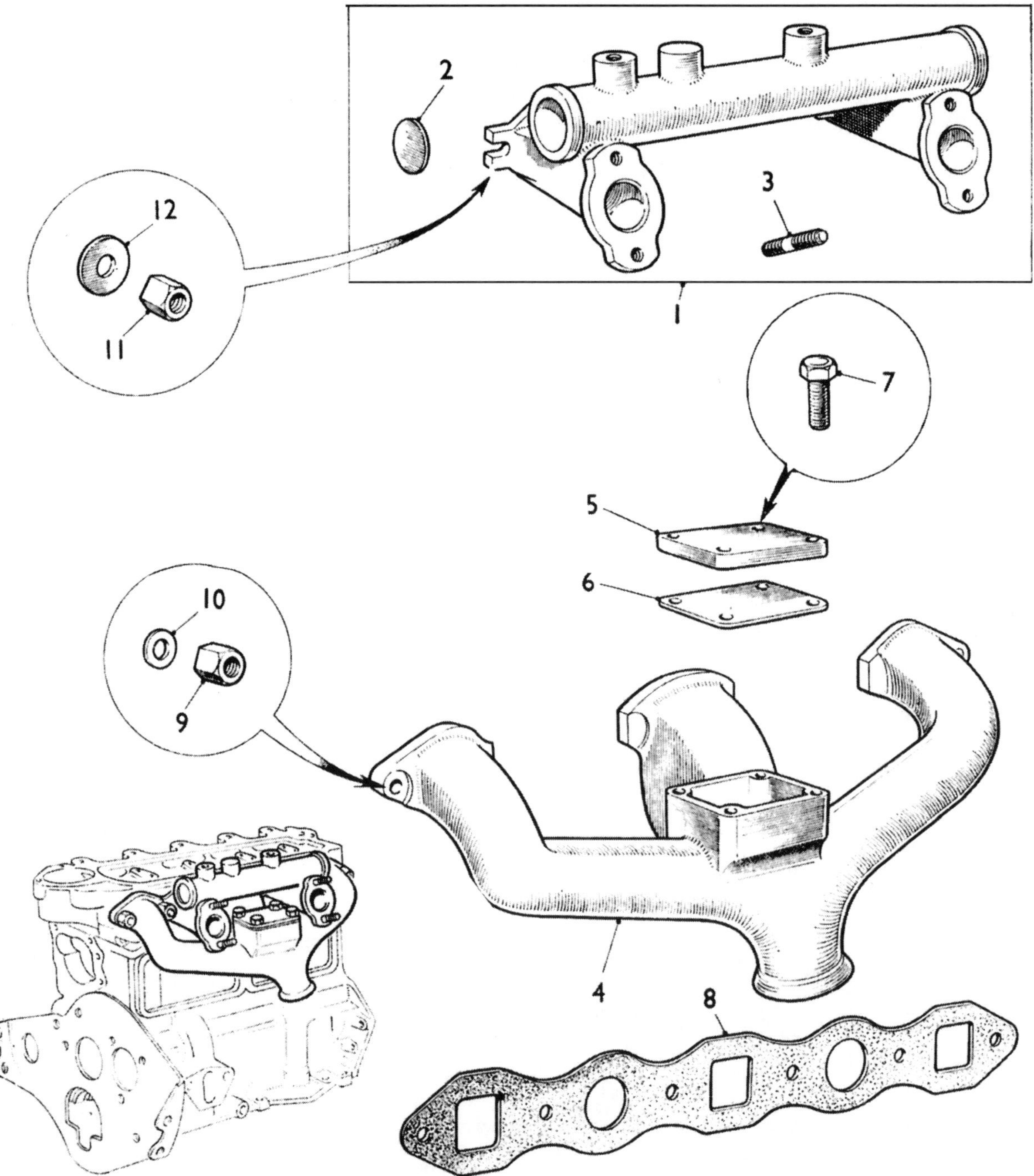

ENGINE MA

		Pages
950-cc	9CG/Da/H	MA 18 to MA 31

950-cc 9CG ENGINE

	Page	Plate
CAMSHAFT	MA 21	A 11
CONNECTING RODS	MA 21	A 11
CONTROLS—ENGINE	MA 48, MA 49	A 30
COVER—VALVE ROCKER	MA 24	A 13
COVERS—CYLINDER	MA 25	A 14
CRANKSHAFT	MA 21	A 11
CYLINDER HEAD	MA 23	A 12
DISTRIBUTOR HOUSING—SPINDLE	MA 22	A 11
ELBOW—WATER OUTLET—THERMOSTAT ...	MA 24	A 13
ENGINE UNIT	MA 19	A 10
EXHAUST SYSTEM	MA 47	A 29
FAN—FAN BELT	MA 29	A 17
FILTER—OIL	MA 27	A 16
FLYWHEEL	MA 22	A 11
MANIFOLDS	MA 31	A 18
MOUNTINGS—DYNAMO	MA 29	A 17
MOUNTINGS—ENGINE	MA 46	A 28
PISTONS—ASSEMBLY—RINGS	MA 20	A 10
PLATE—ENGINE MOUNTING—FRONT	MA 21	A 11
PLATE—ENGINE MOUNTING—REAR	MA 25	A 14
PLUGS—SPARKING	MA 24	A 13
PUMP—OIL—STRAINER	MA 26	A 15
PUMP WATER—FAN PULLEY	MA 28	A 17
SERVICE KITS—ENGINE	MA 30	
SHAFT—VALVE ROCKER	MA 23	A 12
SUMP—OIL DIPPER ROD	MA 26	A 15
TAP—CYLINDER DRAIN	MA 25	A 14
TAPPETS	MA 22	A 11

† Revised Information.

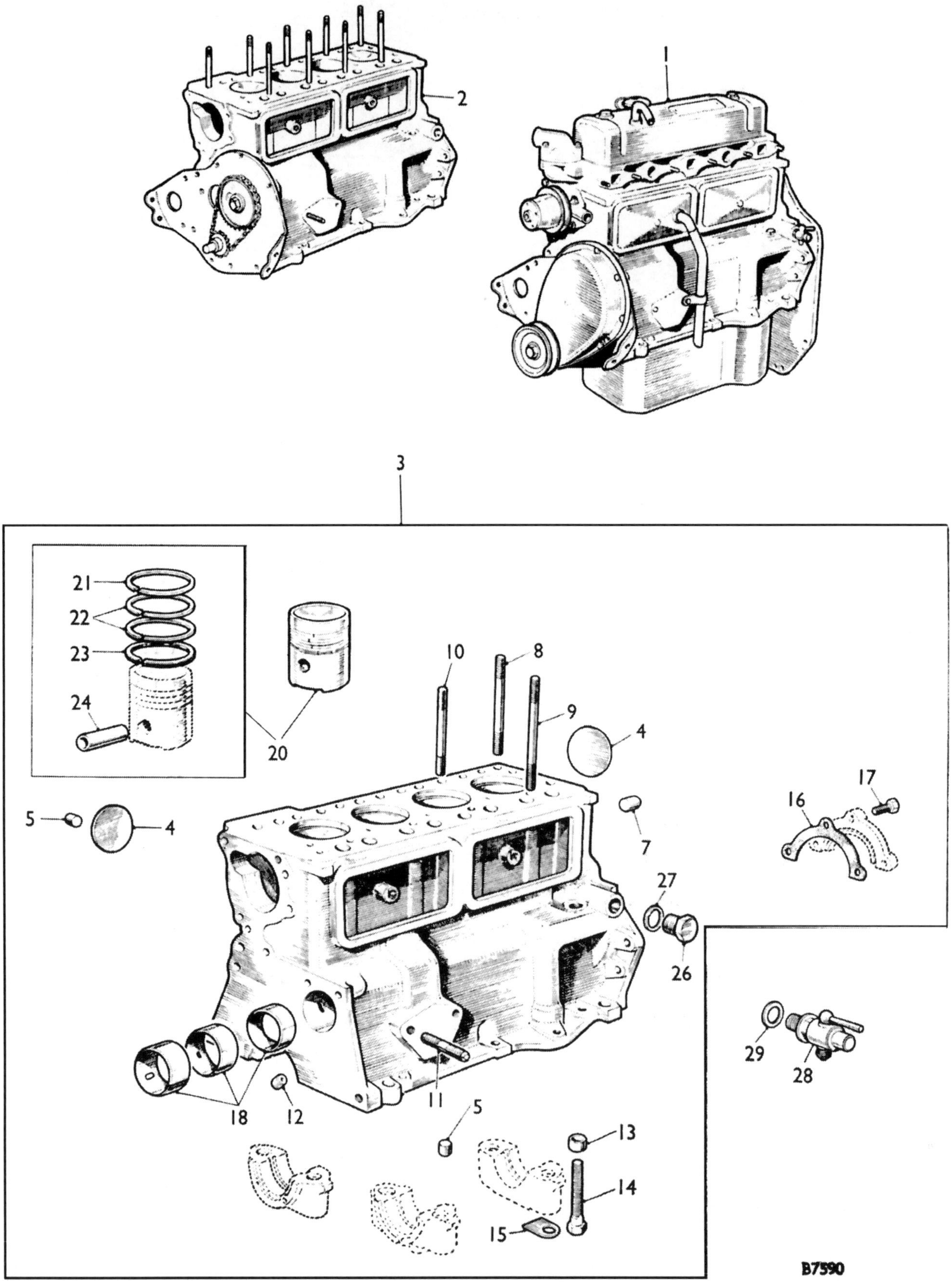

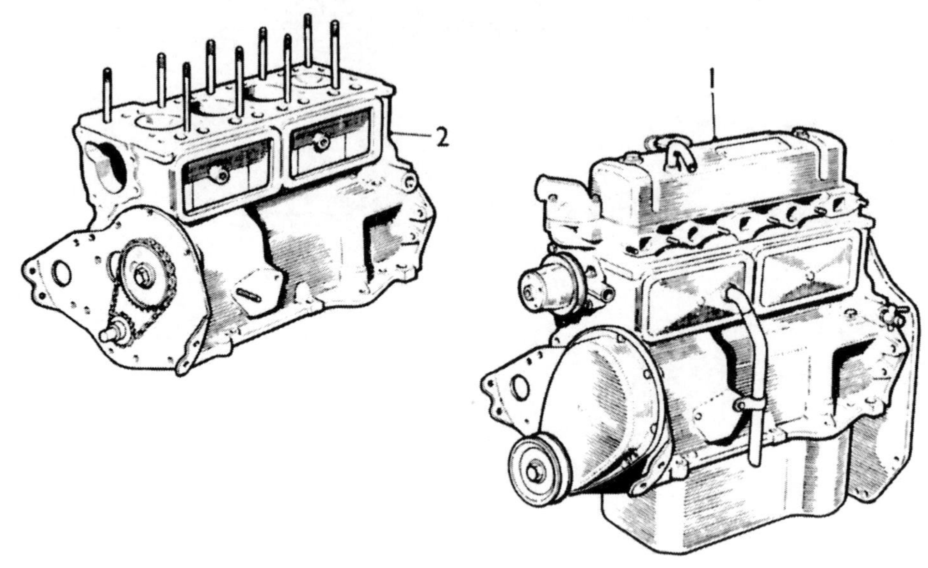

B7590

DESCRIPTION		Part No.	Illus. No.	Quantity	Change Point	REMARKS
ENGINE						
9CG ENGINE UNIT						
Engine unit—stripped	**HC**	8G 16	1	1		
Engine unit—stripped	**LC**	8G 17	1	1		
Engine unit—half	**HC**	28G 130	2	1		
Engine unit—half	**LC**	28G 140	2	1		
Block assembly—cylinder	**HC**	28G 131	3	1		
Block assembly—cylinder	**LC**	28G 139	3	1		
Plug						
Welch		2K 8169	4	4		
Oil release valve passage		2K 1345	5	2		
Oil gallery		2K 8623	7	2		
Oil gallery		†2K 8623	7	1		W.S.E. use 12H 1734
Oil gallery		12H 1734	7	1		
Stud						
Cylinder head		51K 254	8	1		Use 51K 256 for this application
Cylinder head—long		51K 255	9	4		
Cylinder head—short		51K 256	10	5/4		
Fuel pump		53K 525	11	2		
Cap—main bearing						
Front		NSP		1		
Centre		NSP		1		
Rear		NSP		1		
Restrictor—camshaft bearing—oil feed		1A 1964	12	1		
Screw—main bearing cap		2A 53	14	6		
Washer—lock		6K 927	15	6		
Dowel—main bearing cap		2A 54	13	6		
Cover—crankcase—rear		NSP		1		
Gasket		2A 127	16	1		
Screw		53K 1028	17	3		
Liner—camshaft bearings		28G 133	18	1 set		
Plug—drain		2K 4993	26	1		
Washer		6K 638	27	1		
Tap—drain		3H 576	28	1		For service purposes only
Washer		2K 4975	29	1		For service purposes only

† Revised Information.

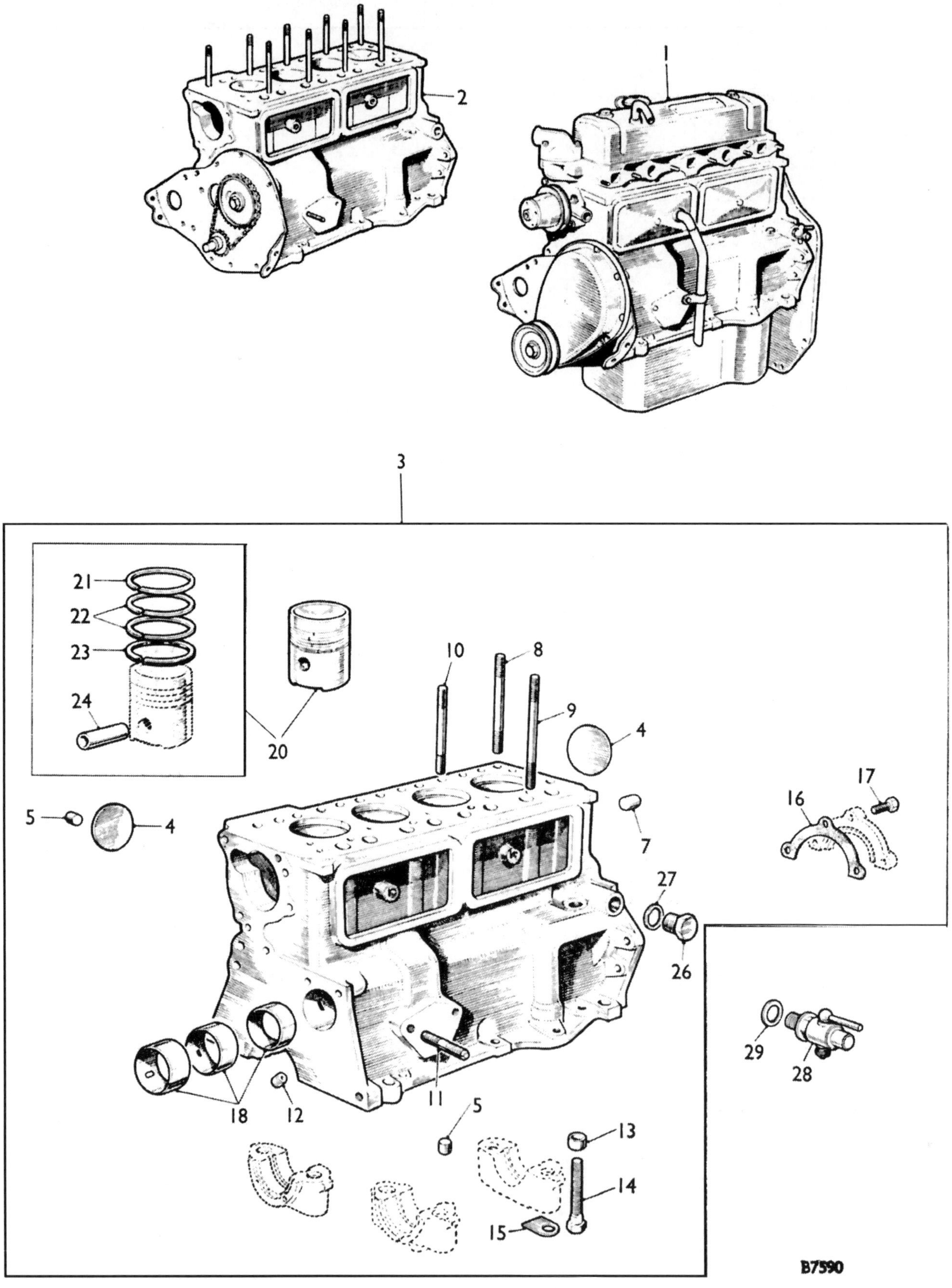

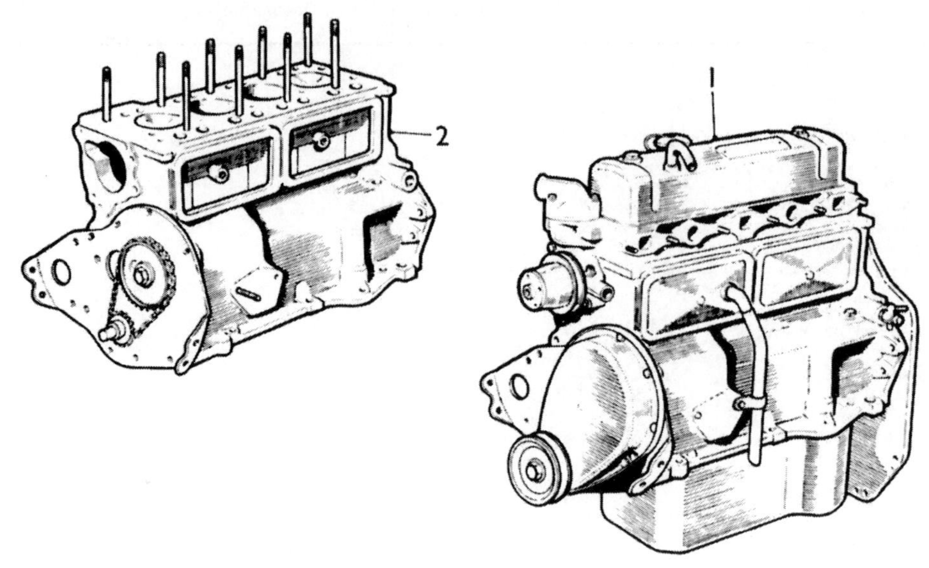
2
1

3
21
22
23
24
20
10
8
9
4
5
4
7
16
17
27
26
29
28
18
12
11
5
13
14
15
B7590

DESCRIPTION	Part No.	Illus. No.	Quantity	Change Point	REMARKS
9CG Engine—*continued*					
Piston assembly—Grade 3 (HC)					
Standard	12A 0187 03	19	4		
·010″ (·254 mm) O/S	12A 0187 13	19	4		
·020″ (·508 mm) O/S	12A 0187 23	19	4		
·030″ (·762 mm) O/S	12A 0187 33	19	4		
·040″ (1·016 mm) O/S	12A 0187 43	19	4		
Piston assembly—Grade 6 (HC)					
Standard	12A 0187 06	19	4		
·010″ (·254 mm) O/S	12A 0187 16	19	4		
·020″ (·508 mm) O/S	12A 0187 26	19	4		
·030″ (·762 mm) O/S	12A 0187 36	19	4		
·040″ (1·016 mm) O/S	12A 0187 46	19	4		
Piston assembly—Grade 3 (LC)					
Standard	12A 0280 03	19	4		
·010″ (·254 mm) O/S	12A 0280 13	19	4		
·020″ (·508 mm) O/S	12A 0280 23	19	4		
·030″ (·762 mm) O/S	12A 0280 33	19	4		
·040″ (1·016 mm) O/S	12A 0280 43	19	4		
Piston assembly—Grade 6 (LC)					
Standard	12A 0280 06	19	4		
·010″ (·254 mm) O/S	12A 0280 16	19	4		
·020″ (·508 mm) O/S	12A 0280 26	19	4		
·030″ (·762 mm) O/S	12A 0280 36	19	4		
·040″ (1·016 mm) O/S	12A 0280 46	19	4		
Ring—piston—top					
Standard	12A 66	20	4		
·010″ (·254 mm) O/S	12A 0066 10	20	4		
·020″ (·508 mm) O/S	12A 0066 20	20	4		
·030″ (·762 mm) O/S	12A 0066 30	20	4		
·040″ (1·016 mm) O/S	12A 0066 40	20	4		
Ring—piston—2nd and 3rd					
Standard	12A 67	21	8		
·010″ (·254 mm) O/S	12A 0067 10	21	8		
·020″ (·508 mm) O/S	12A 0067 20	21	8		
·030″ (·762 mm) O/S	12A 0067 30	21	8		
·040″ (1·016 mm) O/S	12A 0067 40	21	8		
Ring—piston—scraper					
Standard	12A 68	22	4		
·010″ (·254 mm) O/S	12A 0068 10	22	4		
·020″ (·508 mm) O/S	12A 0068 20	22	4		
·030″ (·762 mm) O/S	12A 0068 30	22	4		
·040″ (1·016 mm) O/S	12A 0068 40	22	4		
Pin—gudgeon					
Standard	2A 837	23	4		
·002″ (·0508 mm) O/S	2A 0837 02	23	4		
·004″ (·1016 mm) O/S	2A 0837 04	23	4		
·006″ (·1524 mm) O/S	2A 0837 06	23	4		

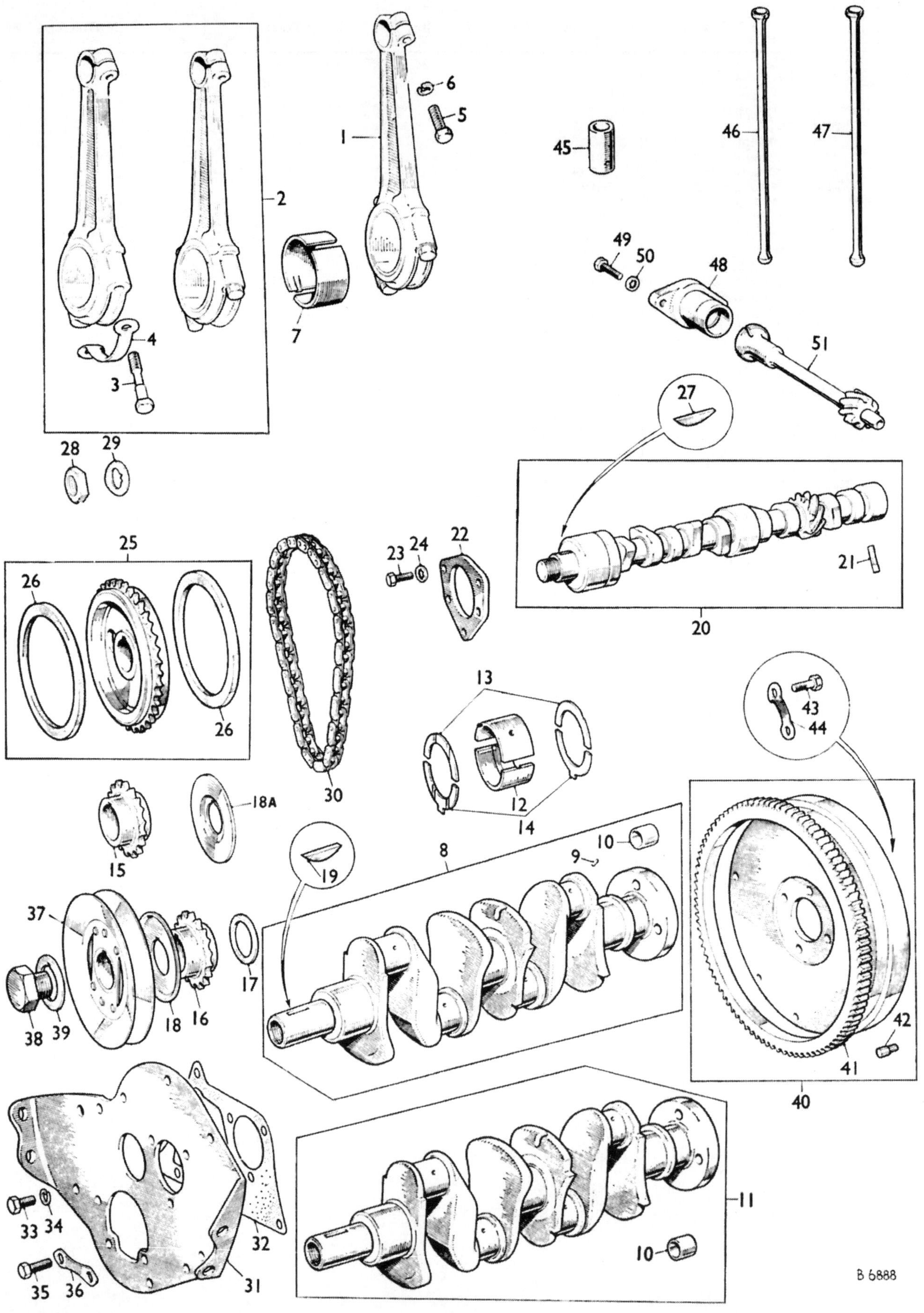
1
2
3
4
5
6
7
8
9
10
11
12
13
14
15
16
17
18
18A
19
20
21
22
23
24
25
26
27
28
29
30
31
32
33
34
35
36
37
38
39
40
41
42
43
44
45
46
47
48
49
50
51
B 6888

DESCRIPTION	Part No.	Illus. No.	Quantity	Change Point	REMARKS
9CG Engine—*continued*					
Rod—connecting—Nos. 1 and 3 cylinders	2A 656	1	2		
Rod—connecting—Nos. 2 and 4 cylinders	2A 654	2	2		
Screw—cap	2A 659	3	8		
Washer—lock	2A 660	4	4		
Screw	51K 1382	5	4		
Washer—spring	LWN 305	6	4		
Bearing—big-end—connecting rod					
Standard	8G 2198	7	1 set		
·010″ (·254 mm) U/S	8G 2198 10	7	1 set		
·020″ (·508 mm) U/S	8G 2198 20	7	1 set		
·030″ (·762 mm) U/S	8G 2198 30	7	1 set		
·040″ (1·016 mm) U/S	8G 2198 40	7	1 set		
CRANKSHAFT AND GEAR					
Crankshaft	88G 225	8	1		Part No. change; was 2A 828 and 2A 830
Crankshaft (with bearings)	28G 95		1		UK market Exchange Unit Scheme only
Bush—1st motion shaft	1A 1559	10	1		
Restrictor—oil	1G 1167	9	1		For use with 2A 828 only
Bearing—main					
Standard	8G 2222	12	1 set		
·010″ (·254 mm) U/S	8G 2222 10	12	1 set		
·020″ (·508 mm) U/S	8G 2222 20	12	1 set		
·030″ (·762 mm) U/S	8G 2222 30	12	1 set		
·040″ (1·016 mm) U/S	8G 2222 40	12	1 set		
Washer—thrust					
Upper—standard	1A 1716	13	2		
Upper—·003″ (·076 mm) O/S	1A 1716 03	13	2		
Lower—standard	1A 1717	14	2		
Lower—·003″ (·076 mm) O/S	1A 1717 03	14	2		
Gear—crankshaft	8G 725	15	1	(E) 9CG/Da/H101 to H5092	
Gear—crankshaft	AEA 538	16	1	(E) 9CG/Da/H5093 on	
Washer—packing	6K 628	17	1		
Thrower—oil—front	2A 1015	18	1		For service with front cover 2A 937
Thrower—oil—front	12A 1148	18A	1		For service with front cover 12G 791
Key—gear and crankshaft	6K 836	19	1		
CAMSHAFT					
Camshaft (with oil pump driving pin)	AEA 630	20	1		
Pin—oil pump driving	2A 299	21	1		
Plate—locating	2A 84	22	1		
Screw	HNS 0406	23	3		
Washer—shakeproof	LWN 404	24	3		
Gear—camshaft (with tensioner rings)	†2A 85	25	1		Correction; was 8A 85
Ring—tensioner	8G 549	26	2		
Key	WKN 505	27	1		
Nut	6K 629	28	1		
Washer—lock	2A 759	29	1		
Chain—camshaft drive	3H 2127	30	1		
FRONT MOUNTING PLATE					
Plate—engine mounting—front	2A 125	31	1		
Gasket—plate to crankcase	2A 126	32	1		W.S.E. use 12G 619
Gasket—plate to crankcase	12G 619	32	1		
Screw	HZS 0505	33	2		
Washer—spring	LWZ 305	34	2		
Screw	53K 2016	35	2		
Plate—lock	6K 831	36	1		
CRANKSHAFT PULLEY					
Pulley—crankshaft	2A 940	37	1		
Bolt—pulley retaining	AEA 312	38	1		
Washer—lock	1G 1319	39	1		

† Revised Information.

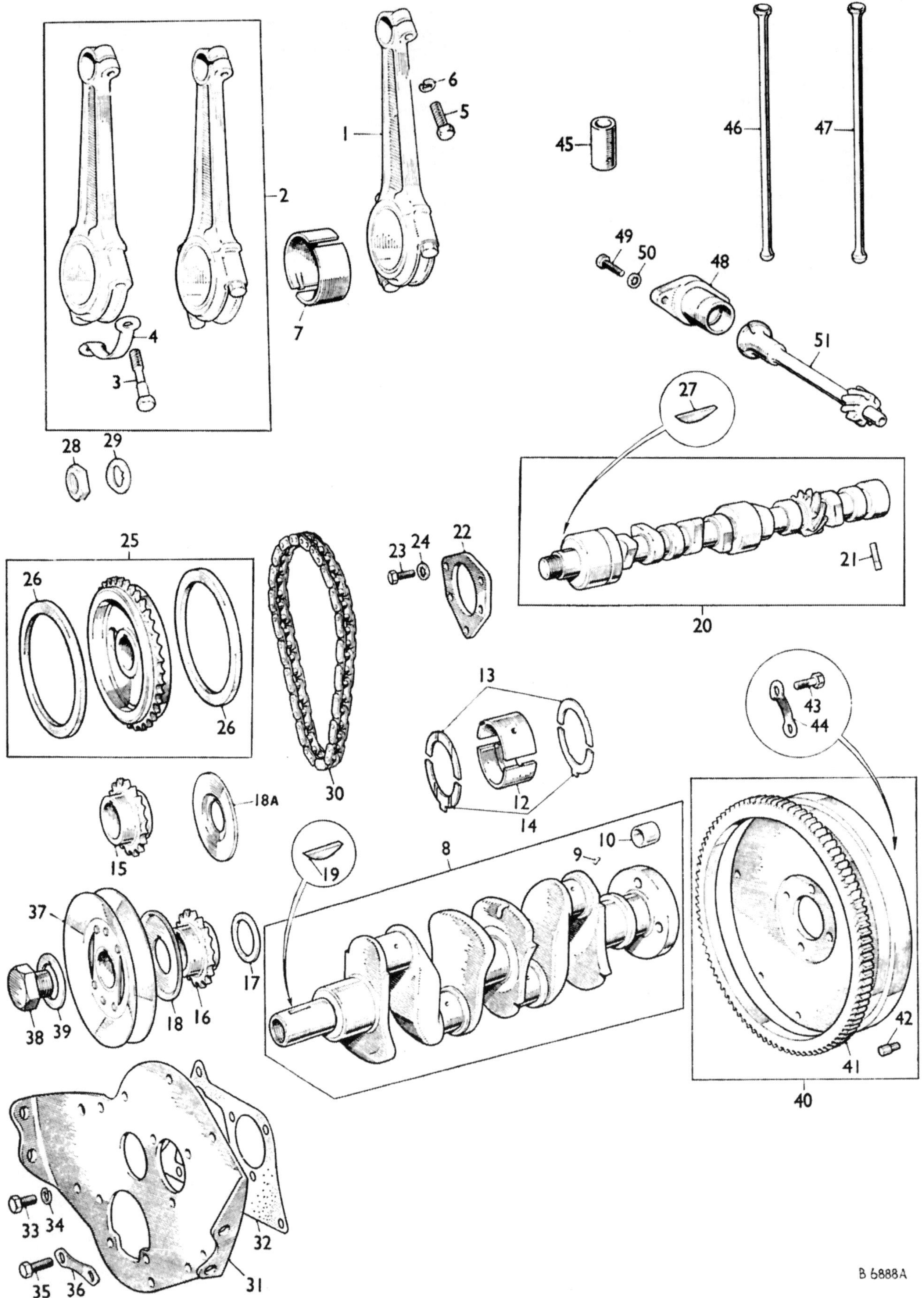
1
2
3
4
5
6
7
8
9
10
12
13
14
15
16
17
18
18A
19
20
21
22
23
24
25
26
26
27
28
29
30
31
32
33
34
35
36
37
38
39
40
41
42
43
44
45
46
47
48
49
50
51
B 6888A

DESCRIPTION	Part No.	Illus. No.	Quantity	Change Point	REMARKS
9CG Engine—*continued*					
FLYWHEEL					
Flywheel assembly	88G 227	40	1		Part No. change; was 12A 182 or AEA 594
Gear—ring—starter	†12A 183	41	1		W.S.E. use AEA 596
Gear—ring—starter	†AEA 596	41	1		
Dowel—clutch to flywheel	1G 2984	42	2		
Screw—flywheel to crankshaft	6K 630	43	4		
Washer—lock	2K 7816	44	2		
TAPPETS AND PUSH-RODS					
Tappet					
Standard	2A 13	45	8		
·010″ (·254 mm) O/S	2A 0013 10	45	8		
·020″ (·508 mm) O/S	2A 0013 20	45	8		
Push-rod	†12A 189	46	8		W.S.E. use 2A 14, 12A 250, or 12A 747
	2A 14	46	8		Alternatives in sets
	12A 250	46	8		Alternatives in sets
	†12A 747	46	8		
DISTRIBUTOR HOUSING AND SPINDLE					
Housing—distributor	†2A 612	48	1		W.S.E. use 12A 1136 together with 'O' ring 13H 2792
Housing—distributor	12A 1136	48	1		
'O' ring—seal	13H 2792		1		
Screw	HZS 0406	49	1		
Washer—shakeproof	LWN 404	50	1		
Spindle—distributor driving	†2A 139	51	1		Alternatives. W.S.E. use 1G 2062 for this application
	†2A 847	52	1		Alternatives. W.S.E. use 1G 2062 for this application
	1G 2062	53	1		

† Revised Information.

1
2
3
22
23
24
25
26
27
28
29
30
31
32
33
34
35
36
37
38
39
21
20
17
19
16
15
18
13
14
41
40
8
42
43
9
10
4
6
5
7
50
51
48
49
12
11
45
46
47
44
B 6943 C

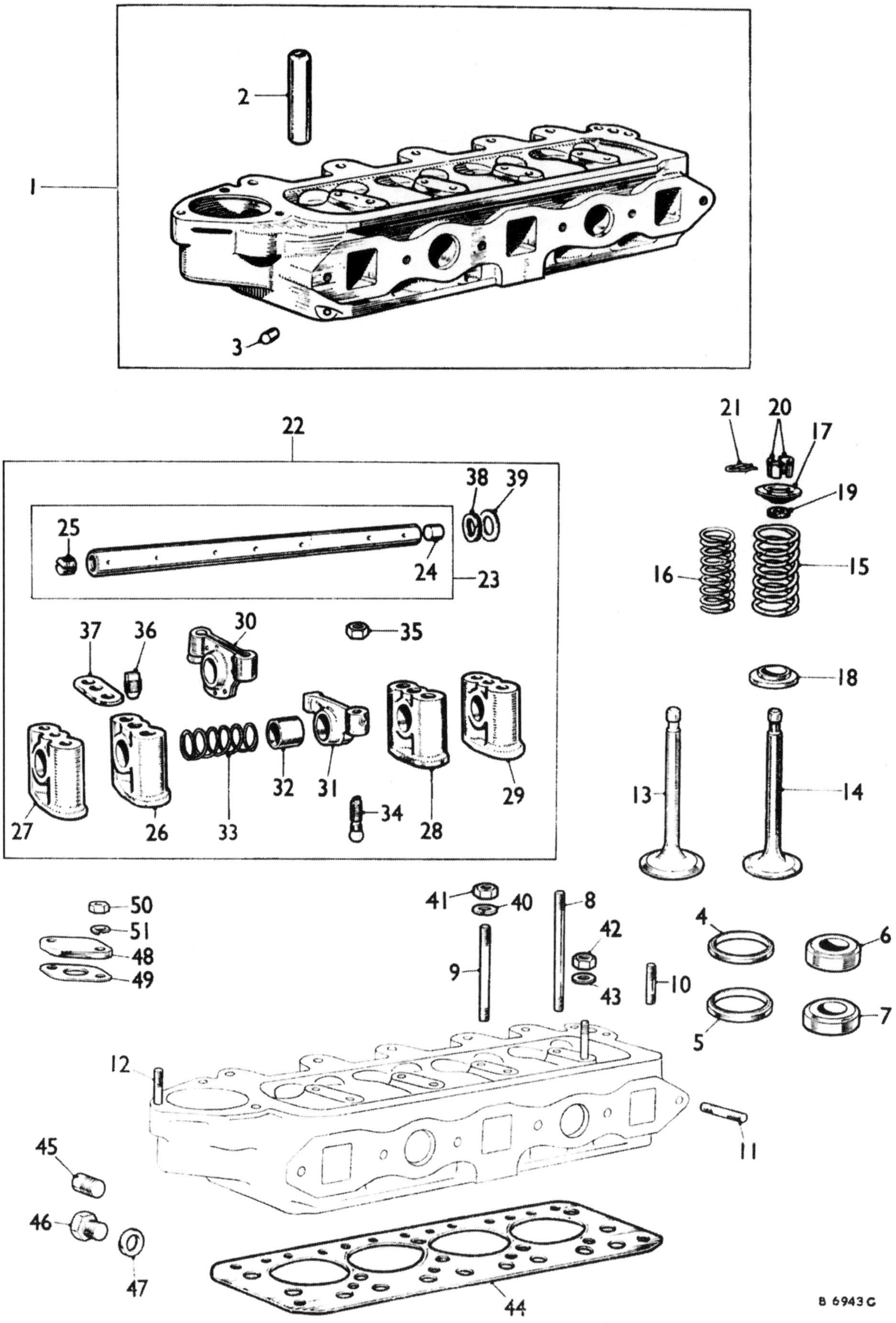

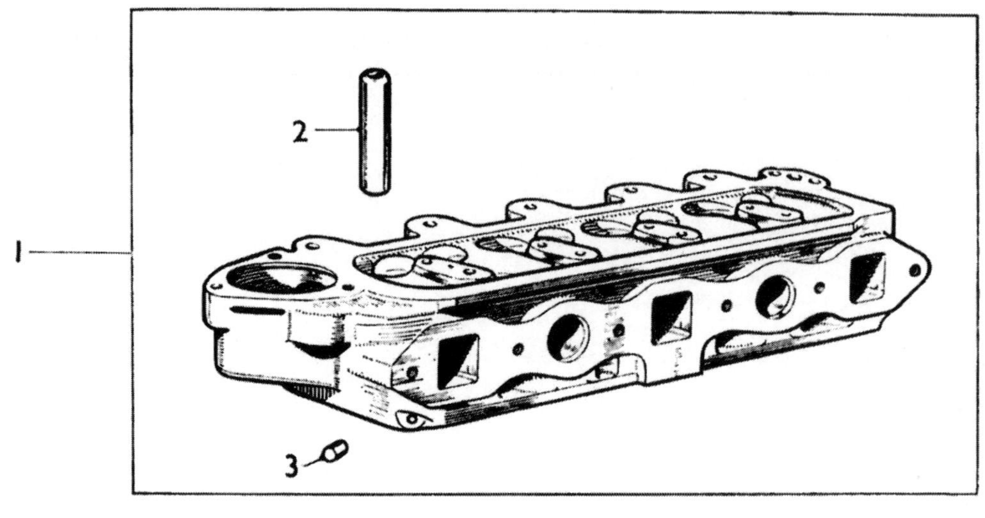

9CG Engine—*continued*

DESCRIPTION	Part No.	Illus. No.	Quantity	Change Point	REMARKS
CYLINDER HEAD DETAILS					
Cylinder head assembly	NSP		1		Was 28G 132
Cylinder head (with guides and plugs)	12A 184	1	1		
Guide—inlet and exhaust valve	12A 186	2	8		
Plug—oil hole	†6K 808	3	1		W.S.E. use 2K 1345
Plug—oil hole	†2K 1345	3	1		
Insert—valve seat					
Inlet—standard	2A 639	4	4		For service purposes only
Inlet—$\frac{1}{16}$" (1·58 mm) O/S	AEA 762	5	4		For service purposes only
Exhaust—standard	2A 660	6	4		For service purposes only
Exhaust—$\frac{1}{16}$" (1·58 mm) O/S	AEA 763	7	4		For service purposes only
Stud					
Rocker bracket—long	51K 885	8	2		
Rocker bracket—short	51K 1473	9	2		
Cover plate	53K 402	10	2		
Inlet and exhaust manifold	53K 487	11	6		
Water outlet elbow	53K 530	12	3		
Plate—cover—heater tap facing	2A 180	48	1		
Gasket—cover plate	88G 221	49	1		Part No. change; was 2A 179 and 12A 82
Nut	FNN 104	50	2		
Washer—spring	LWN 304	51	2		
Valve					
Inlet	AEA 574	13	4		
Exhaust	AEA 434	14	4		Use AEA 400 for this application
Exhaust	AEA 400	14	4		
Spring—valve—outer	AEA 311	15	8		
Spring—valve—inner	AEA 401	16	8		
Collar—valve spring—top	AEA 402	17	8		
Cup—valve spring—bottom	AEA 403	18	8		
Ring—valve packing (rubber)	2A 879	19	8		
Cotter—valve	2A 11	20	16		
Circlip—valve cotter	2A 12	21	8		
Shaft assembly—valve rocker	2A 15	22	1	See (1) foot of page	Use AEA 90 for this application
Shaft assembly—valve rocker	AEA 90	22	1	See (2) foot of page	
Shaft—valve rocker—plugged	2A 16	23	1		
Plug—plain	6K 878	24	1		
Plug—screwed	2K 4608	25	1		
Bracket—rocker shaft					
Tapped	2A 22	26	1		Use 12A 210 for this application
Tapped	†12A 210	27	1		W.S.E. use 12G 1109
Tapped	†12G 1109	27	1		
Plain	2A 23	28	3		Use 12A 211 for this application
Plain	†12A 211	29	3		W.S.E. use 12G 1110
Plain	†12G 1110	29	3		
Rocker—valve—bushed	2H 964	23	8		Alternatives; interchangeable in sets only
Rocker—valve—bushed	2A 533	31	8		Alternatives; interchangeable in sets only
Bush—valve rocker	2A 21	32	8		
Spring—rocker spacing	6K 556	33	3		
Screw—tappet adjusting	†2A 535	34	8		W.S.E. use 12A 1215
Screw—tappet adjusting	12A 1215	34	8		
Locknut—screw	6K 654	35	8		
Screw—rocker shaft locating	2A 258	36	1		
Plate—rocker shaft bracket	2A 515	37	4		
Washer—spring—rocker shaft	2A 18	38	2		
Washer—plain—rocker shaft	6K 555	39	2		
Washer—spring	LWN 205	40	4		
Nut	FNN 105	41	4		
Nut—cylinder head stud	51K 371	42	9		
Washer—cylinder head stud	PWN 106	43	5		
Gasket—cylinder head	12A 190	44	1		Use 12G 293 for this application
Gasket—cylinder head	12G 293	44	1		
Plug—thermal transmitter boss	AEC 997	45	1		Use ADP 210 for this application
Plug—thermal transmitter boss	ADP 210	46	1		
Washer—plug	1B 3664	47	1		

CHANGE POINTS

(1) (E) 9CG/Da/101 to H12255 and L10995
(2) (E) 9CG/Da/H12256 on and L10996 on

† Revised Information.

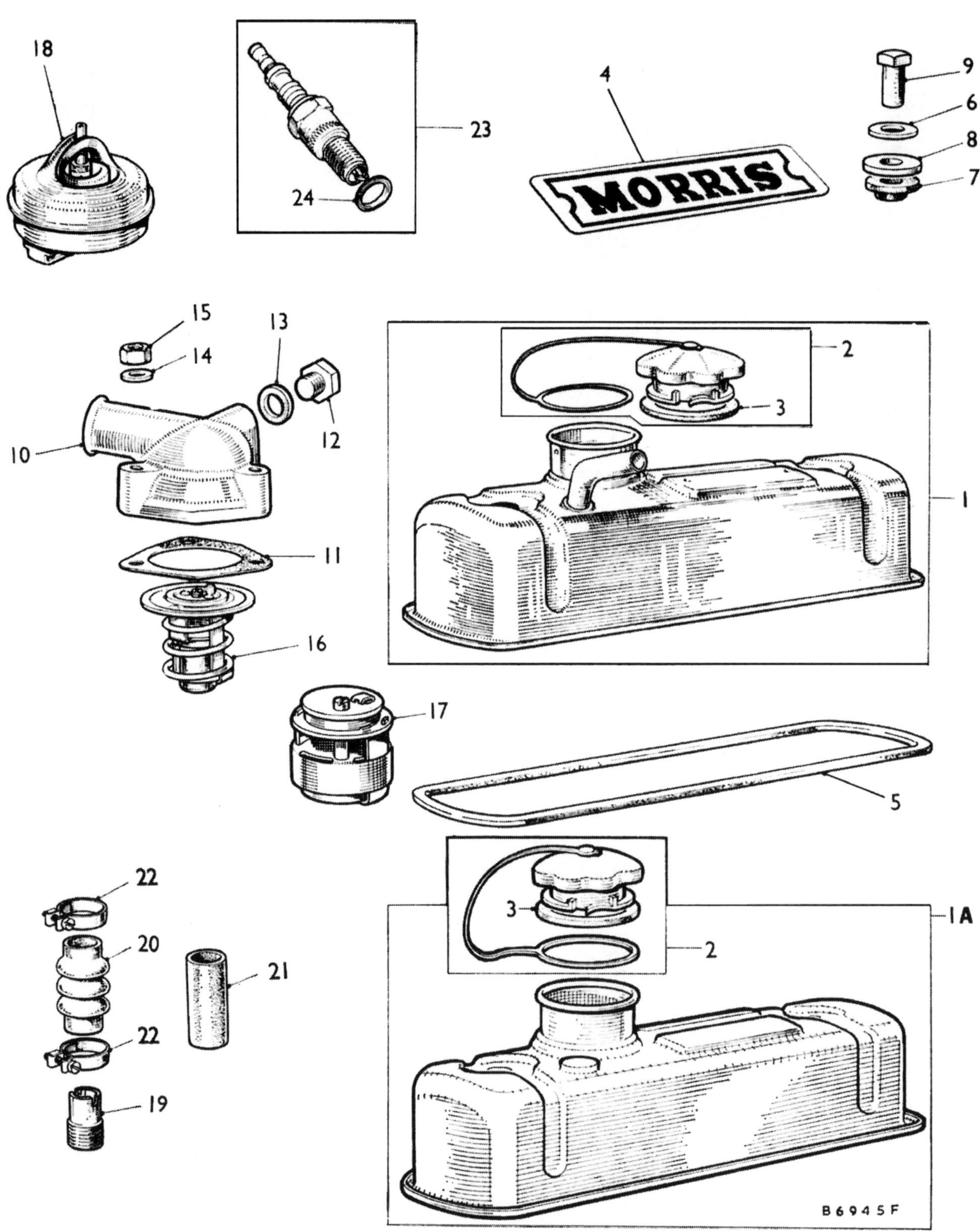
18
23
24
4
MORRIS
9
6
8
7
15
14
13
12
10
11
16
2
3
1
17
5
22
20
21
22
19
3
1A
2
B 6 9 4 5 F

DESCRIPTION	Part No.	Illus. No.	Quantity	Change Point	REMARKS
9CG Engine—*continued*					
VALVE ROCKER COVER AND OIL FILLER					
Cover—valve rocker	AEA 601	1	1		Use 12A 501 for this application
Cover—valve rocker	12A 501	1A	1		
Cap and cable—oil filler	8G 612	2	1		Use 12A 402 for this application
Cap and strap—oil filler	12A 402	3	1		
Washer—oil filler cap	12A 403	25	1		
Bush (rubber)	†2K 8568	4	2		W.S.E. use 12A 1358
Bush (rubber)	†12A 1358	4	2		
Nut	2A 150	5	2		
Piece—distance	1B 2925	6	2		
Washer—cap	1A 2156	7	2		
Washer—joint	12A 14	8	1		
WATER OUTLET ELBOW THERMOSTAT, AND COVER PLATE					
Elbow—water outlet	AEA 306	9	1		
Gasket	12A 29	10	1		Use 12G 330 for this application
Gasket	12G 330	10	1		
Nut	FNZ 105	11	3		
Washer—spring	LWZ 205	12	3		
Thermostat					
Bellows-type—73° C (163° F)	†11G 291	13	1		W.S.E. use 13H 3727 — Hot climates
Bellows-type—73° C (163° F)	†11K 399	13	1		W.S.E. use 13H 3727 — Hot climates
Wax-type—74° C (165° F)	†13H 1412	14	1		W.S.E. use 13H 3727 — Hot climates
Wax-type—74° C (165° F)	†13H 2526	14	1		W.S.E. use 13H 3727 — Hot climates
Wax-type—74° C (165° F)	†13H 3584	14	1		W.S.E. use 13H 3727 — Hot climates
Wax-type—74° C (165° F)	†13H 3727	14	1		Hot climates
Wax-type—82° C (180° F)	†13H 2317	14	1		W.S.E. use 13H 4070 — Temperate climates
Wax-type—82° C (180° F)	†13H 3585	14	1		W.S.E. use 13H 4070 — Temperate climates
Wax-type—82° C (180° F)	†13H 4070	14	1		Temperate climates
Wax-type—88° C (190° F)	†13H 2316	14	1		W.S.E. use 13H 3586 — Cold climates
Wax-type—88° C (190° F)	†13H 3586	14	1		Cold climates
Adaptor—by-pass	2A 243	15	1		
Connection—by-pass (rubber)	2A 242	16	1		Use 12A 1098 for this application
Connection—by-pass (rubber)	12A 1098	17	1		
Clip—connection	3H 2963	18	2		
SPARKING PLUGS					
Plug—sparking (N5)	3H 2006	23	4		
Plug—sparking (XN8)	2A 375	23	4		For use when short-wave radio is fitted
Gasket	2K 5211	24	4		

† Revised Information.

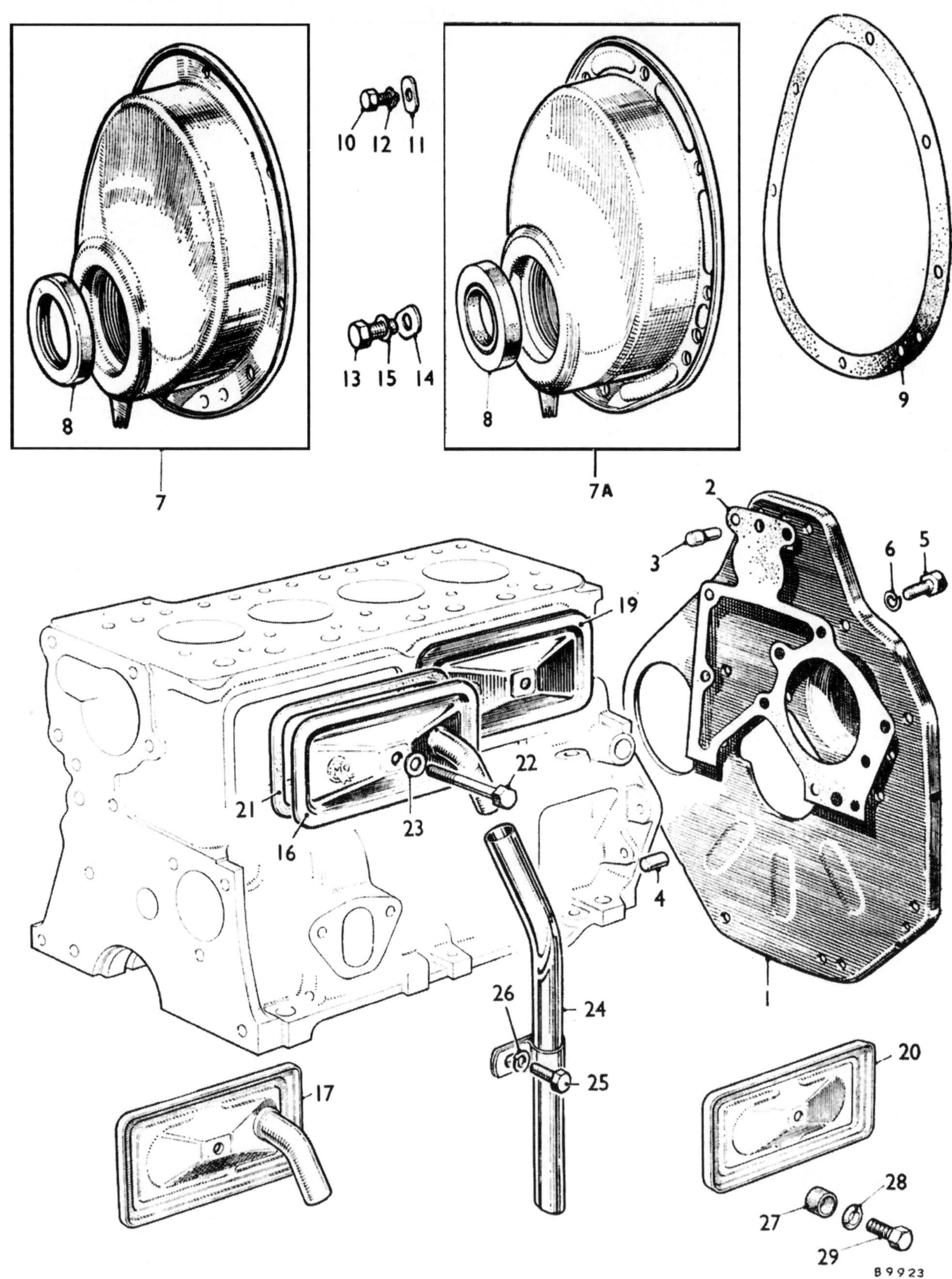
10
12
11
13
15
14
8
8
9
7
7A
2
3
6
5
19
22
21
23
16
4
1
26
24
25
17
20
28
27
29
B9923

DESCRIPTION	Part No.	Illus. No.	Quantity	Change Point	REMARKS
9CG Engine—*continued*					
REAR MOUNTING PLATE					
Plate—engine mounting rear	88G 226	1	1		Part No. change; was 2A 300 and 2A 569
Gasket	†2A 123	2	1		W.S.E. use 12A 22
Gasket	12A 22	2	1		
Dowel—top	1K 52	3	1		
Dowel—bottom	1G 752	4	1		
Screw	HZS 0505	5	7		
Washer—spring	LWZ 305	6	7		
CYLINDER FRONT AND SIDE COVERS					
Cover—front	†2A 937	7	1		W.S.E. use 12G 791 together with oil thrower 12A 1148 on page MA 21
	†12G 791	7A	1		W.S.E. use 12A 1419
	†12A 1419	7A	1		
Seal—oil	†2A 939	8	1		W.S.E. use 13H 4061
Seal—oil	†13H 4061	8	1		
Gasket	1A 2093	9	1		Use 12A 956 for this application
Gasket	12A 956	9	1		
Screw	HZS 0403	10	6		
Washer—plain	2K 5197	11	6		
Washer—spring	LWN 204	12	6		
Screw	HZS 0505	13	4		
Washer—plain	2K 7440	14	4		
Washer—spring	LWZ 305	15	4		
Cover—cylinder side					
Front (with vent pipe)	12H 155	16	1		W.S.E. use 12H 948
Front (with vent pipe)	12H 948	17	1		
Rear	12H 152	19	1		W.S.E. use 12A 1170 together with 1 off each joint 12A 1175, bush 12A 1176, cup 12A 1177, and screw HZS 0509
Rear	12H 941	19	1		
Rear	12A 1170	20	1		
Gasket	†12A 24	21	2		W.S.E. use 12A 1139
Gasket	12A 1139	21	2		For service with side covers 12H 155, 12H 948, 12H 152, and 12H 941
Screw—cover to crankcase	HBZ 0515	22	2		
Washer (fibre)	2K 4958	23	2		
Washer—joint	12A 1175	21	1		For service with side cover 12A 1170
Bush (rubber)	12A 1176	27	1		
Washer—cup	12A 1177	28	1		
Screw—cover to crankcase	HZS 0509	29	1		
Pipe—vent—lower	2A 118	24	1		
Screw	HZS 0505	25	1		
Washer—spring	LWZ 205	26	1		

† Revised Information.

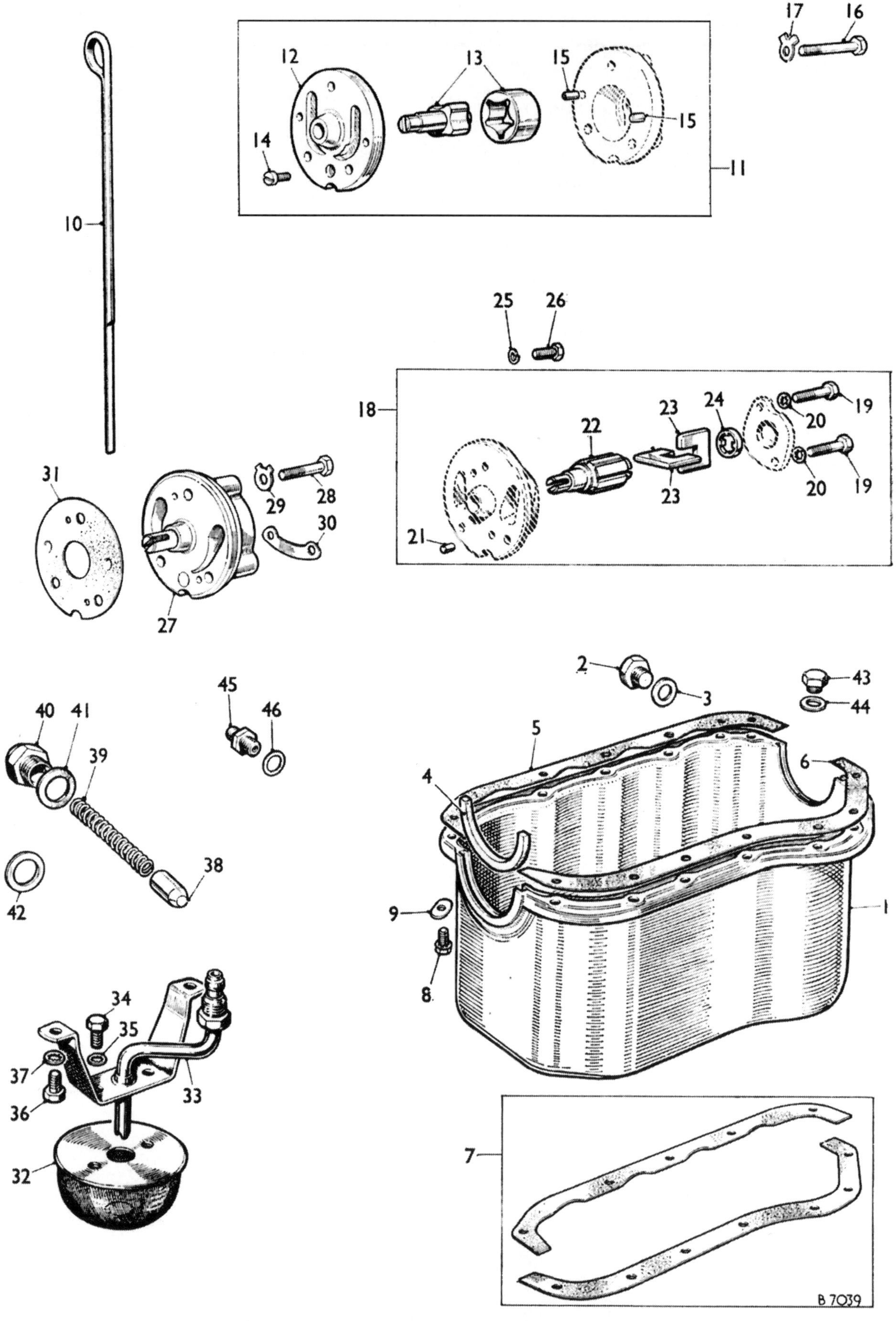
17
16
12
13
15
15
14
11
10
25
26
18
23
24
22
19
20
23
20
19
31
29
28
30
21
27
2
43
3
44
45
40
41
46
5
39
6
4
38
42
9
1
8
34
35
37
33
36
7
32
B 7039

9CG Engine—*continued*

DESCRIPTION	Part No.	Illus. No.	Quantity	Change Point	REMARKS
SUMP AND DIPPER ROD					
Sump—oil	†2A 704	1	1		W.S.E. use 12G 173
Sump—oil	12G 173	1	1		
Plug—drain—sump	88G 257	2	1		Part No. change; was 2A 380 and 2F 4249
Washer (copper)	6K 638	3	1		
Seal—oil—main bearing cap	2A 280	4	2		
Gasket—sump to crankcase					
Right-hand	†12A 20	5	1		W.S.E. use 8G 731
Left-hand	†12A 19	6	1		W.S.E. use 8G 731
	†8G 716	7	1 set		W.S.E. use 8G 731
	†8G 722	7	1 set		W.S.E. use 8G 731
	†8G 731	7	1 set		
Screw (with captive washer)	6K 639	8	14		
Washer	2K 5197	9	14		
Rod—oil dipper	2A 294	10	1		
OIL PUMP, STRAINER, AND RELEASE VALVE					
Pump—oil (Hobourn)	†2A 962	11	1		Alternative to 12G 793
Body	NSP		1		
Cover	17H 6427	12	1		
Shaft—driving (with rotors)	17H 1965	13	1		
Screw	AJD 3204 Z	14	1		
Dowel	17H 1964	15	2		
Screw	HBN 0414	16	3		
Washer—lock	2A 339	17	1		
Pump—oil (Burman)	†2A 819	18	1	(E) 9CG/Da/H101 to H15258 and L101 to L14245	W.S.E. use 2A 962 or 12G 50
Body and cover	NSP		1	(E) 9CG/Da/H101 to H15258 and L101 to L14245	
Screw	HBN 0411	19	2	(E) 9CG/Da/H101 to H15258 and L101 to L14245	
Washer—shakeproof	LWN 404	20	2	(E) 9CG/Da/H101 to H15258 and L101 to L14245	
Dowel	7H 6813	21	2	(E) 9CG/Da/H101 to H15258 and L101 to L14245	
Rotor	7H 6810	22	1	(E) 9CG/Da/H101 to H15258 and L101 to L14245	
Vane—rotor	7H 6807	23	2	(E) 9CG/Da/H101 to H15258 and L101 to L14245	
Sleeve—rotor	7H 6808	24	1	(E) 9CG/Da/H101 to H15258 and L101 to L14245	
Screw	HZS 0405	25	3	(E) 9CG/Da/H101 to H15258 and L101 to L14245	
Washer—spring	LWN 304	26	1	(E) 9CG/Da/H101 to H15258 and L101 to L14245	
Pump—oil (Concentric)	†12A 107	27	1		W.S.E. use 12G 793
	†12A 198	27	1		W.S.E. use 12G 793
	†12G 50	27	1		W.S.E. use 12G 793
	†12G 793	27	1		Alternative to 2A 962
Screw	HBN 0414	28	3		
Washer—lock	2A 339	29	1		
Plate—lock	2A 522	30	1		
Gasket	†2A 494	31	1		W.S.E. use 12G 69
Gasket	†12G 69	31	1		W.S.E. use 88G 411
Gasket	†88G 411	31	1		
Strainer—oil	2A 668	32	1		
Pipe—suction (with bracket)	2A 957	33	1		
Screw—bracket to oil strainer	HNS 0404	34	2		
Washer—shakeproof	LWN 404	35	2		
Screw	HNS 0404	36	2		
Washer—shakeproof	LWN 404	37	2		
Valve—oil release	†1G 1452	38	1		W.S.E. use 12H 865
Valve—oil release	12H 865	38	1		
Spring—oil release valve	6K 853	39	1		
Nut—cap	1A 2206	40	1		
Washer (fibre)	2K 4982	41	2		Use 1 off 6K 431 for this application
Washer (copper)	6K 431	42	1		
Plug—oil priming	2K 4994	43	1		
Washer—plug (copper)	6K 464	44	1		
Union—oil pressure	2A 269	45	1		
Washer—union (fibre)	2K 4956	46	1		

† Revised Information.

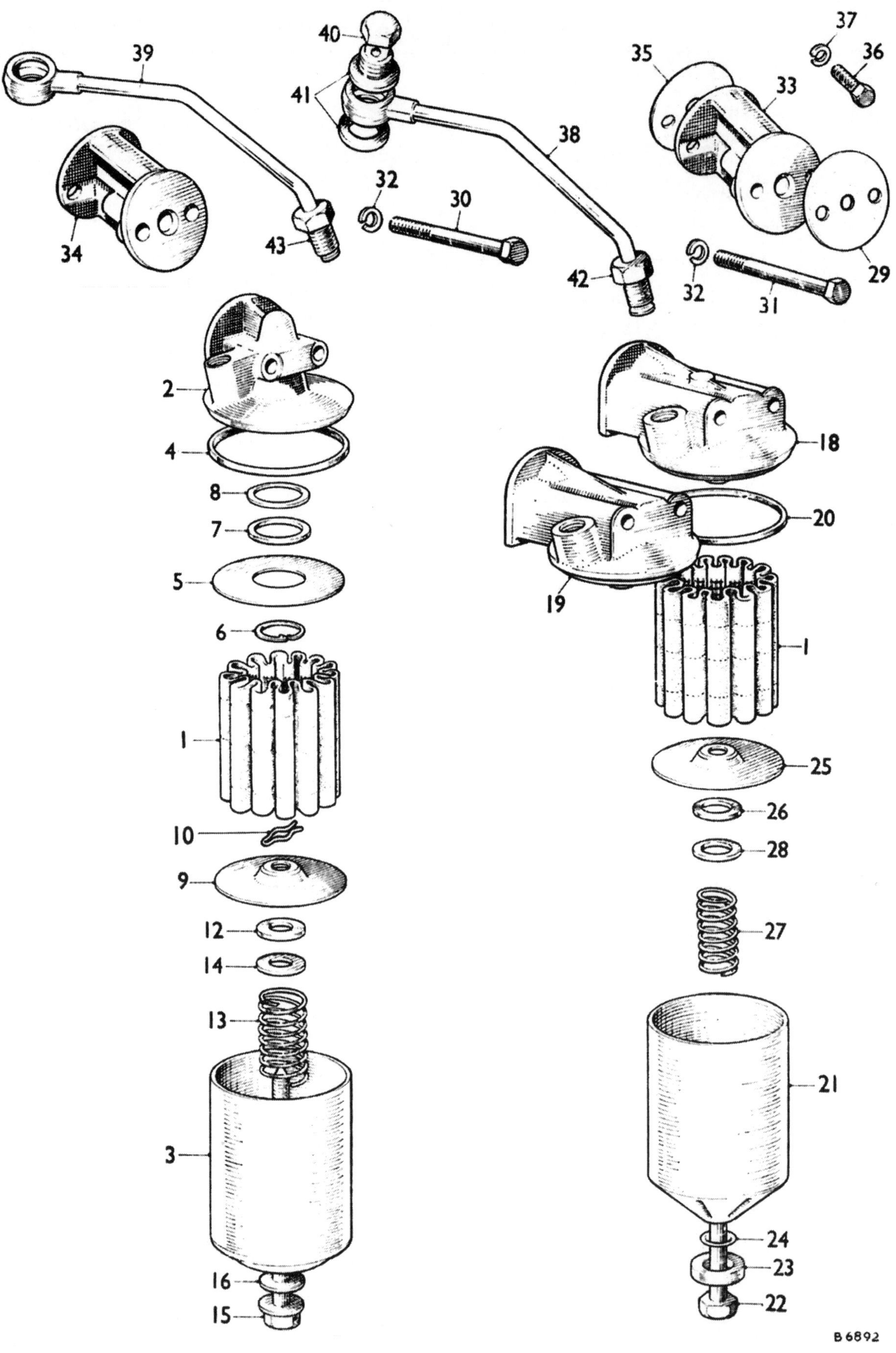
39
40
41
37
35
36
33
38
32
30
34
43
42
32
31
29
2
18
4
8
20
7
5
19
6
1
1
25
10
26
28
9
27
12
14
13
21
3
24
23
16
22
15
B 6892

DESCRIPTION	Part No.	Illus. No.	Quantity	Change Point	REMARKS
9CG Engine—*continued*					
OIL FILTER					
Filter—oil (Tecalemit)	NSP		1		Alternative to Purolator filter
Element	8G 684	1	1		
Head	17H 945	2	1		
Sump	37H 436	3	1		
Seal—sump to head	†17H 4	4	1		W.S.E. use 13H 998
Seal—sump to head	†13H 998	4	1		
Plate—element clamp	7H 147	5	1		
Circlip—plate to head	2A 700	6	1		
Washer—clamp plate (felt)	7H 1756	7	1		
Washer—dished—clamp plate	7H 1761	8	1	Finished at (C) 3807	
Plate—pressure	17H 942	9	1		
Circlip—plate to centre bolt	†7H 1840	10	1		W.S.E. use 17H 2877
Circlip—plate to centre bolt	17H 2877	11	1		
Washer—pressure plate (felt)	7H 1758	12	1		
Spring—pressure plate	7H 1764	13	1		
Washer—spring	7H 1765	14	1		
Bolt—centre	17H 943	15	1		
Seal—bolt to sump	7H 1759	16	1		
Filter—oil (Purolator)	NSP		1		Alternative to Tecalemit filter
Element	8G 684	17	1		
Head assembly	37H 690	18	1		Use 17H 9463 for this application
	17H 9463	19	1		
Plate—clamping	NSP		1		
Seal—sump to head	†27H 1983	20	1		W.S.E. use 12A 1591
	†13H 3249	20	1		W.S.E. use 12A 1591
	†12A 1591	20	1		
Sump	17H 1169	21	1		
Bolt—centre	37H 689	22	1		
Collar—centre bolt	17H 1172	23	1		
Seal—centre bolt collar	17H 1173	24	1		
Plate—pressure	17H 1148	25	1		
Seal—pressure plate	7H 28	26	1		
Spring—pressure plate	7H 25	27	1		
Washer—pressure plate spring	7H 7553	28	1		
Gasket—oil filter to adaptor	88G 205	29	1		Part No. change; was 12A 143, 12A 394, and 12G 148. Use 88G 402 for this application
Gasket—filter to adaptor	88G 402	29	1		
Bolt	HCZ 0628	30	2	(E) 9CG/Da/H101 to H5066	
Bolt	HCZ 0630	31	2	(E) 9CG/Da/H5067 on	
Washer—spring	LWZ 206	32	2		
Adaptor—oil filter	†AEA 305	33	1	(E) 9CG/Da/H101 to H5066	W.S.E. use AEA 657 together with 2 off bolt HCZ 0630 and 1 off pipe AEA 658
Adaptor—oil filter	AEA 657	34	1	(E) 9CG/Da/H5067 on	
Gasket—adaptor to crankcase	88G 205	35	1		Part No. change; was 12A 143, 12A 394, and 12G 148. Use 88G 402 for this application
Gasket—adaptor to crankcase	88G 402	35	1		
Screw	NCS 0608	36	2		
Washer—spring	LWN 206	37	2		
Pipe—oil	†AEA 813	38	1	(E) 9CG/Da/H101 to H5066	W.S.E. use AEA 658 together with 2 off bolt HCZ 0630 and 1 off adaptor AEA 657
Pipe—oil	AEA 658	39	1	(E) 9CG/Da/H5067 on	
Screw—banjo union	2A 715	40	1		
Washer (copper)	AED 172	41	2		
Connection	TCN 206	42	1		Use AEA 678 for this application
Connection	AEA 678	43	1		

† Revised Information.

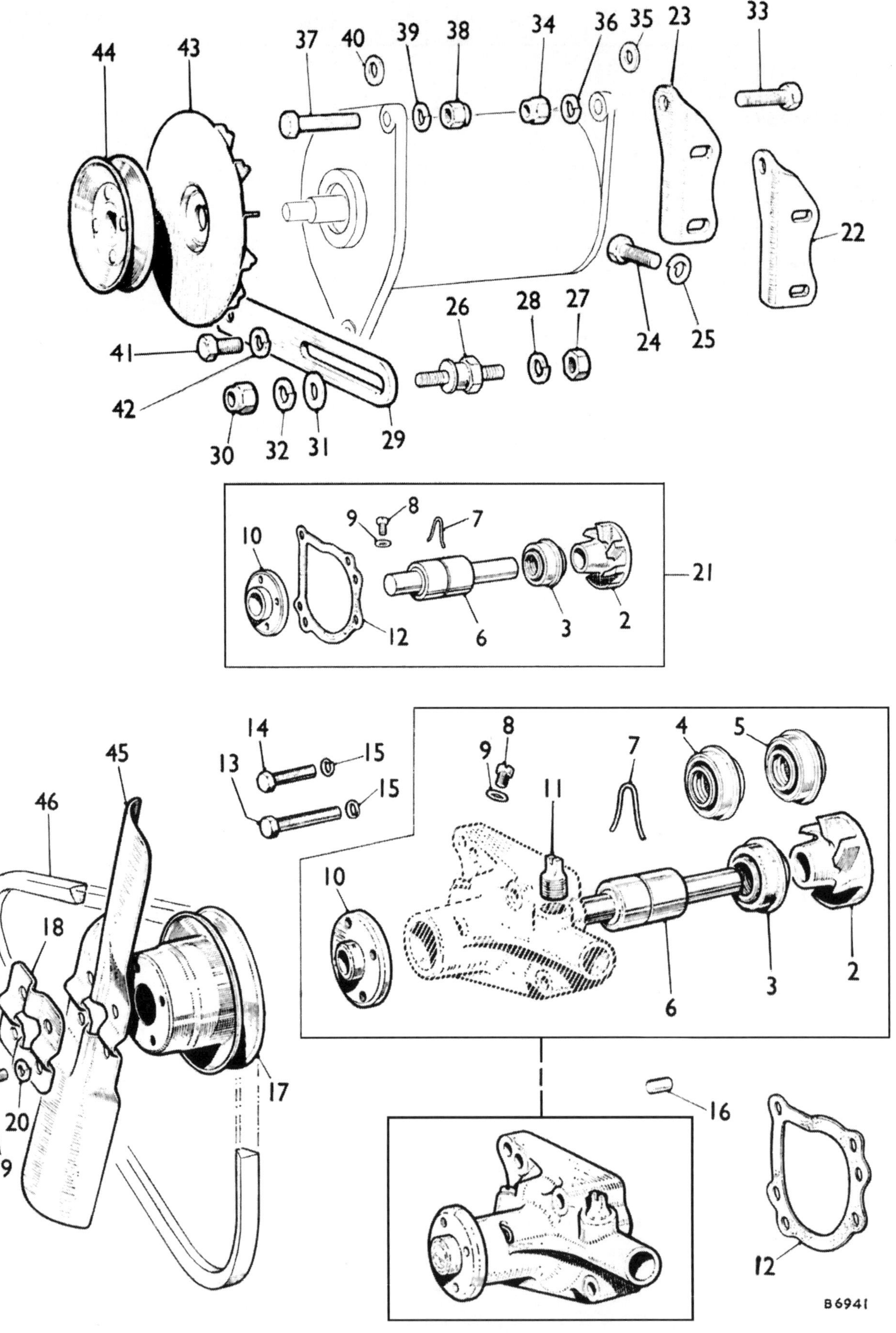
44
43
37
40
39
38
34
36
35
23
33
22
24
25
26
28
27
41
42
30
32
31
29
10
9
8
7
21
12
6
3
2
14
15
13
15
45
46
18
8
9
11
7
4
5
10
6
3
2
17
20
19
16
12
B6941

DESCRIPTION	Part No.	Illus. No.	Quantity	Change Point	REMARKS
9CG Engine—*continued*					
WATER PUMP AND FAN PULLEY					
Pump assembly—water	†2A 774	1	1	(E) 9CG/Da/H101 to H32735 and L101 to L26632	W.S.E. use 12G 120
	†12G 120	1	1	(E) 9CG/Da/H32735 on and L26633 on	W.S.E. use 12A 1332
	†12A 1332	1	1		W.S.E. use 12G 1284
	†12G 1284	1	1		
Body	NSP		1		
Vane	2A 664	2	1		
Seal	†8G 698	3	1		W.S.E. use 13H 591
	†8G 697	3	1		W.S.E. use 13H 591
	13H 591	4	1		For use with 2A 774
	†13H 772	5	1		For use with 12G 120. W.S.E. use 88G 446
	88G 446	5	1		
Bearing (with spindle)	†2A 777	6	1		W.S.E. use 12A 1328
	†12A 1328	6	1		W.S.E. use 12A 1389
	†12A 1389	6	1		
Wire—bearing locating	†2A 778	7	1		For use with water pumps 2A 774, 12G 120 and 12A 1332
Screw—lubricating point	†53K 1433	8	1		For use with water pumps 2A 774, 12G 120 and 12A 1332
Washer (fibre)	2K 4974	9	1		
Hub—pulley	2A 665	10	1		Use 8G 733 for this application
Hub—pulley	8G 733	10	1		
Adaptor—by-pass	2A 243	11	1		
Gasket	88G 215	12	1		Part No. change; was 2A 667 and 12A 31
Screw—long	HZS 0515	13	2		
Screw—short	HZS 0510	14	2		
Washer—spring	LWN 305	15	4		
Dowel	2K 6124	16	2		
Pulley—fan and water pump	2A 601	17	1		
Stiffener—fan blade	2A 803	18	1		
Screw	HZS 0406	19	4		
Washer—spring	LWN 204	20	4		
Kit—repair—water pump	†8G 2361	21	1		Part No. change; was 8G 2312. W.S.E. use 8G 2570
Kit—repair—water pump	†8G 2570	21	1		
Vane	2A 664	2	1		
Seal	88G 446	3	1		
Bearing (with spindle)	12A 1328	6	1		
Wire—bearing locating	2A 778	7	1		
Screw—lubricating point	53K 1433	8	1		
Washer (fibre)	2K 4974	9	1		
Hub—pulley	8G 733	10	1		
Gasket—pump body to crankcase	88G 215	12	1		

† Revised Information.

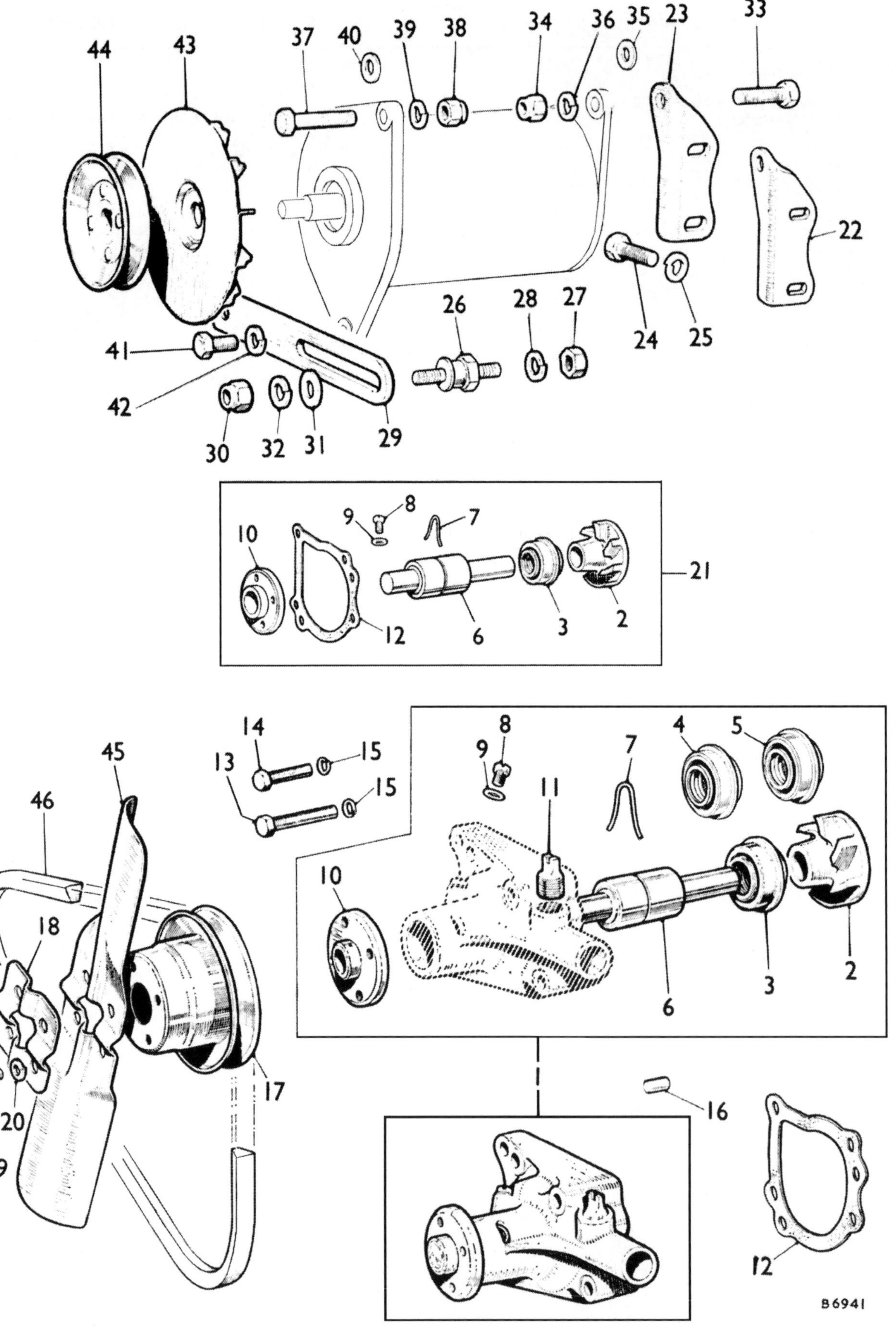
44
43
37
40
39
38
34
36
35
23
33
22
24
25
26
28
27
41
42
30
32
31
29
10
9
8
7
21
12
6
3
2
14
13
15
15
45
46
18
20
19
17
11
4
5
16
12
B6941

DESCRIPTION	Part No.	Illus. No.	Quantity	Change Point	REMARKS
9CG Engine—*continued*					
DYNAMO MOUNTING					
Bracket—dynamo—rear	†2A 758	22	1		W.S.E. use 12A 526
Bracket—dynamo—rear	12A 526	23	1		
Screw	HZS 0507	24	2		
Washer—spring	LWZ 305	25	2		
Pillar—dynamo adjusting link	2A 128	26	1		
Nut	FNZ 106	27	1		
Washer—spring	LWZ 306	28	1		
Link—dynamo adjusting	AEA 325	29	1		
Nut	†LNZ 206	30	1		
Washer—plain	PWN 106	31	1		
Washer—spring	LWZ 306	32	1		
Bolt	HZS 0509	33	1		Use HZS 0510 for this application
Bolt	HZS 0510	33	1		
Nut	LNZ 205	34	1		
Washer					
Plain	PWZ 305	35	1		
Spring	†2K 5319	36	1		W.S.E. use LWN 305
Spring	LWN 305	36	1		
Bolt	HBZ 0513	37	1		Use HZS 0514 for this application
Bolt	HZS 0514	37	1		
Nut	LNZ 204	38	1		
Washer—spring	LWZ 305	39	1		
Washer—plain	PWZ 305	40	1		
Screw—adjusting link to dynamo	†3H 2098	41	1		W.S.E. use ZCS 0505
Screw—adjusting link to dynamo	ZCS 0505	41	1		
Washer—spring	LWZ 305	42	1		
Fan—dynamo	†1G 1783	43	1		W.S.E. use AEC 82
Fan—dynamo	AEC 82	43	1		
Pulley—dynamo	1H 998	44	1		
FAN AND FAN BELT					
Blade—fan	AEA 301	45	2		
Belt—fan—wedge-type	†AEA 849	46	1	Fitted up to change over to AEJ 63	W.S.E. use 13H 1329
	†AEJ 63	46	1	(E) 9CG/Da/H22851 and L15656 on	W.S.E. use 13H 1329
	13H 1329	46	1		

DESCRIPTION	Part No.	Illus. No.	Quantity	Change Point	REMARKS
ENGINE SERVICE KITS					
Set—gasket—engine decarbonizing	8G 2320		1		W.S.E. use 8G 2402
Set—gasket—engine decarbonizing	8G 2402		1		
Gasket					
Cylinder head	12G 293		1		
Manifold	†AEG 181		1		
Water outlet elbow	†12G 330		1		
Rocker cover	12A 14		1		
Cover plate	†88G 221		1		
Carburetter	1G 2624		6		
Air cleaner	†12H 862		2		
Ring—valve packing	2A 879		8		
Set—gasket—supplementary	8G 2232		1		Use with 8G 2402 for complete engine overhaul
Gasket					
Front mounting plate	12G 619		1		
Cylinder front cover	12A 956		1		
Cylinder side cover	12A 1139		2		
Oil pump	†88G 411		1		
Sump	†8G 731		1		
Water pump	†88G 215		1		
Petrol pump	2A 113		1		
Rear mounting plate	12A 22		1		
Crankcase rear cover	2A 127		1		
Oil filter to crankcase	†88G 402		2		
Seal—oil—main bearing cap	2A 280		2		
Washer					
Oil priming plug	6K 464		1		
Sump drain plug	6K 638		1		
Drain tap	2K 4954		1		Alternatives
Drain tap	†2K 4975		1		Alternatives

† Revised Information.

DESCRIPTION	Part No.	Illus. No.	Quantity	Change Point	REMARKS
9CG Engine—*continued*					
INLET AND EXHAUST MANIFOLDS					
Manifold—inlet (with plug and studs)	†AEA 576	1	1	(E) 9CG/Da/H101 to H8169	W.S.E. use AEA 683
Manifold—inlet (with plug and studs)	AEA 683	2	1	(E) 9CG/Da/H8170 on	
Plug—inlet manifold	2K 8159	3	2	(E) 9CG/Da/H101 to H8169	
Plug—inlet manifold	AEA 685	4	2	(E) 9CG/Da/H8170 on	
Stud—carburetter to manifold	CHS 2620	5	4		
Manifold—exhaust	12A 191	6	1		
Gasket—inlet and exhaust manifold	12A 192	7	1		Use 12G 300 for this application
Gasket—inlet and exhaust manifold	12G 300	7	1		
Nut—inlet and exhaust manifold stud	BNN 105	8	6		
Washer—clamping	2A 110	9	4		
Washer	PWN 105	10	2		

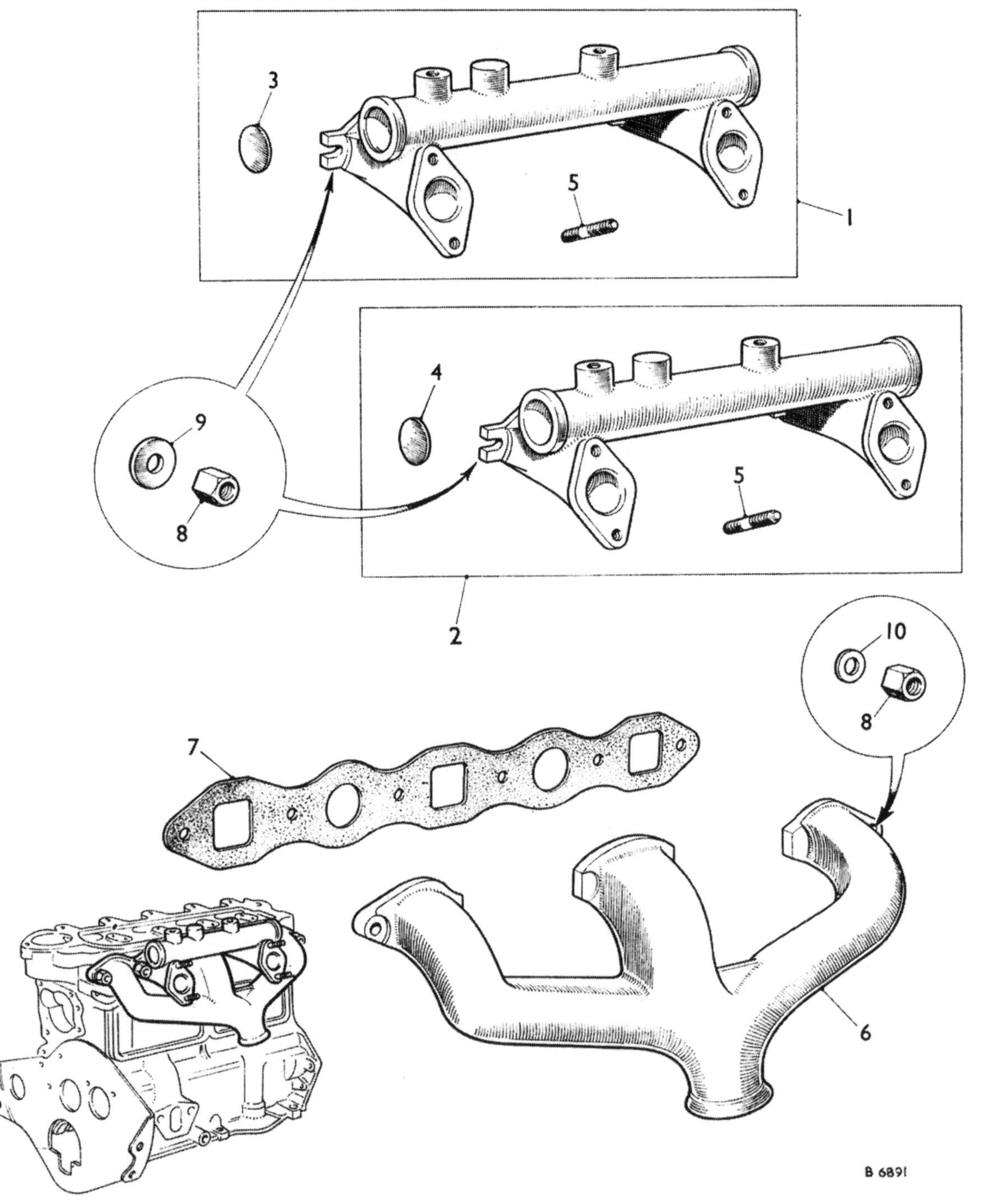

ENGINE MA

		Pages
1098-cc	10CG/Da/H	MA 32 to MA 48

1098-cc 10CG ENGINE

	Page	Plate
CAMSHAFT	MA 35	A 20
CONNECTING RODS	MA 35	A 20
CONTROLS—ENGINE	MA 48, MA 49	A 30
COVERS—CYLINDER	MA 39	A 23
COVER—VALVE ROCKER	MA 38	A 22
CRANKSHAFT—PULLEY	MA 35	A 20
CYLINDER HEAD	MA 37	A 21
DISTRIBUTOR HOUSING—SPINDLE	MA 36	A 20
ELBOW—WATER OUTLET—THERMOSTAT ...	MA 38	A 22
ENGINE UNIT	MA 33	A 19
EXHAUST SYSTEM	MA 47	A 29
FAN—FAN BELT	MA 43	A 26
FILTER—OIL	MA 41	A 25
FLYWHEEL	MA 36	A 20
MANIFOLDS	MA 45	A 27
MOUNTINGS—DYNAMO	MA 43	A 26
MOUNTINGS—ENGINE	MA 46	A 28
PISTONS	MA 34	A 19
PLATE—ENGINE MOUNTING—FRONT	MA 35	A 20
PLATE—ENGINE MOUNTING—REAR	MA 39	A 23
PLUGS—SPARKING	MA 38	A 22
PUMP—OIL	MA 40	A 24
PUMP—WATER—FAN PULLEY	MA 42	A 26
SERVICE KITS—ENGINE	MA 44	
SHAFT—VALVE ROCKER	MA 37	A 21
SUMP—OIL—DIPPER ROD	MA 40	A 24
TAPPETS	MA 36	A 20

† Revised Information.

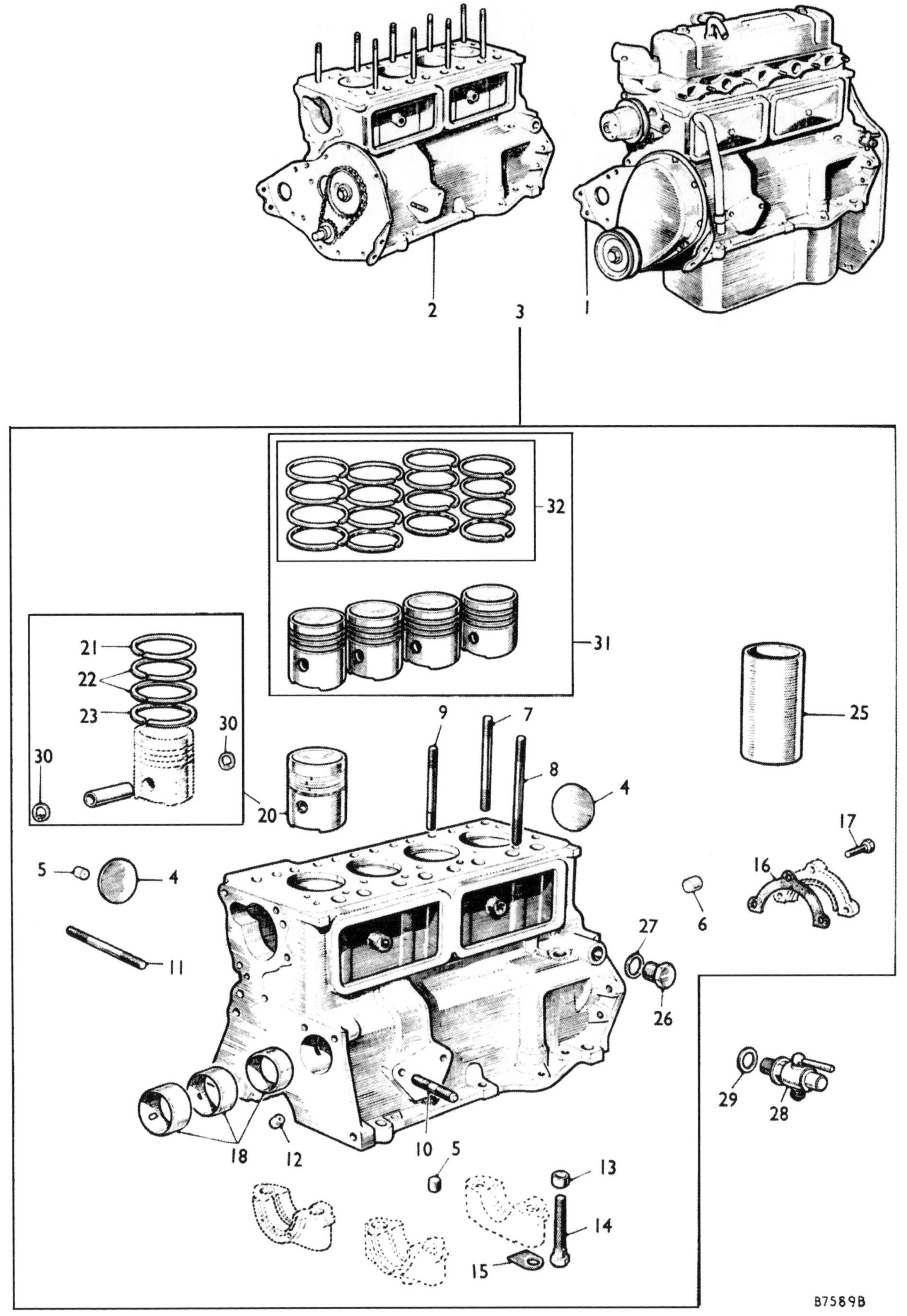
2
3
1
32
31
21
22
23
30
30
20
9
7
8
4
25
17
16
5
4
6
27
11
26
29
28
18
12
10
5
13
14
15
B7589B

DESCRIPTION	Part No.	Illus. No.	Quantity	Change Point	REMARKS
ENGINE					
10CG ENGINE UNIT					
Engine unit—stripped					
HC	8G 124	1	1	(E) 10CG/Da/H101 to H14877	
LC	8G 125	1	1	(E) 10CG/Da/H101 to H14877	
Modified head **HC**	8G 135	1	1	(E) 10CG/Da/H14878 on	
Modified head **LC**	8G 136	1	1	(E) 10CG/Da/H14878 on	
Engine unit—half **HC**	88G 310	2	1		
Engine unit—half **LC**	88G 311	2	1		
Block assembly—cylinder **HC**	†38G 306	3	1		W.S.E. use 38G 336
LC	†38G 307	3	1		W.S.E. use 88G 337
HC	38G 336	3	1		
LC	37G 337	3	1		
Plug					
Welch	2K 8169	4	4		
Oil release valve passage	2K 1345	5	2		
Oil gallery	†2K 8623	6	2		W.S.E. use **12H 1734**
Oil gallery	12H 1734	6	2		
Stud					
Cylinder head—medium	51K 254	7	1		Use **51K 256** for this application
Cylinder head—long	51K 255	8	4		
Cylinder head—short	51K 256	9	5		
Petrol pump	53K 525	10	2		
Oil filter	53K 524	11	2		
Restrictor—camshaft oil feed	1A 1964	12	1		
Cap—main bearing					
Front	NSP		1		
Centre	NSP		1		
Rear	NSP		1		
Dowel—main bearing cap	2A 54	13	6		
Screw—main bearing cap	2A 53	14	6		
Washer—lock—main bearing cap	6K 927	15	6		
Cover—crankcase—rear	NSP		1		
Gasket	2A 127	16	1		
Screw	53K 1028	17	1		
Liner—camshaft bearing	28G 133	18	1 set		
Plug—drain	2K 4993	26	1		
Washer	6K 638	27	1		
Tap—drain	3H 576	28	1		For service purposes only
Washer	2K 4975	29	1		For service purposes only
Liner—cylinder block	†12G 164	25	1		For service purposes only

† Revised Information.

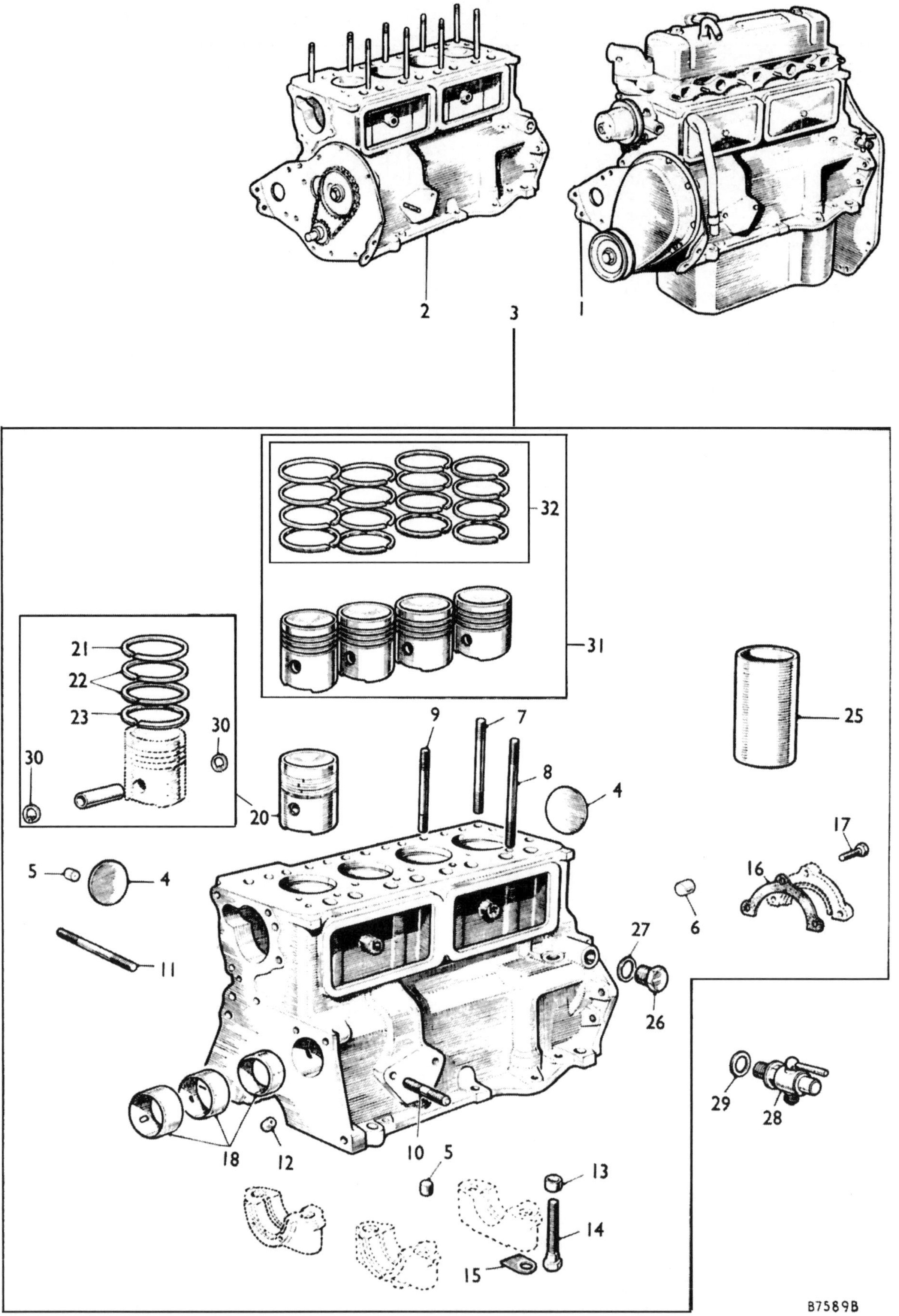
1
2
3
4
5
6
7
8
9
10
11
12
13
14
15
16
17
18
20
21
22
23
25
26
27
28
29
30
31
32
B7589B

DESCRIPTION		Part No.	Illus. No.	Quantity	Change Point	REMARKS
10CG Engine—*continued*						
Piston and connecting rod assembly		NSP				Piston and connecting rods are no longer supplied as assemblies; Service Bulletin GN/157 refers
Piston assembly—Grade 3						
Standard	HC	†12G 0306 03	20	4		W.S.E. use piston assembly—engine set 8G 2441 03 with oversizes
·010″ (·254 mm) O/S	HC	†12G 0306 13	20	4		
·020″ (·508 mm) O/S	HC	†12G 0306 23	20	4		
Standard	LC	†12G 0303 03	20	4		W.S.E. use piston assembly—engine set 8G 2443 03 with oversizes
·010″ (·254 mm) O/S	LC	†12G 0303 13	20	4		
·020″ (·508 mm) O/S	LC	†12G 0303 23	20	4		
Piston assembly—Grade 6						
Standard	HC	†12G 0306 06	20	4		W.S.E. use piston assembly—engine set 8G 2441 06 with oversizes
·010″ (·254 mm) O/S	HC	†12G 0306 16	20	4		
·020″ (·508 mm) O/S	HC	†12G 0306 26	20	4		
Standard	LC	†12G 0303 06	20	4		W.S.E. use piston assembly—engine set 8G 2443 06 with oversizes
·010″ (·254 mm) O/S	LC	†12G 0303 16	20	4		
·020″ (·508 mm) O/S	LC	†12G 0303 26	20	4		
Piston assembly—engine set—Grade 3						
Standard	HC	†8G 2441 02	31	1 set		
·010″ (·254 mm) O/S	HC	†8G 2441 13	31	1 set		
·020″ (·508 mm) O/S	HC	†8G 2441 23	31	1 set		
Standard	LC	†8G 2443 03	31	1 set		
·010″ (·254 mm) O/S	LC	†8G 2443 13	31	1 set		
·020″ (·508 mm) O/S	LC	†8G 2443 23	31	1 set		
Piston assembly—engine set—Grade 6						
Standard	HC	†8G 2441 06	31	1 set		
·010″ (·254 mm)	HC	†8G 2441 16	31	1 set		
·020″ (·508 mm)	HC	†8G 2441 26	31	1 set		
Standard	LC	†8G 2443 06	31	1 set		
·010″ (·254 mm)	LC	†8G 2443 16	31	1 set		
·020″ (·508 mm)	LC	†8G 2443 26	31	1 set		
Ring—piston						
Top—standard		†12G 55	21	4		W.S.E. use ring—piston—engine set 8G 745 with oversizes
·010″ (·254 mm) O/S		†12G 0055 10	21	4		
·020″ (·508 mm) O/S		†12G 0055 20	21	4		
2nd and 3rd—standard		†12G 56	22	8		
·010″ (·254 mm) O/S		†12G 0056 10	22	8		
·020″ (·508 mm) O/S		†12G 0056 20	22	8		
Scraper—standard		†12G 57	23	4		
·010″ (·254 mm) O/S		†12G 0057 10	23	4		
·020″ (·508 mm) O/S		†12G 0057 20	23	4		
Scraper—standard		†12G 270	23	4		
·010″ (·254 mm) O/S		†12G 0270 10	23	4		
·020″ (·508 mm) O/S		†12G 0270 20	23	4		
Ring—piston—engine set						
Standard		†8G 745	32	1 set		
·010″ (·254 mm) O/S		†8G 0745 10	32	1 set		
·020″ (·508 mm) O/S		†8G 0745 20	32	1 set		
Pin—gudgeon		NSP		4		
Circlip—gudgeon pin		CCN 210	30	8		

† Revised Information.

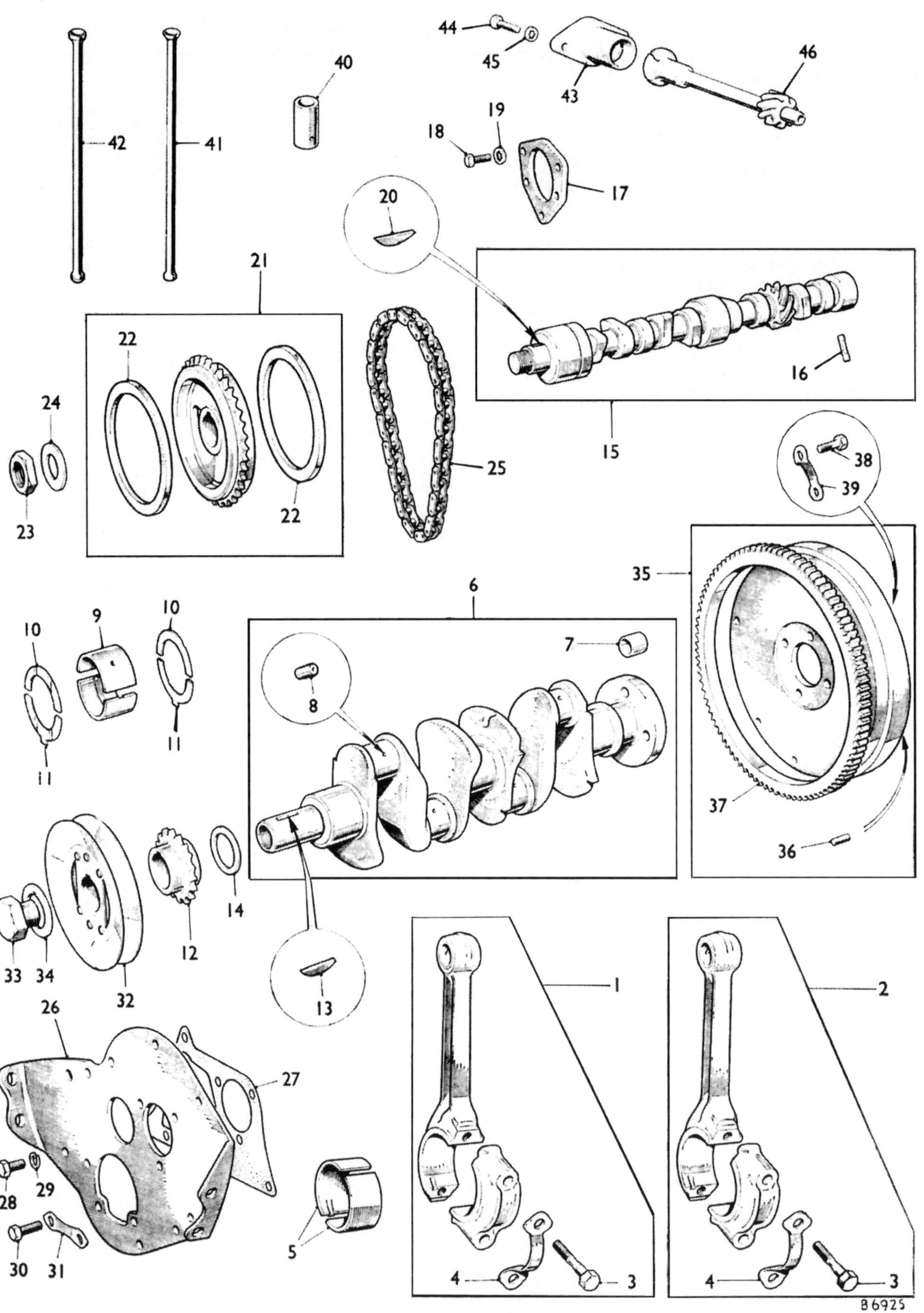
44
45
40
43
46
19
18
42
41
17
20
21
15
16
22
24
25
23
22
38
39
6
35
10
9
10
7
8
11
11
37
36
14
12
33 34
32
13
26
1
2
27
28
29
30 31
5
4
3
4
3
B 6925

	DESCRIPTION	Part No.	Illus. No.	Quantity	Change Point	REMARKS
	10CG Engine—*continued*					
	CONNECTING RODS AND BEARINGS					
	Rod—connecting—Nos. 1 and 3 cylinders	12G 126	1	2		
	Rod—connecting—Nos. 2 and 4 cylinders	12G 123	2	2		
	Screw—connecting rod cap	12G 93	3	8		
	Washer—lock-screw	2A 660	4	4		
	Bush—connecting rod	NSP		4		
	Bearing—connecting rod					
	Standard	8G 2198	5	1 set		
	·010″ (·254 mm) U/S	8G 2198 10	5	1 set		
	·020″ (·508 mm) U/S	8G 2198 20	5	1 set		
	·030″ (·762 mm) U/S	8G 2198 30	5	1 set		
	·040″ (1·016 mm) U/S	8G 2198 40	5	1 set		
	CRANKSHAFT AND GEAR					
	Crankshaft	88G 202	6	1		Part No. change; was 12G 178 and 12G 246
	Bush—1st motion shaft	1A 1559	7	1		
	Restrictor—oil	1G 1167	8	1		
	Crankshaft—reground (with bearings)	38G 319		1		UK market Exchange Unit Scheme only
	Bearing—main					
	Standard	8G 2332	9	1 set		
	·010″ (·254 mm) U/S	8G 2332 10	9	1 set		
	·020″ (·508 mm) U/S	8G 2332 20	9	1 set		
	·030″ (·762 mm) U/S	8G 2332 30	9	1 set		
	·040″ (1·016 mm) U/S	8G 2332 40	9	1 set		
	Washer—thrust					
	Upper	8G 2422	10	2		Part No. change; was 12A 208
	Upper—·003″ (·076 mm) O/S	8G 2422 03	10	2		Part No. change; was 12A 0206 03
	Upper—·030″ (·762 mm) O/S	8G 2422 30	10	2		
	Lower	8G 2423	11	2		Part No. change; was 12A 209
	Lower—·003″ (·076 mm) O/S	8G 2423 03	11	2		Part No. change; was 12A 6209 03
	Lower—·030″ (·762 mm) O/S	8G 2423 30	11	2		
	Gear—crankshaft	AEA 538	12	1		
	Key	6K 836	13	1		
	Washer—packing	6K 628	14	1 or A/R		
	CAMSHAFT AND GEAR					
	Camshaft	†12G 165	15	1		Alternatives
	Camshaft	†AEA 630	15	1		Alternatives
	Pin—oil pump driving	2A 299	16	1		
	Plate—camshaft locating	2A 84	17	1		
	Screw	HNS 0406	18	8		
	Washer	LWN 404	19	3		
	Key	WKN 505	20	1		
	Gear—camshaft	2A 85	21	1		
	Ring—tensioner	8G 549	22	2		
	Nut	6K 629	23	1		
	Washer—lock	2A 759	24	1		
	Chain—camshaft drive	3H 2127	25	1		
	FRONT MOUNTING PLATE					
	Plate—engine mounting—front	2A 125	25	1		Use 12G 312 together with pillar—dynamo adjusting link 12G 314 for this application
	Plate—engine mounting—front	12G 312	26	1		Use together with pillar—dynamo adjusting link 12G 314
	Gasket—plate to crankcase	12A 413	27	1		
	Screw	HZS 0505	28	2		
	Washer—spring	LWZ 305	29	2		
	Screw—plate to bearing cap	53K 2016	30	2		
	Plate—locking—plate to bearing cap screw	6K 831	31	1		
	CRANKSHAFT PULLEY					
	Pulley—crankshaft	2A 940	32	1		
	Bolt—pulley retaining	AEA 312	33	1		
	Washer—lock—starting nut	1G 1319	34	1		

† Revised Information.

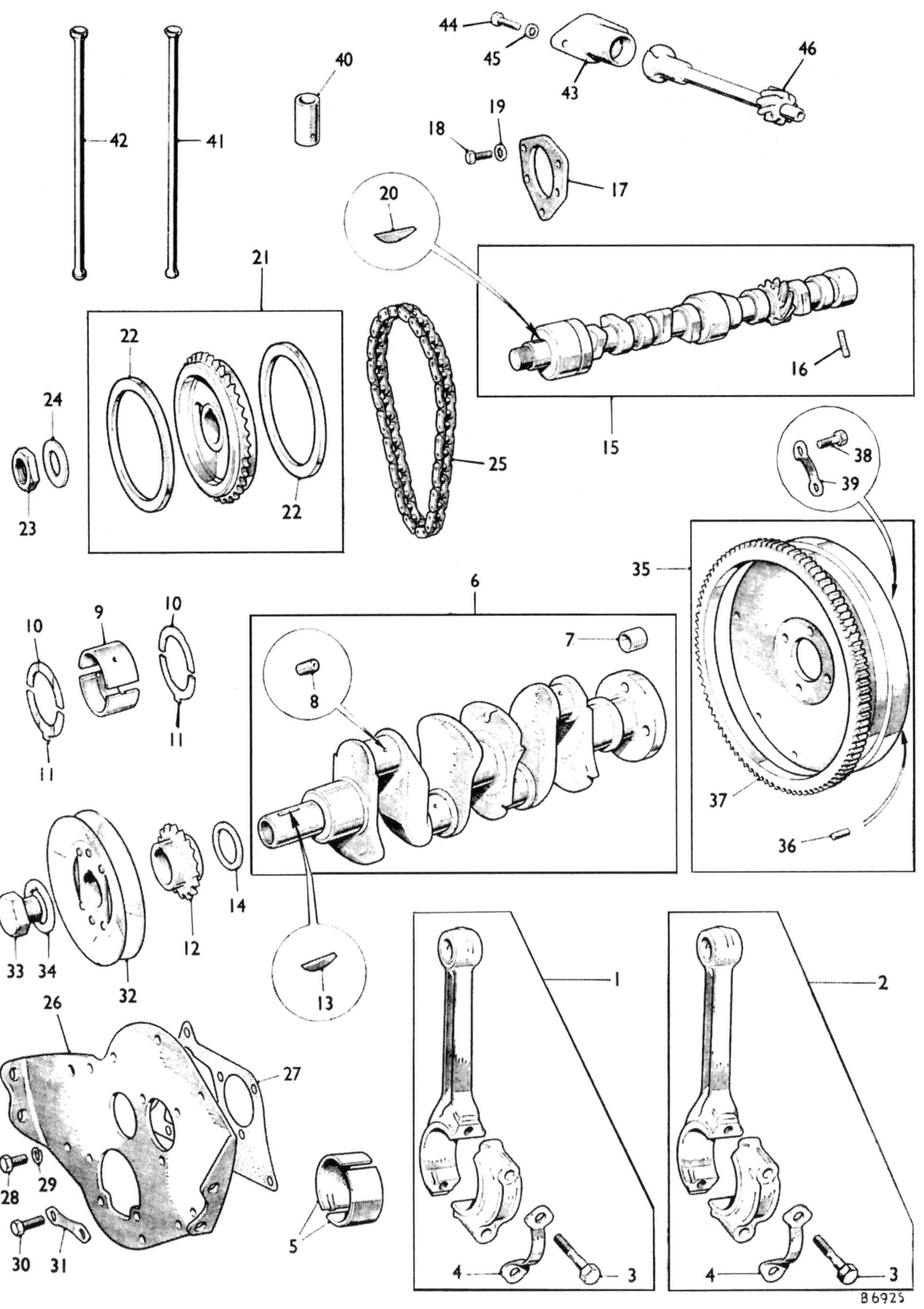

1
2
3
4
5
6
7
8
9
10
11
12
13
14
15
16
17
18
19
20
21
22
23
24
25
26
27
28
29
30
31
32
33
34
35
36
37
38
39
40
41
42
43
44
45
46
B 6925

DESCRIPTION	Part No.	Illus. No.	Quantity	Change Point	REMARKS
10CG Engine—*continued*					
FLYWHEEL					
Flywheel assembly	12G 180	35	1		
Dowel—flywheel to clutch	1G 2984	36	2		
Gear—ring—starter	12G 290	37	1		
Screw	6K 630	38	4		
Washer—lock	2K 7816	39	2		
TAPPETS AND PUSH-RODS					
Tappet					
Standard	2A 13	40	8		
·010" (·254 mm) O/S	2A 0013 10	40	8		
·020" (·508 mm) O/S	2A 0013 20	40	8		
Push-rod	2A 14	41	8		Alternatives in sets
	12A 250	41	8		
	12A 747	42	8		
DISTRIBUTOR HOUSING AND SPINDLE					
Housing—distributor	†2A 612	43	1		W.S.E. use 12A 1136 together with 'O' ring 13H 2792
Housing—distributor	12A 1136	43	1		
'O' ring—seal	13H 2792		1		
Screw	HZS 0406	44	1		
Washer—shakeproof	LWN 404	45	1		
Spindle—distributor driving	†2A 139	46	1		Alternatives. W.S.E. use 1G 2062
	†2A 847	46	1		
	†1G 2062	46	1		

† Revised Information.

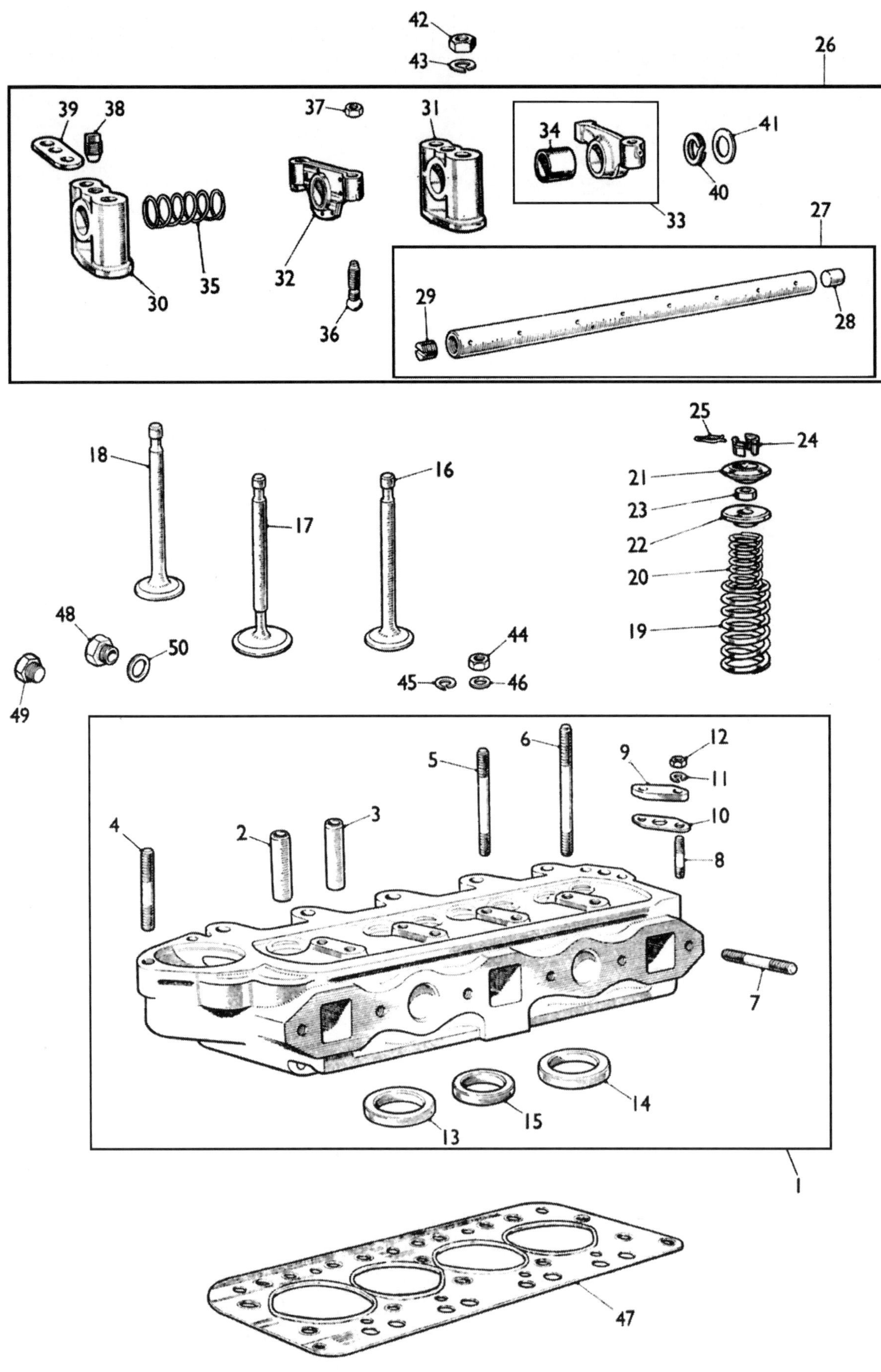
42
43
26
39 38
37
31
34
41
40
33
27
35
32
30
29
28
36
25
24
18
16
21
17
23
22
20
19
48
44
50
49
45
46
6
12
5
9
11
3
10
4
2
8
7
14
15
13
1
47

DESCRIPTION	Part No.	Illus. No.	Quantity	Change Point	REMARKS
10CG Engine—*continued*					
CYLINDER HEAD DETAILS					
Head assembly—cylinder	NSP		1		
Head—cylinder (with guides, plugs, and studs)	28G 191	1	1	(E) 10CG/Da/H101 to 14877	
Head—cylinder (with guides, plugs, and studs)	28G 222	1	1	(E) 10CG/Da/H14878 on	
Guide					
Inlet—standard	12A 186	2	4		
Inlet—·010″ (·254 mm) O/S	12A 0186 10	2	4		
Exhaust—standard	12A 186	3	4		
Exhaust—·010″ (·254 mm) O/S	12A 0186 10	3	4		
Plug—oil hole	†6K 808		1		W.S.E. use 2K 1345
Plug—oil hole	†2K 1345		1		
Stud					
Water outlet elbow	CHS 2515	4	3		
Rocker bracket—short	51K 1473	5	2		
Rocker bracket—long	51K 885	6	2		
Inlet and exhaust manifold	53K 487	7	6		
Cover plate or heater control tap	53K 402	8	2		
Plate—cover—heater tap facing	2A 180	9	1		
Gasket	88G 221	10	1		Part No. change; was 2A 179 and 12A 32
Washer—spring	LWN 304	11	2		
Nut	FNN 104	12	2		
Insert—valve seat					
Inlet	12G 267	13	4	(E) 10CG/Da/H101 to 14877	For service purposes only. Inserts to be all standard or all oversize, not mixed
Inlet	12G 721	14	4	(E) 10CG/Da/H14878 on	
Exhaust	2A 640	15	4		
Exhaust—$\frac{1}{16}$″ (1·58 mm) O/S	AEA 763	15	4		
Valve					
Inlet	12G 209	16	4	(E) 10CG/Da/H101 to 14877	
Inlet	12G 296	17	4	(E) 10CG/Da/H14878 on	
Exhaust	AEA 400	18	4		
Spring—valve—outer	AEA 311	19	8		
Spring—valve—inner	AEA 401	20	8		
Collar—valve spring—top	AEA 402	21	8		
Cup—valve spring—bottom	AEA 403	22	8		
Ring—valve packing	2A 879	23	8		
Cotter—valve—halves	2A 11	24	8 prs		
Circlip—valve cotters	2A 12	25	8		
Shaft assembly—valve rocker	AEA 90	26	1		
Shaft—valve rocker—plugged	2A 16	27	1		
Plug—plain	6K 878	28	1		
Plug—screwed	2K 4608	29	1		
Bracket—rocker shaft					
Plain	†12A 211	31	3		W.S.E. use 12G 1110
Plain	†12G 1110	31	3		
Tapped	†12A 210	30	1		W.S.E. use 12G 1109
Tapped	†12G 1109	30	1		
Rocker—valve—bushed (pressed steel)	2A 964	32	8		Alternatives; interchangeable in sets
Rocker—valve—bushed	2A 533	33	8		
Bush—valve rocker	2A 21	34	8		
Spring—valve rocker spacing	6K 556	35	3		
Screw—tappet adjusting	2A 535	36	8		W.S.E. use 12A 1215
Screw—tappet adjusting	12A 1215	36	8		
Nut—lock	6K 654	37	8		
Screw—rocker shaft locating	2A 258	38	1		
Plate—rocker shaft bracket	2A 515	39	4		
Washer—spring—rocker shaft	2A 18	40	2		
Washer—plain—rocker shaft	6K 555	41	2		
Nut—rocker cover stud	FNN 105	42	4		
Washer—spring	LWN 205	43	4		
Nut—cylinder head stud	51K 371	44	9		
Washer—spring—cylinder head nut	LWN 205	45	4		
Washer—plain—cylinder head nut	PWN 106	46	5		Use 8 off PWN 106 together with 1 off plate 2A 515 for this application
Gasket—cylinder head	†12A 190	47	1		W.S.E. use 12G 293
Gasket—cylinder head	†12G 293	47	1		Correction; was 12G 293
Plug—thermal transmitter boss	AEC 997	48	1		Use ADP 210 together with 1 off washer 1B 3664 for this application
Plug—thermal transmitter boss	ADP 210	49	1		
Washer	1B 3664	50	1		

† Revised Information.

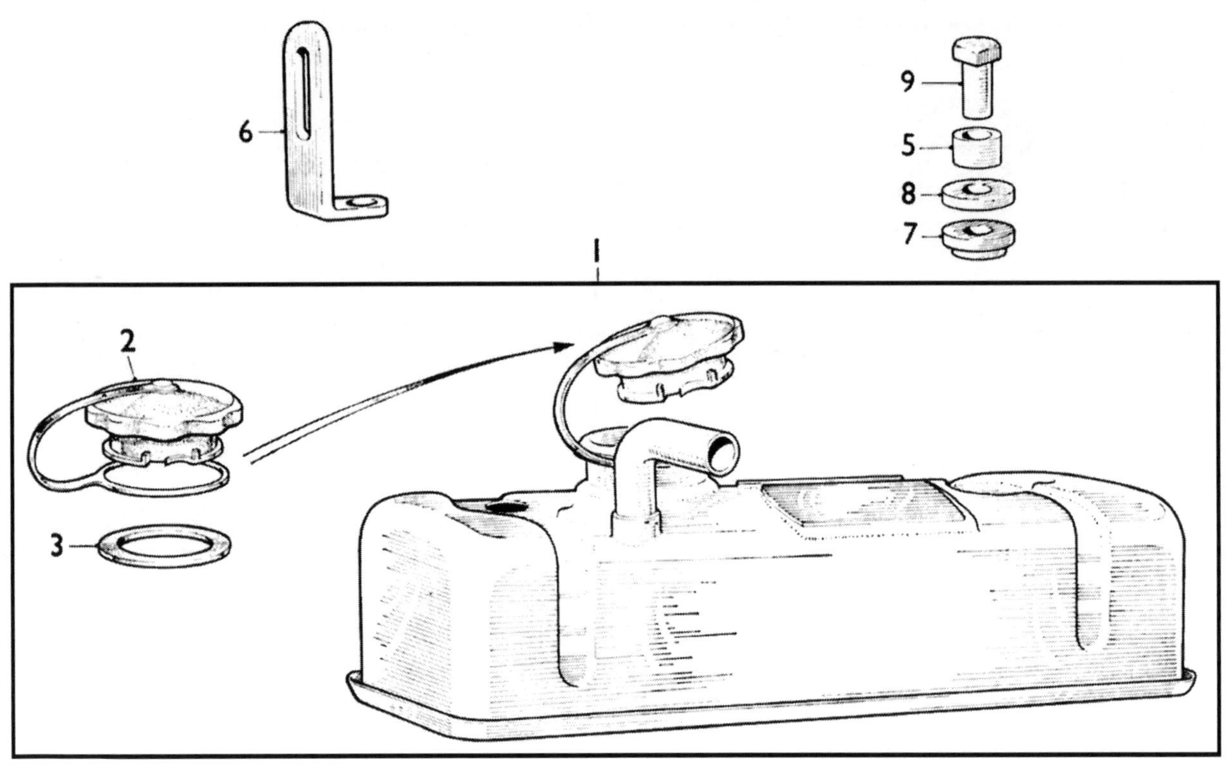

1
2
3
6
9
5
8
7

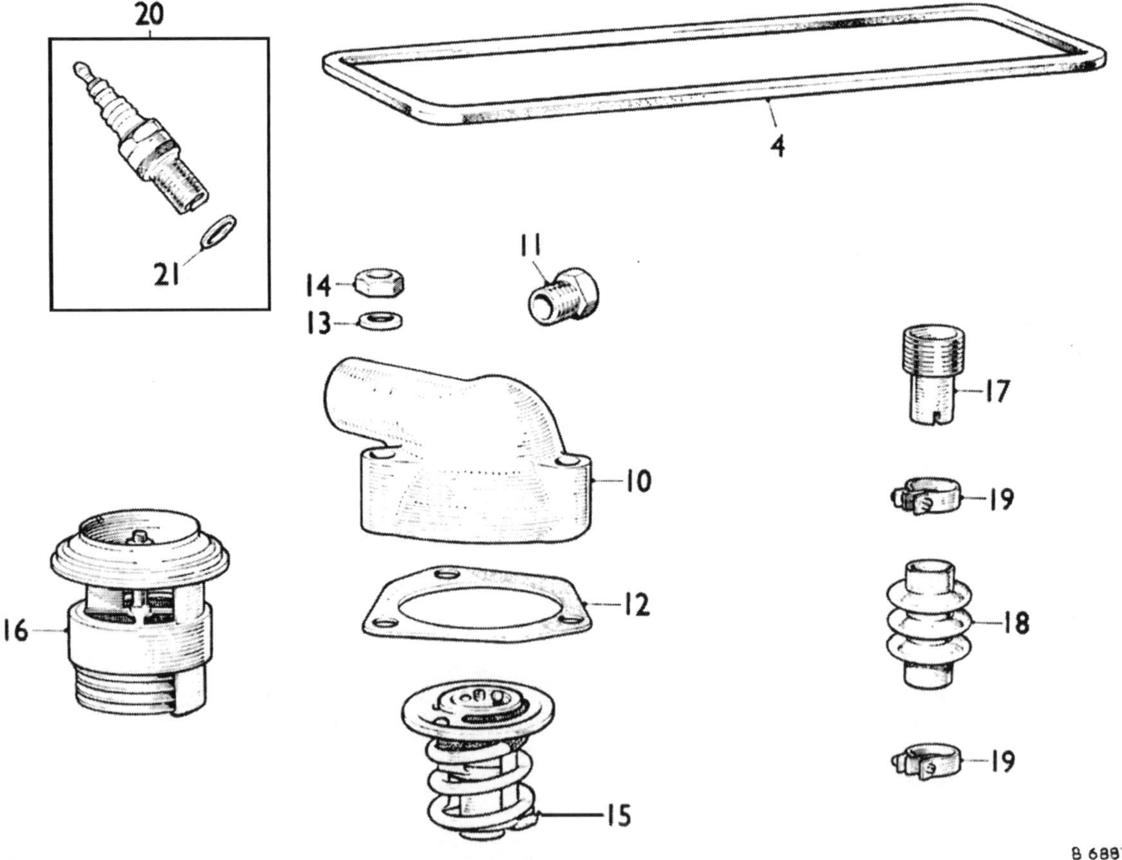

20
21
4
11
14
13
10
12
15
16
17
19
18
19
B 6887

DESCRIPTION	Part No.	Illus. No.	Quantity	Change Point	REMARKS
10CG Engine—*continued*					
VALVE ROCKER COVER AND OIL FILLER					
Cover—valve rocker assembly	12A 501	1	1		
Cap assembly—oil filler	12A 402	2	1		
Washer—oil filler cap (rubber)	12A 403	3	1		
Gasket—valve rocker cover	12A 14	4	1		
Piece—distance—valve rocker cover and cap nut	1B 2925	5	2		
Bracket—engine sling	2A 829	6	2		Slave items. Replace with 2 off piece—distance 1B 2925
Bush—valve rocker cover (rubber)	†2K 8568	7	2		W.S.E. use 12A 1358
Bush—valve rocker cover (rubber)	†12A 1358	7	2		
Washer—cup—cap nut	1A 2156	8	2		
Nut—cap	2A 150	9	2		
WATER OUTLET ELBOW AND THERMOSTAT					
Elbow—water outlet	12G 243	10	1		
Plug—thermal transmitter tapping	ADP 210	11	1		
Gasket—elbow to cylinder head	†12G 114	12	1		W.S.E. use 12G 330
Gasket—elbow to cylinder head	12G 330	12	1		
Washer—plain	PWZ 104	13	3		
Nut	FNZ 105	14	3		
Thermostat					
Wax-type—74° C. (165° F.)	†13H 1452	15	1		W.S.E. use 13H 3727 — Hot Climates
Wax-type—74° C. (165° F.)	†13H 2526	15	1		W.S.E. use 13H 3727 — Hot Climates
Wax-type—74° C. (165° F.)	†13H 3584	15	1		W.S.E. use 13H 3727 — Hot Climates
Wax-type—74° C. (165° F.)	†13H 3727	15	1		Hot Climates
Bellows-type—82° C. (180° F.)	†11G 214	16	1		W.S.E. use 13H 4070 — Temperate climates
Bellows-type—82° C. (180° F.)	†11G 292	16	1		W.S.E. use 13H 4070 — Temperate climates
Wax-type—82° C. (180° F.)	†13H 630	15	1		W.S.E. use 13H 4070 — Temperate climates
Wax-type—82° C. (180° F.)	†13H 957	15	1		W.S.E. use 13H 4070 — Temperate climates
Wax-type—82° C. (180° F.)	†13H 3585	15	1		W.S.E. use 13H 4070 — Temperate climates
Wax-type—82° C. (180° F.)	†13H 4070	15	1		Temperate climates
Wax-type—88° C. (190° F.)	†13H 956	15	1		W.S.E. use 13H 3586 — Cold climates
Wax-type—88° C. (190° F.)	†13H 3586	15	1		Cold climates
Adaptor—by-pass	2A 243	17	1		
Connection—by-pass (rubber)	2A 242	18	1		
Clip—by-pass connection	3H 2963	19	2		
SPARKING PLUGS					
Plug—sparking (N5)	3H 2006	20	4		
Gasket—sparking plug	11G 145	21	4		Alternatives
Gasket—sparking plug	2K 5211	21	4		Alternatives

† Revised Information.

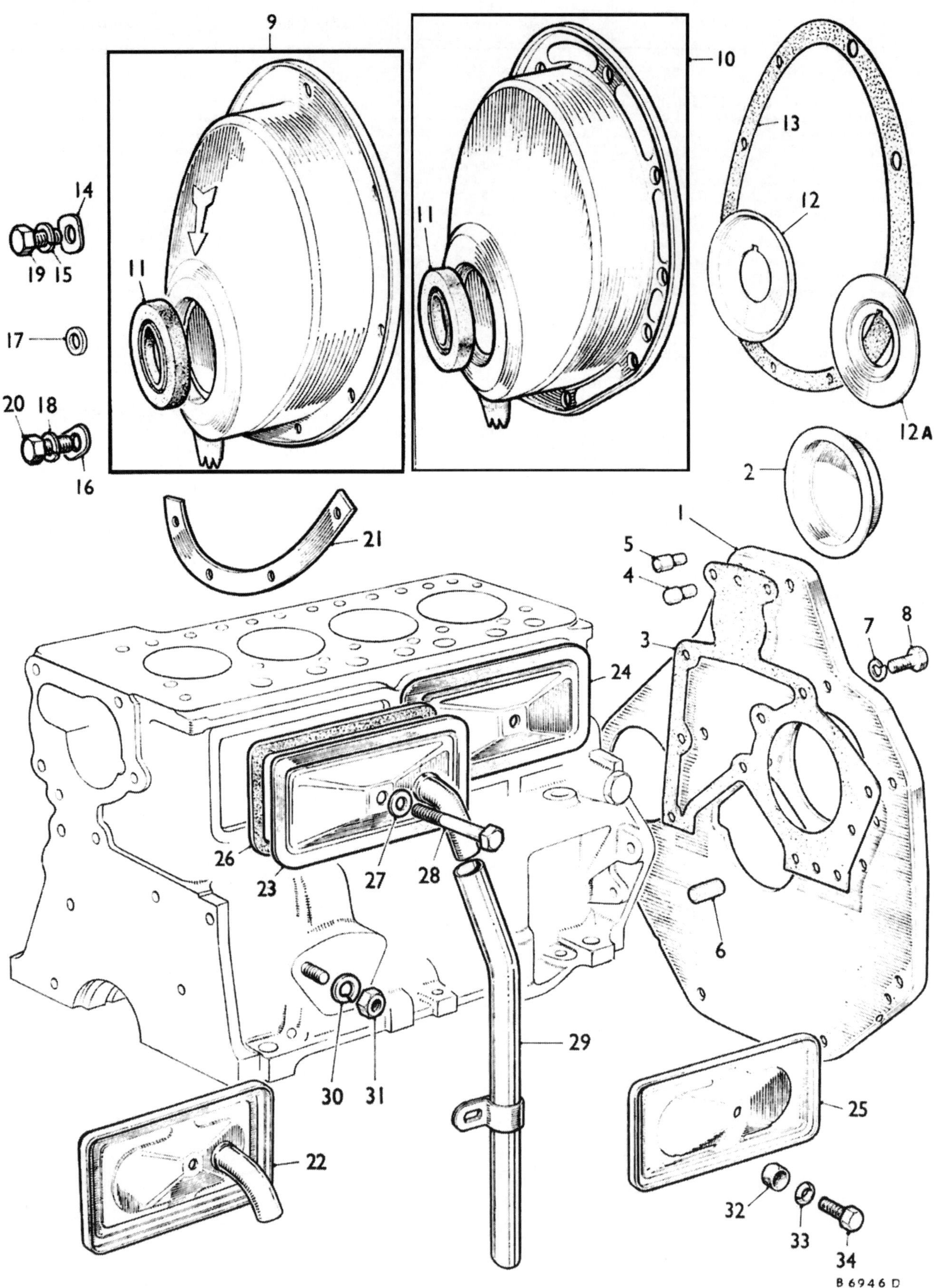
9
10
13
12
14
19 15
11
11
17
20 18
16
12A
2
21
1
5
4
3
7
8
24
26
23
27
28
6
29
30
31
25
22
32
33
34
B 6946 D

DESCRIPTION	Part No.	Illus. No.	Quantity	Change Point	REMARKS
10CG Engine—*continued*					
REAR MOUNTING PLATE					
Plate—rear—engine mounting	12G 275	1	1		
Cover—oil pump	12G 276	2	1		
Gasket—plate to crankcase	12A 22	3	1		
Dowel—mounting plate					
Top	†12G 278	4	1		W.S.E. use 12G 422
Top	12G 422	5	1		
Bottom	1G 752	6	1		
Washer—spring	LWZ 305	7	7		
Screw	HZS 0505	8	7		
CYLINDER FRONT AND SIDE COVERS					
Cover—front	†12A 937	9	1		W.S.E. use 12G 791 together with oil thrower 12A 1148
(With stiffener)	12A 723	9	1		(as above)
(With timing pointer)	†12G 791	10	1		W.S.E. use 12A 1419
	†12A 1419	10	1		
Seal—oil	†2A 939	11	1		W.S.E. use 13H 4061
Seal—oil	†13H 4061	11	1		
Thrower—oil—crankshaft	2A 1015	12	1		For service with front covers 2A 937, 12A 723
Thrower—oil—crankshaft	12A 1148	12A	1		For service with front cover 12G 791
Gasket—front cover	†1A 2093	13	1		W.S.E. use 12A 956
Gasket—front cover	†12A 956	13	1		
Washer					
Plain	2K 5197	14	3		Use PWZ 104 for this application
Plain	PWZ 104	14	3		
Spring	LWN 204	15	3		
Plain	2K 7440	16	3		Use PWZ 105 for this application
Plain	PWZ 105	17	3		
Spring	LWZ 305	18	3		
Screw	HZS 0408	19	3		
Screw	HZS 0505	20	3		
Stiffener—front cover	12A 666	21	1		For use with 2A 937
Cover—cylinder side					
Front (with vent pipe)	†12G 152	23	1		W.S.E. use 12H 948
Front (with vent pipe)	12H 948	22	1		
Rear	†12H 152	24	1		W.S.E. use 12A 1170 together with 1 off each joint 12A 1175, bush 12A 1176, cup 12A 1177, and screw HZS 0509
Rear	†12H 941	24	1		(as above)
Rear	12A 1170	25	1		
Gasket	†12A 24	26	2		W.S.E. use 12A 1139
Gasket	12A 1139	26	2		For service with side covers 12G 152, 12H 948, 12H 152, and 12H 941
Screw—cover to crankcase	HBZ 0515	28	2		(as above)
Washer (fibre)	2K 4958	27	2		(as above)
Gasket	12A 1175	26	1		
Bush (rubber)	12A 1176	32	1		
Washer—cup	12A 1177	33	1		
Screw—cover to crankcase	HZS 0509	34	1		
Pipe—vent—lower	2A 118	29	1		
Washer—spring	LWZ 305	30	1		
Nut	FNZ 105	31	1		

† Revised Information.

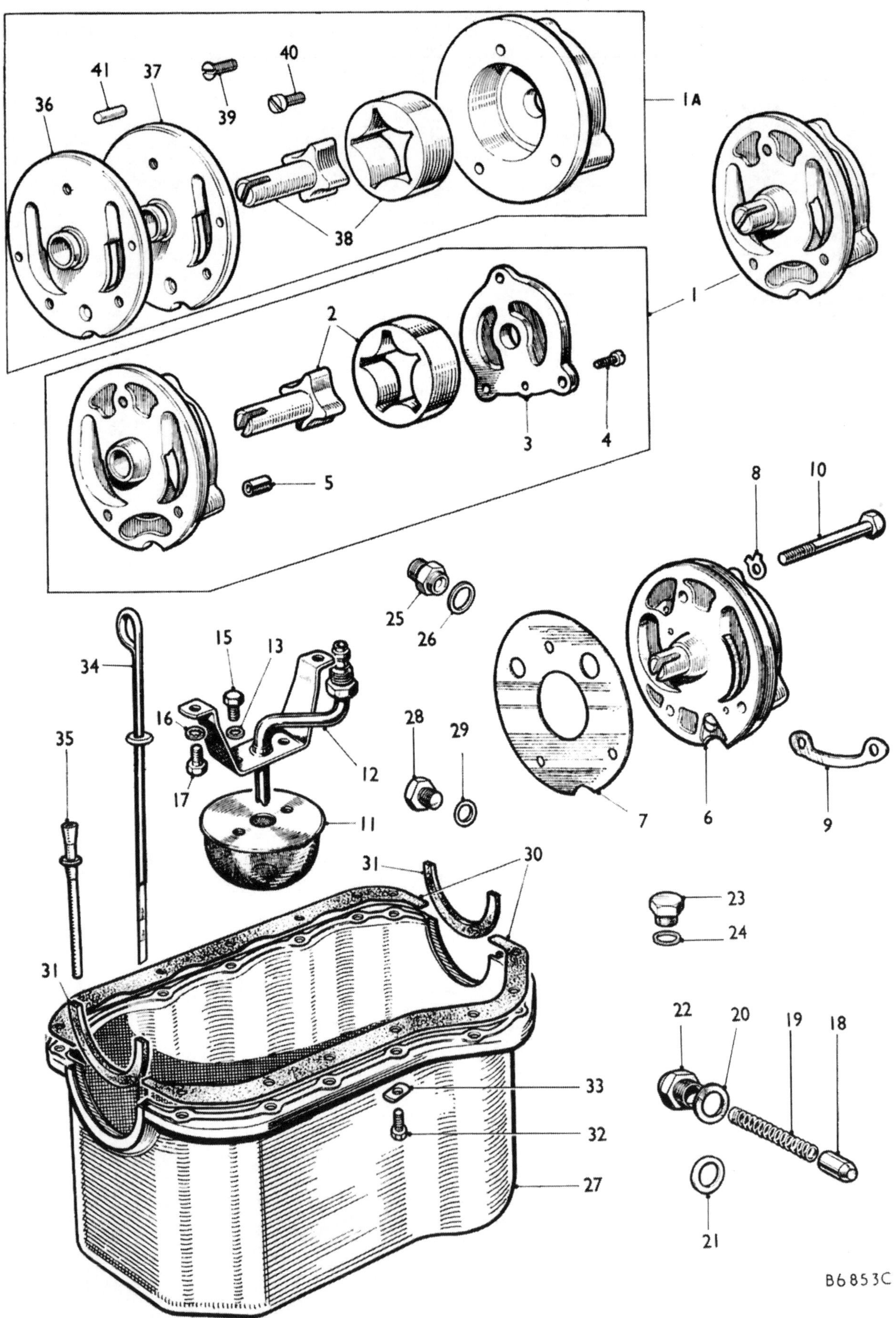
41
37
40
39
36
1A
38
2
1
3
4
5
8
10
25
26
15
13
34
16
35
28
29
12
17
11
7
6
9
31
30
23
24
31
22
20
19
18
33
32
27
21
B6853C

DESCRIPTION	Part No.	Illus. No.	Quantity	Change Point	REMARKS
10CG Engine—*continued*					
OIL PUMPS, STRAINER, AND RELEASE VALVE					
Pump—oil (Hobourn-Eaton)	†12A 303	1	1		Alternative to 12G 50. W.S.E. use 2A 962
Shaft and outer rotor	37H 861	2	1		
Body	NSP		1		
Cover	37H 863	3	1		
Screw	AJD 3204 Z	4	1		
Dowel—spring	†37H 864	5	2		
Pump—oil (Hobourn-Eaton)	†2A 962	1A	1		Alternative to 12G 793
Body	NSP				
Cover (countersunk holes)	†17H 1963	36	1		
Cover (plain holes)	†17H 6427	37	1		
Shaft—driving (with rotors)	†17H 1965	38	1		
Screw—countersunk	AJD 4205 Z	39	1		
Screw—cheese-head	AJD 3204 Z	40	1		
Dowel	17H 1964	41	2		
Pump—oil (Concentric)	12G 50	6	1		W.S.E. use 12G 793
Pump—oil (Concentric)	†12G 793	6	1		Alternative to 12A 962
Gasket	12G 69	7	1		Use 88G 411 for this application
Gasket	88G 411	7	1		
Washer—lock—oil pump screw	2A 339	8	1		
Plate—locking—oil pump screw	2A 522	9	1		
Screw	HBN 0414	10	3		
Strainer—oil	2A 668	11	1		
Pipe—oil suction (with strainer bracket)	12A 451	12	1		
Washer—shake-proof	LWN 404	13	2		
Screw	HNS 0404	15	2		
Washer—shakeproof	LWN 404	16	2		
Screw	HNS 0404	17	2		
Valve—oil release	†1G 1452	18	1		W.S.E. use 12H 865
Valve—oil release	12H 865	18	1		
Spring—oil release	6K 853	19	1		
Washer	2K 4982	20	2		Use 6K 431 for this application
Washer (copper)	6K 431	21	1		
Nut—cap—oil release valve	1A 2206	22	1		
Plug—oil priming	2K 4994	23	1		
Washer—oil priming plug	6K 464	24	1		
Union—oil pressure	2A 269	25	1		
Washer—oil pressure union	2K 4956	26	1		
OIL SUMP AND DIPPER ROD					
Sump—oil	12G 173	27	1		
Plug—drain	88G 257	28	1		
Washer—sump drain plug (copper)	6K 638	29	1		
Gasket—sump to crankcase	8G 731	30	1		
Seal—oil—main bearing cap	2A 280	31	2		
Screw (with captive washer)	6K 639	32	14		
Washer—screw	2K 5197	33	14		
Rod—oil dipper	12G 175	34	1		
Tube—oil dipper rod	12G 107	35	1		

† Revised Information.

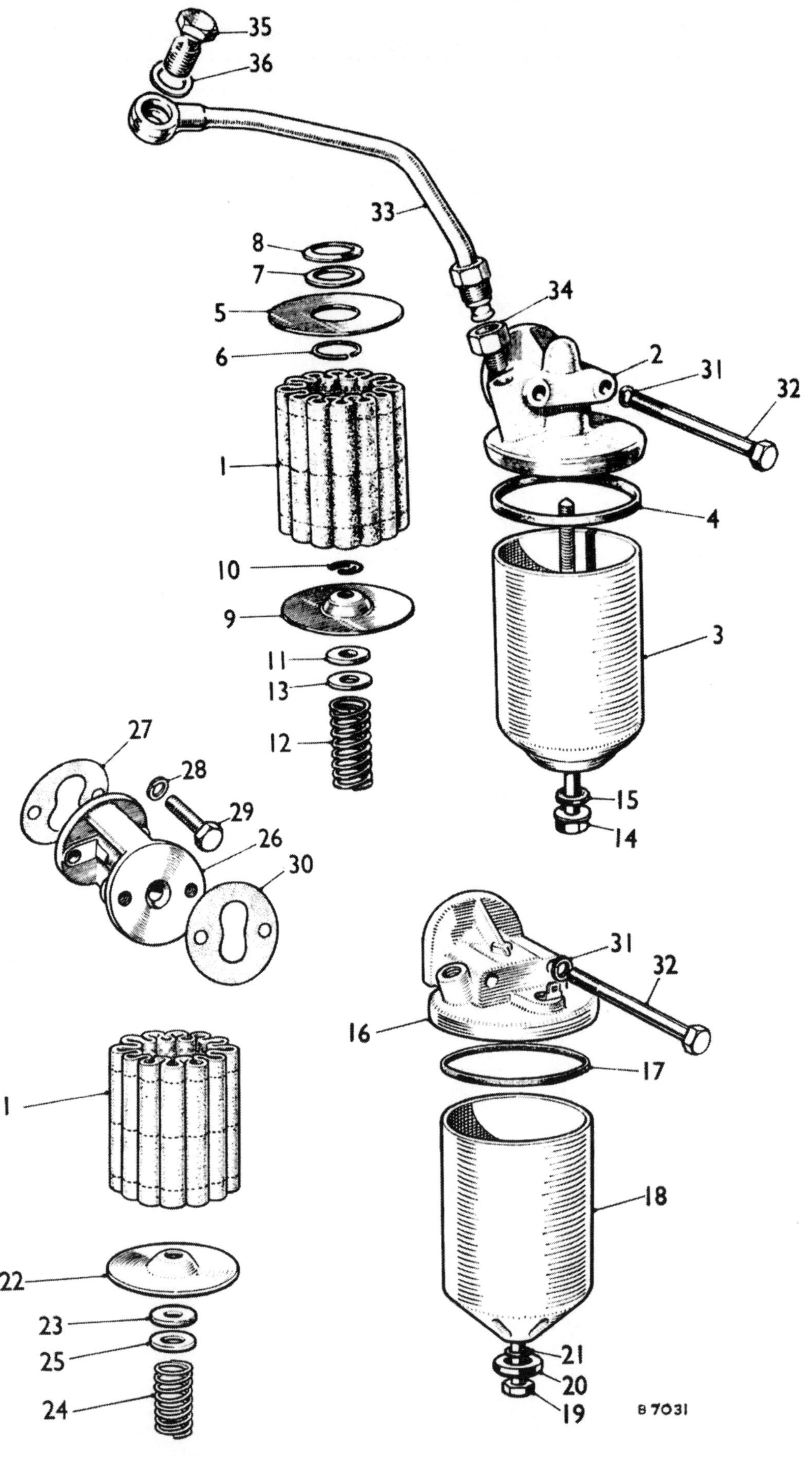
35
36
33
8
7
5
6
34
2
31
32
1
4
10
9
3
11
13
12
27
28
29
26
30
15
14
31
32
16
17
1
18
22
23
25
24
21
20
19
B 7031

10CG Engine—*continued*

DESCRIPTION	Part No.	Illus. No.	Quantity	Change Point	REMARKS
OIL FILTER					
Filter—oil (Tecalemit)	NSP		1		Alternative to Purolator filter
Element	8G 684	1	1		
Head	17H 945	2	1		
Sump	37H 436	3	1		
Seal—sump to head	†17H 4	4	1		W.S.E. use 13H 998
Seal—sump to head	†13H 998	4	1		
Plate—element clamp	7H 147	5	1		
Circlip—plate to head	2A 700	6	1		
Washer—clamp plate (felt)	7H 1756	7	1		
Washer—dished—clamp plate	7H 1761	8	1		
Plate—pressure	17H 942	9	1		
Circlip—plate to centre bolt	7H 1840	10	1		
Washer—pressure plate (felt)	7H 1758	11	1		
Spring—pressure plate	7H 1764	12	1		
Washer—pressure plate spring	7H 1765	13	1		
Bolt—centre	17H 943	14	1		
Seal—bolt to sump	7H 1759	15	1		
Filter—oil (Purolator)	NSP				Alternative to Tecalemit filter
Element	8G 684	1	1		
Head assembly (with switch)	†27H 3496	16	1		W.S.E. use 37H 1528
	†27H 6503	16	1		
	†37H 1528	16	1		
Plate—clamping	NSP		1		
Ball—relief valve	NSP		1		
Seal—sump to head	†27H 1983	17	1		W.S.E. use 12A 1591
	†13H 3249	17	1		
	†12A 1591	17	1		
Sump	17H 1169	18	1		
Bolt—centre	37H 689	19	1		
Collar—centre bolt	17H 1172	20	1		
Seal—centre bolt	17H 1173	21	1		
Plate—pressure	17H 1148	22	1		
Seal—pressure plate	7H 28	23	1		
Spring—pressure plate	7H 25	24	1		
Washer	PWN 106	25	1		
Adaptor—oil filter	AEA 657	26	1		
Gasket—adaptor to crankcase	†12G 148	27	1		W.S.E. use 88G 402
Gasket—adaptor to crankcase	†88G 402	27	1		
Washer—spring	LWZ 206	28	1		
Screw—adaptor to crankcase	NCS 0608	29	2		
Gasket—filter to adaptor	†12A 394	30	1		Alternatives. W.S.E. use 12G 148
	†12A 143	30	1		
	†12G 148	30	1		W.S.E. use 88G 402
	†88G 402	30	1		
Washer—spring	LWZ 206	31			
Bolt	HCZ 0630	32	2		
Pipe—oil	AEA 658	33	1		
Connection—flared-type	AEA 678	34	1		
Screw—banjo union	2A 715	35	2		
Washer—banjo union screw (copper)	AED 172	36	1		

† Revised Information.

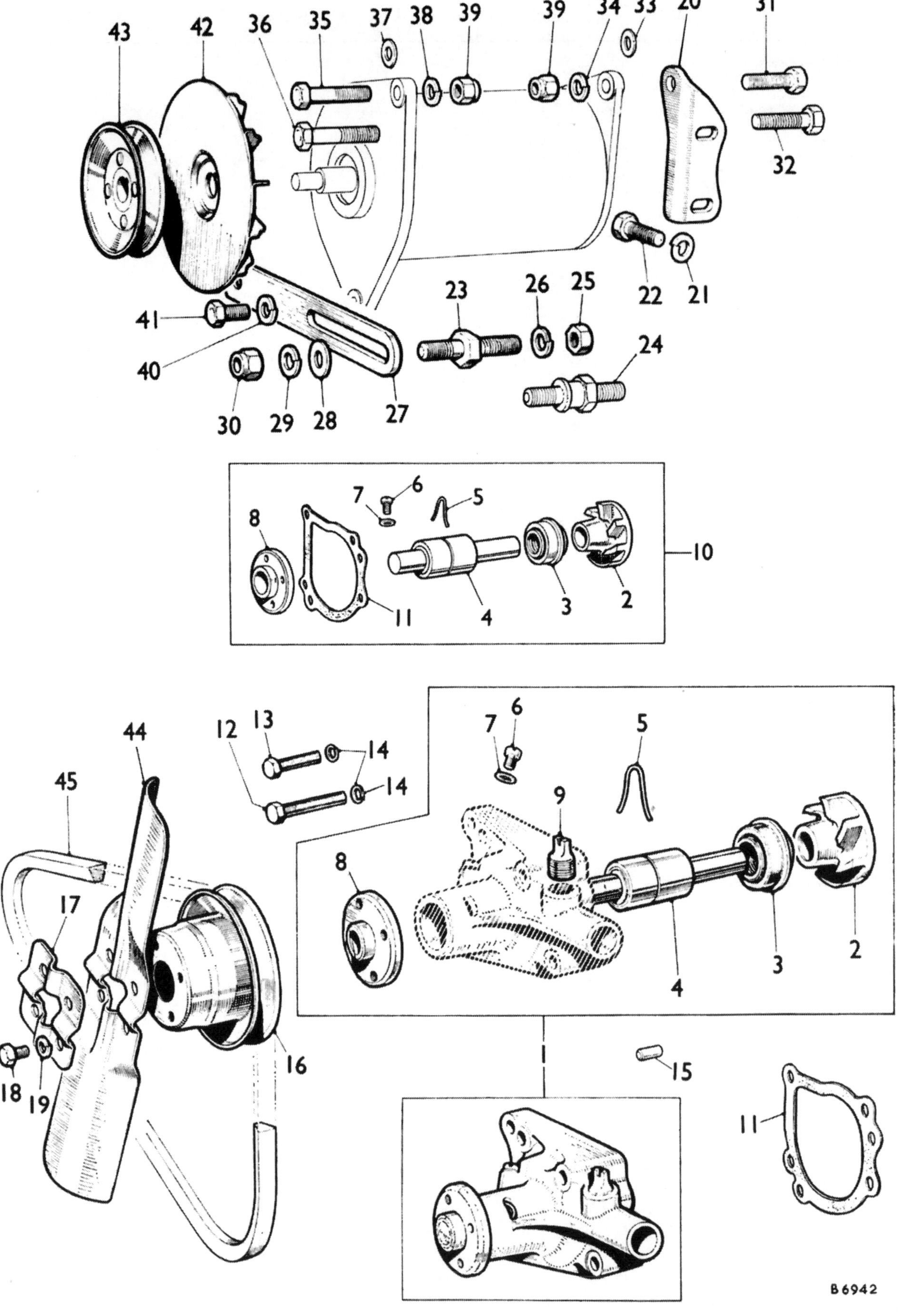
43
42
36
35
37
38
39
39
34
33
20
31
32
22
21
41
40
23
26
25
24
30
29
28
27
7
6
5
8
10
11
4
3
2
44
12
13
14
14
45
17
18
19
16
9
1
15
11
B 6942

10CG Engine—*continued*

WATER PUMP AND FAN PULLEY

DESCRIPTION	Part No.	Illus. No.	Quantity	Change Point	REMARKS
Pump assembly—water	†12G 120	1	1		W.S.E. use 12A 1332
	†12A 1332	1	1		W.S.E. use 12G 1284
	†12G 1284	1	1		
Body	NSP		1		
Vane	2A 664	2	1		
Seal	13H 772	3	1		Use 88G 446 for this application
Seal	88G 446	3	1		
Bearing (with spindle)	2A 777	4	1		W.S.E. use 12A 1328
	†12A 1328	4	1		W.S.E. use 12A 1389
	†12A 1389	4	1		
Wire—bearing locating	†2A 778	5	1		For use with water pumps 12G 120 and 12A 1332
Screw—lubricating point	†53K 1433	6	1		
Washer (fibre)	2K 4974	7	1		
Hub—pulley	8G 733	8	1		
Adaptor—by-pass	2A 243	9	1		
Kit—water pump repair	†8G 2361	10	1		W.S.E. use 8G 2570
Kit—water pump repair	†8G 2570	10	1		
Vane	2A 664	2	1		
Seal	88G 446	3	1		
Bearing (with spindle)	†12A 1328	4	1		
Wire—bearing locating	2A 778	5	1		
Screw—lubricating point	53K 1433	6	1		
Washer (fibre)	2K 4974	7	1		
Hub—pulley	8G 733	8	1		
Gasket	88G 215	9			
Gasket	88G 215	11	1		Part No. change; was 2A 667 and 12A 31
Screw	HZS 0515	12	2		
Screw	HZS 0510	13	2		
Washer—spring	LWN 305	14	4		
Dowel—water pump	2K 6124	15	2		
Pulley—fan and water pump	2A 601	16	1		
Stiffener—fan blade	2A 803	17	1		
Screw	HZS 0406	18	4		
Washer—spring	LWZ 204	19	4		

† Revised Information.

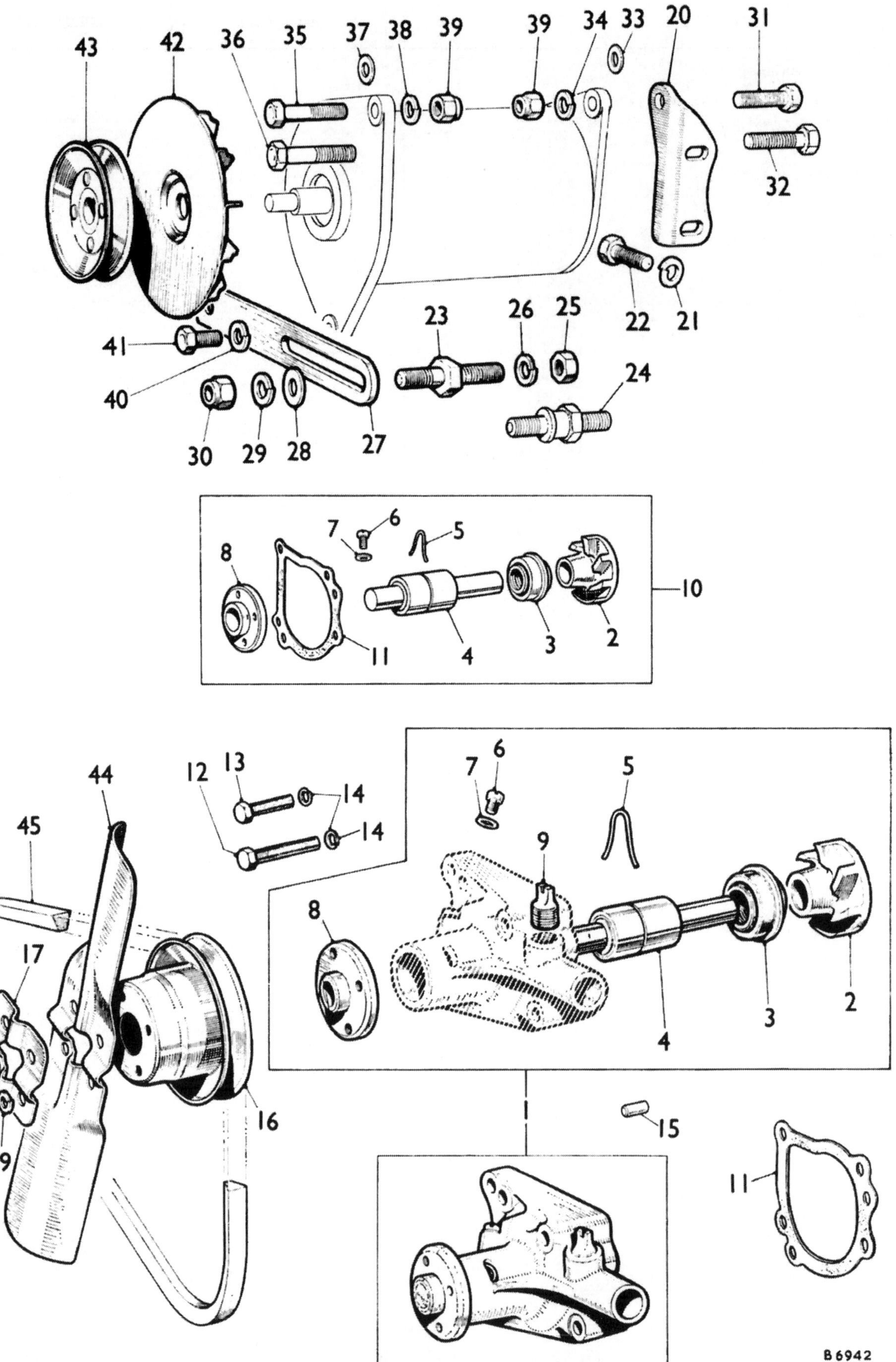
43
42
36
35
37
38
39
39
34
33
20
31
32
22
21
41
40
23
26
25
24
30
29
28
27
7
6
5
8
10
11
4
3
2
44
45
12
13
14
14
9
17
16
18
19
15
11
B 6942

DESCRIPTION	Part No.	Illus. No.	Quantity	Change Point	REMARKS
10CG Engine—*continued*					
DYNAMO MOUNTING AND PULLEY					
Bracket—dynamo—rear	12A 526	20	1		
Washer—spring	LWZ 305	21	2		
Screw	HZS 0507	22	2		
Pillar—dynamo adjusting link	AEA 643	23	1	(E) 10CG/Da/H101 to H2571	
	12G 289	24	1	(E) 10CG/Da/H2572 on	
	12G 314	24	1		For service with 12G 312
Washer—spring	LWZ 306	25	1		
Nut	FNZ 105	26	1		
Link—dynamo adjusting	AEA 679	27	1		
Washer—plain	1B 8806	28	1		
Washer—spring	LWZ 306	29	1		
Nut	†LNZ 206	30	1		Correction; was LHZ 206
Screw	HZS 0509	31	1	(E) 10CG/Da/H101 to 2571	
Screw	HZS 0510	32	1	(E) 10CG/Da/H2572 on	
Washer—plain	PWZ 305	33	1		
Washer—spring	LWN 305	34	1		
Bolt	HBZ 0513	35	1	(E) 10CG/Da/H101 to 2571	
Bolt	HBZ 0515	36	1	(E) 10CG/Da/H2578 on	
Washer—plain	PWZ 305	37			
Washer—spring	LWZ 305	38	1		
Nut	LNZ 205	39	1		
Washer—spring	LWZ 305	40	1		
Screw	ZCS 0505	41	1		
Fan—dynamo	17D 11	42	1		
Pulley—dynamo	1H 998	43	1		
FAN AND FAN BELT					
Blade—fan	AEA 301	44	1		
Belt—fan (wedge-type)	†AEJ 63	45	1	(E) 10CG/Da/H101 to H17772	W.S.E. use 13H 1329
Belt—fan (wedge-type)	13H 1329	45	1	(E) 10CG/Da/H17773 on	

DESCRIPTION	Part No.	Illus. No.	Quantity	Change Point	REMARKS
ENGINE SERVICE KITS					
Set—gasket—engine decarbonizing	8G 2402		1		
Gasket					
Cylinder head	12G 293		1		
Manifold	†AEG 181		1		
Water outlet elbow	12G 330		1		
Rocker cover	12A 14		1		
Cover plate	†88G 221		1		
Carburetter	1G 2624		6		
Air cleaner	†12H 862		2		
Ring—valve packing	2A 879		8		
Set—gasket—supplementary	8G 2282		1		Use with 8G 2402 for complete engine overhaul
Gasket					
Front mounting plate	12G 619		1		
Cylinder front cover	12A 956		1		
Cylinder side cover	12A 1189		2		
Oil pump	†88G 411		1		
Sump	8G 731		1		
Water pump	88G 215		1		
Petrol pump	2A 113		1		
Rear mounting plate	12A 22		1		
Crankcase rear cover	2A 127		1		
Oil filter to crankcase	†88G 402		2		
Seal—oil—main bearing cap	2A 280		2		
Washer					
Oil priming plug	6K 464		1		
Sump drain plug	6K 638		1		
Drain tap	2K 4954		1		Alternatives
Drain tap	†2K 4975		1		Alternatives

† Revised Information.

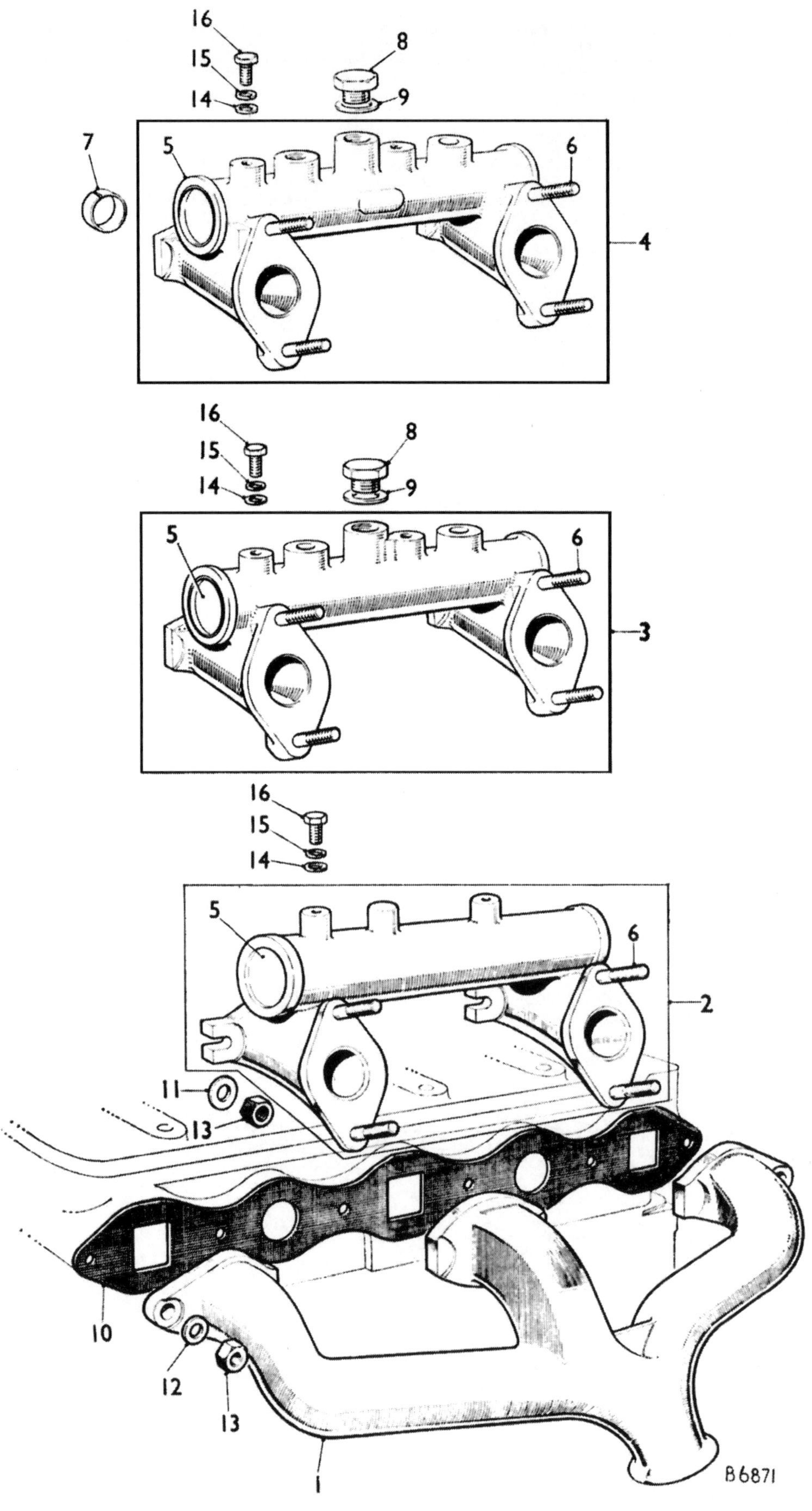
16
15
14
8
9
7
5
6
4
16
15
14
8
9
5
6
3
16
15
14
5
6
2
11
13
10
12
13
1
B6871

10CG Engine—*continued*

INLET AND EXHAUST MANIFOLDS

DESCRIPTION	Part No.	Illus. No.	Quantity	Change Point	REMARKS
Manifold					
Exhaust	12A 191	1	1		
Inlet (with plug and studs)	†AEA 633	2	1	(E) 10CG/101 to 18627	W.S.E. use 12G 583
Inlet (with plug and studs)	†12G 301	3	1	(E) 10CG/H18628 on	W.S.E. use 12G 583
Inlet (with plug and studs)	12G 583	4	1		Use together with 1 off plug ADP 210 and washer 1B 3664
Plug—inlet manifold	AEA 635	5	2		
Stud—carburetter to inlet manifold	CHS 2620	6	4		
Ferrule—inlet port	12G 297	7	2	(E) 10CG/H18628 on	
Plug—inlet manifold	ADP 210	8	1		For use when 12G 583 replaces 12G 301
Washer—plug—inlet manifold	1B 3664	9	1		For use when 12G 583 replaces 12G 301
Gasket—manifold to cylinder head	†12A 192	10	1		W.S.E. use 12G 300
Gasket—manifold to cylinder head	12G 300	10	1		
Washer—clamping	2A 110	11	4		
Washer—plain	PWZ 105	12	2		
Nut	BNN 105	13	6		
Washer—plain	PWZ 104	14	2		
Washer—spring	LWZ 204	15	2		
Screw	ZCS 0404	16	2		

† Revised Information.

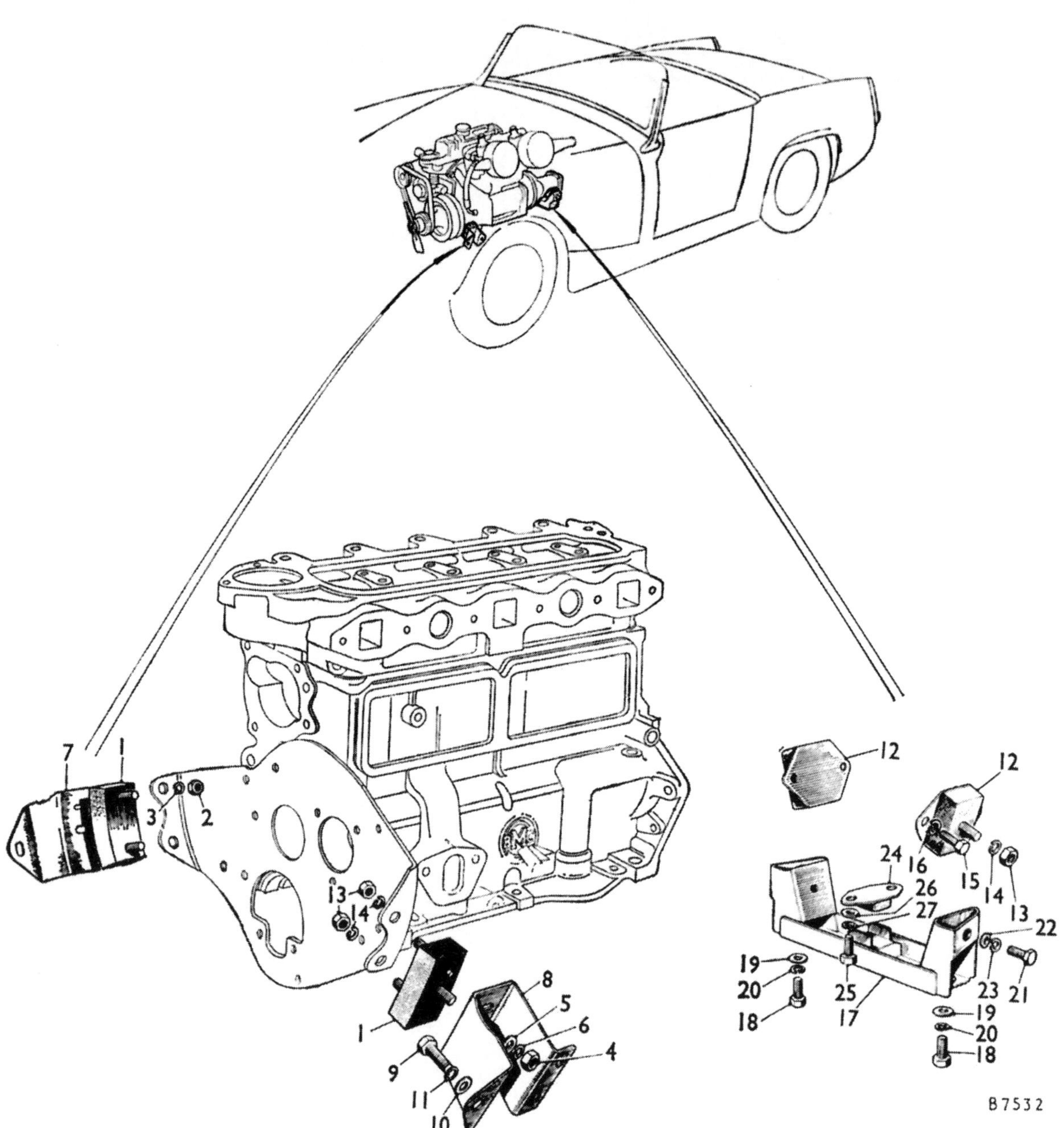
7
1
3
2
13
14
1
8
5
6
4
9
11
10
12
12
24
16
15
14
13
26
27
22
19
20
18
25
17
23
21
19
20
18
B7532

DESCRIPTION	Part No.	Illus. No.	Quantity	Change Point	REMARKS
ENGINE MOUNTING					
Mounting—front	2A 305	1	2	(E) 9C/U/H101 to 15304	Use AHA 5484 for this application
Mounting—front	AHA 5484	1	2	(E) 9C/U/H15305 to 49201 (E) 9CG/Da/H101 to 36711 (E) 10CG/Da/H101 on	
Nut	FNZ 105	2	4		
Washer—spring	LWZ 305	3	4		
Nut	FNZ 106	4	2		
Washer—plain	PWZ 106	5	2		
Washer—spring	LWZ 306	6	2		
Bracket—mounting—RH	2A 5570	7	1		
Bracket—mounting—LH	2A 5571	8	1		
Screw	HZS 0505	9	5		
Screw	HZS 0506	9	1		
Washer					
Plain	PWZ 105	10	6		
Spring	2K 5319	11	6		W.S.E. use LWN 305
Spring	LWN 305	11	6		
Mounting—rear	2A 5422	12	2		
Nut	FNZ 106	13	2		
Washer—spring	LWZ 206	14	2		
Screw	ZCS 0506	15	4		Part No. change; was 53K 154
Washer—spring	LWZ 205	16	4		
Plate—rear mounting support	2A 5552	17	1		
Bolt	HBZ 0626	18	2		
Washer—plain	PWZ 106	19	2		
Washer—spring	LWZ 206	20	2		
Screw	HZS 0506	21	2		
Washer—plain	PWZ 205	22	2		
Washer—spring	LWZ 205	23	2		
Rubber—tie—rear mounting	2A 5420	24	1		
Screw	ZCS 0506	25	2		Part No. change; was 53K 154
Washer—plain	PWZ 105	26	2		
Washer—spring	LWZ 205	27	2		

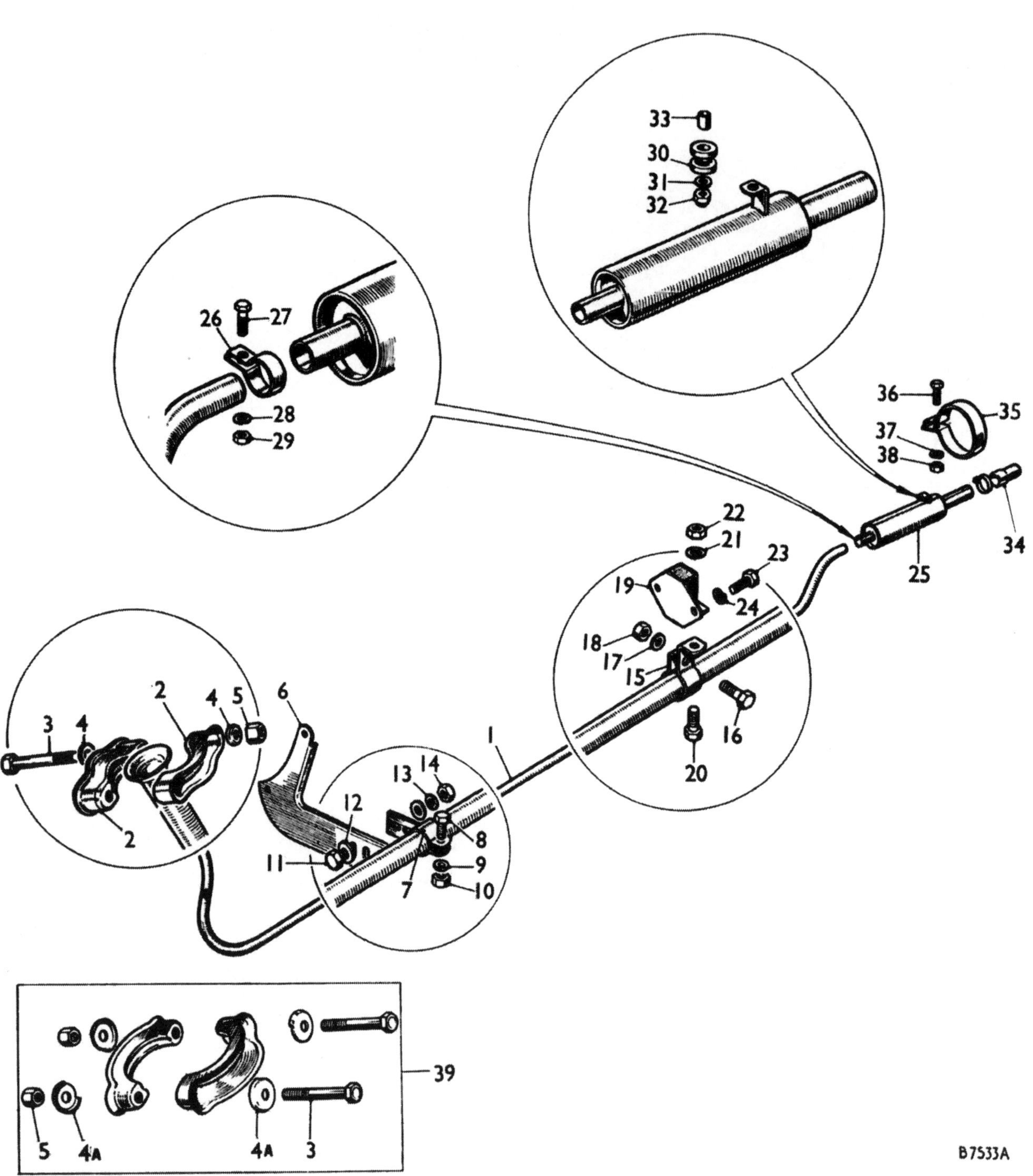
33
30
31
32
26
27
28
29
36
35
37
38
34
25
22
21
23
19
24
18
17
15
16
20
2
3
4
5
6
1
13
14
12
8
9
10
11
7
2
39
5
4A
4A
3
B7533A

DESCRIPTION	Part No.	Illus. No.	Quantity	Change Point	REMARKS
EXHAUST SYSTEM					
Pipe—exhaust	2A 2089	1	1	(C) H-AN5-501 to 5476 (less 5137, 5287, and 5288)	
	AHA 5860	1	1	(C) H-AN5-5477 to 50116 (plus 5137, 5287, and 5288)	
				(C) H-AN6-101 to 24731	
				(C) H-AN7-24732 on	
				(C) G-AN1-101 to 16183	
				(C) G-AN2-16184 on	
Europe	AHA 5688	1	1	(C) H-AN6-101 to 24731	
				(C) H-AN7-24732 on	
				(C) G-AN1-101 to 16183	
				(C) G-AN2-16184 on	
Clamp—pipe to manifold	†2A 237	2	2		W.S.E. use 18G 8581
Kit—exhaust clamp	†18G 8581	39	1		
Clamp—exhaust	†NSP		2		
Bolt	†HBZ 0518	40	2		
Washer	†37H 3800	41	2		
Nut	†BNN 105	42	2		
Screw	HZS 0518	3	2		
Washer—plain	2K 5806	4	4		
Nut	AHH 5171	5	2		
Bracket—pipe mounting	AHA 5238	6	1	(C) H-AN5-501 to 5476 (less 5137, 5287, and 5288)	
Bracket—pipe mounting	AHA 5361	6	1	(C) H-AN5-5477 to 50116 (plus 5137, 5287, and 5288)	
				(C) H-AN6-101 to 24731	
				(C) H-AN7-24732 on	
				(C) G-AN1-101 to 16183	
				(C) G-AN2-16184 on	
Clip—pipe	AHA 5239	7	1		
Screw	HZS 0508	8	1		
Washer—spring	LWZ 205	9	1		
Nut	FNZ 105	10	1		
Screw	HZS 0506	11	2		
Washer—plain	PWZ 105	12	2		
Washer—spring	LWZ 205	13	2		
Nut	FNZ 105	14	2		
Clip—pipe support—rear	2A 2091	15	1		
Screw	HZS 0407	16	1		
Washer—spring	LWZ 204	17	1		
Nut	FNZ 104	18	1		
Mounting—pipe (rubber)	8H 3076	19	1		
Screw	HZS 0505	20	1		
Washer—spring	LWZ 205	21	1		
Nut	FNZ 105	22	1		
Screw	HZS 0505	23	1		
Washer—spring	LWZ 205	24	1		
Silencer	88G 292	25	1	(C) H-AN5-501 to 50116	Part No. change; was 2A 2090 and ARA 79
	ARA 184	25	1	(C) H-AN6-101 to 24731	
Europe	ARA 116	25	1	(C) H-AN7-24732 on	
				(C) G-AN1-101 to 16183	
				(C) G-AN2-16184 on	
Clip—silencer to pipe	AHA 5354	26	1		
Screw	HZS 0508	27	1		
Washer—spring	LWZ 205	28	1		
Nut	FNZ 105	29	1		
Bush—silencer support (rubber)	2A 2092	30	2		
Washer—plain	PWZ 205	31	2	(C) H-AN5-501 to 50116	
Locknut	LNZ 205	32	1		
Bush—silencer support (rubber)	AHA 5689	30	2		
Spacer—bush	AHA 5690	33	1		
Washer—plain	PWZ 205	31	1		
Locknut	LNZ 105	32	1	(C) H-AN6-101 to 24731	Alternatives
Locknut	LNZ 205	32	1	(C) H-AN7-24732 on	
Extension—tail pipe	AHA 6172	34	1	(C) G-AN1-101 to 16183	
Clip—extension	AHA 6173	35	1	(C) G-AN2-16184	
Screw	HZS 0507	36	1		
Washer—spring	LWZ 205	37	1		
Nut	FNZ 105	38	1		

† Revised Information.

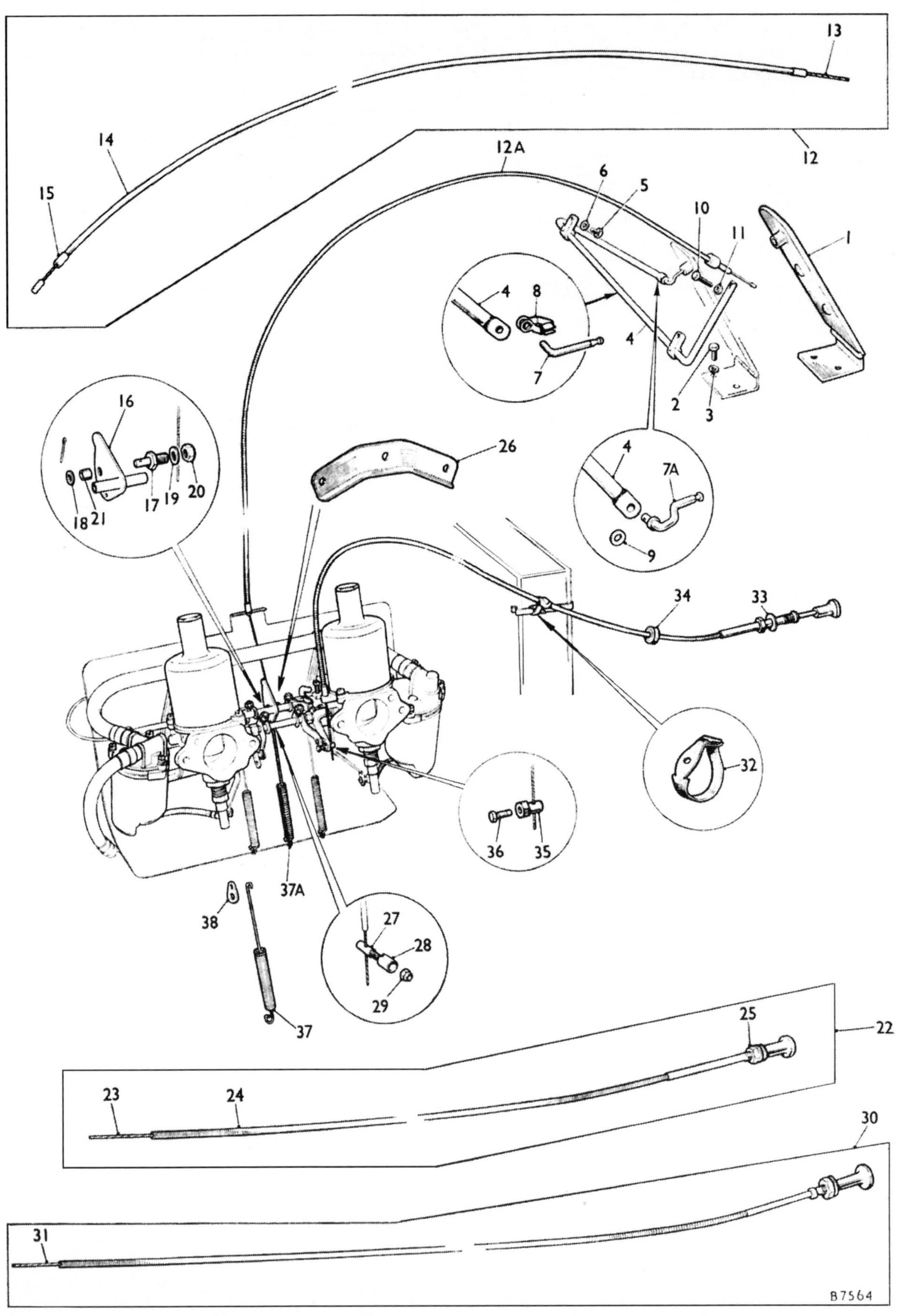
13
14
12A
12
15
6
5
10
11
1
4
8
7
4
2
3
16
26
4
7A
17
19
20
18
21
9
34
33
32
36
35
37A
38
27
28
29
37
25
22
23
24
30
31
B7564

DESCRIPTION	Part No.	Illus. No.	Quantity	Change Point	REMARKS
ENGINE CONTROLS					
Pedal—accelerator	11G 2034	1	1	(C) H-AN5-501 to 50116	
				(C) H-AN6-101 to 10719	
				(C) G-AN1-101-6020	
Pedal—accelerator	AHA 6256	1	1	(C) H-AN6-10720 to 24731	
				(C) H-AN7-24732 on	
				(C) G-AN1-6021 to 16183	
				(C) G-AN2-16184 on	
Screw	HZS 0404	2	2		
Washer—spring	LWZ 204	3	2		
Lever—pedal	2A 2077	4	1		
Screw	HZS 0407	5	2		
Washer—spring	LWZ 204	6	2		
Link—pedal	2A 2079	7	1	(C) H-AN5-501 to 50116	
				(C) H-AN6-101 to 10719	
				(C) G-AN1-101 to 6020	
Link—pedal	AHA 6255	7A	1	(C) H-AN6-10720 to 24731	
				(C) H-AN7-24732 on	
				(C) G-AN1-6021 to 16183	
				(C) G-AN2-16184 on	
Clip—link to lever	13H 72	8	1	(C) H-AN5-501 to 50116	
				(C) H-AN6-101 to 10719	
				(C) G-AN1-101 to 6020	
Washer—plain	PWZ 104	9	1	(C) H-AN6-10720 to 24731	
				(C) H-AN7-24732 on	
				(C) G-AN1-6021 to 16183	
				(C) G-AN2-16184 on	
Screw—pedal lever stop	HZS 0407	10	1		
Locknut	FNZ 204	11	1		
Cable assembly—accelerator control	21G 5077	12	1		W.S.E. use AAA 1768
Cable assembly—accelerator control	AAA 1768	12	1		
Cable—inner	21G 5078	13	1	(C) H-AN5-501 to 50116	
Cable—outer	†ACA 5322	14	1		W.S.E. use AAA 1768
Ferrule—cable	88G 349	15	2		Part No. change; was ACA 5416
Cable—accelerator control	AHA 5746	12A	1	(C) H-AN6-101 to 24731	
Lever—throttle	AEA 597	16	1	(C) H-AN7-24732 on	
				(C) G-AN1-101 to 16183	
				(C) G-AN2-16184 on	
Pin—cable to lever	ACC 5062	17	1		
Washer—plain	PWZ 203	18	1		
Washer—plain	PWZ 104	19	1		
Nut	FNZ 104	20	1		
Piece—distance	AEA 606	21	3	(C) H-AN6-101 to 24731	W.S.E. use AJD 7032
Piece—distance	AJD 7032	21	3	(C) H-AN7-24732 on	
				(C) G-AN1-101 to 16183	
				(C) G-AN2-16184 on	
Cable assembly—mixture control	†2A 2086	22	1		
Cable—inner	97H 2074	23	1		
Cable—outer	97H 2075	24	1		
Nut	†97H 2076	25	1		W.S.E. use FNZ 206
Nut	FNZ 206	25	1	(C) H-AN5-501 to 50116	
Bracket—control to carburetter	2A 850	26	1		
Trunnion—control to bracket	11B 542	27	1		
Piece—distance	11B 543	28	1		
Locknut—trunnion	53K 1392	29	1		
Cable assembly—mixture control **RHD**	†AHA 5676	30	1	(C) H-AN6-101 to 24731	
Cable—inner **RHD**	27H 3363	31	1	(C) H-AN7-24732 on	
Cable assembly—mixture control **LHD**	†AHA 6203	30	1	(C) G-AN1-101 to 16183	
Cable—inner **LHD**	27H 3364	31	1	(C) G-AN2-16184 on	
Strap—cable to heater clip	ACH 8979	32	1		
Washer—plain	PWZ 106	33	1		
Grommet	RFN 303	34	1		
Trunnion—cable	1B 2697	35	1	(C) H-AN5-501 to 50116	
	ACH 9042	35	1	(C) H-AN6-101 to 12437	
				(C) G-AN1-101 to 7703	
	AHA 6367	35	1	(C) H-AN6-12438 to 24731	
				(C) H-AN7-24732 on	
				(C) G-AN1-7704 to 16183	
				(C) G-AN2-16184 on	
Screw—trunnion	53K 1023	36	1	(C) H-AN5-501 to 50116	
	†ACA 5453	36	1	(C) H-AN6-101 to 24731	W.S.E. use 53K 3503
	†53K 3503	36	1	(C) H-AN7-24732 on	
				(C) G-AN1-101 to 16183	
				(C) G-AN2-16184 on	
Spring—return Accelerator cable	ACH 8393	37	1	(C) H-AN5-501 to 11030	
Accelerator cable	AHA 5454	37	1	(C) H-AN5-11031 to 50116	
Accelerator and choke cable	AEA 602	37A	3	(C) H-AN6-101 to 24731	
				(C) H-AN7-24732 on	
				(C) G-AN1-101 to 16183	
				(C) G-AN2-16184 on	
Bracket—return spring	AAA 649	38	1	(C) H-AN5-11031 to 50116	

† Revised Information.

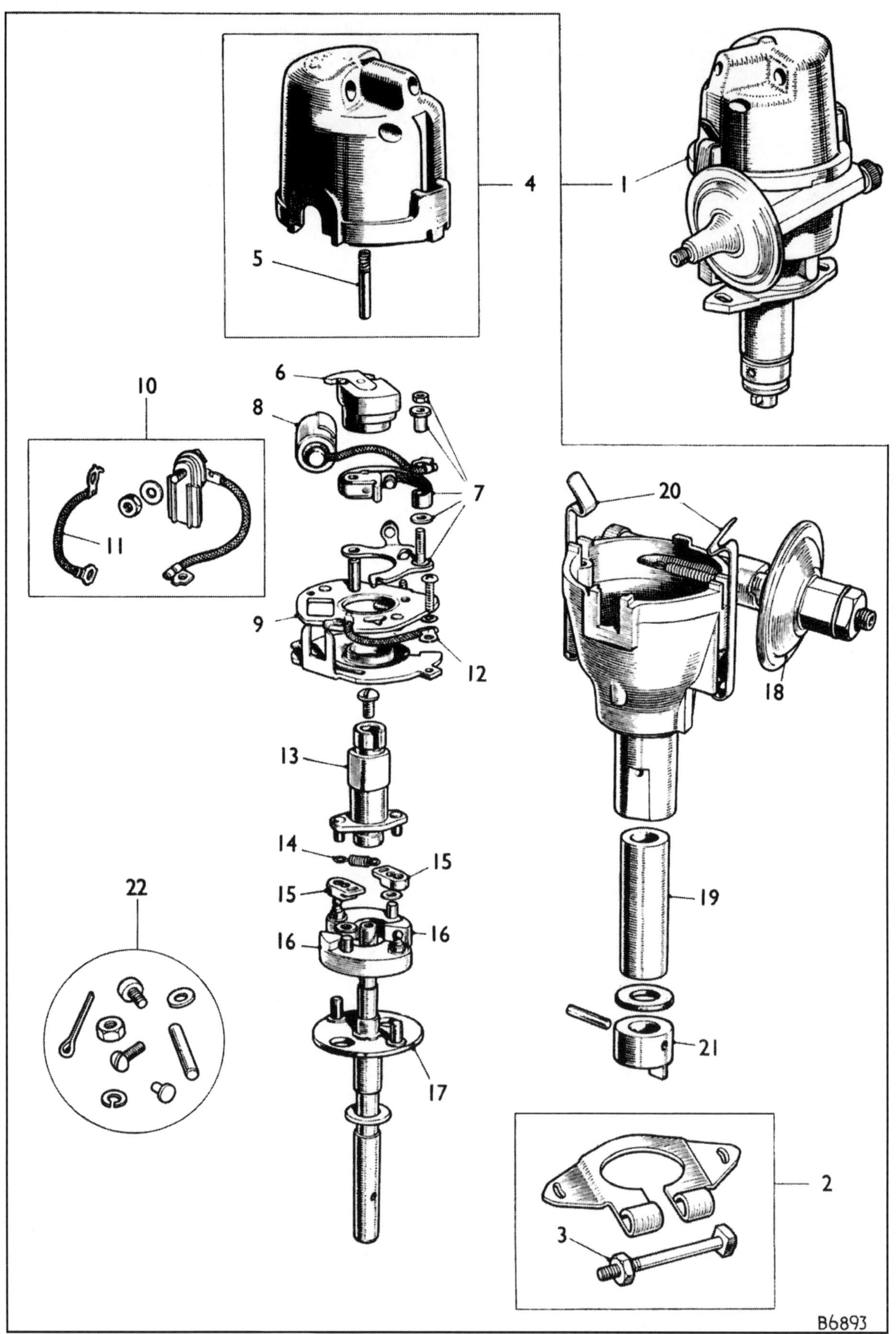

4
1
5
6
8
7
10
11
9
12
13
14
15
15
16
16
17
20
18
19
21
22
2
3
B6893

DESCRIPTION	Part No.	Illus. No.	Quantity	Change Point	REMARKS

950-cc 9C/U/H IGNITION EQUIPMENT

	Page	Plate
DISTRIBUTOR	MB 3–MB 4	B 1, B 2
VACUUM IGNITION CONTROL PIPE—IGNITION COIL IGNITION CABLES	MB 5	B 3

IGNITION EQUIPMENT

9C

DISTRIBUTOR

DESCRIPTION	Part No.	Illus. No.	Quantity	Change Point	REMARKS
Distributor	†2A 721	1	1		W.S.E. use 12A 419. See page MB 4
Plate assembly—clamping	3H 2138	2	1		
Screw—clamping plate	†NSP	3	1		Was 37H 5063
Cover	†17H 5422	4	1		W.S.E. use 57H 5477
	57H 5477	4	1		
Brush and spring	17H 5065	5	1		
Arm—rotor	7H 5086	6	1		
Contact	17H 5423	7	1 set		
Condenser	†17H 5421	8	1		W.S.E. use 47H 5250
Condenser	47H 5250	8	1		
Plate—contact breaker base	17H 5469	9	1		
Terminal—low tension (with bush and lead)	37H 5409	10	1		
Lead—low tension	17H 5532	11	1		
Lead—earth	17H 5531	12	1		
Cam	17H 5066	13	1		
Spring—automatic advance	†37H 5440	14	1 set		W.S.E. use 27H 5519
Spring—automatic advance	27H 5519	14	1 set		
Toggle	17H 5069	15	2		
Weight	17H 5095	16	2		
Shaft and action plate	37H 5439	17	1		
Unit—vacuum (with actuating arm)	†37H 5438	18	1		W.S.E. use 47H 5520
Unit—vacuum (with actuating arm)	47H 5520	18	1		
Bushing	17H 5071	19	1		
Clip—cap retaining	17H 5064	20	2		
Dog—driving	17H 5118	21	1		
Sundry parts	17H 5106	22	1 set		

† Revised Information.

1
2
3
4
5
6
7
8
9
10
11
12
13
14
15
16
17
18
19
20
21
22
B6894

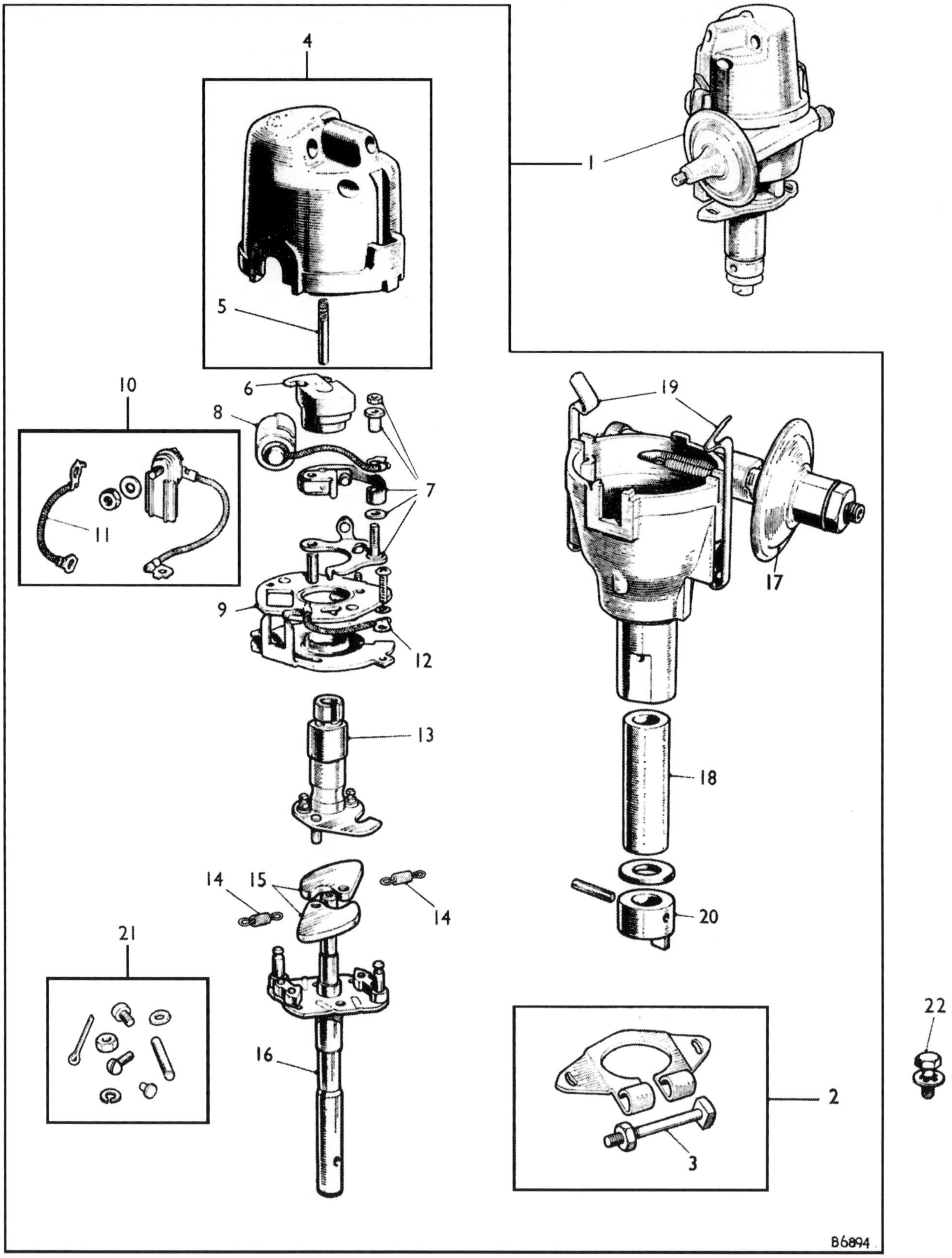

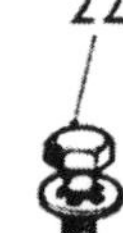

DESCRIPTION	Part No.	Illus. No.	Quantity	Change Point	REMARKS
9C Ignition Equipment—*continued*					
Distributor	†12A 165	1	1		W.S.E. use **12A 419**
Plate assembly—clamping	3H 2138	2	1		
Screw—clamping plate	†NSP	3	1		Was **37H 5063**
Cover	†17H 5422	4	1		W.S.E. use **57H 5477**
Cover	†57H 5477	4	1		
Brush and spring	17H 5065	5	1		
Arm—rotor	7H 5086	6	1		
Contact	17H 5423	7	1 set		
Condenser	47H 5250	8	1		
Plate—contact breaker base	17H 5469	9	1		
Terminal—low tension (with bush and lead)	37H 5409	10	1		
Lead—low tension	17H 5532	11	1		
Lead—earth	17H 5531	12	1		
Cam	57H 5184	13	1		
Spring—automatic advance	57H 5185	14	1 set		
Weight	57H 5049	15	2		
Shaft and action plate	57H 5050	16	1		
Unit—vacuum (with actuating arm)	47H 5520	17	1		
Bushing	47H 5164	18	1		
Clip—cap retaining	37H 5445	19	2		
Dog—driving	47H 5249	20	1		
Sundry parts	17H 5106	21	1 set		
Distributor	12A 419	1	1		
Plate assembly—clamping	3H 2138	2	1		
Screw—clamping plate	†NSP	3	1		Was **37H 5063**
Cover	57H 5477	4	1		
Brush and spring	17H 5065	5	1		
Arm—rotor	7H 5086	6	1		
Contact	17H 5423	7	1 set		
Condenser	47H 5250	8	1		
Plate—contact breaker base	17H 5469	9	1		
Terminal—low tension (with bush and lead)	17H 2639	10	1		
Lead—low tension	17H 5532	11	1		
Lead—earth	17H 5531	12	1		
Cam	57H 5184	13	1		
Spring—automatic advance	57H 5185	14	1 set		
Weight	57H 5420	15	2		
Shaft and action plate	57H 5050	16	1		
Unit—vacuum	47H 5520	17	1		
Bush—body bearing	47H 5164	18	1		
Clip—cover retaining	37H 5445	19	2		
Dog—driving	47H 5249	20	1		
Sundry parts	17H 5106	21	1 set		
Screw—distributor to housing	†6K 639	22	2		W.S.E. use **2** off screw **HZS 0404** together with **2** off washer **LWZ 404**
Screw—distributor to housing	†HZS 0404	22	2		
Washer	†LWZ 404		2		

† Revised Information.

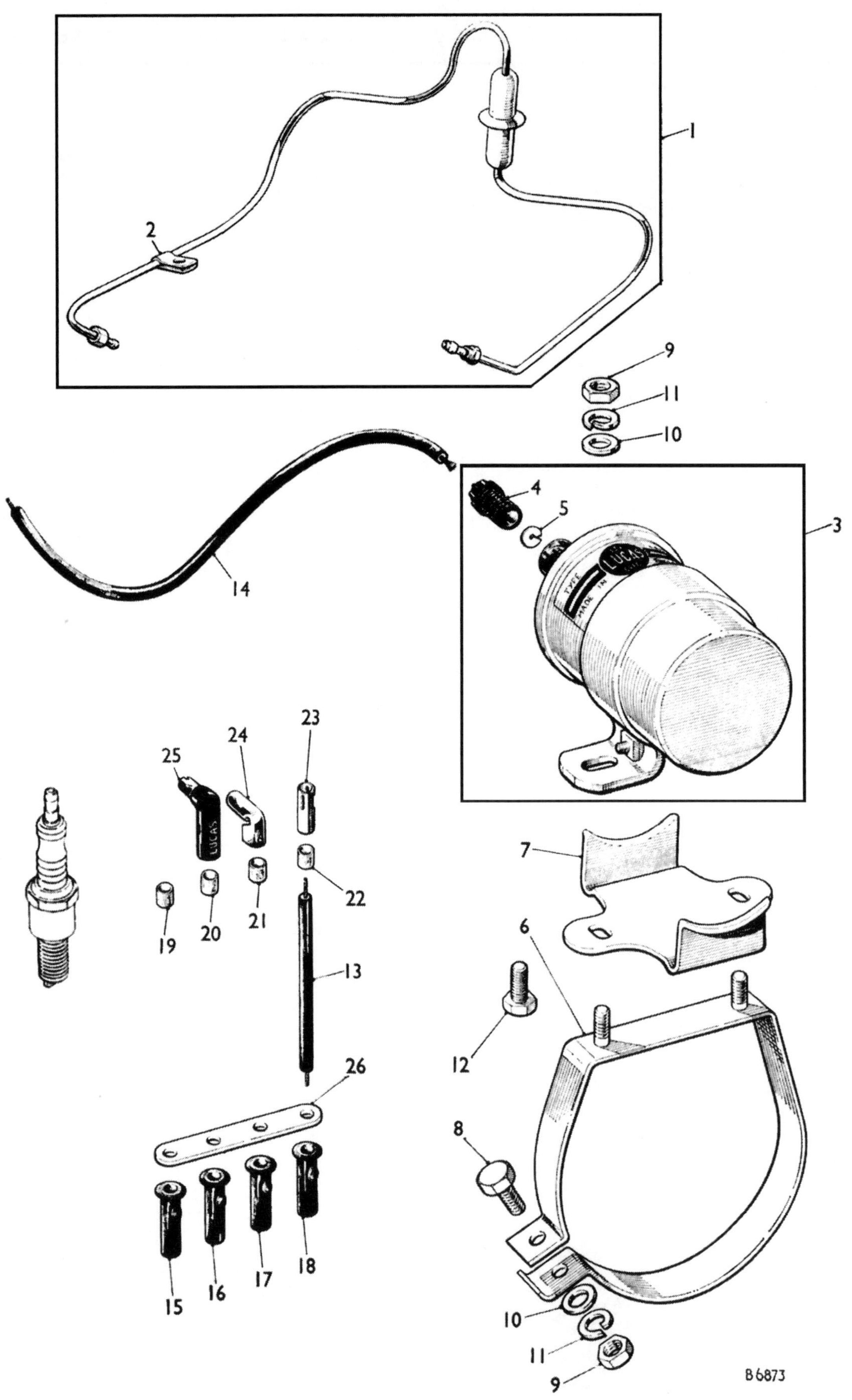
1
2
9
11
10
4
5
3
LUCAS
14
23
24
25
LUCAS
22
7
19
20
21
6
13
12
26
8
15
16
17
18
10
11
9
B6873

DESCRIPTION	Part No.	Illus. No.	Quantity	Change Point	REMARKS
9C Ignition Equipment—*continued*					
VACUUM CONTROL PIPE					
Pipe—vacuum control	†AEA 346	1	1	Fitted up to change over to AEA 447	W.S.E. use AEA 447
Pipe—vacuum control	AEA 447	1	1	(E) 9C/U/H82663 on	
Clip	†1B 2121	2	1		W.S.E. use ACH 9009
Clip	ACH 9009	2	1		
IGNITION COIL					
Coil—ignition	†2A 536	3	1		W.S.E. use 17H 9171
	†17H 9171	3	1		W.S.E. use 37H 2883
	†37H 2883	3	1		
Terminal—high tension	3H 2695	4	1		
Washer—spring	3H 2696	5	1		
Bracket—coil to dynamo	88G 203	6	1	(E) 9C/U/H101 to H11888	Part No. change; was 1H 1070 and 1H 1302
Plate—coil—steady	11G 221	7	1	(E) 9C/U/H101 to H11888	
Bolt	HZS 0406	8	1	(E) 9C/U/H101 to H11888	
Nut	FNZ 104	9	3	(E) 9C/U/H101 to H11888	
Washer—plain	PWN 204	10	3	(E) 9C/U/H101 to H11888	
Washer—spring	LWN 304	11	3	(E) 9C/U/H101 to H11888	
Screw	HZS 0405	12	2	(E) 9C/U/H11889 on	
Nut	FNZ 104	9	2	(E) 9C/U/H11889 on	
Washer—plain	PWZ 204	10	2	(E) 9C/U/H11889 on	
Washer—spring	LWZ 204	11	2	(E) 9C/U/H11889 on	
IGNITION CABLES					
Cable—ignition	AAA 5981	13	A/R		Supplied in 100′ (30·4 m) rolls
No. 1—12″ (30·48 cm)			1		
No. 2—11″ (27·94 cm)			1		
No. 3—8½″ (21·59 cm)			1		
No. 4—9⅝″ (24·44 cm)			1		
Cable—coil to distributor—9⅝″ (24·44 cm)	AAA 5981	14	1		
Ferrule—cable					
No. 1	3H 1655	15	1	(E) 9C/U/H101 to H4795	
No. 2	3H 1656	16	1	(E) 9C/U/H101 to H4795	
No. 3	3H 1657	17	1	(E) 9C/U/H101 to H4795	
No. 4	3H 1658	18	1	(E) 9C/U/H101 to H4795	
Sleeve—identification—plug lead					
No. 1	2H 4243	19	1	(E) 9C/U/H4796 on	
No. 2	2H 4244	20	1	(E) 9C/U/H4796 on	
No. 3	2H 4245	21	1	(E) 9C/U/H4796 on	
No. 4	2H 4246	22	1	(E) 9C/U/H4796 on	
Connector—sparking plug	8G 616	23	4	(E) 9C/U/H101 to H4795	
Connector—sparking plug	13H 184	24	4	(E) 9C/U/H4796 on	
Suppressor—sparking plug	3H 1422	25	4	(E) 9C/U/H25484 on	
Spacer—4-way—HT cables	1G 2673	26	1		
Terminal—ignition cable	8G 2565		1 set		

† Revised Information.

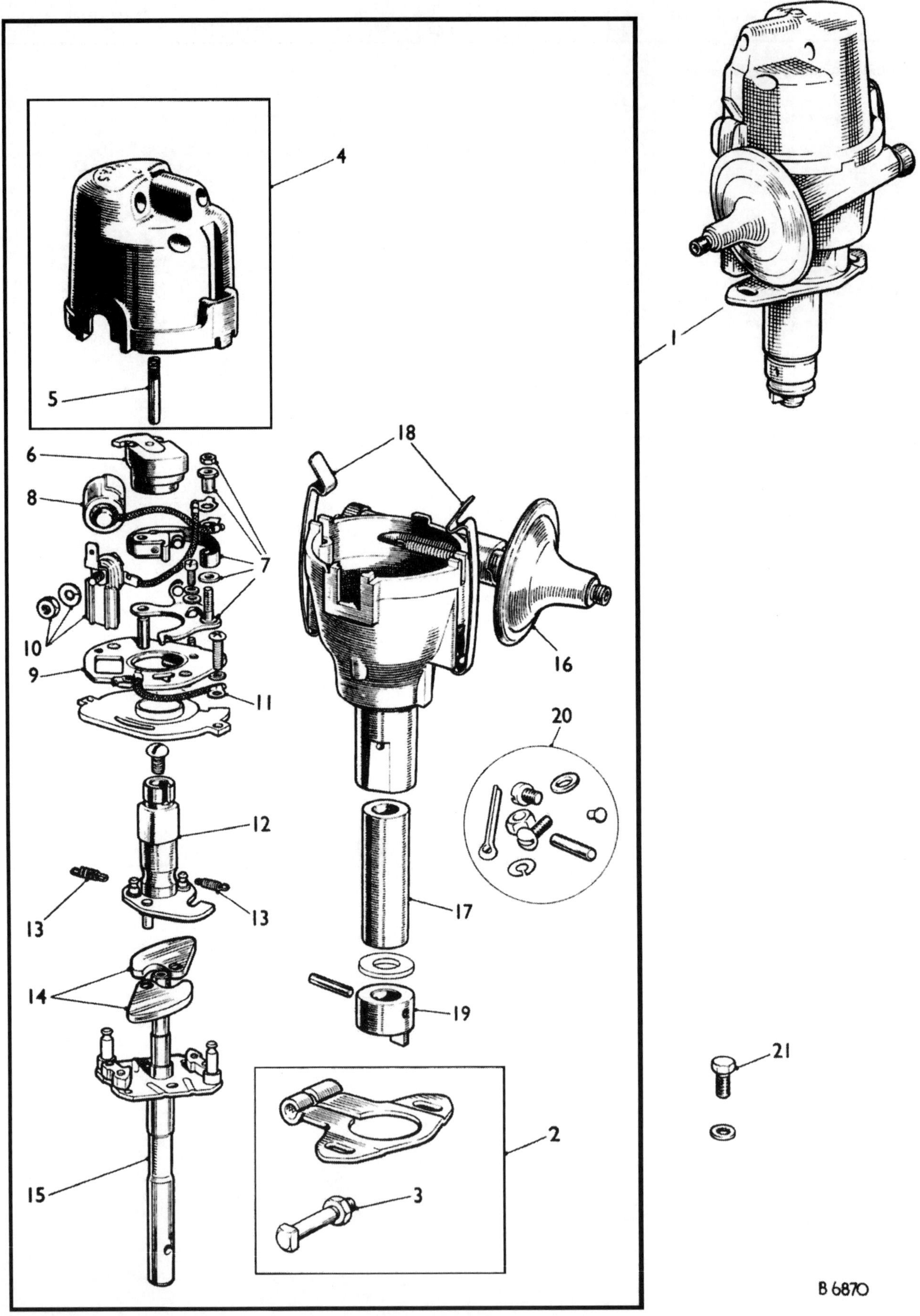
1
2
3
4
5
6
7
8
9
10
11
12
13
13
14
15
16
17
18
19
20
21
B 6870

950-cc 9CG/Da/H IGNITION EQUIPMENT

	Page	Plate
DISTRIBUTOR	MB 7	B 4
VACUUM IGNITION CONTROL PIPE—IGNITION COIL—IGNITION CABLES	MB 8	B 5

IGNITION EQUIPMENT

9CG

DISTRIBUTOR

DESCRIPTION	Part No.	Illus. No.	Quantity	Change Point	REMARKS
Distributor	AEJ 48	1	1	See (1) foot of page	
Distributor	AEJ 78	1	1	See (2) foot of page	
Plate assembly—clamping	8H 2138	2	1		
Screw—clamping plate	†NSP	3	1		Was 37H 5063
Cover	†17H 5422	4	1	See (1) foot of page	W.S.E. use 57H 5477
Cover	57H 5477	4	1	See (2) foot of page	
Brush and spring	17H 5065	5	1		
Arm—rotor	7H 5086	6	1		
Contact	17H 5423	7	1 set		
Condenser	47H 5250	8	1		
Plate—contact breaker base	17H 5469	9	1		
Terminal (with bush and lead)	57H 5346	10	1	See (1) foot of page	
Terminal (with bush and lead)	57H 5478	10		See (2) foot of page	
Lead—earth	17H 5531	11	1		
Cam	57H 5362	12	1		
Spring—automatic advance	57H 5363	13	1		
Weight	57H 5049	14	2	See (1) foot of page	
Weight	57H 5420	14	2	See (2) foot of page	
Shaft and action plate	57H 5050	15	1		
Unit—vacuum	47H 5520	16	1		
Bush—body bearing	47H 5164	17	1		
Clip—cover retaining	37H 5445	18	2		
Dog—driving	47H 5249	19	1		
Sundry parts	17H 5106	20	1 set		
Screw—distributor to housing	†6K 639	21	2		W.S.E. use 2 off screw HZS 0404 together with 2 off washer LWZ 404
Screw—distributor to housing	†HZS 0404	21	2		
Washer	†LWZ 404		2		

CHANGE POINTS

(1) 9CG/Da/101 to H27444 and L16948
(2) 9CG/Da/H27445 on and L16949 on

† Revised Information.

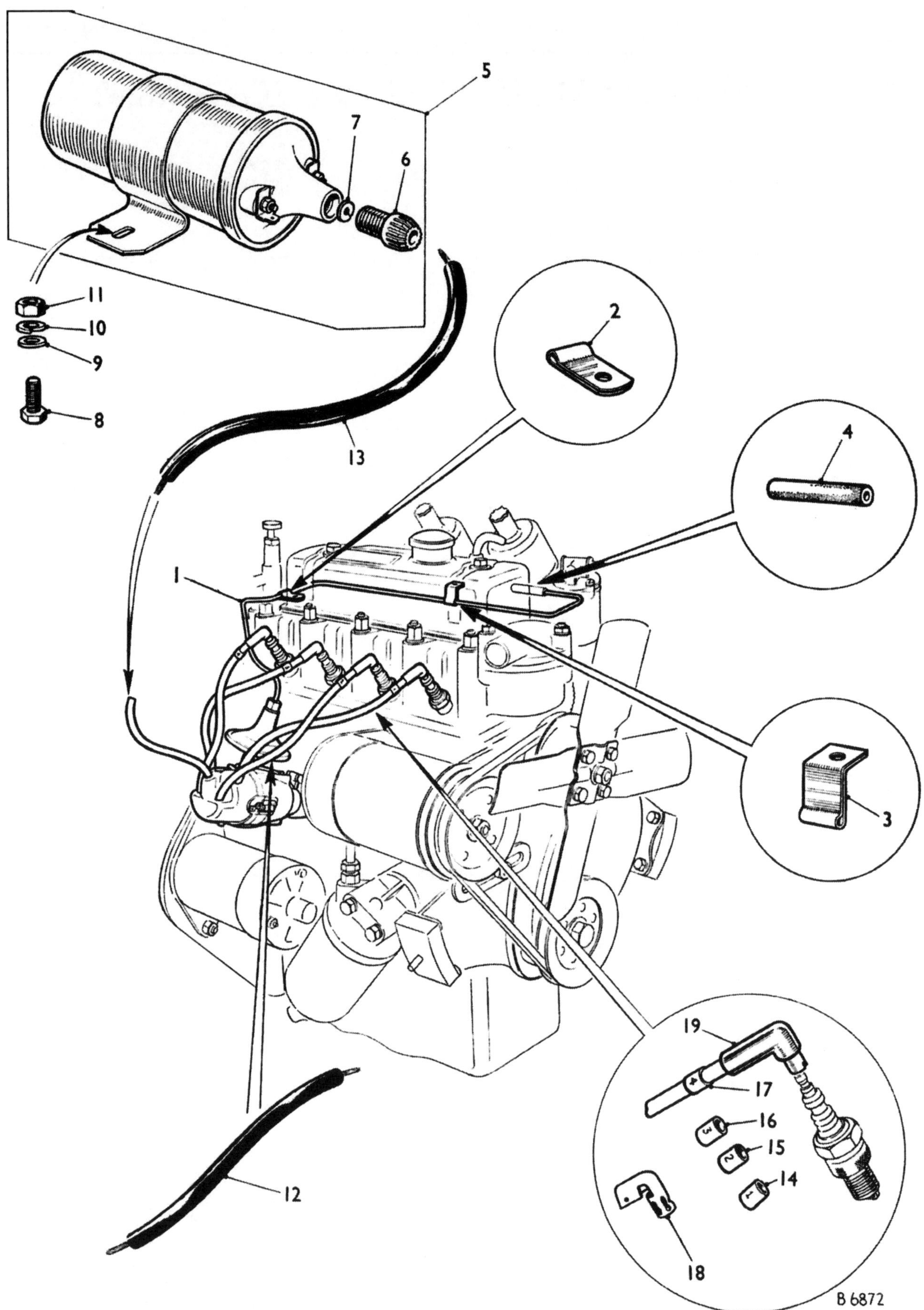
5
7
6
11
10
9
8
13
2
4
1
3
19
17
16
15
14
18
12
B 6872

DESCRIPTION	Part No.	Illus. No.	Quantity	Change Point	REMARKS
9CG Ignition Equipment—*continued*					
VACUUM CONTROL PIPE					
Pipe—vacuum control	AEA 579	1	1	(E) 9CG/Da/101 to H8984 (less H8690 to H8700) and L1042	
Pipe—vacuum control	†AEA 663	1	1	(E) 9CG/Da/H8985 on (plus H8690 to H8700) and L1043 on	W.S.E. use AEA 579
Clip—pipe to inlet manifold	AEA 581	2	1		
Clip—pipe to cylinder head	ACH 9009	3	1		
Connection—pipe to carburetter (rubber)	ACH 9041	4	1		
IGNITION COIL					
Coil—ignition	BMK 356	5	1		Use 17H 8100 for this application
	†17H 8100	5	1		W.S.E. use 37H 2883
	†37H 2883	5	1		
Terminal—high tension	3H 2695	6	1		
Washer—spring	3H 2696	7	1		
Screw	HZS 0405	8	2		
Washer—plain	PWZ 204	9	2		
Washer—spring	LWZ 204	10	2		
Nut	FNZ 104	11	2		
IGNITION CABLES					
Cable—ignition	AAA 5981	12	A/R		Supplied in 100′ (30·4 m) rolls
No. 1—12″ (30·48 cm)			1	(E) 9CG/Da/101 to H8984 (less H8690 to H8700) and L1042	
No. 2—11″ (27·94 cm)			1		
No. 3—8½″ (21·59 cm)			1		
No. 4—9⅝″ (24·44 cm)			1		
No. 1—14″ (35·56 cm)			1	(E) 9CG/Da/H8985 on (plus H8690 to H8700) and L1043 on	
No. 2—14″ (35·56 cm)			1		
No. 3—10″ (25·4 cm)			1		
No. 4—9½″ (24·44 cm)			1		
Cable—coil to distributor—9⅝″ (24·44 cm)	AAA 5981	13	1		
Sleeve—identification—plug lead					
No. 1	2H 4243	14	1		
No. 2	2H 4244	15	1		
No. 3	2H 4245	16	1		
No. 4	2H 4246	17	1		
Connector—sparking plug	13H 184	18	4		
Suppressor—sparking plug **RHD**	3H 1422	19	4		
Terminal—ignition cable	8G 2565		1 set		

† Revised Information.

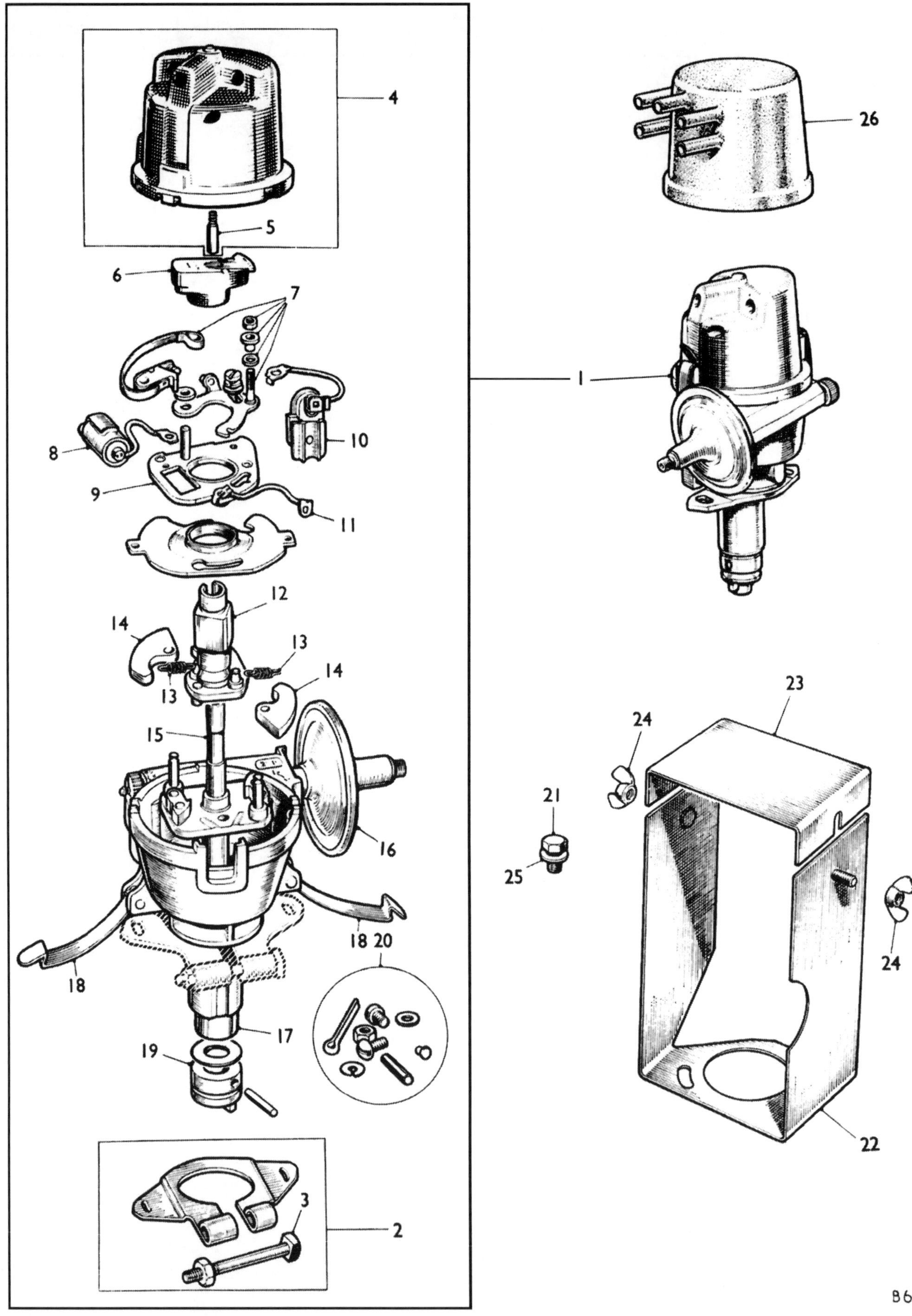
4
5
6
7
8
9
10
11
12
13
14
15
16
17
18
19
20
2
3
26
1
23
24
21
25
22
B68

	DESCRIPTION	Part No.	Illus. No.	Quantity	Change Point	REMARKS

1098-cc 10CG/Da/H IGNITION EQUIPMENT

	Page	Plate
DISTRIBUTOR	MB 10	B 6
VACUUM IGNITION CONTROL PIPE—IGNITION COIL—IGNITION CABLES	MB 11	B 7

IGNITION EQUIPMENT

10CG

DISTRIBUTOR

DESCRIPTION	Part No.	Illus. No.	Quantity	Change Point	REMARKS
Distributor assembly	†12G 233	1	1	Fitted up to change over to 12G 437	W.S.E. use 12G 695
	12G 437	1	1	(E) 10CG/Da/ ▼ on	
	12G 695	1	1		
Plate—clamping	3H 2138	2	1		
Screw	†NSP	3	1		Was 37H 5063
Cover—moulded	57H 5477	4	1		
Brush and spring	17H 5065	5	1		
Arm—rotor	†7H 5086	6	1		Correction; was 7H 5208
Contact	17H 5423	7	1 set		
Condenser	47H 5250	8	1		
Plate—contact breaker base	17H 5469	9	1		
Terminal—bush and lead	57H 5478	10	1		
Lead—earth	17H 5531	11	1		
Cam	17H 6626	12	1		
Spring—automatic advance	17H 6657	13	1 set		
Weight	57H 5420	14	2		
Shaft and action plate	17H 9416	15	1		
Unit—vacuum	17H 6656	16	1		
Bushing—body bearing	47H 5164	17	1		
Clip—retaining cover	37H 5445	18	2		
Dog—driving	47H 5249	19	1		
Sundry parts	17H 5106	20	1 set		
Screw—distributor to housing	†6K 639	21	2		W.S.E. use 2 off HZS 0404 together with 2 off washer LWZ 404
Screw—distributor to housing	†HZS 0404	21	2		
Washer	†LWZ 404	25	2		
Body—suppression screen (**France**)	12G 335	22	1		
Cover (**France**)	12G 337	23	1		
Nut—wing (**France**)	WNZ 103	24	2		
Cover—waterproof (**Canada**)	†8G 726	26	1		

▼ Change point not available

† Revised Information.

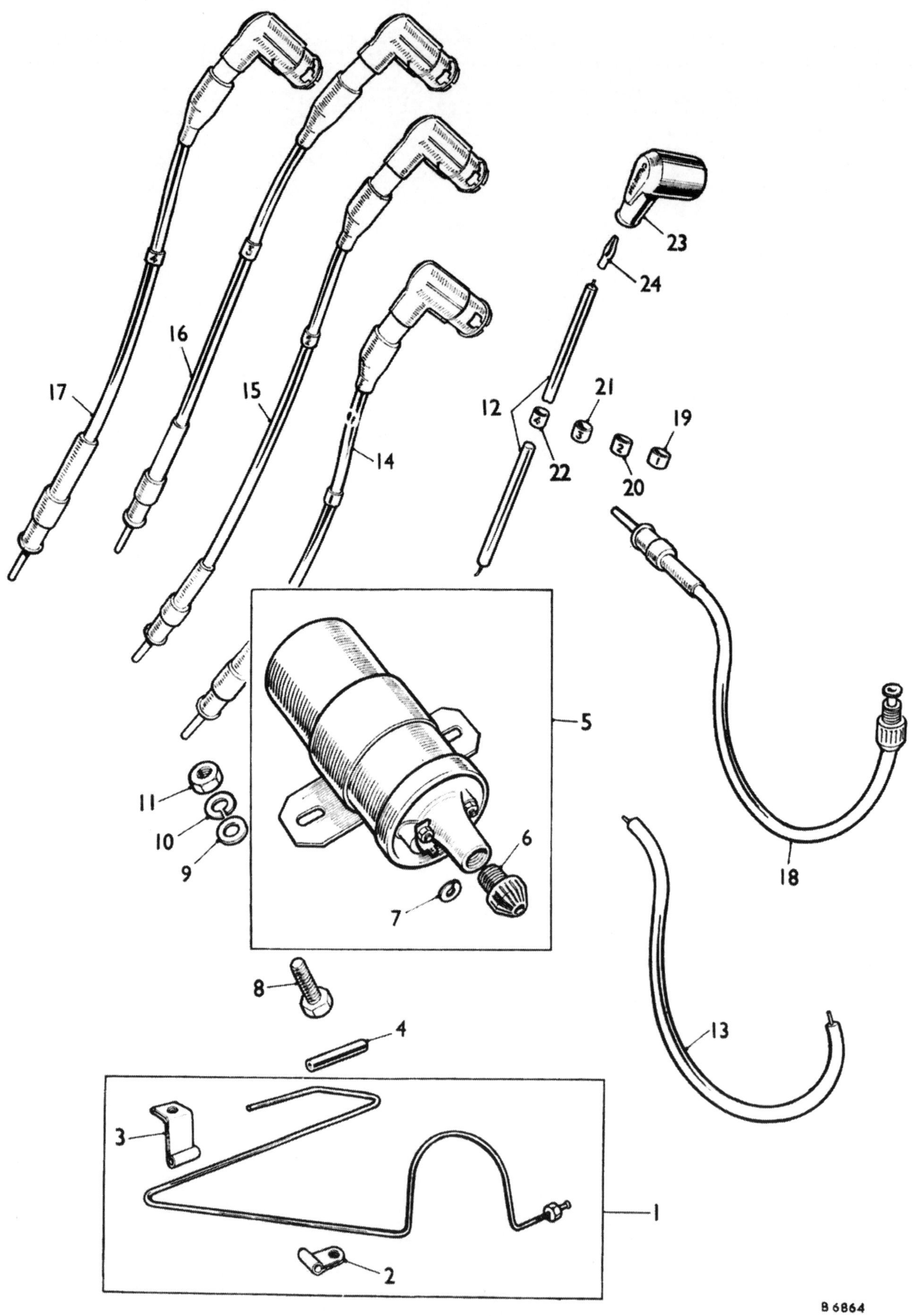
1
2
3
4
5
6
7
8
9
10
11
12
13
14
15
16
17
18
19
20
21
22
23
24
B 6864

DESCRIPTION	Part No.	Illus. No.	Quantity	Change Point	REMARKS
10CG Ignition Equipment—*continued*					
VACUUM CONTROL PIPE					
Pipe—vacuum control	†AEA 663	1	1	(E) 10CG/Da/H101 to 10969	W.S.E. use AEA 579
Pipe—vacuum control	AEA 579	1	1	(E) 10CG/Da/H10970 on	
Clip—pipe to manifold	AEA 581	2	1		
Clip—pipe to cylinder head	ACH 9009	3	1		
Connection—pipe to carburetter (rubber)	ACH 9041	4	1		
IGNITION COIL					
Coil—ignition	†17H 8100	5	1		W.S.E. use 37H 2883
Terminal—high tension	3H 2695	6	1		
Washer—spring	3H 2696	7	1		
Coil—ignition	†37H 2883	5	1		
Screw	HZS 0405	8	2		
Washer—plain	PWZ 204	9	2		
Washer—spring	LWZ 204	10	2		
Nut	FNZ 104	11	2		
IGNITION CABLES					
Cable—ignition	AAA 5981	12	A/R		Supplied in 100′ (30·4 m) rolls
No. 1—12″ (30·48 cm)			1		
No. 2—11″ (27·94 cm)			1		
No. 3—8½″ (21·59 cm)			1		
No. 4—9⅝″ (24·44 cm)			1		
Cable—coil to distributor—9⅝″ (24·44 cm)	AAA 5981	13	1		
Cable—ignition (with connectors)					
No. 1—12″ (30·48 cm) (France)	12G 346	14	1		
No. 2—12″ (30·48 cm) (France)	12G 347	15	1		
No. 3—9½″ (24·13 cm) (France)	12G 348	16	1		
No. 4—9½″ (24·13 cm) (France)	12G 349	17	1		
Cable—coil to distributor (with connector)—10½″ (26·27 cm) (France)	12G 350	18	1		
Sleeve—identification					
No. 1	2H 4243	19	1		
No. 2	2H 4244	20	1		
No. 3	2H 4245	21	1		
No. 4	2H 4246	22	1		
Connector—sparking plug	8G 576	23	4		
Clip—cable end	7H 6894	24	4		
Terminal—ignition cable	†8G 2565		1 set		

† Revised Information.

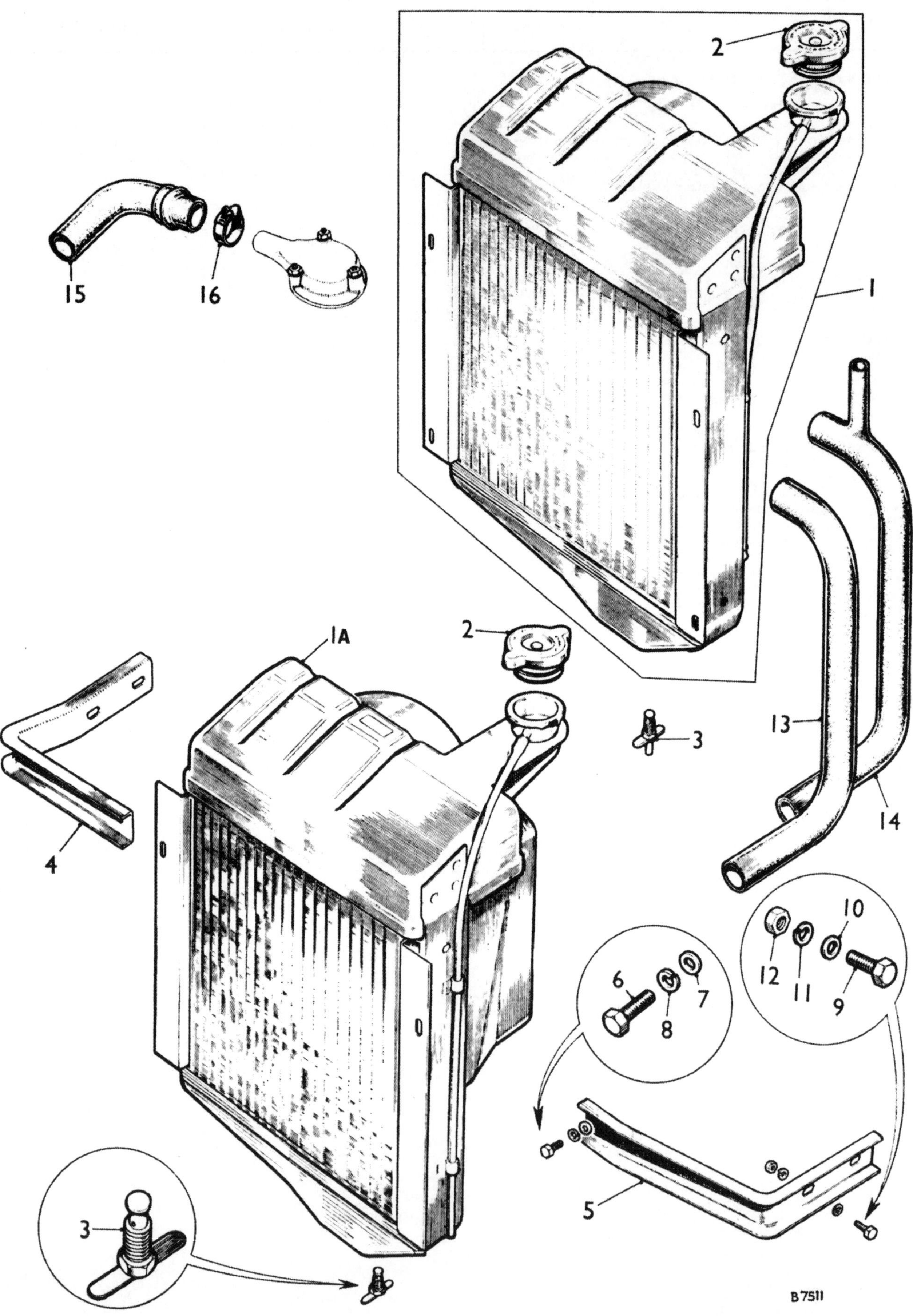
2
1
15
16
1A
2
3
13
14
4
10
12
11
9
6
7
8
5
3
B7511

	DESCRIPTION	Part No.	Illus. No.	Quantity	Change Point	REMARKS

RADIATOR AND FITTINGS

	Page	Plate
HOSES—WATER	MC 1	C 1
RADIATOR	MC 1	C 1

RADIATOR AND FITTINGS

DESCRIPTION	Part No.	Illus. No.	Quantity	Change Point	REMARKS
Radiator assembly	†ARA 73	1	1	(C) H-AN5-501 to 6888	W.S.E. use ARA 92
Cap—filler	†ARH 1039	2	1		W.S.E. use ARH 1662
Radiator	†ARA 92	1A	1	(C) H-AN5-6889 to 50116	W.S.E. use ARA 241
Radiator	ARA 241	1A	1	(C) H-AN6-101 to 24731 (C) H-AN7-24732 on (C) G-AN1-101 to 16183 (C) G-AN2-16184 on	
Cap—filler	†ARH 1039	2	1	(C) H-AN5-6889 to 35054	W.S.E. use ARH 1662
	†ARH 1542	2	1	(C) H-AN5-35005 to 50116	W.S.E. use ARH 1662
	†ARH 1662	2	1	(C) H-AN6-101 to 24731 (C) H-AN7-24732 on (C) G-AN1-101 to 16183 (C) G-AN2-16184 on	
Tap—drain	88G 291	3	1		Part No. change; was 3H 2724 and 13H 82
Bracket—radiator mounting—RH	2A 5591	4	1		
Bracket—radiator mounting—LH	2A 5592	5	1		
Screw	HZS 0405	6	4/3		Quantity reduced when windscreen washer is fitted
Washer—plain	PWZ 204	7	4/3		Quantity reduced when windscreen washer is fitted
Washer—spring	LWZ 204	8	4/3		Quantity reduced when windscreen washer is fitted
Screw	HZS 0406	9	4		
Washer—plain	PWZ 104	10	4		
Washer—spring	LWZ 304	11	4		
Nut	FNZ 104	12	4	(C) H-AN5-501 to 50116	
Hose					
Radiator to pump	†2A 2083	13	1		W.S.E. use AHA 7983 — When heater is not fitted
Radiator to pump	AHA 7983	13	1		When heater is not fitted
Radiator to pump	†2A 2084	14	1		W.S.E. use AHA 7984 — When heater is fitted
Radiator to pump	AHA 7984	14	1		When heater is fitted
Radiator to outlet elbow	†2A 2082	15	1		W.S.E. use AHA 7911
Radiator to outlet elbow	†AHA 7911	15	1		W.S.E. use AHA 7981
Radiator to outlet elbow	†AHA 7981	15	1		
Clip	†8G 550	16	1		W.S.E. use HCS 0913
Clip	HCS 0913	16	1		

† Revised Information.

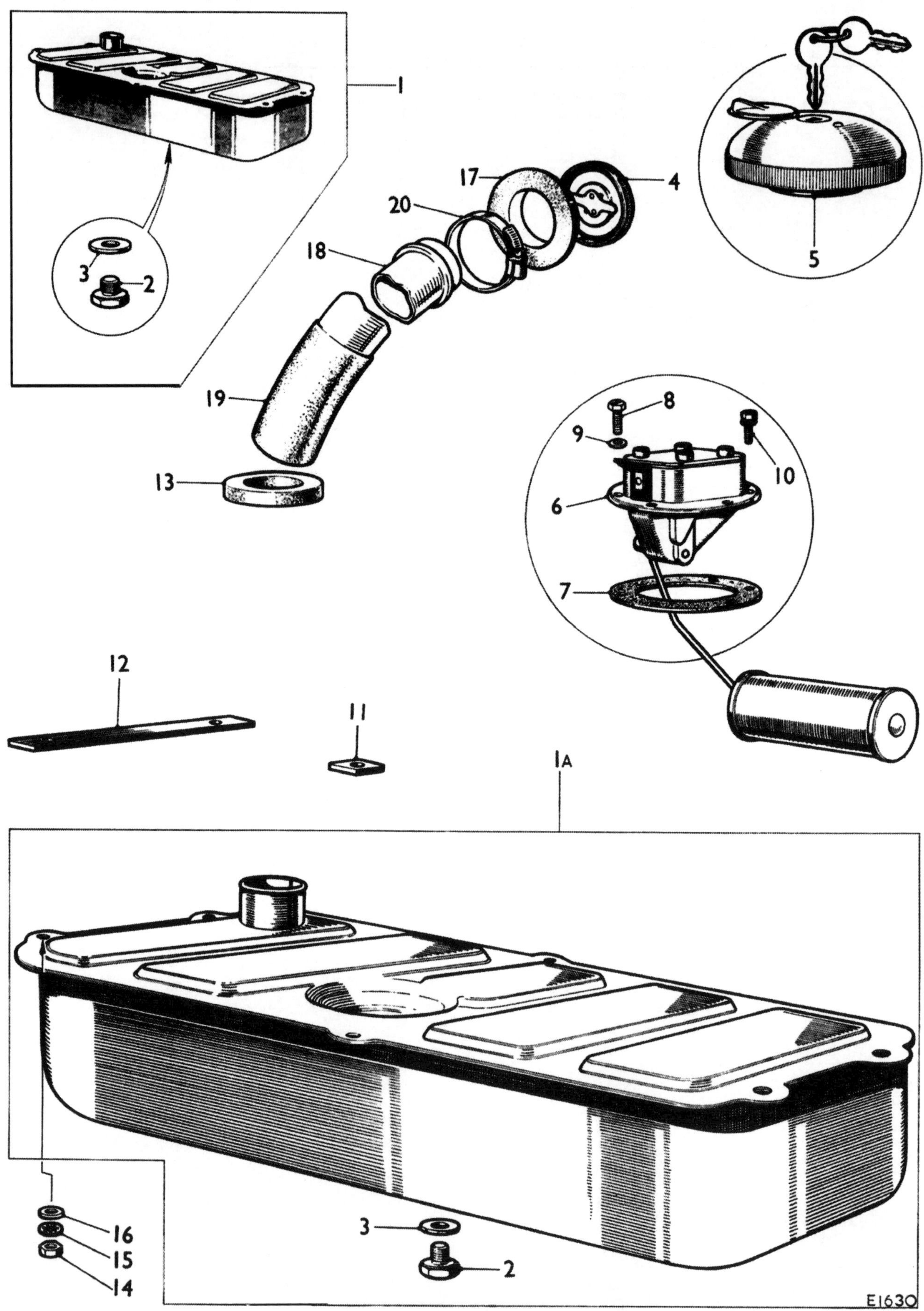
1
3
2
17
4
20
18
5
19
8
9
10
13
6
7
12
11
1A
16
15
14
3
2
E1630

FUEL SYSTEM

	Page	Plate
CLEANER—AIR	MD 5	D 4
PIPES—FUEL	MD 3	D 2
PUMP—FUEL	MD 4	D 3
SHIELD—HEAT	MD 5	D 4
TANK—FUEL	MD 2	D 1

FOR CARBURETTER DETAILS USE THE 'S.U. CARBURETTER SERVICE PARTS LIST', PART NUMBER AKD 5036.

FUEL SYSTEM

FUEL TANK

DESCRIPTION	Part No.	Illus. No.	Quantity	Change Point	REMARKS
Tank assembly—fuel (with filler tube)	ARA 77	1	1	(C) H-AN5-501 to 50116	
Tank assembly—fuel	ARA 114	1A	1	(C) H-AN6-101 to 24731 (C) H-AN7-24732 on (C) G-AN1-101 to 16183 (C) G-AN2-16184 on	
Plug—drain	ARH 672	2	1		
Washer—plug	†ARA 949	3	1		W.S.E. use ARA 967
	†ARH 673	3	1		W.S.E. use ARA 967
	ARA 967	3	1		
Cap assembly—filler	8G 654	4	1		
Seal—filler cap	27H 3573		1		
Cap—filler (locking)	2A 504	5	1		Optional extra. W.S.E. use AKE 1439
Cap—filler (locking)	AKF 1439	5	1		
Unit—fuel gauge	2A 404	6	1	(C) H-AN5-501 to 50116	
Unit—fuel gauge	21A 168	6	1	(C) H-AN6-101 to 24731 (C) H-AN7-24732 on (C) G-AN1-101 to 16183 (C) G-AN2-16184 on	
Washer—joint	2H 1082	7	1		
Screw	53K 165	8	6	(C) H-AN5-501 to 50116	
Washer	2A 2088	9	6	(C) H-AN5-501 to 50116	
Screw—unit to tank (with washer)	ARG 923	10	6	(C) H-AN6-101 to 24731 (C) H-AN7-24732 on (C) G-AN1-101 to 16183 (C) G-AN2-16184 on	
Washer—small—tank mounting	2A 2070	11	1		
Washer—large—tank mounting	2A 2071	12	1		
Ring—sealing—tank to floor	2A 2069	13	1		
Nut	FNZ 105	14	6		
Washer—shakeproof	LWN 405	15	6		
Washer—plain	PWZ 105	16	6		
Collar—tank filler (rubber)	ALH 2459	17	1	(C) H-AN5-501 to 11759	Use AHA 5445 for this application
Grommet—tank filler	AHA 5445	17	1	(C) H-AN5-11760 to 50116 (C) H-AN6-101 to 24731 (C) H-AN7-24732 on (C) G-AN1-101 to 16183 (C) G-AN2-16184 on	
Tube—filler	AHA 5662	18	1	(C) H-AN6-101 to 24731 (C) H-AN7-24732 on (C) G-AN1-101 to 16183 (C) G-AN2-16184 on	
Hose—filler tube neck (rubber)	AHA 5663	19	1	(C) H-AN6-101 to 24731 (C) H-AN7-24732 on (C) G-AN1-101 to 16183 (C) G-AN2-16184 on	
Clip—hose	8G 505	20	2	(C) H-AN6-101 to 24731 (C) H-AN7-24732 on (C) G-AN1-101 to 16183 (C) G-AN2-16184 on	W.S.E. use HCS 1622
Clip	HCS 1622	20	2	(C) H-AN6-101 to 24731 (C) H-AN7-24732 on (C) G-AN1-101 to 16183 (C) G-AN2-16184 on	

† Revised Information.

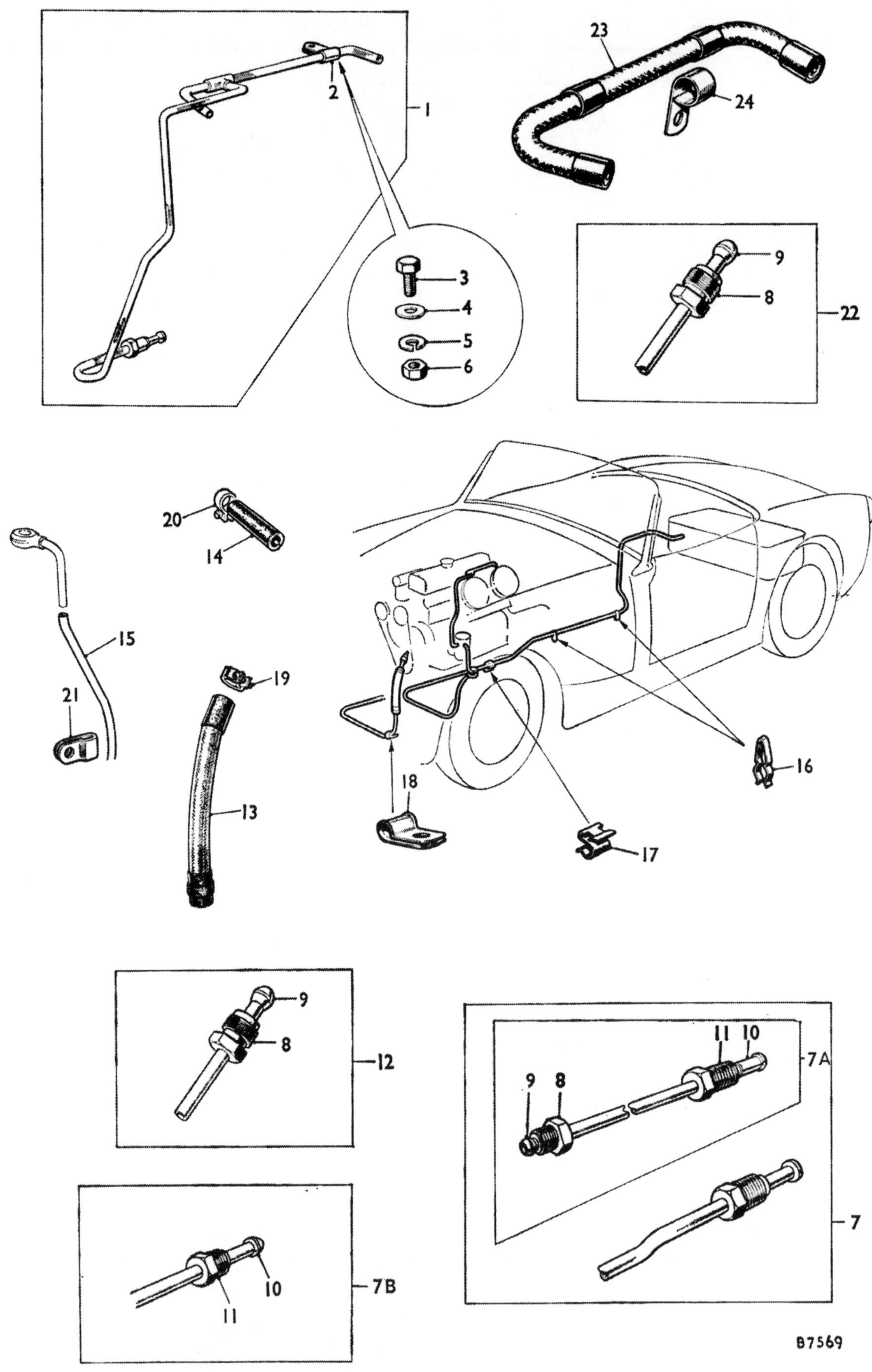
1
2
3
4
5
6
23
24
9
8
22
20
14
15
21
19
13
18
17
16
9
8
12
11 10
9 8
7A
7
10
11
7B
B7569

DESCRIPTION	Part No.	Illus. No.	Quantity	Change Point	REMARKS
Fuel System—*continued*					
FUEL PIPES (SPRITE H-AN5)					
Pipe assembly—pump outlet	AEA 342	1	1	(E) 9C/U/H101 to 18479	W.S.E. use AEA 393
Pipe assembly—pump outlet	AEA 393	1	1	(E) 9C/U/H18480 on	
Clip	PCR 0409	2	2/1		Quantity reduced at (E) 9C/U/H18480
Screw	ZCS 0404	3	2	(E) 9C/U/H101 to 18479	
Screw	HZS 0404	3	1	(E) 9C/U/H18480 on	
Washer—plain	PWZ 104	4	2/1		Quantity reduced at
Washer—spring	LWZ 204	5	2/1		(E) 9C/U/H18480
Nut	FNZ 104	6	1	(E) 9C/U/H18480 on	
Pipe assembly—tank to pump	2A 5638	7	1	(C) H-AN5-501 to 15400	Use AHA 5469 for this application
Pipe assembly—tank to pump	AHA 5469	7A	1	(C) H-AN5-15401 to 41015	W.S.E. use AHA 5536 together with 1 off pipe BRT 2413, 1 off pipe AHA 5535, 1 off clip PCR 0411, and 2 off clip ACH 5854
Nut	6K 648	8	2/1	(C) H-AN5-501 to 41015	Quantity reduced at
Olive	6K 685	9	2/1		(C) H-AN5-15401
Nipple (tank end)	ACA 5129	10	1	(C) H-AN5-15401 to 41015	
Nut (tank end)	ACA 5128	11	1		
Pipe assembly—tank to flexible pipe	AHA 5536	7B	1		
Nipple	ACA 5129	10	1		
Nut	ACA 5128	11	1	(C) H-AN5-41016 on	
Pipe assembly—flexible pipe to pump	AHA 5535	12	1		
Nut	6K 648	8	1		
Olive	6K 685	9	1		
Pipe					
Flexible	BRT 2413	13	1	(C) H-AN5-41016 on	Part No. change; was 21A 206
Pump outlet pipe to carburetter	AEA 338	14	2	(E) 9C/U/H101 to 35640	
Pump outlet pipe to carburetter	AEC 992	14	2	(E) 9C/U/H35641 on	
Overflow (nylon)	AEC 985	15	2	(E) 9C/U/H28914 on	
Clip					
Pipe to underframe	6K 35	16	2		
Pipe to underframe	†17H 9525	17	3		W.S.E. use 17H 9603
Pipe to underframe	†17H 9603	17	3		
Pipe to LH engine mounting bracket	PCR 0411	18	1	(C) H-AN5-41016 on	
Flexible pipe	ACH 5854	19	2		
Pipe to pump outlet pipe and carburetter	AEA 443	20	4	(E) 9C/U/H23012 to 35640	W.S.E. use HCS 0304
Pipe to pump outlet pipe and carburetter	HCZ 0304	20	4		
Pipe to pump outlet pipe and carburetter	AEC 2003	20	4	(E) 9C/U/H35641 on	
Overflow pipe	AEH 550	21	1	(E) 9C/U/H1551 to 28913	
FUEL PIPES (SPRITE Mk. II AND MIDGET)					
Pipe assembly—tank to flexible pipe	AHA 5536	7B	1		
Nipple	ACA 5129	10	1		
Nut	ACA 5128	11	1		
Pipe assembly—flexible pipe to pump	AHA 5535	12	1		
Nut	6K 648	8	1		
Olive	6K 685	9	1		
Pipe assembly—pump outlet	AEA 582	22	1		
Nut	6K 648	8	1		
Olive	6K 685	9	1		
Pipe—flexible					
Main pipe to pump inlet pipe	BRT 2413	13	1		Part No. change; was 21A 206
Pump outlet pipe to carburetter	1H 2181	14	1		W.S.E. use 11H 127
Pump outlet pipe to carburetter	11H 127	14	1		
Carburetter to carburetter	AEA 588	23	1		
Clip					
Pipe to underframe	6K 35	16	2		
Pipe to underframe	†17H 9525	17	3		W.S.E. use 17H 9603
Pipe to underframe	†17H 9603	17	3		
Pipe to LH engine mounting bracket	PCR 0411	18	1		
Flexible pipe	ACH 5854	19	6		
Flexible pipe support	AEA 589	24	2		W.S.E. use 12H 1001
Flexible pipe support	12H 1001	24	2		

† Revised Information.

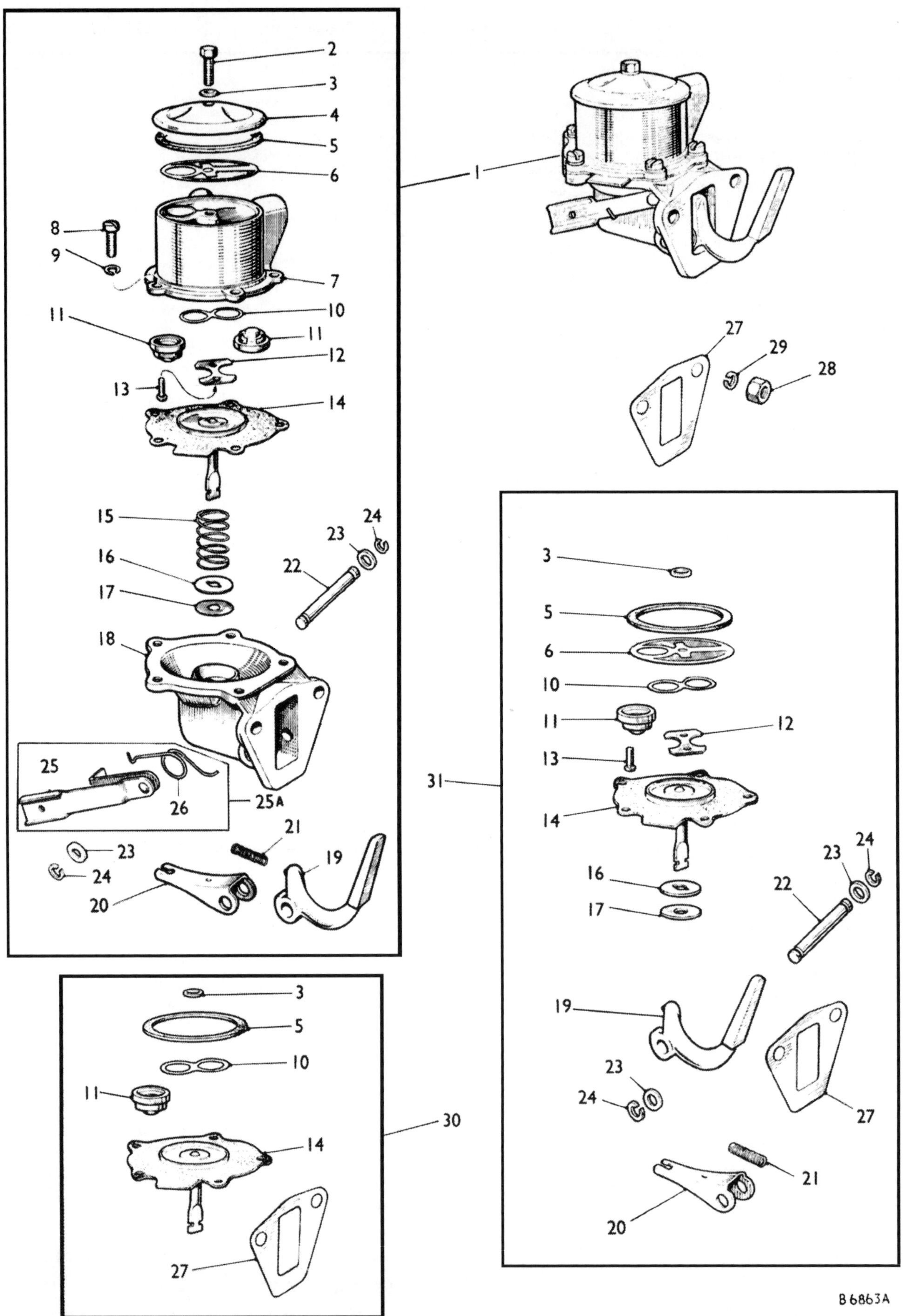

1
2
3
4
5
6
7
8
9
10
11
12
13
14
15
16
17
18
19
20
21
22
23
24
25
25A
26
27
28
29
30
31
B 6863A

DESCRIPTION	Part No.	Illus. No.	Quantity	Change Point	REMARKS
Fuel System—*continued*					
FUEL PUMP					
Pump—fuel	17H 98	1	1		
Screw—cover fixing	7H 1390	2	1		
Washer	†7H 1384	3	1		
Washer	†2K 4961	3	1		
Cover—filter	7H 1381	4	1		
Gasket	17H 856	6	1		
Gauze—filter	7H 1382	6	1		
Casting—upper	†27H 1170	u	1		W.S.E. use 27H 6542
Casting—upper (cover and valve)	27H 6542	7	1		
Screw	7H 1391	8	5		
Washer—lock	LWN 303	9	5		
Gasket—valve	†7H 816	10	1		W.S.E. use 2 off 37H 1255
Gasket—valve	37H 1255	10	2		
Valve	†7H 1561	11	2		W.S.E. use 27H 4568
Valve	27H 4568	11	2		
Retainer	7H 1670	12	1		For service with 27H 1170
Screw	7H 1483	13	2		For service with 27H 1170
Diaphragm	7H 1379	14	1		
Spring	7H 1392	15	1		
Washer—oil seal (metal)	17H 860	16	1		
Washer—oil seal (fabric)	17H 861	17	1		
Body—pump	7H 1679	18	1		
Arm—rocker	7H 1387	19	1		
Link	7H 1386	20	1		
Spring	7H 1393	21	1		
Pin	7H 813	22	1		
Washer—plain	7H 1389	23	2		
Clip	7H 1388	24	2		
Set—primer parts	†17H 3619	25A	1		
Lever—priming	†7H 1667	25	1		W.S.E. use 17H 3619
Spring	7H 1666	26	1		
Gasket—fuel pump mounting	2A 113	27	1		
Nut	12A 1	28	2		
Washer—spring	LWN 205	29	2		
Kit—fuel pump repair—primary	8G 2205	30	1		
Gasket					
Cover—screw	†2K 4961	3	1		
Filter cover	17H 856	5	1		
Valve	†37H 1255	10	2		
Fuel pump mounting	2A 113	27	1		
Valve	†27H 4568	11	2		
Diaphragm	†37H 1821	14	1		
Kit—fuel pump repair—major	8G 2206	31	1		
Gasket					
Cover screw	†2K 4961	3	1		
Filter cover	17H 856	5	1		
Filter	7H 1382	6	1		
Valve	†37H 1255	10	1		
Fuel pump mounting	2A 113	27	1		
Valve	†27H 4568	11	1		
Diaphragm	†37H 1821	14	1		
Retainer—valve	7H 1670	12	1		
Screw—retainer	7H 1483	13	2		
Washer—oil seal (metal)	17H 860	16	1		
Washer—oil seal (fabric)	17H 861	17	1		
Arm—rocker	7H 1387	18	1		
Link	7H 1386	20	1		
Spring	7H 1393	21	1		
Pin	7H 813	22	1		
Washer—plain	7H 1389	23	2		
Clip	7H 1388	24	2		

† Revised Information.

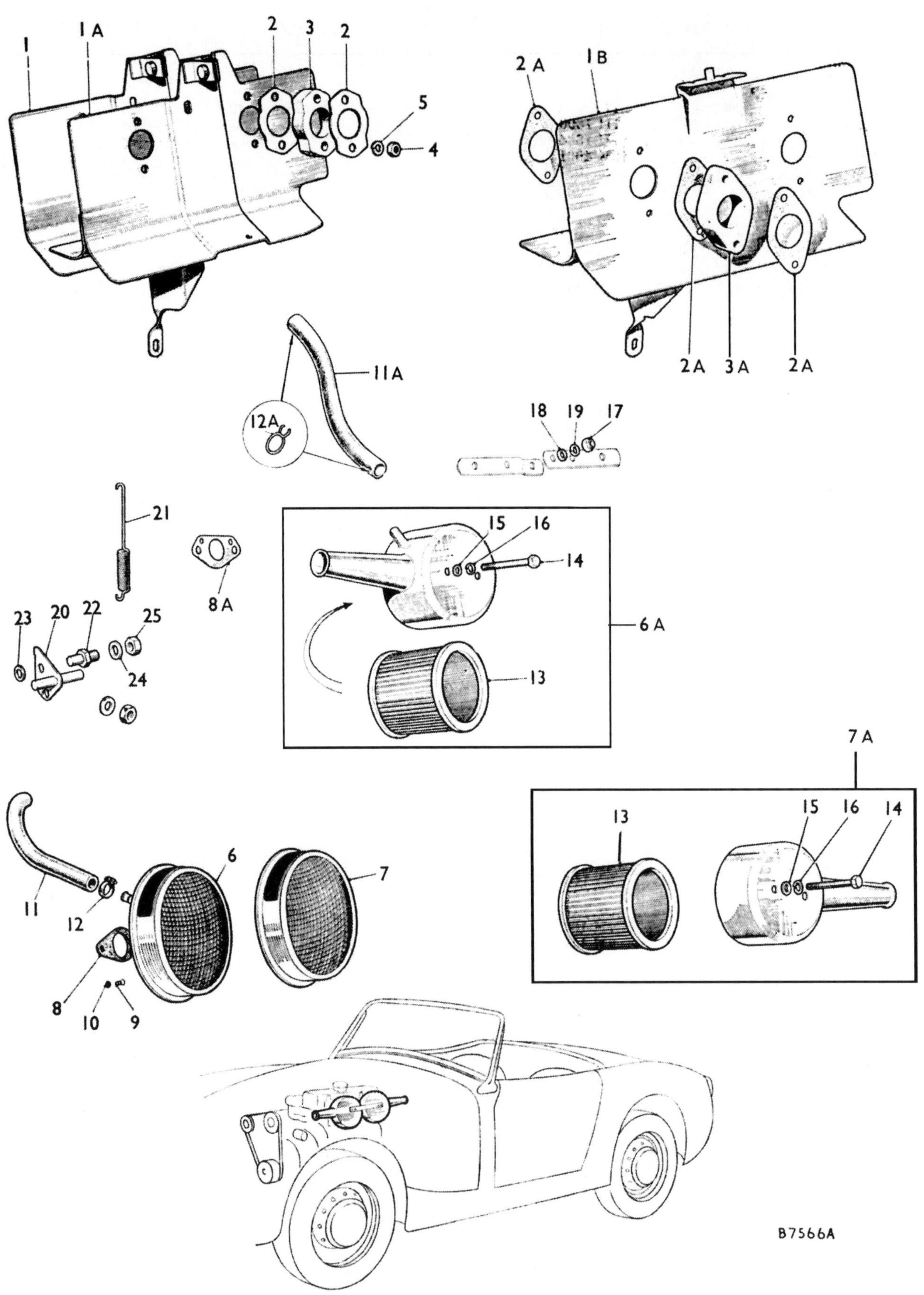
1
1 A
2
3
2
5
4
2 A
1 B
2 A
3 A
2 A
11 A
12 A
18
19
17
21
8 A
15
16
14
6 A
13
23
20
22
25
24
7 A
13
15
16
14
6
7
11
12
8
10
9
B7566A

DESCRIPTION	Part No.	Illus. No.	Quantity	Change Point	REMARKS
Fuel System—*continued*					
HEAT SHIELD					
Shield—heat	†AEA 339	1	1	(E) 9C/U/H101 to 17364	W.S.E. use AEA 395
Shield—heat	AEA 395	1A	1	(E) 9C/U/H17365 to 49201	
Gasket—carburetter and heat shield	3H 2687	2	6	(C) H-AN5-501 to 50116	
Piece—distance—insulating	3H 2686	3	1		
Nut—carburetter stud	FNZ 104	4	2		
Washer—spring	LWZ 204	5	2		
Shield—heat	AEA 592	1B	1	(C) H-AN6-101 to 24731	
Gasket—carburetter and heat shield	1G 2624	2A	6	(C) H-AN7-24732 on	
Piece—distance—insulating	AEA 586	3A	1	(C) G-AN1-101 to 16183	
Nut—carburetter stud	†FNZ 206	4	2	(C) G-AN2-16184 on	Correction; was FNZ 106
Washer—spring	†PWZ 106	5	2		Correction; was LWZ 206
Lever—throttle	AEA 597	20	1		
Spring—throttle return	AEA 602	21	2		
Spring—throttle cable return	AEA 602	21	1		
Pin—clamp—throttle cable	ACC 5062	22	1		
Piece—distance—clamp pins	AEA 606	23	1		
Washer—plain	PWZ 104	24	1		
Nut	FNZ 104	25	1		
Pipe—carburetter overflow (Nylon)	†AEC 985		2		
AIR CLEANER					
Cleaner—air					
Front	†2A 835	6	1	(C) H-AN5-501 to 50116	W.S.E. use 2A 848 — Alternatives
Front	2A 848	6	1		
Rear	†2A 836	7	1		W.S.E. use 2A 849 — Alternatives
Rear	2A 849	7	1		
Gasket—cleaner to carburetter	ACA 5071	8	2		
Screw	HZS 0506	9	4		
Washer—spring	LWZ 305	10	4		
Hose—cleaner to rocker cover	1H 529	11	1		
Clip—hose	†8G 531	12	2		W.S.E. use HCS 0507
Clip—hose	HCS 0507	12	2		
Cleaner assembly—air—front	AHA 5873	6A	1	(C) H-AN6-101 to 24731 (C) H-AN7-24732 on (C) G-AN1-101 to 16183 (C) G-AN2-16184 on	
Cleaner assembly—air—rear	AHA 5874	7A	1		
Element	37H 732	13	2		
Bolt—air cleaner	HCZ 0536	14	4		
Washer—plain	PWZ 105	15	4		
Washer—spring	LWZ 205	16	4		
Gasket—cleaner to carburetter	ACA 8014	8A	2		
Nut—Nyloc	LNZ 205	17	1		
Washer—plain	PWZ 205	18	1		
Washer—spring	LWZ 205	19	1		
Hose—cleaner to rocker cover	AHA 5930	11A	1		
Clip—hose	ACA 5290	12A	2		

† Revised Information.

15
16
17
19
18
2
1
5
6
3
4
7
9
10
12
11
8
13
14
B 6971

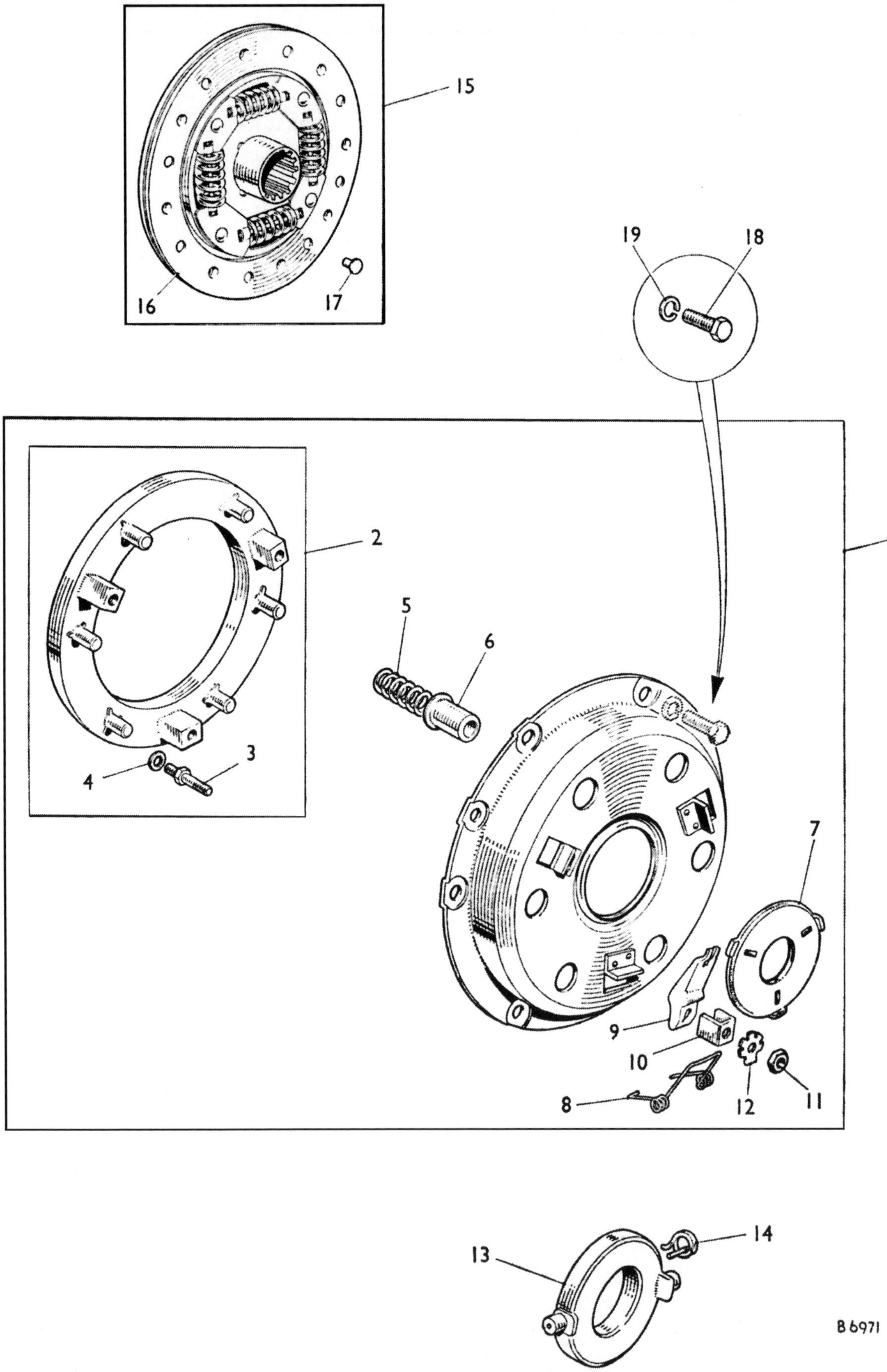

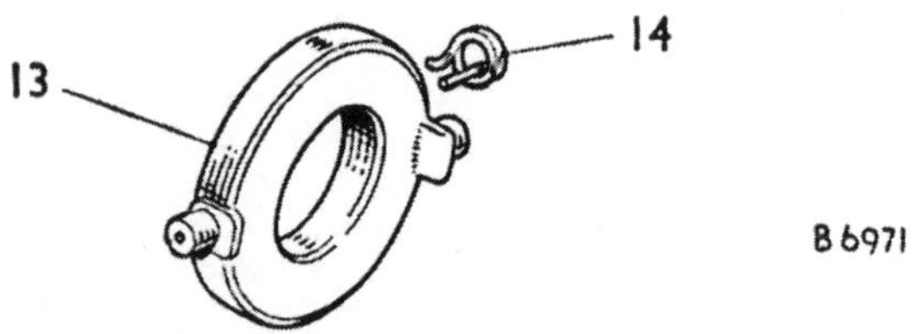

950-cc 9C/U/H CLUTCH AND CONTROLS

	Page	Plate
CLUTCH	ME 3	E 1
CLUTCH CYLINDER	ME 8	E 3
CLUTCH PEDAL AND LINKAGE	ME 8	E 3

CLUTCH AND CONTROLS

DESCRIPTION	Part No.	Illus. No.	Quantity	Change Point	REMARKS
9C CLUTCH					
Cover assembly	AEA 355	1	1		
Plate—pressure (with studs)	7H 3036	2	1		
Stud—pressure plate	7H 3028	3	3		
Washer—shakeproof	LWN 405	4	3		
Springs—thrust—Yellow and Dark Green	27H 3101	5	6		
Cup—thrust spring	7H 3221	6	6		
Plate—thrust	27H 3177	7	1		
Retainer—thrust plate	7H 3025	8	3		
Lever—release	7H 3029	9	3		
Plate—bearing—release lever	7H 3181	10	3		
Nut—pressure plate stud	7H 3031	11	3		
Washer—tab—nut	7H 3222	12	3		
Bearing and cup assembly—release	7H 3166	13	1		
Ring (carbon)	NSP		1		Was X 31404
Spring—release bearing retaining	7H 3185	14	2		
Plate assembly—driven	27H 3102	15	1		Use 27H 3231 for this application
Plate assembly—driven	27H 3231	15	1		
Linings and rivets—friction plate	8G 8345	16	1 set		Part No. change; was 27H 3103
Rivet	7H 3004	17	18		
Screw—clutch to flywheel	51K 2036	18	6		Use HZS 0506 for this application
Screw—clutch to flywheel	HZS 0506	18	6		
Washer—spring	†2K 5319	19	6		W.S.E. use LWN 305
Washer—spring	†LWN 305	19	6		

950-cc 9CG/U/H CLUTCH AND CONTROLS

	Page	Plate
CLUTCH	ME 5	E 1
CLUTCH CYLINDER	ME 8	E 3

Clutch and Controls—*continued*

DESCRIPTION	Part No.	Illus. No.	Quantity	Change Point	REMARKS
9CG CLUTCH					
Cover assembly	AEA 355	1	1	(E) 9CG/Da/H101 to H2139	
Cover assembly	22A 218	1	1	(E) 9CG/Da/H2140 on	
Plate—pressure	7H 3036	2	1	(E) 9CG/Da/H101 to H2139	
Plate—pressure	27H 3275	2	1	(E) 9CG/Da/H2140 on	
Stud—pressure plate	†7H 3028	3	3		W.S.E. use 27H 3276
Stud—pressure plate	27H 3276	3	3		
Washer—shakeproof	LWN 405	4	3		
Spring—thrust—Yellow and Dark Green	27H 3101	5	6		
Cup—thrust—spring	7H 3221	6	6		
Plate—thrust	27H 3177	7	1		
Retainer—thrust plate	7H 3025	8	3		
Lever—release	7H 3029	9	3		
Plate—bearing—release lever	7H 3181	10	3		
Nut—pressure plate stud	7H 3031	11	3		
Washer—tab—nut	7H 3222	12	3		
Bearing and cap—release	7H 3166	13	1		
Spring—release bearing retaining	7H 3185	14	2		
Plate assembly—driven	27H 3231	15	1		
Lining and rivets	8G 8345	16	1 set		
Rivet	7H 3004	17	18		
Screw—clutch to flywheel	†51K 2036	18	6		Use HZS 0506 for this application
Screw—clutch to flywheel	†HZS 0506	18	6		
Washer—spring	†2K 5319	19	6		W.S.E. use LWN 305
Washer—spring	LWN 305	19	6		

† Revised Information.

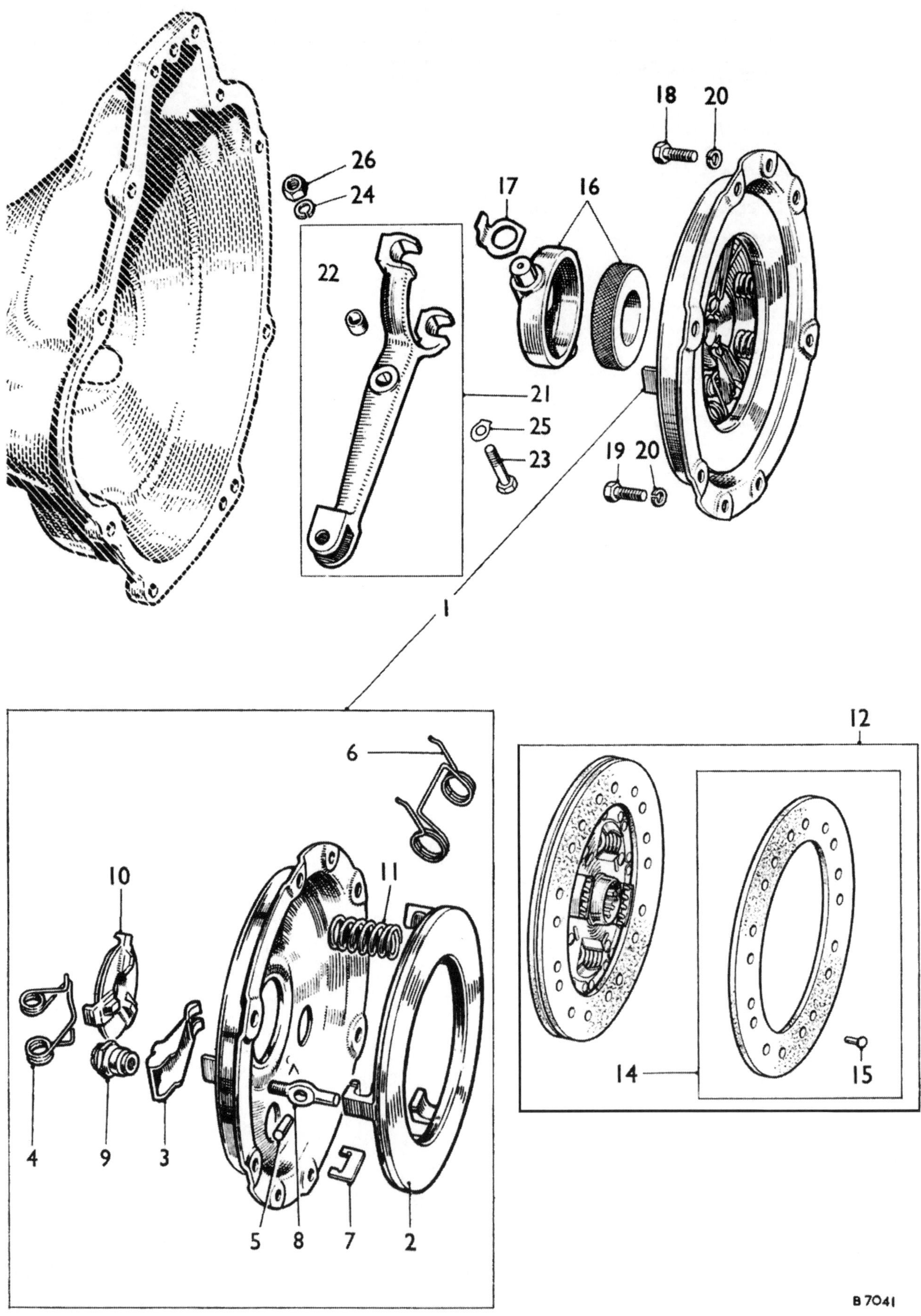
18
20
26
24
17
16
22
21
25
23
19
20
1
12
6
10
11
4
9
3
5
8
7
2
14
15
B 7041

	DESCRIPTION	Part No.	Illus. No.	Quantity	Change Point	REMARKS

1098-cc 10CG/Da/H CLUTCH AND CONTROLS

	Page	Plate
CLUTCH	ME 7	E 2
CLUTCH CYLINDER	ME 8	E 3
CLUTCH PEDAL AND LINKAGE	ME 8	E 3
CLUTCH WITHDRAWAL LEVER	ME 7	E 2

Clutch and Controls—*continued*

DESCRIPTION	Part No.	Illus. No.	Quantity	Change Point	REMARKS
10CG CLUTCH					
Cover assembly—clutch	13H 815	1	1	(E) 10CG/Da/H101 to H10344	
Cover assembly—clutch	13H 988	1	1	(E) 10CG/Da/H10345 on	
Cover	NSP				
Plate—pressure	7H 3057	2	1		
Lever—release	7H 3209	3	3		
Retainer—lever	7H 3009	4	3		
Pin—lever	7H 3061	5	3		
Spring—anti-rattle	7H 3008	6	3		
Strut—release lever	7H 3060	7	3		
Eyebolt	7H 3207	8	3		
Nut—eyebolt	17H 2721	9	3		
Plate—release lever	7H 3043	10	1		
Spring—pressure plate—Yellow	†2H 4927	11	6	(E) 10CG/Da/H101 to H10344	Correction; was 12H 4927
Spring—pressure plate—Red	13H 989	11	6	(E) 10CG/Da/H10345 on	
Plate assembly—driven	†12G 200	12	1		W.S.E. use 13H 8741
	†13H 1501	12	1		W.S.E. use 13H 8741
	13H 8741	12	1		
Lining and rivets	8G 8847	14	1 set		
Rivet	7H 3078	15	20		
Bearing assembly—release	17H 8719	16	1		
Bearing	NSP		1		
Retainer—bearing to clutch fork	13H 788	17	1		
Screw—clutch to flywheel	51K 2036	18	6		Use HZS 0506 for this application
Screw—clutch to flywheel	HZS 0506	19	6		
Washer—spring	LWN 305	20	6		
CLUTCH WITHDRAWAL LEVER					
Lever—clutch withdrawal	22G 168	21	1		
Bush	2A 3006	22	1		
Bolt	2A 3289	23	1		
Washer—spring	LWN 305	24	1		
Washer—lock	2K 5813	25	1		
Nut	FNZ 105	26	1		

† Revised Information.

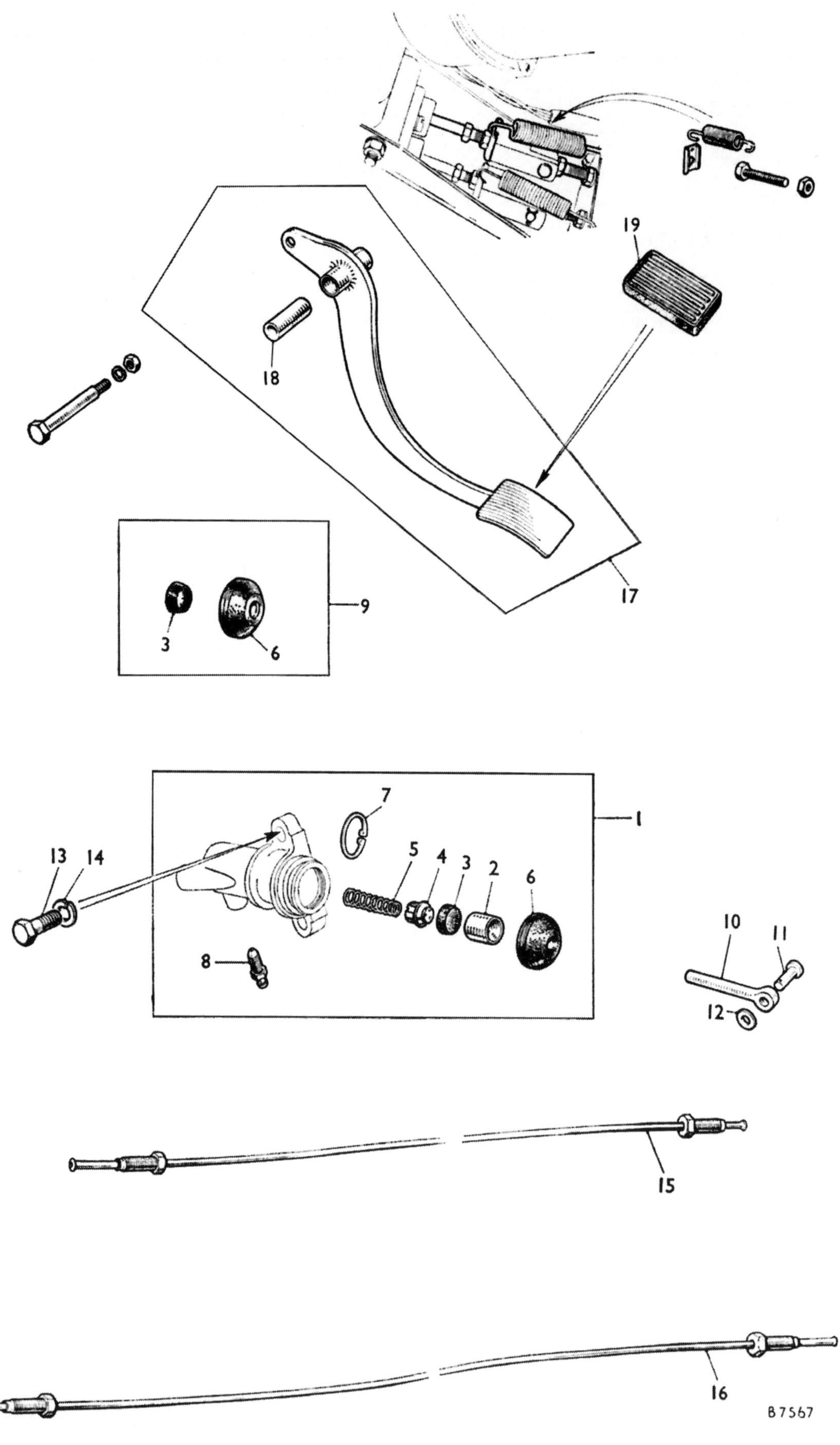
19
18
17
9
3
6
7
1
13
14
5
4
3
2
6
8
10
11
12
15
16
B7567

DESCRIPTION	Part No.	Illus. No.	Quantity	Change Point	REMARKS
Clutch and Controls—*continued*					
CLUTCH CYLINDER					
Cylinder assembly—clutch operating	18H 80	1	1	(C) H-AN5-501 to 6695	
	18H 135	1	1	(C) H-AN5-6696 to 50116	Not available; use 22A 283
				(E) 9CG/Da/H101 to 2139	
	22A 283	1	1	(E) 9CG/Da/H2140 to 36711	
				(E) 10CG/Da/H101 on	
Body	NSP		1		
Piston	17H 7539	2	1	(E) 9C/U/H101 to 49201	Not available; use 17H 7841
				(E) 9CG/Da/H101 to 2139	
Piston	17H 7841	2	1	(E) 9CG/Da/H2140 to 36711	
				(E) 10CG/Da/H101 on	
Cup—piston	7H 7928	3	1	(E) 9C/U/H101 to 49201	Not available; use 17H 7868
				(E) 9CG/Da/H101 to 2139	
Cup—piston	17H 7868	3	1	(E) 9CG/Da/H2140 to 36711	
				(E) 10CG/Da/H101 on	
Filler—cup	17H 7540	4	1		
Spring—filler	17H 7541	5	1		Not available; use 17H 7580
Spring—filler	17H 7580	5	1		
Boot	17H 7268	6	1		
Circlip	CCN 214	7	1	(C) H-AN5-501 to 6695	Part No. change; was 17H 7266
Circlip	AAA 81	7	1	(C) H-AN5-6696 to 50116	Part No. change; was 37831
				(E) 9CG/Da/H101 to 36711	
				(E) 10CG/Da/H101 on	
Screw—bleeder	3H 2428	8	1		
Kit—cylinder repair	8G 8146	9	1		Not available; use 8G 8446
Cup—piston	7H 7928	3	1		
Boot	17H 7268	6	1		
Kit—cylinder repair	8G 8446	9	1		
Cup—piston	17H 7868	3	1		
Boot	17H 7268	6	1		
Push-rod	18H 21	10	1		
Pin—clevis	CLZ 0517	11	1		
Washer—plain	PWZ 105	12	1		
Bolt	53K 152	13	2		
Washer—spring	LWZ 305	14	2		
Pipe—master cylinder to operating cylinder **RHD**	2A 5615	15	1		For fixing details see page MM 8
LHD	2A 5617	16	1	(C) H-AN5-501 to 50116	
LHD	AHA 5508	16	1	(C) H-AN6-101 to 24731	
				(C) H-AN7-24732 on	
				(C) G-AN1-101 to 16183	
				(C) G-AN2-16184 on	
CLUTCH PEDAL AND LINKAGE					
Pedal assembly—clutch	2A 5566	17	1	(C) H-AN5-501 to 4995	Not available; use AHA 5431
	AHA 5431	17	1	(C) H-AN5-4996 to 50116	Not available; use AHA 6408
				(C) H-AN6-101 to 20092	
				(C) G-AN1-101 to 13403	
	AHA 6408	17	1	(C) H-AN6-20093 to 24731	
				(C) H-AN7-24732 on	
				(C) G-AN1-13404 to 16183	
				(C) G-AN2-16184 on	
Bush	2A 5564	18	1		
Pad—pedal (rubber)	AHA 5326	19	1		
Screw—pedal adjustment	HZS 0408	20	1		
Locknut—screw	FNZ 204	21	1		
Spring—pedal return	2A 5574	22	1		
Retainer—spring	2A 5573	23	1		
Bolt—clutch and brake pedal					See page MM 1
Washer—spring					
Nut					
Push-rod—master cylinder					
Locknut—push-rod					
Fork end—push-rod					
Pin—clevis—fork end to pedal					
Circlip—pin					

† Revised Information.

GEARBOX

	Pages
9C/U/H101 to H49201	MF 2 to MF 7
9CG/Da/H101 to H36711	MF 8 to MF 12
10CG/Da/101 to H21048 and L17082	MF 13 to MF 17

GEARBOX

950-cc—9C

	Page	Plate
CASE ASSEMBLY...	MF 3	F 1
CONTROL—REMOTE	MF 6	F 3
COVERS—SIDE AND FRONT	MF 3	F 1
EXTENSION—GEARBOX	MF 6	F 3
GEARBOX ASSEMBLY	MF 3	F 1
GEARS—2nd AND 3rd SPEED	MF 5	F 2
†LAYGEAR—LAYSHAFT	MF 5	F 2
LEVER—CHANGE SPEED	MF 7	F 3
PINION—SPEEDOMETER	MF 6	F 3
RODS—FORK	MF 3	F 1
SELECTORS	MF 6	F 3
SHAFTS—1st AND 3rd MOTION	MF 4	F 2
SYNCHRONIZERS	MF 4	F 2
WHEEL—REVERSE	MF 5	F 2

† Revised Information.

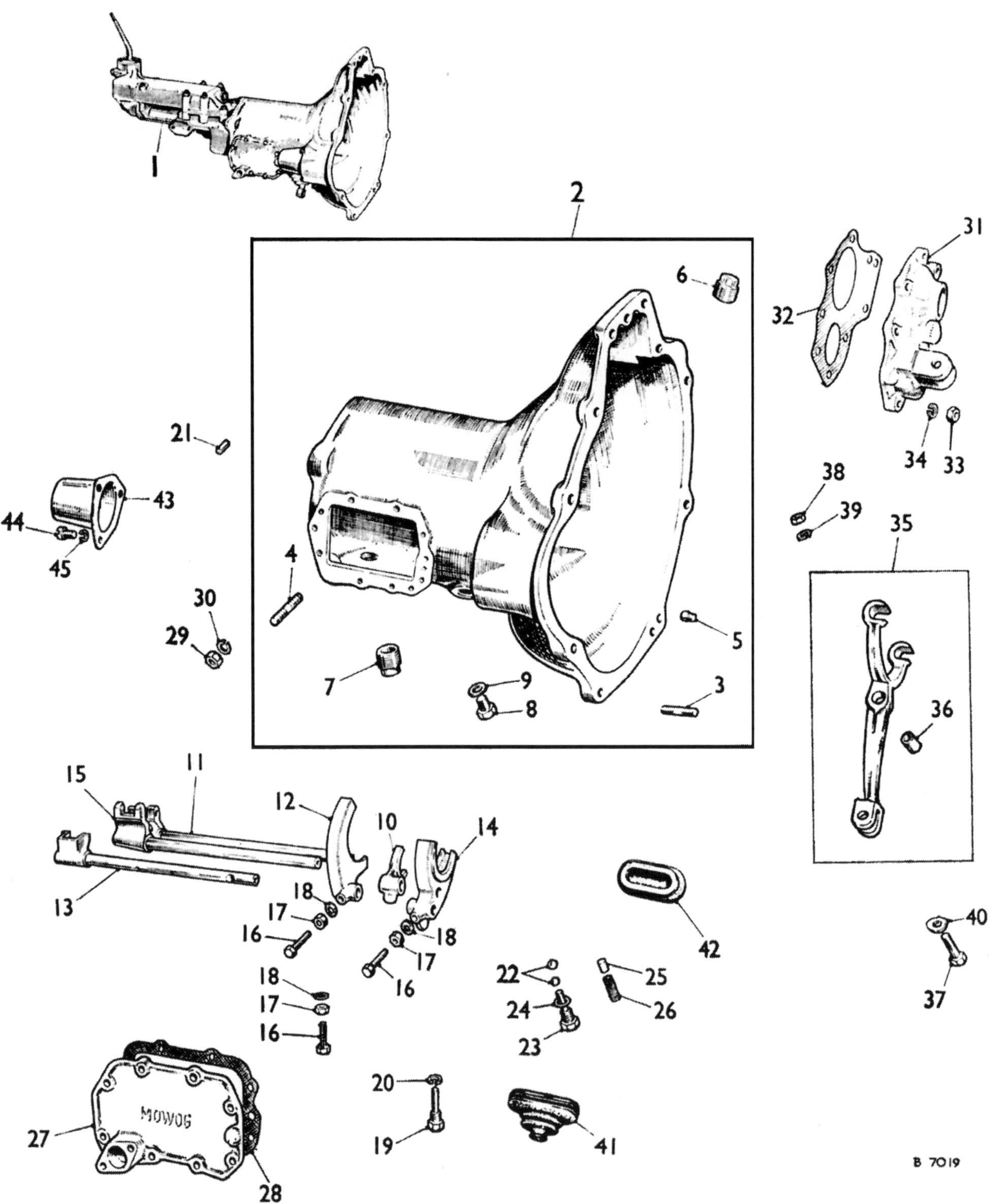
1
2
3
4
5
6
7
8
9
10
11
12
13
14
15
16
17
18
19
20
21
22
23
24
25
26
27
28
29
30
31
32
33
34
35
36
37
38
39
40
41
42
43
44
45
MOWOG
B 7019

9C GEARBOX

* Cones are machine-finished after being shrunk on gears, supplied loose where facilities for these operations exist. (Assemblies must always be supplied for Export.)

DESCRIPTION	Part No.	Illus. No.	Quantity	Change Point	REMARKS
Gearbox assembly	†2A 3413	1	1		W.S.E. use 28G 111
Gearbox assembly	†28G 111	1	1		
Case assembly	28G 87	2	1		
Stud—front cover	53K 463	3	7		
Stud—side cover	53K 463	4	8		
Dowel	1G 752	5	1		
Plug—filler	2K 5830	6	1		
Plug—drain	2K 5830	7	1		
Plug—reverse plunger spring	6K 643	8	1		
Washer—plug	2K 4956	9	1		
Fork—reverse	2A 3284	10	1		
Rod—reverse fork	†2A 3357	11	1	(G) 101 to 1145	W.S.E. use 22A 198
Rod—reverse fork	22A 198	11	1	(G) 1146 on	
Fork—1st and 2nd speed	2A 3019	12	1		
Rod—1st and 2nd speed fork	2A 3305	13	1		
Fork—3rd and 4th speed	2A 3021	14	1		
Rod—3rd and 4th speed fork	2A 3347	15	1		
Screw—fork locating	2A 3141	16	3		
Nut	†51K 1671	17	3		W.S.E. use FNN 504
Washer—shakeproof	LWN 404	18	3		Part No. change; was 2K 8607 and LWN 604
Screw—locking—reverse shaft	2A 3028	19	1		
Washer—spring	LWN 204	20	1		
Plunger—interlock	2A 3110	21	1		
Ball—interlock	BLS 110	22	2		
Plug—interlock ball hole	2A 3253	23	1		
Washer—plug	2K 4956	24	1		
Plunger—fork rods	2A 3108	25	3		
Spring—plunger	†2K 4909	26	3		W.S.E. use 22A 75
Spring—plunger	22A 75	26	3		
Cover—side	88G 214	27	1		Part No. change; was 2A 3285 and 22A 170
Gasket—side cover	2A 3286	28	1		
Nut	FNZ 104	29	8		
Washer—spring	LWN 204	30	8		
Cover—front	2A 3087	31	1		
Gasket	2A 3007	32	1		
Nut	FNZ 104	33	7		
Washer—spring	LWN 304	34	7		
Lever—clutch withdrawal	2A 3406	35	1		
Bush	2A 3006	36	1		
Bolt—clutch withdrawal lever	2A 3289	37	1		
Nut	FNZ 105	38	1		
Washer—spring	LWN 305	39	1		
Washer—lock	2K 5813	40	1		
Cover—dust—clutch withdrawal lever	2A 3084	41	1	Fitted up to change over to 1G 3667	
Cover—dust—clutch withdrawal lever	1G 3667	41	1	(E) 9C/U/H320 on	
Cover—dust—bell housing	2A 3076	42	1		
Cover—starter pinion	1B 3346	43	1		
Screw	53K 1435	44	3		
Washer—spring	LWN 204	45	3		

† Revised Information.

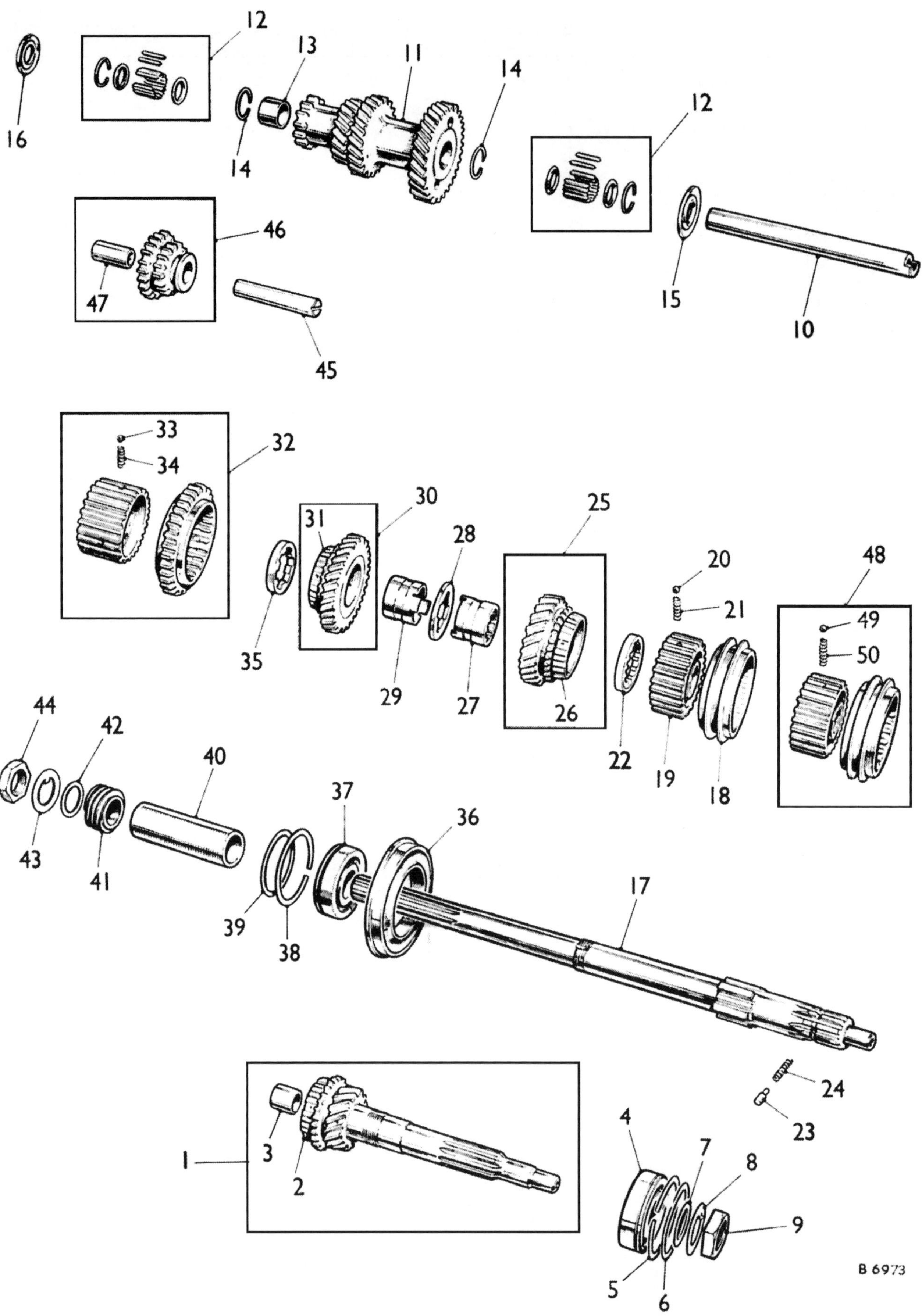
1
2
3
4
5
6
7
8
9
10
11
12
12
13
14
14
15
16
17
18
19
20
21
22
23
24
25
26
27
28
29
30
31
32
33
34
35
36
37
38
39
40
41
42
43
44
45
46
47
48
49
50
B 6973

9C Gearbox—*continued*

* Cones are machine-finished after being shrunk on gears, supplied loose where facilities for these operations exist. (Assemblies must always be supplied for Export.)

	DESCRIPTION	Part No.	Illus. No.	Quantity	Change Point	REMARKS
	Shaft—1st motion (with cone)	†2A 3359	1	1		W.S.E. use 22A 141
	Shaft—1st motion (with cone)	22A 141	1	1		
*	Cone—synchronizing	†2A 3147	2	1		W.S.E. use 22A 138
*	Cone—synchronizing	22A 138	2	1		
	Bush—3rd motion shaft	2A 3034	3	1		
	Washer—packing—bearing					
	·004″ (·1016 mm)	2K 8737	6	A/R		Alternative sizes
	·006″ (·1524 mm)	2K 8738	6	A/R		Alternative sizes
	·010″ (·254 mm)	2K 8739	6	A/R		Alternative sizes
	Washer—plain—shaft	6K 559	7	1		
	Washer—lock—shaft	2A 3035	8	1		
	Nut	2K 6677	9	1		
	Layshaft	8G 664	10	1		
	Laygear	†2A 3358	11	1		Alternatives. W.S.E. use 22A 287
		†22A 203	11	1		Alternatives. W.S.E. use 22A 287
		22A 287	11	1		
	Bearing—needle roller	88G 396	12	2		Part No. change; was 3H 2113
	Piece—distance	†2A 3168	13	1		W.S.E. use 22G 277
	Piece—distance	22G 277	13	1		
	Ring—spring	2A 3366	14	2		W.S.E. use 22G 278
	Ring—spring	22G 278	14	2		
	Washer—thrust					
	Front	2A 3023	15	1		
	Rear — ·123 to ·124″ (3·12 to 3·14 mm)	2A 3024	16	1		Alternative sizes
	Rear — ·125 to ·126″ (3·17 to 3·20 mm)	2A 3025	16	1		Alternative sizes
	Rear — ·127 to ·128″ (3·22 to 3·25 mm)	2A 3026	16	1		Alternative sizes
	Rear — ·130 to ·131″ (3·30 to 3·32 mm)	2A 3027	16	1		Alternative sizes
	Shaft—3rd motion	†2A 3224	17	1		W.S.E. use 22A 213
	Shaft—3rd motion	22A 213	17	1		
	Sleeve—3rd and 4th speed coupling	†2A 3145	18	1		W.S.E. use synchronizer assembly 2A 3226
	Synchronizer—3rd and 4th speed	2A 3220	19	1	(G) 101 to 945	
	Ball—synchronizer	BLS 107	20	3	(G) 101 to 945	
	Spring—synchronizer ball	2A 3142	21	3	(G) 101 to 945	
	Synchronizer assembly—3rd and 4th speed	2A 3226	48	1	(G) 946 on	
	Ball—synchronizer	BLS 107	49	3	(G) 946 on	
	Spring—synchronizer ball	2A 3142	50	3	(G) 946 on	
	Washer—thrust—front					
	·212 to ·213″ (5·38 to 5·41 mm)	22A 550	22	1		Alternative sizes
	·214 to ·215″ (5·43 to 5·46 mm)	†2A 3217	22	1		W.S.E. use 22A 536; Alternative sizes
		†22A 525	22	1		W.S.E. use 22A 536; Alternative sizes
		22A 536	22	1		Alternative sizes
	·216 to ·217″ (5·48 to 5·51 mm)	†2A 3218	22	1		W.S.E. use 22A 537; Alternative sizes
		†22A 526	22	1		W.S.E. use 22A 537; Alternative sizes
		22A 537	22	1		Alternative sizes
	·218 to ·219″ (5·53 to 5·56 mm)	†2A 3219	22	1		W.S.E. use 22A 538; Alternative sizes
		†22A 527	22	1		W.S.E. use 22A 538; Alternative sizes
		22A 538	22	1		Alternative sizes
	Peg—thrust washer	†2A 3160	23	1		W.S.E. use 22A 495
	Peg—thrust washer	22A 495	23	1		
	Spring—peg	†2A 3161	24	1		W.S.E. use 22A 528
	Spring—peg	22A 528	24	1		

† Revised Information.

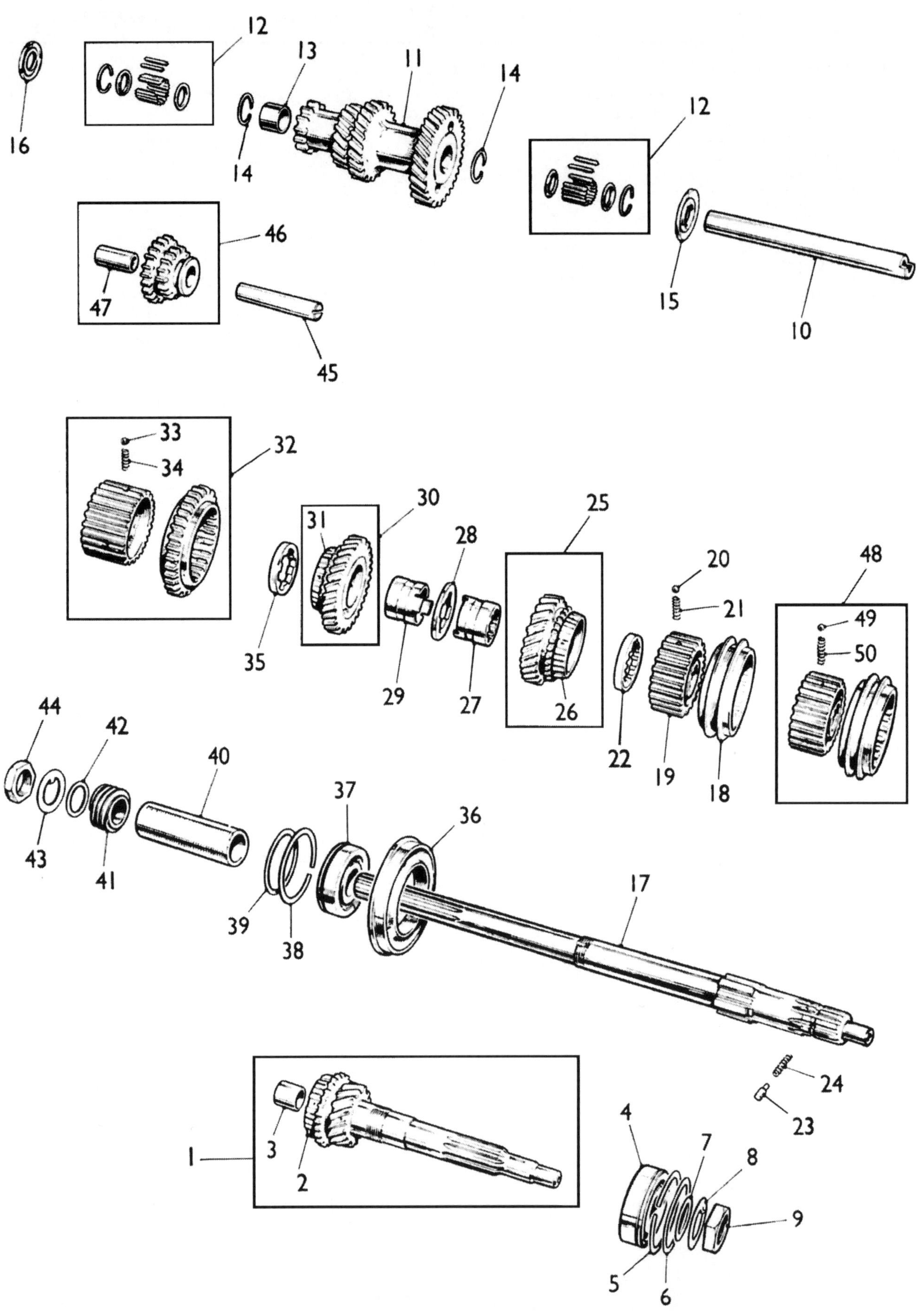
12
13
11
14
16
14
12
46
47
45
15
10
33
32
34
30
25
31
28
20
48
21
49
50
35
29
27
26
22
19
18
44
42
40
37
36
43
41
39
38
17
24
23
4
7
8
1
3
2
9
5
6

	DESCRIPTION	Part No.	Illus. No.	Quantity	Change Point	REMARKS

9C Gearbox—*continued*

* Cones are machine-finished after being shrunk on gears, supplied loose where facilities for these operations exist. (Assemblies must always be supplied for Export.)

DESCRIPTION	Part No.	Illus. No.	Quantity	Change Point	REMARKS
Gear—3rd speed (with cone)	†2A 3361	25	1		W.S.E. use 22A 140
Gear—3rd speed (with cone)	22A 140	25	1		
* Cone—synchronizing	†2A 3147	26	1		W.S.E. use 22A 138
* Cone—synchronizing	22A 138	26	1		
Bush—3rd speed gear	2A 3290	27	1		
Ring—interlocking—2nd and 3rd speed gear bush	†2A 3045	28	1		W.S.E. use 22G 374
	†2A 3401	28	1		W.S.E. use 22G 374
	†22G 242	28	1		W.S.E. use 22G 374
	22G 374	28	1		
Bush—2nd speed gear	2A 3298	29	1		
Gear—2nd speed (with cone)	†2A 3330	30	1		W.S.E. use 22A 139
Gear—2nd speed (with cone)	22A 139	30	1		
* Cone—synchronizing	†2A 3147	31	1		W.S.E. use 22A 138
* Cone—synchronizing	22A 138	31	1		
1st speed wheel and 2nd speed synchronizer	2A 3333	32	1		Use AEA 3030 for this application
1st speed wheel and 2nd speed synchronizer	AEA 3030	32	1		
1st speed wheel	NSP		1		
Synchronizer	NSP		1		
Ball—synchronizer	BLS 107	33	3		
Spring—ball	†2A 3142	34	3		Correction; was 2A 3412; W.S.E. use 22A 332
Washer—thrust—rear	2A 3042	35	1		
Housing—bearing	2A 3085	36	1		
Bearing—ball—3rd motion shaft	2A 3245	37	1		
Ring—spring—bearing	6K 558	38	1		
Washer—packing					
·004″ (·1016 mm)	2K 8737	39	A/R		Alternative sizes
·006″ (·1524 mm)	2K 8738	39	A/R		Alternative sizes
·010″ (·254 mm)	2K 8739	39	A/R		Alternative sizes
Piece—distance—3rd motion shaft	2A 3057	40	1		
Wheel—speedometer	2A 3371	41	1		
Washer	6K 559	42	1		
Washer—lock	2A 3035	43	1		
Nut—3rd motion shaft	2K 6677	44	1		
Shaft—reverse	88G 216	45	1		Part No. change; was 2A 3283 and 22A 131
Wheel—reverse and bush	†2A 3363	46	1		Alternatives. W.S.E. use 22A 204
	†22A 200	46	1		Alternatives. W.S.E. use 22A 204
	22A 204	46	1		
Bush—reverse wheel	2A 3282	47	1		

† Revised Information.

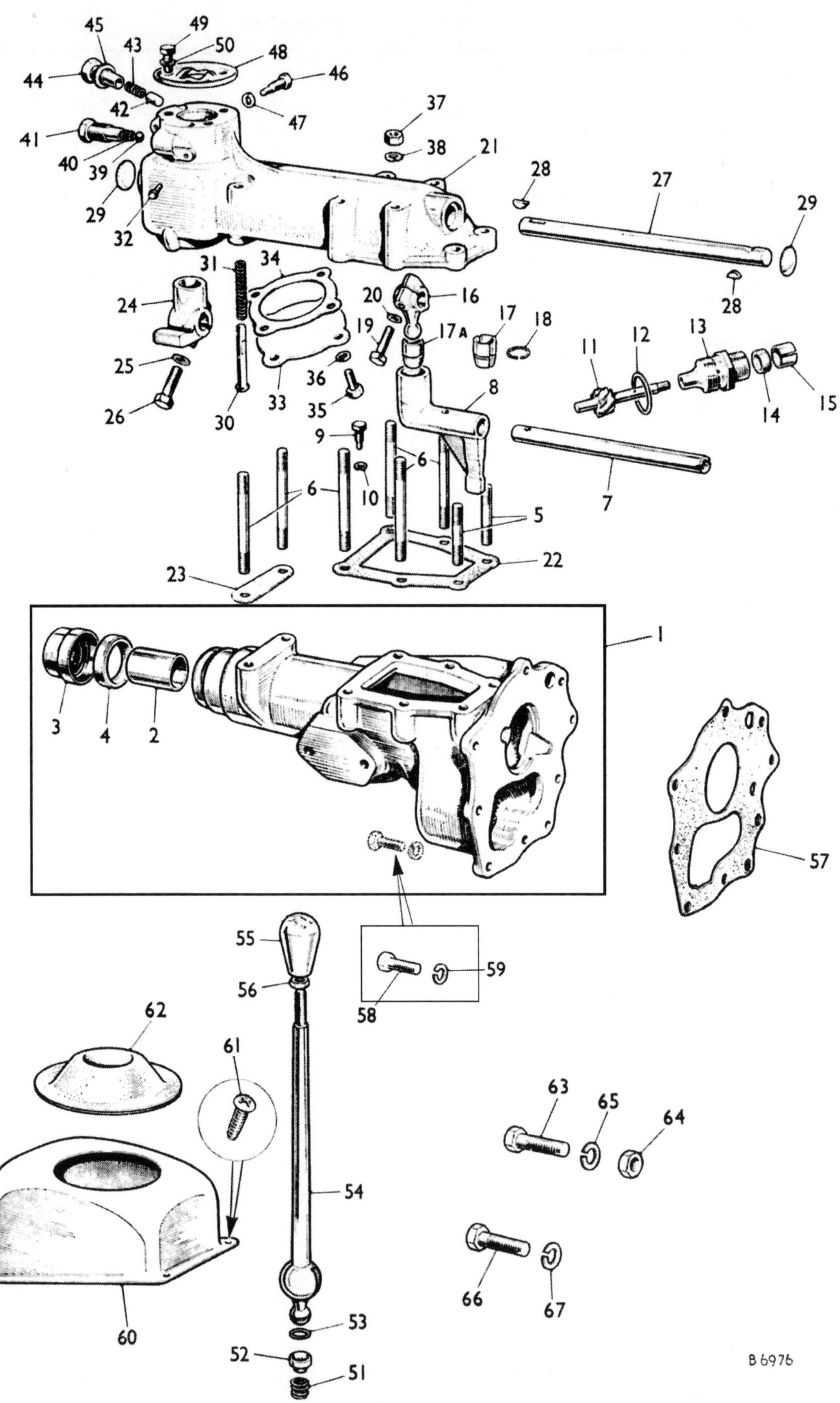
1
2
3
4
5
6
7
8
9
10
11
12
13
14
15
16
17
17A
18
19
20
21
22
23
24
25
26
27
28
29
30
31
32
33
34
35
36
37
38
39
40
41
42
43
44
45
46
47
48
49
50
51
52
53
54
55
56
57
58
59
60
61
62
63
64
65
66
67
B 6976

DESCRIPTION	Part No.	Illus. No.	Quantity	Change Point	REMARKS
9C Gearbox—*continued*					
Extension—gearbox (with bush, seal, and felt ring)	2A 3367	1	1		
Bush	2A 3325	2	1		
Seal—oil	2A 3061	3	1		
Gasket—oil seal	2A 3278	4	1		Use 3H 2110 for this application
Gasket—oil seal	3H 2110	4	1		
Stud—remote control housing—short	53K 528	5	2		
Stud—remote control housing—long	53K 535	6	6		
Shaft—control	88G 217	7	1		Part No. change; was 2A 3350 and 22A 183
Lever—control	2A 3384	8	1		
Peg—lever locating	1H 3101	9	1		
Washer—spring	LWZ 204	10	1		
Pinion—speedometer	†2A 3372	11	1	(E) 9C/U/H101 to H5678	W.S.E. use 2A 3420
Pinion—speedometer	2A 3420	11	1	(C) 9C/U/H5679 on	
Gasket—pinion bush (copper)	88G 208	12	1		Part No. change; was 51K 3169 and 11G 3084
Bush—pinion (brass)	2A 3256	13	1	(G) 101 to 21266	
Bush—pinion (Nylon)	2A 3664	13	1	(G) 21267 on	
Seal—oil pinion	2A 3254	14	1		
Ring—oil seal retaining	2A 3255	15	1		
Lever—front selector	2A 3385	16	1		
Bush—selector—in halves	2A 3377	17	1	(G) 101 to 14494	W.S.E. use 2A 3468
Circlip—bush	1G 3709	18	1	(G) 101 to 14494	W.S.E. use 2A 3468
Bush—selector	2A 3468	17A	1	(G) 14495 on	
Screw	2A 3352	19	1		
Washer—spring	LWZ 204	20	1		
Casing—remote control	88G 218	21	1		Part No. change; was 2A 3380 and 2A 3411
Gasket—casing to extension—front	2A 3344	22	1		
Gasket—casing to extension—rear	2A 3345	23	1		
Lever—selector—rear	2A 3388	24	1		
Screw	2A 3335	26	1		
Washer—spring	LWZ 205	25	1		
Shaft—remote control	2A 3375	27	1		
Key	WKN 404	28	2		
Plug—welch—remote control housing	2K 8158	29	2		
Plunger—reverse selector	1G 3707	30	1		
Spring—plunger	1G 3863	31	1		
Pin—locating—reverse selector plunger	2A 3378	32	1		

† Revised Information.

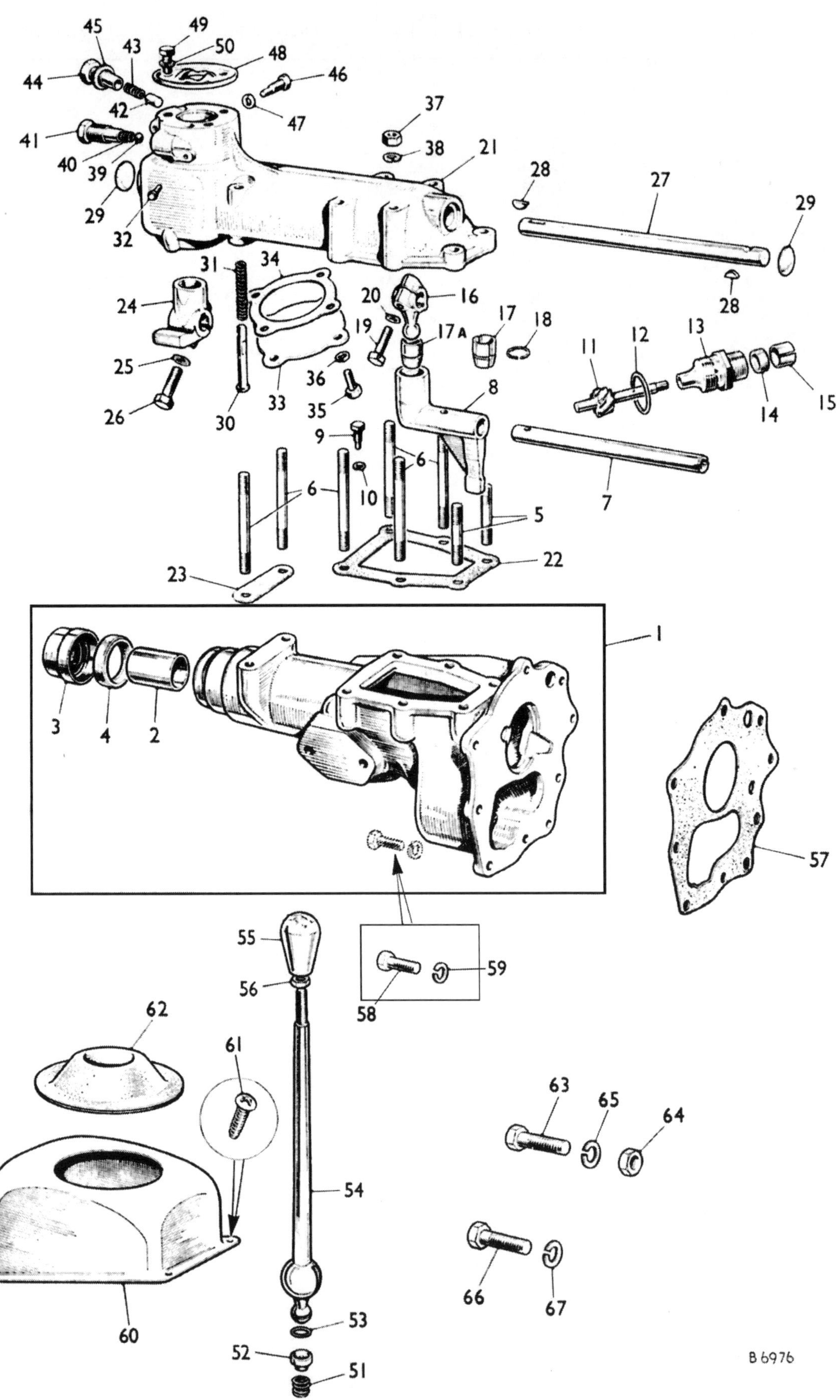
45
49
43
50
48
44
46
42
47
37
41
38
21
40
39
28
27
29
29
32
28
31
34
24
20
16
17
18
19
17A
11
12
13
25
36
33
35
8
14
15
26
30
9
6
10
6
7
5
23
22
1
3
4
2
57
55
59
56
58
62
61
63
65
64
54
66
67
60
53
52
51
B 6976

	DESCRIPTION	Part No.	Illus. No.	Quantity	Change Point	REMARKS
	9C Gearbox—*continued*					
	Cover—change speed lever tower—bottom	2A 3340	33	1		
	Gasket	†2A 3341	34	1		
	Screw	HZS 0404	35	4		
	Washer—spring	LWZ 204	36	4		
	Nut—stud—casing to extension	FNZ 105	37	8		
	Washer—spring	LWZ 305	38	8		
	Ball—reverse selector plunger	BLS 110	39	1		
	Spring—plunger	†2K 4909	40	1		W.S.E. use 22A 75
	Spring—plunger	22A 75	40	1		
	Plug—reverse plunger	2A 3379	41	1		
	Plunger—anti-rattle	AEG 3124	42	2	(E) 9C/U/H101 to H25508	
	Plunger—anti-rattle	22A 84	42	2	(E) 9C/U/H25509 on	
	Spring—plunger	AEG 3123	43	2		
	Cap—spring—retaining	2A 3354	44	2	(E) 9C/U/H101 to H25508	
	Cap—spring—retaining	22A 85	44	2	(E) 9C/U/H25509 on	
	Washer—spring	AEG 3122	45	2		
	Peg—change speed lever locating	1H 3101	46	1		
	Washer—spring	LWZ 304	47	1		
	Cover—change speed lever seat	2A 3339	48	1		
	Screw	HZS 0405	49	3		
	Washer—spring	LWZ 305	50	3		
	Spring—thrust button	2A 3390	51	1		
	Button—thrust—change speed lever	†2A 3389	52	1		W.S.E. use 2A 3467
	Button—thrust—change speed lever	2A 3467	52	1		
	Ring—change speed lever (rubber)	TRS 0710	53	1		
	Lever—change speed	2A 3416	54	1		
	Knob—lever	†2A 3383	55	1	(G) 101 to 11521	] W.S.E. use 22G 110
		†AEA 3188	55	1		]
		†22G 110	55	1		Correction; was 22G 210
	Nut—lock	53K 1722	56	1		For use with knob 2A 3383
	Gasket—extension to gearbox	†2A 3295	57	1		
	Screw—extension to gearbox	HZS 0407	58	9		
	Washer—spring	LWN 204	59	9		
	Cover—remote control	BLA 768	60	1		
	Screw	PTZ 803	61	4		
	Grommet	ACA 5208	62	1		
	Bolt—gearbox to mounting plate	HZS 0509	63	3		
	Nut	FNZ 105	64	3		
	Washer—spring	LWN 305	65	8		
	Screw—gearbox to mounting plate	HZS 0509	66	5		
	Washer—spring	LWN 305	67	5		

† Revised Information.

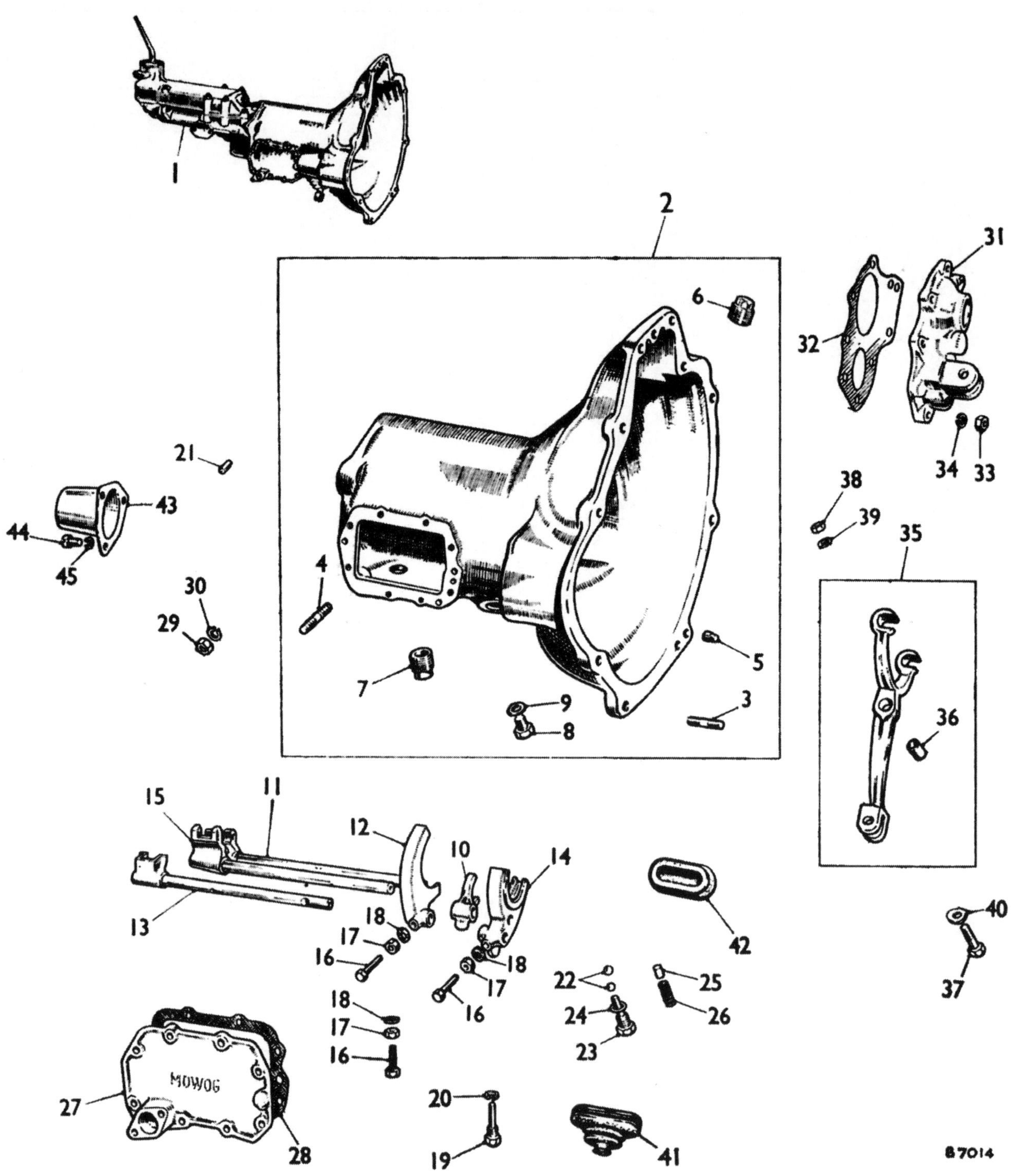
1
2
3
4
5
6
7
8
9
10
11
12
13
14
15
16
17
18
19
20
21
22
23
24
25
26
27
MOWOG
28
29
30
31
32
33
34
35
36
37
38
39
40
41
42
43
44
45
87014

GEARBOX 950-cc—9CG

	Page	Plate
CASE ASSEMBLY...	MF 9	F 4
CONTROL—REMOTE	MF 12	F 6
COVERS—SIDE AND FRONT	MF 9	F 4
EXTENSION—GEARBOX	MF 12	F 6
GEARBOX ASSEMBLY	MF 9	F 4
GEARS—2nd and 3rd SPEED	MF 11	F 5
†LAYGEAR—LAYSHAFT	MF 10	F 5
LEVER—CHANGE SPEED	MF 12	F 6
PINION—SPEEDOMETER	MF 12	F 6
RODS—FORK	MF 9	F 4
SELECTORS	MF 12	F 6
SHAFTS—1st AND 3rd MOTION	MF 10	F 5
SYNCHRONIZERS	MF 11	F 5
WHEEL—REVERSE	MF 11	F 5

9CG GEARBOX

* Cones are machine-finished after being shrunk on gears, supplied loose where facilities for these operations exist. (Assemblies must always be supplied for Export.)

DESCRIPTION	Part No.	Illus. No.	Quantity	Change Point	REMARKS
Gearbox assembly	AEA 3031	1	1	(E) 9CG/Da/H101 to H2140	
Gearbox assembly	AEA 3021	1	1	(E) 9CG/Da/H2141 on	
Case assembly	†28G 87	2	1	(E) 9CG/Da/H101 to H2140	W.S.E. use 28G 152
Case assembly	28G 152	2	1	(E) 9CG/Da/H2141 on	
Stud—front cover	53K 468	3	7		
Stud—side cover	53K 468	4	8		
Dowel	1G 752	5	1		
Plug					
Filler	2K 5830	6	1		
Drain	2K 5830	7	1		
Reverse plunger spring	6K 643	8	1		
Washer—plug	2K 4956	9	1		
Fork—reverse	2A 3284	10	1		
Rod—reverse fork	22A 198	11	1		
Fork—1st and 2nd speed	2A 3019	12	1		
Rod—1st and 2nd speed fork	2A 3305	13	1		
Fork—3rd and 4th speed	2A 3021	14	1		
Rod—3rd and 4th speed fork	2A 3347	15	1		
Screw—fork locating	2A 3141	16	3		
Nut	FNN 504	17	3		
Washer—shakeproof	LWN 404	18	3		
Screw—locking—reverse shaft	2A 3023	19	1		
Washer—spring	LWN 204	20	1		
Plunger—interlock	2A 3110	21	1		
Ball—interlock	BLS 110	22	2		
Plug—interlock ball hole	2A 3253	23	1		
Washer—plug	2K 4956	24	1		
Plunger—fork rod	2A 3108	25	3		
Spring—plunger	22A 75	26	3		
Cover—side	88G 214	27	1		Part No. change; was 2A 3285 and 22A 170
Washer—joint—side cover	2A 3286	28	1		
Nut—side cover stud	FNZ 104	29	8		
Washer—spring	LWN 204	30	8		
Cover—front	2A 3087	31	1	(E) 9CG/Da/H101 to H2140	
Cover—front	22A 224	31	1	(E) 9CG/Da/H2141 on	
Gasket	2A 3007	32	1		
Nut—front cover stud	FNZ 104	33	7		
Washer—spring	LWN 304	34	7		
Lever—clutch withdrawal	2A 3406	35	1	(E) 9CG/Da/H101 to H2140	
Lever—clutch withdrawal	22A 219	35	1	(E) 9CG/Da/H2141 on	
Bush	2A 3006	36	1		
Bolt—clutch withdrawal lever	2A 3289	37	1		
Nut	FNZ 105	38	1		
Washer—spring	LWN 305	39	1		
Washer—lock	2K 5813	40	1		
Cover—dust—clutch withdrawal lever	1G 3667	41	1		
Cover—dust—bell housing	2A 3076	42	1		
Cover—starter pinion	1B 3346	43	1		
Screw	53K 1435	44	3		
Washer—spring	LWZ 304	45	3		

† Revised Information.

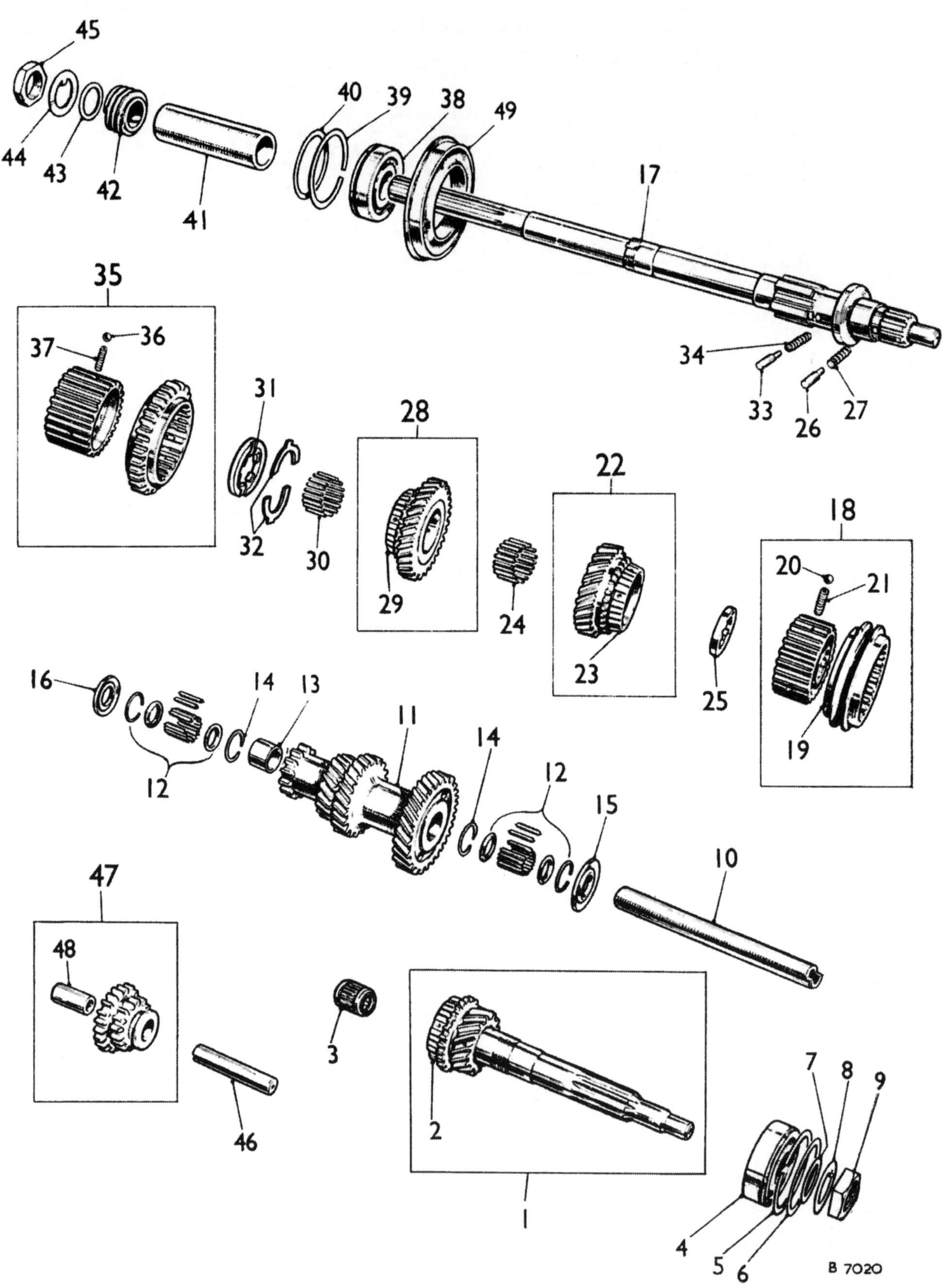
45
44
43
42
41
40
39
38
49
17
35
37
36
34
33
26
27
31
28
22
18
32
30
29
24
23
20
21
25
19
16
14
13
11
12
14
12
15
10
47
48
3
2
1
46
7
8
9
4
5
6
B 7020

9CG Gearbox—*continued*

* Cones are machined-finished after being shrunk on gears, supplied loose where facilities for these operations exist. (Assemblies must always be supplied for Export.)

DESCRIPTION	Part No.	Illus. No.	Quantity	Change Point	REMARKS
Shaft—1st motion (with cone)	†AEA 3022	1	1	(G) 101 to 20329	W.S.E. use AEA 3032
* Cone—synchronizing	†2A 3147	2	1		W.S.E. use 22A 138
Shaft—1st motion (with cone)	AEA 3032	1	1	(G) 20330 on	
* Cone—synchronizing	22A 138	2	1		
Bearing—3rd motion shaft	88G 409	3	1		Part No. change; was AEA 3203
Bearing—ball journal—1st motion shaft	2A 3245	4	1		
Ring—spring—bearing	6K 558	5	1		
Washer—packing—bearing					
·004″ (·1016 mm)	2K 8737	6	A/R		
·006″ (·1524 mm)	2K 8738	6	A/R		
·010″ (·254 mm)	2K 8739	6	A/R		
Washer—plain—shaft	6K 559	7	1		
Washer—lock—shaft	2A 3035	8	1		
Nut	2K 6677	9	1		
Layshaft	8G 664	10	1		
Laygear	22A 207	11	1		
Bearing—needle-roller	88G 396	12	2		Part No. change; was 3H 2113
Piece—distance—bearing	†2A 3168	13	1		W.S.E. use 22G 277
Piece—distance—bearing	22G 277	13	1		
Ring—spring—bearing	†2A 3366	14	2		W.S.E. use 22G 278
Ring—spring—bearing	22G 278	14	2		
Washer—thrust					
Front	2A 3023	15	1		
Rear—·123 to ·124″ (3·12 to 3·14 mm)	2A 3024	16	1		Alternative sizes
Rear—·125 to ·126″ (3·17 to 3·20 mm)	2A 3025	16	1		Alternative sizes
Rear—·127 to ·128″ (3·22 to 3·25 mm)	2A 3026	16	1		Alternative sizes
Rear—·130 to ·131″ (3·30 to 3·32 mm)	2A 3027	16	1		Alternative sizes
Shaft—3rd motion	AEA 3196	17	1		
Synchronizer assembly—3rd and 4th speed	28G 134	18	1		
Sleeve—3rd and 4th speed couplings	2A 3145	19	1		
Ball	BLS 107	20	3		
Spring	†2A 3142	21	3		W.S.E. use 22A 332
Spring	22A 332	21	3		

† Revised Information.

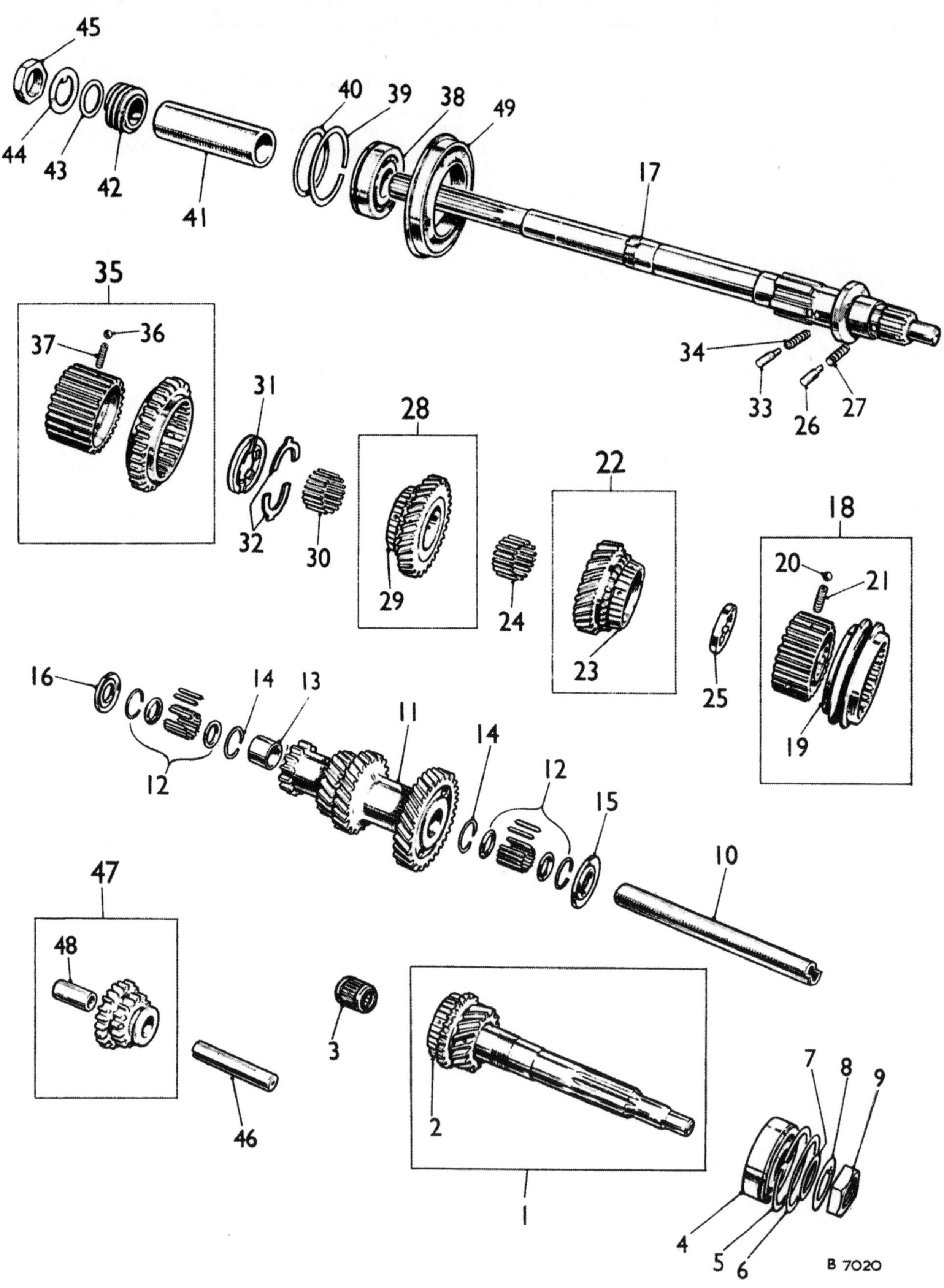
45
44
43
42
41
40
39
38
49
17
35
37
36
34
33
26
27
31
32
30
28
29
22
23
24
18
20
21
19
25
16
14
13
11
12
14
12
15
10
47
48
46
3
2
1
7
8
9
4
5
6
B 7020

9CG Gearbox—*continued*

* Cones are machined-finished after being shrunk on gears, supplied loose where facilities for these operations exist. (Assemblies must always be supplied for Export.)

	DESCRIPTION	Part No.	Illus. No.	Quantity	Change Point	REMARKS
	Gear—3rd speed (with cone)	†AEA 3025	22	1	(G) 101 to 20329	W.S.E. use AEA 3034
*	Cone—synchronizer	†2A 3147	23	1		W.S.E. use 22A 138
	Gear—3rd speed (with cone)	AEA 3304	22	1	(G) 20330 on	
*	Cone—synchronizer	22A 138	23	1		
	Bearing—needle roller	AEA 3201	24	28		
	Collar—locking	AEA 3204	25	1		
	Peg	AEA 3207	26	1		
	Spring—peg	2A 3161	27			
	Gear—2nd speed (with cone)	†AEA 3024	28	1	(G) 101 to 20329	W.S.E. use AEA 3033
*	Cone—synchronizing	†2A 3147	29	1		W.S.E. use 22A 138
	Gear—2nd speed (with cone)	AEA 3033	28	1	(G) 20330 on	
*	Cone—synchronizing	22A 138	29	1		
	Bearing—needle roller	AEA 3201	30	28		
	Collar—locking	AEA 3199	31	1		
	Washer	AEA 3200	32	2		
	Peg	2A 3160	33	1	(E) 9CG/Da/H101 to H33512 and L26637	
	Peg	22A 495	33	1	(E) 9CG/Da/H33513 on and L26638 on	
	Spring	2A 3161	34	1		
	1st speed wheel—2nd speed synchronizer assembly	AEA 3028	35	1		
	Wheel—1st speed	NSP		1		
	Synchronizer—2nd speed	NSP		1		
	Ball	BLS 107	36	3		
	Spring	†2A 3142	37	3		W.S.E. use 22A 332
	Spring	22A 332	37	3		
	Housing—bearing	2A 3085	37	1		
	Bearing—ball journal—3rd motion shaft	2A 3245	38	1		
	Ring—spring—bearing	6K 558	39	1		
	Washer—packing					
	·004″ (·1016 mm)	2K 8737	40	A/R		
	·006″ (·1524 mm)	2K 8738	40	A/R		
	·010″ (·254 mm)	2K 8739	40	A/R		
	Piece—distance—3rd motion shaft	2A 3057	41	1		
	Wheel—speedometer	2A 3371	42	1		
	Washer—plain	6K 559	43	1		
	Washer—lock	2A 3035	44	1		
	Nut	2K 6677	45	1		
	Shaft—reverse	88G 216	46	1		Part No. change; was 2A 3283 and 22A 131
	Wheel—reverse and bush	22A 204	47	1		
	Bush	2A 3282	48	1		

† Revised Information.

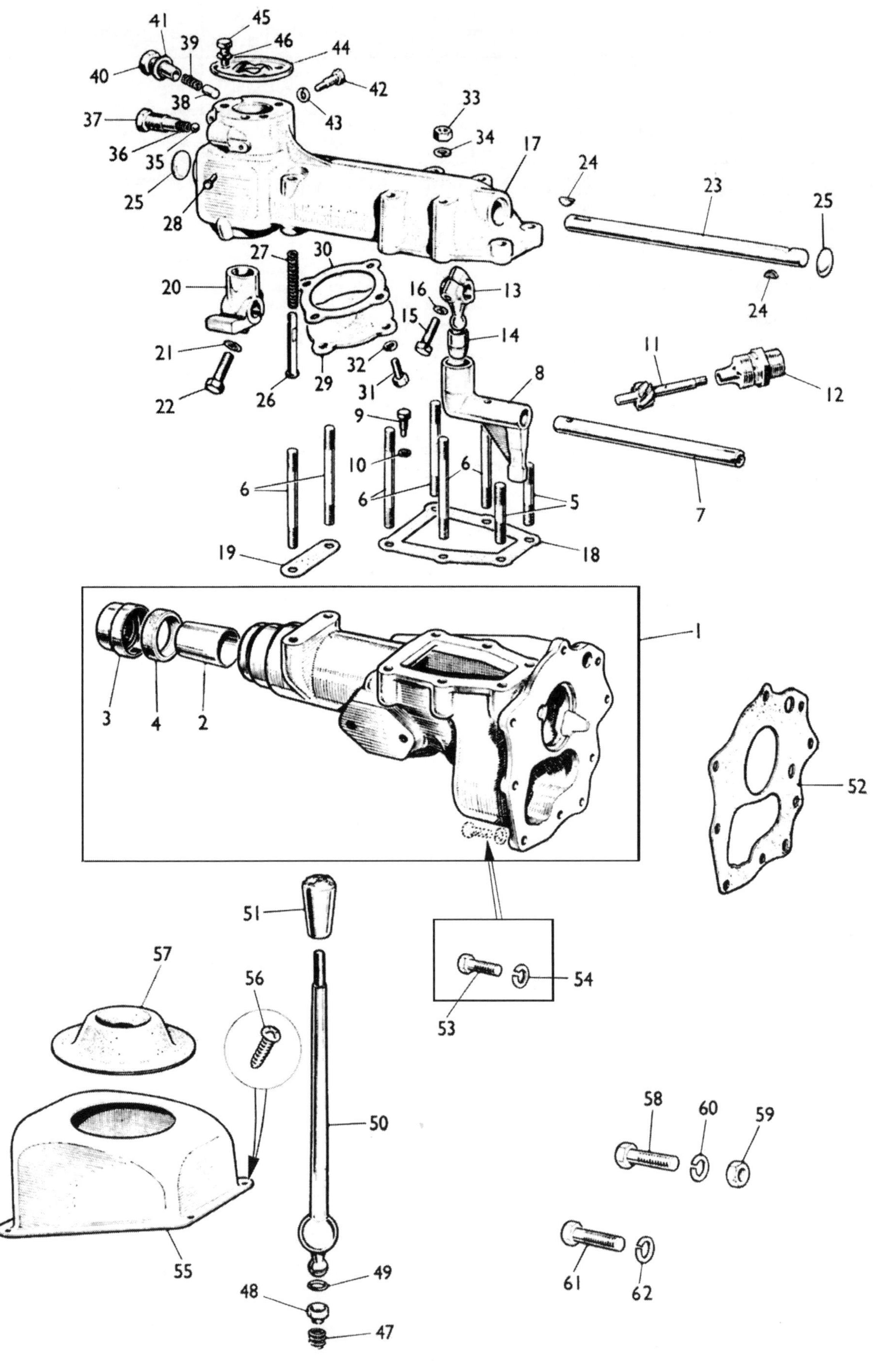

41
45
39
46
44
40
42
38
33
37
43
34
17
36
35
24
25
23
25
28
27
30
20
16
13
24
15
14
11
21
32
12
22
29
26
31
8
9
10
6
6
6
5
7
19
18
1
3
4
2
52
51
57
54
56
53
58
60
59
50
55
61
62
49
48
47

DESCRIPTION	Part No.	Illus. No.	Quantity	Change Point	REMARKS
9CG Gearbox—*continued*					
Extension—gearbox (with bush and seal)	2A 3367	1	1		
Bush	2A 3325	2	1		
Seal—oil	2A 3061	3	1		
Washer—joint—oil seal	3H 2110	4	1		
Stud—remote control housing—short	53K 528	5	2		
Stud—remote control housing—long	53K 535	6	6		
Shaft—control	88G 217	7	1		Part No. change; was 2A 3350 and 22A 183
Lever—control	2A 3384	8	1		
Peg—lever locating	1H 3101	9	1		
Washer—spring	LWZ 304	10	1		
Pinion—speedometer	2A 3420	11	1		
Seal—oil—pinion	22A 71	12	1		
Lever—selector—front	2A 3385	13	1		
Bush—selector	2A 3468	14	1		
Screw	2A 3352	15	1		
Washer—spring	LWZ 204	16	1		
Casing—remote control	88G 218	17	1		
Gasket—casing to extension—front	2A 3344	18	1		
Gasket—casing to extension—rear	2A 3345	19	1		
Lever—selector—rear	2A 3388	20	1		
Washer—spring	LWZ 205	21	1		
Screw	2A 3335	22	1		
Shaft—remote control	2A 3375	23	1		
Key	WKN 404	24	2		
Plug—welch—remote control housing	2K 8158	25	2		
Plunger—reverse selector	1G 3707	26	1		
Spring—plunger	1G 3863	27	1		
Pin—locating—plunger	2A 3378	28	1		
Cover—change speed tower—bottom	2A 3340	29	1		
Gasket	2A 3341	30	1		
Screw	HZS 0404	31	4		
Washer—spring	LWZ 204	32	4		
Nut	FNZ 105	33	8		
Washer—spring	LWZ 305	34	8		
Ball—reverse selector plunger	BLS 110	35	1		
Spring	22A 75	36	1		
Plug—detent—reverse selector plunger	2A 3379	37	1		
Plunger—control shaft damper	22A 84	38	2		
Spring	AEG 3123	39	2		
Cap—spring retaining	22A 85	40	2		
Washer—plain	AEG 3122	41	2		
Peg—change speed lever locating	1H 3101	42	1		
Washer—spring	LWZ 304	43	1		
Cover—change speed lever seat	2A 3339	44	1		
Screw	HZS 0405	45	3		
Washer—spring	LWZ 304	46	3		
Spring—thrust button	2A 3390	47	1		
Button—thrust	2A 3467	48	1		
Ring—change speed lever	TRS 0710	49	1		
Lever—change speed	2A 3416	50	1		
Knob—lever	†AEA 3188	51	1		W.S.E. use 22G 110
Knob—lever	†22G 110	51	1		Correction; was 22G 210
Gasket—extension to gearbox	2A 3295	52	1		
Screw—extension to gearbox	HZS 0407	52	9		
Washer—spring	LWN 304	54	9		
Cover—remote control	BLA 768	55	1		
Screw	PTZ 803	56	4		
Grommet—gear lever	ACA 5208	57	1		
Bolt—gearbox to mounting plate	HZS 0509	58	3		
Nut	FNZ 105	59	3		
Washer—spring	LWN 305	60	3		
Screw—gearbox to mounting plate	HZS 0509	61	5		
Washer—spring	LWN 305	62	5		

† Revised Information.

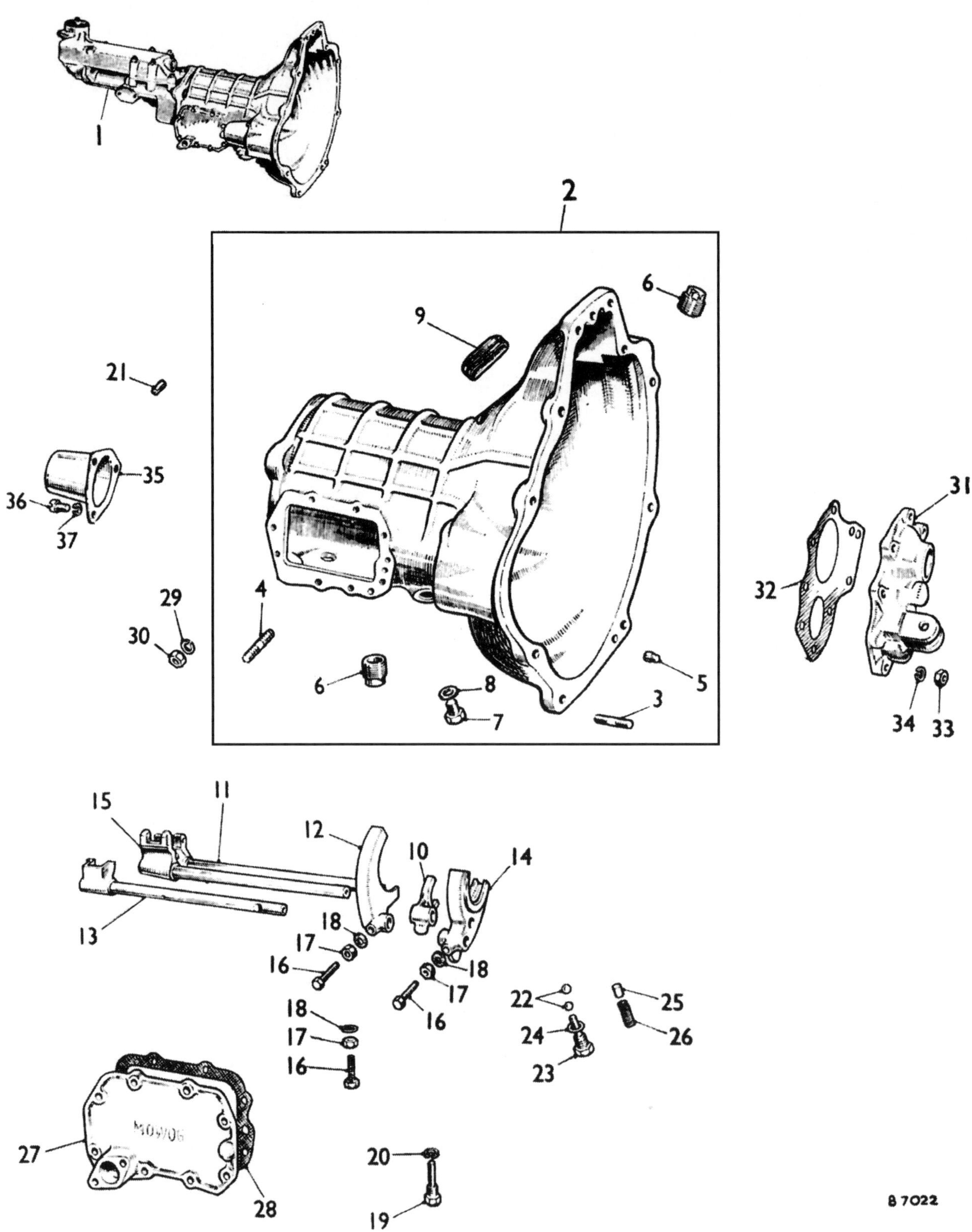
1
2
3
4
5
6
6
7
8
9
10
11
12
13
14
15
16
16
16
17
17
17
18
18
18
19
20
21
22
23
24
25
26
27
28
29
30
31
32
33
34
35
36
37
B 7022

GEARBOX 1098-cc—10CG

	Page	Plate
CASE ASSEMBLY...	MF 14	F 7
CONTROL—REMOTE	MF 17	F 9
COVERS—SIDE AND FRONT	MF 14	F 7
EXTENSION—GEARBOX	MF 17	F 9
GEARBOX ASSEMBLY	MF 14	F 7
GEARS—2nd AND 3rd SPEED	MF 16	F 8
†LAYGEAR—LAYSHAFT	MF 15	F 8
LEVER—CHANGE SPEED	MF 17	F 9
PINION—SPEEDOMETER	MF 17	F 9
RODS—FORK	MF 14	F 7
SELECTORS	MF 17	F 9
SHAFTS—1st AND 3rd MOTION	MF 15	F 7
SYNCHRONIZERS	MF 16	F 8
WHEEL—REVERSE	MF 16	F 8

10CG GEARBOX

DESCRIPTION	Part No.	Illus. No.	Quantity	Change Point	REMARKS
Gearbox assembly	38G 316	1	1		
Case assembly	38G 313	2	1		
Stud—front cover	53K 463	3	7		
Stud—side cover	53K 463	4	8		
Dowel	1G 752	5	1		
Plug—filler and drain	2K 5830	6	2		
Plug—reverse plunger spring	6K 643	7	1		
Washer—plug	2K 4956	8	1		
Cover—dust—bell housing	22G 199	9	1		
Fork—reverse	2A 3284	10	1		
Rod—reverse fork	22A 468	11	1		
Fork—1st and 2nd speed	22A 469	12	1		
Rod—1st and 2nd speed fork	22A 470	13	1		
Fork—3rd and 4th speed	22A 471	14	1		
Rod—3rd and 4th speed fork	22A 472	15	1		
Screw—fork locating	2A 3141	16	3		
Nut	FNN 504	17	3		
Washer—shakeproof	LWN 404	18	3		
Screw—locking—reverse shaft	2A 3028	19	1		
Washer—spring	LWN 204	20	1		
Plunger—interlocking	2A 3110	21	1		
Ball—interlocking	BLS 110	22	2		
Plug—interlocking—ball hole	2A 3253	23	1		
Washer—plain	2K 4856	24	1		
Plunger—fork rod	2A 3108	25	1		
Spring—plunger	22A 75	25	1		
Cover—side	88G 214	27	1		Part No. change; was 2A 3285 and 22A 170
Gasket—side cover	†2A 3286	28	1		
Washer—spring	LWN 304	29	8		
Nut	FNZ 104	30	8		
Cover—front	22G 118	31	1		
Gasket	†22G 165	32	1		
Nut	FNZ 104	33	7		
Washer—spring	LWN 304	34	7		
Cover—starter pinion	1B 3346	35	1		
Screw	53K 1435	36	3		
Washer—spring	LWN 204	37	3		

† Revised Information.

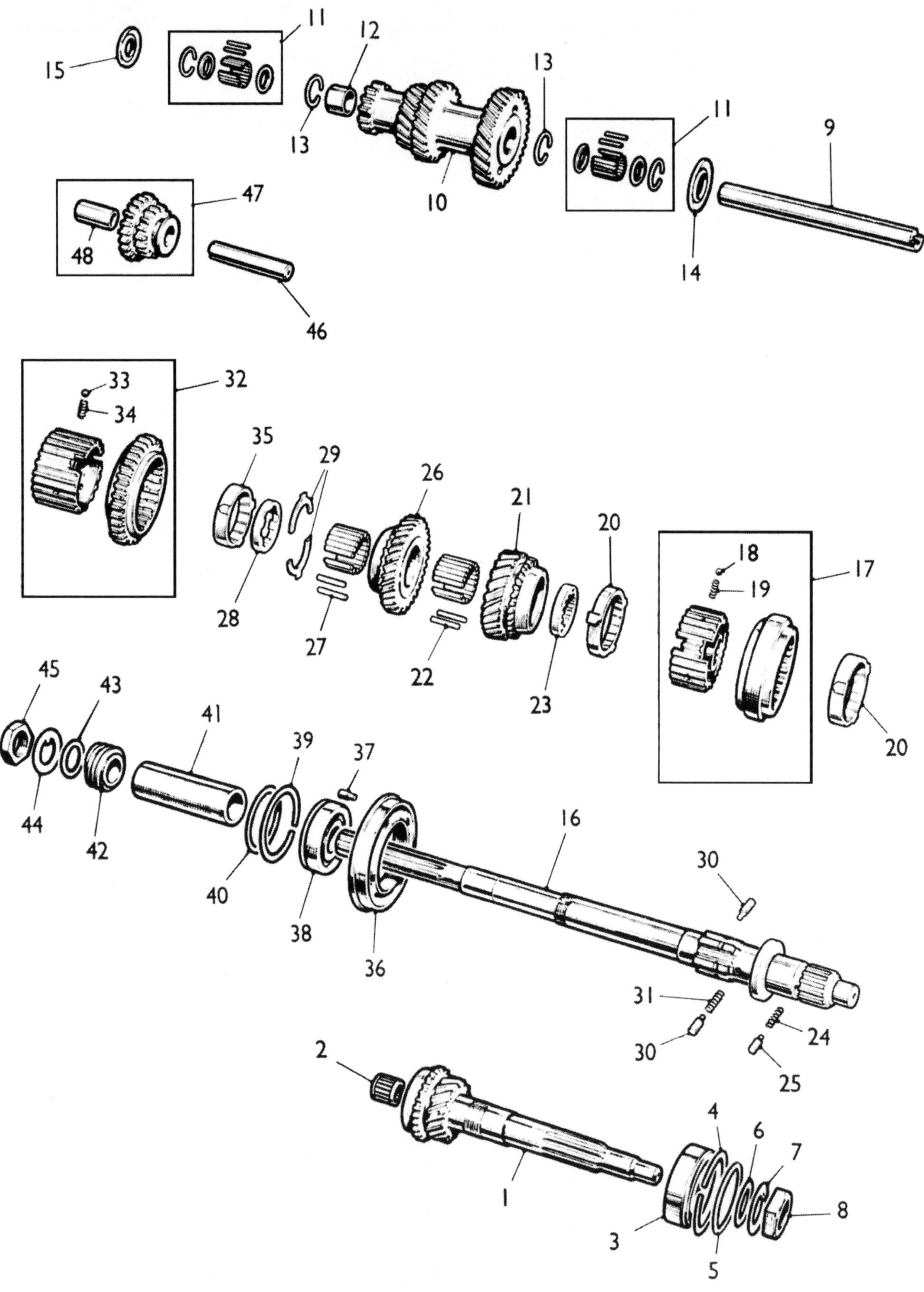
11
12
15
13
13
11
9
10
47
48
14
46
33
32
34
35
29
26
21
20
18
17
19
28
27
22
23
20
45
43
41
39
37
44
42
40
38
36
16
30
31
30
24
25
2
4
6
7
1
8
3
5

DESCRIPTION	Part No.	Illus. No.	Quantity	Change Point	REMARKS
10CG Gearbox—*continued*					
Shaft—1st motion	22G 172	1	1		
Bearing—3rd motion shaft	88G 409	2	1		Part No. change; was AEA 3203
Bearing—ball—1st motion shaft	2A 3245	3	1		
Ring—spring—bearing	6K 558	4	1		
Washer—packing					
·004″ (·1016 mm)	2K 8737	5	A/R		
·006″ (·1524 mm)	2K 8738	5	A/R		
·010″ (·254 mm)	2K 8739	5	A/R		
Washer—plain	6K 559	6	1		
Washer—lock	2A 3035	7	1		
Nut	2K 6677	8	1		
Layshaft	8G 664	9	1		
Laygear	22G 76	10	1		
Bearing—needle roller	88G 396	11	2		Part No. change; was 3H 2113
Piece—distance	†2A 3168	12	1		W.S.E. use 22G 277
Piece—distance	22G 277	12	1		
Ring—spring—bearing	2A 3366	13	2		W.S.E. use 22G 378
Ring—spring—bearing	†22G 278	13	2		
Washer—thrust					
Front	2A 3023	14	1		
Rear—·123 to ·124″ (3·12 to 3·14 mm)	2A 3024	15	1		Alternative sizes
Rear—·125 to ·126″ (3·17 to 3·20 mm)	2A 3025	15	1		Alternative sizes
Rear—·127 to ·128″ (3·22 to 3·25 mm)	2A 3026	15	1		Alternative sizes
Rear—·130 to ·131″ (3·30 to 3·32 mm)	2A 3027	15	1		Alternative sizes
Shaft—3rd motion	22G 146	16	1		
Synchronizer assembly—3rd and 4th speed	†22G 150	17	1		W.S.E. use 22G 318
Synchronizer assembly—3rd and 4th speed	22G 318	17	1		
Synchronizer—3rd and 4th speed	NSP		1		
Sleeve—coupling	NSP		1		
Ball	BLS 107	18	3		
Spring	22A 367	19	3		Use together with synchronizer assembly 22G 150
Spring	22G 317	19	3		Use together with synchronizer assembly 22G 318
Ring—baulk	†22G 64	20	2		W.S.E. use 22G 220
	†22A 517	20	2		W.S.E. use 22G 220
	†8G 743	20	2		W.S.E. use 22G 220
	22G 220	20	2		

† Revised Information.

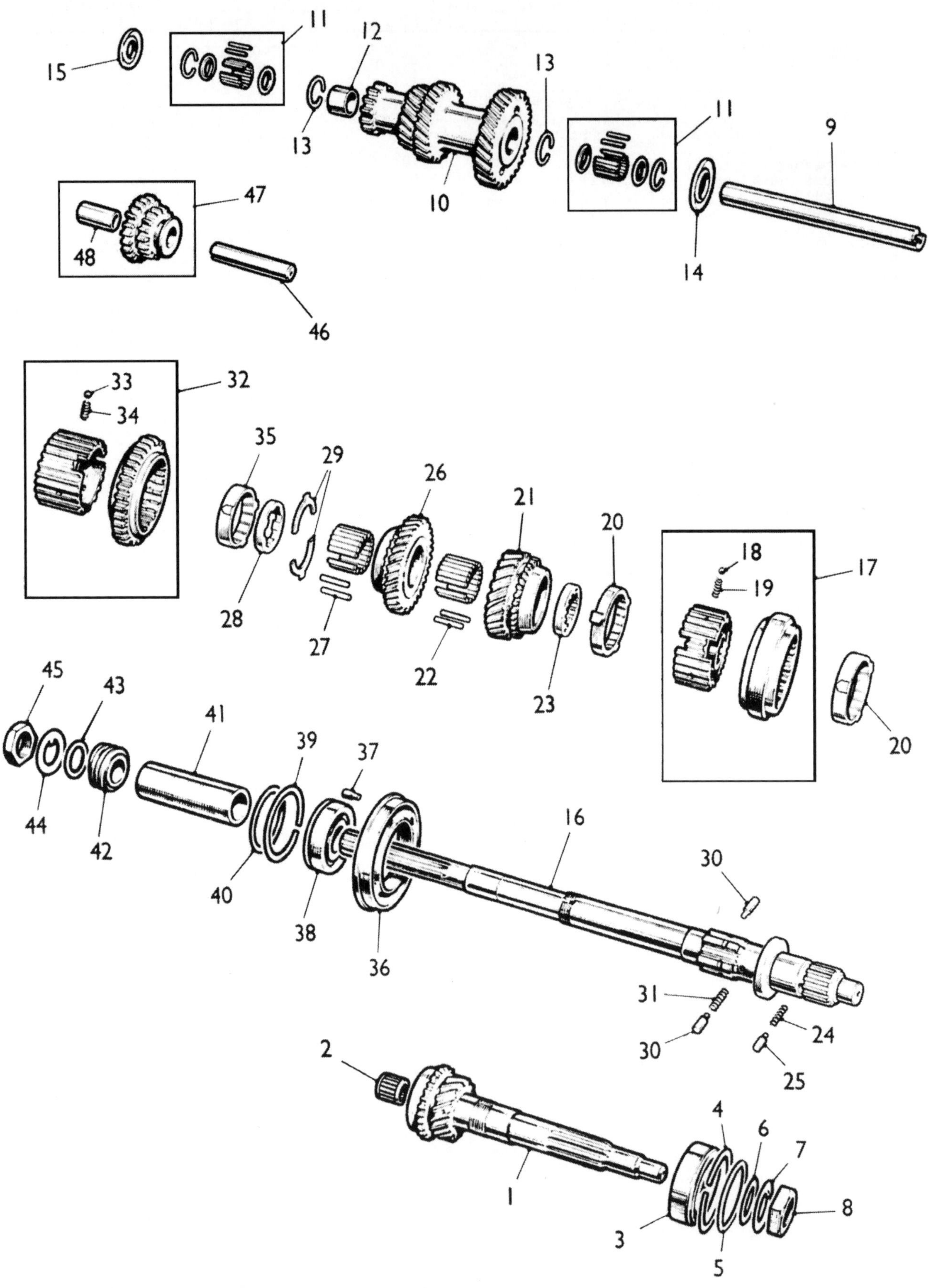
15
11
12
13
13
11
9
10
47
48
14
46
32
33
34
35
29
26
21
20
18
17
19
28
27
22
23
20
45
43
41
39
37
44
42
40
38
36
16
30
31
24
30
25
2
4
6
7
1
8
3
5

DESCRIPTION	Part No.	Illus. No.	Quantity	Change Point	REMARKS
10CG Gearbox—*continued*					
Gear—3rd speed	22G 148	21	1		
Bearing—needle roller	22G 149	22	26		
Collar—locking	22G 155	23	1		
Peg	22A 495	24	1		
Spring	22G 154	25	1		
Gear—2nd speed	22G 147	26	1		
Bearing—needle roller	22G 149	27	26		
Collar—locking	22G 156	28	1		
Washer—locking collar	22G 157	29	2		
Peg	22A 495	30	2		
Spring	22G 154	31	1		
1st speed wheel—2nd speed synchronizer assembly	†22G 161	32	1		W.S.E. use 22G 257
1st speed wheel—2nd speed synchronizer assembly	22G 257	32	1		
Wheel—1st speed	NSP		1		
Synchronizer—2nd speed	NSP		1		
Ball	BLS 107	33	3		
Spring	22A 367	34	3		Use together with synchronizer assembly 22G 161
Spring	22G 317	34	3		Use together with synchronizer assembly 22G 257
Ring—baulk	†22G 64	35	1		W.S.E. use 8G 743
	†22A 517	35	1		W.S.E. use 8G 743
	8G 743	35	1		
Housing—bearing	†22A463	36	1		
Peg—locating	1G 3530	37	1		
Bearing—ball—3rd motion shaft	22A 465	38	1		
Ring—spring	6K 558	39	1		
Washer—packing					
·004″ (·1016 mm)	2K 8737	40	A/R		
·006″ (·1524 mm)	2K 8738	40	A/R		
·010″ (·254 mm)	2K 8739	40	A/R		
Piece—distance—3rd motion shaft	22A 466	41	1		
Wheel—speedometer	2A 3371	42	1		
Washer—plain	6K 559	43	1		
Washer—lock	2A 3035	44	1		
Nut	2K 6677	45	1		
Shaft—reverse	88G 216	46	1		Part No. change; was 2A 3283 and 22A 131
Wheel—reverse	22A 453	47	1		
Bush	2A 3282	48	1		

† Revised Information.

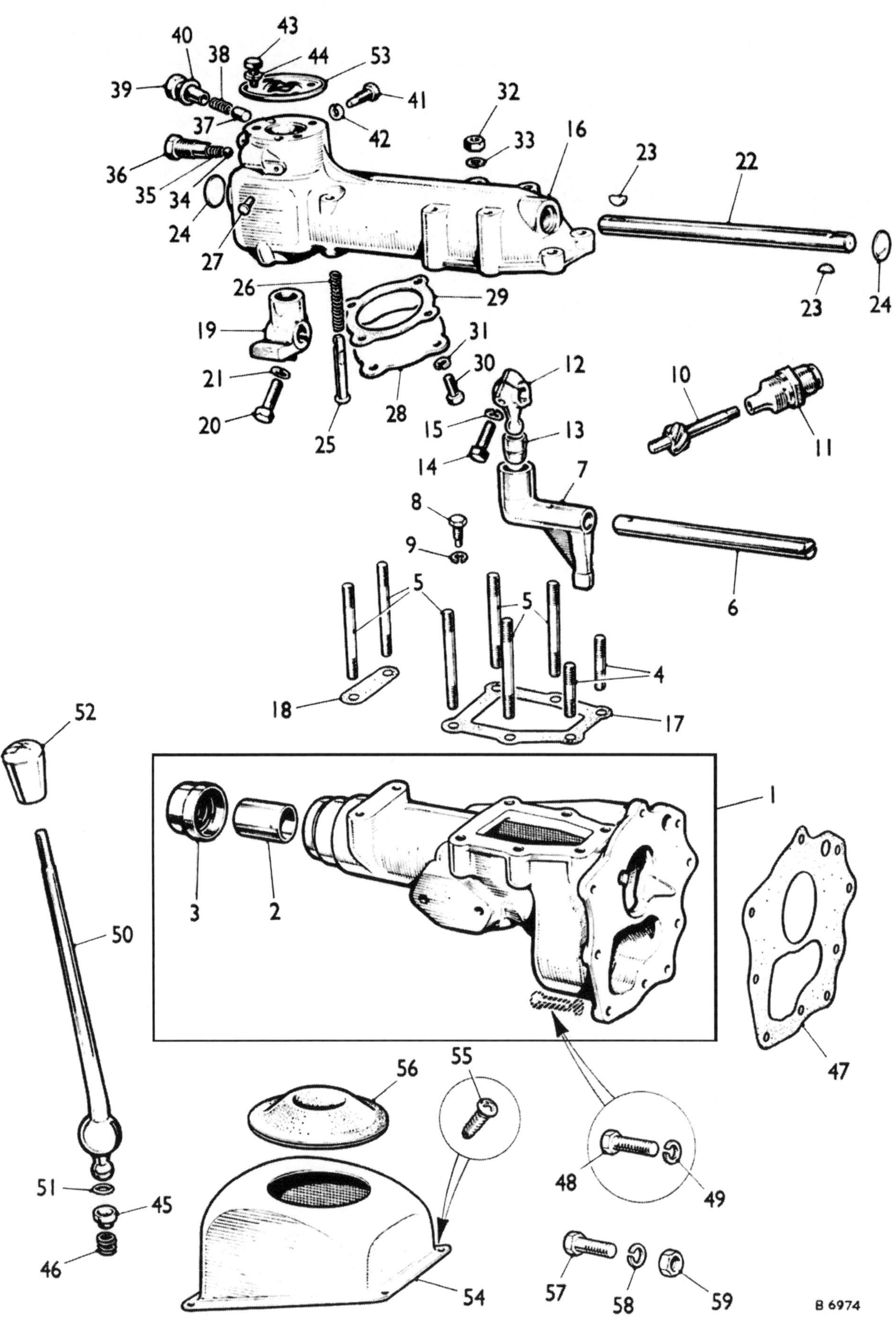
1
2
3
4
5
6
7
8
9
10
11
12
13
14
15
16
17
18
19
20
21
22
23
24
25
26
27
28
29
30
31
32
33
34
35
36
37
38
39
40
41
42
43
44
45
46
47
48
49
50
51
52
53
54
55
56
57
58
59
B 6974

DESCRIPTION	Part No.	Illus. No.	Quantity	Change Point	REMARKS
10CG Gearbox—*continued*					
Extension—gearbox (with bulb and seal)	22A 474	1	1		
Bush	2A 3325	2	1		
Seal—oil	2A 3061	3	1		
Stud—remote control housing—short	53K 528	4	2		
Stud—remote control housing—long	53K 538	5	6		
Shaft—control	22A 475	6	1		
Lever—control	22A 476	7	1		
Peg—lever locating	1H 3101	8	1		
Washer—spring	LWZ 304	9	1		
Pinion—speedometer	2A 3420	10	1		
Seal—oil—pinion	22A 71	11	1		
Lever—selector—front	2A 3385	12	1		
Bush—selector	2A 3468	13	1		
Screw	2A 3352	14	1		
Washer—spring	LWZ 204	15	1		
Casing—remote control	22A 480	16	1		
Gasket—casing to extension—front	2A 3344	17	1		
Gasket—casing to extension—rear	2A 3345	18	1		
Lever—selector—rear	2A 3388	19	1		
Screw	2A 3335	20	1		
Washer—spring	LWZ 205	21	1		
Shaft—remote control	2A 3375	22	1		
Key	WKN 404	23	2		
Plug—welch—remote control housing	2K 8158	24	2		
Plunger—reverse selector	1G 3707	25	1		
Spring	1G 3863	26	1		
Pin—locating—plunger	2A 3378	27	1		
Cover—change speed tower—bottom	2A 3340	28	1		
Gasket	2A 3341	29	1		
Screw	HZS 0404	30	4		
Washer—spring	LWZ 204	31	4		
Nut—stud—casing to extension	FNZ 105	32	8		
Washer—spring	LWZ 305	33	8		
Ball—reverse selector plunger	BLS 110	34	1		
Spring	22A 75	35	1		
Plug—reverse plunger	2A 3379	36	1		
Plunger—control shaft damper	22A 84	37	2		
Spring	AEG 3123	38	2		
Cap—spring retaining	22A 85	39	2		
Washer—plain	AEG 3122	40	2		
Peg—change speed lever—locating	1H 3101	41	1		
Washer—spring	LWZ 304	42	1		
Screw—change speed seat	HZS 0405	43	3		
Washer—spring	LWZ 304	44	3		
Button—thrust	2A 3467	45	1		
Spring—button	2A 3390	46	1		
Gasket—extension to gearbox	22A 481	47	1		
Screw	HZS 0407	48	9		
Washer—spring	LWN 304	49	9		
Lever—change speed	†22G 152	50	1		W.S.E. use 22G 328
Lever—change speed	†22G 328	50	1		
Ring—lever (rubber)	TRS 0710	51	1		
Knob—lever	22G 110	52	1		
Cover—change speed lever seat	2A 3339	53	1		
Cover—remote control	BLA 768	54	1		
Screw	PTZ 803	55	4		
Grommet—change speed lever	ACA 5208	56	1		
Bolt—gearbox to mounting plate	22G 173	57	8		
Washer—spring	LWN 305	58	8		
Nut	FNZ 105	59	3		

† Revised Information.

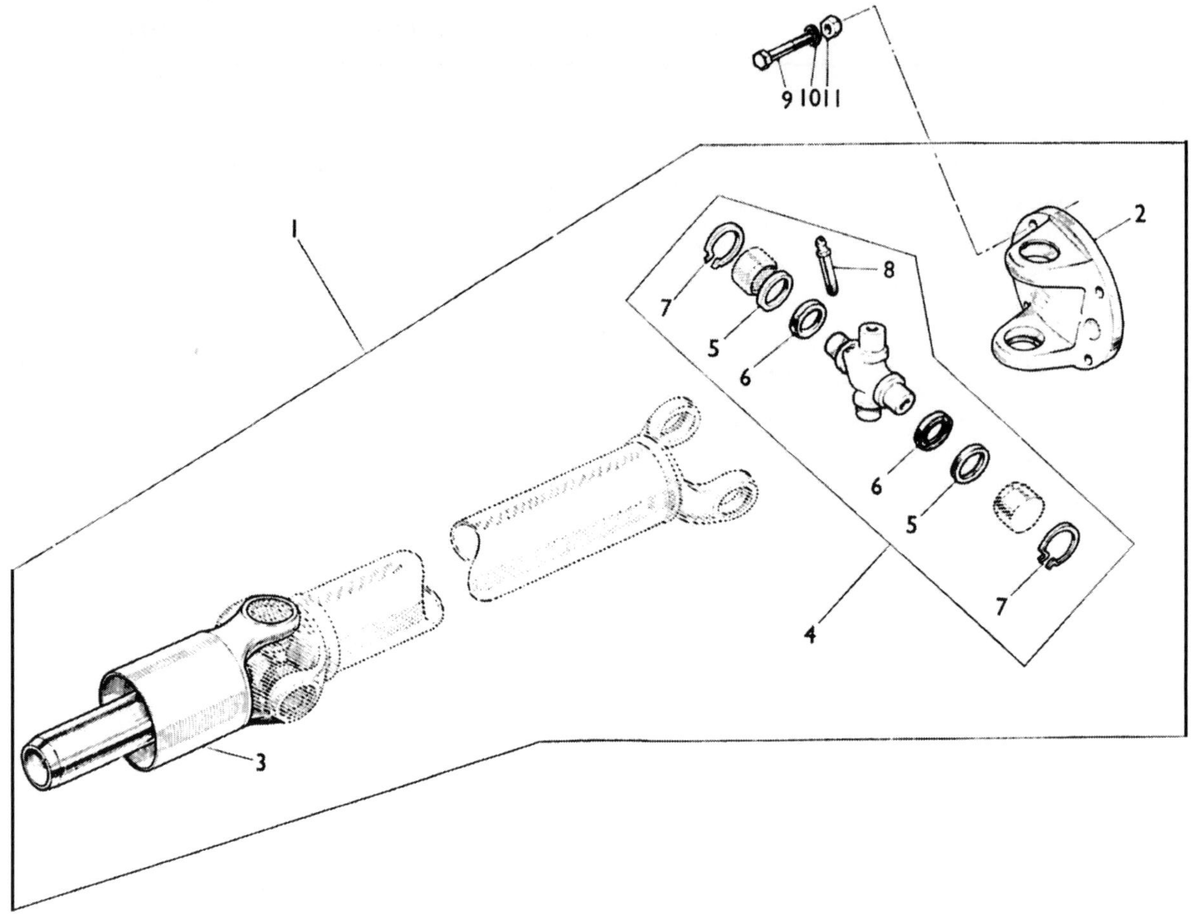
9 10 11
1
2
8
7
5
6
6
5
7
4
3

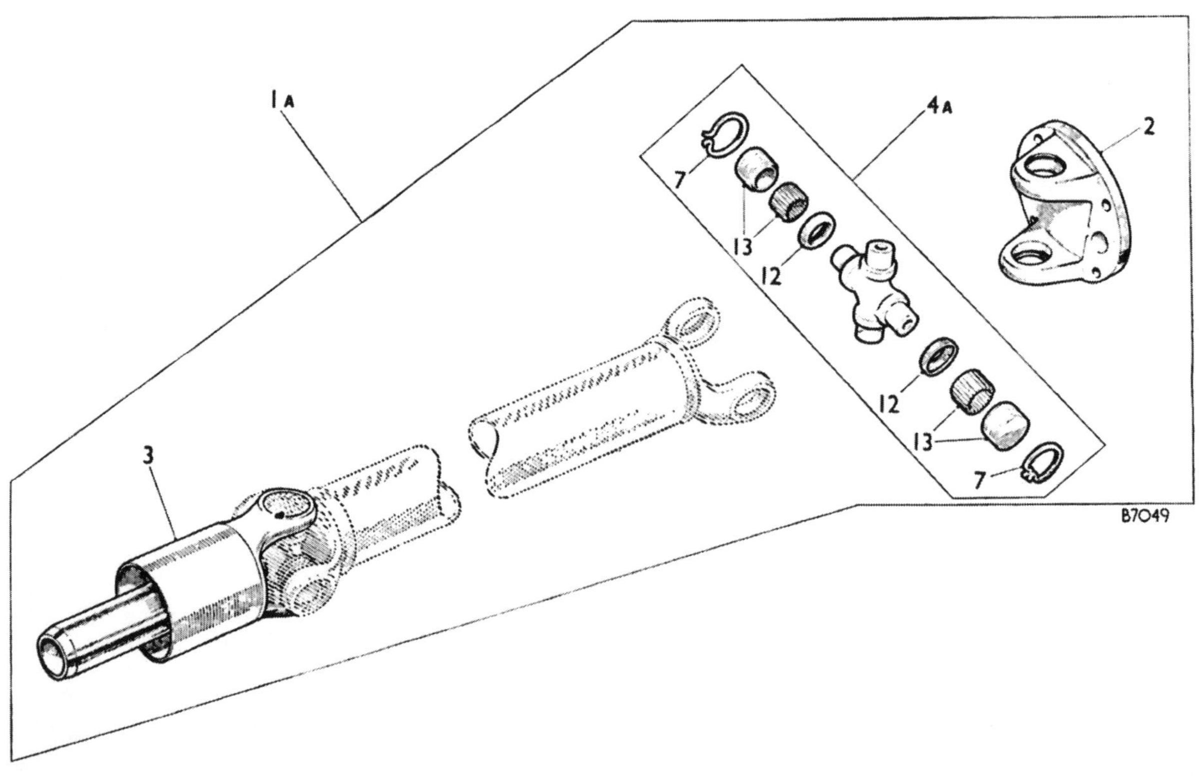
1A
4A
2
7
13
12
12
13
7
3
B7049

PROPELLER SHAFT

	Page	Plate
SHAFT—PROPELLER	MG 1	G 1

PROPELLER SHAFT

DESCRIPTION	Part No.	Illus. No.	Quantity	Change Point	REMARKS
Shaft assembly—propeller	2A 7272	1	1		Not available; use AHA 7928
Shaft	†NSP		1		Was 17H 3919
Flange—yoke	†17H 3828	2	1		
Sleeve—yoke	†17H 3894	3	1		
Journal assembly	†8G 3000	4	2		Not available; use 8G 8979
Gasket—journal	†17H 3818	5	8		
Retainer—gasket	†17H 3819	6	8		
Bearing—needle	7H 3874		8		
Circlip	†7H 3877	7	8		
Lubricator—journal	†7H 3858	8	2		
Shaft assembly—propeller	†AHA 7928	1A	1		
Flange—yoke	†17H 3828	2	1		
Sleeve—yoke	†17H 3894	3	1		
Journal assembly	†8G 8979	4A	2		
Seal—lip	†27H 4230	12	8		
Bearing—needle	†27H 4228	13	8		
Circlip	†7H 3877	7	8		
Bolt	†HBZ 0510	9	4		
Washer—spring	†LWZ 305	10	4		
Nut	†LNZ 205	11	4		Alternatives
Nut	†LNZ 105	11	4		Alternatives

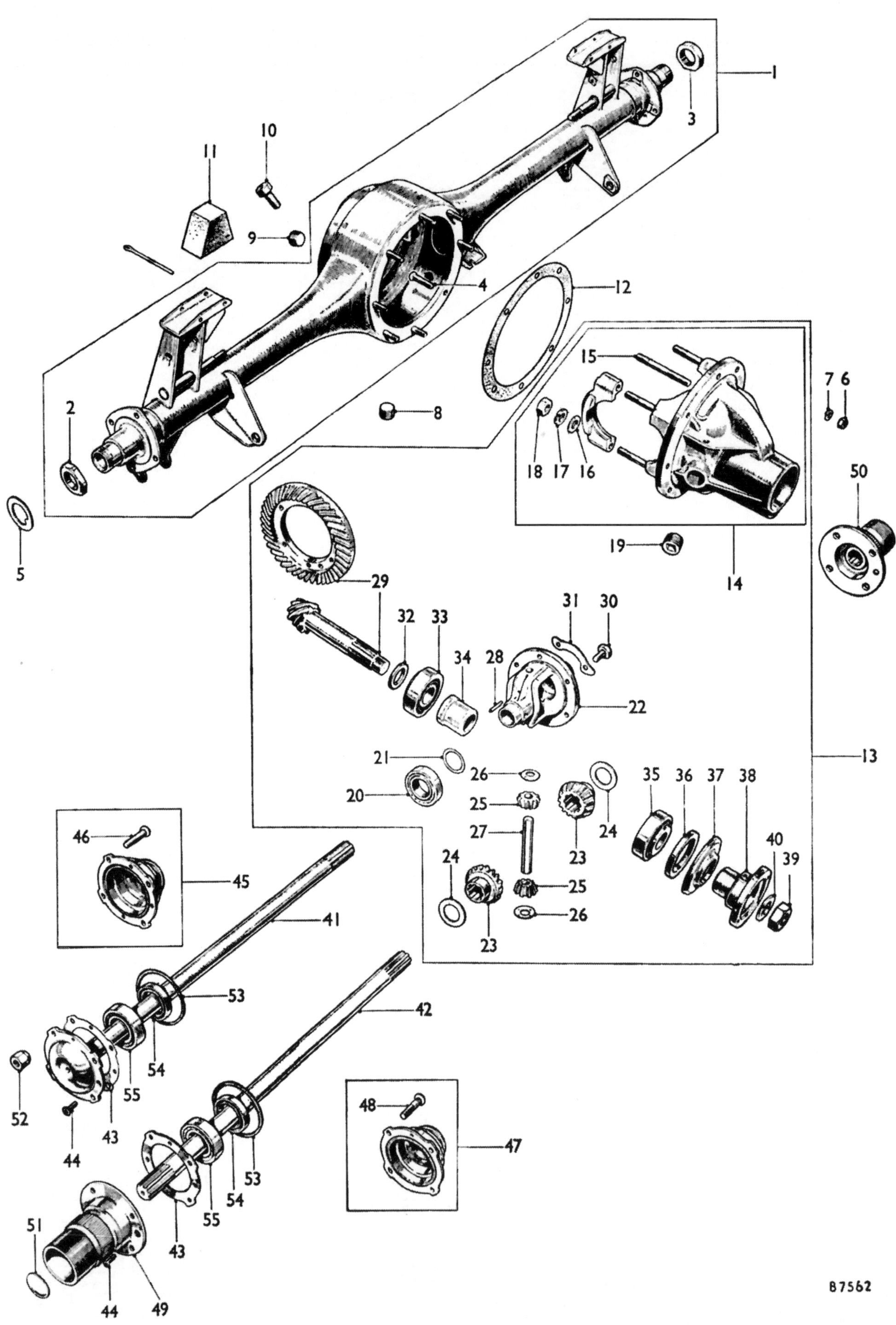
1
2
3
4
5
6
7
8
9
10
11
12
13
14
15
16
17
18
19
20
21
22
23
24
25
26
27
28
29
30
31
32
33
34
35
36
37
38
39
40
41
42
43
44
45
46
47
48
49
50
51
52
53
54
55
B7562

DESCRIPTION	Part No.	Illus. No.	Quantity	Change Point	REMARKS

REAR AXLE AND REAR SUSPENSION

	Page	Plate
BRAKE—REAR	MH 4	H 2
CASE—AXLE	MH 2	H 1
CROWN WHEEL AND PINION	MH 3	H 1
CYLINDER—WHEEL	MH 4	H 2
DIFFERENTIAL	MH 2	H 1
HUB	MH 3	H 1
SHAFT—AXLE	MH 3	H 1
SPRING—ROAD	MH 6	H 3

REAR AXLE AND REAR SUSPENSION

DESCRIPTION	Part No.	Illus. No.	Quantity	Change Point	REMARKS
Axle assembly	NSP		1		
Case assembly	ATA 7329	1	1	Fitted up to change over to ATA 7618	Not available; use ATA 7618
	ATA 7618	1	1	(C) H–AN5–4333 to 50116 (less 4471, 4622, 4680, and 4684) (C) H–AN6–see (1) foot of page (C) G–AN1–101 to 13554	
	BTA 568	1	1	(C) H–AN6–see (3) foot of page (C) G–AN1–13555 on	Disc wheels only
	BTA 569	1	1	(C) H–AN6–20812 on (C) G–AN2–16790 on	Wire wheels only
Nut—bearing retaining—RHT	2A 7103	2	1		
Nut—bearing retaining—LHT	1G 3584	3	1		
Stud—gear carrier	2A 7226	4	8		
Washer—lock—bearing retaining	2A 7250	5	2		
Nut—gear carrier to axle case	FNZ 105	6	8		
Washer—spring	LWZ 205	7	8		
Plug—drain	6K 499	8	1		
Plug—filler	6K 499	9	1		
Breather	1H 3364	10	1		
Bump (rubber)	2A 7142	11	2		
Washer—joint—axle case	2A 7027	12	1		
Differential assembly—9 × 38 teeth (4·222 to 1 ratio)	ATA 7326	13	1	(C) H–AN5–501 to 50116 (C) H–AN6–101 to 24731 (C) G–AN1–101 to 16183	
Carrier assembly	ATA 7082	14			
Differential assembly—9 × 38 teeth (4·222 to 1 ratio)	BTA 550	13	1	(C) H–AN7–24732 on (C) G–AN2–16184 on	
Carrier assembly	BTA 549	14	1		
Stud—bearing cap	51K 886	15	4		
Nut—stud	FNN 107	16	4		
Washer—plain	PWN 107	17	4		
Washer—spring	LWN 307	18	4		
Plug—filler	6K 499	19	1	(C) H–AN5–501 to 50116 (C) H–AN6–101 to 24731 (C) G–AN1–101 to 16183	
Bearing—differential	2K 5943	20	2		
Washer—bearing packing ·002″ (·0508 mm)	2K 7779	21	A/R		
·003″ (·0760 mm)	ATA 7269	21	A/R		
·004″ (·1016 mm)	2K 7778	21	A/R		
·010″ (·2540 mm)	2A 7271	21	A/R		
Cage—differential	ATA 7086	22	1		
Wheel—differential	ATA 7037	23	2		
Washer—thrust—differential wheel	ATA 7296	24	2	(C) H–AN5–501 to 50116 (C) H–AN6–101 to 24731 (C) G–AN1–101 to 16183	
Washer—thrust—differential wheel	ATA 7039	24	2	(C) H–AN7–24732 on (C) G–AN2–16184 on	
Pinion—differential	2A 7015	25	2		
Washer—thrust—pinion	ATA 7297	26	2	(C) H–AN5–501 to 50116 (C) H–AN6–101 to 24731 (C) G–AN1–101 to 16183	
Washer—thrust—pinion	2A 7062	26	2	(C) H–AN7–24732 on (C) G–AN2–16184 on	
Pin—pinion	2A 7016	27	1		
Peg—pinion pin	6K 631	28	1		

CHANGE POINTS

(1) (C) H–AN6–101 to 20544 (plus 20580, 20582, 20583, 20595, 20596, 20692 to 20696, 20741 to 20757, 20760, and 20788 to 20792)
(2) (C) H–AN6–12868 to 20544 (plus 20580, 20582, 20583, 20595, 20596, 20692 to 20696, 20741 to 20757, 20760, and 20788 to 20792)
(3) (C) H–AN6–20545 on (less 20580, 20582, 20583, 20595, 20596, 20692 to 20696, 20741 to 20757, 20760, and 20788 to 20792)
(4) (C) H–AN6–20545 to 24731 (less 20580, 20582, 20583, 20595, 20596, 20692 to 20696, 20741 to 20757, 20760, and 20788 to 20792)

† Revised Information.

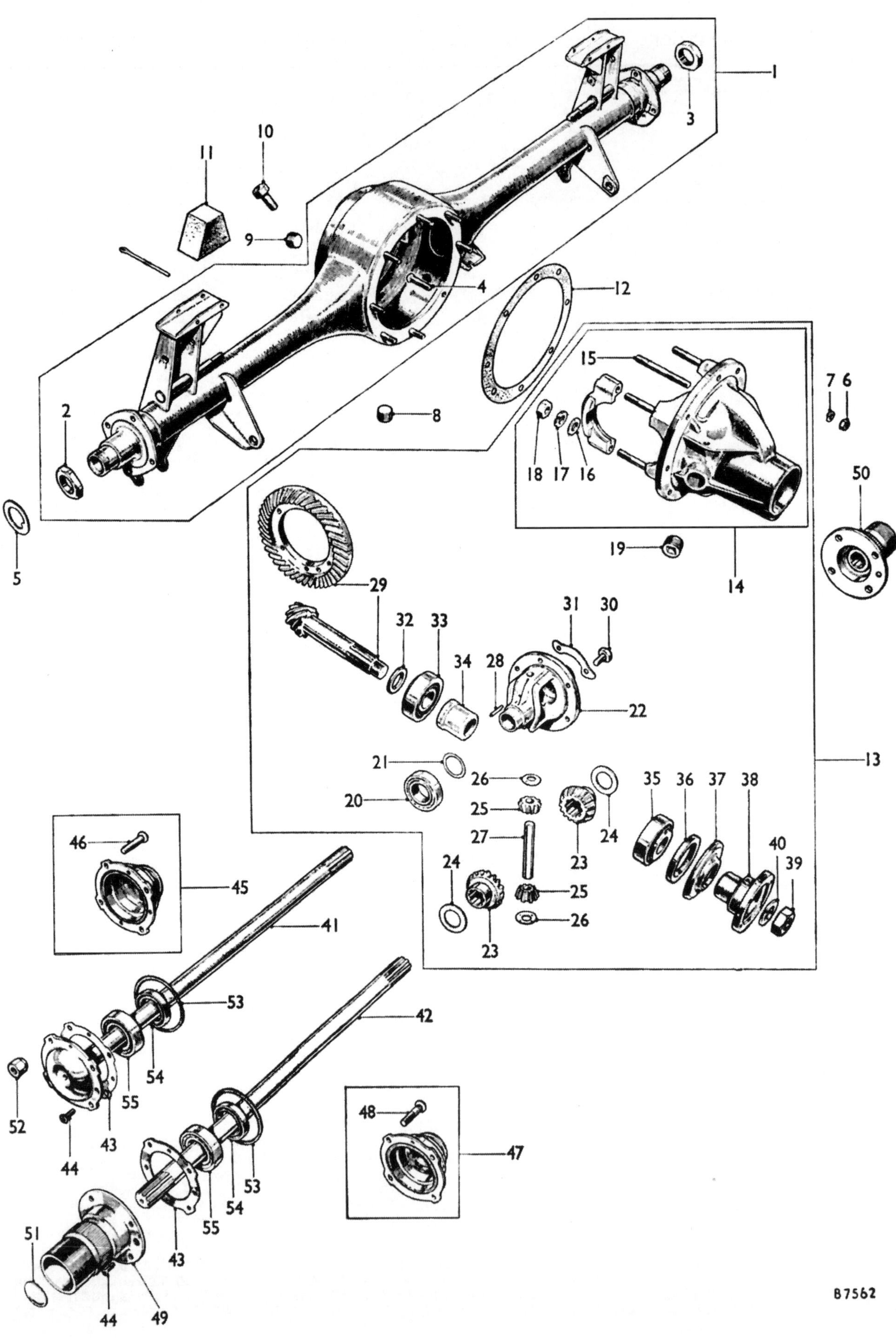
1
2
3
4
5
6
7
8
9
10
11
12
13
14
15
16
17
18
19
20
21
22
23
24
25
26
27
28
29
30
31
32
33
34
35
36
37
38
39
40
41
42
43
44
45
46
47
48
49
50
51
52
53
54
55
B7562

DESCRIPTION	Part No.	Illus. No.	Quantity	Change Point	REMARKS
Rear Axle and Rear Suspension—*continued*					
Crown wheel and pinion—9×38 teeth (4·222 to 1 ratio)	ATA 7266	29	1	(C) H-AN5-501 to 50116 (C) H-AN6-101 to 24731 (C) G-AN1-101 to 16183	
Crown wheel and pinion—9×38 teeth (4·222 to 1 ratio)	BTA 539	29	1	(C) H-AN7-24732 on (C) G-AN2-16184 on	
Bolt—crown wheel to differential cage	ATA 7043	30	6		W.S.E. use ATA 7232
Bolt—crown wheel to differential cage	ATA 7232	30	6		
Washer—tab	ATA 7044	31	3		
Washer—pinion thrust					
·130″ (3·301 mm)	ATA 7123	32	1		One used of selected size
·128″ (3·251 mm)	ATA 7124	32	1		One used of selected size
·126″ (3·200 mm)	ATA 7125	32	1		One used of selected size
·124″ (3·149 mm)	ATA 7126	32	1		One used of selected size
·122″ (3·098 mm)	ATA 7127	32	1		One used of selected size
·120″ (3·048 mm)	ATA 7128	32	1		One used of selected size
·118″ (2·996 mm)	ATA 7129	32	1		One used of selected size
·116″ (2·945 mm)	ATA 7130	32	1		One used of selected size
Bearing—pinion—inner	ATA 7328	33	1	(C) H-AN5-501 to 50116 (C) H-AN6-101 to 24731 (C) G-AN1-101 to 16183	
Spacer—bearing	ATA 7219	34	1	(C) H-AN5-501 to 50116 (C) H-AN6-101 to 24731 (C) G-AN1-101 to 16183	
Bearing—pinion—outer	2A 7213	35	1	(C) H-AN5-501 to 50116 (C) H-AN6-101 to 24731 (C) G-AN1-101 to 16183	
Bearing—pinion—inner	ATA 7166	33	1	(C) H-AN7-24732 on (C) G-AN2-16184 on	
Spacer—bearing	BTA 532	34	1	(C) H-AN7-24732 on (C) G-AN2-16184 on	
Bearing—pinion—outer	BTB 440	35	1	(C) H-AN7-24732 on (C) G-AN2-16184 on	
Seal—oil	88G 320	36	1		Part No. change; was ATA 7047
Cover—dust	†1G 7439	37	1		Correction; was 1G 7639
Flange—universal joint	ATA 7056	38	1		
Nut—pinion	FNN 612	39	1		
Washer—spring	LWZ 212	40	1		
Shaft—axle	2A 7085	41	2		W.S.E. use BTA 501
	2A 7242	41	2		Use BTA 501 for this application
	BTA 501	41	2		Disc wheels only
	BTA 491	42	2	(B) H-AN7-20812 on (B) G-AN1-16780 on	Wire wheels only
Washer—joint—shaft to hub	2A 7091	43	2		
Screw—shaft to hub	CMZ 0410	44	2		
Hub assembly	2A 7087	45	2		Disc wheels only
Stud—wheel	2A 7089	46	8		Disc wheels only
Hub assembly	BTA 490	47	2	(B) H-AN7-20812 on (B) G-AN1-16780 on	Wire wheels only
Stud—wheel	BTA 492	48	8	(B) H-AN7-20812 on (B) G-AN1-16780 on	Wire wheels only
Extension—hub—RH	BTA 488	49	1	(B) H-AN7-20812 on (B) G-AN1-16780 on	Wire wheels only
Extension—hub—LH	BTA 489	50	1	(B) H-AN7-20812 on (B) G-AN1-16780 on	Wire wheels only
Plug—welch	2K 8160	51	2	(B) H-AN7-20812 on (B) G-AN1-16780 on	Wire wheels only
Nut—wheel stud	88G 322	52	8		Part No. change; was 2A 8012 and ATA 7499
Ring—oil seal	ATA 7225	53	2		
Seal—oil	3H 2118	54	2		W.S.E. use BTA 108
Seal—oil	BTA 108	54	2		
Bearing—hub	AMK 777	55	2		Part No. change; was 6K 584

† Revised Information.

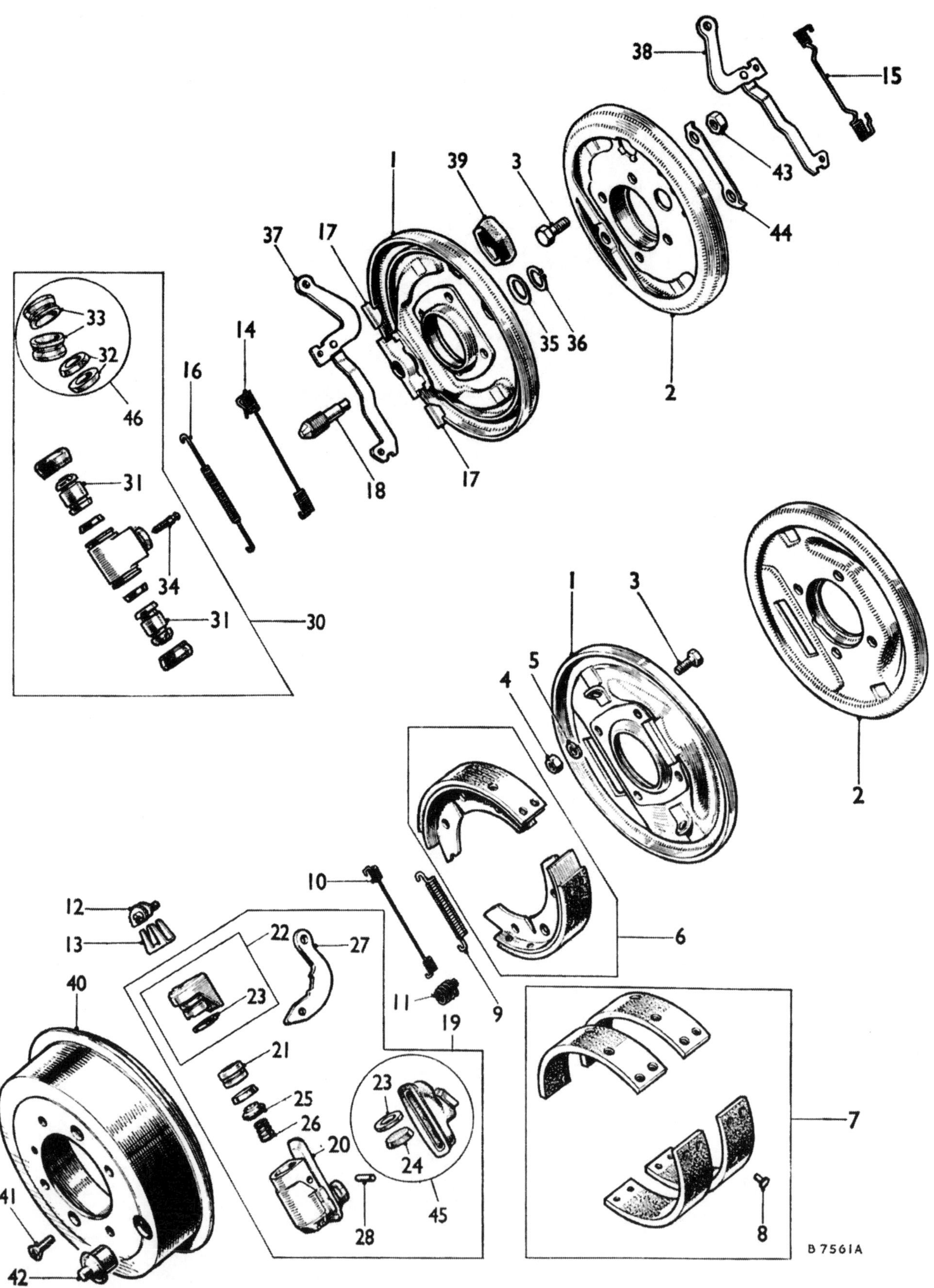
1
2
3
4
5
6
7
8
9
10
11
12
13
14
15
16
17
18
19
20
21
22
23
24
25
26
27
28
30
31
32
33
34
35
36
37
38
39
40
41
42
43
44
45
46
B 7561A

DESCRIPTION	Part No.	Illus. No.	Quantity	Change Point	REMARKS
Rear Axle and Rear Suspension—*continued*					
Plate—brake					
Right-hand	ATA 7076	1	1	(C) H–AN5–501 to 50116	
Left-hand	ATA 7077	2	1	(C) H–AN6 see (1) foot of page MH 2	
				(C) G–AN1–101 to 18554	
Right-hand	BTA 466	1	1	(C) H–AN6 see (4) foot of	
Left-hand	BTA 467	2	1	page MH 2	
				(C) H–AN7–24732 to 26912	
				(C) G–AN1–18555 to 16183	
				(C) G–AN2–16184 to 17834	
Right-hand	BTA 566	1	1	(C) H–AN7–26913 on	
Left-hand	BTA 567	2	1	(C) G–AN2–17835 on	
Screw	HZS 0506	3	8		
Nut	FNZ 105	4	8		
Washer—spring	LWZ 305	5	8		
Shoe assembly—brake (Not USA)	AJA 5086	6	2 sets	(C) H–AN5–501 to 50116	
Lining assembly (Not USA)	AAA 4692	7	1 box	(C) H–AN6–101 to 12867	
Rivet (Not USA)	7H 7398	8	28	(C) G–AN1–101 to 7897	
Shoe assembly—brake (Not USA)	8G 8671	6	2 sets	(C) H–AN6 see (2) foot of	
Lining assembly (Not USA)	8G 8672	7	1 box	page MH 2	
Rivet (Not USA)	7H 7398	8	28	(C) G–AN1–7898 to 12554	
Shoe assembly—brake (Not USA)	8G 8646	6	2 sets	(C) H–AN6 see (4) foot of	
Lining assembly (Not USA)	8G 8647	7	1 box	page MH 2	
Rivet (Not USA)	7H 7398	8	28	(C) G–AN1–18555 to 16183	
Shoe assembly—brake (Not USA)	8G 8762	6	2 sets		W.S.E. use 18G 8328
Lining assembly (Not USA)	†8G 8763	7	1 box		W.S.E. use 18G 8329
Rivet (Not USA)	7H 7398	8	28	(C) H–AN7–24732 on	
Shoe assembly—brake (USA)	18G 8328	6	2 sets	(C) G–AN2–16184 on	
Lining assembly (USA)	18G 8329	7	1 box		
Rivet (USA)	7H 7398	8	28		
Spring					
Shoe return—abutment end	AAA 4777	9	2	(C) H–AN5–501 to 50116	
Shoe return—cylinder end	AAA 4778	10	2	(C) H–AN6 see (1) foot of	
Brake shoe steady	AAA 4714	11	4	page MH 2	
Adjuster	AAA 423	12	2	(C) G–AN1–101 to 13554	
Mask—adjuster	AAA 421	13	2		
Spring—shoe return					
Cylinder end—RH	17H 7947	14	1	(C) H–AN6 see (4) foot of	
Cylinder end—LH	17H 7948	15	1	page MH 2	
Adjuster end	17H 7621	16	2	(C) H–AN7–24732 on	
Tappet	17H 7618	17	4	(C) G–AN1–13555 to 16183	
Wedge	17H 7619	18	2	(C) G–AN2–16184 on	

† Revised Information.

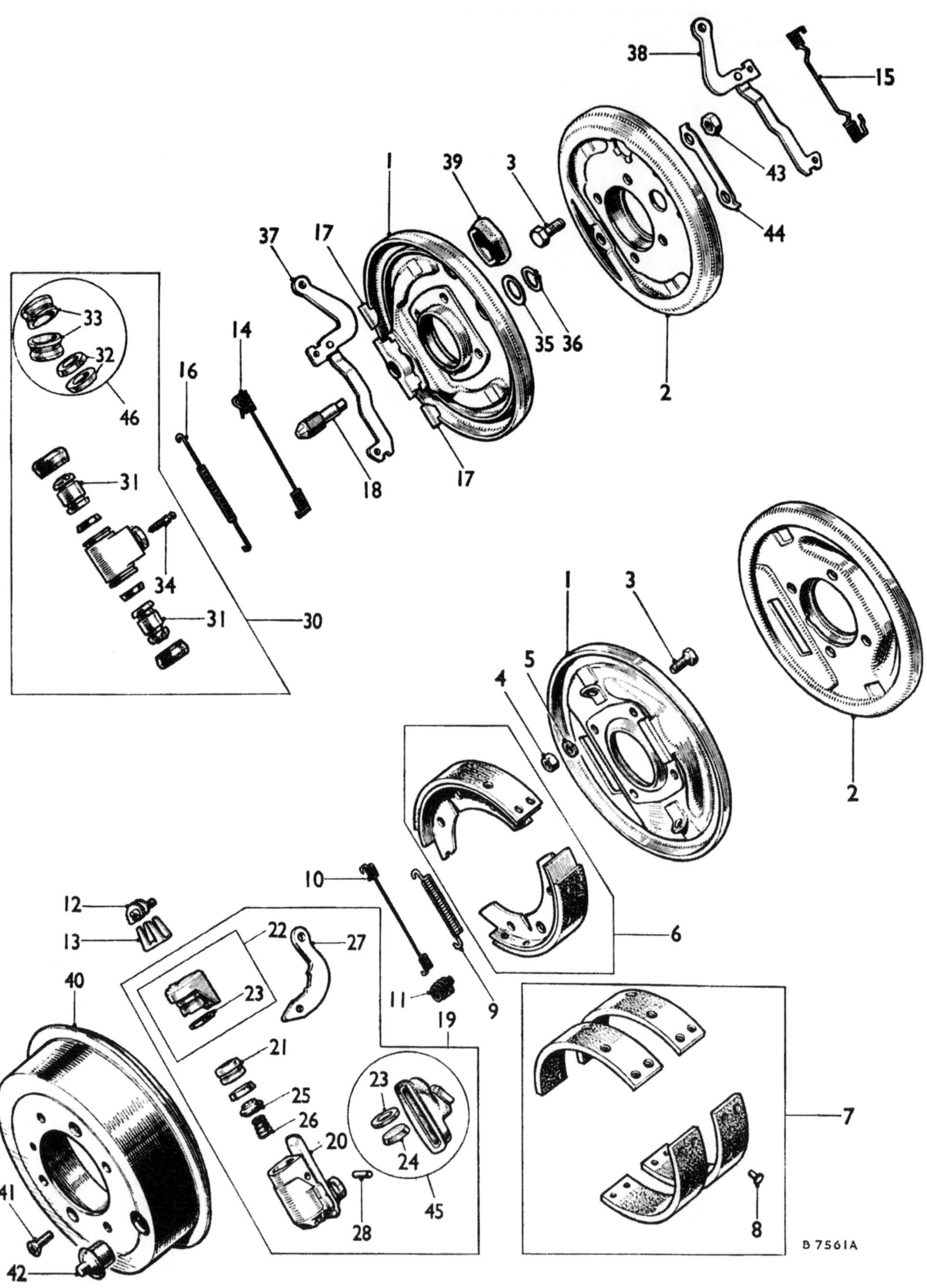
38
15
1
39
3
43
44
37
17
33
32
46
14
16
35 36
2
18
17
31
34
31
30
1
3
5
4
2
10
12
13
22
27
6
40
23
11
19
9
21
23
25
26
20
24
7
41
28
45
8
42
B 7561A

Rear Axle and Rear Suspension—*continued*

DESCRIPTION	Part No.	Illus. No.	Quantity	Change Point	REMARKS
Cylinder assembly—wheel	AAA 4775	19	2		
Body	7H 7942	20	2		
Piston—hydraulic	7H 7928	21	2		
Piston assembly (with dust cover)	AJA 5008	21	2		W.S.E. use AJA 5002
Piston assembly (with dust cover)	AJA 5002	22	2		
Seal	17H 7707	23	2		Also an included part
				(C) H-AN5-501 to 50116	of kit 8G 8243
Filler—cup	7H 7940	25	2	(C) H-AN6 see (1) foot of	
Spring—cup filler	7H 7939	26	2	page MH 2	
Lever—hand brake	27H 7395	27	2		
Pin—lever pivot	17H 7203	28	2		
Kit—repair—wheel cylinder	8G 8243	45	2		
Seal	17H 7707	23	2		
Cup	7H 7923	24	2		
Boot	NSP		2		Was 7H 7943
Boot—wheel cylinder	NSP		2		Was 7H 7943
Cylinder assembly—wheel	17H 2826	30	2		
Body	NSP		2		
Piston	17H 2827	31	4	(C) H-AN6 see (4) foot of	
Screw—bleed	17H 7623	34	2	page MH 2	
Kit—repair—wheel cylinder	8G 8741	46	2	(C) G-AN1-13555 to 16183	W.S.E. use 17H 7511
Seal	17H 7515	32	4		
Boot	17H 7766	33	4		W.S.E. use 17H 7511
Cylinder assembly—wheel	†17H 7861	30	2	(C) H-AN7-26732 to 26912	W.S.E. use 17H 8152
				(C) G-AN2-16184 to 17834	
	†7H 6993	30	2	(C) H-AN7-26913 to 29225	
				(C) G-AN2-17835 to 19299	
	17H 8152	30	2	(C) H-AN7-29226 on	
				(C) G-AN2-19300 on	
Body	NSP		2		
Piston	†17H 7626	31	4	(C) H-AN7-24732 to 29225	W.S.E. use 17H 8399
				(C) G-AN2-16184 to 19299	
Piston	17H 8399	31	4	(C) H-AN7-29226 on	
				(C) G-AN2-192300 on	
Screw—bleed	17H 7623	34	2		
Kit—repair—wheel cylinder	8G 8255	46	2	(C) H-AN7-24732 on	
Seal	NSP		4	(C) G-AN2-16184 on	Was 17H 7739
Boot	17H 7511	33	4		
Washer—Belleville	17H 7613	35	2	(C) H-AN6 see (4) foot of	
				page MH 2	
				(C) G-AN1-13555 to 16183	
Circlip—wheel cylinder fixing	17H 7622	36	2	(C) H-AN6 see (4) foot of	
Lever—hand brake—RH	17H 2824	37	1	page MH 2	
Lever—hand brake—LH	17H 2825	38	1	(C) H-AN7-24732 on	
Boot—lever	17H 7612	39	2	(C) G-AN1-13555 to 16183	
				(C) G-AN2-16184 on	
Drum—brake	2A 7168	40	2		
Screw	CMZ 0410	41	4		
Plug—drum (rubber)	2A 7228	42	2		
Nut—drum to hub	FNZ 506	43	8		Wire wheels only
Washer—tab	BTA 493	44	4		

† Revised Information.

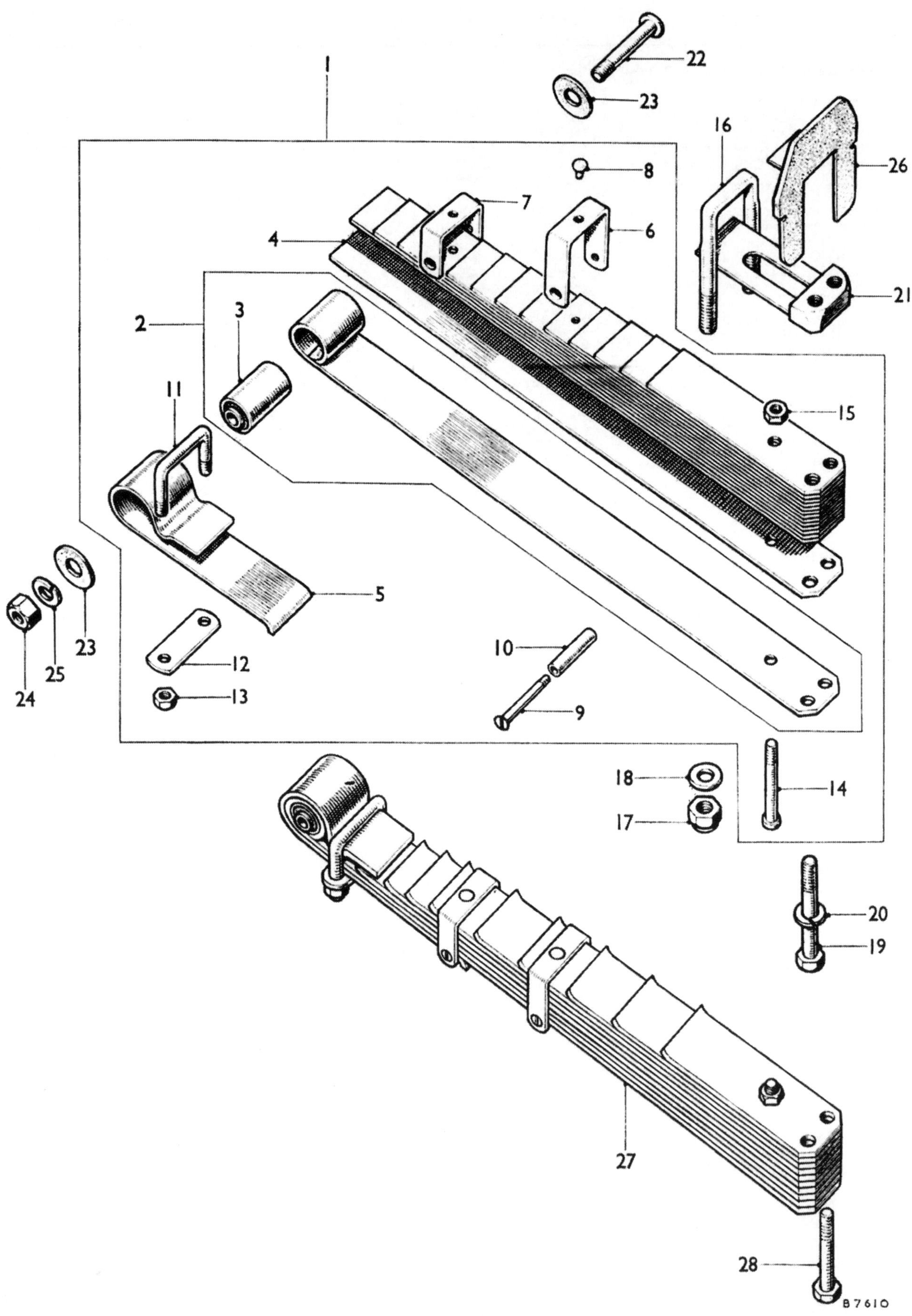
1
2
3
4
5
6
7
8
9
10
11
12
13
14
15
16
17
18
19
20
21
22
23
24
25
26
27
28
B 7610

DESCRIPTION	Part No.	Illus. No.	Quantity	Change Point	REMARKS
Rear Axle and Rear Suspension—*continued*					
Spring assembly	2A 7309	1	2		
Leaf—main	AHA 5331	2	2		
Bush	88G 278	3	2		Part No. change; was 2H 4605
Leaf—second	AHA 5332	4	2		
Clip					
Safety	AHA 5350	5	2		
Spring—long	AHA 5346	6	2		
Spring—short	AHA 5347	7	2		
Rivet—clip	RRS 0405	8	4		
Screw—spring clip	AHA 5348	9	4		Alternatives for service
Screw—spring clip	27H 2421	9	4		Alternatives for service
Tube—distance—clip	AHA 5349	10	4		
'U' bolt—safety clip to spring	AHA 5351	11	2		
Plate—'U' bolt	AHA 5352	12	2		
Nut—'U' bolt	FNZ 105	13	4		
Bolt—locating	AHA 5353	14	2		
Locknut	FNZ 205	15	2		
Clip—spring to frame	AHA 5221	16	2		
Nut	LNZ 108	17	4		
Washer—plain	PWZ 108	18	4		
Bolt—spring to frame	HBZ 0626	19	4		
Washer—spring	LWZ 306	20	4		
Plate—spring attachment	AHA 5222	21	2		
Pin—spring	2A 7279	22	2		
Washer—spring to rear axle (fibre)	AHA 6370	23	4	(C) H-AN6-12068 to 24731 (C) H-AN7-24732 on (C) G-AN1-7442 to 16183 (C) G-AN2-16184 on	
Nut—pin	FNZ 107	24	2		
Washer—spring	LWZ 307	25	2		
Seal—spring housing	AHA 6418	26	2	(C) H-AN6-22907 to 24731 (C) H-AN7-24732 on (C) G-AN1-14527 to 16183 (C) G-AN2-16184 on	
Spring—heavy duty	AHA 5468	27	2		Optional extra
Bolt—spring to frame	HBZ 0624	28	4		Optional extra

STEERING

	Page	Plate
COLUMN—STEERING	MJ 3	J 2
LOCK—STEERING	MJ 3	J 2
PINION	MJ 2	J 1
RACK	MJ 2	J 1
SOCKET—BALL	MJ 2	J 1
TIE-ROD	MJ 2	J 1
WHEEL—STEERING	MJ 3	J 2

† Revised Information.

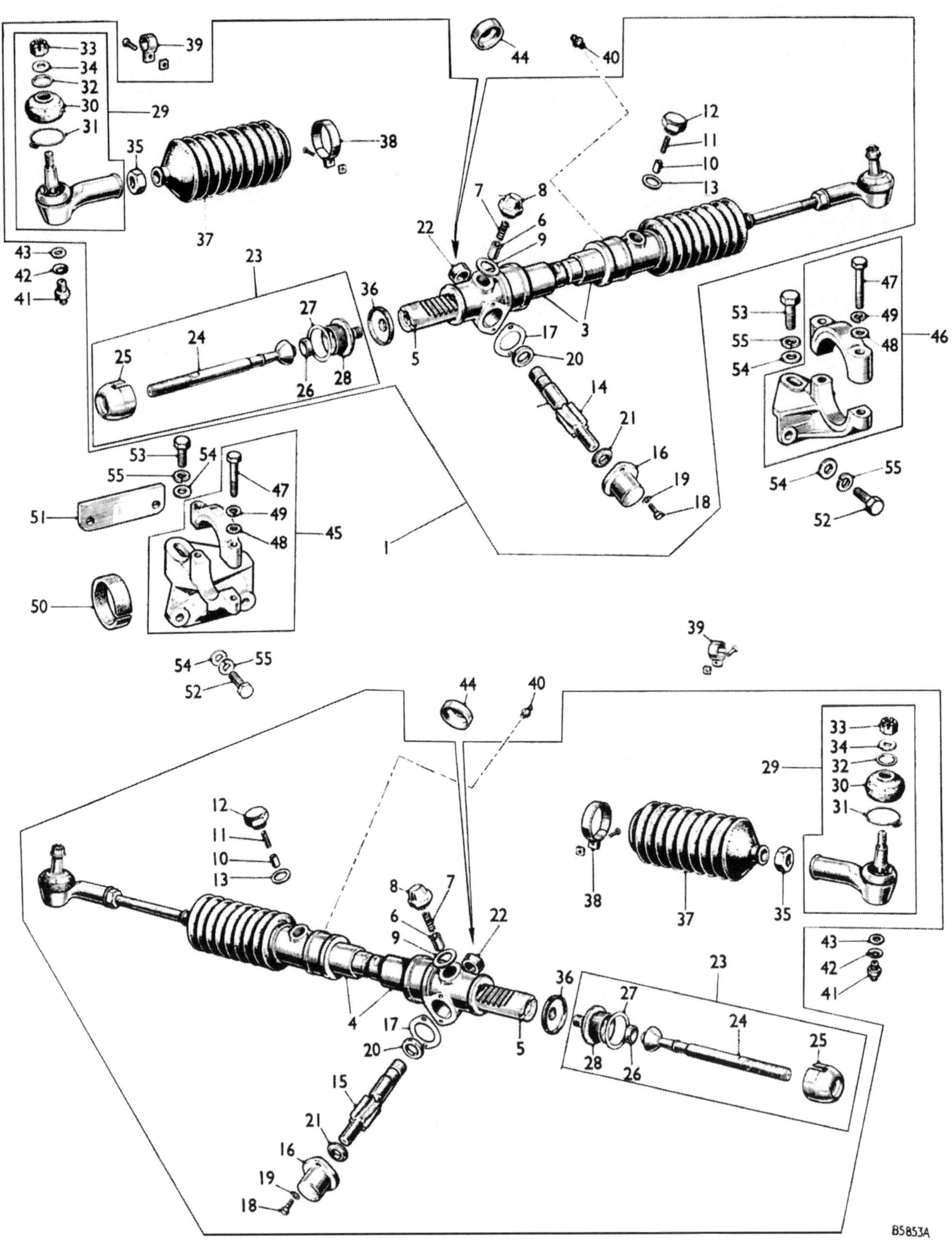

33
34
32
30
31
29
39
35
37
38
44
40
12
11
10
13
7
8
6
9
22
23
36
27
24
25
26
28
5
3
17
20
14
21
16
19
18
43
42
41
53
54
55
47
49
48
45
51
50
1
46
52
4
15
B5853A

STEERING

DESCRIPTION		Part No.	Illus. No.	Quantity	Change Point	REMARKS
Rack assembly	**RHD**	ACG 6010	1	1		
Rack assembly	**LHD**	ACG 6009	2	1		
Housing	**RHD**	ACA 6020	3	1		
Housing	**LHD**	ACA 6019	4	1		
Rack		ACA 6026	5	2		
Pad—damper		ACA 5244	6	1		
Spring—pad		ACA 5248	7	1		
Housing—pad		ACA 5245	8	1		
Shim—housing—·003″ (·076 mm)		ACA 5249	9	A/R		
Shim—housing—·010″ (·254 mm)		ACA 5275	9	A/R		
Pad—secondary damper		ACA 5284	10	1		
Spring—pad		ACA 5286	11	1		
Housing—pad		ACA 5285	12	1		
Washer—housing		ACA 5283	13	1		
Pinion	**RHD**	ACA 6028	14	1		
Pinion	**LHD**	ACA 6027	15	1		
Bearing—pinion tail		ACA 5307	16	1		
Shim—tail bearing						
·003″ (·076 mm)		ACA 5259	17	A/R		
·005″ (·127 mm)		ACA 5260	17	A/R		
·010″ (·254 mm)		ACA 5320	17	A/R		
Screw—bearing to rack housing		AJD 6155 Z	18	2		
Washer						
Spring		LWZ 204	19	2		
Thrust—pinion—top		ACA 5257	20	1		
Thrust—pinion—bottom		ACA 5258	21	1		
Seal—pinion		ACA 5261	22	1		
Tie-rod assembly		ACA 6018	23	2		
Tie-rod		ACA 6015	24	2		
Ball housing—female		ACA 5304	25	2		
Seat—ball		ACA 5246	26	2		
Shim						
·002″ (·058 mm)		ACA 6017	27	A/R		
·003″ (·076 mm)		ACA 5301	27	A/R		
·005″ (·127 mm)		ACA 5302	27	A/R		
·010″ (·254 mm)		ACA 5303	27	A/R		
Ball housing—male		ACA 6031	28	2		
Socket assembly—ball		†8G 8452	29	2		W.S.E. use 88G 414
Socket assembly—ball		†88G 414	29	2		
Boot		7H 3762	30	2		
Clip—boot		7H 3565	31	2		
Ring—boot		7H 3763	32	2		
Nut—ball pin		FNZ 407	33	2		
Washer—plain		PWZ 107	34	2		
Locknut—ball socket		FNZ 210	35	2		
Washer—lock—ball housing		ACA 5247	36	2		
Seal—rack housing		ACA 6029	37	2		
Clip—inner—seal		ACA 6030	38	2		
Clip—seal—outer		†ACA 5118	39	2		W.S.E. use 3H 2963
Clip—seal—outer		3H 2963	39	2		
Lubricator—rack		UHH 305	40	1		
Lubricator—ball socket		UHN 305	41	2		
Washer—dished		ACH 6170	42	2		
Washer (fibre)		ACH 6173	43	2		
Retainer—pinion oil seal		AHA 5496	44	1	(C) H-AN5-22583 to 50116 (C) H-AN6-101 to 24731 (C) H-AN7-24732 on (C) G-AN1-101 to 16183 (C) G-AN2-16184 on	
Bracket assembly—mounting						
Right-hand		†2A 6145	45	1		W.S.E. use AHA 5391
Right-hand		AHA 5391	45	1		
Left-hand		†2A 6146	46	1		W.S.E. use AHA 5392
Left-hand		AHA 5392	46	1		
Bolt—cap to bracket		HCZ 0512	47	4		
Washer—plain		PWZ 105	48	4	(C) H-AN5-501 to 4967	
Washer—spring		LWZ 205	49	4		
Seating—rack to bracket		2A 6128	50	2		
Packing—bracket to frame						
·094″ (2·38 mm)		2A 6129	51	A/R		
·156″ (3·97 mm)		2A 6130	51	A/R		
·218″ (5·54 mm)		2A 6131	51	A/R		
Screw—bracket to frame		HZS 0506	52	4		
Screw—bracket to frame		HZS 0508	53	2		
Washer—plain		PWZ 105	54	6		
Washer—spring		LWZ 205	55	6		

† Revised Information.

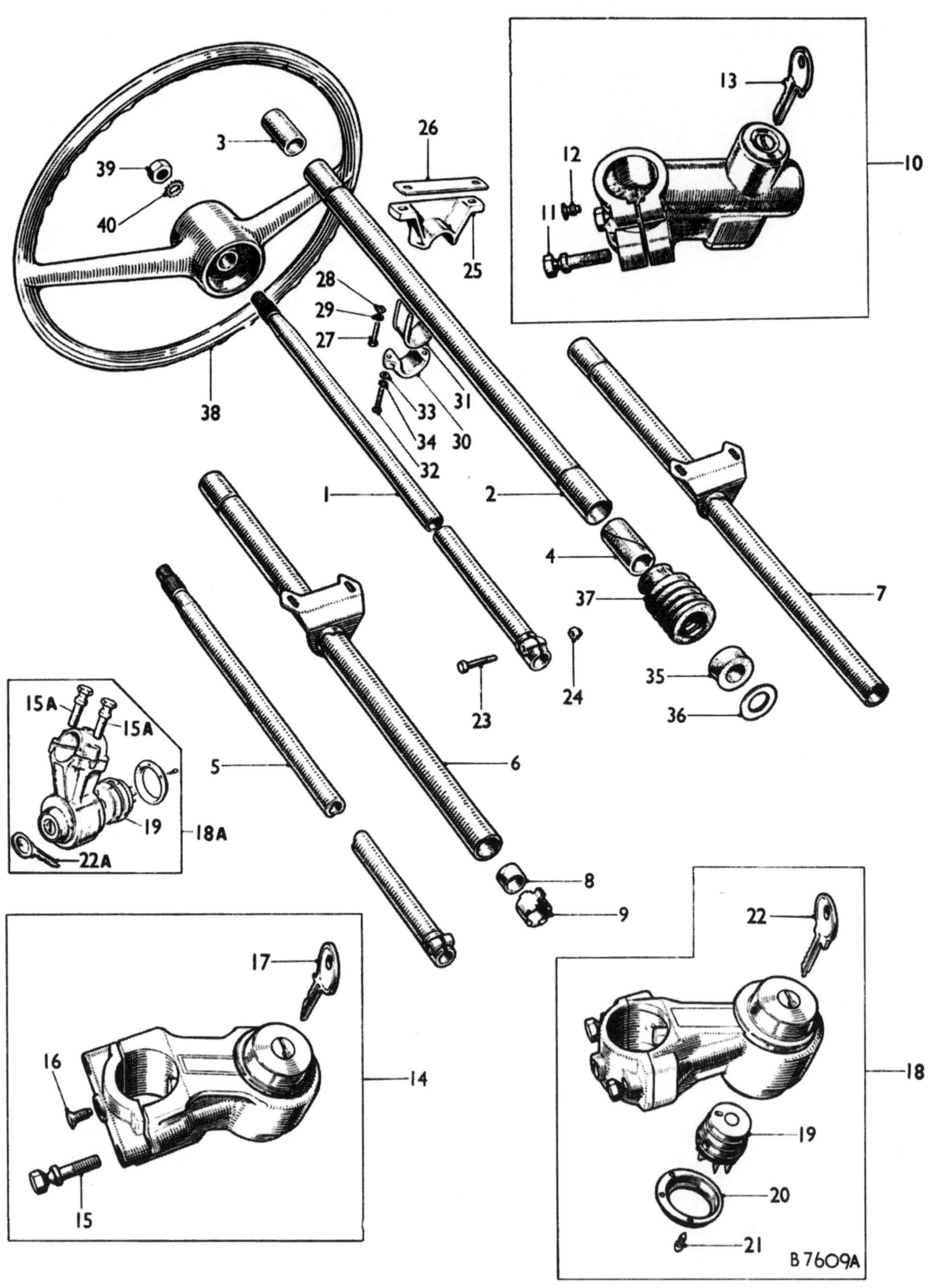
1
2
3
4
5
6
7
8
9
10
11
12
13
14
15
15A
15A
16
17
18
18A
19
19
20
21
22
22A
23
24
25
26
27
28
29
30
31
32
33
34
35
36
37
38
39
40
B 7609A

DESCRIPTION	Part No.	Illus. No.	Quantity	Change Point	REMARKS
Steering—*continued*					
Column—inner	2A 6136	1	1		
Column—outer	2A 6140	2	1	(C) H-AN5-501 to 48626	W.S.E. use AHA 5967 with AHA 5893
Bush—upper (felt)	ACA 5297	3	1		
Bush—lower (felt)	ACA 5398	4	1		W.S.E. use AHA 6166
Column—outer	AHA 5967	2	1	(C) H-AN5-48627 to 50166	
Bush—upper (felt)	AHA 5893	3	1	(C) H-AN6-101 to 24731	
Bush—lower (felt)	AHA 6166	4	1	(C) H-AN7-24732 on	
				(C) G-AN1-101 to 16183	
				(C) G-AN2-16184 on	
Column					
Inner	17H 6541	5	1		Required when steering lock is fitted
Outer **RHD**	17H 6552	6	1		
Outer **LHD**	17H 6540	7	1		
Bush—lower (felt)	13H 569	8	1		
Clip—bush retaining	13H 568	9	1		
Lock assembly (with ignition switch)	†ACB 9425	10	1	(C) H-AN6-101 to 24731	W.S.E. use 13H 4180
Bolt—shear	ACB 9427	11	2	(C) H-AN7-24732 to 34273	
Screw—locating	ACB 9428	12	1	(C) G-AN1-101 to 16183	
Key—cut	97H 2797	13	2	(C) G-AN2-16184 to 22616	Quote key or car No.
Lock assembly (with ignition switch)	13H 709	14	1		W.S.E. use 13H 2972
Bolt—shear	17H 2805	15	2	(C) H-AN7-34274 to ▼	
Screw—locating	17H 8659	16	1	(C) G-AN2-22617 to ▼	
Key—cut	17H 2807	17	2		Quote key or car No.
Lock assembly (with ignition switch)	13H 2972	18	1		W.S.E. use 13H 4180
Switch	27H 6237	19	1		
Cap—switch	27H 6236	20	1		
Screw	27H 6238	21	2	(C) H-AN7- ▼ on	
Key—cut	27H 6245	22	2	(C) G-AN2- ▼ on	Quote key or car No.
Lock assembly (with ignition switch)	13H 4180	18A	1		
Switch	27H 6237	19	1		
Bolt—shear	27H 9394	15A	2		
Key—cut	27H 9391	22A	2		Always quote key or car No.
Bolt—column to rack	53K 1013	23	1		
Nut	LNZ 104	24	1		
Bracket—column to foot-well	2A 6132	25	1		
Piece—packing—bracket	2A 6144	26	A/R		
Screw	HBZ 0408	27	2		
Washer—plain	PWZ 104	28	2		
Washer—spring	LWZ 204	29	2		
Cap—bracket	2A 6133	30	1		
Seating—column to bracket	4B 2502	31	1		
Screw—cap to bracket	53K 2599	32	2		
Washer—plain	PWZ 104	33	2		
Washer—spring	LWZ 204	34	2		
Seal—dust—column to toe-board	2A 6141	35	1	(C) H-AN5-501 to 7432	
Washer—retaining—dust seal	AHA 5272	36	1		
Excluder—draught—column to toe-board	AHA 5435	37	1	(C) H-AN5-7433 to 50116	
				(C) H-AN6-101 to 24731	
				(C) H-AN7-24732 on	
				(C) G-AN1-101 to 16183	
				(C) G-AN2-16184 on	
Wheel—steering **Sprite**	2A 6156	38	1		
Midget	AHA 5682	38	1	(C) G-AN1-101 to 5033	
Midget	AHA 6372	38	1	(C) G-AN1-5034 to 16183	
				(C) G-AN2-16184 on	
Nut—wheel to column	2A 6142	39	1		
Washer—shakeproof	LWN 509	40	1		

▼ Change point not available

† Revised Information.

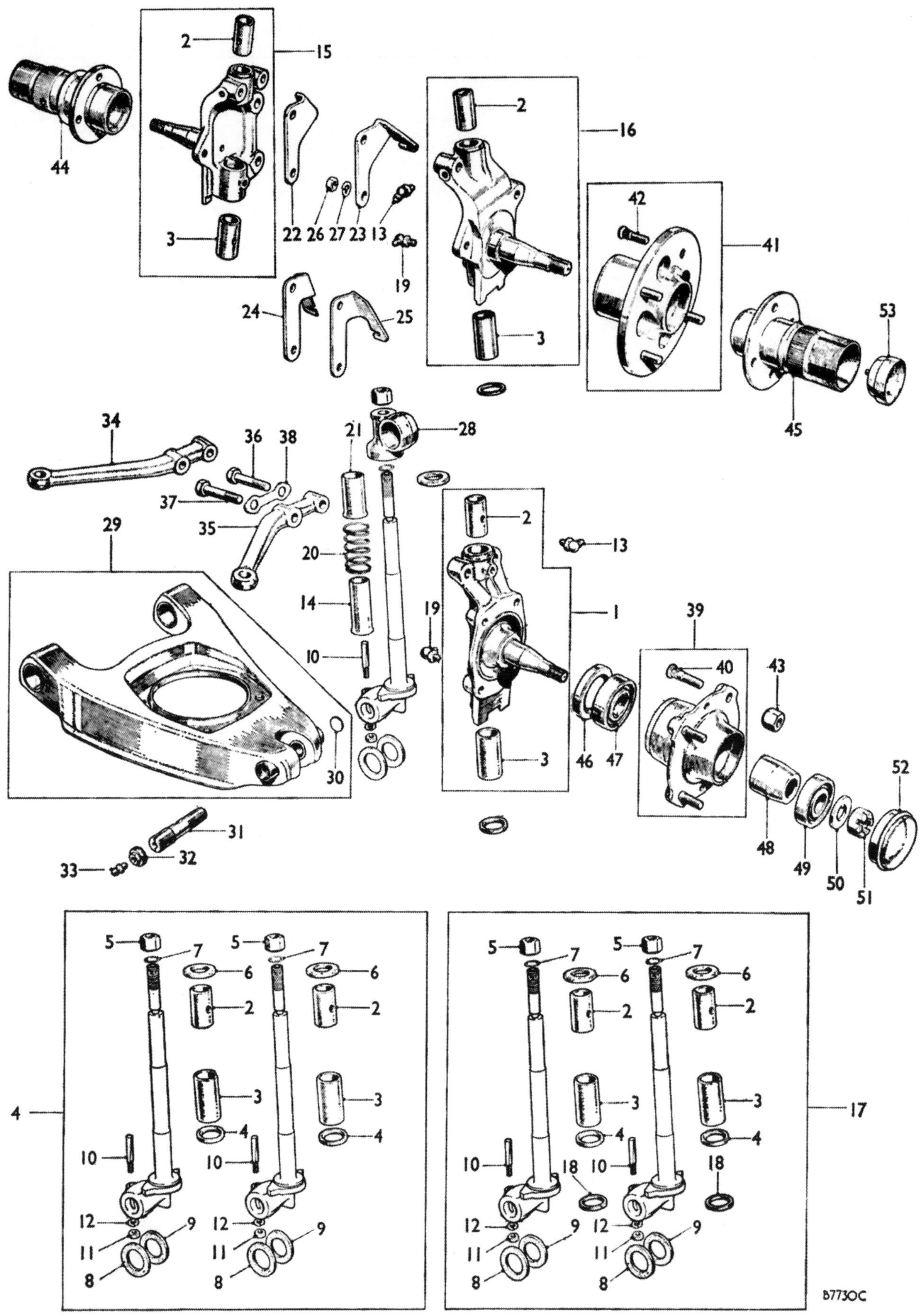
B7730C

FRONT SUSPENSION

	Page	Plate
ABSORBER—SHOCK	MK 5	K 3
AXLE—SWIVEL	MK 2	K 1
BRAKE—FRONT	MK 4	K 2
HUB	MK 3	K 1
†KIT—REPAIR	MK 2, MK 4, MK 4·1	K 1, K 2
LEVER—STEERING	MK 2	K 1
†LINK—LOWER	MK 3	K 1
PIN—SWIVEL	MK 2	K 1
SPRING—ROAD	MK 5	K 3

FRONT SUSPENSION

DESCRIPTION	Part No.	Illus. No.	Quantity	Change Point	REMARKS
Suspension assembly—RH	NSP		1		
Suspension assembly—LH	NSP		1		
Axle assembly—swivel	†2A 4129	1	2	(C) H-AN5-501 to 6432	
				(less 6118, 6121, 6232, 6234,	
				6235, 6312, 6326, 6329, 6366,	
				6374, 6395, 6406, and 6408)	
Axle assembly—swivel	†2A 4304	1	2	(C) H-AN5-6433 to 50116	
Bush—top	†2A 4176	2	2	(plus 6118, 6121, 6232, 6234,	Also included in kit
Bush—bottom	†1A 4744	3	2	6235, 6312, 6326, 6329, 6366,	8G 4208
Lubricator—bush	†UHN 490	13	4	6374, 6395, 6406, and 6408)	
Tube—dust excluder—bottom	†2A 4011	14	2	(C) H-AN6-101 to 24731	
				(C) G-AN1 to 16183	
Kit—repair—swivel pin	†8G 4177	4	1 set		W.S.E. use 8G 4208
Kit—repair—swivel pin	†8G 4208	4	2 sets		
Pin—swivel	†NSP		2		Was 21A 1160
Bush—top	†2A 4176	2	2		
Bush—bottom	†1A 4744	3	2		
Ring—sealing	†2A 4009	4	2		
Nut—swivel pin	†FNZ 307	5	2		
Washer—thrust	†2A 4006	6	2	(C) H-AN5-501 to 50116	
Shim—adjusting				(C) H-AN6-101 to 24731	
·012″ (·305 mm)	†2A 4008	7	A/R	(C) G-AN1-101 to 16183	
·008″ (·203 mm)	†2A 4007	7	A/R		1 off of each included in
·003″ (·076 mm)	†2A 4168	7	A/R		kit 8G 4208
Ring—fulcrum pin—large	†2A 4206	8	2		
Ring—fulcrum pin—small	†2A 4205	9	2		
Pin—cotter	†51K 1769	10	2		
Nut—cotter pin	†FNZ 103	11	2		
Washer—spring	†LWZ 203	12	2		
Axle assembly—swivel					
Right-hand	†BTA 600	15	1		W.S.E. use BTA 744
Left-hand	†BTA 601	16	1		W.S.E. use BTA 745
Right-hand	†BTA 744	15	1		
Left-hand	†BTA 745	16	1		
Bush—top	†BTA 382	2	2		Also included in kit
Bush—bottom	†ATC 4246	3	2		8G 4195
Kit—repair—swivel pin	†8G 4195	17	1 set		
Pin—swivel	†NSP		2		Was BTA 605
Bush—top	†BTA 382	2	2		
Bush—bottom	†ATC 4246	3	2		
Ring—sealing	†BTA 613	4	2		
Nut—swivel pin	†FNZ 307	5	2	(C) H-AN7-24732 on	
Washer—thrust	†2A 4006	6	2	(C) G-AN2-16184 on	
Shim—adjusting					
·012″ (·305 mm)	†2A 4008	7	A/R		
·008″ (·203 mm)	†2A 4007	7	A/R		1 off of each included in
·003″ (·076 mm)	†2A 4168	7	A/R		kit 8G 4195
Ring—fulcrum pin—large	†2A 4206	8	2		
Ring—fulcrum pin—small	†2A 4205	9	2		
Pin—cotter	†51K 1769	10	2		
Nut	†FNZ 103	11	2		
Washer—spring	†LWZ 203	12	2		
Ring—dust excluder tube	†BTA 607	18	2		
Lubricator—top bush	†UHN 490	13	2		
Lubricator—bottom bush	†UHN 445	19	2		
Tube—dust excluder—bottom	†BTA 606	14	2		
Spring—dust excluder tube	†6K 653	20	2		
Tube—dust excluder—top	†2A 4010	21	2		

† Revised Information.

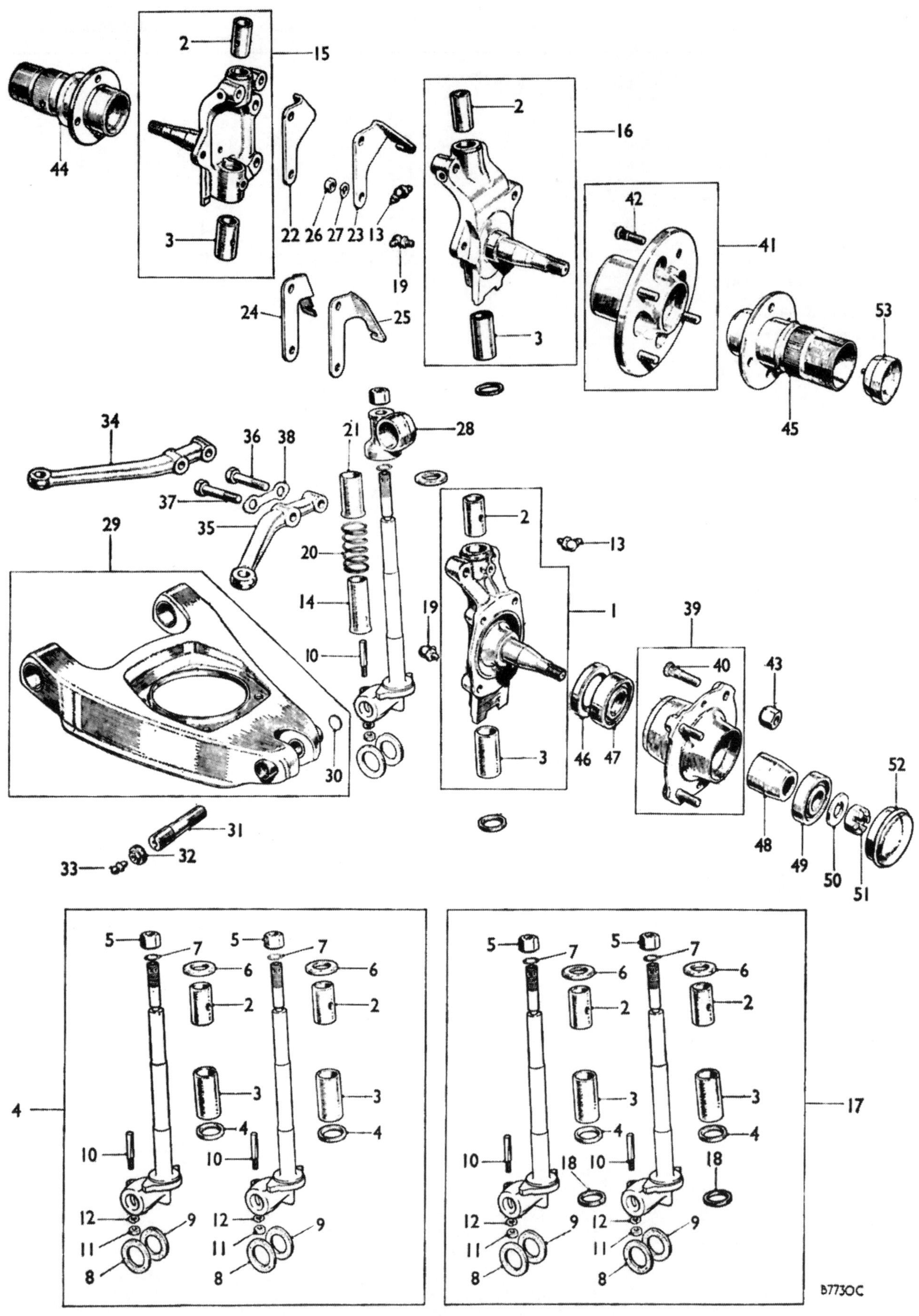
B7730C

DESCRIPTION	Part No.	Illus. No.	Quantity	Change Point	REMARKS
Front Suspension—*continued*					
Lock plate—brake hose					
Right-hand	†BTA 442	22	1		
Left-hand	†BTA 443	23	1		
Right-hand	†BTA 792	24	1	(C) H–AN7–24732 on	For use with bolt—calliper mounting BTA 789
Left-hand	†BTA 793	25	1	(C) G–AN2–16184 on	
Nut	†FNZ 105	26	4		
Washer—spring	†LWZ 305	27	4		
Trunnion—suspension link	†2A 4005	28	2		
Link assembly—lower	†2A 4169	29	2	(C) H–AN5–501 to 27911	W.S.E. use 21A 153
Link assembly—lower	21A 153	29	2	(C) H–AN5–27912 to 50116 (C) H–AN6–101 to 24731 (C) H–AN7–24732 on (C) G–AN1–101 to 16183 (C) G–AN2–16184 on	
Plug—blanking	51K 3424	30	2		
Pin—fulcrum	2A 4020	31	2		
Pin—cotter—fulcrum pin to swivel pin—oversize	51K 2751	10	2		
Plug—adaptor	8G 589	32	2		
Lubricator	UHN 400	33	2		
Lever—steering					
Right-hand	2A 4212	34	1	(C) H–AN5–501 to 4799	W.S.E. use BTA 648 RH and BTA 649 LH in pairs only
Left-hand	2A 4213	35	1		
Right-hand	ATA 4130	34	1	(C) H–AN5–4800 to 50116 (C) H–AN6–101 to 24731 (C) H–AN7–24732 to 28367 (C) G–AN1–101 to 16183 (C) G–AN2–16184 to 18471	
Left-hand	ATA 4131	35	1		
Right-hand	BTA 648	34	1	(C) H–AN7–28368 on	
Left-hand	BTA 649	35	1	(C) G–AN2–18472 on	
Screw—lever to swivel axle—short	53K 1370	36	4/2		Quantity reduced at (C) H–AN5–4800
Screw—lever to swivel axle—long	ATA 4132	37	2	(C) H–AN5–4800 to 50116 (C) H–AN6–101 to 24731 (C) H–AN7–24732 on (C) G–AN1–101 to 16183 (C) G–AN2–16184 on	
Washer—lock	2K 5377	38	2		
Hub assembly	2A 4137	39	2		Use 2H 4348 for this application. Disc wheels only
Hub assembly	2A 4348	39	2	(C) H–AN5–501 to 50116 (C) H–AN6–101 to 24731 (C) G–AN1–101 to 16183	Disc wheels only
Stud—wheel	2A 4066	40	8		
Hub assembly	BTA 384	41	2	(C) H–AN7–24732 on (C) G–AN2–16184 on	Disc wheels only
Stud—wheel	BTA 839	42	8		
Nut—wheel stud	88G 322	43	8		Part No. change; was 2A 8012 and ATA 7499. Disc wheels only
Hub—RH	BTA 470	44	1	(B) H–AN7–20812 on	Wire wheels only
Hub—LH	BTA 471	45	1	(B) G–AN2–16780 on	
Seal—oil	ACA 4000	46	2		
Bearing—inner	2A 4147	47	2		W.S.E. use 2A 4299
Bearing—inner	2A 4299	47	2		
Piece—distance—bearing	88G 321	48	2		Part No. change; was 2A 4146 and ATA 4064
Bearing—outer	2A 4148	49	2		
Washer—bearing retaining	2A 4003	50	2		
Nut—swivel axle	51K 828	51	2		
Cap—grease retaining	2A 4067	52	2		Disc wheels only
Cap—grease retaining	1B 4316	53	2	(B) H–AN7–20812 on (B) G–AN2–16780 on	Wire wheels only

† Revised Information.

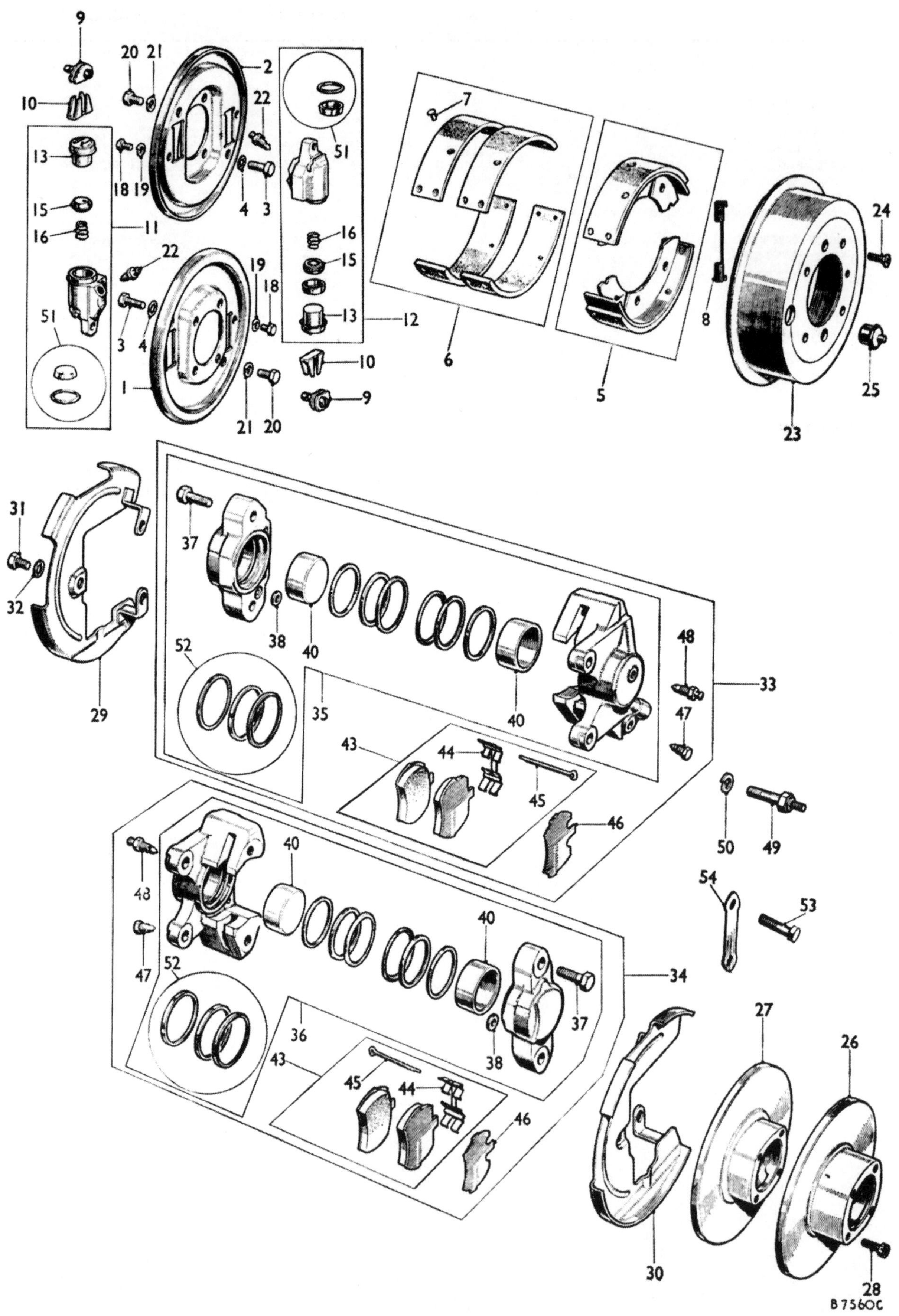
9
20 21
2
10
22
13
18 19
4 3
15
16
11
22
19
18
51
3 4
1
21 20
51
16
15
13
12
10
9
7
6
5
8
24
25
23
31
32
29
37
38
40
52
40
35
40
48
33
47
43
44
45
46
50 49
54
53
48
47
52
40
40
34
37
38
36
43
45
44
46
27
26
30
28
B7560C

DESCRIPTION	Part No.	Illus. No.	Quantity	Change Point	REMARKS
Front Suspension—*continued*					
Plate—brake—RH	17H 7543	1	1	(C) H-AN5-501 to 50116	
Plate—brake—LH	17H 7544	2	1	(C) H-AN6-101 to 24731	
Screw—brake plate to swivel axle	51K 1368	3	8	(C) G-AN1-101 to 16183	
Washer—shakeproof	LWZ 405	4	8		
Shoe assembly—brake	AJA 5085	5	2 sets	(C) H-AN5-501 to 50116	
Lining assembly	AAA 4692	6	1 box	(C) H-AN6-101 to 21867	
Rivet	7H 7398	7	28	(C) G-AN1-101 to 7897	
Shoe assembly—brake	8G 8670	5	2 sets	(C) H-AN6-12868 to 24731	
Lining assembly	8G 8672	6	1 box	(C) G-AN1-7898 to 16183	
Rivet	7H 7398	7	28		
Spring—brake shoe return	AAA 4776	8	4		
Adjuster—micram	68640	9	4		W.S.E. use 17H 7576
Adjuster—micram	17H 7576	9	4		
Mask—adjuster	AAA 421	10	4		
Cylinder assembly—wheel—RH	7H 7949	11	2		
Cylinder assembly—wheel—LH	7H 7950	12	2		
Body	NSP		4		
Piston (with dust cover)	7H 7941	13	4		
Filler—cup	7H 7938	15	4		
Spring—cup filler	7H 7939	16	4	(C) H-AN5-510 to 50116	
				(C) H-AN6-101 to 24731	
Kit—repair—wheel cylinder	8G 8245	51	4	(C) G-AN1-101 to 16183	
Cup	NSP		4		Was 7H 7924
Ring—sealing	NSP		4		
Screw—wheel cylinder—short	7H 7520	18	4		
Washer—spring	LWN 204	19	4		
Screw	HNS 0505	20	4		
Washer—spring	7H 7368	21	4		W.S.E. use LWN 305
Washer—spring	LWN 305	21	4		
Screw—bleed	3H 2428	22	2		
Drum—brake	2A 7168	23	2		
Screw	CMZ 0407	24	4		
Plug—brake drum	2A 7228	25	2		
Disc—brake	BTA 383	26	2	(C) H-AN7-24732 on	Disc wheels only
				(C) G-AN2-16184 on	
Disc—brake	BTA 469	27	2	(B) H-AN7-20812 on	Wire wheels only
				(B) G-AN2-16780 on	
Bolt—disc to hub	BTA 370	28	8		
Cover—dust—brake disc—RH	BTA 472	29	1	(C) H-AN7-24732 on	
Cover—dust—brake disc—LH	BTA 473	30	1	(C) G-AN2-16184 on	
Bolt	HZS 0503	31	2		
Washer—shakeproof	LWZ 505	32	2		

† Revised Information.

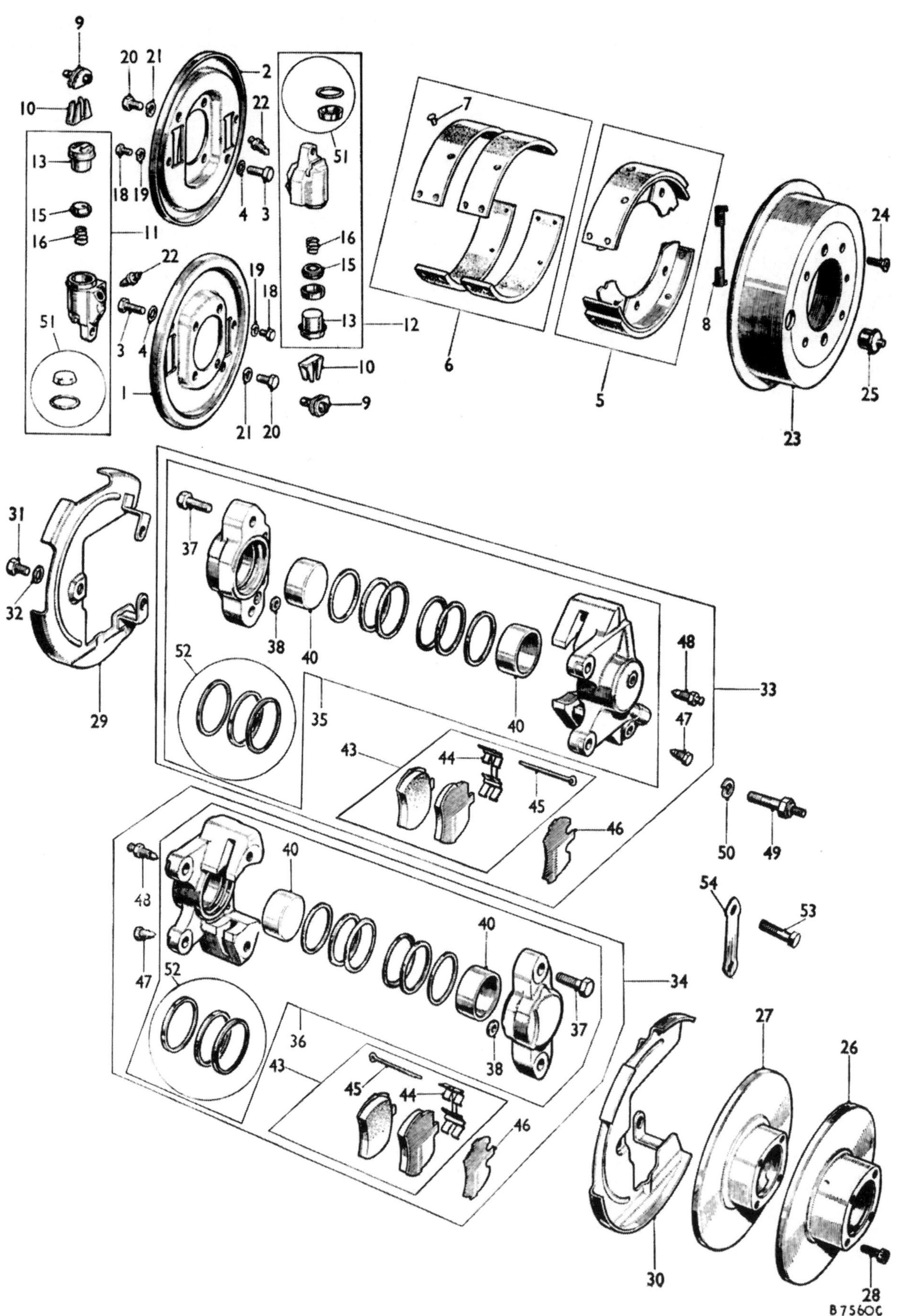
9
10
20 21
2
22
13
18 19
4 3
51
7
15
16
11
22
19
18
16
15
13
12
6
5
8
24
23
25
51
3 4
1
21 20
10
9
31
32
29
37
38
40
52
35
40
48
33
47
43
44
45
46
50
49
54
53
40
48
47
52
40
37
38
34
36
43
45
44
46
27
26
30
28
B 7560C

DESCRIPTION	Part No.	Illus. No.	Quantity	Change Point	REMARKS
Front Suspension—*continued*					
Unit assembly—calliper					
Right-hand	†BTA 373	33	1	(C) H-AN7-24732 to 30514 (C) G-AN2-16184 to 19981	W.S.E. use 17H 9439 together with 1 off pad 8G 8813 and 2 off shim 17H 2460
Left-hand	†BTA 372	34	1		W.S.E. use 17H 9438 together with 1 off pad 8G 8813 and 2 off shim 17H 2460
Right-hand	BTA 653	33	1	(C) H-AN7-30515 on	
Left-hand	BTA 652	34	1	(C) G-AN2-19982 on	W.S.E. use 17H 9438 together with 1 off pad 8G 8813 and 2 off shim 17H 2460
Unit assembly—calliper (less pads and shims)—LH	†17H 9438	35	1		
Unit assembly—calliper (less pads and shims)—RH	†17H 9439	36	1		
Calliper assembly—RH	NSP		1	(C) H-AN7-24732 on (C) G-AN2-16184 on	Was 17H 7959
Calliper assembly—LH	NSP		1		Was 17H 7958
Bolt—bridge	17H 8250	37	4		
Seal—fluid channel	17H 7679	38	2		
Piston	17H 7960	40	4		
Kit—repair—calliper unit	8G 8668	52	2		
Seal—inner	†NSP		4		Was 17H 7961
Seal and retainer—dust	†NSP		4		Was 17H 7962
Pad assembly	8G 8667	43	1 set	(C) H-AN7-24732 to 30514 (C) G-AN2-16154 to 19981	W.S.E. use 8G 8813
Spring—pad retaining	17H 7963	44	2		
Pin—split cotter	17H 2461	45	4		W.S.E. use ZPS 0524
Pad assembly	8G 8813	43	1 set	(C) H-AN7-30515 on (C) G-AN2-19982 on	
Spring—pad retaining	17H 7963	44	4		
Pin—split cotter	ZPS 0524	45	4		
Shim—anti-squeal	17H 2460	46	4	(C) H-AN7-24732 on (C) G-AN2-16184 on	
Plug	17H 7917	47	2		
Screw—bleed	3H 2428	48	2		
Bolt—calliper mounting	BTA 444	49	4		W.S.E. use BTA 789 and BTC 114 together with 1 off lockplate RH BTA 792 or 1 off lockplate LH BTA 793
Bolt—calliper mounting	BTA 789	53	4		
Washer—tab	BTC 114	54	2		
Washer—spring	LWZ 307	50	4		

† Revised Information.

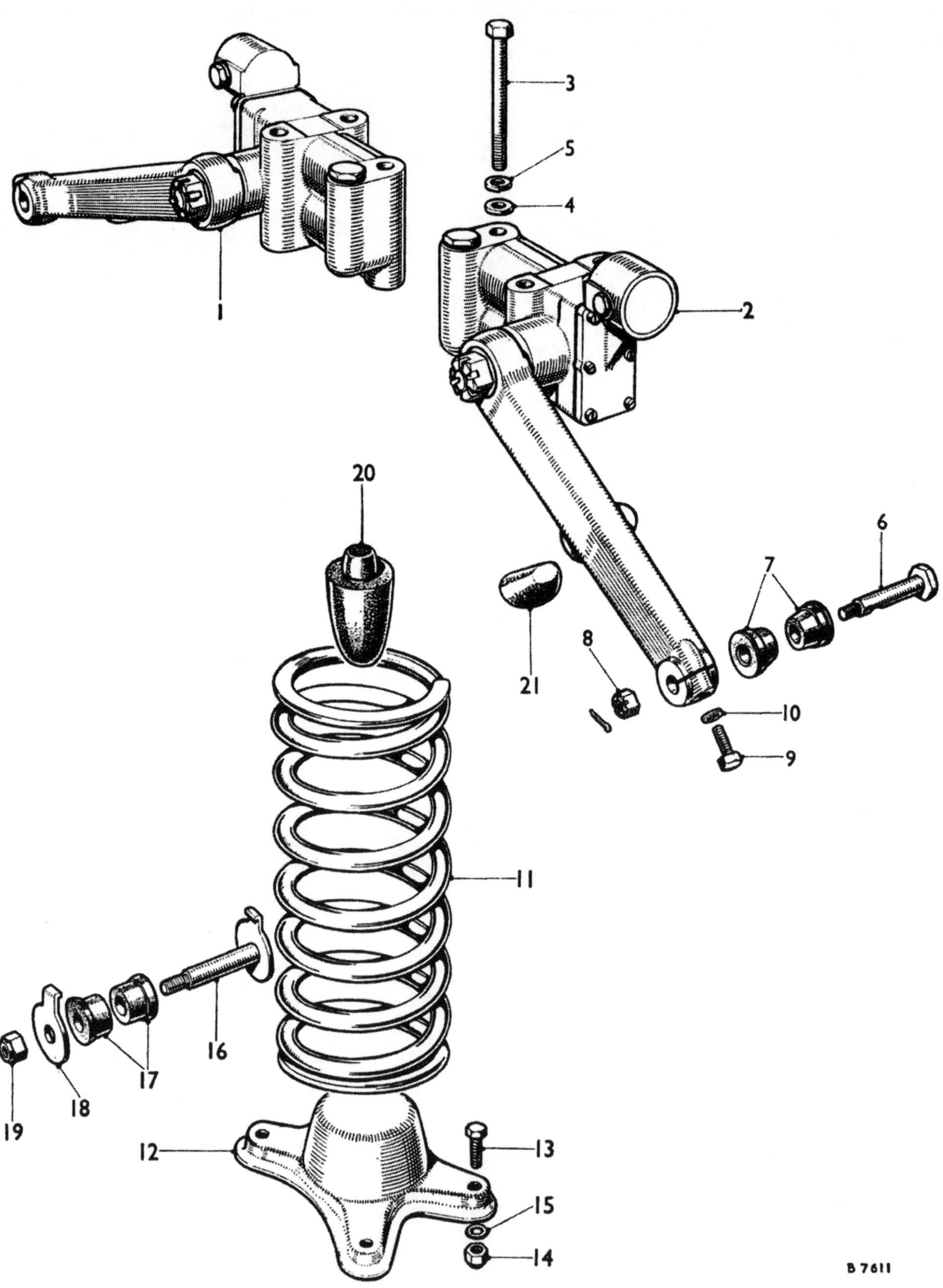
1
2
3
4
5
6
7
8
9
10
11
12
13
14
15
16
17
18
19
20
21
B 7611

DESCRIPTION	Part No.	Illus. No.	Quantity	Change Point	REMARKS
Front Suspension—*continued*					
Absorber—shock—RH	2A 4172	1	1		
Absorber—shock—LH	2A 4174	2	1		
Screw—shock absorber to frame	53K 1364	3	6		
Washer—plain	PWZ 106	4	6		
Washer—spring	LWZ 306	5	6		
Pin—fulcrum—shock absorber	2A 4028	6	2		
Bearing—fulcrum pin	88G 274	7	4		Part No. change; was 2A 4027 and 2A 4163
Nut	FNZ 306	8	2		
Bolt—clamping—fulcrum pin	53K 1389	9	2		
Washer—shakeproof	LWN 405	10	2		
Spring—road	2A 4214	11	2		
Seat—spring	2A 4031	12	2	(C) H–AN5–501 to 48337	Not available; use 21A 137
Seat—spring	21A 137	12	2	(C) H–AN5–48338 to 50116	
				(C) H–AN6–101 to 24731	
				(C) H–AN7–24732 on	
				(C) G–AN1–101–16183	
				(C) G–AN2–16184 on	
Bolt—seat to lower link	53K 1368	13	8		
Nut	LNZ 205	14	8		
Washer—shakeproof	LWN 405	15	8		
Pin—fulcrum—lower link to frame	2A 4021	16	4	(C) H–AN5–501 to 11125	Not available; use 2A 4272 with LNZ 206
Pin—fulcrum—lower link to frame	2A 4272	16	4	(C) H–AN5–11126 to 50116	
				(C) H–AN6–101 to 24731	
				(C) H–AN7–24732 on	
				(C) G–AN1–101 to 16183	
Bearing—lower—link	8G 621	17	8		
Washer—special—fulcrum pin	2A 4024	18	4		
Nut—fulcrum pin	FNZ 306	19	4	(C) H–AN5–501 to 11125	
Nut—fulcrum pin	LNZ 206	19	4	(C) H–AN5–11126 to 50116	
				(C) H–AN6–101 to 24731	
				(C) H–AN7–24732 on	
				(C) G–AN1–101 to 16183	
				(C) G–AN2–16184 on	
Buffer					
Suspension	2A 4029	20	2		Use AHA 6378 in pairs for this application
Suspension	AHA 6378	20	2		
Rebound	2A 4082	21	2		

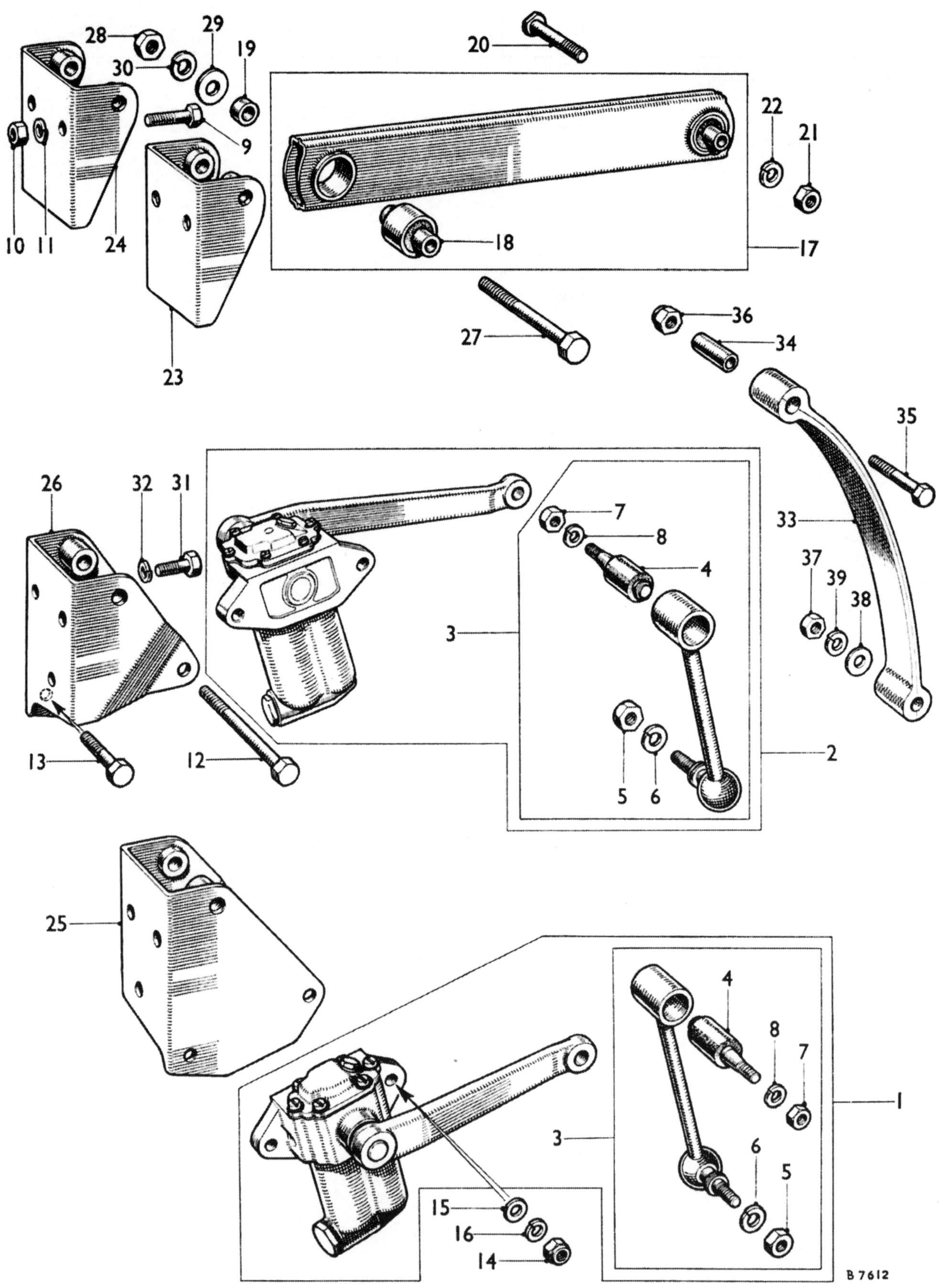
28
29
19
30
20
22
21
9
10 11
24
18
17
27
36
34
23
35
26
32 31
7
8
33
4
37
39
38
3
13
12
5 6
2
25
4
8
7
1
3
6
5
15
16
14
B 7612

SHOCK ABSORBERS

SHOCK ABSORBERS

DESCRIPTION	Part No.	Illus. No.	Quantity	Change Point	REMARKS
REAR SHOCK ABSORBERS					
Absorber assembly—shock—RH	2A 7298	1	1		
Absorber assembly—shock—LH	2A 7299	2	1		
Link assembly	2A 7303	3	2		
Bush (rubber)	97H 222	4	2		
Nut	FNZ 107	5	2	(C) H-AN5-501 to 4332 (plus	
Washer—spring	LWZ 307	6	2	4471, 4622, 4680, and 4684)	
Nut	FNZ 106	7	2		
Washer—spring	LWZ 306	8	2		
Screw	HZS 0609	9	4		
Nut	FNZ 106	10	4		
Washer—spring	LWZ 306	11	4		
Absorber assembly—shock—RH	AHA 5312	1	1		
Absorber assembly—shock—LH	AHA 5311	2	1		
Link assembly	AHA 5313	3	2		
Bush (rubber)	97H 222	4	2	(C) H-AN5-4333 to 50116	
Nut	FNZ 107	5	2	(less 4471, 4622, 4680, and	
Washer—spring	LWZ 307	6	2	4684)	
Nut	FNZ 106	7	2	(C) H-AN6-101 to 24731	
Washer—spring	LWZ 306	8	2	(C) H-AN7-24732 on	
Bolt	HBZ 0630	12	2	(C) G-AN1-101 to 16183	
Bolt	HBZ 0612	13	2	(C) G-AN2-16184 on	
Nut	LNZ 106	14	4		
Washer—plain	PWZ 106	15	4		
Washer—spring	LWZ 306	16	4		
Link assembly—top	2A 7310	17	2		
Bush (rubber)	2A 7278	18	4		
Piece—distance—bush	AHA 5224	19	4		
Pin—top link to axle bracket	2A 7279	20	2		
Nut	FNZ 107	21	2		
Washer—spring	LWZ 307	22	2		
Bracket—mounting					
Link—RH	2A 7314	23	1	(C) H-AN5-501 to 4322	
Link—LH	2A 7315	24	1	(plus 4471, 4622, 4680, and 4684)	
Link and absorber—RH	AHA 5305	25	1	(C) H-AN5-4333 to 50116	
Link and absorber—LH	AHA 5306	26	1	(less 4471, 4622, 4680, and 4684)	
				(C) H-AN6-101 to 24731	
				(C) H-AN7-24732 on	
				(C) G-AN1-101 to 16183	
				(C) G-AN2-16184 on	
Bolt	HBZ 0732	27	2		
Nut	FNZ 107	28	2		
Washer—plain	PWZ 107	29	2		
Washer—spring	LWZ 307	30	2		
Screw	HZS 0610	31	6		
Washer—spring	LWZ 206	32	6		
Strap—axle check	†AHH 5081	33	2		Correction; was AHA 5081
Tube—distance—strap	2A 7306	34	2		
Bolt	HBZ 0618	35	2		
Nut	LNZ 206	36	2		
Nut	FNZ 106	37	2		
Washer—plain	PWZ 206	38	2		
Washer—spring	LWZ 206	39	2		

† Revised Information.

22
23
21
24
13
14
12
10
9
8
15
11
16
6
2
7
5
4
3
1
18
19
17
24
20
B.7534

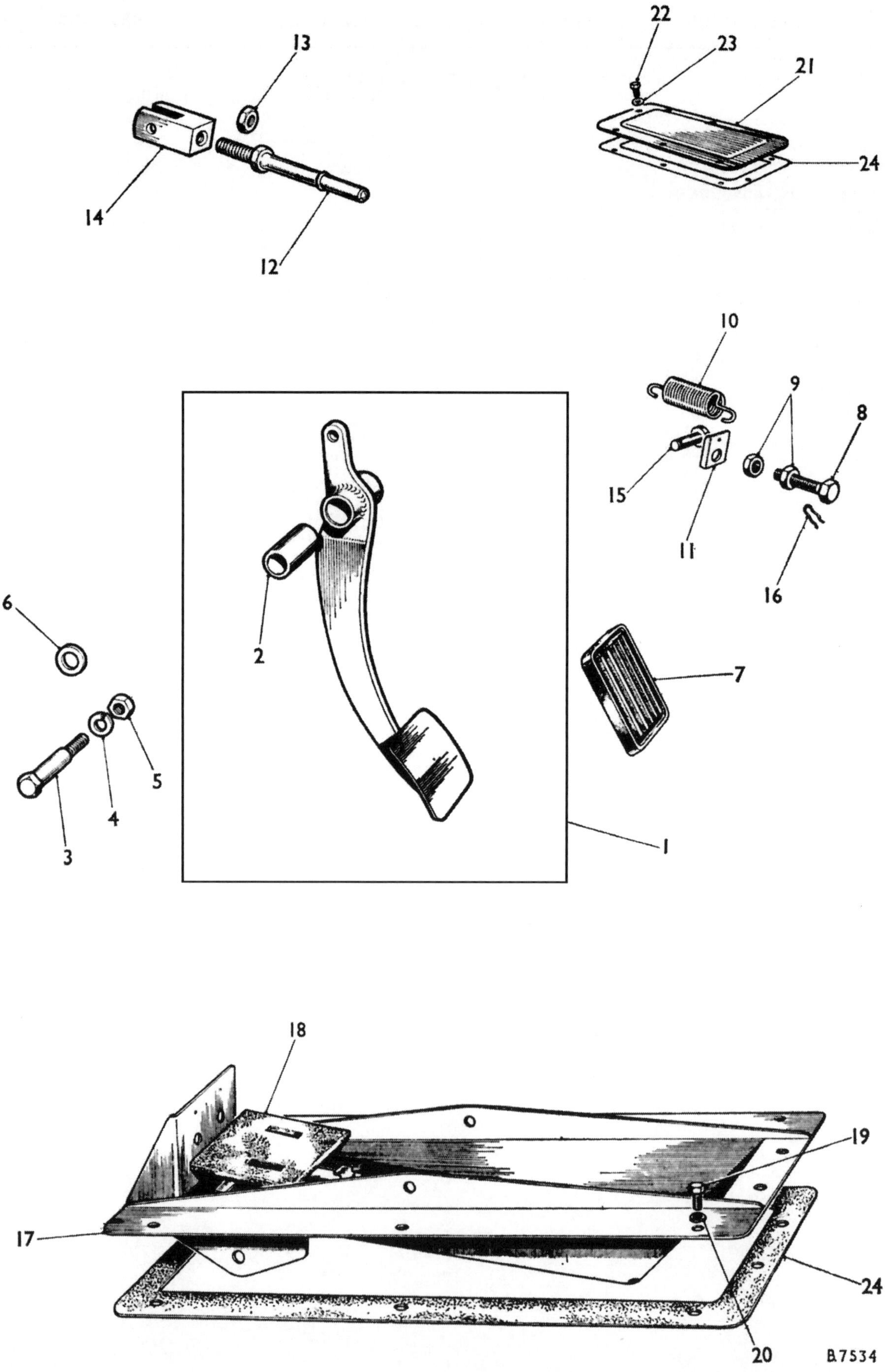

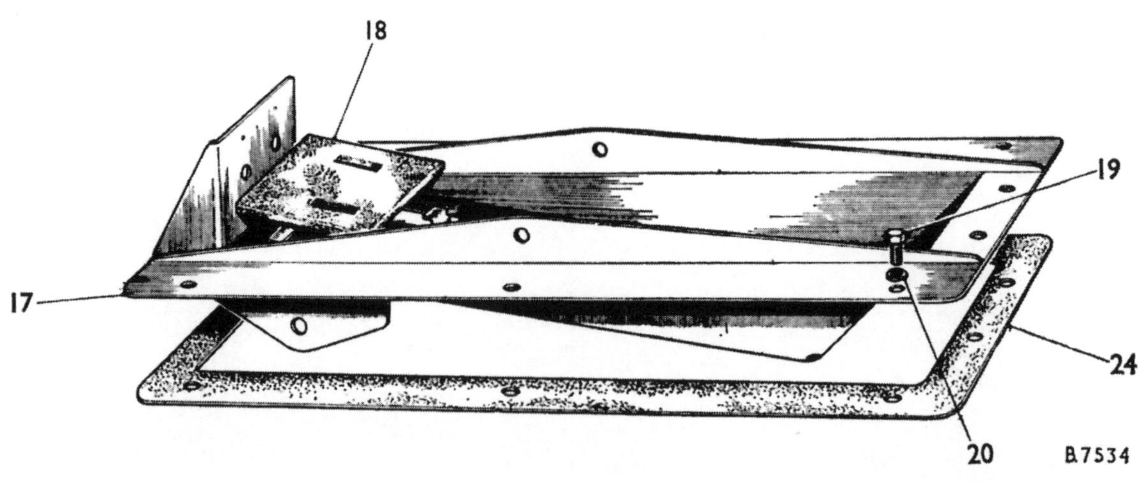

	DESCRIPTION	Part No.	Illus. No.	Quantity	Change Point	REMARKS

BRAKE CONTROLS

	Page	Plate
BOX—PEDAL	MM 2	M 1
CROSS-RODS—BRAKE	MM 6	M 4
CYLINDER AND SUPPLY TANK—MASTER	MM 3	M 2
HAND BRAKE	MM 6	M 4
HOSES—BRAKE	MM 4	M 3
PEDAL—BRAKE	MM 2	M 1
PIPES—BRAKE	MM 4	M 3
PUSH-ROD—MASTER CYLINDER	MM 2	M 1
SWITCH—STOP LIGHT	MM 5	M 3

BRAKE CONTROLS

BRAKE PEDAL AND LINKAGE

DESCRIPTION	Part No.	Illus. No.	Quantity	Change Point	REMARKS
Pedal assembly—brake	†2A 5559	1	1	(C) H-AN5-501 to 50116	W.S.E. use AHA 6407
				(C) H-AN6-101 to 20092	
				(C) G-AN1-101 to 13403	
Pedal assembly—brake	AHA 6407	1	1	(C) H-AN6-20093 to 24731	
				(C) H-AN7-24732 on	
				(C) G-AN1-13404 to 16183	
				(C) G-AN2-16184 on	
Bush	2A 5564	2	1		
Bolt	2A 5568	3	1		
Washer—spring	LWZ 205	4	1		
Nut	FNZ 105	5	1		
Washer—distance	2A 5565	6	1		
Pad—pedal (rubber)	AHA 5326	7	1		
Screw—pedal adjustment	HZS 0408	8	1		
Locknut	FNZ 204	9	2		
Spring—pedal return	2A 5574	10	1		
Retainer	2A 5573	11	1		
Push-rod—master cylinder					
Brake	2A 5587	12	1	(C) H-AN5-501 to 50116	
				(C) H-AN6-101 to 24731	
				(C) G-AN1-101 to 16183	
Clutch	2A 5588	12	1	(C) H-AN5-501 to 4995	
Clutch	2A 5587	12	1	(C) H-AN5-4996 to 50116	
				(C) H-AN6-101 to 24731	
				(C) G-AN1-101 to 16183	
Brake and clutch	AHA 6409	12	2	(C) H-AN7-24732 on	
				(C) G-AN2-16184 on	
Locknut	FNZ 205	13	2		
Fork-end	2A 5576	14	2		
Pin—clevis	2A 5575	15	2		
Circlip	1B 3498	16	2		
Box—pedal	2A 5538	17	1		
Excluder—draught	2A 5572	18	1		
Screw—short	HZS 0405	19	9		
Screw—long	HZS 0408	19	1		
Washer—spring	LWZ 304	20	10		
Plate—blanking—foot-well	2A 5589	21	1		
Screw	HZS 0405	22	8		
Washer—spring	LWZ 304	23	8		
Washer—joint—pedal box and blanking plate	2A 5549	24	2	(C) H-AN5-501 to 50116	W.S.E. use AHA 6366
				(C) H-AN6-101 to 11011	
				(C) G-AN1-101 to 6178	
Washer—joint	AHA 6366	24	2	(C) H-AN6-11012 to 24731	
				(C) H-AN7-24732 on	
				(C) G-AN1-6179 to 16183	
				(C) G-AN2-16184 on	

† Revised Information.

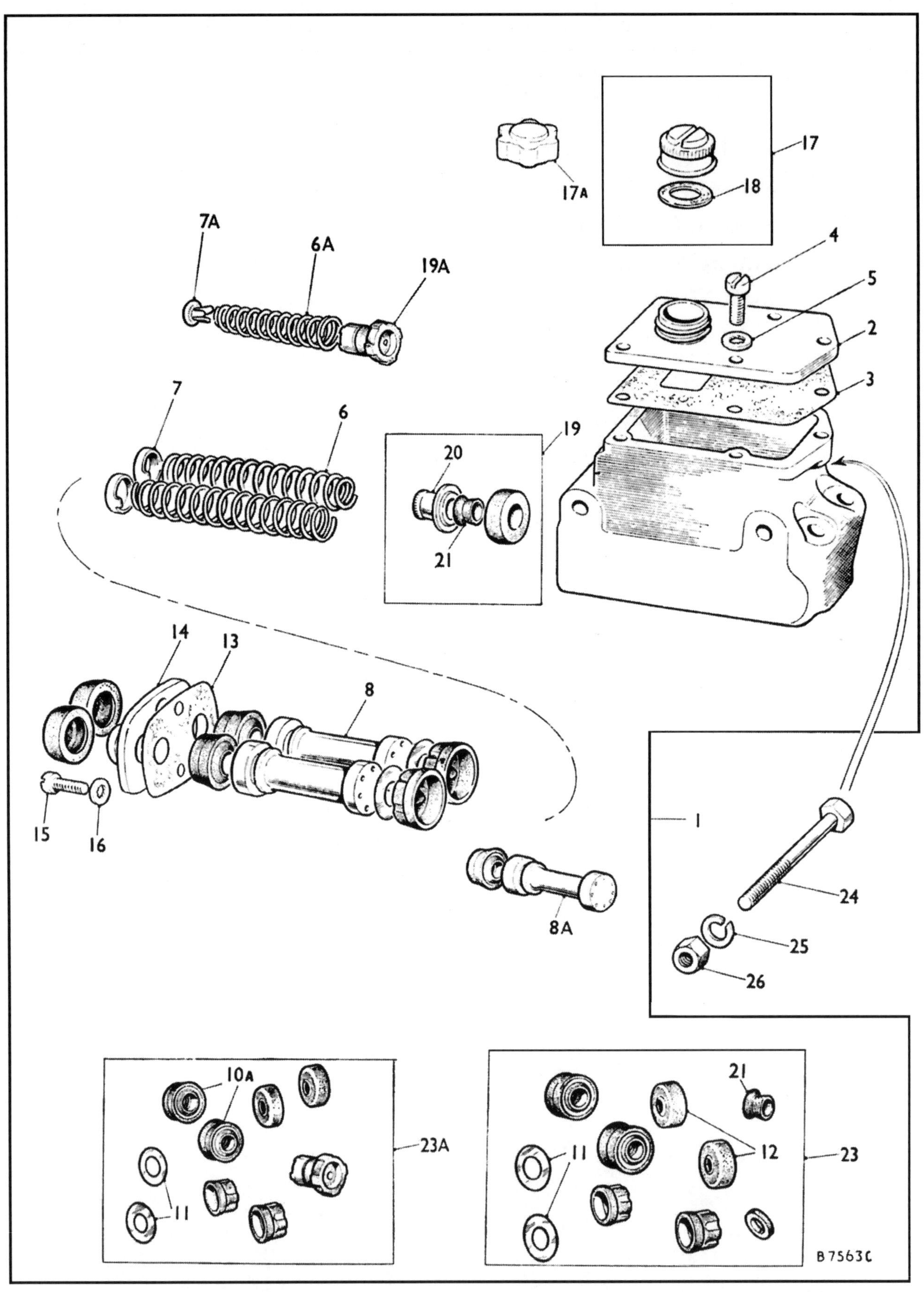
17
17A
18
4
7A
6A
19A
5
2
3
7
6
19
20
21
1
14
13
8
15
16
8A
24
25
26
10A
23A
11
21
11
12
23
B 7563C

DESCRIPTION	Part No.	Illus. No.	Quantity	Change Point	REMARKS
Brake Controls—*continued*					
BRAKE MASTER CYLINDER					
Cylinder assembly—master	AJH 5128	1	1		W.S.E. use BHA 4365
Body	NSP		1		
Cover—body	AJH 5085	2	1		W.S.E. use 17H 3721
Gasket—cover	†AJH 5086	3	1		W.S.E. use 37H 2496
Gasket—cover	†37H 2496	3	1		
Screw—cover to body	AAA 4758	4	5		Part No. change; was 301551
Washer—shakeproof	LWZ 404	5	5		
Spring—piston return	AJH 5083	6	2		
Retainer—spring	7H 7487	7	2		W.S.E. use 17H 7571
Retainer—spring	17H 7571	7	2		
Piston	7H 7925	8	2		
Gasket—boot plate	AAA 4757	13	1		Part No. change; was 301550
Plate—boot	AAA 4756	14	1		Part No. change; was 301549
Screw—plate	AAA 4758	15	2		Part No. change; was 301551
Washer—shakeproof	LWZ 404	16	2		
Cap assembly—filler	AJG 5006	17	1		W.S.E. use 17H 7480
	17H 7480	17	1		W.S.E. use 17H 3723
	17H 3723	17	1	(C) H-AN5-501 to 50116	W.S.E. use 17H 6861
Seal	AJG 5016	18	1	(C) H-AN6-101 to 24731	W.S.E. use 17H 7408
Cap—filler (plastic)	17H 6861	17A	1	(C) G-AN1-101 to 16183	
Valve assembly	39731	19	1		W.S.E. use component parts
Body	7H 7488	20	1		
Cup	7H 7022	21	1		W.S.E. use 17H 7886] Also included in kit 8G 8224
Cup	†17H 7886	21	1		
Washer	NSP		1		Was 7H 7489
Kit—master cylinder repair	8G 8224	23	1		
Cup					
Primary—piston	†NSP		2		Was 7H 7485
Secondary—piston	NSP		2		Was 17H 7109
Valve	7H 7022	21	1		W.S.E. use 17H 7886
Valve	17H 7886	21	1		
Washer—primary cup to piston	7H 7484	11	2		W.S.E. use 7H 8355
Washer—primary cup to piston	7H 8355	11	2		
Boot—push-rod	AJH 5084	12	2		
Washer—valve	NSP		1		Was 7H 7489
Cylinder assembly—master	BHA 4365	1	1		
Body	NSP		1		
Cover—body	17H 3721	2	1		
Gasket—cover	†AJH 5086	3	1		W.S.E. use 37H 2496
Gasket—cover	†37H 2496	3	1		
Screw—cover	AAA 4758	4	5		
Washer—shakeproof	LWZ 404	5	5		
Spring—piston return	17H 7981	6A	2		
Retainer—return spring	17H 7554	7A	2		
Piston	17H 3687	8A	2		
Gasket—boot plate	AAA 4757	13	1	(C) H-AN7-24732 on	
Plate—boot	AAA 4756	14	1	(C) G-AN2-16184 on	
Screw—plate	AAA 4758	15	2		
Washer—shakeproof	LWZ 404	16	2		
Kit—master cylinder repair	8G 8766	23A	1		
Cup—primary—piston	NSP		2		Was 17H 7122
Cup—secondary—piston	17H 7123	10A	2		
Washer—primary cup to piston	17H 7984	11	2		
Boot—push-rod	†NSP		2		Was AJH 5084
Valve	17H 7629	19A	1		
Cap assembly—filler	17H 3723	17	1	(C) H-AN7-24732 to ▼	W.S.E. use 17H 6861
Seal	17H 7408	18	1	(C) G-AN2-16184 to ▼	
Cap—filler (plastic)	17H 6861		1	(C) H-AN7- ▼ on (C) G-AN2- ▼ on	
Valve	†NSP		1	(C) H-AN7-24732 on (C) G-AN2-16184 on	Was 17H 7629
Bolt—short	HBZ 0624	24	1		
Bolt—long	HBZ 0626	24	1		
Washer—spring	LWZ 206	25	2		
Nut	FNZ 106	26	2		

▼ Change point not available

† Revised Information.

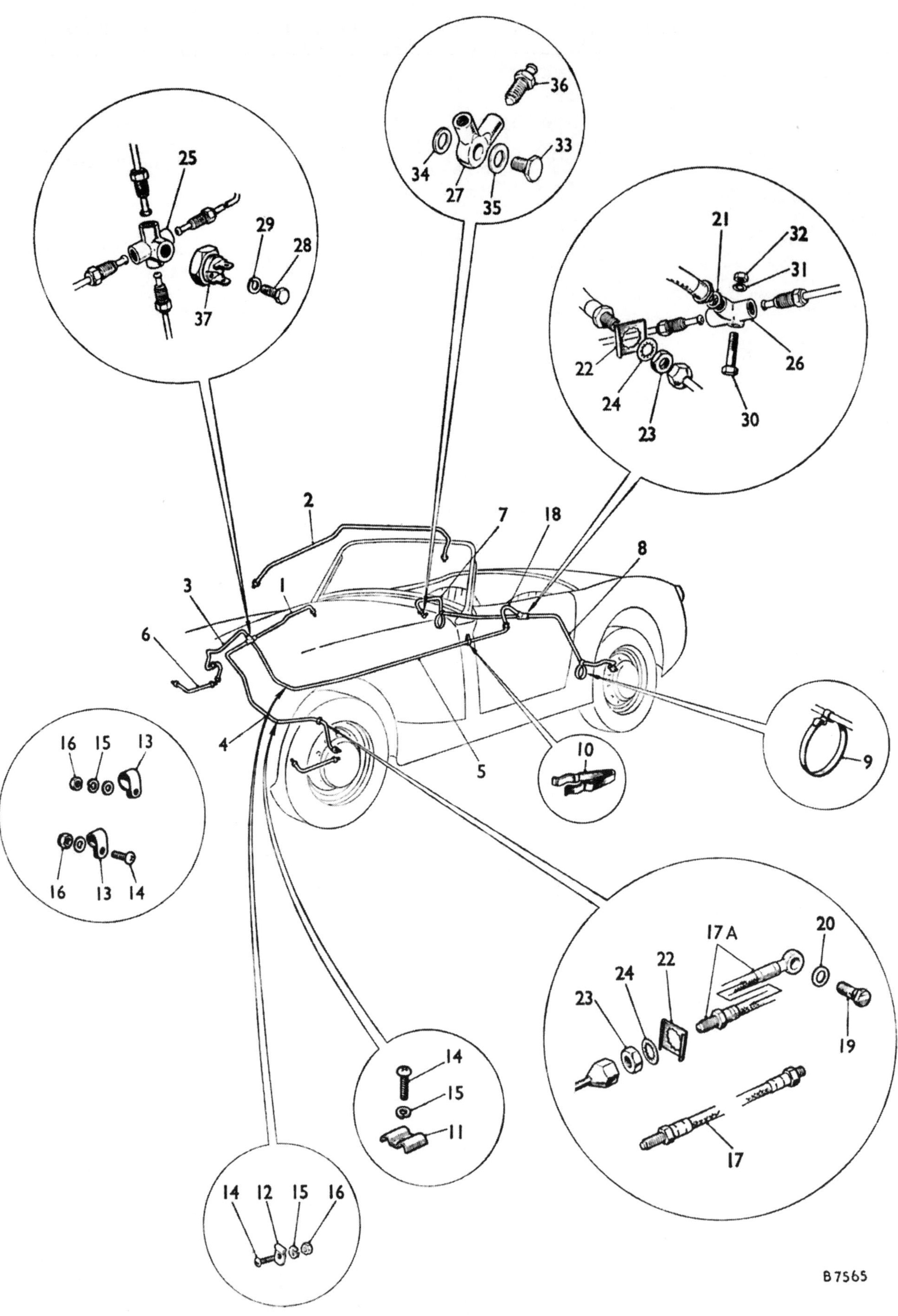
25
29
28
37
36
33
34
27
35
21
32
31
22
26
24
30
23
2
7
18
8
3
1
6
4
5
10
9
16 15 13
16 13 14
17 A
20
24
22
23
19
17
14
15
11
14 12 15 16
B 7565

DESCRIPTION	Part No.	Illus. No.	Quantity	Change Point	REMARKS
Brake Controls—*continued*					
BRAKE PIPES					
Pipe					
Master cylinder to 4-way connection—28" (71·12 cm) long **RHD**	2A 5605	1	1		
Master cylinder to 4-way connection—63" (160·02 cm) long **LHD**	2A 5619	2	1	(C) H-AN5-501 to 50116	
Master cylinder to 4-way connection—64" (162·56 cm) long **LHD**	AHA 5507	2	1	(C) H-AN6-101 to 24731 (C) H-AN7-24732 on (C) G-AN1-101 to 16183 (C) G-AN2-16184 on	
4-way connection to RH front brake hose—14" (33·02 cm) long	2A 5607	3	1		
4-way connection to LH front brake hose—47" (119·38 cm) long	2A 5609	4	1		
4-way connection to rear brake hose—74" (187·96 cm) long	2A 5611	5	1		
Bridge—front wheel cylinder—9" (22·86 cm) long	21D 69	6	2	(C) H-AN5-501 to 50116 (C) H-AN6-101 to 24731 (C) G-AN1-101 to 16183	Part No. change; was AHA 5198
3-way connection to RH rear brake—23" (58·42 cm) long	17H 7531	7	1	See (1) on page MM 8	
3-way connection to LH rear brake—31" (78·74 cm) long	2A 2181	8	1	See (1) on page MM 8	Part No. change; was 17H 7532
3-way connection to RH rear brake—22" (55·88 cm) long	AHA 6482	7	1	See (2) on page MM 8	
3-way connection to LH rear brake—30" (76·20 cm) long	ACB 9162	8	1	See (2) on page MM 8	
Strap—pipe	ACA 5375	9	1		
Clip					
Pipe to frame	6K 35	10	5		
Pipe to foot-well **RHD**	2H 400	11	1		
Pipe to dash **LHD**	CHR 0307	12	4		
Pipe to cover-plate bolt **LHD**	PCR 0311	13	3		
Screw **RHD**	PMZ 0305	14	1		
Washer—spring **RHD**	LWZ 203	15	1		
Screw **LHD**	PMZ 0305	14	4		
Washer—spring **LHD**	LWZ 203	15	4		
Nut **LHD**	FNZ 106	16	4		
Hose					
Front brake	13H 83	17	2	(C) H-AN5-501 to 50116 (C) H-AN6-101 to 24731 (C) G-AN1-101 to 16183	
Front brake	BHA 4311	17A	2	(C) H-AN7-24732 on (C) G-AN2-16184 on	W.S.E. use BHA 4543
Front brake **Except USA**	BHA 4543	17A	2	(C) H-AN7-24732 on (C) G-AN2-16184 on	
Rear brake **Except USA**	BCA 4031	18	1		
Front brake **USA**	AHA 8781	17A	2		
Rear brake **USA**	†AHH 8925	18	1		Correction; was AHA 8925
Bolt—banjo—front brake hose	11D 5264	19	2	(C) H-AN7-24732 on (C) G-AN2-16184 on	
Gasket—bolt	3H 550	20	2	(C) H-AN7-24732 on (C) G-AN2-16184 on	
Gasket—brake hose	3H 2287	21	3		
Plate—locking—brake hose	1G 9198	22	3		
Nut	FNZ 106	23	3		
Washer—shakeproof	LWN 406	24	3		Part No. change; was 2K 7131 and LWN 606
Connection					
4-way	17H 7108	25	1		Part No. change; was AHH 5288
3-way	3H 2424	26	1		
Banjo	AHH 5684	27	1	See (1) on page MM 8	
Screw	HBZ 0408	28	1		
Washer—spring	LWZ 204	29	1		
Bolt	HBZ 0409	30	1		
Washer—spring	LWZ 204	31	1		
Nut	FNZ 104	32	1		
Bolt—banjo connection	7H 7847	33	2	See (1) on page MM 8	
Gasket—small	3H 2287	34	2	See (1) on page MM 8	
Gasket—large	3H 550	35	2	See (1) on page MM 8	
Screw—bleeder	3H 2428	36	2	See (1) on page MM 8	
Switch—stop light	3H 1894	37	1	(C) H-AN5-501 to 50116	
Switch—stop light	13H 1781	37	1	(C) H-AN6-101 to 24731 (C) H-AN7-24732 on (C) G-AN1-101 to 16183 (C) G-AN2-16184 on	Part No. change; was 2A 5740

† Revised Information.

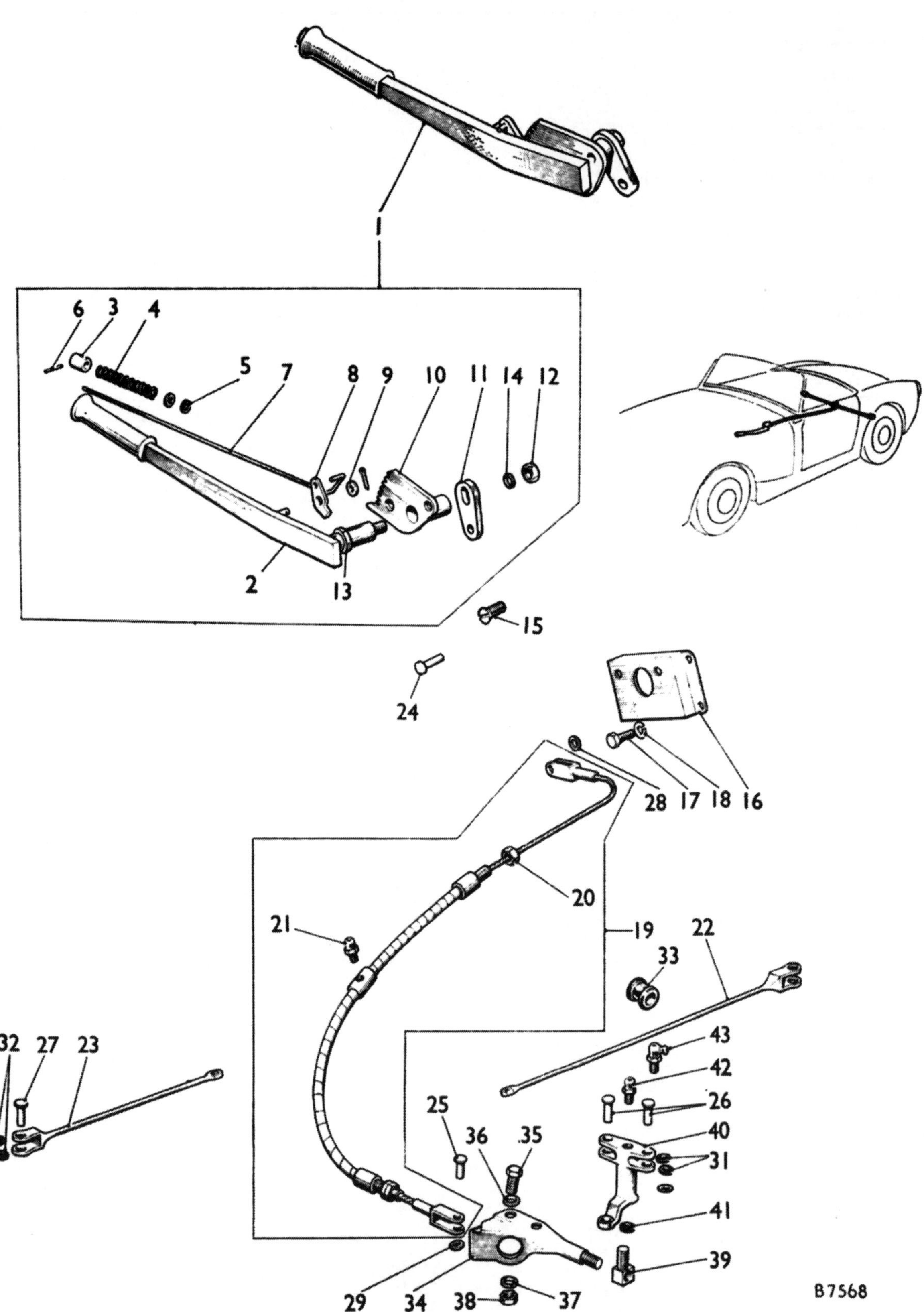
1
6
3
4
5
7
8
9
10
11
14
12
2
13
15
24
28
17
18
16
20
21
19
22
33
43
42
26
32
27
23
25
36
35
40
31
41
39
29
34
38
37
B7568

DESCRIPTION	Part No.	Illus. No.	Quantity	Change Point	REMARKS
Brake Controls—*continued*					
HAND BRAKE MECHANISM					
Hand brake assembly	2A 7290	1	1	See (1) foot of page	W.S.E. use AHA 6406
Hand brake assembly	AHA 6406	1	1	See (2) foot of page	
Handle	7H 5944	2	1	See (1) foot of page	
Handle	17H 2095	2	1	See (2) foot of page	
Plunger—thumb	7H 5948	3	1		
Spring—plunger	7H 5950	4	1		
Washer—plunger (rubber)	7H 5951	5	1		
Pin—plunger	MPS 4304	6	1		Part No. change; was 7H 5952
Rod—pawl	7H 5945	7	1	See (1) foot of page	
Rod—pawl	17H 2098	7	1	See (2) foot of page	
Pawl	7H 5946	8	1		
Washer—anti-rattle	†AWZ 104	9	1		Correction; was AWN 104
Ratchet	7H 5947	10	1		
Link—main spindle	7H 5949	11	1		
Nut	FNZ 106	12	1		
Washer—anti-rattle	17H 2091	13	1		
Washer—shakeproof	LWZ 406	14	1		
Screw—hand brake to bracket	88G 295	15	2		
Bracket—mounting	2A 7291	16	1		
Screw	HZS 0505	17	3		
Washer—spring	LWZ 205	18	3		
Cable assembly—hand brake	2A 7308	19	1		
Locknut	1B 7364	20	3		
Lubricator	UHN 105	21	1		
Cross-rod					
Right-hand	ATA 7458	22	1	See (1) on page MM 8	Disc wheels
Left-hand	ATA 7459	23	1	See (1) on page MM 8	Disc wheels
Right-hand	BTA 498	22	1	See (2) on page MM 8	Disc wheels
Left-hand	BTA 497	23	1	See (2) on page MM 8	Disc wheels
Right-hand	BTA 494	22	1	(B) H-AN7-20812	Wire wheels
Left-hand	BTA 495	23	1	(B) G-AN2-16780	Wire wheels
Pin—clevis					
Cable to hand brake lever	CLZ 0515	24	1		
Cable to balance lever	CLZ 0514	25	1		
Cross-rod to balance lever—long	6K 870	26	1	See (1) on page MM 8	
Cross-rod to balance lever—short	6K 689	26	1	See (1) on page MM 8	
Cross-rod to brake	CLZ 0514	27	2	See (1) on page MM 8	
Cross-rod to balance lever	CLZ 0814	26	2	See (2) on page MM 8	
Cross-rod to brake	2K 6930	27	2	See (2) on page MM 8	

CHANGE POINTS

(1) (C) H-AN5-501 to 50116, (C) H-AN6-101 to 21045, (C) G-AN1-101 to 13867
(2) (C) H-AN6-21046 to 24731, (C) H-AN7-24732 on, (C) G-AN1-13868 to 16183, (C) G-AN2-16184 on

DESCRIPTION	Part No.	Illus. No.	Quantity	Change Point	REMARKS
Washer—plain—pin					
Cable to hand brake	PWZ 105	28	1		
Cable to balance lever	PWZ 104	29	1		
Cross-rod to balance lever	AJD 7082	30	1	See (1) on page MM 8	Part No. change; was 6K 9695
Washer—pin (felt)					
Cross-rod to balance lever	6K 690	31	4		
Cross-rod to brake	ATA 7187	32	4	See (1) on page MM 8	
Cross-rod to brake	2K 5291	32	4	See (2) on page MM 8	
Ferrule—cross-rod steady	1B 5329	33	1	(C) H-AN5-501 to 50116	
Support—balance lever	ATA 7320	34	1		
Screw	HZS 0506	35	2		
Washer—plain	PWZ 105	36	2		
Washer—spring	LWZ 305	37	2		
Nut	FNZ 105	38	2		
Carrier—balance lever	2A 7058	39	1		
Lever—balance	2A 7057	40	1		
Washer—balance lever (felt)	2K 5820	41	1		
Lubricator—balance lever	8H 2192	42	1		Not available; use UHN 490
Lubricator—balance lever	UHN 490	43	1		

CHANGE POINTS

(1) (C) H-AN5-501 to 50116
(C) H-AN6-101 to 20792 (less 20545 to 20579, 20581, 20584 to 20594, 20597 to 20691, 20697 to 20740, 20758, 20759, and 20761 to 20787)
(C) G-AN1-101 to 13554

(2) (C) H-AN6-20793 to 24731 (plus 20545 to 20579, 20581, 20584 to 20594, 20597 to 20691, 20697 to 20740, 20758, 20759, and 20761 to 20787)
(C) H-AN7-24732 on
(C) G-AN1-13554 to 16183
(C) G-AN2-16184 on

† Revised Information.

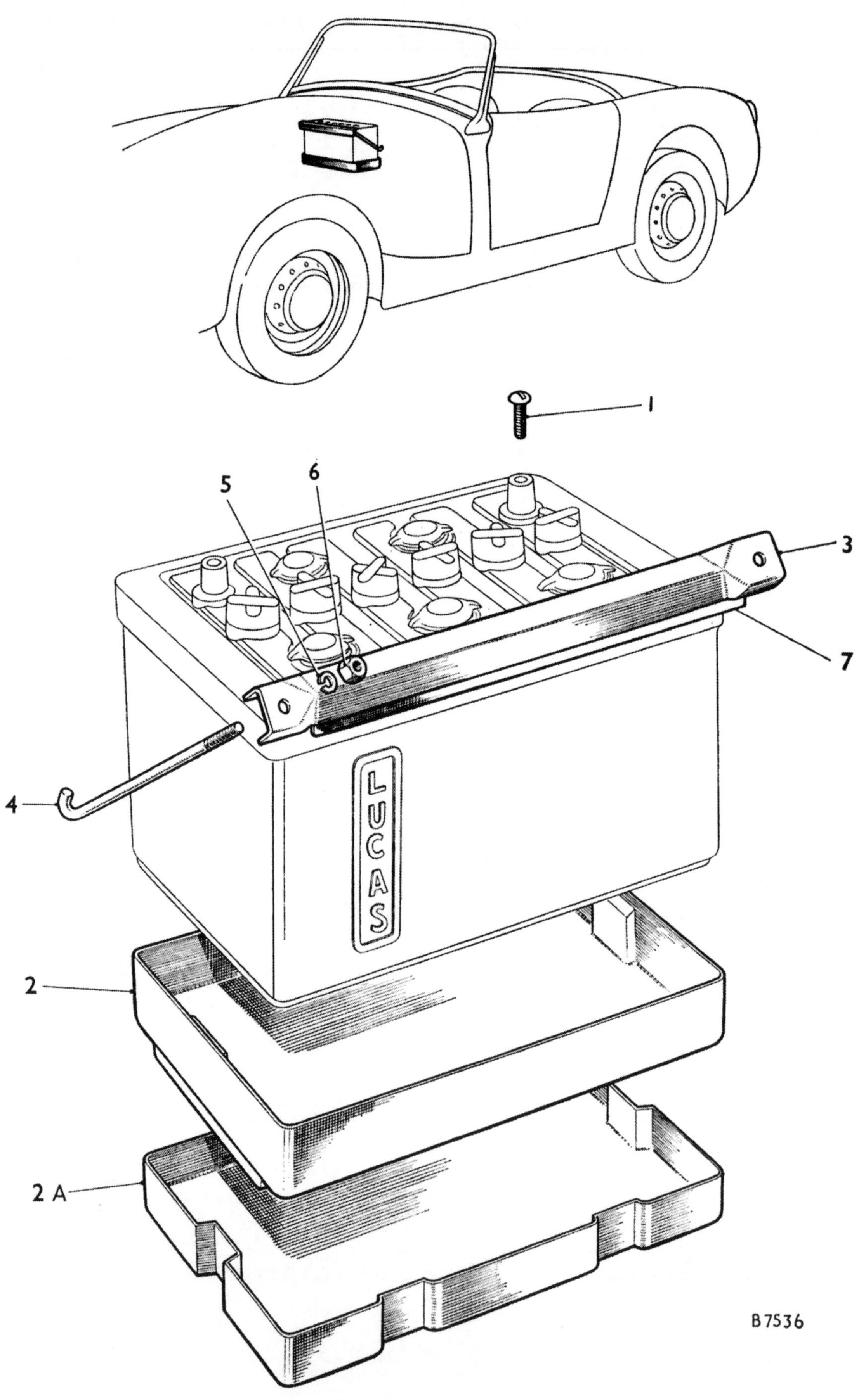
1
5
6
3
7
4
LUCAS
2
2 A
B7536

ELECTRICAL EQUIPMENT

	Page	Plate
BATTERY	MN 2	N 1
CABLES—WIRING	MN 22–MN 25	N 15, N 16
CONTROL BOX	MN 5, MN 6	N 4, N 5
DYNAMO	MN 3	N 2
FLASHER UNIT	MN 5, MN 6	N 4, N 5
FUSEBOX	MN 5, MN 6	N 4, N 5
HEADLAMPS (SPRITE AN5)	MN 7–MN 9	N 6
HEADLAMPS (SPRITE Mk. II & MIDGET Mk. I)	MN 11–MN 15	N 8, N 9
HORNS	MN 18, MN 19	N 11, N 12
LAMPS—SIDE, STOP/TAIL FLASHER, NUMBER-PLATE, AND FOG (SPRITE AN5)	MN 10	N 7
LAMPS—SIDE, STOP/TAIL FLASHER, NUMBER-PLATE, AND FOG (SPRITE Mk. II & MIDGET Mk. I)	MN 16, MN 17	N 10
SLIP-RING	MN 18, MN 19	N 11, N 12
STARTER	MN 4	N 3
SWITCH—DIRECTION INDICATOR	MN 5, MN 6	N 4, N 5
SWITCHES	MN 5, MN 6	N 4, N 5
WINDSCREEN WIPER	MN 20, MN 21	N 13, N 14

ELECTRICAL EQUIPMENT

BATTERY AND FIXINGS

DESCRIPTION	Part No.	Illus. No.	Quantity	Change Point	REMARKS
Battery	NSP		1		
Screw—terminal	2K 8645	1	2		
Tray—battery	4G 6680	2	1	(C) H-AN5-501 to 50116	
				(C) H-AN6-101 to 7959	
				(C) G-AN1-101 to 3733	
Tray—battery	AHA 6305	2A	1	(C) H-AN6-7960 to 24731	
				(C) H-AN7-24732 on	
				(C) G-AN1-3734 to 16183	
				(C) G-AN2-16184 on	
Bar—battery fixing	14G 5508	3	1	(C) H-AN5-501 to 50116	
Rod—battery fixing	88G 294	4	2	(C) H-AN6-101 to 24731	Part No. change; was 14A 4667
				(C) H-AN7-24732 to 27755	
				(C) G-AN1-101 to 16183	
				(C) G-AN2-16184 to 18219	
Bar—battery fixing	AHA 6934	3	1	(C) H-AN7-27756 on	
Rod—battery fixing	AHA 6935	4	2	(C) G-AN2-18220 on	W.S.E. use AHA 7769
Rod—battery fixing	AHA 7769	4	2		
Washer—spring	LWZ 204	5	2		
Nut	FNZ 104	6	2		
Packing—bar to battery—9¼″ (24 cm)	†14G 7532	7	1		W.S.E. use 27H 4149
Packing—bar to battery	†27H 4149		A/R		Supplied in multiples of feet

† Revised Information.

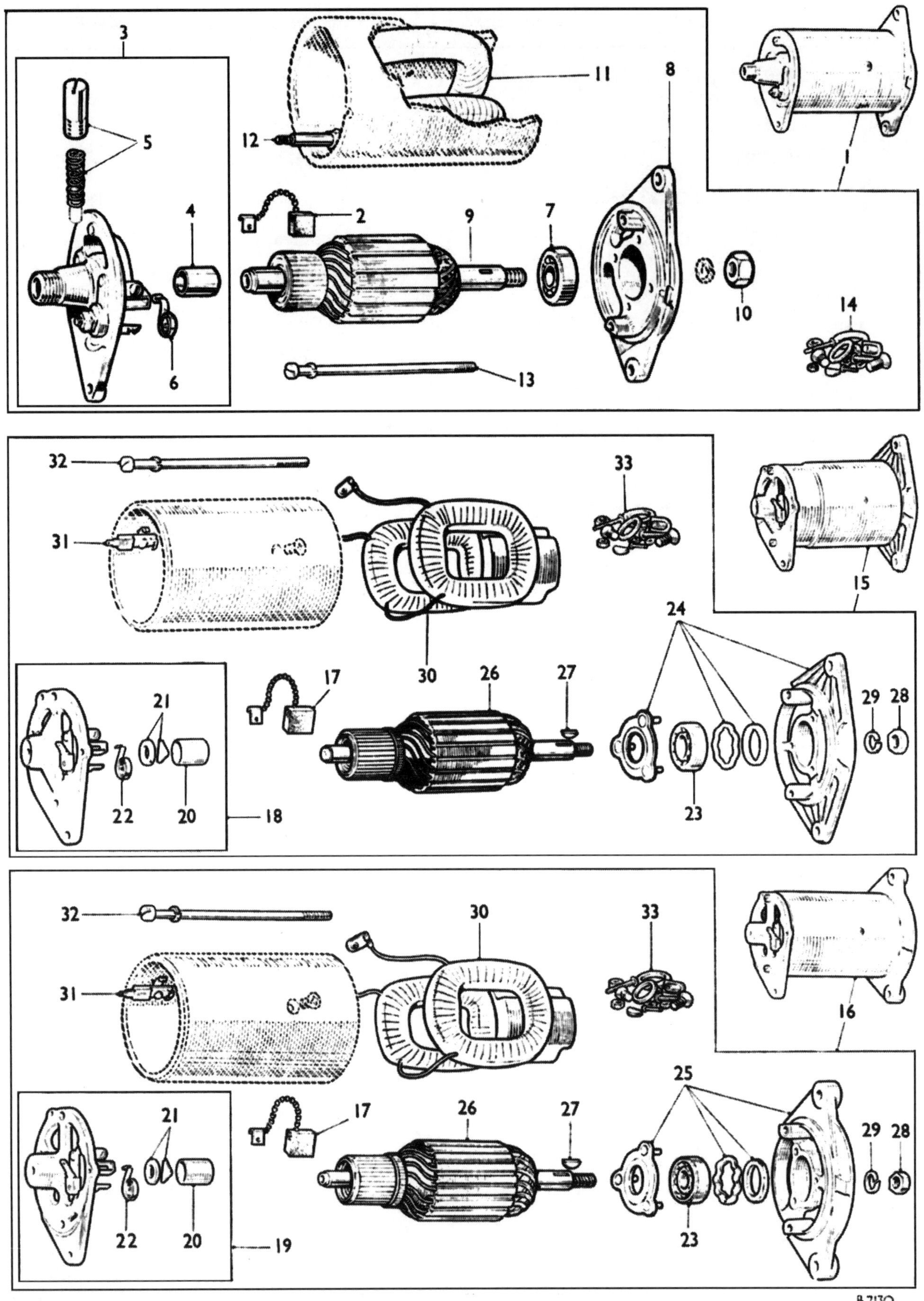
3
5
4
6
12
11
8
2
9
7
10
14
13
1
32
33
31
30
15
24
17
26
27
29
28
21
22
20
18
23
32
30
33
31
16
25
17
26
27
29
28
21
22
20
19
23
B 7130

Electrical Equipment—*continued*

DESCRIPTION	Part No.	Illus. No.	Quantity	Change Point	REMARKS
DYNAMO					
Dynamo assembly	†AEA 309	1	1		W.S.E. use 13H 219
Brush	7H 5028	2	1 set		
Bracket assembly—commutator end	27H 5420	3	1		
Bearing—bushing	7H 5390	4	1		
Oiler	7H 5527	5	1		
Spring—brush tension	7H 5031	6	1 set		
Bearing—drive end	97H 626	7	1		
Bracket—drive end	7H 5388	8	1	(E) 9C/U/H101 to H49201	
Armature	37H 5207	9	1	(E) 9CG/Da/H101 to 36711	
Nut	7H 5034	10	1		Use FNN 207 for this application
Nut	FNN 207	10	1		
Coil—field	7H 5071	11	1 set		
Terminal	17H 5433	12	1		
Bolt—through-fixing	17H 5217	13	2		
Sundry parts	7H 5376	14	1 set		
Dynamo assembly	AEJ 49	1	1		
Brush	47H 5388	2	1 set		
Bracket assembly—commutator end	57H 5338	3	1		
Bearing—bushing	7H 5390	4	1		
Oiler	7H 5527	5	1		
Spring—brush tension	47H 5389	6	1 set		
Bearing—drive end	97H 626	7	1	See (2) page MN 26	
Bracket—drive end	57H 5339	8	1		
Armature	57H 5340	9	1		
Nut	FNN 207	10	1		
Coil—field	57H 5341	11	1 set		
Terminal	57H 5084	12	1		
Bolt—through-fixing	17H 5217	13	2		
Sundry parts	57H 5085	14	1 set		
Dynamo assembly	13H 219	15	1	(E) 10CG/Da/H101 to H2570	
Dynamo assembly	13H 826	16	1	(E) 10CG/Da/H2571 on	
Brush	47H 5388	17	1 set		
Bracket assembly—commutator end	47H 5395	18	1	(E) 10CG/Da/H101 to H2570	
Bracket assembly—commutator end	17H 6821	19	1	(E) 10CG/Da/H2571 on	
Bearing—bushing	7H 5390	20	1		
Oiler	47H 5394	21	1		
Spring—brush tension	47H 5389	22	1 set		
Bearing—drive end	97H 626	23	1		
Bracket—drive end	47H 5393	24	1	(E) 10CG/Da/H101 to H2570	
Bracket—drive end	17H 6822	25	1	(E) 10CG/Da/H2571 on	
Armature	47H 5391	26	1	(E) 10CG/Da/H101 to H2570	
	†17H 6823	26	1	(E) 10CG/Da/H2571 on	W.S.E. use 27H 3574
	27H 3574	26	1		
Key	WKN 404	27	1		
Nut	FNN 207	28	1		
Washer—spring	LWZ 207	29	1		
Coil—field	57H 5341	30	1 set		
Terminal	57H 5084	31	1 set		
Bolt—through-fixing	17H 5217	32	2		
Sundry parts	57H 5085	33	1 set		

† Revised Information.

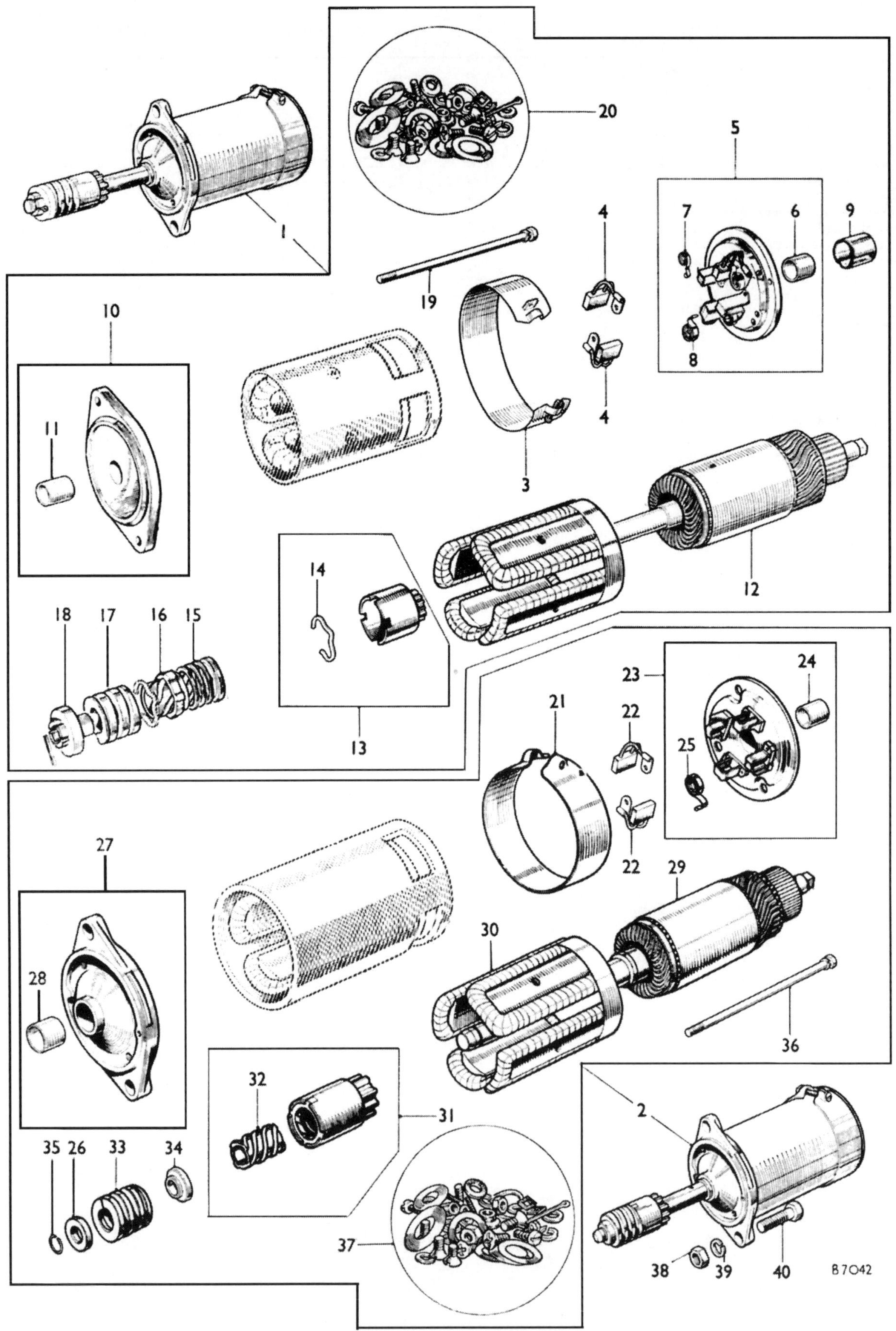
1
2
3
4
4
4
5
6
7
8
9
10
11
12
13
14
15
16
17
18
19
20
21
22
22
23
24
25
26
27
28
29
30
31
32
33
34
35
36
37
38
39
40
B7042

Electrical Equipment—*continued*

STARTER

DESCRIPTION	Part No.	Illus. No.	Quantity	Change Point	REMARKS
Starter	3H 952	1	1		Not available; use 13H 559
Band—cover	7H 5038	3	1		
Brush	7H 5040	4	1 set		
Bracket—commutator end	7H 5041	5	1		
Bush	7H 5042	6	1		
Spring—brush tension—split support post	7H 5043	7	1 set		See Austin Service Journal A/337
Spring—brush tension	47H 5341	8	1 set		
Cap—shaft	7H 5039	9	1	(E) 9C/U/H101 to H49201	
Bracket assembly—drive end	7H 5048	10	1	(E) 9CG/Da/H101 to ▼	
Bush	7H 5049	11	1		
Armature	7H 5050	12	1		
Pinion and barrel assembly	7H 5046	13	1		
Circlip—spring and control nut retaining	47H 5100	14	1		
Spring	7H 5047	15	1		
Sleeve—screwed (with control nut)	7H 5529	16	1		
Spring—main	7H 5045	17	1		
Nut—armature shaft	47H 5342	18	1		
Bolt—through-fixing	17H 5444	19	2		
Sundry parts	7H 5156	20	1 set		
Starter assembly	13H 559	2	1		
Band—cover	7H 5038	21	1		
Brushes	7H 5040	22	1 set		
Bracket assembly—commutator end	47H 5339	23	1		
Bush	47H 5340	24	1		
Spring—brush tension	47H 5341	25	1 set		
Cap—shaft	67H 5008	26	1		
Bracket assembly—drive end	67H 5014	27	1		
Bush	47H 5346	28	1	(E) 9CG/Da/H ▼ to H36711	
Armature	67H 5012	29	1	(E) 10CG/Da/101 on	
Coil—field	7H 5051	30	1 set		
Pinion and barrel assembly	67H 5010	31	1		
Sleeve—screwed	67H 5013	32	1		
Spring—main	7H 5045	33	1		
Cup—spring	67H 5008	34	1		Not available; use 27H 3755
Cup—spring	27H 3755	34	1		
Circlip—cup retaining	7H 6887	35	1		
Bolt—through-fixing	17H 5444	36	2		
Sundry parts	7H 5156	37	1 set		
Bolt	HBZ 0613	38	2		
Washer—spring	LWZ 306	39	2		
Nut	FNZ 106	40	2		

▼ Change point not available

† Revised Information.

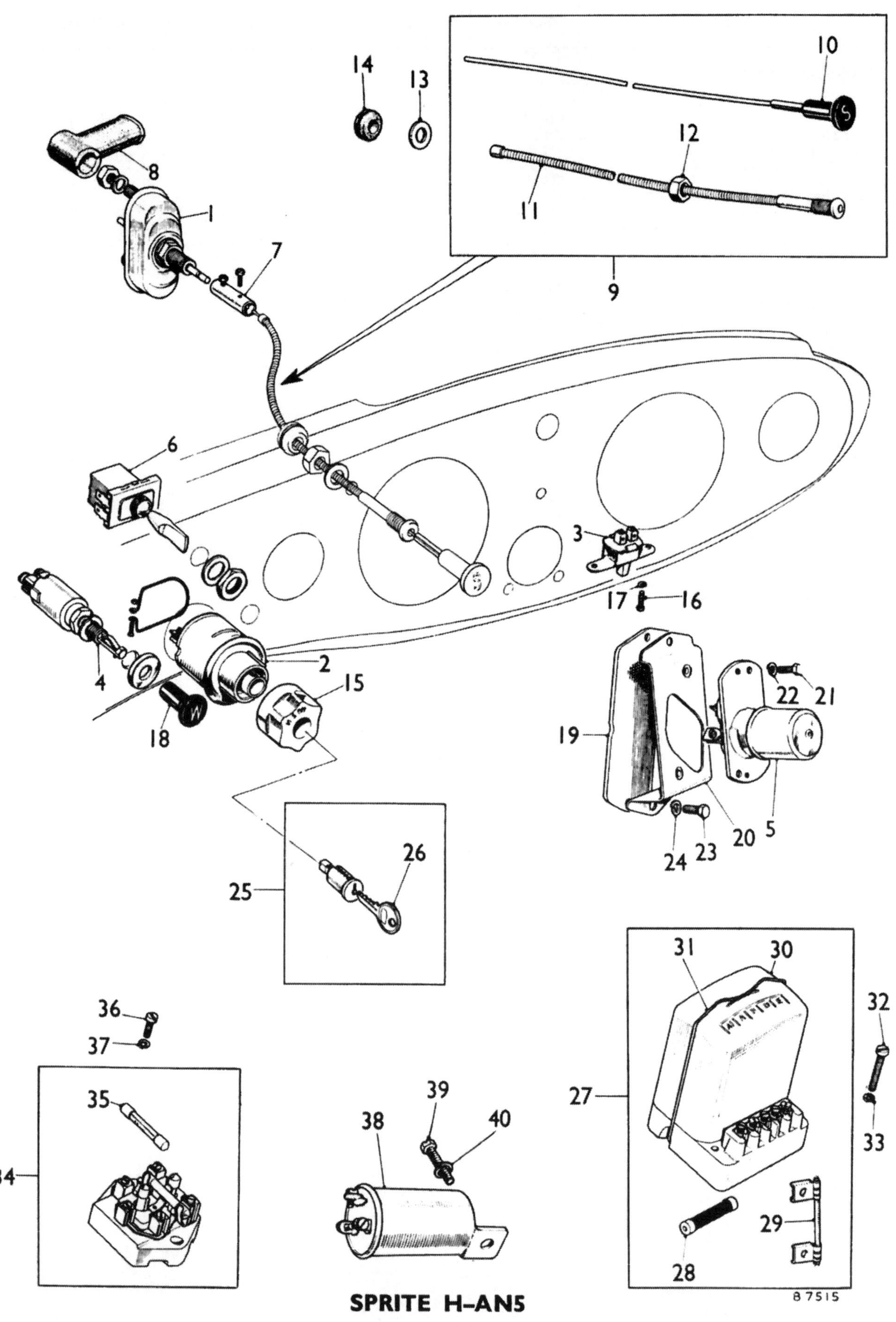

14
13
10
12
11
9
8
1
7
6
3
17
16
4
2
15
18
19
22
21
5
20
24
23
26
25
31
30
32
36
37
27
35
39
40
38
33
34
29
28
8 7515

SPRITE H-AN5

Electrical Equipment—*continued*

SWITCHES, CONTROL BOX, AND FUSEBOX (SPRITE H-AN5)

DESCRIPTION	Part No.	Illus. No.	Quantity	Change Point	REMARKS
Switch					
Starter	3H 949	1	1		
Lighting and ignition	3H 1557	2	1		
Panel light	3H 3100	3	1		
Windscreen wiper	3H 3095	4	1		Not available; use 27H 5278
Windscreen wiper	27H 5278	4	1		
Headlamp dipper	11G 2007	5	1		
Direction indicator	2A 9074	6	1		
Coupling—starter switch to control	3H 950	7	1		
Bootee—starter switch terminal	8G 548	8	1		
Cable assembly—starter control	2A 2085	9	1		
Cable—inner (with knob)	97H 2071	10	1		
Cable—outer	97H 2072	11	1		
Nut	97H 2073	12	1		Not available; use FNZ 206
Nut	FNZ 206	12	1		
Washer—plain	PWZ 106	13	1		
Grommet—cable through dash	RFN 303	14	1		
Knob—lighting and ignition switch	3H 1558	15	1		
Screw—panel light switch to fascia	AJD 1703 N	16	2		Part No. change; was 6K 9588
Washer—spring	LWZ 202	17	2		
Knob—windscreen wiper switch	11K 9101	18	1		
Pad—insulating—dipper switch	AHA 5285	19	1		
Bracket—dipper switch	2A 9102	20	1		
Screw	PMZ 0307	21	2		
Washer—spring	LWZ 203	22	2		
Screw	PMZ 0408	23	2		
Washer—spring	LWZ 204	24	2		
Barrel assembly—lock—ignition switch	7H 9830	25	1		Not available; use 2H 4185
	2H 4185	25	1		Not available; use 24G 1345
	24G 1345	25	1		
Key	ANK 4646	26	2		
Box assembly—control	3H 1885	27	1		
Resistance—63 ohms (carbon-type)	7H 5066	28	1		See Austin Service Journal A/826
Resistance—60 ohms (wire-wound)	47H 5589	29	1		See Austin Service Journal A/826
Cover	7H 5522	30	1		
Clip—cover	7H 5128	31	1		
Screw	PMZ 0820	32	2		
Washer—spring	LWZ 203	33	2		
Box assembly—fuse	1G 2613	32	1		
Fuse—35-amp	7H 5067	35	4		
Screw	PMZ 0310	36	2		
Washer—spring	LWZ 203	37	2		
Unit—flasher	11G 9093	38	1		
Screw	PMZ 0406	39	1		
Washer—spring	LWZ 204	40	1		

† Revised Information.

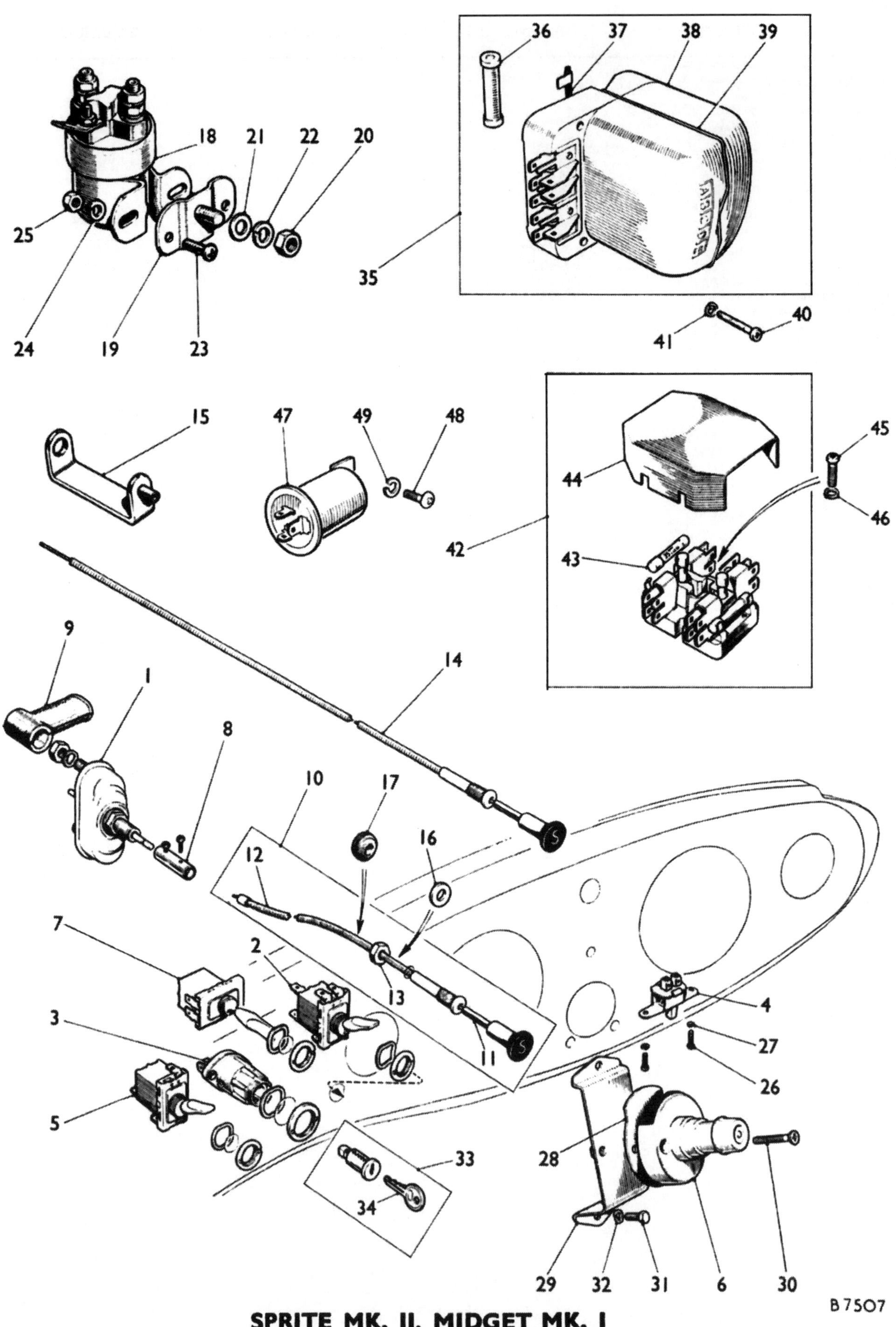

SPRITE MK. II, MIDGET MK. I

DESCRIPTION	Part No.	Illus. No.	Quantity	Change Point	REMARKS
Electrical Equipment—*continued*					
SWITCHES, CONTROL BOX, AND FUSEBOX (SPRITE MK. II AND MIDGET)					
Switch					
Starter	3H 949	1	1		
Lighting	BCA 4294	2	1		
Ignition	BHA 4234	3	1		Required when steering lock is not fitted
Panel light	3H 3100	4	1		
Windscreen wiper	BHA 4237	5	1		
Headlamp dipper	13H 176	6	1		
Flasher	2A 9074	7	1		Part No. change; was BHA 4188
Fog lamp	BCA 4294	2	1		Optional extra
Coupling—starter switch to control	3H 950	8	1		
Bootee—starter switch terminal	†8G 548	9	2		Correction; was 8G 584
Cable assembly—starter control **RHD**	2A 2085	10	1		
Cable—inner (with knob)	97H 2071	11	1		
Cable—outer	†97H 2072	12	1		W.S.E. use 2A 2085
Nut	†97H 2073	13	1		W.S.E. use FNZ 206
Nut	FNZ 206	13	1		
Cable—starter control } **LHD**	AHA 6202	14	1		
Bracket—cable } **LHD**	AAA 1534	15	1		Part No. change; was 129039
Washer—plain	PWZ 106	16	1		
Solenoid—starter	BHA 4265	18	1		For use when steering lock is fitted
Bracket—solenoid mounting	AHA 6269	19	1		For use when steering lock is fitted
Nut	FNZ 105	20	1		For use when steering lock is fitted
Washer—plain	PWZ 205	21	1		For use when steering lock is fitted
Washer—spring	LWZ 205	22	1		For use when steering lock is fitted
Screw	PMZ 0308	23	2		For use when steering lock is fitted
Washer—spring	LWZ 203	24	2		For use when steering lock is fitted
Nut	FNZ 103	25	2		For use when steering lock is fitted
Grommet—cable through dash	RFN 303	17	1		
Screw—panel light switch to fascia	AJD 1703 N	26	2		
Washer—spring	LWZ 202	27	2		
Pad—insulating—dipper switch	57H 5591	28	1		
Bracket—mounting—dipper switch	AHA 5516	29	1		
Screw	CMZ 0318	30	2		
Screw	PMZ 0408	31	2		
Washer—spring	LWZ 204	32	2		
Barrel assembly—lock—ignition switch	†7H 9830	33	1		W.S.E. use 24G 1345; Required when steering lock is not fitted
	†2H 4185	33	1		W.S.E. use 24G 1345; Required when steering lock is not fitted
	24G 1345	33	1		Required when steering lock is not fitted
Key	ANK 4646	34	2		Required when steering lock is not fitted
Box assembly—control	13H 142	35	1	See (1) on page MN 26	
Box assembly—control	BCA 4308	35	1	See (2) on page MN 26	
Resistance—63 ohms (carbon-type)	7H 5066	36	1		See Austin Service Journal A/326 and Service Memorandum MG/324
Resistance—60 ohms (wire-wound)	47H 5589	37	1		See Austin Service Journal A/326 and Service Memorandum MG/324
Cover	7H 5522	38	1		
Clip—cover	7H 5128	39	1		
Screw	PMZ 0320	40	2		
Washer—spring	LWZ 203	41	2		
Box assembly—fuse	†13H 252	42	1		
Fuse—35-amp	7H 5067	43	4		
Cover	47H 5212	44	1		
Screw	PMZ 0310	45	1		
Washer—spring	LWZ 203	46	1		
Unit—flasher	13H 110	47	1		
Screw	PMZ 0408	48	1		
Washer—spring	LWZ 204	49	1		

† Revised Information.

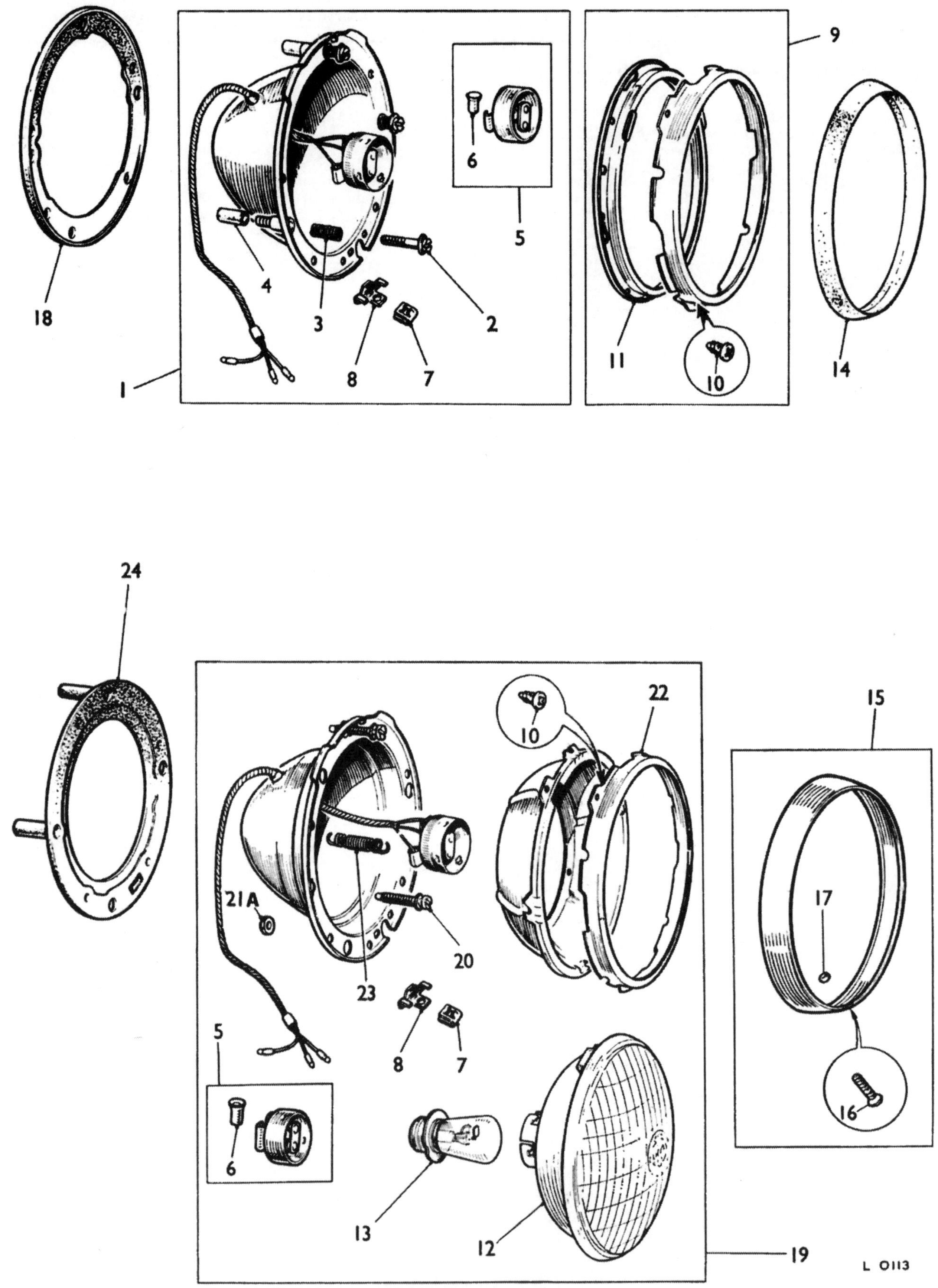

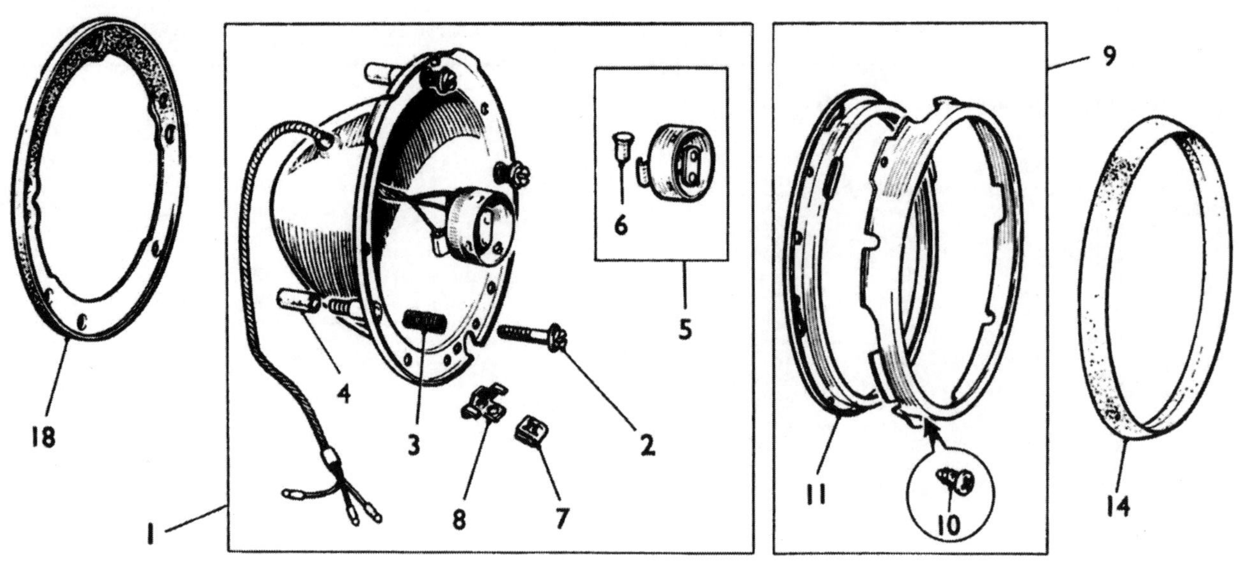

L O113

SPRITE H-AN5

Electrical Equipment—*continued*

DESCRIPTION	Part No.	Illus. No.	Quantity	Change Point	REMARKS
LAMPS—ROAD (SPRITE H-AN5)					
Headlamp assembly complete—left dip—Mk. VI	†8H 2518		2		W.S.E. use 27H 8209 together with 1 off rim 17H 5147 and 1 off gasket 13H 565
Headlamp assembly complete—left dip—Mk. VI	†47H 5365		2		W.S.E. use 27H 8209 together with 1 off rim 17H 5147 and 1 off gasket 13H 565
Body assembly	7H 6838	1	2		W.S.E. use 27H 8209 together with 1 off gasket 13H 565
Screw—trimmer	17H 5394	2	6		
Spring—trimmer screw	17H 5231	3	6		
Sleeve—sealing	27H 5253	4	6		
Adaptor (with cable)	17H 5145		2		W.S.E. use 17H 5306
	37H 5588		2		W.S.E. use 17H 5306
	27H 2333		2		W.S.E. use 17H 5306
Adaptor assembly	17H 5306	5	2		
Sleeve—terminal	27H 6713	6	6		Part No. change; was 7H 5582 and 37H 5271
Nut—rim fixing screw	27H 5354	7	2		
Bracket—rim fixing screw	37H 5190	8	2		
Plate assembly—light unit retaining	17H 5205	9	2		
Screw	PJZ 602	10	6		
Rim—light unit retaining	**RHD** 17H 5395	11	2		
Unit—light	**except** 7H 5483	12	2		
Bulb	**Europe** BFS 414	13	2		Part No. change; was 13H 140
Excluder—dust	8H 2962	14	2		
Rim assembly	17H 5147	15	2		
Screw	AJA 5081	16	2		
Washer (rubber)	21G 9057	17	2		
Gasket (rubber)	8H 1031	18	2		
Headlamp assembly—left dip—Mk. X	†27H 8209	19	2		W.S.E. use 27H 8495
Headlamp assembly—left dip—Mk. X	†27H 8495	19	2		
Screw—trimmer	67H 5025	20	4		
Nut—trimmer screw	27H 6482	21A	4		
Adaptor assembly	17H 5306	5	2		
Sleeve—terminal	27H 6713	6	6		
Nut—rim fixing screw	27H 5354	7	2		
Bracket—rim fixing screw	37H 5190	8	2		
Plate—light unit retaining	27H 3338	22	2		
Screw	PJZ 602	10	6		
Spring—unit seating rim	67H 5026	23	2		
Unit—light	7H 5483	12	2		
Bulb	BFS 414	13	2		
Rim assembly	17H 5147	15	2		
Screw	AJA 5081	16	2		
Washer (rubber)	21G 9057	17	2		
Gasket (rubber)	13H 565	24	2		

See T.I.B. 1B45 F18 for identification of Mk. VI and Mk. X headlamps

† Revised Information.

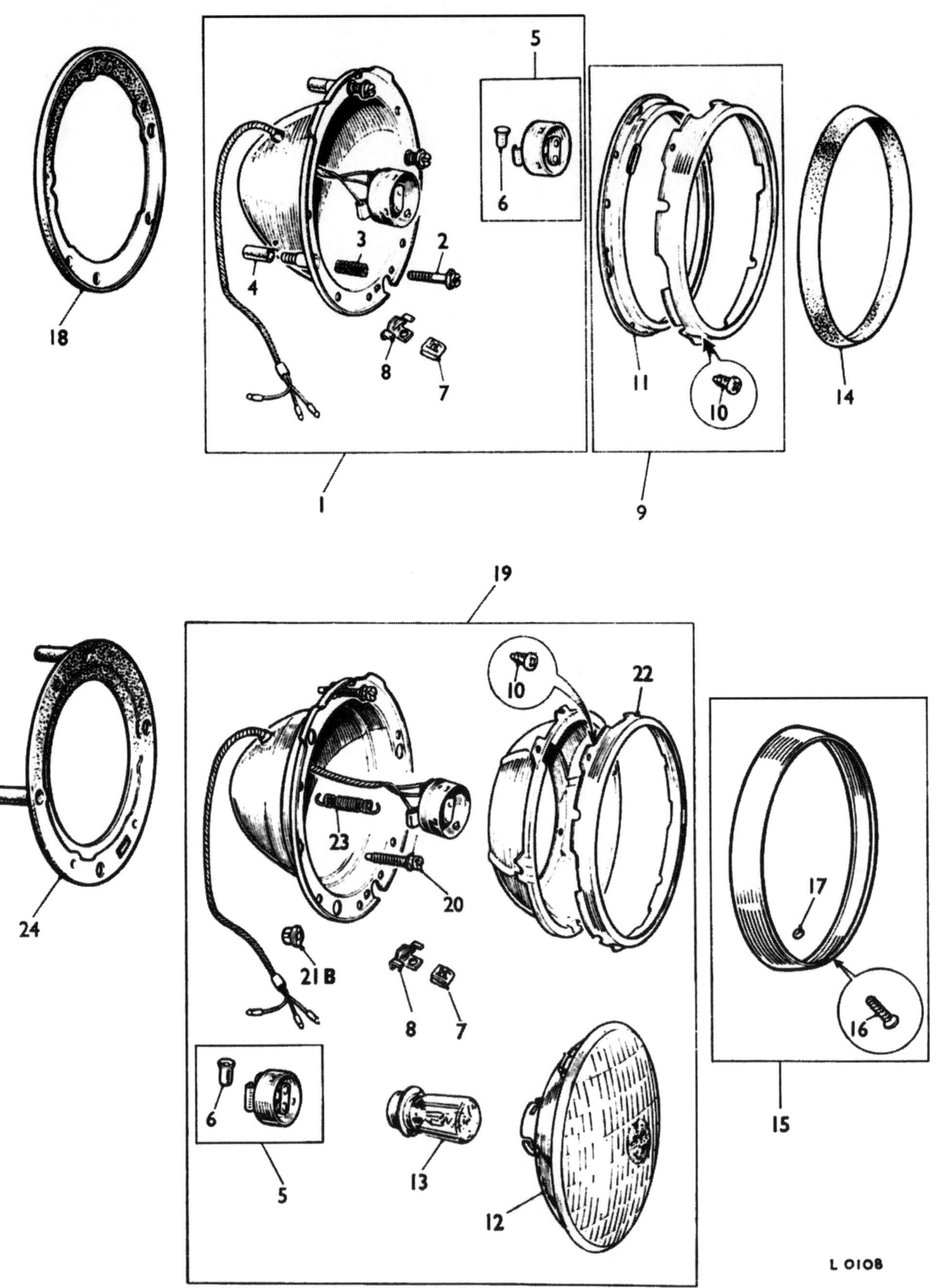
5
6
3
2
4
18
8
7
11
10
14
1
9
19
10
22
24
23
20
21 B
8
7
17
16
15
6
5
13
12
L 0108

Electrical Equipment—*continued*
Lamps—Road (Sprite H-AN5)—*continued*

DESCRIPTION		Part No.	Illus. No.	Quantity	Change Point	REMARKS
Headlamp complete—vertical dip—Mk. VI		8H 2520		2		Not available; use 27H 7971 together with 1 off rim 17H 5147 and 1 off gasket 57H 5358
Body assembly		7H 6838	1	2		Not available; use 27H 7971 together with 1 off gasket 57H 5358
Screw—trimmer		17H 5394	2	6		
Spring—trimmer screw		17H 5231	3	6		
Sleeve—sealing		27H 5253	4	6		Correction; was 27H 6253
Adaptor (with cable)		17H 5145		2		Not available; use 17H 5306
		37H 5588		2		Not available; use 17H 5306
		27H 2388		2		Not available; use 17H 5306
Adaptor assembly		17H 5306	5	2		
Sleeve—terminal		27H 6713	6	6		Part No. change; was 7H 5582 and 37H 5271
Nut—rim fixing screw		27H 5354	7	2		
Bracket—rim fixing screw		37H 5190	8	2		
Plate assembly—light unit retaining		17H 5205	9	2		
Screw	**LHD**	PJZ 602	10	6		
Rim—light unit retaining	**Europe**	17H 5395	11	2	(C) H-AN5-501 to 10488	
Unit—light	**except**	7H 5485	12	2		
Bulb	**France**	BFS 370	13	2		Part No. change; was 8H 921
Excluder—dust		8H 2962	14	2		
Rim assembly		17H 5147	15	2		
Screw		AJA 5081	16	2		
Washer (rubber)		21G 9057	17	2		
Gasket (rubber)		8H 1031	18	2		
Headlamp assembly—vertical dip—Mk. X		27H 7971	19	2		
Screw—trimmer		67H 5025	20	4		
Retainer—trimmer screw		27H 7824	21B	4		
Adaptor assembly		17H 5306	5	2		
Sleeve—terminal		27H 6713	6	6		
Nut—rim fixing screw		27H 5354	7	2		
Bracket—rim fixing screw		37H 5190	8	2		
Plate—light unit retaining		27H 3338	22	2		
Screw		PJZ 602	10	6		
Spring—unit seating rim		67H 5026	23	2		
Unit—light		7H 5485	12	2		
Bulb		BFS 370	13	2		
Rim assembly		17H 5147	15	2		
Screw		AJA 5081	16	2		
Washer (rubber)		21G 9057	17	2		
Gasket (rubber)		57H 5358	24	2		

See T.I.B. 1B45 F18 for identification of Mk. VI and Mk. X headlamps

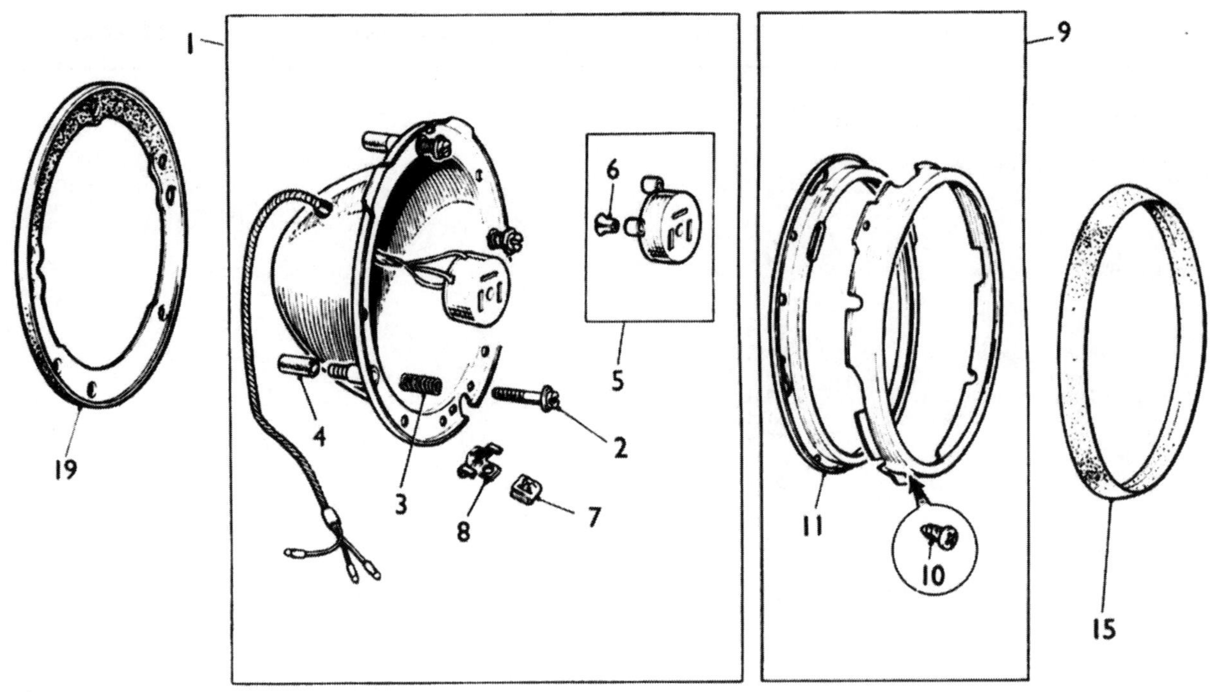
1
9
6
5
19
4
2
3
8
7
11
10
15

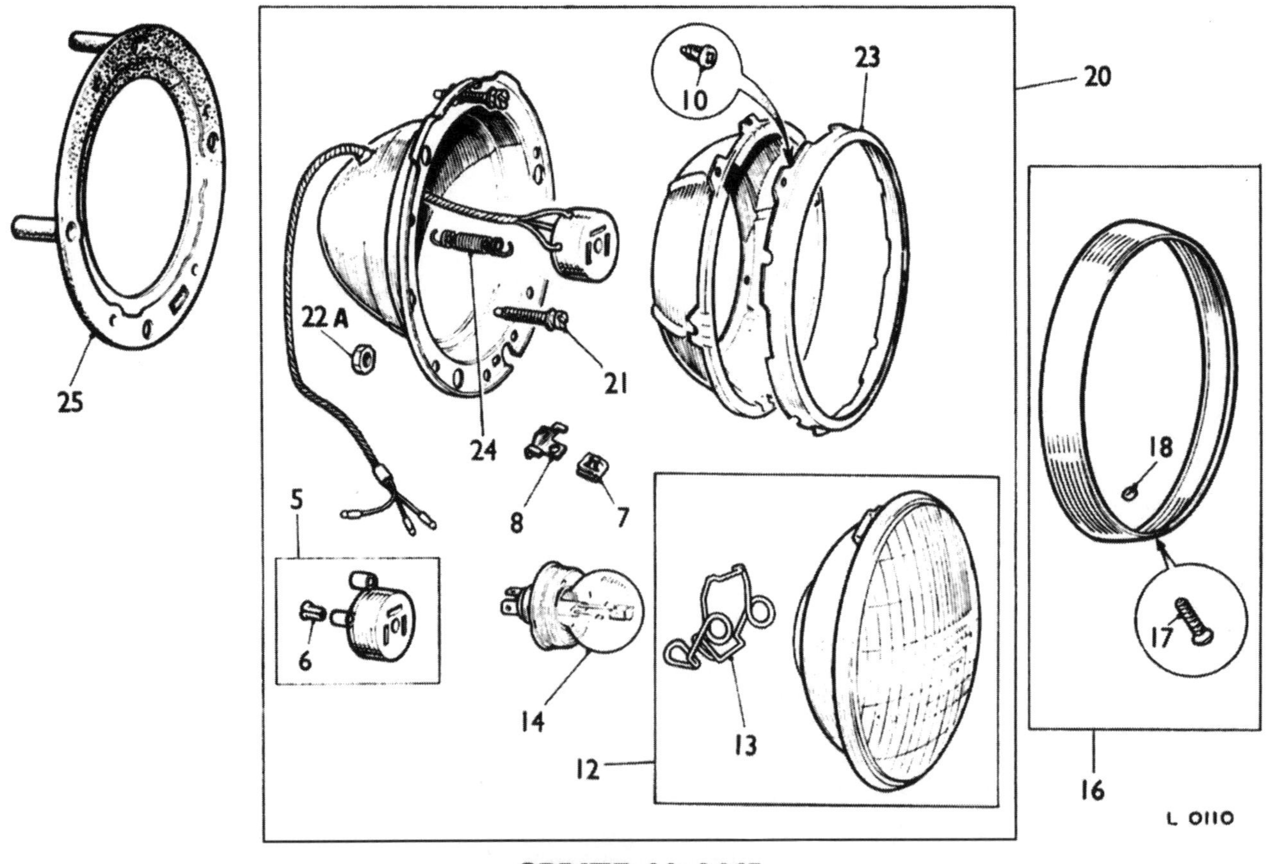
10
23
20
25
22 A
21
24
18
5
8
7
6
14
13
17
12
16
L 0110

SPRITE H-AN5

Electrical Equipment—*continued*
Lamps—Road (Sprite H-AN5)—*continued*

DESCRIPTION	Part No.	Illus. No.	Quantity	Change Point	REMARKS
Headlamp complete—vertical dip—Mk. VI	BHA 4092		2		Not available; use 27H 8204 together with 1 off rim 17H 5147 and 1 off gasket 13H 565
Body assembly	67H 5028	1	2		Not available; use 27H 8204 together with 1 off gasket 13H 565
Screw—trimmer	17H 5394	2	6		
Spring—trimmer screw	17H 5231	3	6		
Sleeve—sealing	27H 5253	4	6		
Adaptor (with cable)	BHA 4235		2		Not available; use 47H 5126
Adaptor assembly	47H 5126	5	2		
Sleeve—terminal	27H 6713	6	6		Part No. change; was 7H 5582 and 37H 5271
Nut—rim fixing screw	27H 5354	7	2		
Bracket—rim fixing screw	37H 5190	8	2		
Plate assembly—light unit retaining	17H 5205	9	2		
Screw	PJZ 602	10	6		
Rim—light unit retaining	17H 5395	11	2		
Unit assembly—light	47H 5124	12	2		Not available; use 27H 4146
Unit assembly—light	**LHD** 27H 4146	12	2		
Spring—bulb retaining	**Europe** 47H 5125	13	2	(C) H-AN5-**10489** on	
Bulb	**except** BFS 410	14	2	(except Sweden), 10489 to	Part No. change; was 13H 138
	France			21117 (Sweden)	
Excluder—dust	3H 2962	15	2		
Rim assembly	17H 5147	16	2		
Screw	AJA 5081	17	2		
Washer (rubber)	21G 9057	18	2		
Gasket (rubber)	3H 1031	19	2		
Headlamp assembly—vertical dip—Mk. X	27H 8204	20	2		
Screw—trimmer	67H 5025	21	4		
Nut—trimmer screw	27H 6482	22A	4		
Adaptor assembly	47H 5126	5	2		
Sleeve—terminal	27H 6713	6	6		
Nut—rim fixing screw	27H 5354	7	2		
Bracket—rim fixing screw	37H 5190	8	2		
Plate—light unit retaining	27H 3338	23	2		
Screw	PJZ 602	10	6		
Spring—unit seating rim	67H 5026	24	2		
Unit assembly—light	27H 4146	12	2		
Spring—bulb retaining	47H 5125	13	2		
Bulb	BFS 410	14	2		
Rim assembly	17H 5147	16	2		
Screw	AJA 5081	17	2		
Washer (rubber)	21G 9057	18	2		
Gasket (rubber)	13H 565	25	2		

See T.I.B. 1B45 F18 for identification of Mk. VI and Mk. X headlamps

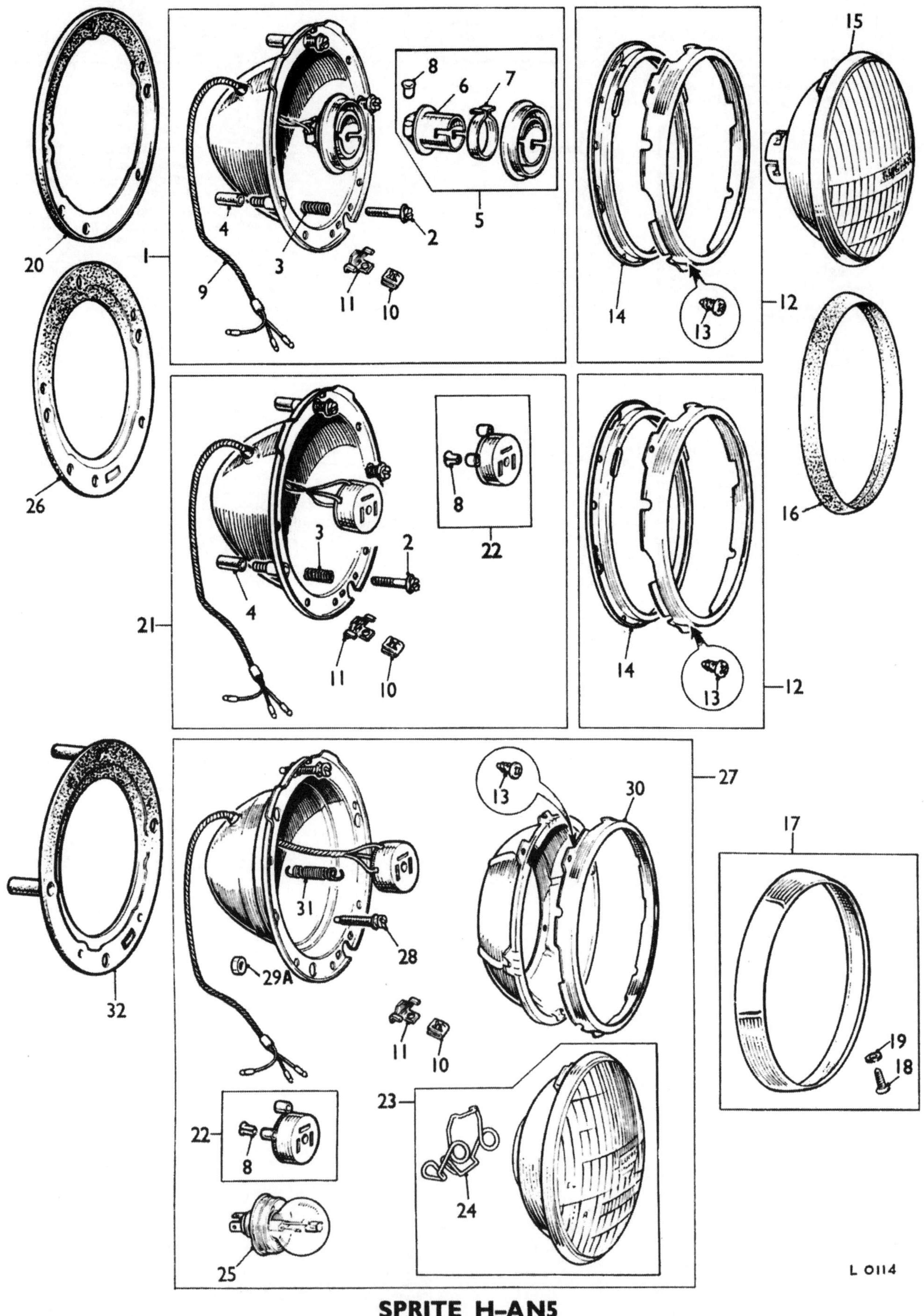

1
2
3
4
5
6
7
8
9
10
11
12
13
14
15
16
17
18
19
20
21
22
23
24
25
26
27
28
29A
30
31
32
L 0114

SPRITE H-AN5

DESCRIPTION	Part No.	Illus. No.	Quantity	Change Point	REMARKS
Electrical Equipment—*continued*					
Lamps—Road (Sprite H-AN5)—*continued*					
Headlamp complete (less bulb) — Mk. VI	8H 2521		2		Part No. change; was 17H 5530. W.S.E. use 37H 1368 together with 1 off rim 17H 5147 and 1 off gasket 57H 5358
Body assembly	7H 6915	1	2		W.S.E. use 37H 1368 together with 1 off gasket 57H 5358
Screw—trimmer	17H 5394	2	6		
Spring—trimmer screw	17H 5231	3	6		
Sleeve—sealing	27H 5253	4	6		
Back-shell assembly	17H 5146	5	2		
Holder—bulb	7H 5062	6	2		
Clip and screw	37H 5192	7	2	(C) H-AN5-501 to 7781	
Sleeve—terminal	27H 6713	8	6		Part No. change; was 7H 5582 and 37H 5271
Cable	†NSP		2		Was 7H 6916
Nut—rim fixing screw	27H 5354	10	2		
Bracket—rim fixing screw	37H 5190	11	2		
Plate assembly—light unit retaining	17H 5205	12	2		
Screw	PJZ 602	13	6		
Rim—light unit retaining	17H 5395	14	2		
Unit—light	7H 5486	15	2		
Excluder—dust	8H 2962	16	2		
Rim assembly	17H 5147	17	2		
Screw	AJA 5081	18	2		
Washer (rubber)	21G 9057	19	2		
Gasket (rubber)	8H 1031	20	2		
Headlamp complete—vertical dip—Mk. VI	**France** BHA 4098		2		W.S.E. use 37H 1368 together with 1 off rim 17H 5147 and 1 off gasket 13H 565
Body assembly	67H 5028	21	2		W.S.E. use 37H 1368 together with 1 off gasket 13H 565
Screw—trimmer	17H 5394	2	6		
Spring—trimmer screw	17H 5231	3	6		
Sleeve—sealing	27H 5253	4	6		
Adaptor (with cable)	BHA 4235		2		W.S.E. use 47H 5126
Adaptor assembly	47H 5126	22	2		
Sleeve—terminal	27H 6713	8	6		Part No. change; was 7H 5582 and 37H 5271
Nut—rim fixing screw	27H 5354	10	2		
Bracket—rim fixing screw	37H 5190	11	2	(C) H-AN5-7782 on	
Plate assembly—light unit retaining	17H 5205	12	2		
Screw	PJZ 602	13	6		
Rim—light unit retaining	17H 5395	14	2		
Unit assembly—light	47H 5124	23	2		W.S.E. use 27H 4146
Unit assembly—light	27H 4146	23	2		
Spring—bulb retaining	47H 5125	24	2		
Bulb	BFS 411	25	2		Part No. change; was 13H 139
Excluder—dust	8H 2962	16	2		Used with gasket 8H 1031 only
Rim assembly	17H 5147	17	2		
Screw	AJA 5081	18	2		
Washer (rubber)	21G 9057	19	2		
Gasket (rubber)	8H 1031	20	2		
Gasket (rubber)	7H 8338	26	2		Fitted to later headlamps

See T.I.B. 1B45 F18 for identification of Mk. VI and Mk. X headlamps

† Revised Information.

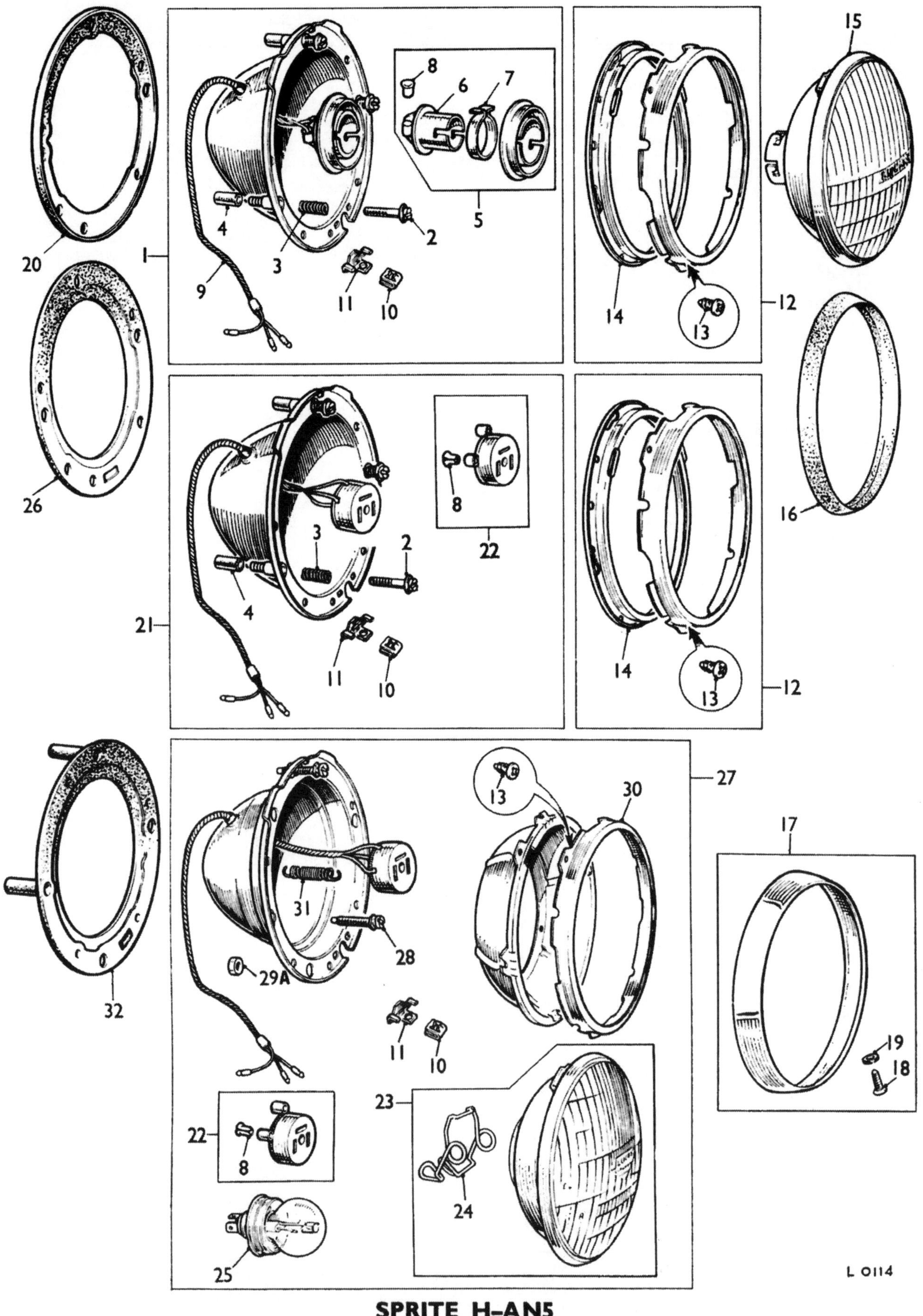
8
6
7
5
1
2
3
4
9
10
11
20
15
12
13
14
16
26
22
21
17
27
30
31
28
29A
32
19
18
23
24
25
L 0114

SPRITE H-AN5

DESCRIPTION		Part No.	Illus. No.	Quantity	Change Point	REMARKS
Electrical Equipment—*continued*						
Lamps—Road (Sprite H-AN5)—*continued*						
Headlamp assembly—vertical dip—Mk. X		37H 1368	27	2		
Screw—trimmer		67H 5025	28	4		
Nut—trimmer screw		27H 6482	29A	4		
Adaptor assembly		47H 5126	22	2		
Sleeve—terminal		27H 6713	8	6		
Nut—rim fixing screw		27H 5354	10	2		
Bracket—rim fixing screw		37H 5190	11	2		
Plate—light unit retaining		27H 3338	30	2		
Screw	**France**	PJZ 602	18	6		
Spring—unit seating rim		67H 5026	31	2		
Unit assembly—light		27H 4146	23	2		
Spring—bulb retaining		47H 5125	24	2		
Bulb		BFS 411	25	2		
Rim assembly		17H 5147	17	2		
Screw		AJA 5081	18	2		
Washer (rubber)		21G 9057	19	2		
Gasket (rubber)		57H 5358	32	2	(C) H-AN5-501 to ▼	
Gasket (rubber)		18H 565	32	2	(C) H-AN5-▼ on	

See T.I.B. 1B45 F18 for identification of Mk. VI and Mk. X headlamps

▼ Change point not available

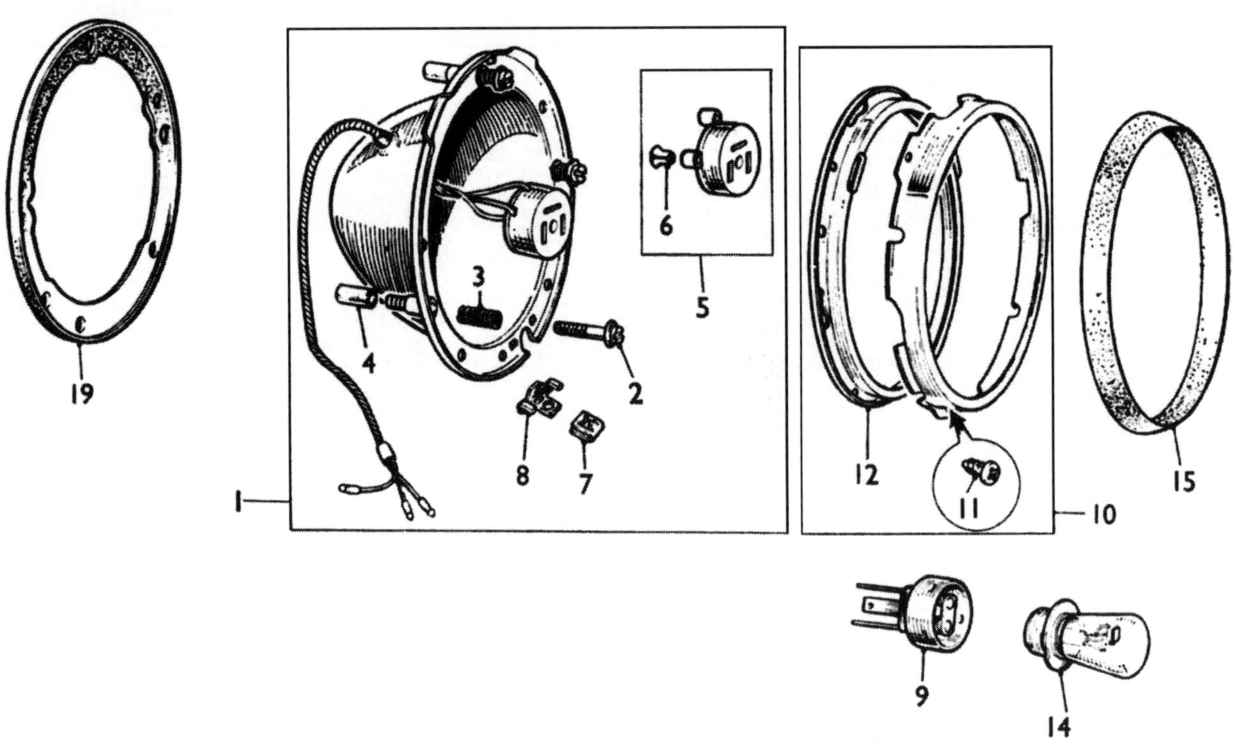
19
1
2
3
4
5
6
7
8
9
10
11
12
14
15

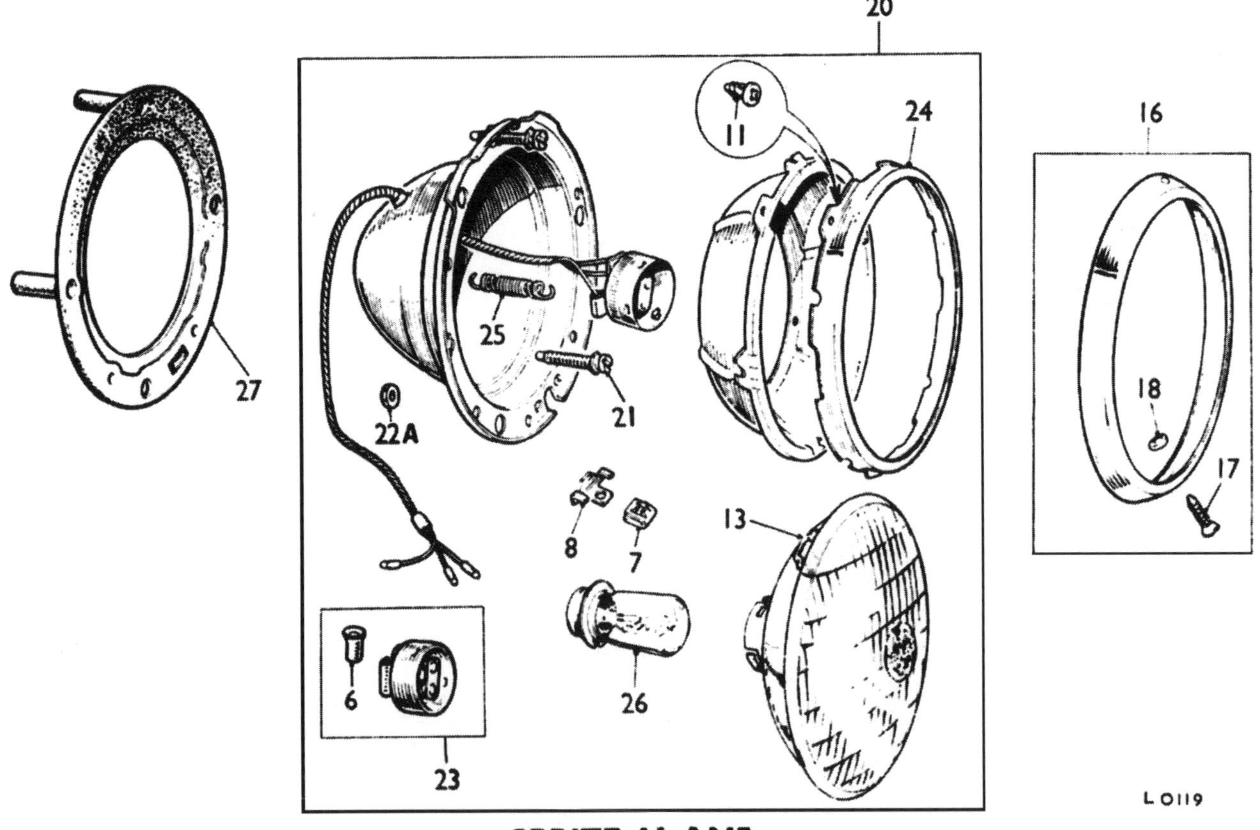
20
11
24
16
27
25
21
22A
18
17
13
8
7
6
26
23
L0119

SPRITE H-AN5

Electrical Equipment—*continued*
Lamps—Road (Sprite H-AN5)—*continued*

DESCRIPTION	Part No.	Illus. No.	Quantity	Change Point	REMARKS
Headlamp complete—vertical dip —Mk. VI	13H 323		2		Not available; use 27H 8287 together with 1 off rim 17H 5147 and 1 off gasket 13H 565
Body assembly	67H 5028	1	2		Not available; use 27H 8287 together with 1 off gasket 13H 565
Screw—trimmer	17H 5394	2	6		
Spring—trimmer screw	17H 5231	3	6		
Sleeve—sealing	27H 5253	4	6		
Adaptor (with cable)	BHA 4235		2		Not available; use 47H 5126
Adaptor assembly	47H 5126	5	2		
Sleeve—terminal	27H 6713	6	6		Part No. change; was 7H 5582 and 37H 5271
Nut—rim fixing screw	27H 5354	7	2		
Bracket—rim fixing screw	37H 5190	8	2		
Plate assembly—light unit retaining	17H 5205	9	2		
Screw	PJZ 602	10	6		
Rim—light unit retaining	17H 5395	11	2		
Unit assembly—light	NSP		2		Serviced by A.G.E.B.E. Sweden
Spring—bulb retaining	47H 5125	12	2		
Bulb **Sweden**	BFS 410	13	2	(C) H-AN5-21118 on	Part No. change; was 13H 138
Excluder—dust	3H 2962	14	2		
Rim assembly	17H 5147	15	2		
Screw	AJA 5081	16	2		
Washer (rubber)	21G 9057	17	2		
Gasket (rubber)	3H 1031	18	2		
Headlamp assembly—vertical dip —Mk. X	27H 8287	19	2		
Screw—trimmer	67H 5025	20	4		
Retainer—trimmer screw	27H 7824	21B	4		
Adaptor assembly	47H 5126	5	2		
Sleeve—terminal	27H 6713	6	6		
Nut—rim fixing screw	27H 5354	7	2		
Bracket—rim fixing screw	37H 5190	8	2		
Plate—light unit retaining	27H 3338	22	2		
Screw	PJZ 602	10	6		
Spring—unit seating rim	67H 5026	23	2		
Unit assembly—light	NSP		2		Serviced by A.G.E.B.E. Sweden
Spring—bulb retaining	47H 5125	12	2		
Bulb	BFS 410	13	2		
Rim assembly	17H 5147	15	2		
Screw	AJA 5081	16	2		
Washer (rubber)	21G 9057	17	2		
Gasket (rubber)	13H 565	24	2		

See T.I.B. 1B45 F18 for identification of Mk. VI and Mk. X headlamps

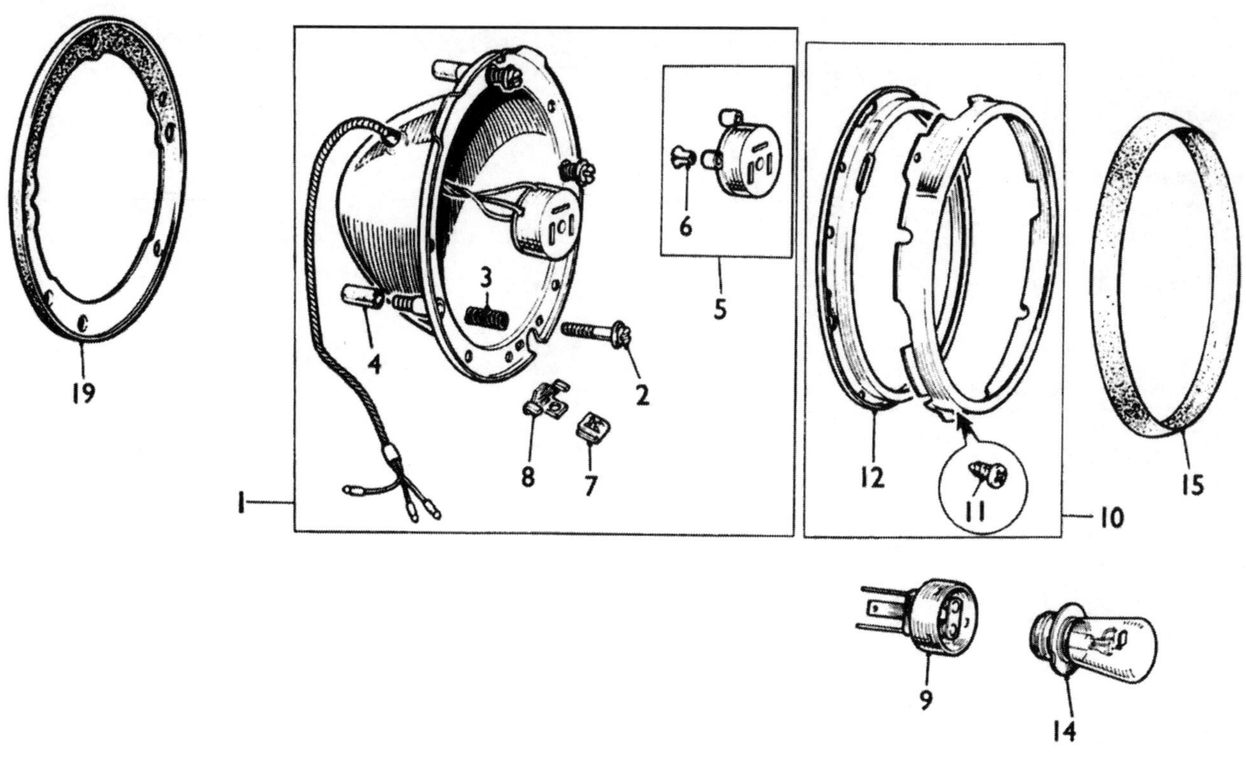
19
1
2
3
4
5
6
7
8
9
10
11
12
14
15

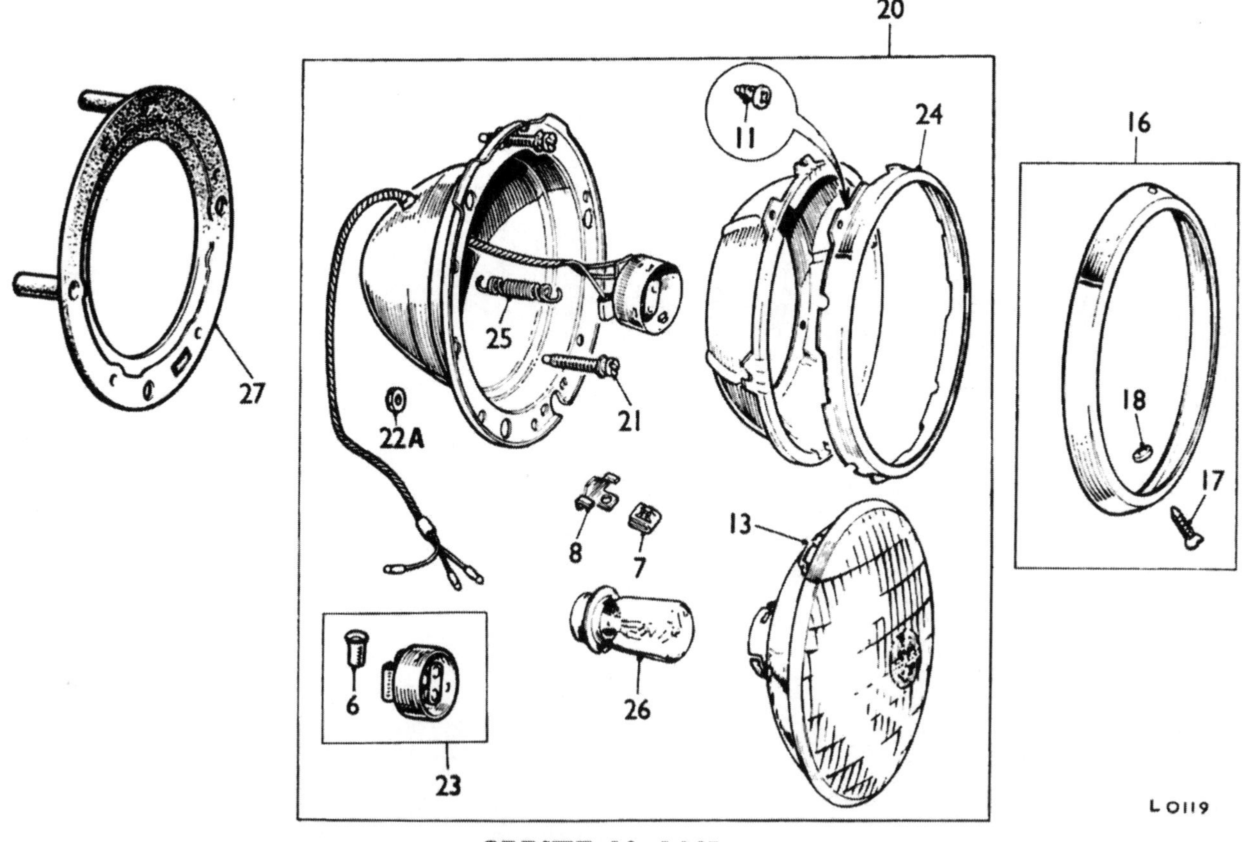
20
11
24
16
27
25
21
22A
8
7
13
18
17
6
23
26
L0119

SPRITE H-AN5

Electrical Equipment—*continued*
Lamps—Road (Sprite H-AN5)—*continued*

DESCRIPTION	Part No.	Illus. No.	Quantity	Change Point	REMARKS
Headlamp complete—right dip—Mk. VI	17H 5548		2		Not available; use 27H 8206 together with 1 off rim 17H 5147 and 1 off gasket 57H 5358
Body assembly	67H 5028	1	2		Not available; use 27H 8207 together with 1 off gasket 57H 5358
Screw—trimmer	17H 5394	2	6		
Spring—trimmer screw	17H 5231	3	6		
Sleeve—sealing	27H 5253	4	6		
Adaptor (with cable)	BHA 4235		2		Not available; use 47H 5126
Adaptor assembly	47H 5126	5	2		
Sleeve—sealing	27H 6713	6	6		Part No. change; was 7H 5582 and 37H 5271
Nut—rim fixing screw	27H 5354	7	2		
Bracket—rim fixing screw	37H 5190	8	2		
Adaptor—conversion	17H 5546	9	2		
Plate assembly—light unit retaining	17H 5205	10	2		
Screw	PJZ 602	11	6		
Rim—light unit retaining	**LHD** 17H 5395	12	2		
Unit—light	**except** 17H 5375	13	2	(C) H-AN5-501 on (except USA) 501 to 19014 (USA)	
Bulb	**Europe** BFS 355	14	2		Part No. change; was 13H 1893
Excluder—dust	3H 2962	15	2		
Rim assembly	17H 5147	16	2		
Screw	AJA 5081	17	2		
Washer (rubber)	21G 9057	18	2		
Gasket (rubber)	3H 1031	19	2		
Headlamp assembly—right dip—Mk. X	27H 8206	20	2		
Screw—trimmer	67H 5025	21	4		
Nut—trimmer screw	27H 6482	22A	4		
Adaptor assembly	17H 5306	23	2		
Sleeve—terminal	27H 6713	6	6		
Nut—rim fixing screw	27H 5354	7	2		
Bracket—rim fixing screw	37H 5190	8	2		
Plate—light unit retaining	27H 3338	24	2		
Screw	PJZ 602	11	6		
Spring—unit seating rim	67H 5026	25	2		
Unit—light	17H 5375	13	2		
Bulb	BFS 415	26	2		
Rim assembly	17H 5147	16	2		
Screw	AJA 5081	17	2		
Washer (rubber)	21G 9057	18	2		
Gasket (rubber)	57H 5358	27	2		

See T.I.B. 1B45 F18 for identification of Mk. VI and Mk. X headlamps

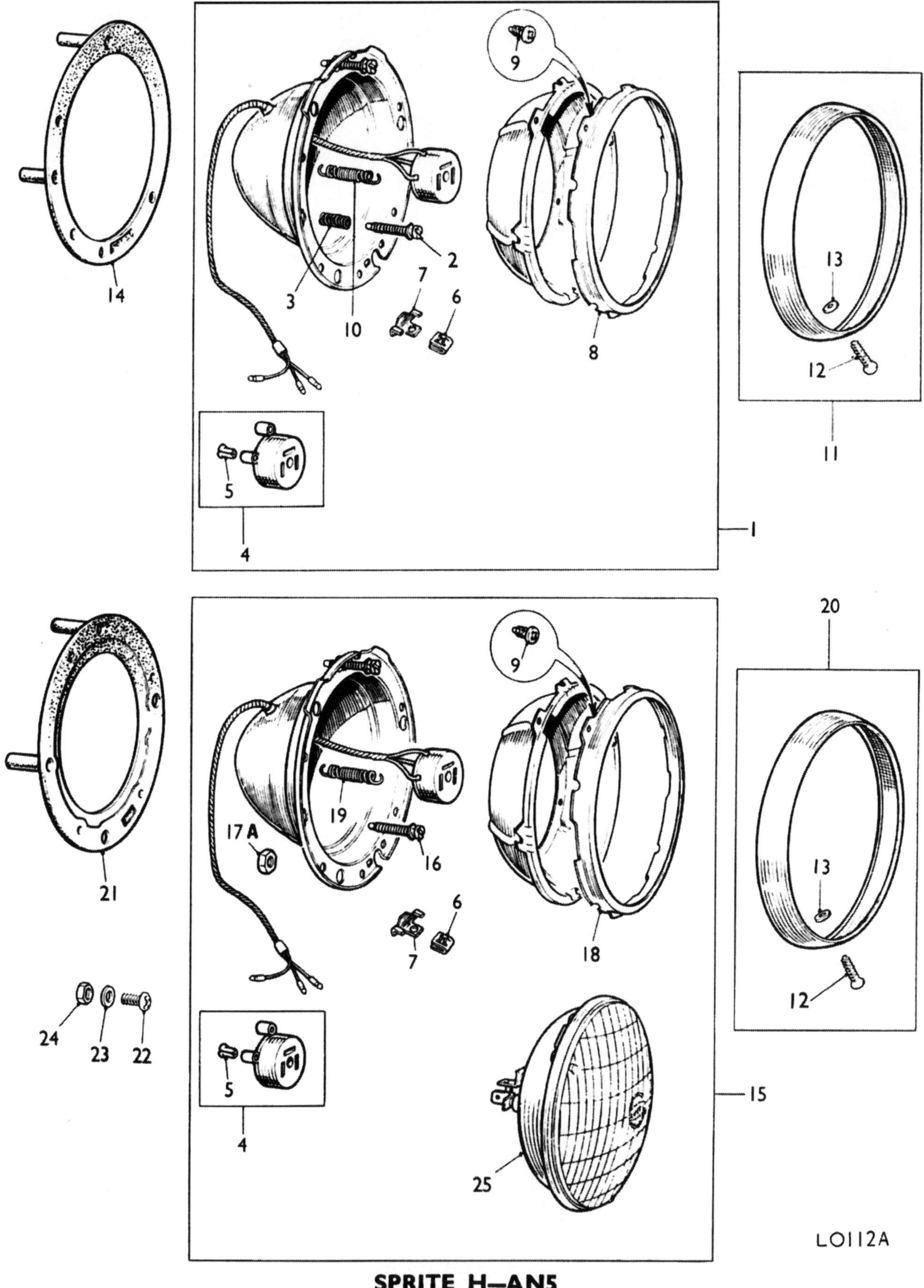

SPRITE H—AN5

Electrical Equipment—*continued*
Lamps—Road (Sprite H-AN5)—*continued*

DESCRIPTION		Part No.	Illus. No.	Quantity	Change Point	REMARKS
Headlamp assembly—Mk. VIII		†57H 5004		2		W.S.E. use 27H 8207 together with 1 off rim 17H 5147 and 1 off gasket 13H 565
Body assembly		†67H 5029	1	2		W.S.E. use 27H 8207 together with 1 off gasket 13H 565
Screw—trimmer		17H 5230	2	4		
Spring—trimmer		17H 5231	3	4		
Adaptor (with cable)		†BHA 4235		2		W.S.E. use 47H 5126
Adaptor assembly		47H 5126	4	2		
Sleeve—terminal		27H 6713	5	6		Part No. change; was 7H 5582 and 37H 5271
Nut—rim fixing screw		27H 5354	6	2		
Bracket—rim fixing screw		37H 5190	7	2		
Plate—light unit retaining		17H 5273	8	2		
Screw		PJZ 602	9	6		
Spring—unit seating rim		17H 5277	10	2	(C) H-AN5-19015 on	
Rim assembly	USA	47H 5564	11	2		
Screw		AJA 5081	12	2		
Washer (rubber)		21G 9057	13	2		
Gasket (rubber)		13H 346	14	2		
Headlamp assembly—Mk. X		27H 8207	15	2		
Screw—trimmer		67H 5025	16	4		
Nut—trimmer		27H 6482	17A	4		
Adaptor assembly		47H 5126	4	2		
Sleeve—terminal		27H 6713	5	6		
Nut—rim fixing screw		27H 5354	6	2		
Bracket—rim fixing screw		37H 5190	7	2		
Plate—light unit retaining		27H 3338	18	2		
Screw		PJZ 602	9	6		
Spring—light unit retaining		67H 5026	19	2		
Unit—light		†17H 9472	25	2		
Rim assembly		17H 5147	20	2		
Screw		AJA 5081	12	2		
Washer (rubber)		21G 9057	13	2		
Gasket (rubber)		13H 565	21	2		
Screw		PMZ 0312	22	8	(C) H-AN5-24400 on	
Washer—plain		PWZ 203	23	4		
Nut		FNZ 103	24	4		

See T.I.B. 1B45 F18 for identification of Mk. VI and Mk. X headlamps

† Revised Information.

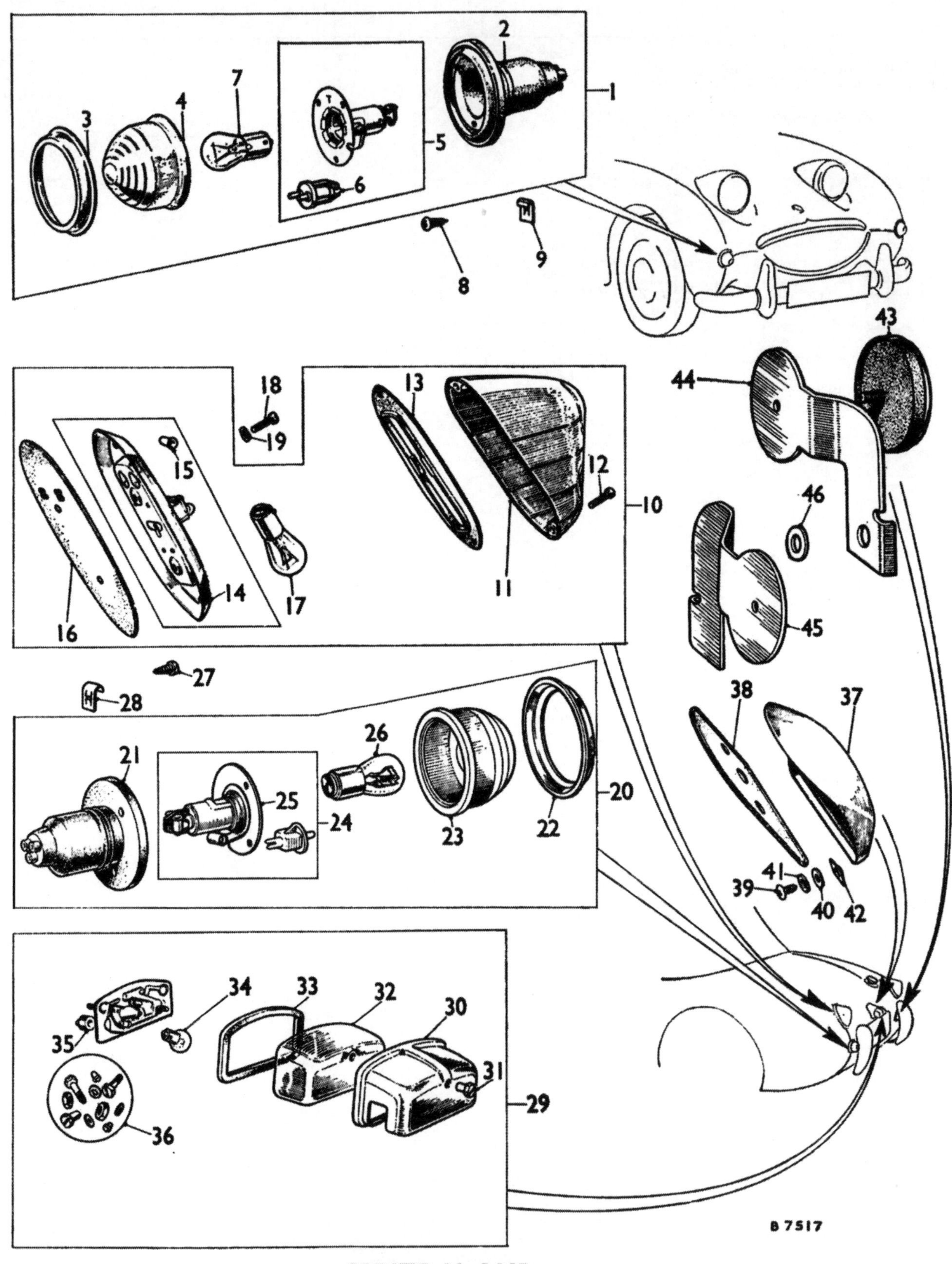
1
2
3
4
5
6
7
8
9
10
11
12
13
14
15
16
17
18
19
20
21
22
23
24
25
26
27
28
29
30
31
32
33
34
35
36
37
38
39
40
41
42
43
44
45
46
B 7517

SPRITE H-AN5

Electrical Equipment—*continued*
Lamps—Road (Sprite H-AN5)—*continued*

DESCRIPTION	Part No.	Illus. No.	Quantity	Change Point	REMARKS
Sidelamp assembly	1B 9100	1	2		
Body (rubber)	37H 5527	2	2		
Rim	7H 5182	3	2		
Lens	37H 5519	4	2		
Holder assembly—bulb	27H 5545	5	2		
Interior	17H 5427	6	2		W.S.E. use 7H 5111
Interior	7H 5111	6	2		
Bulb	BFS 380	7	2		Part No. change; was 1F 9026
Screw	PTZ 604	8	6		
Nut	PFS 326	9	6		
Lamp assembly—stop/tail and reflector	13H 23	10	2		
Lens and reflector	AJA 5069	11	2		
Screws—lens	37H 5410	12	4		
Rubber—lens seating	AJA 5071	13	2		
Rim and bulb holder assembly	AJA 5072	14	2		
Sleeve—terminal	27H 6713	15	6		Part No. change; was 37H 5271
Rubber—lamp seating	AJA 5073	16	2		
Bulb	BFS 380	17	2		Part No. change; was 1F 9026
Screw	PMZ 0308	18	4		
Washer—spring	LWZ 203	19	4		
Lamp assembly—flasher—rear—Amber	2A 9013	20	2		
Lamp assembly—flasher—rear—Red	2A 9040	20	2		
Body (rubber)	37H 5527	21	2		
Rim	7H 5182	22	2		
Lens—Amber	37H 5520	23	2		
Lens—Red	37H 531	23	2		
Holder assembly—bulb	37H 5528	48	2		
Interior	AJH 5100	25	2		W.S.E. use 7H 5202
Interior	7H 5202	25	2		
Bulb	BFS 382	26	2		Part No. change; was 1F 9012
Screw	PTZ 604	27	6		
Nut	PFS 326	28	6		
Lamp assembly—number-plate	†3H 1813	29	1	(C) H-AN5-501 to 36193	W.S.E. use BHA 4153
Lamp assembly—number-plate	BHA 4153	29	1	(C) H-AN5-36194 on	
Cover	7H 5185	30	1		
Screw—cover	17H 5385	31	1		W.S.E. use sundry parts set 7H 5123
Lens	7H 5121	32	1	(C) H-AN5-501 to 36193	W.S.E. use 57H 5128
Lens	57H 5128	32	1	(C) H-AN5-36194 on	
Gasket—lens seating	7H 5122	33	1	(C) H-AN5-501 to 36193	
Gasket—lens seating	57H 5368	33	1	(C) H-AN5-36194 on	
Bulb	BFS 989	34	1/2		Quantity increased at (C) H-AN5-36194. Part No. change; was 2H 4817
Grommet—cable	7H 5164	35	1	(C) H-AN5-501 to ▼	W.S.E. use 5L 321
Grommet—cable	5L 321	35	1		
Sundry parts	7H 5123	36	1 set		
Bracket—lamp mounting	14A 4615	37	1		
Rubber—lamp mounting	14A 4743	38	1		
Screw	PJZ 1006	39	2		
Washer—plain	PWZ 203	40	2		
Washer—spring	LWZ 203	41	2		
Nut—spring	PFS 510	42	2		
Reflector—rear (**Not UK**)	BHA 4148	43	2		
Bracket—reflector mounting—RH (**Not UK**)	AHH 5981	44	1		
Bracket—reflector mounting—LH (**Not UK**)	AHH 5980	45	1		
Washer—plain (**Not UK**)	PWZ 205	46	1		

▼ Change point not available

† Revised Information.

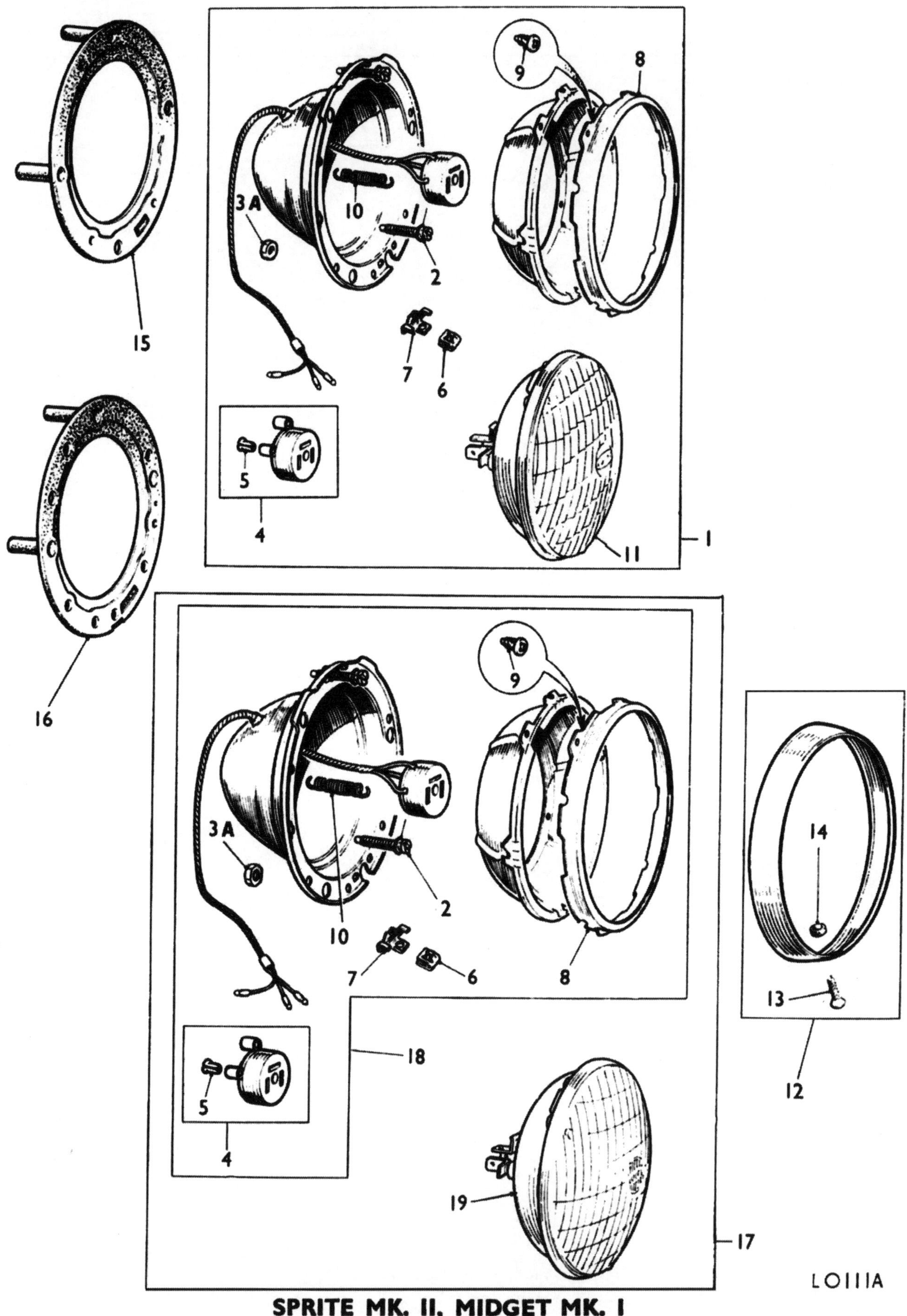

SPRITE MK. II, MIDGET MK. I

Electrical Equipment—*continued*

DESCRIPTION	Part No.	Illus. No.	Quantity	Change Point	REMARKS
LAMPS—ROAD (SPRITE Mk. II AND MIDGET)					
Headlamp assembly complete—Mk. X	†BHA 4247		2	(C) H-AN6-101 to 11768 (C) G-AN1-101 to 6737	W.S.E. use 27H 8203 together with 1 off rim 17H 5147 and 1 off gasket 57H 5353
Headlamp assembly complete—Mk. X	†13H 579		2	(C) H-AN6-11769 to 24731 (C) H-AN7-24732 on (C) G-AN1-6738 to 16183 (C) G-AN2-16184 on	W.S.E. use 27H 8203 together with 1 off rim 17H 5143 and 1 off gasket 57H 5456
Headlamp assembly—Mk. X	27H 8203	1	2		
Screw—trimmer	67H 5025	2	4		
Nut—trimmer screw	27H 6482	3A	4		
Adaptor (with cable)	†BHA 4235		2		W.S.E. use 47H 5126
Adaptor assembly	47H 5126	4	2		
Sleeve—terminal	27H 6713	5	6		Part No. change; was 7H 5582 and 37H 5271
Nut—rim fixing screw	**RHD** 27H 5354	6	2		
Bracket—rim fixing screw	**except** 37H 5190	7	2		
Plate—light unit retaining	**Europe** †57H 5292	8	2		W.S.E. use 27H 3338
Plate—light unit retaining	27H 3338	8	2		
Screw	PJZ 602	9	6		
Spring—unit seating rim	67H 5026	10	2		
Unit—light	13H 496	11	2		
Rim assembly	17H 5147	12	2	(C) H-AN6-101 to 11768 (C) G-AN1-101 to 6737	
Rim assembly	17H 5143	12	2	(C) H-AN6-11769 to 24731 (C) H-AN7-24732 on (C) G-AN1-6738 to 16183 (C) G-AN2-16184 on	
Screw	AJA 5081	13	2		
Washer (rubber)	21G 9057	14	2		
Gasket (rubber)	57H 5353	15	2	(C) H-AN6-101 to 11768 (C) G-AN1-101 to 6737	
Gasket (rubber)	57H 5456	16	2	(C) H-AN6-11769 to 24731 (C) H-AN7-24732 on (C) G-AN1-6738 to 16183 (C) G-AN2-16184 on	
Headlamp assembly complete—Mk. X	†57H 5382		2		W.S.E. use 27H 8207 together with 1 off rim 17H 5147 and 1 off gasket 13H 565
Headlamp assembly—Mk. X	27H 8207	17	2		
Body assembly	†67H 5024	18	2		W.S.E. use 27H 8207
Screw—trimmer	67H 5025	2	4		
Nut—trimmer screw	27H 6482	3A	4		
Adaptor (with cable)	†BHA 4235		2	(C) H-AN6-101 to 8155	W.S.E. use 47H 5126
Adaptor assembly	**USA** 47H 5126	4	2	(less 7220 to 8146)	
Sleeve—terminal	27H 6713	5	6	(C) G-AN1-101 to 4112	Part No. change; was
				(less 3627 to 3858, 3860 to	7H 5582 and 37H 5271
Nut—rim fixing screw	27H 5354	6	2	4060, 4066 to 4078 and 4083 to	
Bracket—rim fixing screw	37H 5190	7	2	4109)	
Plate—light unit retaining	†57H 5292	8	2		W.S.E. use 27H 3338
Plate—light unit retaining	27H 3338	8	2		
Screw	PJZ 602	9	6		
Spring—unit seating rim	67H 5026	10	2		
Unit—light	†17H 9472	19	2		
Rim assembly	17H 5147	12	2		
Screw	AJA 5081	13	2		
Washer (rubber)	21G 9057	14	2		
Gasket (rubber)	†13H 565	15	2		

See T.I.B. **1B45 F18** for identification of Mk. VI and Mk. X headlamps

† Revised Information.

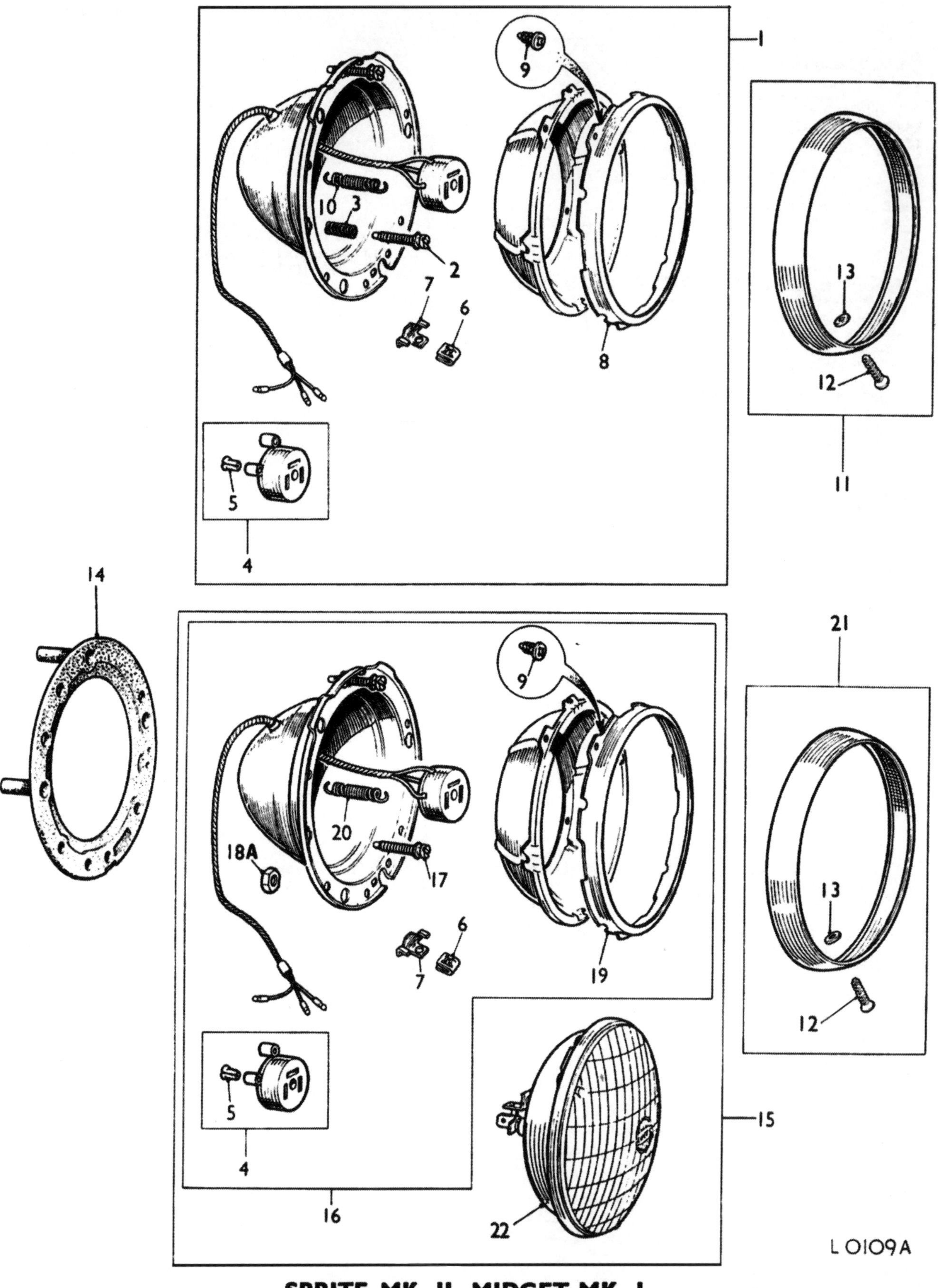

SPRITE MK. II, MIDGET MK. I

DESCRIPTION	Part No.	Illus. No.	Quantity	Change Point	REMARKS
Electrical Equipment—*continued*					
Lamps—Road (Sprite Mk. II and Midget)—*continued*					
Headlamp assembly complete—					
Mk. VIII	†57H 5009		2		W.S.E. use 27H 8207 together with 1 off rim 17H 5143 and 1 off gasket 57H 5456
Body assembly	†67H 5029	1	2		
Screw—trimmer	17H 5230	2	4		
Spring—trimmer screw	17H 5231	3	4		
Adaptor (with cable)	†BHA 4235		2	(C) H-AN6-8156 to 12776	W.S.E. use 47H 5126
Adaptor assembly	47H 5126	4	2	(plus 7220 to 8146)	
Sleeve—terminal	27H 6713	5	6	(C) G-AN1-4113 to 7680 (plus 3627 to 3858, 3860 to	Part No. change; was 7H 5582 and 37H 5271
Nut—rim fixing screw	27H 5354	6	2	4060, 4066 to 4078 and 4083	
Bracket—rim fixing screw	37H 5190	7	2	to 4109)	
Plate—light unit retaining	17H 5273	8	2		
Screw	PJZ 602	9	6		
Spring—unit seating rim	17H 5277	10	2		
Rim assembly	47H 5554	11	2		
Screw	AJA 5081	12	2		
Washer (rubber)	21G 9057	13	2		
Gasket (rubber)	**North** †17H 5214	14	2		W.S.E. use 57H 5456
Gasket (rubber)	**America** 57H 5456	14	2		
Headlamp assembly—Mk. X	27H 8207	15	2		
Body assembly	†67H 5024	16	2		W.S.E. use 27H 8207
Screw—trimmer	67H 5025	17	4		
Nut—trimmer screw	27H 6482	18A	4		
Adaptor (with cable)	†BHA 4235		2		W.S.E. use 47H 5126
Adaptor assembly	47H 5126	4	2		
Sleeve—terminal	27H 6713	5	6	(C) H-AN6-12777 to 24731	Part No. change; was 7H 5582 and 37H 5271
Nut—rim fixing screw	27H 5354	6	2	(C) H-AN7-24732 on	
Bracket—rim fixing screw	37H 5190	7	2	(C) G-AN1-7681 to 16183	
Plate—light unit retaining	†57H 5292	19	2	(C) G-AN2-16184 on	W.S.E. use 27H 3388
Plate—light unit retaining	27H 3388	19	2		
Screw	PJZ 602	9	6		
Spring—unit seating rim	67H 5026	20	2		
Unit—light	†17H 9472	22	2		
Rim assembly	17H 5143	21	2		
Screw	AJA 5081	12	2		
Washer (rubber)	21G 9057	13	2		
Gasket (rubber)	57H 5456	14	2		

See T.I.B. 1B45 F18 for identification of Mk. VI and Mk. X headlamps

† Revised Information.

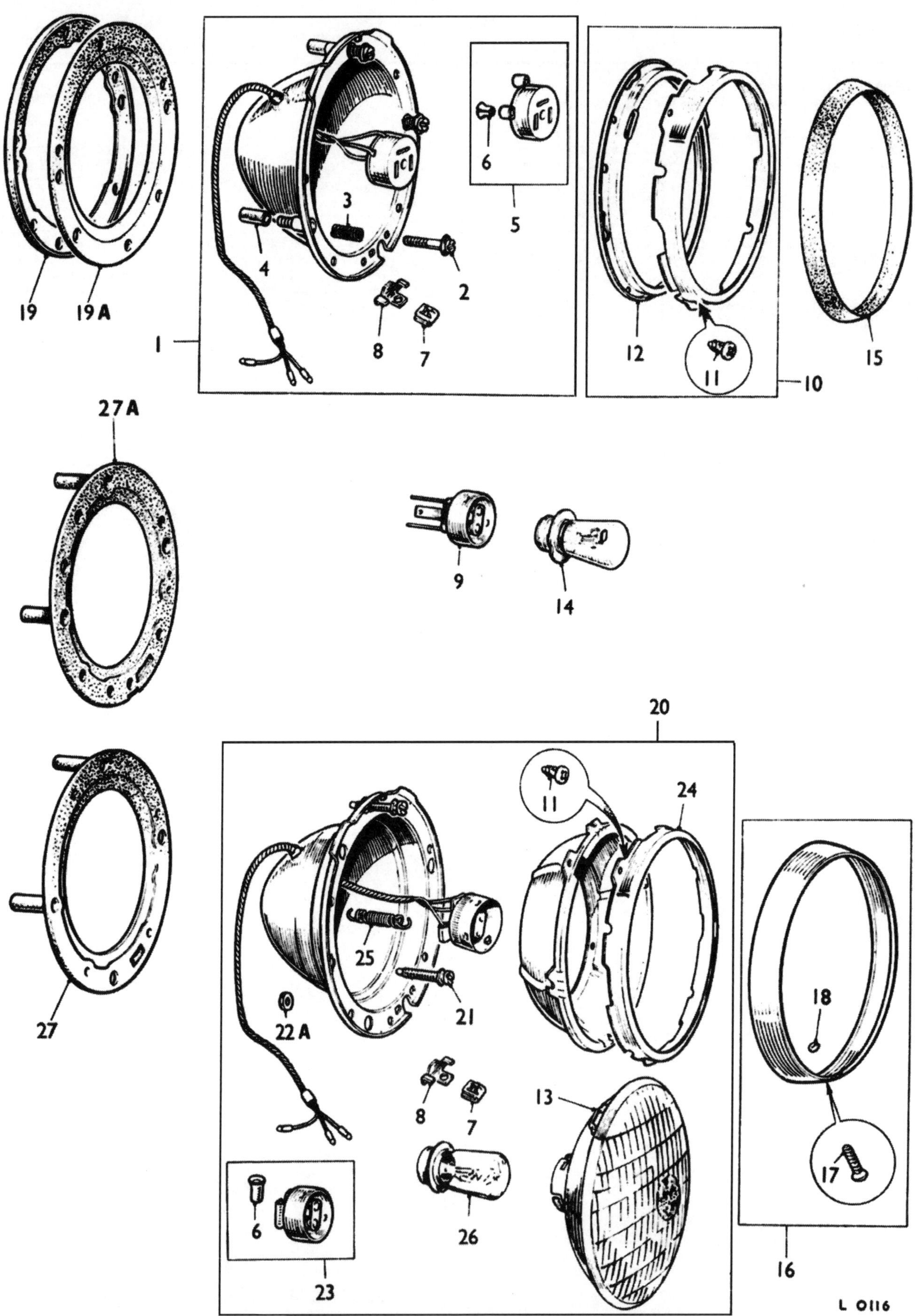

SPRITE MK. II, MIDGET MK. I

DESCRIPTION		Part No.	Illus. No.	Quantity	Change Point	REMARKS
Electrical Equipment—*continued*						
Lamps—Road (Sprite Mk. II and Midget)—*continued*						
Headlamp complete—right dip—Mk. VI		NSP		2	(C) H-AN6-101 to 9475 (C) G-AN1-101 to 4803	Was 17H 5543. Not available; use 27H 8206 together with 1 off rim 17H 5147 and gasket 13H 565
Body assembly		67H 5028	1	2		Not available; use 27H 8206 together with 1 off gasket 13H 565 or 57H 5356
Screw—trimmer		17H 5394	2	6		
Spring—trimmer		17H 5231	3	6		
Sleeve—sealing		27H 5253	4	6		
Adaptor (with cable)		BHA 4285		2		Not available; use 47H 5126
Adaptor assembly		47H 5126	5	2		
Sleeve—terminal		27H 6718	6	6	(C) H-AN6-101 to 12776 (C) G-AN1-101 to 7680	Part No. change; was 7H 5582 and 37H 5271
Nut—rim fixing screw		27H 5354	7	2		
Bracket—rim fixing screw		37H 5190	8	2		
Adaptor—conversion		17H 5546	9	2		
Plate assembly—light unit retaining		17H 5205	10	2		
Screw		PJZ 602	11	6		
Rim—light unit retaining		17H 5395	12	2		
Unit—light		17H 5375	13	2		
Bulb		BFS 355	14	2		
Excluder—dust		3H 2962	15	2	(C) H-AN6-101 to 9475 (C) G-AN1-101 to 4803	
Rim assembly		17H 5147	16	2	(C) H-AN6-101 to 9475 (C) G-AN1-101 to 4803	
Rim assembly	**LHD except**	17H 5148	16	2	(C) H-AN6-9476 to 12776 (C) G-AN1-4804 to 7680	
Screw	**Europe**	AJA 5081	17	2	(C) H-AN6-101 to 12776 (C) G-AN1-101 to 7680	
Washer (rubber)	**and**	21G 9057	18	2	(C) H-AN6-101 to 12776 (C) G-AN1-101 to 7680	
Gasket (rubber)	**USA**	3H 1031	19	2	(C) H-AN6-101 to 9475 (C) G-AN1-101 to 4803	
Gasket (rubber)		57H 5457	19A	2	(C) H-AN6-9476 to 12776 (C) G-AN1-4804 to 7680	
Headlamp assembly—right dip—Mk. X		27H 8206	20	2		
Screw—trimmer		67H 5025	21	4		
Nut—trimmer screw		27H 6482	22A	4		
Adaptor assembly		17H 5306	23	2		
Sleeve—terminal		27H 6718	6	6		
Nut—rim fixing screw		27H 5354	7	2		
Bracket—rim fixing screw		37H 5190	8	2		
Plate—light unit retaining		27H 8388	24	2		
Screw		PJZ 602	11	6		
Spring—unit seating rim		67H 5026	25	2		
Unit—light		17H 5375	13	2		
Bulb		BFS 415	26	2		
Rim assembly		17H 5147	16	2	(C) H-AN6-101 to 9475 (C) G-AN1-101 to 4803	
Rim assembly		17H 5148	16	2	(C) H-AN6-9476 to 12776 (C) G-AN1-4804 to 7680	
Screw		AJA 5081	17	2		
Washer (rubber)		21G 9057	18	2		
Gasket (rubber)		13H 565	27	2	(C) H-AN6-101 to 9475 (C) G-AN1-101 to 4803	
Gasket (rubber)		57H 5456	27A	2	(C) H-AN6-9476 to 12776 (C) G-AN1-4804 to 7680	

See T.I.B. 1B45 F18 for Identification of Mk. VI and Mk. X headlamps

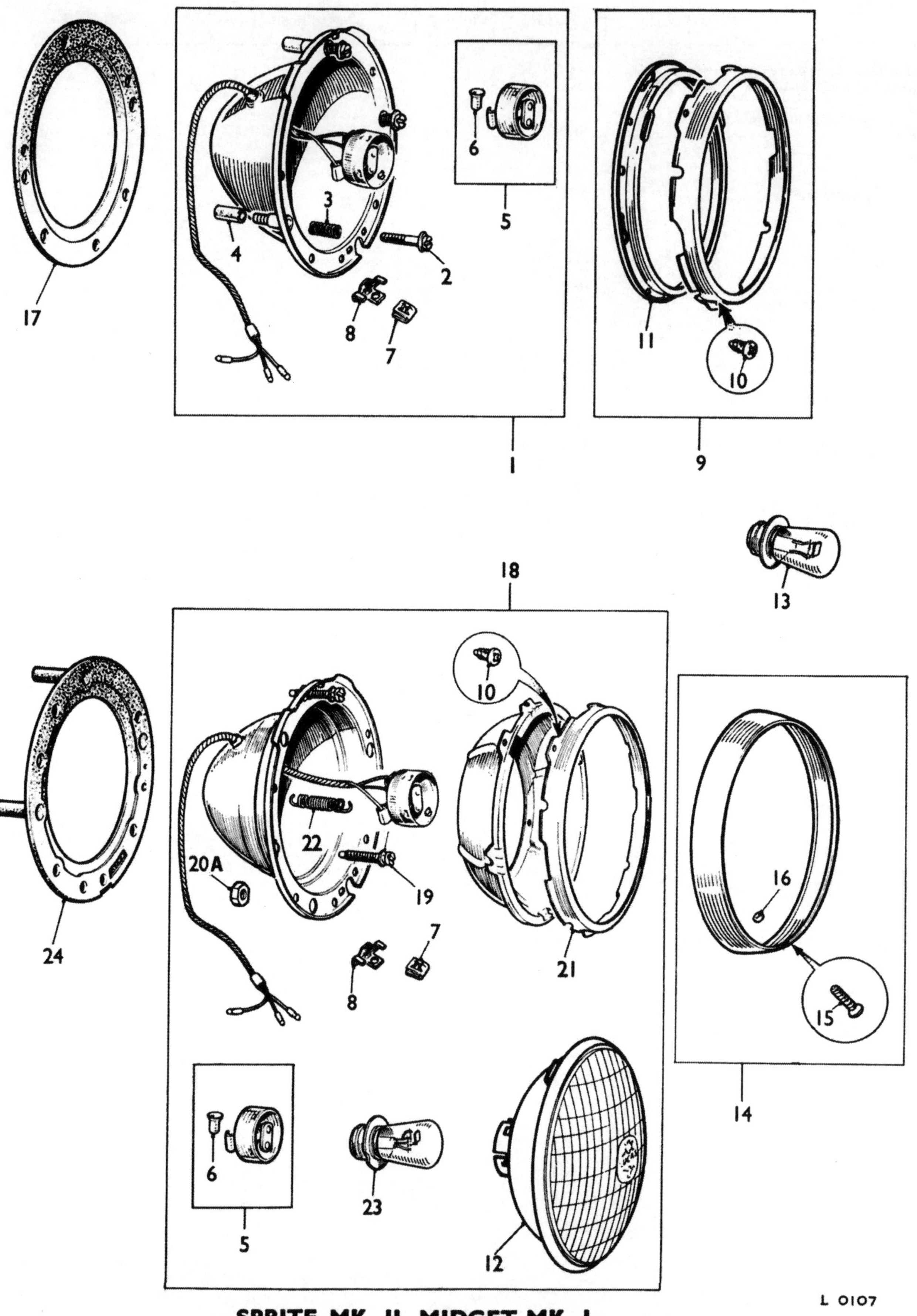

SPRITE MK. II, MIDGET MK. I

Electrical Equipment—*continued*
Lamps—Road (Sprite Mk. II and Midget)—*continued*

DESCRIPTION	Part No.	Illus. No.	Quantity	Change Point	REMARKS
Headlamp complete—right dip—Mk. VI	NSP		2		
Body assembly	7H 6838	1	2		Not available; use 27H 8206 together with 1 off rim 17H 5143 and 1 off gasket 57H 5456
Screw—trimmer	17H 5394	2	6		
Spring—trimmer screw	17H 5231	3	6		Correction; was 17H 6231
Sleeve—sealing	27H 5253	4	6		
Adaptor (with cable)	17H 5145		2		Not available; use 37H 5588
	37H 5588		2		Not available; use 27H 2333
	27H 2333		2		Not available; use 17H 5306
Adaptor assembly	17H 5306	5	2		
Sleeve—terminal	27H 6713	6	6		Part No. change; was 7H 5582 and 37H 5271
Nut—rim fixing screw	27H 5354	7	2		
Bracket—rim fixing screw	37H 5190	8	2		
Plate assembly—light unit retaining	17H 5205	9	2		
Screw	**LHD** PJZ 602	10	6		
Rim—light unit retaining	**except** 17H 5395	11	2	(C) H-AN6-12777 to 24731	
Unit—light	**Europe** 17H 5375	12	2	(C) H-AN7-24732 on	
Bulb	**and** BFS 355	13	2	(C) G-AN1-7681 to 16183	
Rim assembly	**North** 17H 5143	14	2	(C) G-AN2-16184 on	
Screw	**America** AJA 5081	15	2		
Washer (rubber)	21G 9057	16	2		
Gasket (rubber)	57H 5457	17	2		
Headlamp assembly—right dip—Mk. X	27H 8206	18	2		
Screw—trimmer	67H 5025	19	4		
Nut—trimmer	27H 6482	20A	4		
Adaptor assembly	17H 5306	5	2		
Sleeve—terminal	27H 6713	6	6		
Nut—rim fixing screw	27H 5354	7	2		
Bracket—rim fixing screw	37H 5190	8	2		
Plate—light unit retaining	27H 3338	21	2		
Screw	PJZ 602	10	6		
Spring—unit seating rim	67H 5026	22	2		
Unit—light	17H 5375	12	2		
Bulb	BFS 415	23	2		
Rim assembly	17H 5143	14	2		
Screw	AJA 5081	15	2		
Washer (rubber)	21G 9057	16	2		
Gasket (rubber)	57H 5456	24	2		

See T.I.B. 1B45 F18 for identification of Mk. VI and Mk. X headlamps

† Revised Information.

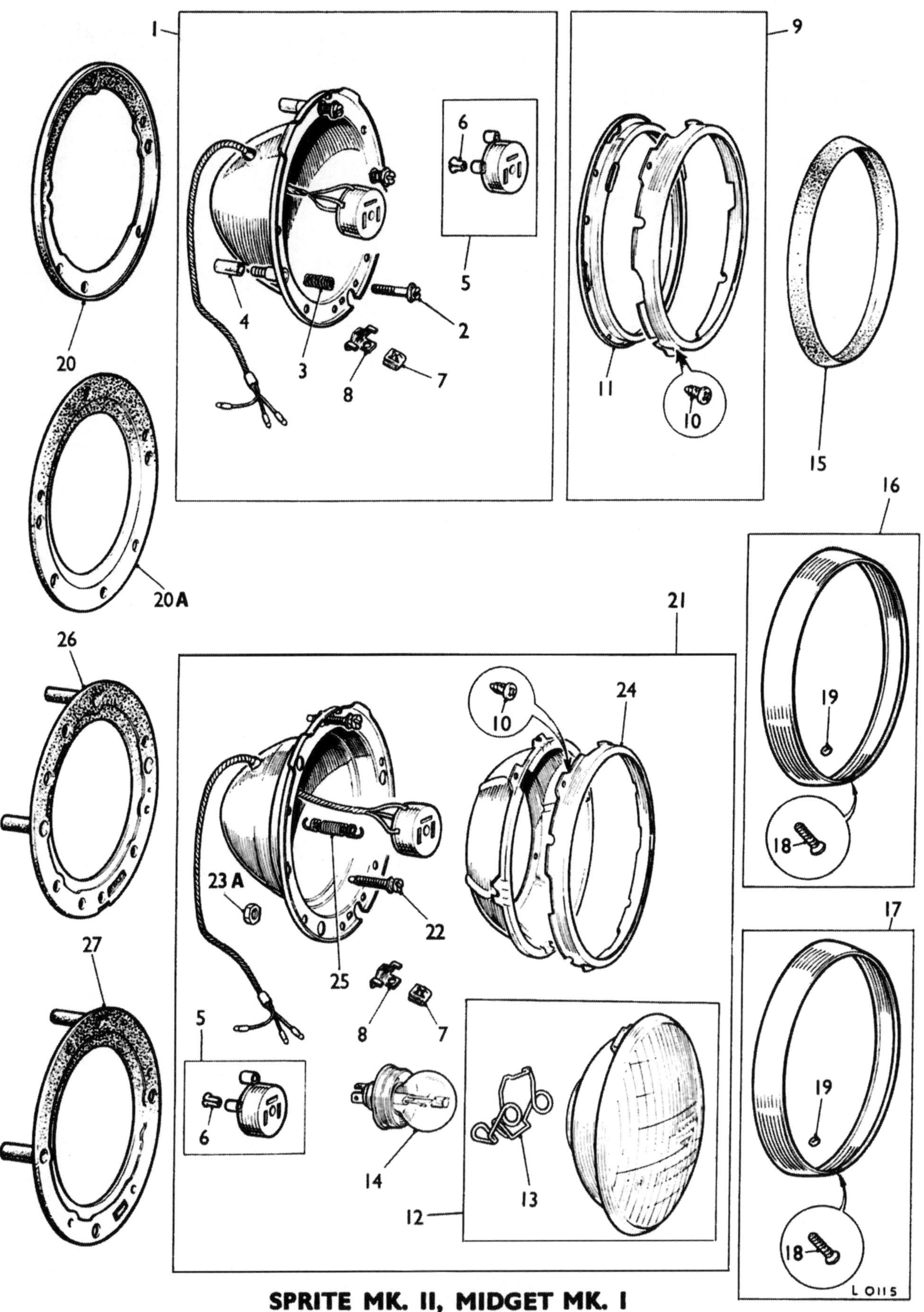

SPRITE MK. II, MIDGET MK. I

Electrical Equipment—*continued*
Lamps—Road (Sprite Mk. II and Midget)—*continued*

DESCRIPTION	Part No.	Illus. No.	Quantity	Change Point	REMARKS
Headlamp complete—vertical dip—Mk. VI	†NSP		2	(C) H-AN6-101 to 10685 (C) G-AN1-101 to 5891	Was BCA 4302. W.S.E. use 27H 8204 together with 1 off rim 17H 5147 and 1 off gasket 13H 565
Body assembly	†67H 5028	1	2		W.S.E. use 27H 8204 together with 1 off gasket 13H 565 or 57H 5456
Screw—trimmer	†17H 5394	2	6		
Spring—trimmer screw	†17H 5231	3	6		
Sleeve—sealing	†27H 5253	4	6		
Adaptor (with cable)	†BHA 4235		2		W.S.E. use 47H 5126
Adaptor assembly	†47H 5126	5	2		
Sleeve—terminal	†27H 6713	6	6		Part No. change; was 7H 5582 and 37H 5271
Nut—rim fixing screw	†27H 5354	7	2		
Bracket—rim fixing screw	†37H 5190	8	2		
Plate assembly—light unit retaining	†17H 5205	9	2		
Screw	†PJZ 602	10	6		
Rim—light unit retaining	†17H 5395	11	2		
Unit assembly—light	†47H 5124	12	2		W.S.E. use 27H 4146
Unit assembly—light	†27H 4146	12	2		
Spring—bulb retaining	†47H 5125	13	2		
Bulb	†BFS 410	14	2		Part No. change; was 13H 188
Excluder—dust	**LHD** †3H 2962	15	2	(C) H-AN6-101 to 10685 (C) G-AN1-101 to 5891	
Rim assembly	**Europe** †17H 5147	16	2		
Rim assembly	**except France** †17H 5143	17	2	(C) H-AN6-10686 to 24731 (C) H-AN7-24732 on (C) G-AN1-5892 to 16183 (C) G-AN2-16184 on	
Screw	†AJA 5081	18	2		
Washer (rubber)	†21G 9057	19	2		
Gasket (rubber)	†3H 1031	20	2	(C) H-AN6-101 to 10685 (C) G-AN1-101 to 5891	
Gasket (rubber)	†57H 5457	20A	2	(C) H-AN6-10686 to 24731 (C) H-AN7-24732 on (C) G-AN1-5892 to 16183 (C) G-AN2-16184 on	
Headlamp assembly—vertical dip—Mk. X	†27H 8204	21	2		
Screw—trimmer	†67H 5025	22	4		
Nut—trimmer screw	†27H 6482	23A	4		
Adaptor assembly	†47H 5126	5	2		
Sleeve—terminal	†27H 6713	6	6		
Nut—rim fixing screw	†27H 5354	7	2		
Bracket—rim fixing screw	†37H 5190	8	2		
Plate—light unit retaining	†27H 3338	24	2		
Screw	†PJZ 602	10	6		
Spring—unit seating rim	†67H 5026	25	2		
Unit assembly—light	†27H 4146	12	2		
Spring—bulb retaining	†47H 5125	13	2		
Bulb	†BFS 410	14	2		
Rim assembly	†17H 5147	16	2	(C) H-AN6-101 to 10685 (C) G-AN1-101 to 5891	
Rim assembly	†17H 5143	17		(C) H-AN6-10686 to 24731 (C) H-AN7-24732 on (C) G-AN1-5892 to 16183 (C) G-AN2-16184 on	
Screw	†AJA 5081	18	2		
Washer (rubber)	†21G 9057	19	2		
Gasket—(rubber)	†13H 565	26	2	(C) H-AN6-101 to 10685 (C) G-AN1-101 to 5891	
Gasket—(rubber)	†57H 5456	27	2	(C) H-AN6-10686 to 24731 (C) H-AN7-24732 on (C) G-AN1-5892 to 16183 (C) G-AN2-16184 on	

See T.I.B. 1B45 F18 for identification of Mk. VI and Mk. X headlamps

† Revised Information.

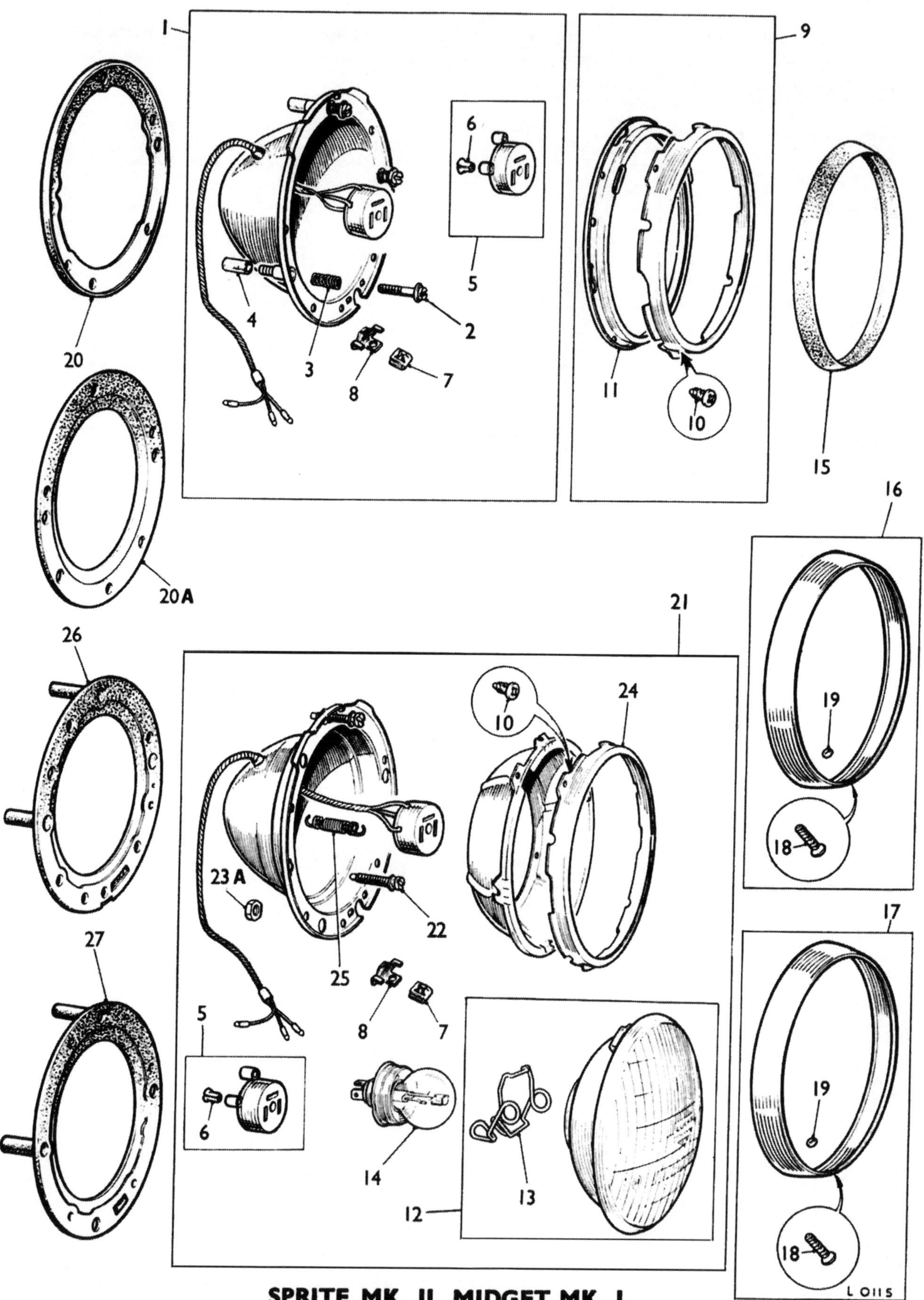

SPRITE MK. II, MIDGET MK. I

Electrical Equipment—*continued*
Lamps—Road (Sprite Mk. II and Midget)—*continued*

DESCRIPTION	Part No.	Illus. No.	Quantity	Change Point	REMARKS
Headlamp complete—vertical dip—Mk. VI	NSP		2	(C) H-AN6-101 to 11690 (C) G-AN1-101 to 6870	Was BCA 4303. Not available; use 37H 1368 together with 1 off rim 17H 5147 and 1 off gasket 13H 565
Body assembly	67H 5028	1	2		Not available; use 37H 1368 together with 1 off gasket 13H 565 or 57H 5456
Screw—trimmer	17H 5394	2	6		
Spring—trimmer screw	17H 5231	3	6		
Sleeve—sealing	27H 5253	4	6		
Adaptor (with cable)	BHA 4235		2		Not available; use 47H 5126
Adaptor assembly	47H 5126	5	2		
Sleeve—terminal	27H 6713	6	6		Part No. change; was 7H 5582 and 37H 5271
Nut—rim fixing screw	27H 5354	7	2		
Bracket—rim fixing screw	37H 5190	8	2		
Plate assembly—light unit retaining	17H 5205	9	2		
Screw	PJZ 602	10	6		
Rim—light unit retaining	17H 5395	11	2		
Unit assembly—light	47H 5124	12	2		Not available; use 27H 4146
Unit assembly—light	27H 4146	12	2		
Spring—bulb retaining	47H 5125	13	2		
Bulb	BFS 411	14	2		
Excluder—dust	3H 2962	15	2	(C) H-AN6-101 to 11690 (C) G-AN1-101 to 6870	
Rim assembly	17H 5147	16	2	(C) H-AN6-101 to 11690 (C) G-AN1-101 to 6870	
Rim assembly	17H 5143	17	2	(C) H-AN6-11691 to 24731 (C) H-AN7-24732 on (C) G-AN1-6871 to 16183 (C) G-AN2-16184 on	
Screw	**France** AJA 5081	18	2		
Washer (rubber)	21G 9057	19	2		
Gasket (rubber)	3H 1031	20	2	(C) H-AN6-101 to 11690 (C) G-AN1-101 to 6870	
Gasket (rubber)	57H 5457	20A	2	(C) H-AN6-11691 to 24731 (C) H-AN7-24732 on (C) G-AN1—6871 to 16183 (C) G-AN2-16184 on	
Headlamp assembly—vertical dip—Mk. X	37H 1368	21	2		
Screw—trimmer	67H 5025	22	4		
Nut—trimmer screw	27H 6482	23A	4		
Adaptor assembly	47H 5126	5	2		
Sleeve—terminal	27H 6713	6	6		
Nut—rim fixing screw	27H 5354	7	2		
Bracket—rim fixing screw	37H 5190	8	2		
Plate—light unit retaining	27H 3338	24	2		
Screw	PJZ 602	10	6		
Spring—unit seating rim	67H 5026	25	2		
Unit assembly—light	27H 4146	12	2		
Spring—bulb retaining	47H 5125	13	2		
Bulb	BFS 411	14	2		
Rim assembly	17H 5147	16	2	(C) H-AN6-101 to 11690 (C) G-AN1-101 to 6870	
Rim assembly	17H 5143	17	2	(C) H-AN6-11691 to 24731 (C) H-AN7-24732 on (C) G-AN1-6871 to 16183 (C) G-AN2-16184 on	
Screw	AJA 5081	18	2		
Washer (rubber)	21G 9057	19	2		
Gasket (rubber)	13H 565	26	2	(C) H-AN6-101 to 11690 (C) G-AN1-101 to 6870	
Gasket (rubber)	57H 5456	27	2	(C) H-AN6-11691 to 24731 (C) H-AN7-24732 on (C) G-AN1-6871 to 16183 (C) G-AN2-16184 on	

See T.I.B. 1B45 F18 for identification of Mk. VI and Mk. X headlamps

† Revised Information.

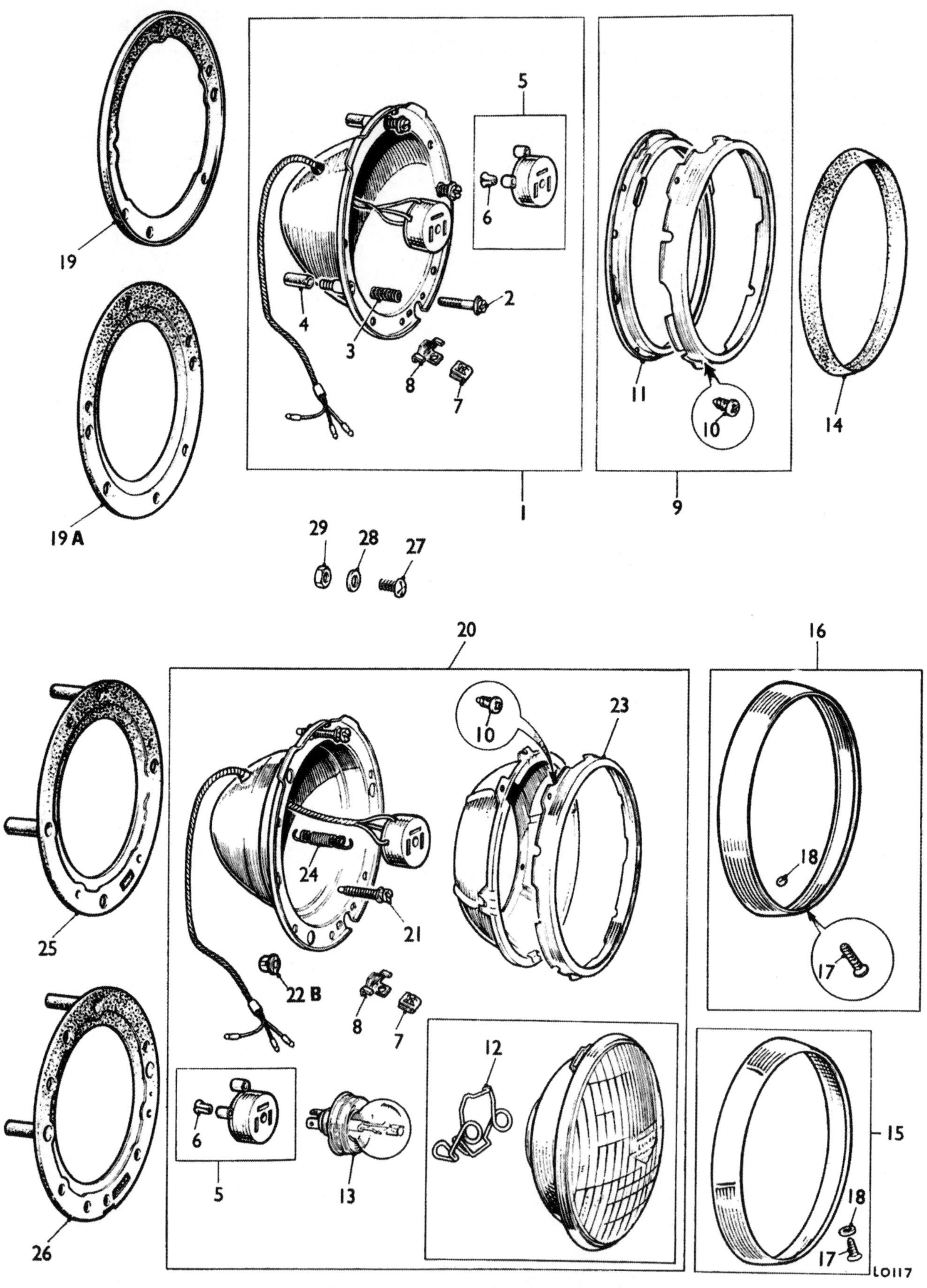

SPRITE MK. II, MIDGET MK. I

Electrical Equipment—*continued*
Lamps—Road (Sprite Mk. II and Midget)—*continued*

DESCRIPTION	Part No.	Illus. No.	Quantity	Change Point	REMARKS
Headlamp complete—vertical dip—Mk. VI	NSP		2	(C) H–AN6–101 to 11690 (C) G–AN1–101 to 6870	Was BCA 4303. W.S.E. use 37H 1368 together with 1 off rim 17H 5147 and 1 off gasket 13H 565
Body assembly	67H 5028	1	2		W.S.E. use 37H 1368 together with 1 off gasket 13H 565 or 57H 5456
Screw—trimmer	17H 5394	2	6		
Spring—trimmer screw	17H 5231	3	6		
Sleeve—sealing	27H 5253	4	6		
Adaptor (with cable)	BHA 4235		2		W.S.E. use 47H 5126
Adaptor assembly	47H 5126	5	2		
Sleeve—terminal	27H 6713	6	6		Part No. change; was 7H 5582 and 37H 5271
Nut—rim fixing screw	27H 5354	7	2		
Bracket—rim fixing screw	37H 5190	8	2		
Plate assembly—light unit retaining	17H 5205	9	2		
Screw	PJZ 602	10	6		
Rim—light unit retaining	17H 5395	11	2		
Unit assembly—light	47H 5124	12	2		W.S.E. use 27H 4146
Unit assembly—light	27H 4146	12	2		
Spring—bulb retaining	47H 5125	13	2		
Bulb	BFS 411	14	2		
Excluder—dust	3H 2962	15	2	(C) H–AN6–101 to 11690	
Rim assembly	17H 5147	16	2	(C) G–AN1–101 to 6870	
Rim assembly	17H 5143	17	2	(C) H–AN6–11691 to 24731 (C) H–AN7–24732 on (C) G–AN1–6871 to 16183 (C) G–AN2–16184 on	
Screw	**France** AJA 5081	18	2		
Washer (rubber)	21G 9057	19	2		
Gasket (rubber)	3H 1031	20	2	(C) H–AN6–101 to 11690 (C) G–AN1–101 to 6870	
Gasket (rubber)	57H 5457	20A	2	(C) H–AN6–11691 to 24731 (C) H–AN7–24732 on (C) G–AN1–6871 to 16183 (C) G–AN2–16184 on	
Headlamp assembly—vertical dip—Mk. X	37H 1368	21	2		
Screw—trimmer	67H 5025	22	4		
Nut—trimmer screw	27H 6482	23A	4		
Adaptor assembly	47H 5126	5	2		
Sleeve—terminal	27H 6713	6	6		
Nut—rim fixing screw	27H 5354	7	2		
Bracket—rim fixing screw	37H 5190	8	2		
Plate—light unit retaining	27H 3388	24	2		
Screw	PJZ 602	10	6		
Spring—unit seating rim	67H 5026	25	2		
Unit assembly—light	27H 4146	12	2		
Spring—bulb retaining	47H 5125	13	2		
Bulb	BFS 411	14	2		
Rim assembly	17H 5147	16	2	(C) H–AN6–101 to 11690 (C) G–AN1–101 to 6870	
Rim assembly	17H 5143	17	2	(C) H–AN6–11691 to 24731 (C) H–AN7–24732 on (C) G–AN1–6871 to 16183 (C) G–AN2–16184 on	
Screw	AJA 5081	18	2		
Washer (rubber)	21G 9057	19	2		
Gasket (rubber)	13H 565	26	2	(C) H–AN6–101 to 11690 (C) G–AN1–101 to 6870	
Gasket (rubber)	57H 5456	27	2	(C) H–AN6–11691 to 24731 (C) H–AN7–24732 on (C) G–AN1–6871 to 16183 (C) G–AN2–16184 on	

See T.I.B. 1B45 F18 for identification of Mk. VI and Mk. X headlamps

† Revised Information.

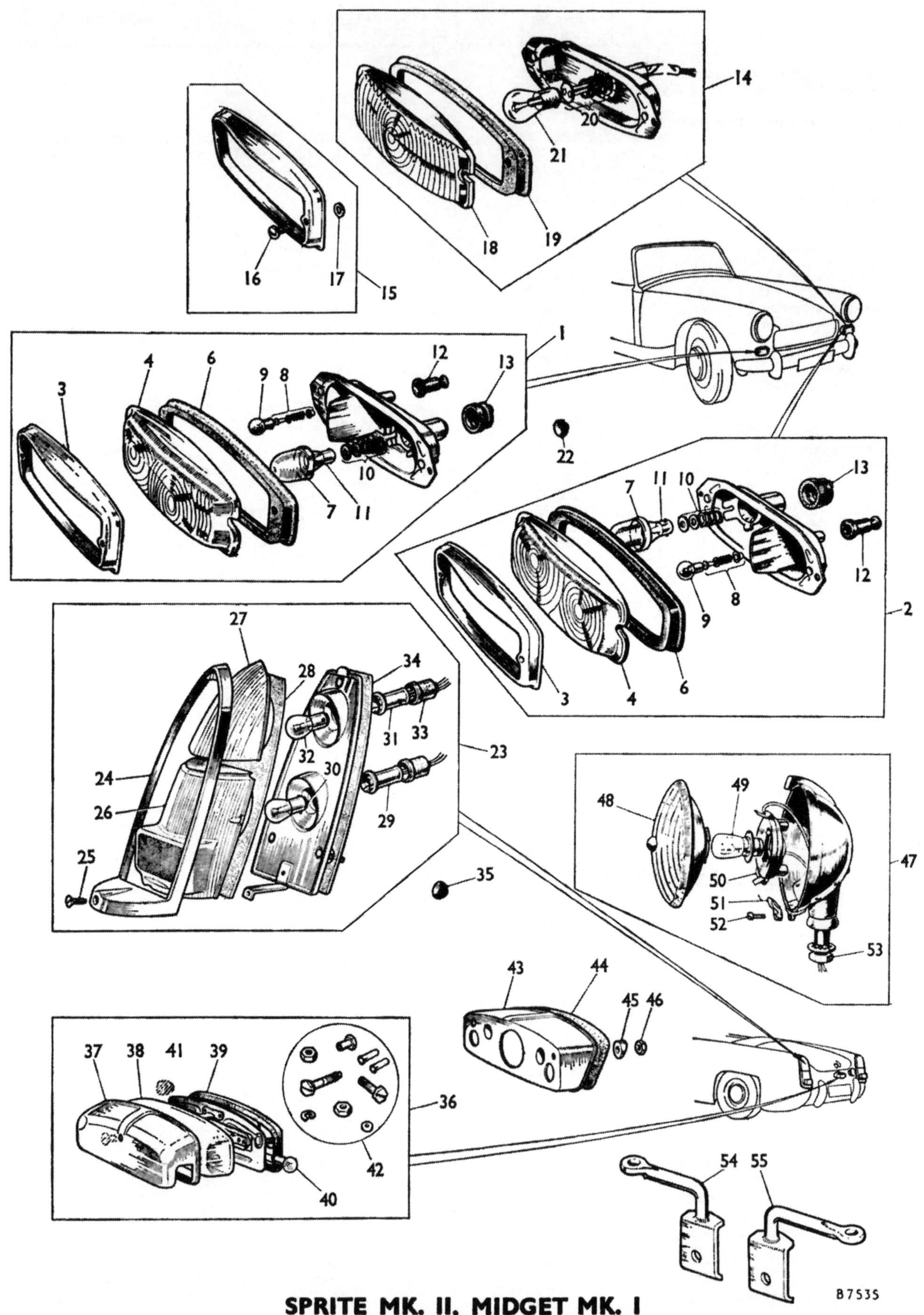

SPRITE MK. II, MIDGET MK. I

DESCRIPTION	Part No.	Illus. No.	Quantity	Change Point	REMARKS
Electrical Equipment—*continued*					
Lamps—Road (Sprite Mk. II and Midget)—*continued*					
Lamp assembly—side and flasher—Amber flasher—RH	13H 429	1	1		
Lamp assembly—side and flasher—Amber flasher—LH	13H 428	2	1		
Rim	57H 5155	3	2		
Lens—RH	57H 5158	4	1		
Lens—LH	57H 5159	5	1		
Gasket—lens seating	57H 5157	6	2		
Shield—flasher bulb	57H 5156	7	2		
Interior—bulb holder—sidelamp	7H 5536	8	2		
Bulb—sidelamp	BFS 222	9	2		Part No. change; was 1D 9081
Interior—bulb holder—flasher lamp	37H 5452	10	2		
Bulb—flasher	BFS 382	11	2		Part No. change; was 1F 9012
Grommet—sidelamp cable	37H 5294	12	2		
Grommet—flasher lamp cable	17H 5216	13	2		
Lamp assembly—side and flasher—White	BHA 4204	14	2		
Rim assembly	57H 5308	15	2		
Screw—rim	57H 5306	16	4		Not available; use AJD 1245 C
Screw—rim	AJD 1245 C	16	4		
Washer—plain	21G 9057	17	4		
Lens	57H 5307	18	2		
Gasket—lens seating	57H 5157	19	2		
Interior—bulb holder	37H 5459	20	2		
Bulb	BFS 380	21	2		Part No. change; was 1F 9026
Nut—earthing—lamp to wing	2A 9156	22	4		
Lamp assembly—stop/tail/flasher and reflex—Amber flasher	BHA 4175	23	2		
Lamp assembly—stop/tail/flasher and reflex—Red flasher	BHA 4176	23	2		
Rim	57H 5355	24	2		
Screw—rim	17H 5425	25	2		Not available; use RMP 0308
Screw—rim	RMP 0308	25	2		
Lens					
Stop/tail	57H 5357	26	2		
Flasher—Amber	57H 5354	27	2		
Flasher—Red	57H 5359	27	2		
Gasket—lens seating	57H 5356	28	2		
Interior—bulb holder—stop/tail	37H 5459	29	2		
Bulb—stop/tail	BFS 380	30	2		Part No. change; was 1F 9026
Interior—bulb holder—flasher	37H 5432	31	2		
Bulb—flasher	BFS 382	32	2		Part No. change; was 1F 9012
Grommet—cable	37H 5525	33	4		
Gasket—lamp seating	57H 5358	34	2		
Nut—earthing—lamp to body	BHA 4242	35	6		
Lamp assembly—number-plate	BHA 4153	36	1		
Cover	7H 5185	37	1		
Lens	57H 5128	38	1		
Gasket—lens seating	57H 5368	39	1		
Bulb	BFS 989	40	2		Part No. change; was 2H 4817
Grommet—cable	†7H 5164	41	1	(C) H-AN6-101 to ▼	W.S.E. use 5L 321
Grommet—cable	5L 321	41	1	(C) G-AN1-101 to ▼	
Sundry parts	7H 5128	42	1 set		
Plinth—number-plate lamp	AHA 5809	43	1		
Seal—plinth to body	AHA 5806	44	1		
Washer—packing—plinth to body	AHA 5805	45	1		
Locknut	LNZ 204	46	2		
Lamp assembly—fog	ADH 785	47	2		Optional extra
Unit—light	ACG 5179	48	2		Optional extra
Bulb	BFS 823	49	2		Optional extra
Adaptor	ACG 5180	50	2		W.S.E. use 57H 5336; Optional extra
Adaptor	57H 5336	50	2		Optional extra
Catch—rim	AJH 5057	51	2		Optional extra
Screw—catch	17H 5400	52	2		Optional extra
Nut—lamp spigot	†17H 5401	53	2		W.S.E. use 27H 6767; Optional extra
Nut—lamp spigot	†27H 6767		2		Optional extra
Bracket—fog lamp mounting—RH	AHA 6368	54	2		Optional extra
Bracket—fog lamp mounting—LH	AHA 6361	55	2		Optional extra

▼ Change point not available

† Revised Information.

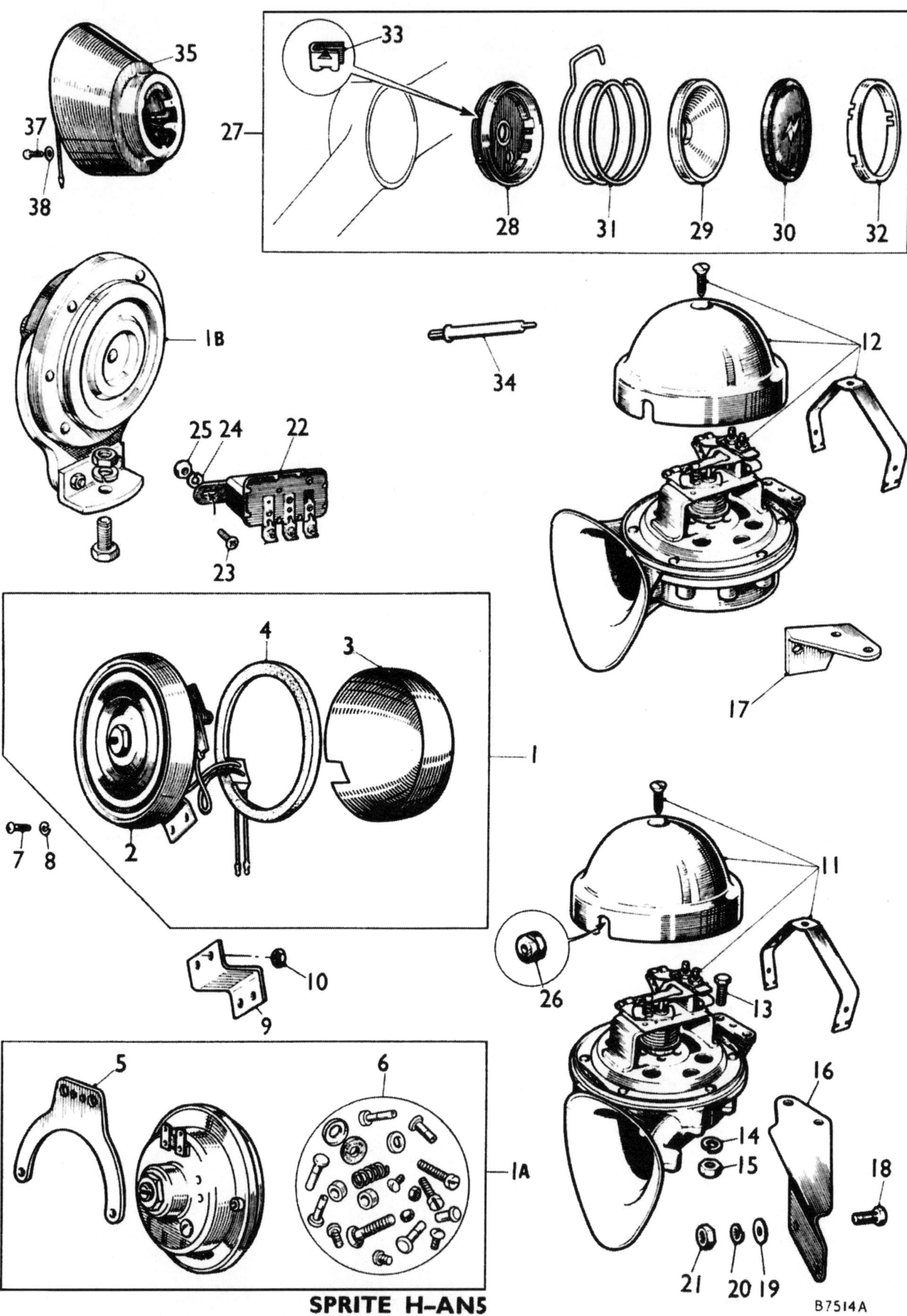
35
37
38
27
33
28
31
29
30
32
1B
34
12
25 24
22
23
17
4
3
1
7 8
2
11
10
9
26
13
5
6
16
14
15
1A
18
21 20 19
B7514A

SPRITE H-AN5

Electrical Equipment—*continued*

HORN AND CONTROL (SPRITE H-AN5)

DESCRIPTION	Part No.	Illus. No.	Quantity	Change Point	REMARKS
Horn assembly	13H 69	1	1		W.S.E. use BHA 4186
Disc—tone	27H 5581	2	1		
Cover	27H 5582	3	1		
Ring—cover sealing	27H 5583	4	2		
Horn assembly	†BHA 4186	1A	1		W.S.E. use 13H 2782
Bracket—horn	57H 5556	5	1		
Sundry parts	57H 5310	6	1 set		
Horn	†13H 2782	1B	1		
Screw	†PMZ 0308	7	2	(C) H-AN5-501 to 6891	
Washer—spring	LWZ 203	8	2	(C) H-AN5-501 to 6891	
Bracket—horn	AHA 5447	9	1	(C) H-AN5-6892 on	
Screw	PMZ 0308	7	4	(C) H-AN5-6892 on	
Washer—spring	LWZ 203	8	4	(C) H-AN5-6892 on	
Nut	FNZ 103	10	2		
Horn—Windtone—high note	1B 9008	11	1		Optional extra
Horn—Windtone—low note	1B 9007	12	1		Optional extra
Screw	HZS 0405	13	4		Optional extra
Washer—spring	LWZ 204	14	4		Optional extra
Nut	FNZ 104	15	4		Optional extra
Bracket—mounting—high note horn	AHA 5458	16	1		Optional extra
Bracket—mounting—low note horn	AHA 5457	17	1		Optional extra
Screw	HZS 0505	18	6		Optional extra
Washer—plain	PWZ 205	19	2		Optional extra
Washer—spring	LWZ 205	20	6		Optional extra
Nut	FNZ 105	21	6		Optional extra
Relay—horn	13H 153	22	1		Optional extra
Screw	PMZ 0206	23	2		Optional extra
Washer—spring	LWZ 203	24	2		Optional extra
Nut	FNZ 103	25	2		Optional extra
Grommet—horn	ADG 1517	26	2		Optional extra
Horn-push assembly	2A 6157	27	1		W.S.E. use AHA 6481
Horn-push assembly	AHA 6481	27	1		
Contact					
Bottom	27H 5572	28	1		For use with 2A 6157
Bottom	NSP	28	1		Was 17H 2074
Top	NSP	29	1		Was 27H 5569
Knob—horn-push	NSP	30	1		Was 27H 5559
Spring	NSP	31	1		Was 27H 5570
Bezel—horn-push	NSP	32	1		Was 27H 5562
Clip—horn-push retaining	57H 5423	33	2		
Brush—horn contact	2A 6162	34	1		
Slip ring and moulding **RHD**	2A 6158	35	1		
Slip ring and moulding **LHD**	†2A 6161	35	1		
Screw	PMZ 0205	37	3		
Washer—plain	6K 9388	38	3		

† Revised Information.

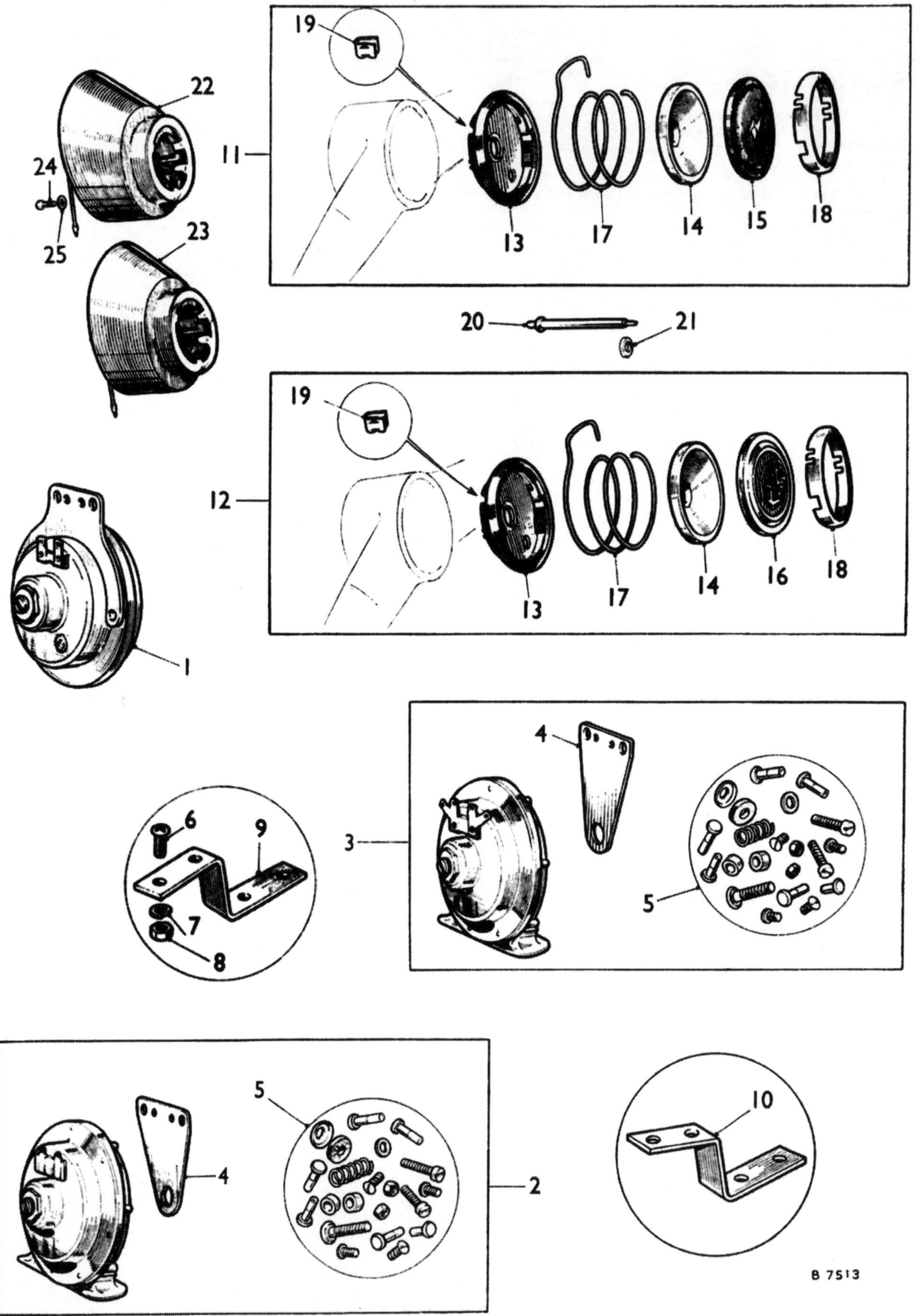

SPRITE MK. II, MIDGET MK. I

Electrical Equipment—*continued*

HORN AND CONTROL (SPRITE MK. II AND MIDGET)

DESCRIPTION	Part No.	Illus. No.	Quantity	Change Point	REMARKS
Horn assembly	†BHA 4186	1	1		Use 13H 472 for this application
Horn assembly—Windtone					
High note	13H 472	2	1		Use BHA 4444 for this application
High note	BHA 4444	2	1		W.S.E. use BHA 4515
Low note	13H 473	3	1		Use BHA 4445 for this application — Optional extra
Low note	BHA 4445	3	1		W.S.E. use BHA 4514 — Optional extra
Low note	BHA 4514	3A	1		Optional extra
Bracket	57H 5309	4	1/2		Quantities increased when twin horns are fitted
Sundry parts	57H 5310	5	1/2 sets		Quantities increased when twin horns are fitted
Screw	PMZ 0410	6	2/4		Quantities increased when twin horns are fitted
Washer—spring	LWZ 204	7	2/4		Quantities increased when twin horns are fitted
Nut	FNZ 104	8	2/4		Quantities increased when twin horns are fitted
Bracket—horn mounting—RH	AHA 6567	9	1	(C) H–AN7–24732 on; (C) G–AN2–16184 on	
Bracket—horn mounting—LH	AHA 6658	10	1	(C) H–AN7–24732 on; (C) G–AN2–16184 on	For use with optional extra horn
Horn-push assembly **Sprite Mk. II**	2A 6157	11	1	(C) H–AN6–101 to 24931	W.S.E. use AHA 6481
				(C) H–AN7–24732 to 26798	
Sprite Mk. II	AHA 6481	11	1	(C) H–AN7–26799 on	
Midget	AHA 5661	12	1	(C) G–AN1–101 to 5033	
Midget	AHA 6371	12	1	(C) G–AN1–5034 to 16183	
				(C) G–AN2–16184 on	
Contact					
Bottom	27H 5572	13	1	(C) H–AN6–101 to 24731	
				(C) H–AN7–24732 to 26798	
Bottom	57H 5411	13	1	(C) G–AN1–101 to 5033	W.S.E. use 17H 2074
Bottom	NSP	13	1	(C) H–AN7–26799 on	Was 17H 2074
				(C) G–AN1–5034 to 16183	
				(C) G–AN2–16184 on	
Top	NSP	14	1		Was 27H 5569
Knob—horn-push **Sprite Mk. II**	NSP	15	1		Was 27H 5559
Knob—horn-push **Midget**	†NSP	16	1		Was 57H 5410
Spring—knob	NSP	17	1		Was 27H 5570
Bezel—horn-push	NSP	18	1		Was 27H 5568
Clip—horn-push retaining	57H 5423	19	2		
Brush—horn contact	2A 6162	20	1		
Washer—insulating—horn contact (fibre)	2K 4960	21	1		
Slip-ring and moulding **RHD**	AHA 5703	22	1	(C) G–AN1–101 to 5033	W.S.E. use 2A 6158
LHD	AHA 5704	23	1	(C) G–AN1–101 to 5033	
RHD	2A 6158	22	1	(C) H–AN6–101 to 24731; (C) H–AN7–24732 on; (C) G–AN1–5034 to 16183; (C) G–AN2–16184 on	
LHD	2A 6161	23	1	(C) H–AN6–101 to 24731; (C) H–AN7–24732 on; (C) G–AN1–5034 to 16183; (C) G–AN2–16184 on	
Screw	PMZ 0205	24	3		
Washer—plain	6K 9388	25	3		

† Revised Information.

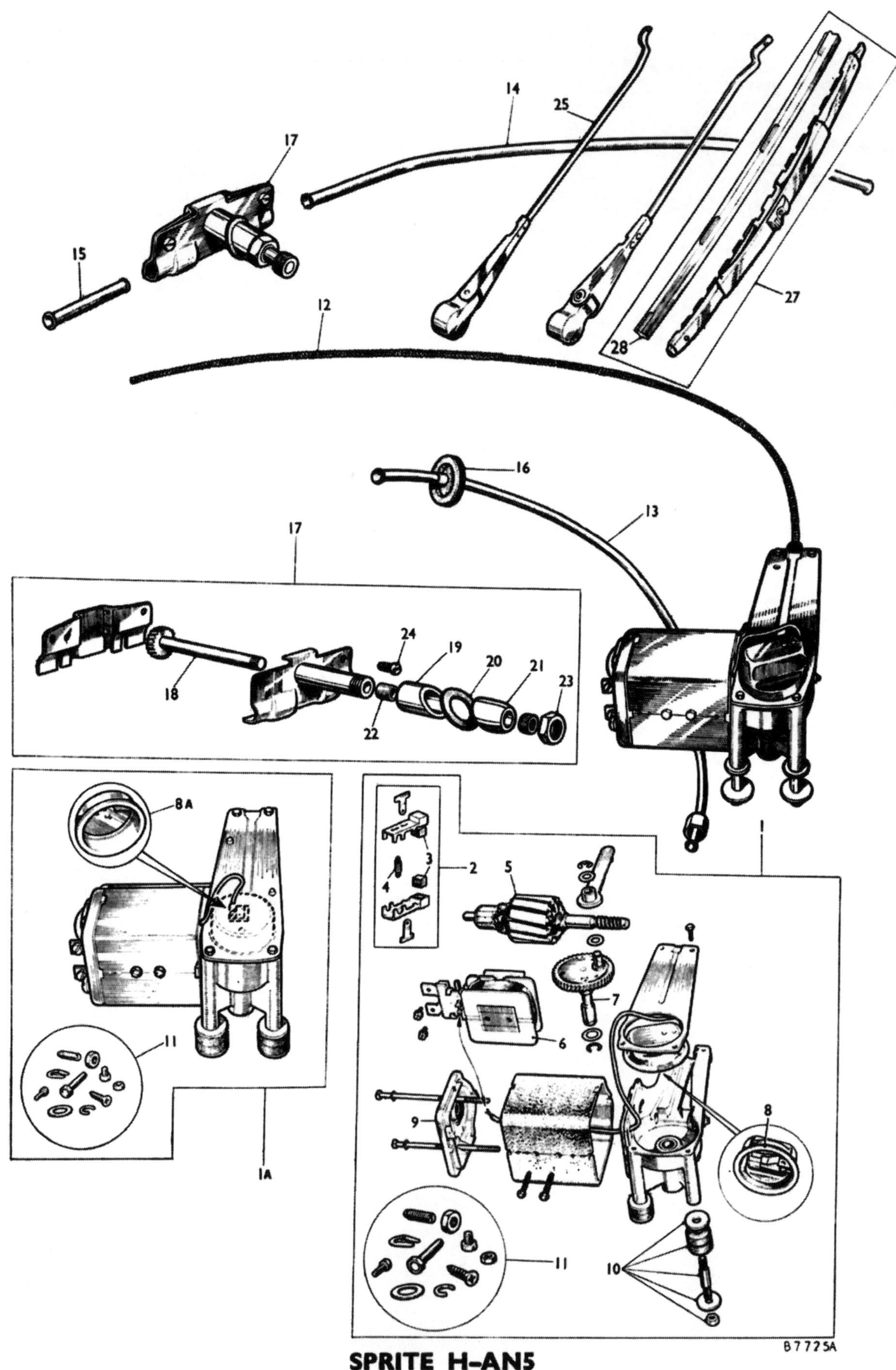
14
25
17
15
12
27
28
16
13
17
24
19
20
21
23
18
22
8A
2
3
4
5
7
6
1
11
9
8
1A
11
10
B7725A

SPRITE H-AN5

DESCRIPTION	Part No.	Illus. No.	Quantity	Change Point	REMARKS
Electrical Equipment—*continued*					
WINDSCREEN WIPER (SPRITE H-AN5)					
Motor assembly—windscreen wiper	†17H 5361	1	1	(C) H-AN5-501 to 5476 (less	W.S.E. use 47H 5012
	47H 5012	1	1	5187, 5287 and 5288)	
	17H 2707	1A	1	(C) H-AN5-5477 to 50116 (plus 5187, 5287, and 5288)	Part No. change; was 37H 5428
Brush gear assembly	17H 5396	2	1		
Brush	7H 5130	3	1 set		
Spring—brush	27H 5309	4	1		
Armature	17H 5255	5	1		
Coil—field	37H 5288	6	1		
Shaft and gear	17H 5443	7	1	(C) H-AN5-501 to 5476 (less	
Switch—parking	17H 5442	8	1	5187, 5287, and 5288)	
Shaft and gear	47H 5315	7	1	(C) H-AN5-5477 to 50116	
Switch—parking	47H 5316	8A	1	plus 5187, 5287, and 5288)	
Cover—end	27H 5554	9	1		
Fixing parts	17H 5431	10	3 sets		
Sundry parts	17H 5441	11	1 set		
Cross-head and rack	†47H 5023	12	1		W.S.E. use 37H 5169
Cross-head and rack	37H 5169	12	1		
Casing—outer					
Motor to wheelbox	14A 4801	13	1		
Wheelbox to wheelbox	14A 4802	14	1		
Wheelbox extension	14G 3722	15	1		
Grommet—casing through dash	8D 5768	16	1		Part No. change; was ADG 1869
Wheelbox assembly	†14B 5588	17	2	(C) H-AN5-501 to 26824	W.S.E. use 13H 4151
Wheelbox assembly	BHA 4151	17	2	(C) H-AN5-26824 to 50116	
Spindle and gear	†17H 5388	18	2		W.S.E. use AJH 5079
Spindle and gear	AJH 5079	18	2		
Bush—rear	AHH 5414	19	2		
Washer (rubber)	ADC 560	20	2		
Bush—front	ADB 826	21	2		
Tube—spindle (rubber)	ANK 3458	22	2		
Nut	ANK 3459	23	2		
Screw—cover	AJD 8202 Z	24	4		
Arm—wiper **RHD**	13H 66	25	2		
Arm—wiper **LHD**	13H 68	26	2		
Blade assembly—wiper	17H 5512	27	2		
Rubber	†27H 9162	28	2		

† Revised Information.

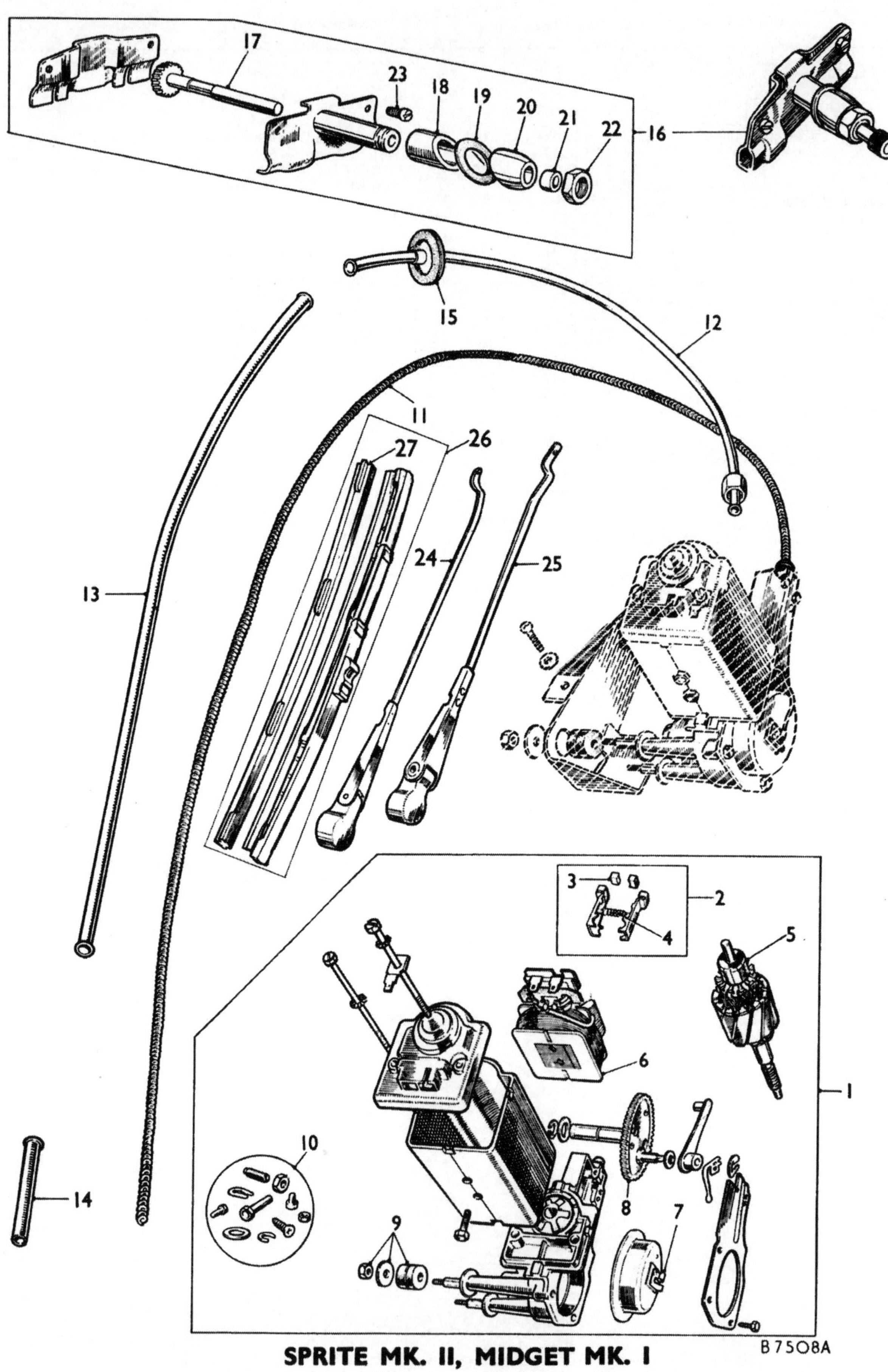

SPRITE MK. II, MIDGET MK. I

Electrical Equipment—*continued*

WINDSCREEN WIPER (SPRITE MK. II AND MIDGET)

DESCRIPTION	Part No.	Illus. No.	Quantity	Change Point	REMARKS
Motor assembly—windscreen wiper	57H 5293	1	1	(C) H-AN6-101 to 6275 RHD, 5659 LHD (C) G-AN1-101 to 3006, RHD, 2205 LHD	W.S.E. use 57H 5555
	57H 5555	1	1	(C) H-AN6-6276 RHD on, 5660 LHD on (C) G-AN1-3007 RHD on, 2206 LHD on	W.S.E. use 27H 3542
	27H 3542	1	1		
Brush gear assembly	17H 5396	2	1		For use with motors 57H 5293 and 57H 5555
Brush	7H 5130	3	1 set		For use with motors 57H 5293 and 57H 5555
Spring—brush	27H 5309	4	1		For use with motors 57H 5293 and 57H 5555
Brush gear assembly	27H 4463	2	1		For use with motor 27H 3542
Brush	27H 4464	3	1 set		For use with motor 27H 3542
Spring—brush	27H 5309	4	1		For use with motor 27H 3542
Armature	17H 5255	5	1	(C) H-AN6-101 to 6275 RHD, 5659 LHD (C) G-AN1-101 to 3006 RHD, 2205 LHD	W.S.E. use 27H 5374
Armature	27H 5374	5	1	(C) H-AN6-6276 RHD on, 5660 LHD on (C) G-AN1-3007 RHD on, 2206 LHD on	
Coil—field	57H 5294	6	1		
Switch—parking	47H 5316	7	1	(C) H-AN6-101 to 6275 RHD, 5659 LHD (C) G-AN1-101 to 3006 RHD, 2205 LHD	W.S.E. use 57H 5559
Shaft—gear	47H 5315	8	1	(C) H-AN6-101 to 6275 RHD, 5659 LHD (C) G-AN1-101 to 3006 RHD, 2205 LHD	W.S.E. use 57H 5589
Switch—parking	57H 5559	7	1	(C) H-AN6-6276 RHD on, 5660 LHD on (C) G-AN1-3007 RHD on, 2206 LHD on	
Shaft and gear	57H 5589	8	1	(C) H-AN6-6276 RHD on, 5660 LHD on (C) G-AN1-3007 RHD on, 2206 LHD on	
Fixing parts	17H 5431	9	3 sets		
Sundry parts	17H 5441	10	1 set		
Cross-head and rack	37H 5169	11	1		
Casing—outer					
Motor to wheelbox	14A 4801	12	1		
Wheelbox to wheelbox	14A 4802	13	1		
Wheelbox extension	14G 3722	14	1		
Grommet—casing through dash	8D 5768	15	1		
Wheelbox assembly	BHA 4151	16	2		
Spindle and gear	AJH 5079	17	2		
Bush—rear	AHH 5414	18	2		
Washer (rubber)	ADC 560	19	2		
Bush—front	ADB 826	20	2		
Tube—spindle (rubber)	ANK 3458	21	2		
Nut	ANK 3459	22	2		
Screw—cover	AJD 3202 Z	23	4		
Arm—wiper **RHD**	13H 66	24	2		
Arm—wiper **LHD**	13H 68	25	2		
Blade assembly—wiper	17H 5512	26	2		
Rubber	†27H 9162	27	2		

† Revised Information.

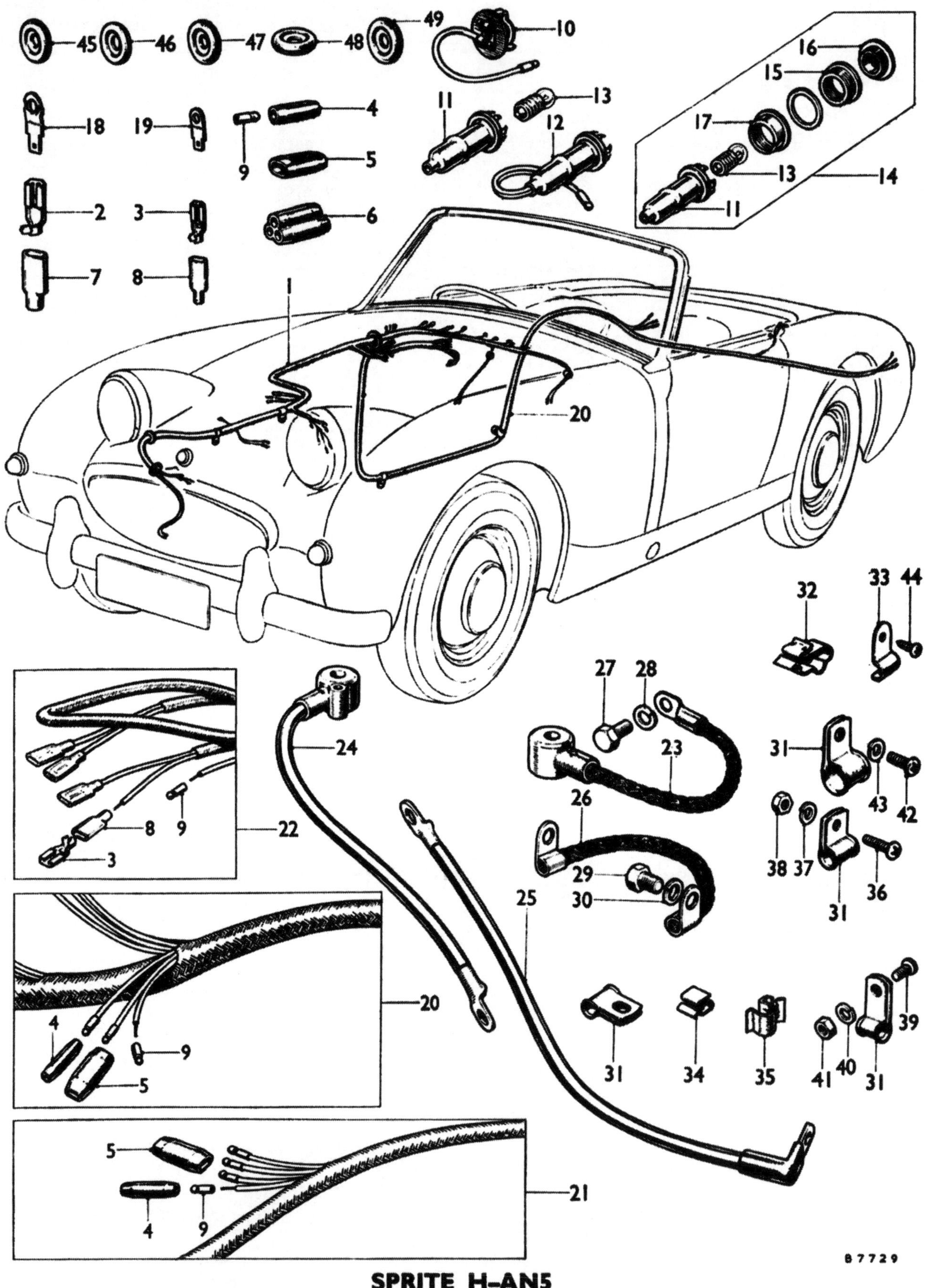
45
46
47
48
49
10
18
19
9
4
5
6
11
12
13
16
15
17
14
2
3
7
8
1
20
32
33
44
27
28
23
26
24
31
43
42
38
37
36
22
29
30
25
39
21
34
35
41
40
B7729

SPRITE H-AN5

DESCRIPTION	Part No.	Illus. No.	Quantity	Change Point	REMARKS
Electrical Equipment—*continued*					
CABLES AND CONNECTIONS (SPRITE H-AN5)					
Cable assembly—main harness	2A 9071	1	1	(C) H-AN5-501 to 22800	Not available; use AHA 5497 together with socket connector blades BMK 403 and 47H 5522
Cable assembly—main harness	AHA 5497	1	1	(C) H-AN5-22801 on	
Connector					
Socket—35-amp	47H 5419	2	A/R	(C) H-AN5-22801 on	
Socket—17·5-amp	47H 5496	3	A/R	(C) H-AN5-22801 on	
Snap—single	2H 3406	4	A/R		
Snap—double	2H 2617	5	A/R		
Snap—treble	2H 4992	6	A/R		
Insulator—socket connector—35-amp	5L 289	7	A/R	(C) H-AN5-22801 on	Part No. change; was 47H 5418
Insulator—socket connector—17·5-amp	5L 286	8	A/R	(C) H-AN5-22801 on	Part No. change; was 47H 5417
Plug—snap connector	2H 2704	9	A/R		
Holder—bulb					
Combined instrument and fuel gauge	3H 914	10	2		
Main-beam warning light, flasher warning light, and speedometer	37H 5181	11	3		
Ignition warning light	47H 5166	12	1		
Bulb	BFS 987	13	6		
Body assembly—main-beam warning light	27H 5562	14	1		Not required when tachometer is fitted
Body	27H 5565	15	1		Not required when tachometer is fitted
Cover and lens—Red	27H 5566	16	1		Not required when tachometer is fitted
Nut	27H 5564	17	1		Not required when tachometer is fitted
Holder—bulb	37H 5181	11	1		Not required when tachometer is fitted
Bulb	BFS 987	13	1		Not required when tachometer is fitted
Body assembly—flasher warning light	27H 5596	14	1		
Body	27H 5565	15	1		
Cover and lens—Green	27H 5597	16	1		
Nut	27H 5564	17	1		
Holder—bulb	37H 5181	11	1		
Bulb	BFS 987	13	1		
Blade—socket connector—35-amp	47H 5522	18	A/R		For use with AHA 5497 when fitted to cars prior to (C) H-AN5-22801
Blade—socket connector—17·5-amp	BMK 403	19	A/R		For use with AHA 5497 when fitted to cars prior to (C) H-AN5-22801
Cable assembly—body harness	2A 9072	20	1		
Connector—snap—single	2H 3406	4	A/R		
Connector—snap—double	2H 2617	5	A/R		
Plug—snap connector	2H 2704	9	A/R		
Cable assembly—forward lighting harness	2A 9073	21	1		
Connector—snap—single	2H 3406	4	A/R		
Connector—snap—double	2H 2617	5	A/R		
Plug—snap connector	2H 2704	9	A/R		
Cable assembly—horn harness	AHA 5470	22	1		For use when Windtone horns are fitted
Connector—socket	47H 5496	3	A/R		For use when Windtone horns are fitted
Insulator—connector	5L 286	8	A/R		For use when Windtone horns are fitted
Plug—snap connector	2H 2704	9	A/R		For use when Windtone horns are fitted
Lead—earth	NSP		2		Was ADH 2610; For use when Windtone horns are fitted
Cable					
Battery positive to earth	1B 2802	23	1		
Battery negative to starter switch	2A 9076	24	1		
Starter switch to starter	2A 9075	25	1		
Engine to earth	2K 6167	26	1		
Screw—positive cable to dash	HZS 0504	27	1		
Washer—spring	LWZ 305	28	1		
Screw—earth cable to frame	HZS 0605	29	1		
Washer—spring	LWZ 306	30	1		

† Revised Information.

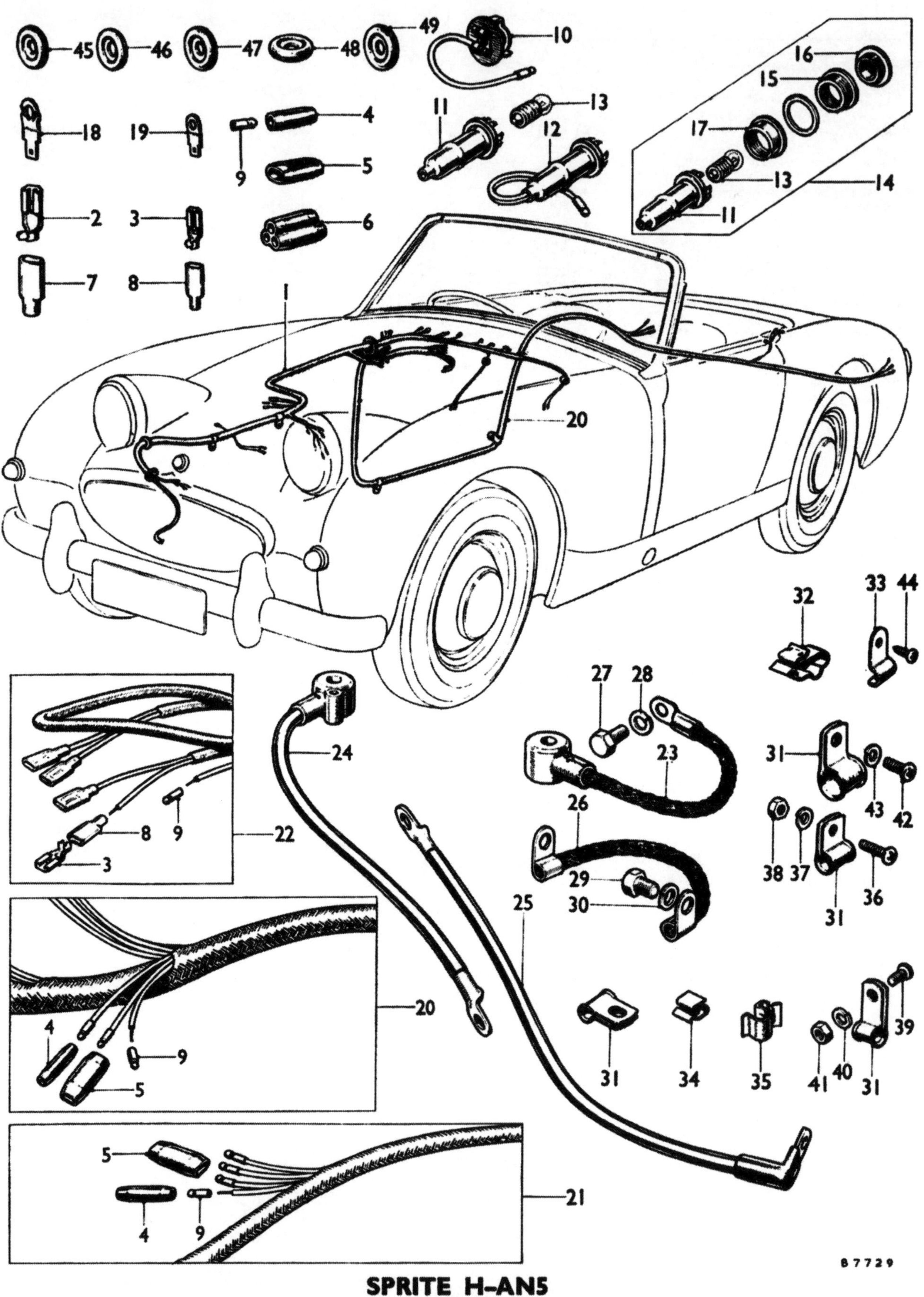
45
46
47
48
49
10
18
19
9
4
5
11
13
12
16
15
17
13
14
11
2
3
6
7
8
1
20
32
33
44
27
28
23
24
26
31
43
42
38
37
36
22
8
9
3
29
30
25
31
20
4
9
5
31
34
35
41
40
31
39
5
4
9
21
B7729

SPRITE H-AN5

DESCRIPTION	Part No.	Illus. No.	Quantity	Change Point	REMARKS
Electrical Equipment—*continued*					
Cables and Connections (Sprite H-AN5)—*continued*					
Clip					
1/4" (6·35 mm) cable dia × 7/32" (5·56 mm) fixing hole dia	PCR 0407	31	A/R		
1/4" (6·35 mm) cable dia × 9/32" (7·14 mm) fixing hole dia	PCR 0409	31	A/R		
3/8" (9·52 mm) cable dia × 7/32" (5·56 mm) fixing hole dia	PCR 0607	31	A/R		
3/8" (9·52 mm) cable dia × 9/32" (7·14 mm) fixing hole dia	PCR 0609	31	A/R		
5/8" (15·87 mm) cable dia × 7/32" (5·56 mm) fixing hole dia	PCR 1007	31	A/R		
Cable to bonnet flange	6K 490	32	2		
Harness to sill	CHR 0405	33	A/R		
Horn harness	BHA 4130	34	3		For use when Windtone horns are fitted
Horn harness	17H 9528	35	1		For use when Windtone horns are fitted
Screw	PMZ 0310	36	1		
Washer—spring	LWZ 203	37	1		
Nut	FNZ 103	38	1		
Screw	PMZ 0306	39	1		
Washer—spring	LWZ 203	40	1		
Nut	FNZ 103	41	1		
Screw	PMZ 0307	42	1		
Washer—spring	LWZ 203	43	1		
Screw—clip to sill	PTZ 603	44	A/R		
Grommet					
Harness through dash	RFN 303	45	1		
Wiper motor cable through dash	RFN 305	46	1		
Dipper switch cable through foot-well	RFN 305	47	1		
Tank unit cable through rear floor	RFN 303	48	1		
Number-plate lamp cable through rear panel	RFN 303	49	1		

† Revised Information.

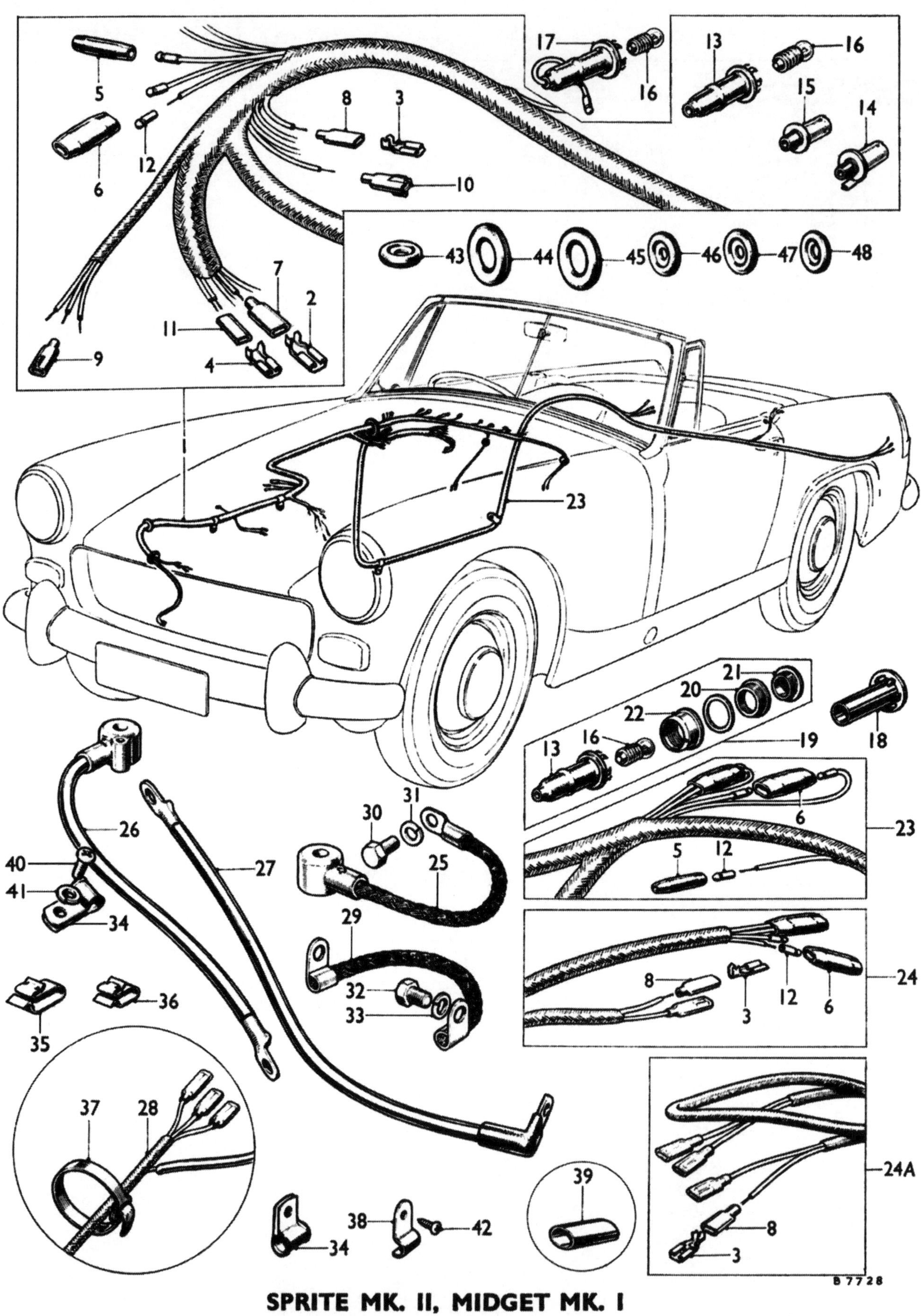

SPRITE MK. II, MIDGET MK. I

DESCRIPTION	Part No.	Illus. No.	Quantity	Change Point	REMARKS
Electrical Equipment—*continued*					
CABLES AND CONNECTIONS (SPRITE MK. 11 AND MIDGET)					
Cable assembly—main harness	AHA 5655	1	1	(C) H-AN6-101 to 24731 (C) G-AN1-101 to 16183	
Cable assembly—main harness	AHA 6980	1	1	(C) H-AN7-24732 on (C) G-AN2-16184 on	
Connector					
Socket—single—35-amp	47H 5419	2	A/R		
Socket—single—17·5-amp	47H 5496	3	A/R		
Socket—double	47H 5499	4	A/R		
Snap—single	2H 3406	5	A/R		
Snap—double	2H 2617	6	A/R		
Insulator—socket connector					
Single—35-amp	5L 289	7	A/R		Part No. change; was 47H 5418
Single—17·5-amp	5L 286	8	A/R		Part No. change; was 47H 5417
Single—17·5-amp	5L 285	9	A/R		Part No. change; was 47H 5316
Single—17·5-amp	BMK 449	10	A/R		
Double	5L 287	11	A/R		Part No. change; was 47H 5500
Plug—snap connector	27H 2704	12	A/R		
Holder—bulb					
Instrument illumination	37H 5181	13	5		
Ignition warning light	†57H 5844	14	1		W.S.E. use 57H 5445
Ignition warning light	57H 5445	14	1		
Main-beam warning light	†57H 5206	15	1		W.S.E. use 13H 1927
Main-beam warning light	†13H 1927	15	1		
Bulb	BFS 987	16	7/8		Part No. change; was 2H 4732 Quantity increased at (C) H-AN7-34274 and (C) G-AN2-22617
Holder and cable—bulb—tachometer illumination	†2A 9097	17	1	(C) H-AN6-101 to 24731 (C) H-AN7-24732 to 34273 (C) G-AN1-101 to 16183 (C) G-AN2-16184 to 22616	W.S.E. use 13H 1924
Bulb	BFS 987	16	1		Part No. change; was 2H 4732
Holder—bulb—tachometer illumination	†13H 1924		1		
Cover and lens—main-beam warning light—Red	AHA 5845	18	1		Required when tachometer is not fitted
Body assembly—flasher warning light	27H 5596	19	1		
Body	27H 5565	20	1		
Cover and lens—Green	27H 5597	21	1		
Nut	27H 5564	22	1		
Holder—bulb	37H 5181	13	1		
Bulb	BFS 987	16	1		Part No. change; was 2H 4732
Cable assembly—body harness	AHA 5656	23	1		
Connector—snap—single	2H 3406	5	A/R		
Connector—snap—double	2H 2617	6	A/R		
Plug—snap connector	2H 2704	12	A/R		
Cable assembly—horn harness	AHA 5692	24	1	(C) H-AN6-101 to 13388 (C) G-AN1-101 to 8976	For use when twin horns are fitted
Connector—socket	47H 5496	3	A/R		
Insulator—connector	5L 286	8	A/R		Part No. change; was 47H 5417
Connector—snap—double	2H 2617	6	A/R		
Plug—snap connector	2H 2704	12	A/R		
Cable assembly—horn harness—horn to horn	AHA 6396	24A	1	(C) H-AN6-13389 to 24731 (C) H-AN7-24732 on (C) G-AN1-8977 to 16183 (C) G-AN2-16184 on	
Connector—socket	47H 5496	3	4		
Insulator—connector	5L 286	8	4		Part No. change; was 47H 5417

† Revised Information.

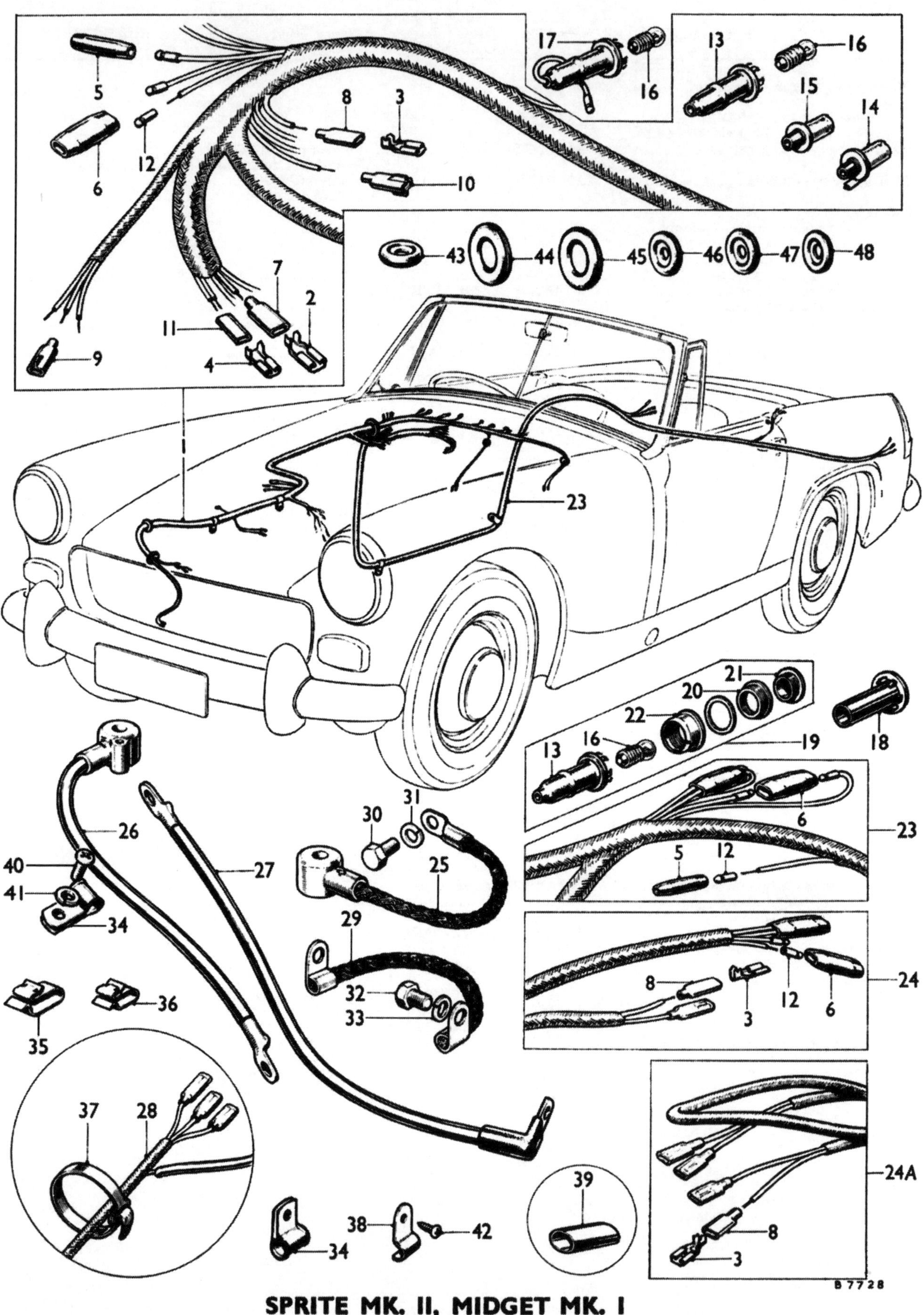

SPRITE MK. II, MIDGET MK. I

DESCRIPTION	Part No.	Illus. No.	Quantity	Change Point	REMARKS
Electrical Equipment—*continued*					
Cables and Connections (Sprite Mk. II and Midget)—*continued*					
Cable					
Battery positive to earth	1B 2802	25	1		
Battery negative to starter switch	2A 9076	26	1		
Starter switch to starter	2A 9075	27	1		
Battery negative to starter solenoid	BHA 4257	26	1		For use when steering lock is fitted
Starter solenoid to starter	AHA 6280	27	1		For use when steering lock is fitted
Steering lock	AHA 6824	28	1		For use when steering lock is fitted
Engine to earth	2K 6167	29	1		
Screw	HZS 0504	30	1		
Washer—spring	LWZ 305	31	1		
Screw	HZS 0605	32	1		
Washer—spring	LWZ 306	33	1		
Clip					
3/8" (9·52 mm) cable dia × 7/32" (5·56 mm) fixing hole dia	PCR 0607	34	A/R		
5/8" (15·87 mm) cable dia × 9/32" (7·14 mm) fixing hole dia	PCR 1009	34	A/R		
Harness to fascia top	BHA 4233	35	1		
Harness to bonnet locking platform	BHA 4232	36	1		
Harness to bonnet locking platform	BHA 4233	35	2		
Cable to column	AHH 7108	37	1		
Harness to sill	CHR 0405	38	A/R		
Sleeve—dipper switch cable clip **LHD**	5L 64	39	6	(C) H-AN6-16489 to 24731 (C) H-AN7-24732 on (C) G-AN1-11081 to 16183 (C) G-AN2-16184 on	
Screw	PMZ 0308	40	1		
Washer—spring	LWZ 203	41	1		
Screw	PTZ 603	42	A/R		
Grommet					
Harness through dash	RFN 308	43	1		
Harness through baffle	RFN 110	44	2		
Harness through mudshield	RFR 110	45	1		
Wiper motor cable through dash	RFN 305	46	1		
Tank unit cable through rear floor	RFN 308	47	1		
Number-plate lamp cable	RFN 308	48	2		

CHANGE POINTS

(1) (C) H-AN6-101 to 10117 (less 7499 to 7685, 7687 to 7771, 7774 to 7849, 7853, 7855 to 7863, 7867, 7871 to 8046, and 8048 to 10116)
(C) G-AN1-101 to 7519 (less 3491 to 3562, 3565 to 3615, 3617 to 3631, 3640 to 3652, 3654, 3660 to 3665, 3669 to 3686, 3688 to 3833, 3835 to 3903, 3905 to 3924, 3926 to 5187, and 5190 to 7507)

(2) (C) H-AN6-10118 to 24731 (plus 7499 to 7685, 7687 to 7771, 7774 to 7849, 7853, 7855 to 7863, 7867, 7871 to 8046, and 8048 to 10116)
(C) H-AN7-24732 on
(C) G-AN1-7520 to 16183 (plus 3491 to 3562, 3565 to 3615, 3617 to 3631, 3640 to 3652, 3654, 3660 to 3665, 3669 to 3686, 3688 to 3833, 3835 to 3903, 3905 to 3924, 3926 to 5187, and 5190 to 7507)
(C) G-AN2-16184 on

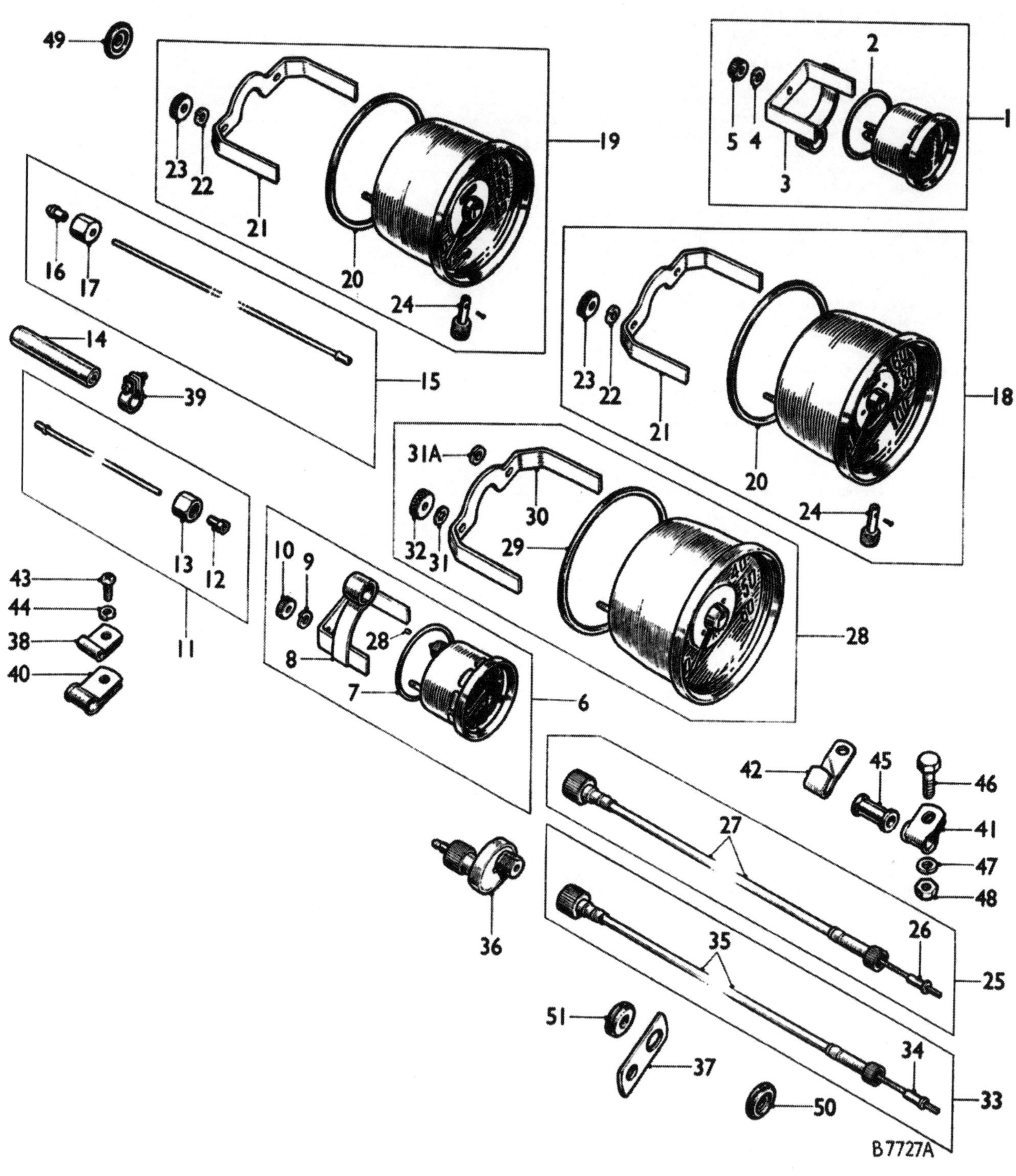
49
2
1
5
4
3
19
23
22
21
20
24
16
17
14
15
39
18
23
22
21
20
24
31A
30
32
31
29
28
10
9
13
12
43
44
38
40
11
28
8
7
6
42
45
46
27
41
47
48
36
26
35
25
51
37
34
33
50
B7727A

SPRITE H-AN5

INSTRUMENTS

SPRITE (AN 5)

	Page	Plate
CABLES—SPEEDOMETER AND TACHOMETER ...	MO 3	O 1
GAUGES—FUEL, OIL, AND WATER	MO 2	O 1
PIPES—OIL GAUGE	MO 2	O 1
SPEEDOMETER	MO 2	O 1
TACHOMETER	MO 3	O 1

INSTRUMENTS

DESCRIPTION	Part No.	Illus. No.	Quantity	Change Point	REMARKS
(SPRITE H-AN5)					
Gauge assembly—fuel	2A 9069	1	1		
Glass	NSP		1		Was 17H 1068
Tube (rubber)	NSP		1		Was 17H 1821
Bezel	NSP		1		Was AJH 5182
Ring (rubber)	17H 1642	2	1		
Strap—fixing	17H 1822	3	1		
Washer—spring	27H 387	4	1		W.S.E. use LWZ 302
Washer—spring	LWZ 302	4	1		
Nut—thumb	17H 932	5	1		
Gauge assembly—oil and temperature	2A 9070	6	1		
Glass	NSP		1		Was 17H 1068
Grommet	NSP		1		Was 17H 1479
Bezel	NSP		1		Was AJH 5182
Strip—window	NSP		1		Was 17H 1481
Ring (rubber)	17H 1642	7	1		
Strap—fixing	17H 1480	8	1		
Restrictor	†27H 7877		1		
Washer—spring	27H 387	9	2		W.S.E. use LWZ 302
Washer—spring	LWZ 302	9	2		
Nut—thumb	17H 932	10	2		
Pipe assembly—gauge to flexible pipe RHD	2A 5635	11	1		
Pipe assembly—gauge to flexible pipe LHD	2A 5640	11	1		
Union	51K 2824	12	1		
Nut	11B 2037	13	1		
Pipe—flexible	ACA 5420	14	1		
Pipe assembly—flexible pipe to engine	2A 5637	15	1		
Nipple	ACA 5422	16	1		
Nut	ACA 5421	17	1		
Speedometer assembly—mph (SN6155/10)	2A 9067	18	1		Final drive ratio 4·22 : 1
Speedometer assembly—kph (SN6155/11)	2A 9077	19	1		Final drive ratio 4·22 : 1
Glass	NSP		1		Was AJH 5177
Ring—slip	NSP		1		Was 27H 406
Bezel	NSP		1		Was 27H 397
Spindle—trip stem	NSP		1		Was 17H 1478
Ring (rubber)	AJH 5178	20	1		
Strap—fixing	AJH 5176	21	1		Part No. change; was 27H 429
Washer—spring	27H 387	22	2		W.S.E. use LWZ 302
Washer—spring	LWZ 302	22	2		
Nut—thumb	17H 1304	23	2		
Stem—trip	37H 613	24	1		Part No. change; was AJH 5179
Cable assembly—speedometer—5′ 2″ (157·48 cm) long RHD	1H 9049	25	1		
Cable—inner RHD	17H 844	26	1		
Cable—outer RHD	17H 1496	27	1		W.S.E. use 1K 9049
Cable assembly—speedometer—4′ 8″ (142·24 cm) long LHD	2A 9039	25	1	(C) H-AN5-501 to 3688	
Cable—inner LHD	17H 689	26	1	(C) H-AN5-501 to 3688	
Cable—outer LHD	†17H 690	27	1	(C) H-AN5-501 to 3688	W.S.E. use 2A 9039
Cable assembly—speedometer—4′ 6″ (137·16 cm) long LHD	1H 9047	25	1	(C) H-AN5-3689 on	
Cable—inner LHD	17H 843	26	1	(C) H-AN5-3689 on	
Cable—outer LHD	17H 1669	27	1	(C) H-AN5-3689 on	W.S.E. use 1H 9047

† Revised Information.

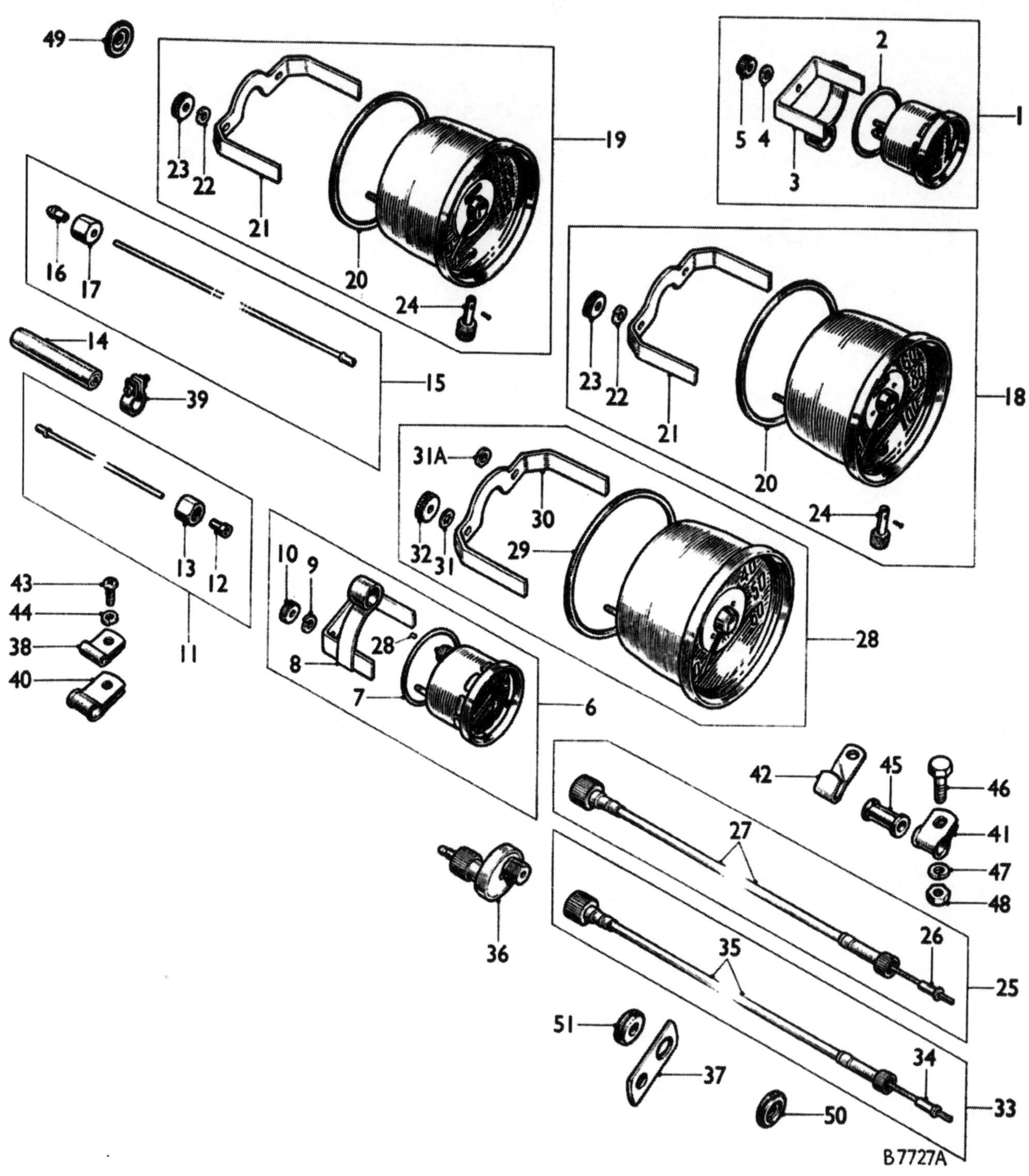
49
2
1
5 4
3
19
23 22
21
20
24
16 17
14
15
39
23 22
21
18
20
24
31A
30
32 31
29
28
10 9
13 12
43
44
38
40
11
28
8
7
6
42
45
46
41
27
47
48
36
26
25
35
51
37
34
33
50
B7727A

SPRITE H-AN5

DESCRIPTION	Part No.	Illus. No.	Quantity	Change Point	REMARKS
Instruments (Sprite H-AN5)—*continued*					
Tachometer assembly	2A 9068	28	1		Optional extra
Glass	NSP		1		Was AJH 5177
Ring—slip	NSP		1		Was 27H 406
Bezel	NSP		1		Was 27H 397
Screw—fixing strap	NSP		2		Was 17H 1544
Ring (rubber)	AJH 5178	29	1		
Strap—fixing	AJH 5176	30	1		Part No. change; was 27H 429
Washer—shakeproof	17H 1341	31	2		W.S.E. use 2K 1369
Washer—spring	2K 1369	31A	2		
Nut—thumb	17H 1304	32	2		
Cable assembly—tachometer—2′ 2″ (66·04 cm) long (RHD)	2A 9104	33	1	(C) H-AN5-501 to 3443	
Cable—inner (RHD)	17H 1499	34	1	(C) H-AN5-501 to 3443	
Cable—outer (RHD)	17H 1497	35	1	(C) H-AN5-501 to 3443	W.S.E. use 2A 9104
Cable assembly—tachometer—2′ 1″ (63·5 cm) long (RHD)	BHA 4086	33	1	(C) H-AN5-3444 on	
Cable—inner (RHD)	17H 1678	34	1	(C) H-AN5-3444 on	
Cable—outer (RHD)	†17H 1679	35	1	(C) H-AN5-3444 on	W.S.E. use BHA 4086
Cable assembly—tachometer—3′ 0″ (91·44 cm) long (LHD)	2A 9108	33	1		
Cable—inner (LHD)	17H 1344	34	1		
Cable—outer (LHD)	17H 1498	35	1		
Box—ratio—cable to dynamo	2A 9105	36	1		W.S.E. use 13H 632
Box—ratio—cable to dynamo	13H 632	36	1		
Bracket—cable	1K 1977	37	1		
Clip					
Oil gauge pipe to foot-well	PCR 0207	38	1		Part No. change; was 1C 166
Oil gauge flexible pipe	88G 308	39	2		Part No. change; was 3H 688
Thermometer capillary	PCR 0307	40	4		
Speedometer cable to bulkhead (RHD)	PCR 0709	41	1		
Speedometer cable to clutch housing (RHD)	1B 9132	42	1		
Screw	PMZ 0306	43	3		
Washer—spring	LWZ 203	44	3		
Sleeve—speedometer cable clip (rubber) (RHD)	ACH 8529	45	1		
Screw (RHD)	HZS 0408	46	1		
Washer—spring (RHD)	LWZ 204	47	1		
Nut (RHD)	FNZ 104	48	1		
Grommet					
Speedometer cable through foot-well	RFN 305	49	1		
Tachometer cable through dash	RFN 305	50	1		
Tachometer cable through bracket	8H 822	51	1		

† Revised Information.

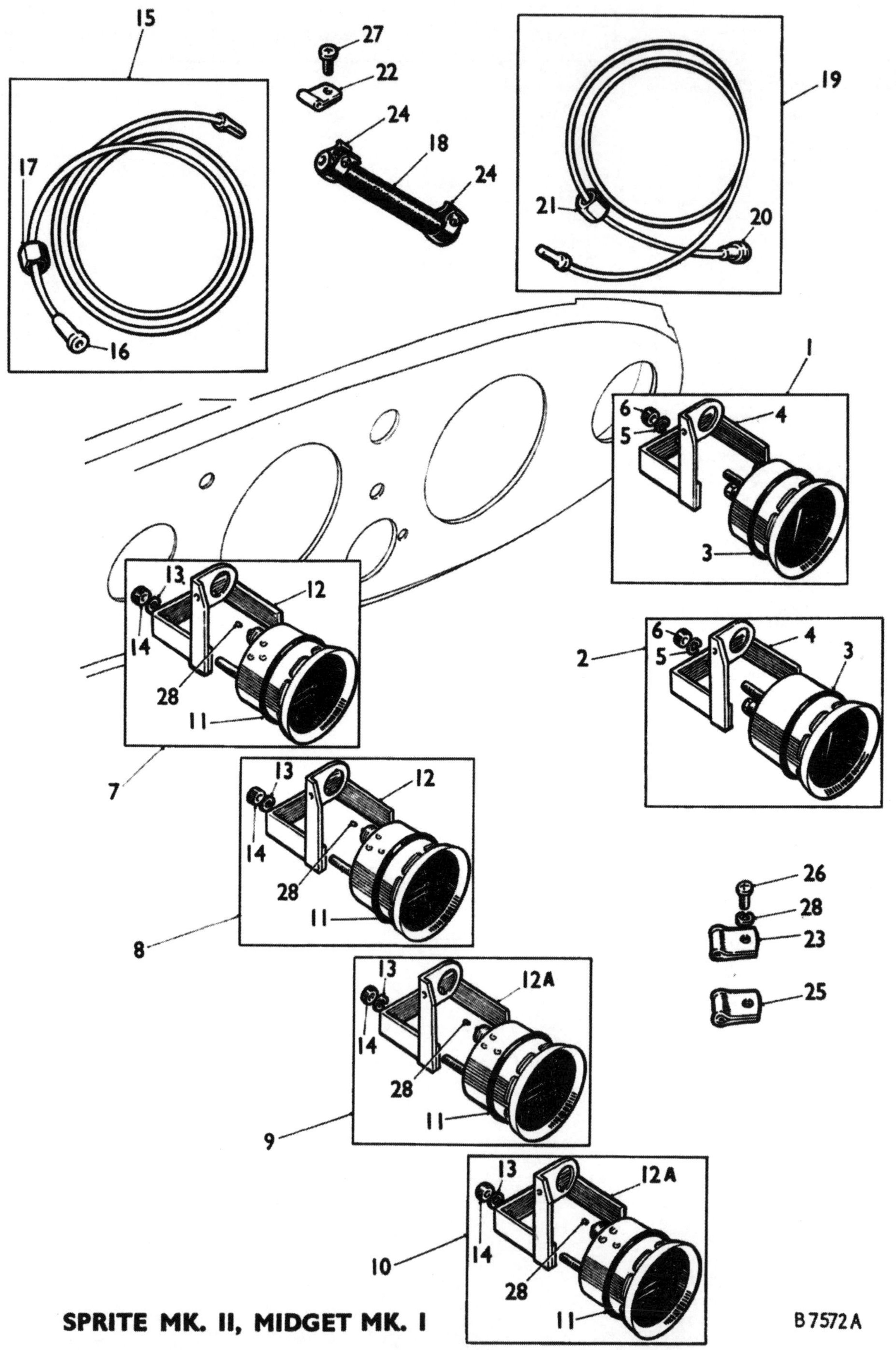

SPRITE MK. II, MIDGET MK. I

INSTRUMENTS

SPRITE Mk. II AND MIDGET Mk. I

CABLES—SPEEDOMETER AND TACHOMETER ... MO 5 O 3

GAUGES—FUEL, OIL, AND WATER ... ... MO 4 O 2

PIPES—OIL GAUGE ... ... MO 4 O 2

SPEEDOMETER ... ... MO 5 O 3

TACHOMETER ... ... MO 5 O 3

Instruments—*continued*

(SPRITE MK. II AND MIDGET)

DESCRIPTION	Part No.	Illus. No.	Quantity	Change Point	REMARKS
Gauge assembly—fuel **Sprite Mk. II**	BHA 4215	1	1	(C) H-AN6-101 to 24781	
Midget	BHA 4214	2	1	(C) G-AN1-101 to 16183	W.S.E. use BHA 4881
	BHA 4881	2	1	(C) H-AN7-24782 on (C) G-AN2-16184 on	
Ring (rubber)	17H 1642	3	1		
Strap—fixing	AJH 5185	4	1		
Washer—spring	27H 387	5	1		W.S.E. use LWZ 302
Washer—spring	LWZ 302	5	1		
Nut—thumb	17H 932	6	1		
Gauge assembly—oil and temperature					
Fahrenheit } **Sprite Mk. II**	BHA 4216	7	1	} (C) H-AN6-101 to 24731	
Centigrade } **Sprite Mk. II**	BHA 4249	8	1		
Fahrenheit } **Midget**	BHA 4217	9	1	} (C) G-AN1-101 to 16183	W.S.E. use BHA 4382
Centigrade } **Midget**	BHA 4250	10	1		W.S.E. use BHA 4383
Fahrenheit	BHA 4382	9	1	} (C) H-AN7-24782 on	
Centigrade	BHA 4383	10	1	} (C) G-AN2-16184 on	
Ring (rubber) } **Sprite Mk. II**	17H 1642	11	1	} (C) H-AN6-101 to 24731	
Strap—fixing } **Sprite Mk. II**	AJH 5186	12	1		
Ring (rubber)	27H 972	11	1	} (C) H-AN7-24782 on	
Strap—fixing	37H 678	12A	1	} (C) G-AN1-101 to 16183 (C) G-AN2-16184 on	
Restrictor	†27H 7877		1		
Washer—spring	27H 387	13	2		W.S.E. use LWZ 302
Washer—spring	LWZ 302	13	2		
Nut—thumb	17H 932	14	2		
Pipe assembly—gauge to flexible pipe **RHD**	2A 5635	15	1		
Pipe assembly—gauge to flexible pipe **LHD**	2A 5640	15	1		
Union	51K 2824	16	1		
Nut	11B 2037	17	1		
Pipe—flexible	ACA 5420	18	1	(C) H-AN6-101 to 10912 (C) G-AN1-101 to 6166	
Pipe—flexible	AHA 6331	18	1	(C) H-AN6-10913 to 24731 (C) H-AN7-24732 on (C) G-AN1-6167 to 16183 (C) G-AN2-16184 on	
Pipe assembly—flexible pipe to engine	2A 5637	19	1	(C) H-AN6-101 to 11702 (C) G-AN1-101 to 6678	
Pipe assembly—flexible pipe to engine	AHA 6392	19	1	(C) H-AN6-11703 to 24731 (C) H-AN7-24732 on (C) G-AN1-6679 to 16183 (C) G-AN2-16184 on	
Nipple	ACA 5422	20	1		
Nut	ACA 5421	21	1		
Clip					
Oil gauge pipe to foot-well	PCR 0207	22	1	(C) H-AN6-101 to 23600 (C) G-AN1-101 to 14686	Part No. change; was 1C 166
Oil gauge pipe to foot-well	PCR 0207	23	1	(C) H-AN6-23601 to 24731 (C) H-AN7-24732 on (C) G-AN1-14687 to 16183 (C) G-AN2-16184 on	
Oil gauge flexible pipe	3H 688	24	2		W.S.E. use 88G 308
Oil gauge flexible pipe	88G 308	24	2		
Thermometer capillary	PCR 0307	25	4		
Screw	PMZ 0308	26	2		
Screw	PMZ 0306	27	1		
Washer—spring	LWZ 203	28	3		

† Revised Information.

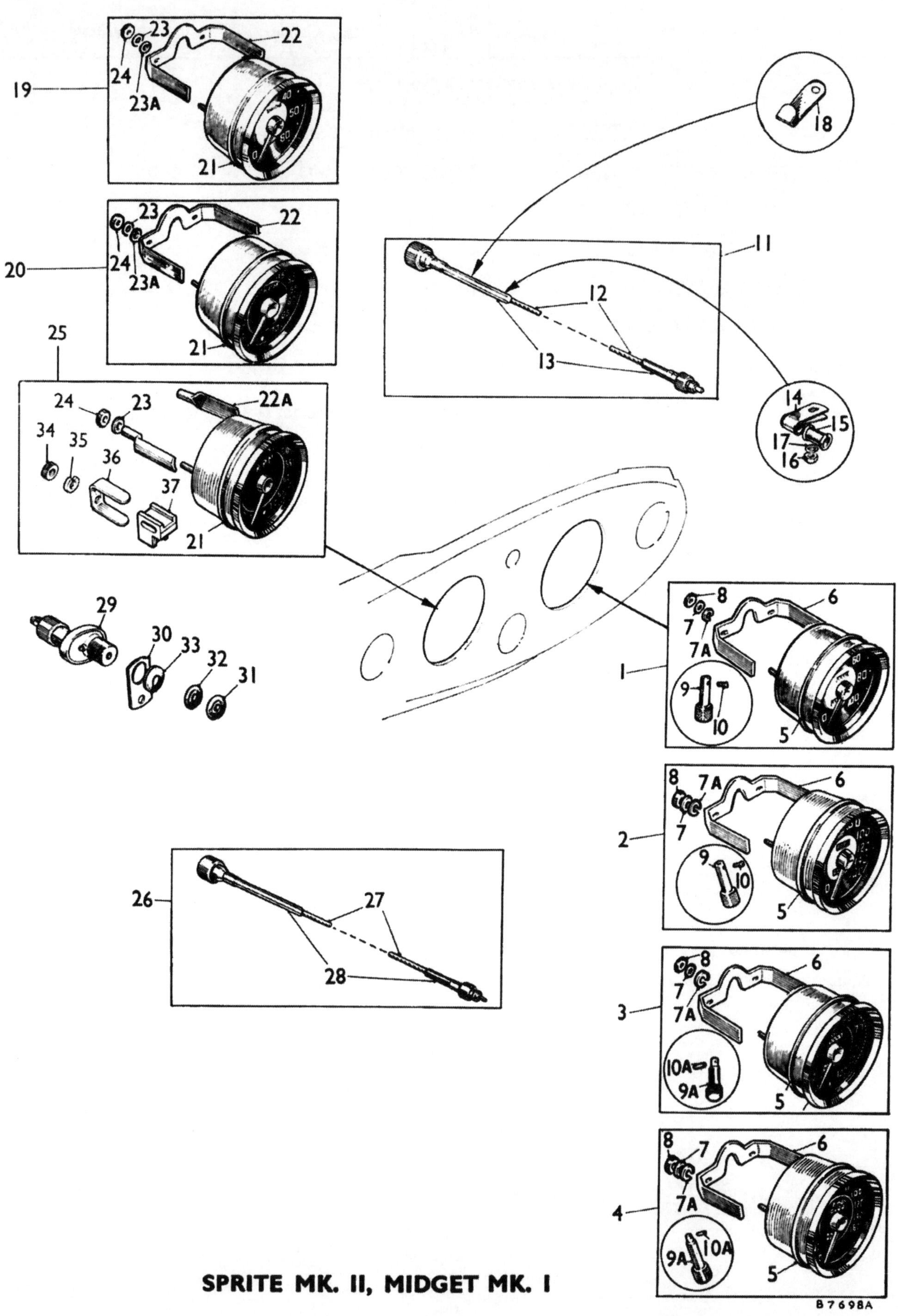

SPRITE MK. II, MIDGET MK. I

Instruments (Sprite Mk. II and Midget)—*continued*

DESCRIPTION	Part No.	Illus. No.	Quantity	Change Point	REMARKS
Speedometer assembly					
MPH (SN6126/00) — **Sprite Mk. II**	BHA 4210	1	1	(C) H-AN6-101 to 24731	Final drive ratio 4·22 : 1
KPH (SN6126/01) — **Sprite Mk. II**	BHA 4211	2	1	(C) H-AN6-101 to 24731	Final drive ratio 4·22 : 1
MPH (SN6125/02) — **Midget**	BHA 4208	3	1	(C) G-AN1-101 to 16183	W.S.E. use BHA 4372; Final drive ratio 4·22 : 1
KPH (SN6125/03) — **Midget**	BHA 4209	4	1	(C) G-AN1-101 to 16183	W.S.E. use BHA 4373; Final drive ratio 4·22 : 1
MPH (SN6135/00)	BHA 4372	3	1	(C) H-AN7-24732 on (C) G-AN2-16184 on	Final drive ratio 4·22 : 1
KPH (SN6135/01)	BHA 4373	4	1	(C) H-AN7-24732 on (C) G-AN2-16184 on	Final drive ratio 4·22 : 1
Ring (rubber)	AJH 5178	5	1		
Strap—fixing	AJH 5176	6	1		
Washer—shakeproof	17H 1341	7	2		W.S.E. use 2K 1369
Washer—spring	2K 1369	7A	2		
Nut—thumb	17H 1304	8	2		
Stem—trip — **Sprite Mk. II**	37H 640	9	1	(C) H-AN6-101 to 24731	
Stem—trip	37H 613	9A	1	(C) H-AN7-24732 on (C) G-AN1-101 to 16183 (C) G-AN2-16184 on	
Screw—trip stem	17H 1658	10	1	(C) H-AN6-101 to 24731 (C) G-AN1-101 to 16183	
Pin—dowel—trip stem	17H 3745	10A	1	(C) H-AN7-24732 on (C) G-AN2-16184 on	
Cable assembly—speedometer—5′ 2″ (157·48 cm) — **RHD**	1H 9049	11	1		
Cable—inner — **RHD**	17H 844	12	1		
Cable—outer — **RHD**	†17H 1496	13	1		W.S.E. use 1H 9049
Clip — **RHD**	PCR 0709	14	1		
Sleeve—clip (rubber) — **RHD**	ACH 8529	15	1		
Nut — **RHD**	FNZ 104	16	1		
Washer—spring — **RHD**	LWZ 204	17	1		
Clip—cable to clutch housing — **RHD**	1B 9132	18	1		
Cable assembly—speedometer—4′ 6″ (137·16 cm) — **LHD**	1H 9047	11	1		
Cable—inner — **LHD**	17H 843	12	1		
Cable—outer — **LHD**	†17H 1669	13	1		W.S.E. use 1H 9047
Tachometer assembly — **Sprite Mk. II**	BHA 4213	19	1	(C) H-AN6-101 to 23781	
Tachometer assembly — **Midget**	BHA 4212	20	1	(C) G-AN1-101 to 16183	
Ring (rubber)	AJH 5178	21	1	(C) H-AN6-101 to 24731 (C) G-AN1-101 to 16183	
Strap—fixing	AJH 5176	22	1	(C) H-AN6-101 to 24731 (C) G-AN1-101 to 16183	
Washer—shakeproof	17H 1341	23	2	(C) H-AN6-101 to 24731 (C) G-AN1-101 to 16183	W.S.E. use 2K 1369
Washer—spring	2K 1369	28A	2	(C) H-AN6-101 to 24731 (C) G-AN1-101 to 16183	
Nut—thumb	17H 1304	24	2	(C) H-AN6-101 to 24731 (C) G-AN1-101 to 16183	
Tachometer assembly—electrical	BHA 4380	25	1	(C) H-AN7-24732 on (C) G-AN2-16184 on	
Thumb nut (small)	†27H 8213	34	1	(C) H-AN7-24732 on (C) G-AN2-16184 on	
Washer	†27H 8214	35	1	(C) H-AN7-24732 on (C) G-AN2-16184 on	
Core (metal)	†27H 8215	36	1	(C) H-AN7-24732 on (C) G-AN2-16184 on	
Loop—sleeve (nylon)	†13H 784	37	1	(C) H-AN7-24732 on (C) G-AN2-16184 on	
Ring (rubber)	AJH 5178	21	1	(C) H-AN7-24732 on (C) G-AN2-16184 on	
Strap—fixing	17H 3744	22A	2	(C) H-AN7-24732 on (C) G-AN2-16184 on	
Washer—shakeproof	LWZ 402	23	2	(C) H-AN7-24732 on (C) G-AN2-16184 on	
Nut—thumb	17H 1304	24	2	(C) H-AN7-24732 on (C) G-AN2-16184 on	
Cable assembly—tachometer—2′ 1″ (63·5 cm) — **RHD**	BHA 4086	26		(C) H-AN6-101 to 3807 (C) G-AN1-101 to 1042	
Cable—inner — **RHD**	17H 1678	27		(C) H-AN6-101 to 3807 (C) G-AN1-101 to 1042	
Cable—outer — **RHD**	17H 1679	28		(C) H-AN6-101 to 3807 (C) G-AN1-101 to 1042	
Cable assembly—tachometer—2′ 2″ (66·04 cm) — **RHD**	2A 9104	26		(C) H-AN6-3808 to 24731 (C) G-AN1-1043 to 16183	
Cable—inner — **RHD**	17H 1499	27		(C) H-AN6-3808 to 24731 (C) G-AN1-1043 to 16183	
Cable—outer — **RHD**	17H 1497	28		(C) H-AN6-3808 to 24731 (C) G-AN1-1043 to 16183	W.S.E. use 2A 9104
Cable assembly—tachometer—3′ 0″ (91·44 cm) — **LHD**	2A 9108	26		(C) H-AN6-101 to 24731 (C) G-AN1-101 to 16183	
Cable—inner — **LHD**	17H 1344	27		(C) H-AN6-101 to 24731 (C) G-AN1-101 to 16183	
Cables—outer — **LHD**	17H 1498	28		(C) H-AN6-101 to 24731 (C) G-AN1-101 to 16183	
Box—ratio—cable to dynamo	2A 9105	29	1	(C) H-AN6-101 to 11161 (C) G-AN1-101 to 6254	W.S.E. use 13H 632
Box—ratio—cable to dynamo	13H 632	29	1	(C) H-AN6-11162 to 24731 (C) G-AN1-6255 to 16183	
Bracket—cable	1K 1977	30	1		
Grommet					
Speedometer cable through foot-well	RFN 805	31	1		
Tachometer cable through dash	RFN 805	32	1		
Tachometer cable through bracket	8H 822	33	1		

† Revised Information.

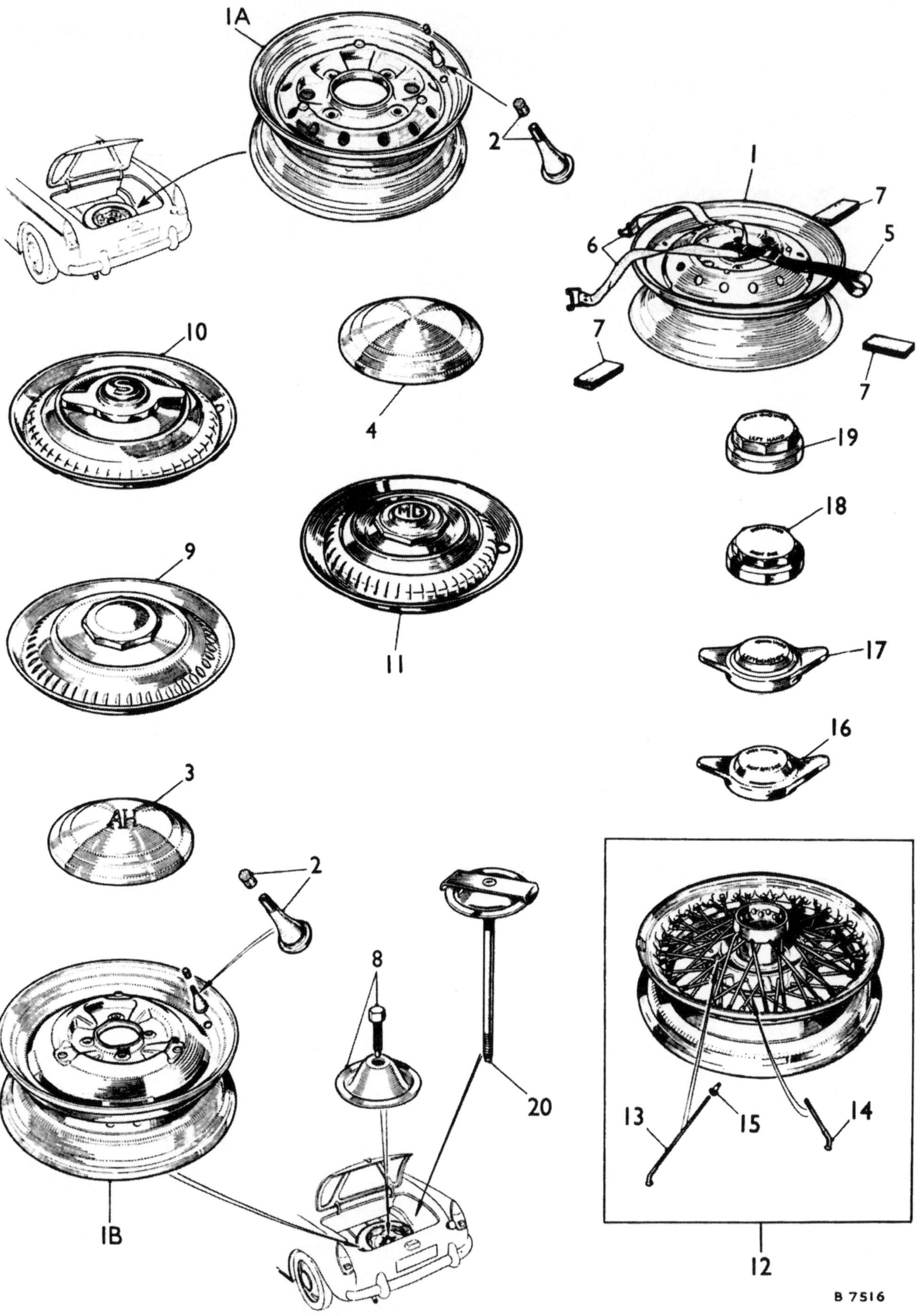
1A
2
1
7
6
5
10
4
7
7
19
18
11
9
17
16
3
2
8
20
13
15
14
1B
12
B 7516

ROAD WHEELS

	Page	Plate
CAPS—HUB	MP 2	P 1
DISCS—LOUVRED	MP 2	P 1
WHEELS	MP 2	P 1

ROAD WHEELS

DESCRIPTION	Part No.	Illus. No.	Quantity	Change Point	REMARKS
Wheel—disc	2A 8060	1	5	(C) H-AN5-501 to 15150	Not available; use AHA 5471 (Disc wheels)
	AHA 5471	1	5	(C) H-AN5-15151 to 39223	Not available; use AHA 5539 (Disc wheels)
	AHA 5539	1A	5	(C) H-AN5-39224 to 50116 (C) H-AN6-101 to 24731 (C) H-AN7-24732 to 26239 (C) G-AN1-101 to 16183 (C) G-AN2-16184 to 17165	Disc wheels
	AHA 6455	1B	5	(C) H-AN7-26240 on (C) G-AN2-17166 on	Disc wheels
Valve—tyre	BCA 4163	2	5	(C) H-AN5-501 to 50116 (C) H-AN6-101 to 8596 (C) G-AN1-101 to 4366	Not available; use 13H 412 (Disc wheels)
Valve—tyre	13H 412	2	5	(C) H-AN6-8597 to 24731 (C) H-AN7-24732 on (C) G-AN1-4367 to 16183 (C) G-AN2-16184 on	Disc wheels
Cap—wheel **Sprite H-AN5 and Sprite Mk. II**	2A 8055	3	5		Disc wheels
Cap—wheel **Midget**	AHA 5660	4	5		Disc wheels
Strap—spare wheel **Sprite H-AN5**	AHA 5217	5	1		Disc wheels
Strap—bracer—spare wheel **Sprite H-AN5**	AHA 5218	6	1		Disc wheels
Packing—spare wheel (felt) **Sprite H-AN5**	AHH 5459	7	3		Disc wheels
Clamp—spare wheel **Sprite Mk. II and Midget**	14A 6511	8	1		Not available; use 24A 1032 (Disc wheels)
Clamp—spare wheel **Sprite Mk. II and Midget**	24A 1032	8	1		Disc wheels
Disc—louvred—wheel					
Right-hand **Sprite Mk. II**	BHA 4163	9	2		Optional extra (Disc wheels)
Left-hand **Sprite Mk. II**	BHA 4164	9	2		Optional extra (Disc wheels)
With centre motif 'S'—RH **Sprite Mk. II**	BHA 4258	10	2		Optional extra (Disc wheels)
With centre motif 'S'—LH **Sprite Mk. II**	BHA 4259	10	2		Optional extra (Disc wheels)
Right-hand **Midget**	BHA 4253	11	2		Optional extra (Disc wheels)
Left-hand **Midget**	BHA 4254	11	2		Optional extra (Disc wheels)
Wheel assembly—wire	AHA 6377	12	5		Optional extra
Spoke—long	17H 3613	13	100		Optional extra
Spoke—short	17H 3984	14	200		Optional extra
Nipple—spoke	7H 1709	15	300		Optional extra
Cap—wheel					
Right-hand	†1B 8077	16	2		Not available; use AHH 7317
Right-hand	†AHH 7317	16	2		
Left-hand	†1B 8078	17	2	(B) H-AN7-20812 on (B) G-AN2-16780 on	Not available; use AHH 7318
Left-hand	†AHH 7318	17	2		
Right-hand **Not UK**	†AHH 8008	18	2		Not available; use AHH 7315
Right-hand **Not UK**	†AHH 7315	18	2		
Left-hand **Not UK**	†AHH 8009	19	2		Not available; use AHH 7316
Left-hand **Not UK**	†AHH 7316	19	2		
Clamp—spare wheel	AHA 6664	20	1		

† Revised Information.

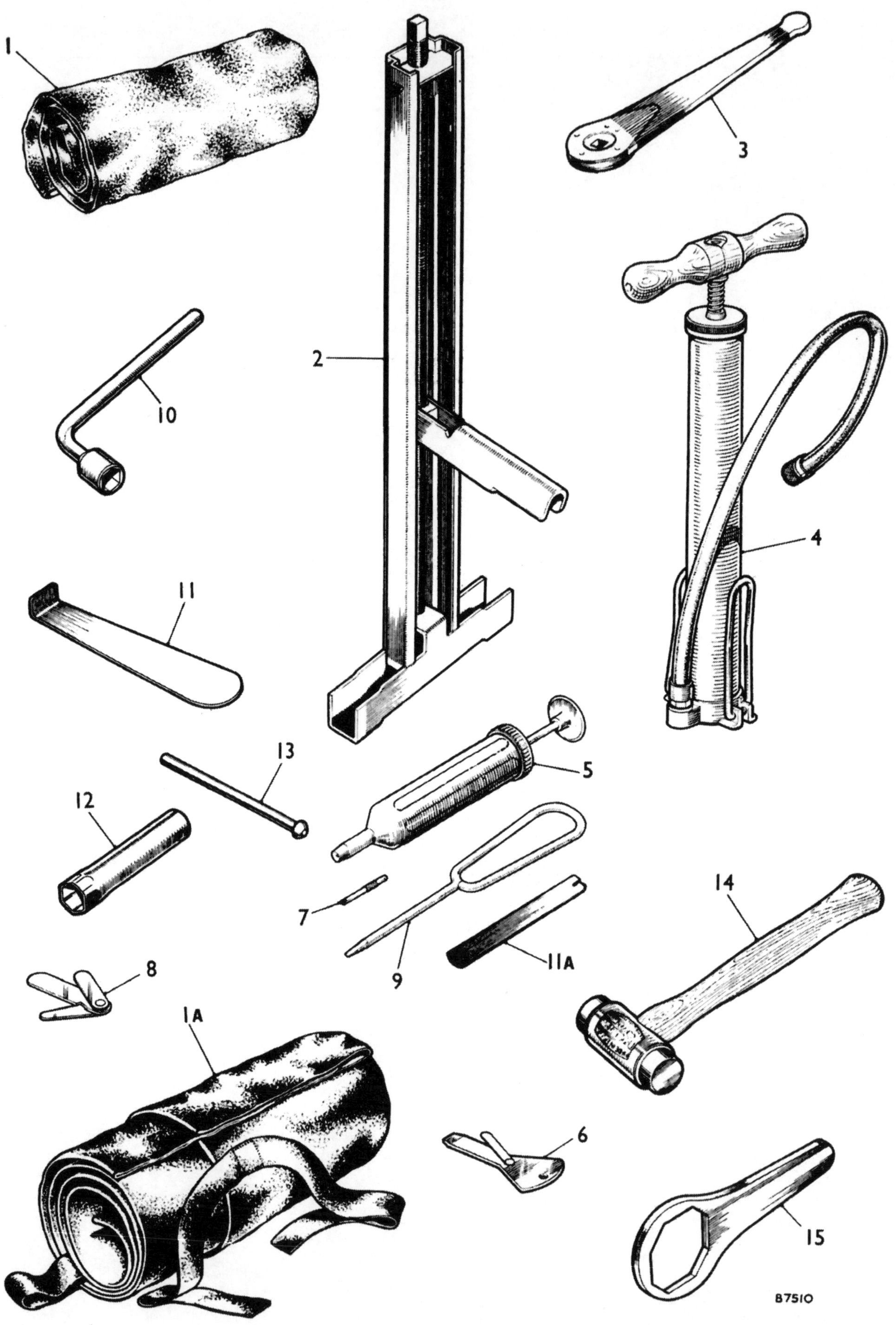
1
2
3
4
5
6
7
8
9
10
11
11A
12
13
14
15
1A
B7510

TOOLS

TOOLS

DESCRIPTION	Part No.	Illus. No.	Quantity	Change Point	REMARKS
Bag—tool	†2A 5412	1	1	(C) H-AN5-501 to 42199	W.S.E. use 11H 169
	11H 169	1	1		
	AHA 5506	1A	1	(C) H-AN5-42200 to 50116	
				(C) H-AN6-101 to 24731	
				(C) H-AN7-24732 on	
				(C) G-AN1-101 to 16183	
				(C) G-AN2-16184 on	
Jack—lifting	2A 5472	2	1	(C) H-AN5-501 to 50116	
Spanner—ratchet—jack	2A 5627	3	1	(C) H-AN6-101 to 24731	
				(C) H-AN7-24732 to 32387	
				(C) G-AN1-101 to 16183	
				(C) G-AN2-16184 to 20932	
Jack—lifting	BHA 4368	2	1	(C) H-AN7-32388 on	
Spanner—ratchet—jack	ACA 9932	3	1	(C) G-AN2-20933 on	Part No. change; was BHA 4367
Pump—tyre	†3H 2274	4	1		W.S.E. use 2H 2649
Pump—tyre	2H 2649				
Gun—grease	13H 50	5	1		
Screwdriver and gauge—ignition	†3H 2648	6	1		W.S.E. use 97H 2724
				(C) H-AN5-501 to 42199	
Screwdriver and gauge—ignition	97H 2724	6	1		
Spanner—tyre valve	2H 1683	7	1		
Gauge—feller—tappet and sparking plug	†2A 5419	8	1		W.S.E. use 97H 2724
Screwdriver	2H 4614	9	1		
Brace—wheel	2A 5626	10	1		
Lever—hub cap removal	†ACA 5432	11	1	(C) H-AN5-42200 to 50116	W.S.E. use 11H 1051
	†11H 1051	11A	1	(C) H-AN6-101 to 24731	
	†11H 1686	11A	1	(C) H-AN7-24732 on	
				(C) G-AN1-101 to 16183	
				(C) G-AN2-16184 on	
Spanner—box—sparking plug	2A 5379	12	1	(C) H-AN5-501 to 42199	
Spanner—box—sparking plug	1B 8995	12	1	(C) H-AN5-52200 to 50116	
Tommy-bar—box spanner	ACA 5216	13	1	(C) H-AN6-101 to 24731	
				(C) H-AN7-24732 on	
				(C) G-AN1-101 to 16183	
				(C) G-AN2-16184 on	
Hammer—hub cap **Not UK**	88G 329	14	1	(B) H-AN7-20812 on	Part No. change; was 11B 5166 — Wire wheels only
Spanner—hub cap	†AHH 5839	15	1	(B) G-AN2-16780 on	

† Revised Information.

BODY DETAILS

FOR BODY DETAILS APPLICABLE TO THESE MODELS REFERENCE SHOULD BE MADE TO THE FOLLOWING PUBLICATION: 'BODY SERVICE PARTS LIST', AKD 3567.

SPECIAL TUNING PARTS
SPRITE/MIDGET

	Page	Plate
BELT—FAN	MT 2	T 1
BODY	MT 12	T 8
BRAKES	MT 12	T 8
CAMSHAFT	MT 2	T 1
CARBURETTER	MT 6-MT 10	T 5, T 6, T 7
CLUTCH	MT 4	T 3
DIFFERENTIAL	MT 4	T 3
DISTRIBUTOR	MT 5	T 4
GASKETS	MT 3	T 2
GEAR—CAMSHAFT	MT 2	T 1
GEARBOX	MT 4	T 3
LITERATURE	MT 12	T 8
MANIFOLD	MT 3	T 2
PISTON	MT 2	T 1
PLUG—SPARKING	MT 2	T 1
PUMP—OIL	MT 3	T 2
ROAD WHEELS	MT 12	T 8
SHAFT—AXLE	MT 4	T 3
SUMP	MT 3	T 2
SUSPENSION	MT 11	T 8
VALVE GEAR	MT 2	T 1

ALL PARTS HAVING THE PREFIX LETTER 'C' IN FRONT OF THE PART No. (EXAMPLE: C-22G 210) MUST BE ORDERED DIRECT FROM BMC SPECIAL TUNING DEPT., ABINGDON-ON-THAMES, BERKSHIRE

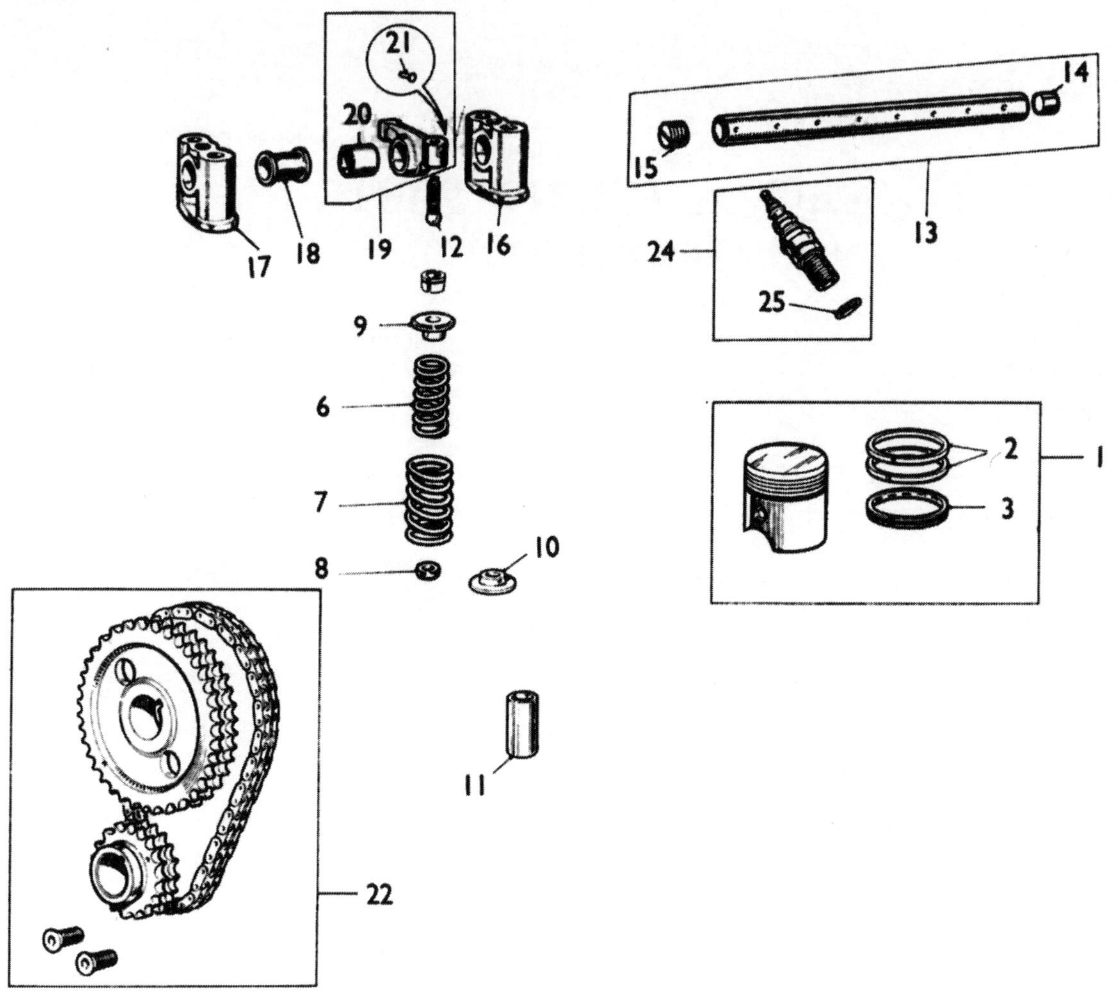
21
20
14
15
13
24
25
17
18
19
12
16
9
6
7
8
10
2
1
3
11
22

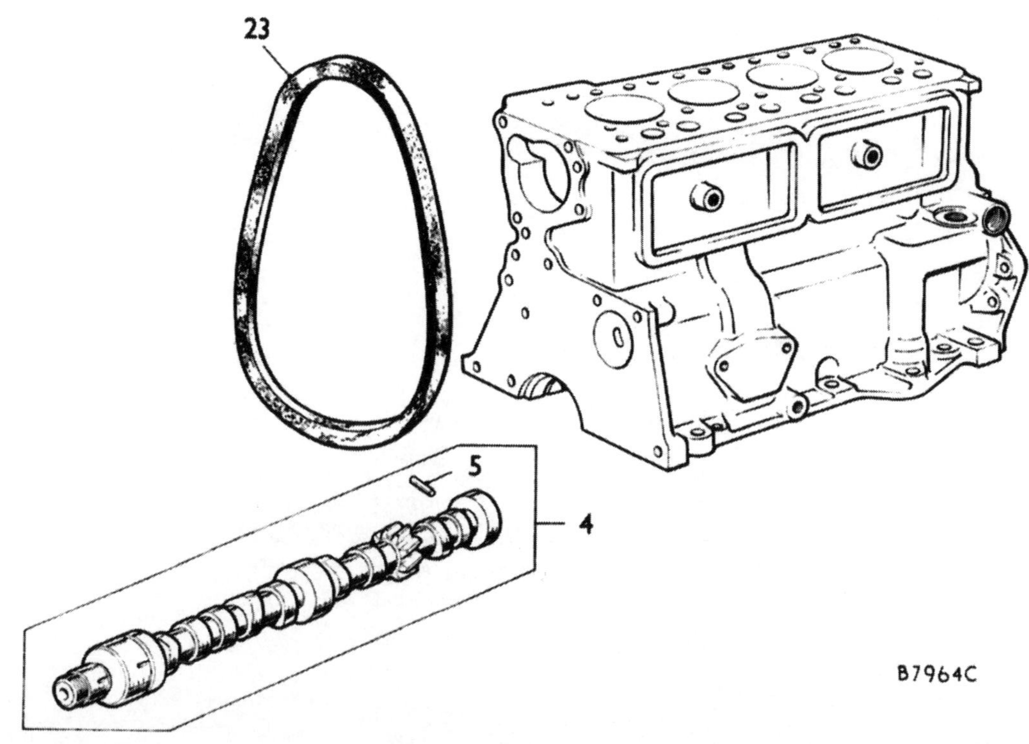
23
5
4
B7964C

DESCRIPTION		Part No.	Illus. No.	Quantity	Change Point	REMARKS
SPECIAL TUNING						
ENGINE						
Piston assembly—flat top						
Standard	948-cc	†C-2A 946	1	4		
·010″ (·254 mm) O/S	948-cc	†C-2A 0946 10	1	4		
·020″ (·508 mm) O/S	948-cc	†C-2A 0946 20	1	4		
·030″ (·762 mm) O/S	948-cc	†C-2A 0946 30	1	4		
·040″ (1·016 mm) O/S	948-cc	†C-2A 0946 40	1	4		
Ring—piston—compression						
Standard	948-cc	†C-2A 954	2	8		
·010″ (·254 mm) O/S	948-cc	†C-2A 0954 10	2	8		
·020″ (·508 mm) O/S	948-cc	†C-2A 0954 20	2	8		
·030″ (·762 mm) O/S	948-cc	†C-2A 0954 30	2	8		
·040″ (1·016 mm) O/S	948-cc	†C-2A 0954 40	2	8		
Ring—piston—scraper						
Standard	948-cc	†C-2A 955	3	4		
·010″ (·254 mm) O/S	948-cc	†C-2A 0955 10	3	4		
·020″ (·508 mm) O/S	948-cc	†C-2A 0954 20	3	4		
·030″ (·762 mm) O/S	948-cc	†C-2A 0955 30	3	4		
·040″ (1·016 mm) O/S	948-cc	†C-2A 0955 40	3	4		
CAMSHAFT						
Camshaft						
Tuning		†88G 229	4	1		
Competition		†C-AEA 731	4	1		
Racing		†C-AEA 648	4	1		
Pin—driving—oil pump		†2A 299	5	1		
VALVE AND VALVE GEAR						
Spring—valve—inner	9C	†AEA 401	6	8		
Spring—valve—outer	9C	†C-2A 950	7	8		
Collar—bottom	9C	†C-AEA 432	8	8		
Cup—top	9C	†AEA 402	9	8		
Spring—valve inner	9G	†C-AEA 494	6	8		
Collar—bottom	9G	†AEA 493	8	8		
Cup—top	9G	†AEA 653	9	8		
Spring—valve						
Inner 140 LB	1098-cc	†AEA 768	6	8		
Outer 140 LB	1098-cc	†AEA 767	7	8		
Inner 165 LB	1098-cc	†C-AEA 494	6	8		
Outer 165 LB	1098-cc	†C-AEA 524	7	8		
Cup—bottom		†AEA 653	10	8		
Tappet—lightened		†C-AEG 579	11	8		
Screw—tappet adjusting		†C-AEA 692	12	8		
Shaft—valve rocker (strengthened)		†AEG 399	13	1		
Plug—plain		†6K 878	14	1		
Plug—screwed		†2K 4608	15	1		
Bracket—rocker shaft						
Plain		†12G 1925	16	2		Use with Shaft AEG 399
With oil hole		†12G 1926	17	1		Use with Shaft AEG 399
Tapped		†12G 1927	17	1		Use with Shaft AEG 399
Spacer—valve rocker		†AEG 392	18	3		
Rocker—valve (forged)	1098-cc	†AEG 425	19	8		
Bush	1098-cc	†2A 21	20	8		
Rivet	1098-cc	†5C 2436	21	8		
Kit—chain timing (Duplex)		†C-AJJ 3325	22	1		
FAN BELT						
Belt—fan (short)		†C-AEA 539	23	1		Use with standard water pump pulley 2A 601 when running without dynamo.
SPARKING PLUG						
Plug—sparking						
N6Y (Rally and road use)		†C-37H 2147	24	4		Was N64Y
N57R		†C-27H 5982	24	4		
N62R		†C-37H 2149	24	4		
N60Y		†C-37H 2148	24	4		
Gasket—plug		†88G 219	25	4		

† Revised Information.

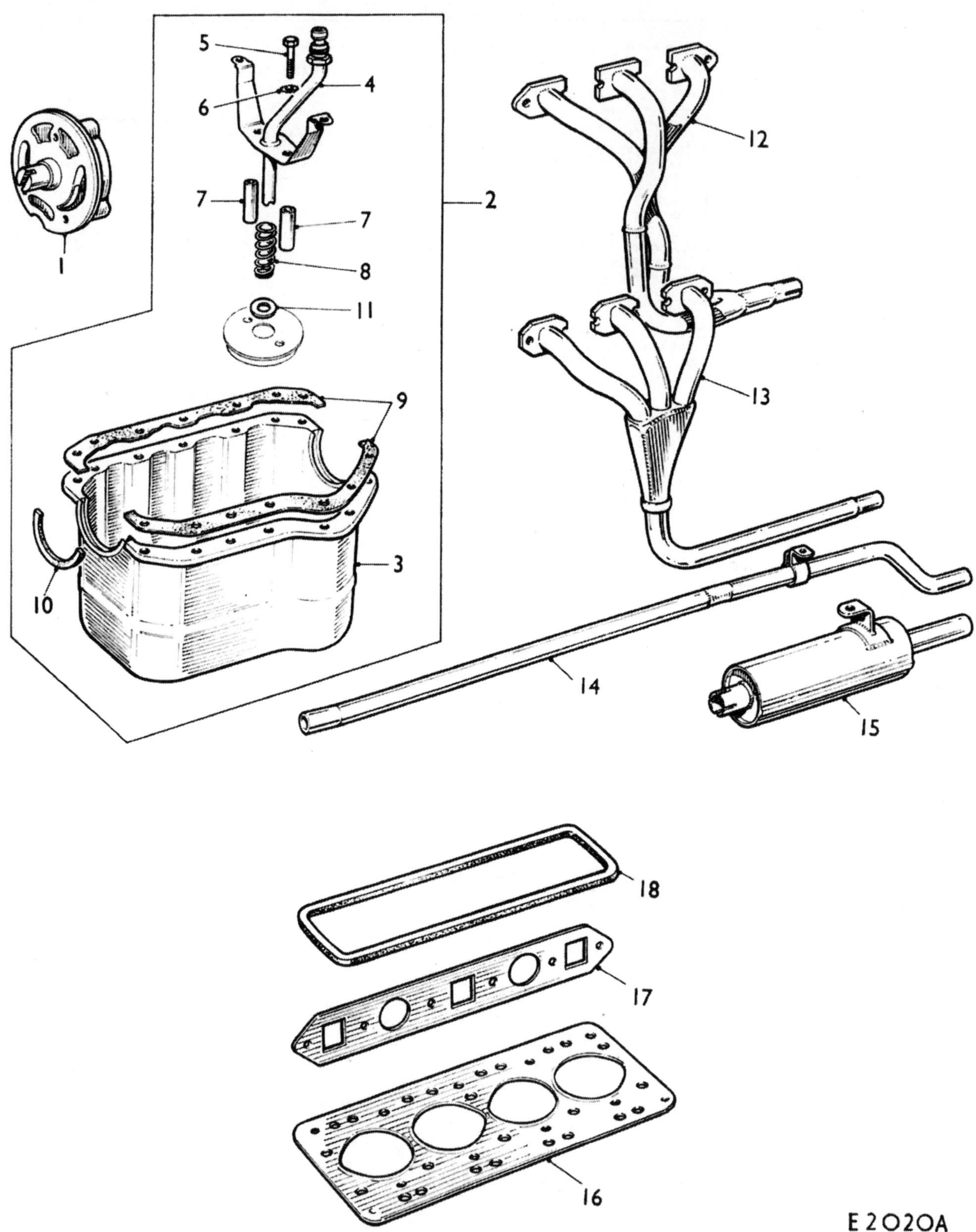
1
2
3
4
5
6
7
7
8
9
10
11
12
13
14
15
16
17
18
E2020A

DESCRIPTION	Part No.	Illus. No.	Quantity	Change Point	REMARKS
Special Tuning—*continued*					
OIL PUMP AND SUMP					
Pump—oil (large capacity) **9C, 9CG**	†12G 793	1	1		
Kit—sump (deep)	†C-AJJ 3324	2	1		
Sump	†C-AHT 12	3	1		
Pipe—oil suction	†C-AHT 14	4	1		
Bolt—bracket to strainer	†HBZ 0414	5	2		
Washer—block	†LWN 504	6	2		
Piece—distance	†AHH 6162	7	2		
Spring	†6K 871	8	1		
Gasket	†8G 781	9	1		
Seal—oil	†2A 280	10	2		
Washer—plain	†2K 6804	11	1		
MANIFOLD					
Manifold—exhaust (large bore)	†C-AHT 11	12	1		
Manifold	†C-AHA 5448	13	1		
Pipe	†C-AHA 5449	14	1		Required only when exhaust manifold C-AHA 5448 is fitted to engines with prefix letter 9C.
Silencer	†C-ARA 135	15	1		
GASKETS					
Gasket					
Cylinder head	†C-AEA 647	16	1		
Manifold	†C-AEA 411	17	1		
Rocker cover	†C-AEA 511	18	1		

† Revised Information.

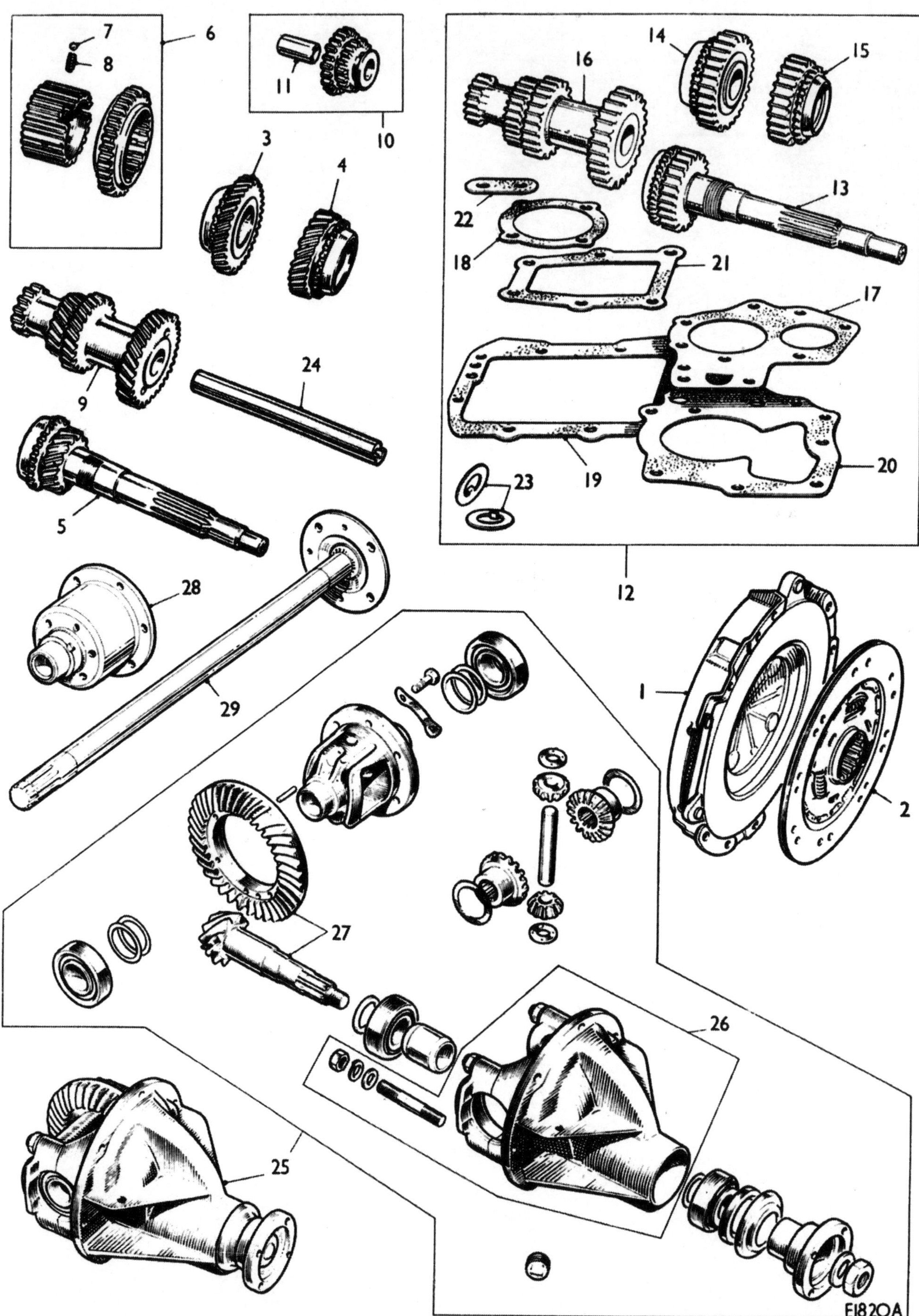
1
2
3
4
5
6
7
8
9
10
11
12
13
14
15
16
17
18
19
20
21
22
23
24
25
26
27
28
29
E1820A

DESCRIPTION	Part No.	Illus. No.	Quantity	Change Point	REMARKS
Special Tuning—*continued*					
CLUTCH					
Cover assembly **10CC**	†C–BHA 4448	1	1		
Plate—driven **10CC**	†C–BHA 4449	2	1		
GEARBOX					
Gear—2nd speed (28 teeth)	†C–22A 226	3	1		Close-ratio for AN5 only; use with 22A 426, 22A 207, and 22A 204
Gear—3rd speed (24 teeth)	†C–22A 227	4	1		
Shaft—1st motion (20 teeth)	†C–22A 228	5	1		
1st speed wheel—2nd speed synchronizer assembly	†22A 426	6	1		
Wheel—1st speed	†NSP		1		
Synchronizer—2nd speed	†NSP		3		
Ball	†BLS 107	7	3		
Spring	†22A 332	8	1		
Laygear (26, 23, 19, 13 teeth)	†22A 207	9	1		
Wheel—reverse	†22A 204	10	1		
Bush	†2A 3282	11	1		
Gears—close ratio—helical cut					
Shaft—1st motion (21 teeth)	†C–22G 304	5	1		Used with gearboxes having 'A' series teeth
Laygear (25, 23, 19, 13 teeth)	†C–22G 305	9	1		
Gear set—close ratio—straight-cut	†C–AJJ 3319	12	1		**Not available; for reference purposes only** Gear set C–AJJ 3319 can also be used on gearboxes fitted to 1098-cc engines prior to change point (i.e. 10CG or 10CC prefix) provided 1st speed wheel and synchronizer 22G 326 and reverse wheel 22G 240 are fitted
Shaft—1st motion	†C–AEG 3138	13	1		
Gear—2nd speed	†C–AEG 3139	14	1		
Gear—3rd speed	†C–AEG 3140	15	1		
Laygear	†C–22G 306	16	1	(E) 10CC/Da/H4643	
Gasket				(E) 10CC/Da/L2857	
Front cover	†22G 165	17	1		
Cover—change speed tower	†2A 3341	18	1		
Side cover	†2A 3286	19	1		
Extension to gearbox	†22A 481	20	1		
Casing to extension—front	†2A 3344	21	1		
Casing to extension—rear	†2A 3345	22	1		
Washer—lock—shaft	†2A 3035	23	2		
1st speed wheel—2nd speed synchronizer assembly	†22G 326	6	1		
Wheel—1st speed	†NSP		1		
Synchronizer—2nd speed	†NSP		1		
Ball	†BLS 107	7	3		
Spring	†22G 317	8	3		
Wheel—reverse	†22G 240	10	1		
Bush	†2A 3282	11	1		
Layshaft	†22G 673	24	1		Use with close-ratio gear set C–AJJ 3319
FINAL DRIVE AND AXLE SHAFT					
Differential assembly **3·727 : 1 ratio**	†ATA 7239	25	1		**Not available; for reference purposes only** — Alternatives for use up to (C) H–AN7–24781 and G–AN2–16183 only
Carrier	†ATA 7167	26	1		
Crown wheel and pinion	†ATA 7240	27	1		
Differential assembly **3·9 : 1 ratio**	†ATA 7353	25	1		
Carrier	†ATA 7167	26	1		
Crown wheel and pinion	†C–ATA 7354	27	1		
Differential assembly **4·222 : 1 ratio**	†ATA 7326	25	1		
Carrier	†ATA 7082	26	1		
Crown wheel and pinion	†ATA 7266	27	1		
Differential assembly **4·555 : 1 ratio**	†ATA 7093	25	1		
Carrier	†ATA 7082	26	1		
Crown wheel and pinion	†8G 7129	27	1		
Differential assembly **4·875 : 1 ratio**	†2A 7230	25	1		
Carrier	†ATA 7082	26	1		
Crown wheel and pinion	†C4 110	27	1		
Differential assembly **5·375 : 1 ratio**	†ATA 7073	25	1		
Carrier	†ATA 7082	26	1		
Crown wheel and pinion	†ATA 7040	27	1		
Crown wheel and pinion **3·727 : 1 ratio**	†BTA 535	27	1	(C) H–AN7–24781 on	Alternatives
Crown wheel and pinion **4·555 : 1 ratio**	†C–BTA 816	27	1	(C) G–AN2–16183 on	
Differential—limited slip	†BTA 881	28	1		Alternatives
Differential—limited slip	†C–BTA 696	28	1		
Shaft—axle—heavy-duty (disc wheels)	†C–BTA 940	29	2		

† Revised Information.

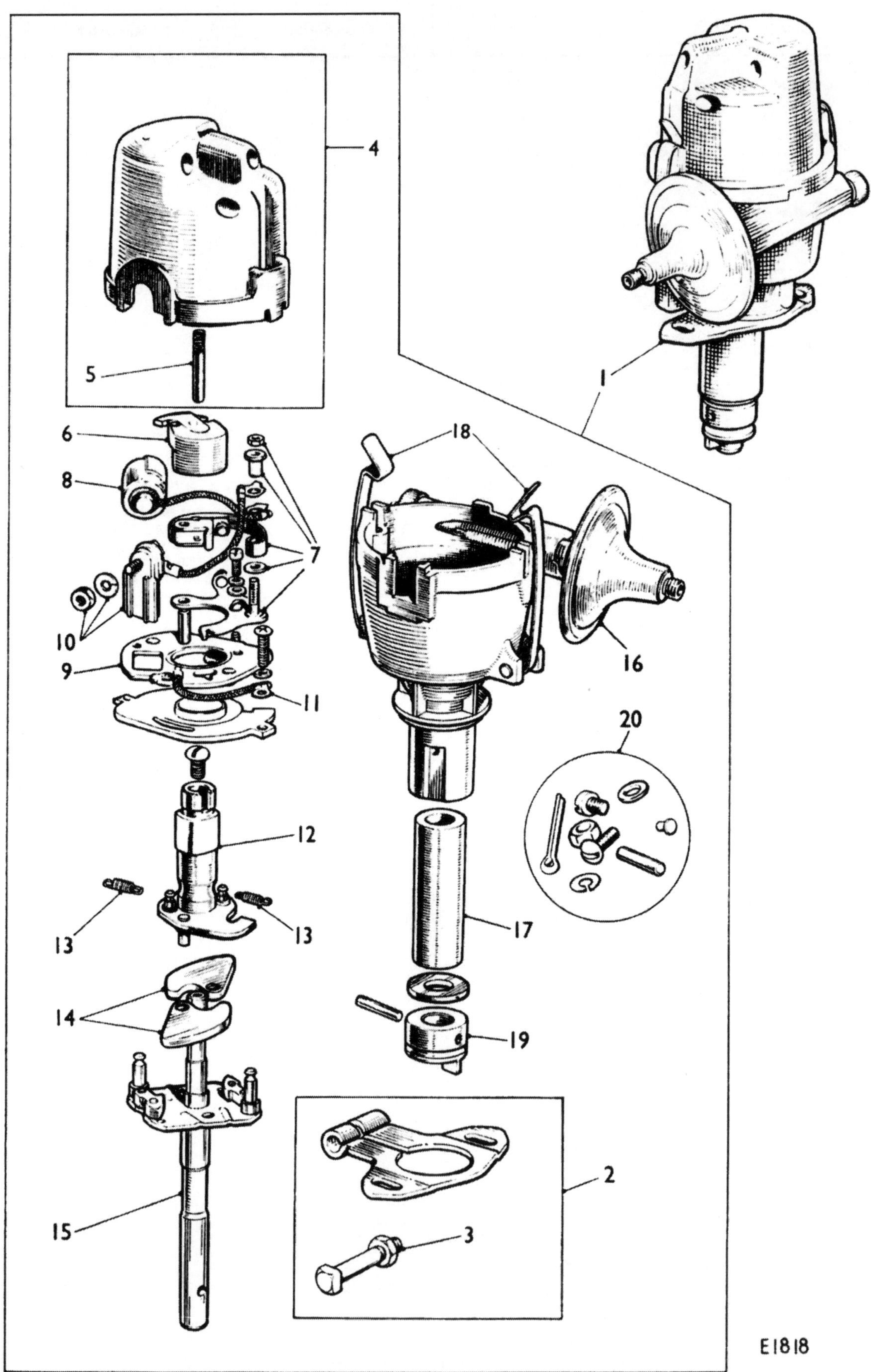
1
2
3
4
5
6
7
8
9
10
11
12
13
13
14
15
16
17
18
19
20
E1818

	DESCRIPTION	Part No.	Illus. No.	Quantity	Change Point	REMARKS
	Special Tuning—*continued*					
	DISTRIBUTOR					
	Distributor	†C-27H 7766	1	1		For use with competition camshafts
	Plate—clamping	†3H 2188	2	1		
	Screw (with nut)	†NSP	3	1		
	Cover	†57H 5477	4	1		
	Brush and spring	†17H 5065	5	1 set		
	Arm—rotor	†7H 5086	6	1		
	Contacts	†17H 5423	7	1 set		
	Condenser	†47H 5250	8	1		
	Plate—contact breaker base	†17H 5469	9	1		
	Terminal—bush and lead	†57H 5478	10	1		
	Lead—earth	†17H 5581	11	1		
	Cam	†57H 5183	12	1		
	Spring—automatic advance	†C-27H 8022	13	1 set		
	Weight	†57H 5420	14	2		
	Shaft and action plate	†57H 5050	15	1		
	Vacuum unit	†47H 5555	16	1		
	Bushing—body bearing	†47H 5164	17	1		
	Clip—cover retaining	†37H 5445	18	2		
	Dog—driving	†47H 5249	19	1		
	Sundry parts	†17H 5106	20	1 set		

† Revised Information.

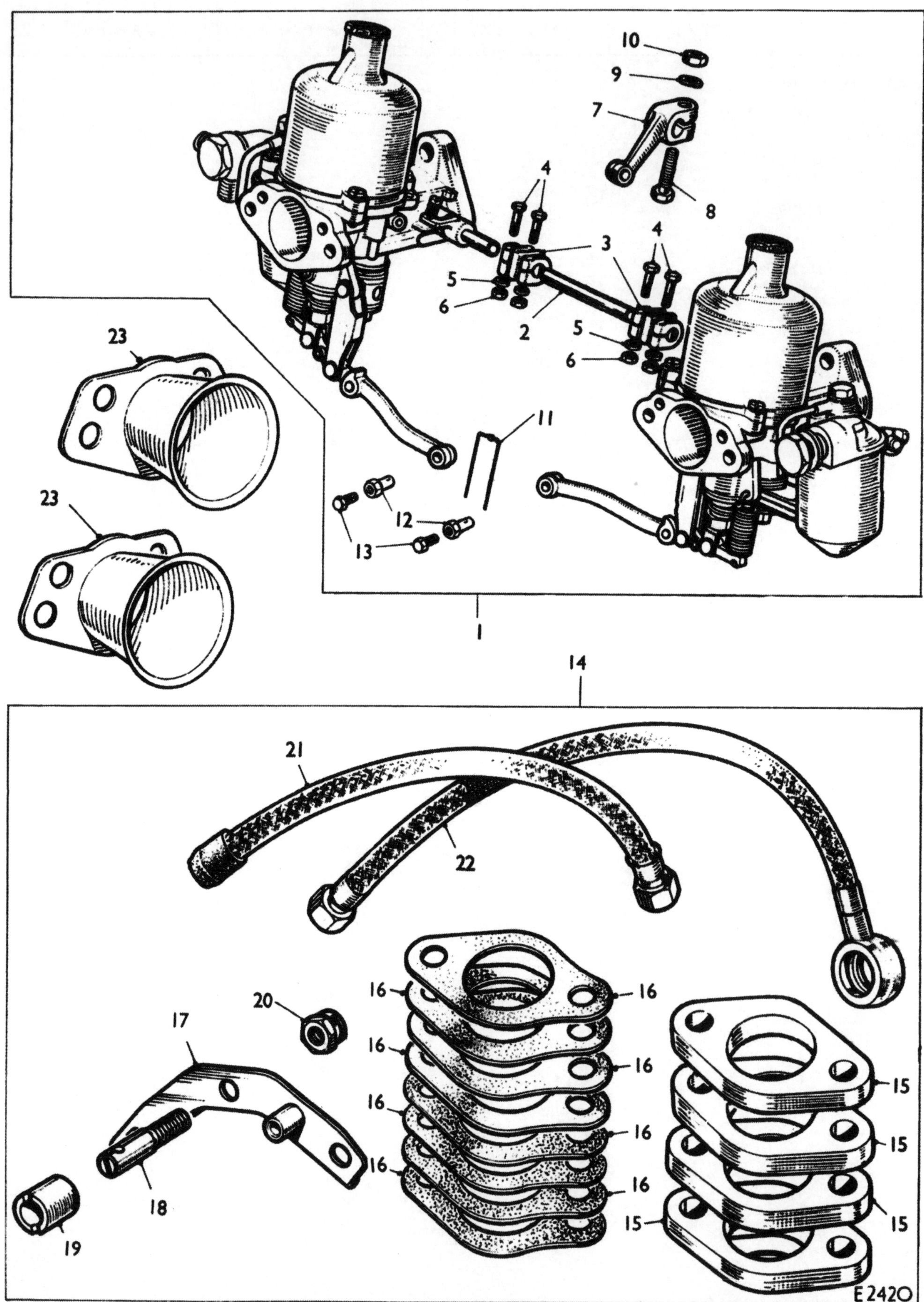
10
9
7
4
8
4
3
5
6
2
5
6
23
11
23
12
13
1
14
21
22
16
16
20
17
16
16
16
15
16
16
15
16
16
15
18
15
15
19
E2420

DESCRIPTION	Part No.	Illus. No.	Quantity	Change Point	REMARKS
Special Tuning—*continued*					
CARBURETTER					
Carburetter installation	†C-AUD 194	1	1 pr		(1½″ twin)
Rod—throttle connecting	†AUC 2402	2	1		
Coupling—rod	†AUC 4334	3	2		
Bolt—coupling	†AUC 2669	4	4		
Washer—plain	†AUC 4612	5	4		
Nut—bolt	†AJD 8014 Z	6	4		
Lever—throttle	†AUC 4454	7	1		
Bolt—lever	†AJD 1042	8	1		
Washer—spring	†LWZ 303	9	1		
Nut—bolt	†AJD 8012 Z	10	1		
Stirrup—jet levers	†AUC 1025	11	1		
Pin—stirrup	†AUC 5058	12	2		
Screw—pin	†AUC 5047	13	2		
Kit installation—carburetter 948-cc, 1098-cc	†C-AJJ 3304	14	1		
Insulator—carburetter flange	†AHH 5713	15	4		
Gasket	†AEH 551	16	8		
Bracket—abutment	†C-AHT 1	17	1		
Pin—cable to bracket	†11B 542	18	1		
Piece—distance—pin	†11B 543	19	1		
Nut—lock	†53K 1392	20	1		
Pipe—petrol—connecting	†ACH 8977	21	1		
Pipe—petrol—feed	†AHB 9059	22	1		
Trumpet—flared (glass fibre)	†C-AHT 10	23	1		Alternatives
Trumpet—flared (steel)	†C-AEA 485	23	1		Alternatives

† Revised Information.

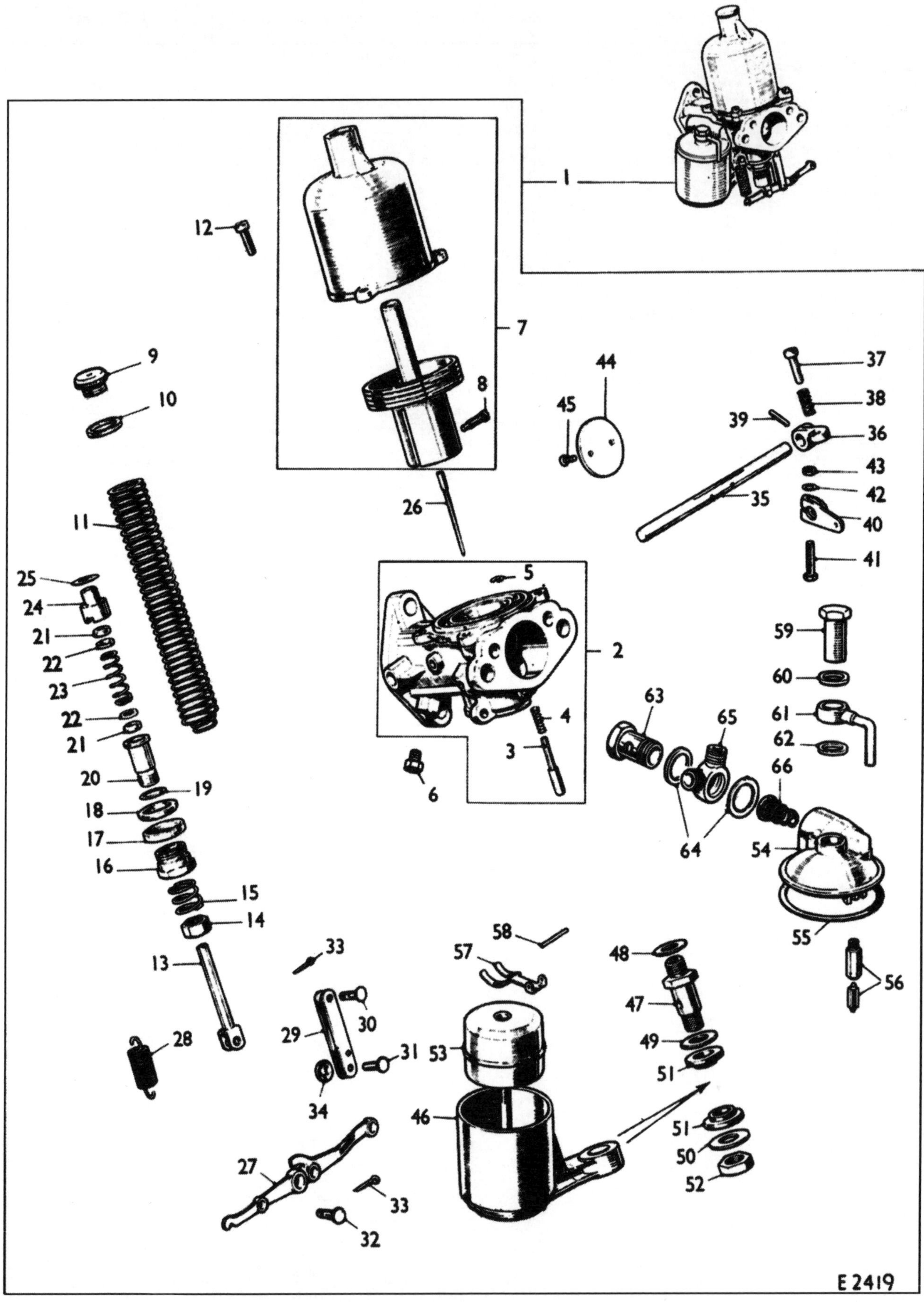
1
2
3
4
5
6
7
8
9
10
11
12
13
14
15
16
17
18
19
20
21
22
23
24
25
26
27
28
29
30
31
32
33
34
35
36
37
38
39
40
41
42
43
44
45
46
47
48
49
50
51
52
53
54
55
56
57
58
59
60
61
62
63
64
65
66
E 2419

DESCRIPTION	Part No.	Illus. No.	Quantity	Change Point	REMARKS
Special Tuning—*continued*					
Carburetter—assembly—front	†C–AUC 9358	1	1		
Body assembly	†AUD 9047	2	1		
Pin—piston lifting	†AUC 1249	3	1		
Spring—pin	†AUC 1151	4	1		
Circlip—pin	†AUC 1250	5	1		
Plug—auto ignition	†AUC 1289	6	1		
Chamber and piston assembly	†AUD 9500	7	1		
Screw—needle locking	†AUC 2057	8	1		
Cap—oil	†AUC 2144	9	1		
Washer (fibre)	†AUC 4900	10	1		
Spring—piston—blue	†AUC 4587	11	1		
Screw—chamber to body	†AUC 2175	12	3		
Jet	†AUC 8182	13	1		
Nut—adjusting	†AUC 2121	14	1		
Spring—adjusting nut	†AUC 2114	15	1		
Nut—gland sealing	†AUC 3232	16	1		
Ring—sealing (aluminium)	†AUC 2117	17	1		
Ring—sealing (cork)	†AUC 2118	18	1		
Washer—bottom bearing (copper)	†AUC 3233	19	1		
Bearing—bottom	†AUC 3231	20	1		
Washer—gland (cork)	†AUC 2120	21	2		
Washer—gland (brass)	†AUC 2119	22	2		
Spring—gland	†AUC 1158	23			
Bearing—top	†AUC 3230	24	1		
Washer—top bearing (copper)	†AUC 2122	25	1		
Needle—jet					
Rich					
Standard (No. 6)	†AUD 1005	26	1		
Weak					
Lever—jet	†AUC 4045	27	1		
Spring—jet lever return	†AUC 4667	28	1		
Link—jet lever	†AUC 4719	29	1		
Pin					
Link to body	†AUC 2381	30	1		
Link to lever	†AUC 5009	31	1		
Lever to jet	†AUC 2381	32	1		
Split	†CPS 0204	33	2		
Washer—Starlock	†AUC 5004	34	1		
Spindle—throttle	†AUC 3212	35	1		
Lever—throttle stop	†AUC 2199	36	1		
Screw—adjusting	†AUC 2521	37	1		
Spring—screw	†AUC 2451	38	1		
Pin—taper	†AUC 2106	39	1		
Lever—return spring	†AUC 8209	40	1		
Bolt—lever	†AJD 1042	41	1		
Washer—plain	†AUC 8396	42	1		
Nut—bolt	†AJD 8012 Z	43	1		
Disc—throttle	†AUC 3116	44	1		
Screw—disc	†AUC 1358	45	2		
Chamber—float	†AUC 3496	46	1		
Pillar—banjo	†AUC 1387	47			
Washer					
Plain—pillar	†AUC 1384	48	1		
Inner—(steel)	†AUC 1389	49	1		
Outer—(steel)	†AUC 1388	50	1		
Grommet (rubber)	†AUC 1534	51	2		
Locknut—pillar	†AJD 8206 Z	52	1		
Float	†AUC 1123	53	1		
Lid—float-chamber	†AUD 2283	54	1		
Gasket—lid	†AUC 1147	55	1		
Needle and seat	†AUD 9096	56	1		
Lever—hinged	†AUD 2285	57	1		
Pin—hinge	†AUC 1152	58	1		
Nut—cap	†AUC 1867	59	1		
Washer (aluminium)	†AUC 1557	60	1		
Pipe—air vent and overflow	†AUC 8200	61	1		
Washer (fibre)	†AUC 1928	62	1		
Bolt—banjo	†AUC 2698	63	1		
Washer (fibre)	†AUC 2141	64	2		
Banjo—double	†AUC 1882	65	1		
Filter	†AUC 2139	66	1		

† Revised Information.

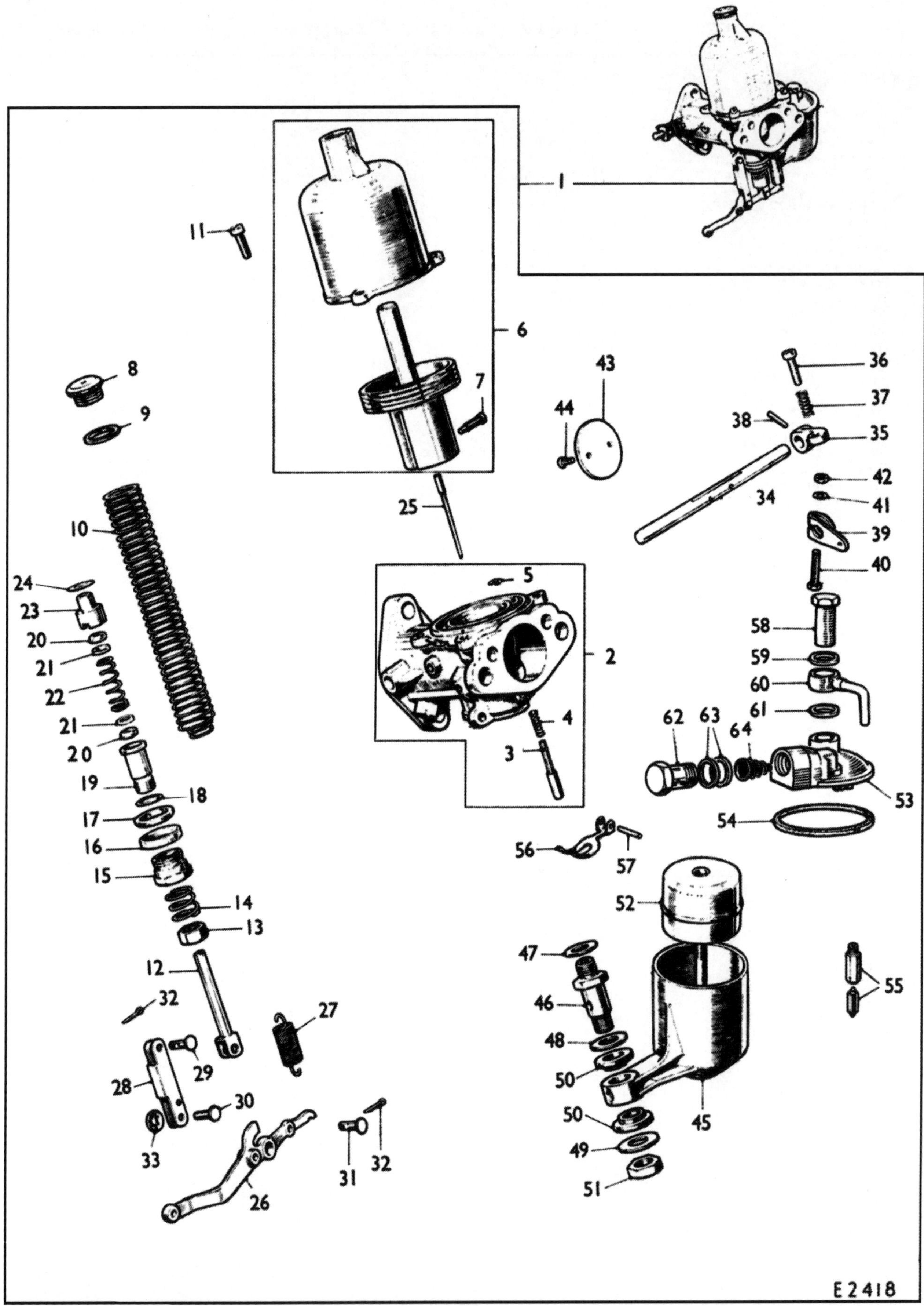
1
2
3
4
5
6
7
8
9
10
11
12
13
14
15
16
17
18
19
20
21
22
23
24
25
26
27
28
29
30
31
32
33
34
35
36
37
38
39
40
41
42
43
44
45
46
47
48
49
50
51
52
53
54
55
56
57
58
59
60
61
62
63
64
E 2418

DESCRIPTION	Part No.	Illus. No.	Quantity	Change Point	REMARKS
Special Tuning—*continued*					
Carburetter assembly—rear	†C-AUC 9854	1	1		
Body assembly	†AUD 9024	2	1		
Pin—piston lifting	†AUC 1249	3	1		
Spring—pin	†AUC 1151	4	1		
Circlip—pin	†AUC 1250	5	1		
Chamber and piston assembly	†AUD 9500	6	1		
Screw—needle locking	†AUC 2057	7	1		
Cap—oil	†AUC 2144	8	1		
Washer (fibre)	†AUC 4900	9	1		
Spring—piston—Blue	†AUC 4587	10	1		
Screw—chamber to body	†AUC 2175	11	3		
Jet	†AUC 8182	12	1		
Nut—adjusting	†AUC 2121	13	1		
Spring—adjusting nut	†AUC 2114	14	1		
Nut—gland sealing	†AUC 3232	15	1		
Ring—sealing (aluminium)	†AUC 2117	16	1		
Ring—sealing (cork)	†AUC 2118	17	1		
Washer—bottom bearing (copper)	†AUC 3233	18	1		
Bearing—bottom	†AUC 3231	19	1		
Washer—gland (cork)	†AUC 2120	20	2		
Washer—gland (brass)	†AUC 2119	21	2		
Spring—gland	†AUC 1158	22	1		
Bearing—top	†AUC 3230	23	1		
Washer—top bearing (copper)	†AUC 2122	24	1		
Needle—jet					
Rich					
Standard (No. 6)	†AUD 1005	25	1		
Weak					
Lever—jet	†AUC 4045	26	1		
Spring—jet lever return	†AUC 4667	27	1		
Link—jet lever	†AUC 4719	28	1		
Pin					
Link to body	†AUC 2381	29	1		
Link to lever	†AUC 5009	30	1		
Lever to jet	†AUC 2381	31	1		
Split	†CPS 0204	32	2		
Washer—Starlock	†AUC 5004	33	1		
Spindle—throttle	†AUC 3513	34	1		
Lever—throttle stop	†AUC 2199	35	1		
Screw—adjusting	†AUC 2521	36	1		
Spring—screw	†AUC 2451	37	1		
Pin—taper	†AUC 2106	38	1		
Lever—return spring	†AUC 8209	39	1		
Bolt—lever	†AJD 1042	40	1		
Washer—plain	†AUC 8396	41	1		
Nut—bolt	†AJD 8012 Z	42	1		
Disc—throttle	†AUC 3116	43	1		
Screw—disc	†AUC 1358	44	2		
Chamber—float	†AUC 3495	45	1		
Pillar—banjo	†AUC 1387	46	1		
Washer					
Plain—pillar	†AUC 1384	47	1		
Inner (steel)	†AUC 1389	48	1		
Outer (steel)	†AUC 1388	49	1		
Grommet (rubber)	†AUC 1534	50	2		
Locknut—pillar	†AJD 8206 Z	51	1		
Float	†AUC 1123	52	1		
Lid—float-chamber	†AUD 2284	53	1		
Gasket—lid	†AUC 1147	54	1		
Needle and seat	†AUD 9096	55	1		
Lever—hinged	†AUD 2285	56	1		
Pin—hinge	†AUC 1152	57	1		
Nut—cap	†AUC 1867	58	1		
Washer (aluminium)	†AUC 1557	59	1		
Pipe—air vent and overflow	†AUC 3200	60	1		
Washer (fibre)	†AUC 1928	61	1		
Bolt—banjo	†AUC 2698	62	1		
Washer (fibre)	†AUC 2141	63	2		
Filter	†AUC 2139	64	1		

† Revised Information.

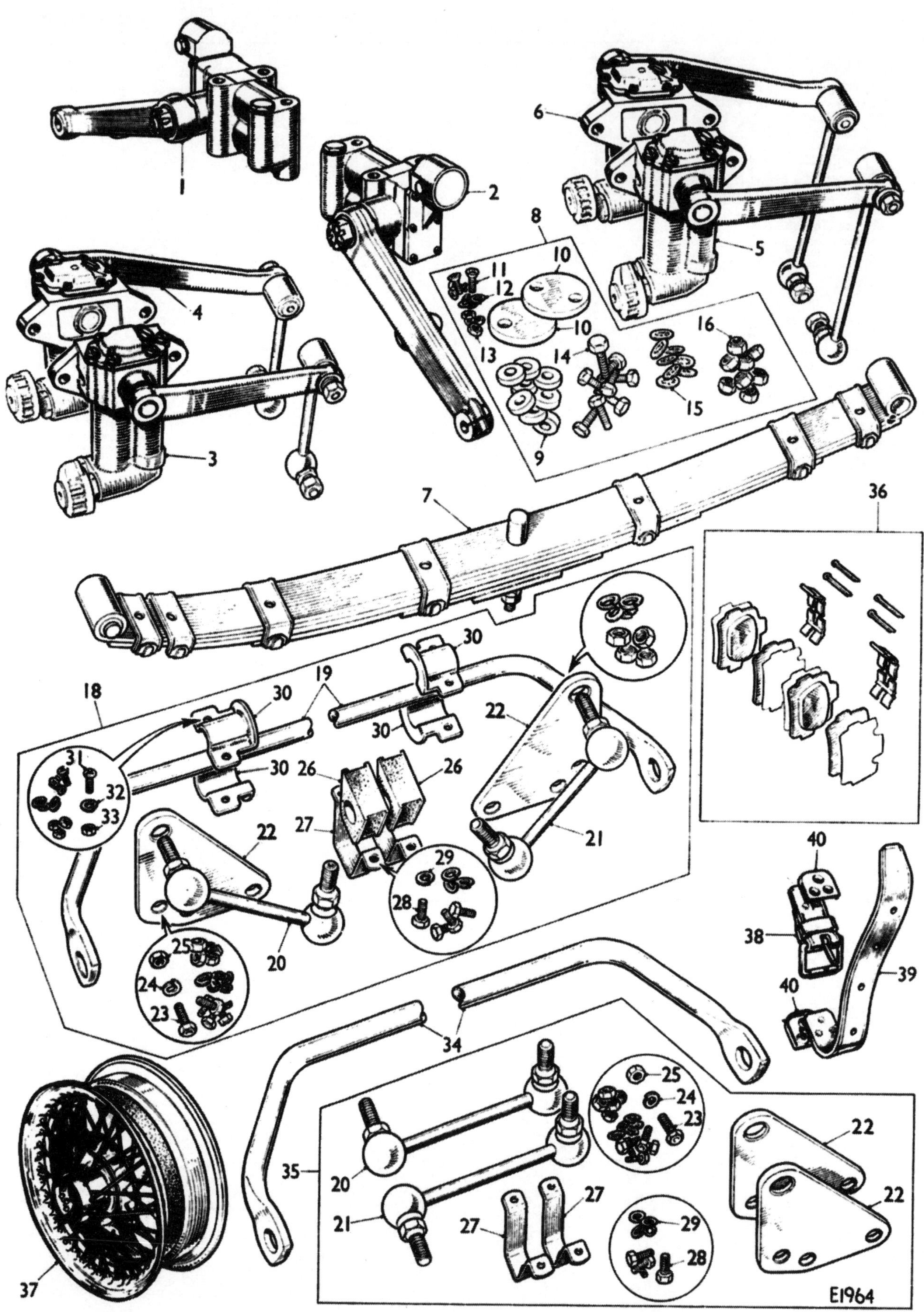
1
2
3
4
5
6
7
8
9
10
11
12
13
14
15
16
18
19
20
21
22
23
24
25
26
27
28
29
30
31
32
33
34
35
36
37
38
39
40
E1964

DESCRIPTION	Part No.	Illus. No.	Quantity	Change Point	REMARKS
Special Tuning—*continued*					
SUSPENSION					
Absorber—shock—competition					
Front—RH	†C-AHA 6451	1	1		
Front—LH	†C-AHA 6452	2	1		
Rear—RH	†C-AHA 6453	3	1		For quarter-elliptic springs only
Rear—LH	†C-AHA 6454	4	1		For quarter-elliptic springs only
Rear—RH (adjustable)	†C-AHA 7906	5	1		For semi-elliptic springs only
Rear—LH (adjustable)	†C-AHA 7907	6	1		For semi-elliptic springs only
Spring—rear road—lowered semi-elliptic	†C-AHA 8272	7	2		
Kit—front suspension—lowering	†C-AJJ 3322	8	1		
Piece—distance	†C-AHA 8277	9	8		
Plate—bump stop	†C-AHA 8278	10	2		
Screw	†CMZ 0210	11	4		
Washer—spring	†LWZ 203	12	4		
Nut	†ANZ 103	13	4		
Bolt	†53K 1369	14	8		
Washer	†LWZ 405	15	8		
Nut	†LNZ 205	16	8		
Kit—anti-roll bar (with $\frac{9}{16}$" [14·3 mm] dia bar)	†C-AJJ 3314	18	1		
Bar—anti-roll	†AHA 7018	19	1		
Link—anti-roll bar—RH	†AHA 7011	20	1		
Link—anti-roll bar—LH	†AHA 7012	21	1		
Bracket—link	†AHA 7028	22	2		
Screw—bracket to lower link	†HZS 0506	23	6		
Washer—spring	†LWZ 205	24	6		
Nut	†FNZ 105	25	6		
Bearing—anti-roll bar	†AHH 6541	26	2		
Strap—bearing	†1B 7356	27	2		
Screw—strap to frame	†HZS 0505	28	4		
Washer—spring	†LWZ 205	29	4		
Stop—end	†AHH 6546	30	4		
Screw—clamping—end top	†PMZ 0307	31	4		
Washer—spring	†LWZ 203	32	4		
Nut	†FNZ 103	33	4		
Bar—anti-roll—$\frac{5}{8}$" (15·9 mm) dia	†C-AHT 57	34	1		
Bar—anti-roll—$\frac{11}{16}$" (17·5 mm) dia	†C-AHT 56	34	1		
Kit—installation—anti-roll bar	†C-AJJ 3356	35	1		For use with C-AHT 56 or C-AHT 57 when no roll bar previously fitted
Link—anti-roll bar—RH	†AHA 7011	20	1		
Link—anti-roll bar—LH	†AHA 7012	21	1		
Bracket—link	†AHA 7028	22	2		
Screw—bracket to lower link	†HZS 0506	23	6		
Washer—spring	†LWZ 205	24	6		
Nut—screw	†FNZ 105	25	6		
Strap—bearing	†1B 7356	27	2		
Screw—strap to frame	†HZS 0506	28	4		
Washer—spring	†LWZ 205	29	4		
BRAKES					
Set—brake—pad (disc brakes only)	†C-AHT 16	36	1		
ROAD WHEELS					
Wheel—wire (60-spoke)	†C-AHA 7573	37	5		
BODY					
Strap—buckle securing	†NSP		A/R		
Buckle—half	†C-AHH 5518	38	1		
Tongue—half	†C-AHH 5519	39	1		
Retainer	†C-AHH 5517	40	2		
LITERATURE					
Special Tuning Booklet					
Sprite Mk. I	†C-AKD 1021 A		1		
948-cc / 1098-cc	†C-AKD 5097		1		
Special Tuning Data Sheet set	†C-AJJ 3333		1		
Binder for Special Tuning Sheets	†C-AKD 5061		1		
Divider set for binder	†C-AKD 5093		1		
Special tuning rosettes	†C-AKD 5100		1 pr.		
Workshop Manual (Sprite Mk. I)	†97H 1585		1		
Workshop Manual (all other models)	†AKD 4021 A		1		

† Revised Information.

Distributed by Brooklands Books Ltd., PO Box 146, Cobham, Surrey KT11 1LG, England Phone: 01932 865051
E-mail: sales@brooklands-books.com www.brooklandsbooks.com

Part No. AKD 3566

S.U. CARBURETTER SERVICE PARTS LIST

	Model Application	Specification No.	Type	Section
AUSTIN-HEALEY	Sprite Mark I (Series AN5) ...	AUC 863	H1	SA
	Sprite Mark II (948 cc)	AUC 990	HS2	SH
	Sprite Mark II (1098 cc)	AUD 73	HS2	SH
M.G.	Midget Mark I (948 cc)	AUC 990	HS2	SH
	Midget Mark I (1098 cc)... ...	AUD 73	HS2	SH

CARBURETTER THROTTLE SIZES

Type	Throttle Diameter
H1	$1\frac{1}{8}$" (2·86 cm)
HS2	$1\frac{1}{4}$" (3·17 cm)

CARBURETTER PISTON SPRING IDENTIFICATION

Paint Colour on End Coil	Load at Length		Part No.
Blue	$2\frac{1}{2}$ oz (70·9 gm)	$2\frac{5}{8}$" (6·67 cm)	AUC 4587
Red	$4\frac{1}{2}$ oz (127·6 gm)	$2\frac{5}{8}$" (6·67 cm)	AUC 4387
Yellow	8 oz (226·8 gm)	$2\frac{3}{4}$" (6·98 cm)	AUC 1167
Green	12 oz (340·2 gm)	3" (7·62 cm)	AUC 1170
Red and Green	$11\frac{1}{4}$ oz (318·9 gm)	$3\frac{7}{8}$" (9·84 cm)	AUC 4826
Red and Light Blue	18 oz (510·3 gm)	$3\frac{7}{8}$" (9·84 cm)	AUC 4818

CARBURETTER JET NEEDLES

On most carburetter specifications that appear in this Service Parts List the rich, standard, and weak jet needles have been listed. In some cases only the rich or weak needles have been listed together with the standard jet needle. The standard jet needle is fitted to all new S.U. carburetter assemblies and installations.

When ordering it is essential to quote the needle code letters and/or numbers together with the appropriate part number.

Example: **Needle—jet**
Rich (RH)....................AUD 1291
Standard (OA6)....................AUD 1276
Weak (OA7)....................AUD 1277

Extract from Part No. AKD 5036

B.M.C. SERVICE LIMITED
COWLEY · OXFORD · ENGLAND

Telephone – – – – – – – – Oxford 77777
Telex – – – – BMC Serv Oxford 83145 and 83146
Telegrams – – – – BMC Serv Telex, Oxford
Cables – – – – BMC Serv Telex Oxford, England
Codes – – Bentley's, Bentley's Second Phrase, A.B.C. (5th and 6th Editions), Western Union and Private

S.U. CARBURETTER SERVICE PARTS LIST

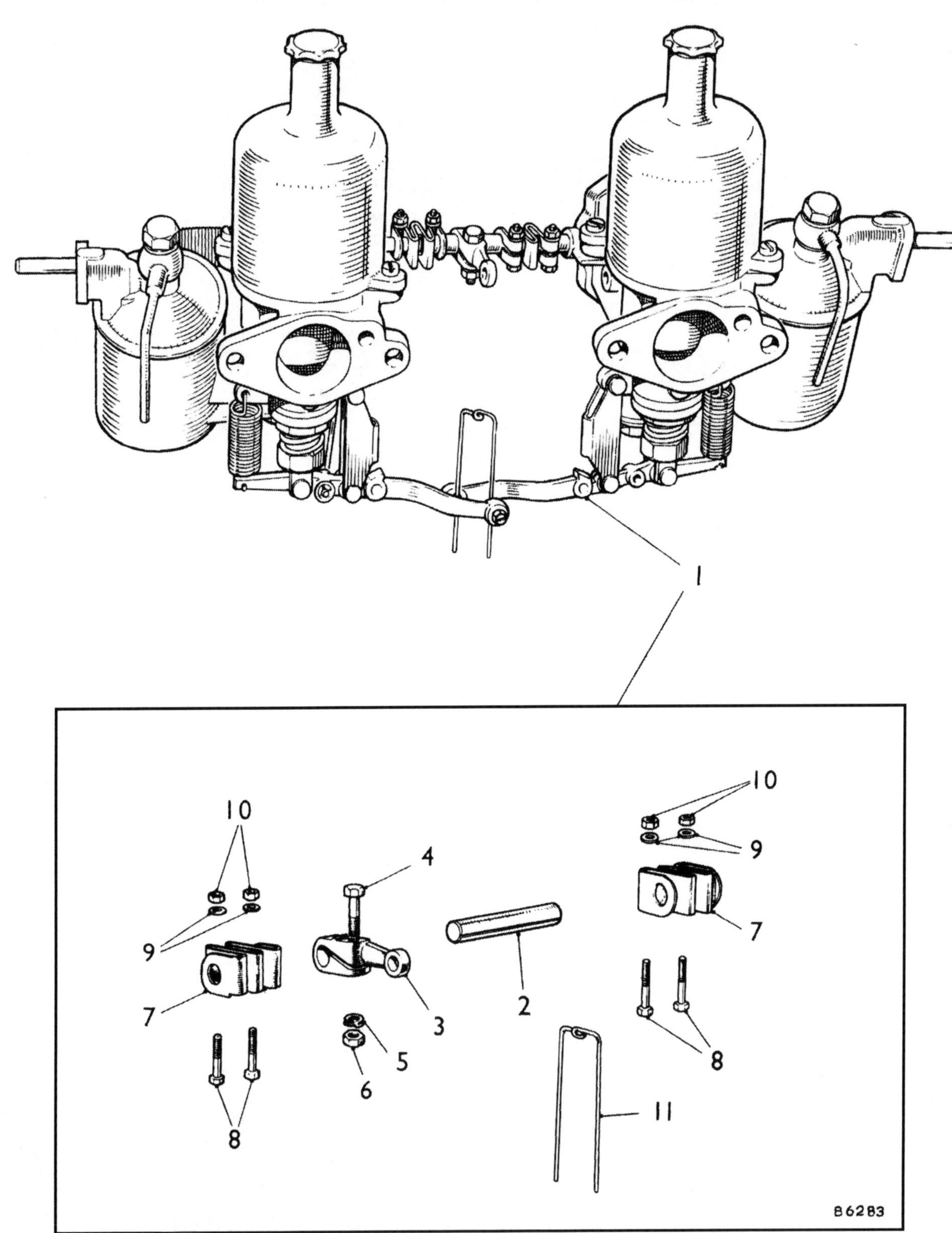

TYPE H1

DESCRIPTION	Part No.	Illus. No.	Quantity	Stock recoms. DIST. Exp.	UK	D	Change Point	REMARKS

CARBURETTERS—TYPE H1

	Page	Plate
TWIN INSTALLATION		
AUC 863	SA 4-SA 7	A 2-A 4

Type H1

TWIN INSTALLATION

DESCRIPTION	Part No.	Illus. No.	Quantity	Exp.	UK	D	Change Point	REMARKS
Carburetter installation	AUC 863	1	1 pr	★	★			
Rod—throttle connecting	AUC 2411	2	1					
Lever—throttle	AUC 1501	3	1					
Bolt—lever	AJD 1042	4	1					Part No. change; was AUC 2694
Washer—spring	LWZ 303	5	1					Part No. change; was AUC 2246
Nut—bolt	AJD 8012 Z	6	1					Part No. change; was AUC 2156
Coupling—rod	AUC 5134	7	2					
Bolt—coupling	AUC 2669	8	4					
Washer—plain	AUC 4612	9	4					
Nut—bolt	AJD 8014 Z	10	4					Part No. change; was AUC 2673
Stirrup—jet lever connecting	AUC 1025	11	1					

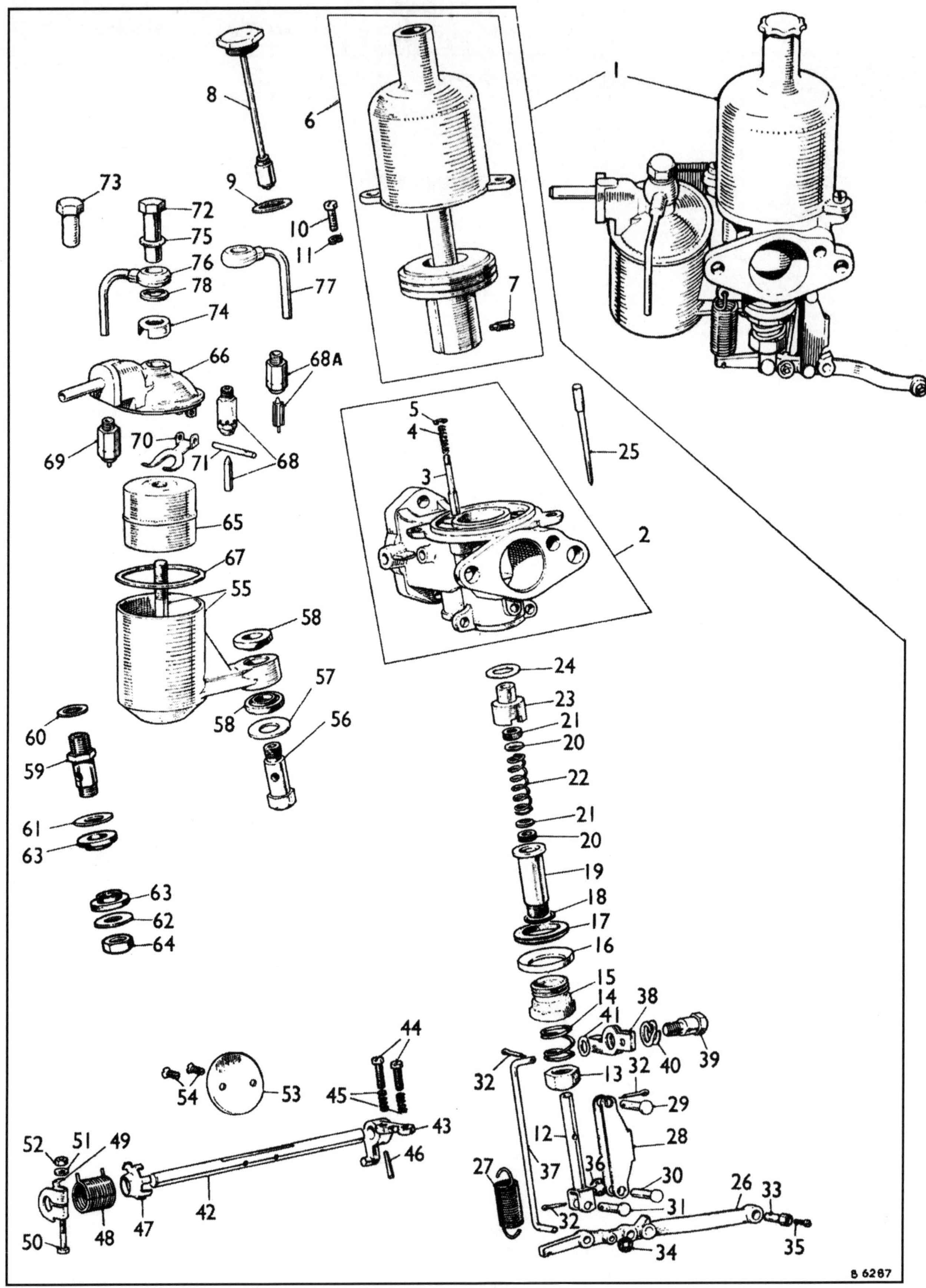
1
2
3
4
5
6
7
8
9
10
11
12
13
14
15
16
17
18
19
20
21
22
23
24
25
26
27
28
29
30
31
32
33
34
35
36
37
38
39
40
41
42
43
44
45
46
47
48
49
50
51
52
53
54
55
56
57
58
59
60
61
62
63
64
65
66
67
68
68A
69
70
71
72
73
74
75
76
77
78
B 6287

TYPE H1

Type H1—*continued*
Twin Installation—*continued*

DESCRIPTION	Part No.	Illus. No.	Quantity	Stock recoms. DIST. Exp.	UK	D	Change Point	REMARKS
Carburetter assembly—front	AUC 9050	1	1					
Body	AUC 6009	2	1					Not available; use AUD 9869
Body assembly	AUD 9369	2	1					
Pin—piston lifting	AUC 1249	3	1	★	★			
Spring—pin	AUC 1151	4	1	★	★			
Circlip—pin	AUC 1250	5	1					
Chamber and piston assembly	AUC 8000	6	1					
Screw—needle locking	AUC 2388	7	1					
Cap and damper	AUC 8114	8	1	★	★			
Washer (fibre)	AUC 4900	9	1	★	★			
Screw—chamber to body	AUC 5156	10	2					
Washer—spring	AUA 1086	11	2					Not available; use AUA 1868
Washer—spring	AUA 1868	11	2					
Jet	AUC 8182	12	1	★	★			
Nut—adjusting	AUC 2121	13	1					
Spring—adjusting nut	AUC 2114	14	1					
Nut—gland sealing	AUC 3232	15	1					
Ring—sealing (aluminium)	AUC 2117	16	1					
Ring—sealing (cork)	AUC 2118	17	1	★	★			
Washer—bottom bearing (copper)	AUC 3233	18	1					
Bearing—bottom	AUC 3231	19	1					
Washer—gland (cork)	AUC 2120	20	2	★	★			
Washer—gland (brass)	AUC 2119	21	2					
Spring—gland	AUC 1158	22	1					
Bearing—top	AUC 3230	23	1					
Washer—top bearing (copper)	AUC 2122	24	1					
Needle—jet								
Rich (EB)	AUD 1149	25	1	★	★			
Standard (GG)	AUD 1211	25	1	★	★			
Weak (MOW)	AUD 1266	25	1	★	★			
Lever—jet	AUC 4045	26	1					
Spring—jet lever return	AUC 4667	27	1	★	★			
Link—jet lever	AUC 4719	28	1					
Pin								
Link to body	AUC 2381	29	1					
Link to lever	AUC 5009	30	1					
Lever to jet	AUC 2381	31	1					
Split	CPS 0204	32	3					Part No. change; was AUC 2109
Pivot	AUC 5058	33	1					
Washer—Starlock	AUC 5002	34	3					
Screw—pivot pin	AUC 5047	35	1					
Washer—Starlock	AUC 5004	36	1					
Link—tension	AUC 3501	37	1					
Lever—rocking	AUC 3508	38	1					
Bolt—pivot	AUC 3471	39	1					
Washer—spring	AUC 3472	40	1					
Washer (aluminium)	AUC 4848	41	1					
Spindle—throttle	AUC 1045	42	1					
Lever—throttle stop	AUC 3446	43	1					
Screw—adjusting—lever	AUC 3464	44	2					
Spring—screw	AUC 3465	45	2					
Pin—taper—lever	AUC 2106	46	1					
Plate—return spring anchor	AUC 4880	47	1					
Spring—spindle return	AUC 4781	48	1					
Clip—end	AUC 4881	49	1					
Bolt—clip	AUC 2669	50	1					
Washer—plain	AUC 4612	51	1					
Nut—bolt	AJD 8014 Z	52	1					Part No. change; was AUC 2678
Disc—throttle	AUC 2103	53	1					
Screw—disc	AUC 1358	54	2					

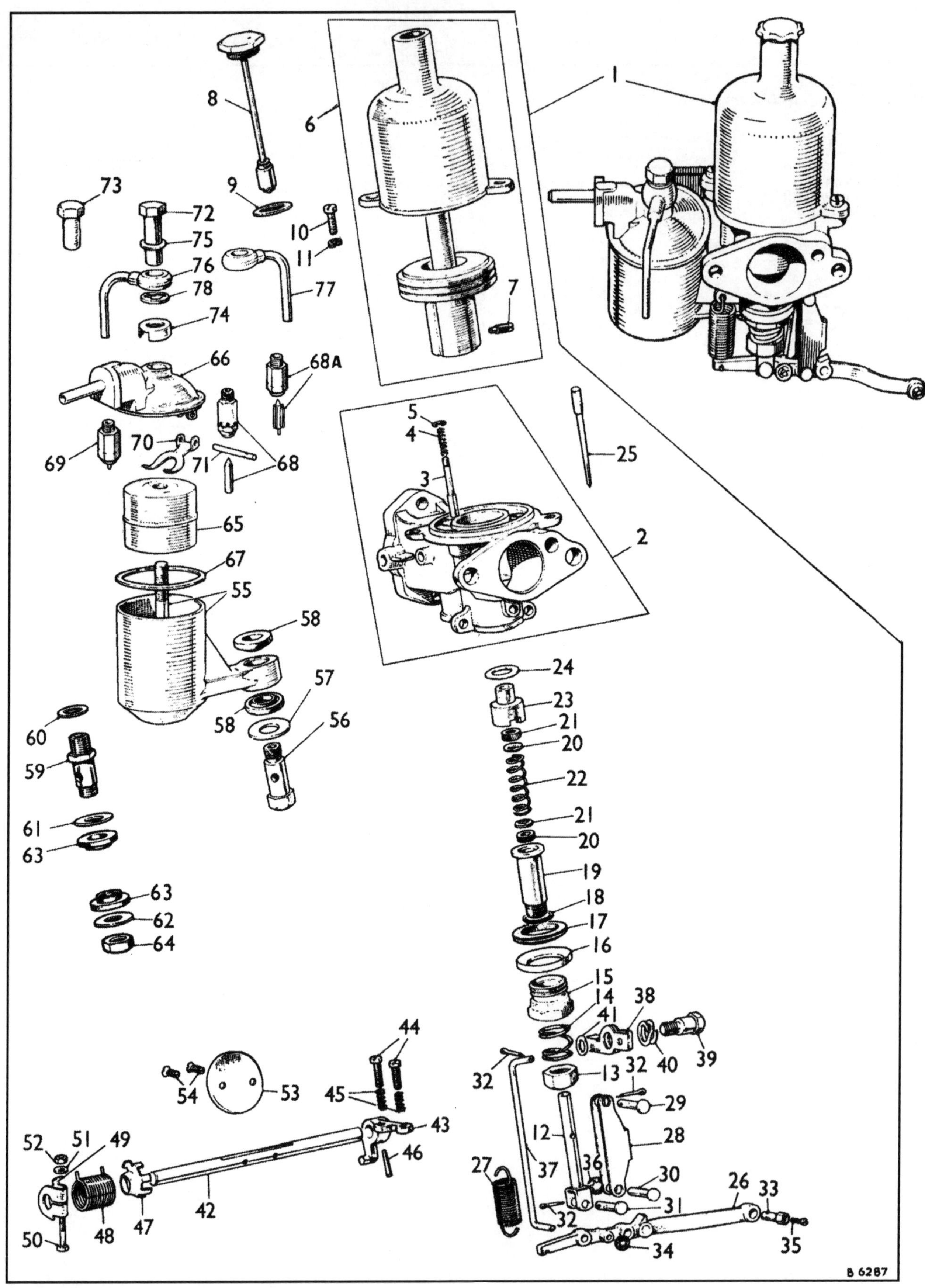
1
2
3
4
5
6
7
8
9
10
11
12
13
14
15
16
17
18
19
20
21
22
23
24
25
26
27
28
29
30
31
32
33
34
35
36
37
38
39
40
41
42
43
44
45
46
47
48
49
50
51
52
53
54
55
56
57
58
59
60
61
62
63
64
65
66
67
68
68A
69
70
71
72
73
74
75
76
77
78
B 6287

TYPE H1

Type H1—*continued*
Twin Installation—*continued*

DESCRIPTION	Part No.	Illus. No.	Quantity	Stock recoms. DIST. Exp.	UK	D	Change Point	REMARKS
Chamber—float	AUC 8402	55	1					
Bolt—chamber to body	AUC 1135	56	1					
Washer—dished—bolt	AUC 1137	57	1					Not available; use AUC 1337
Washer—dished—bolt	AUC 1337	57	1				(E) 9C/U/H101 to ▼	
Grommet (rubber)	AUC 1334	58	2					Not available; use AUC 1534
Grommet (rubber)	AUC 1534	58	2	★	★			
Pillar—banjo	AUC 1387	59	1					
Washer								
Plain—pillar	AUC 1384	60	1					
Inner (steel)	AUC 1389	61	1				(E) 9C/U/H ▼ on	
Outer (steel)	AUC 1388	62	1					
Grommet (rubber)	AUC 1534	63	2	★	★			
Locknut—pillar	AJD 8206 Z	64	1					
Float	AUC 1223	65	1	★	★			
Lid—float chamber	AUC 8208	66	1					
Washer—lid	AUC 1412	67	1	★	★			
Needle and seat	AUC 8170	68	1				(E) 9C/U/H101 to 15304	Not available; use AUD 9096
Needle and seat	AUC 8091	69	1				(E) 9C/U/H15305 on	Not available; use AUD 9096
Needle and seat	AUD 9096	69A	1	★	★			
Lever—hinged	AUC 1981	70	1					
Pin—hinge—lever	AUC 1152	71	1					
Nut—cap—lid	AUC 1163	72	1				(E) 9C/U/H101 to 1550	
Nut—cap—lid	AUC 1867	73	1				(E) 9C/U/H1551 on	
Cover—lid	AUC 1245	74	1				(E) 9C/U/H101 to 1550	
Washer (aluminium)	AUC 1557	75	1					
Pipe—air vent and overflow	AUC 8484	76	1				(E) 9C/U/H101 to ▼	
Pipe—air vent and overflow	AUC 3200	77	1				(E) 9C/U/H ▼ on	
Washer (fibre)	AUC 1928	78	1	★	★			

▼ Change point not available

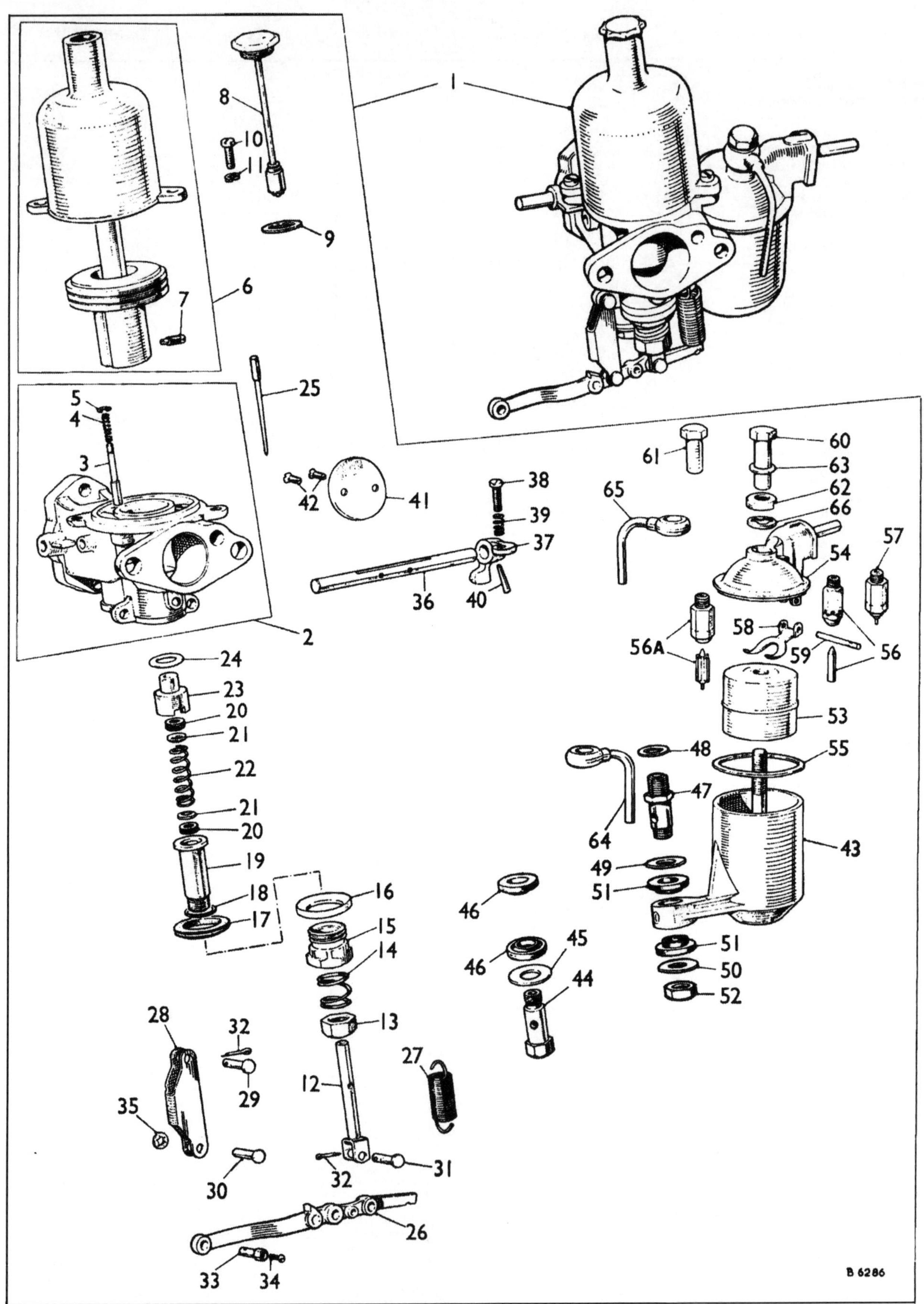
1
2
3
4
5
6
7
8
9
10
11
12
13
14
15
16
17
18
19
20
21
22
21
20
23
24
25
26
27
28
29
30
31
32
32
33
34
35
36
37
38
39
40
41
42
43
44
45
46
46
47
48
49
50
51
51
52
53
54
55
56
56
56A
57
58
59
60
61
62
63
64
65
66
B 6286

TYPE H1

DESCRIPTION	Part No.	Illus. No.	Quantity	Stock recoms. DIST. Exp.	UK	D	Change Point	REMARKS
Type H1—*continued*								
Twin Installation—*continued*								
Carburetter assembly—rear	AUC 9051	1	1					
Body	AUC 6018	2	1					Not available; use AUD 9378
Body assembly	AUD 9378	2	1					
Pin—piston lifting	AUC 1249	3	1	★	★			
Spring—pin	AUC 1151	4	1	★	★			
Circlip—pin	AUC 1250	5	1					
Chamber and piston assembly	AUC 8000	6	1					
Screw—needle locking	AUC 2383	7	1					
Cap and damper	AUC 8114	8	1	★	★			
Washer (fibre)	AUC 4900	9	1	★	★			
Screw—chamber to body	AUC 5156	10	2					
Washer—spring	AUA 1086	11	2					Not available; use AUA 1868
Washer—spring	AUA 1868	11	2					
Jet	AUC 8182	12	1	★	★			
Nut—adjusting	AUC 2121	13	1					
Spring—adjusting nut	AUC 2114	14	1					
Nut—gland sealing	AUC 3232	15	1					
Ring—sealing (aluminium)	AUC 2117	16	1					
Ring—sealing (cork)	AUC 2118	17	1	★	★			
Washer—bottom bearing (copper)	AUC 3233	18	1					
Bearing—bottom	AUC 3231	19	1					
Washer—gland (cork)	AUC 2120	20	2	★	★			
Washer—gland (brass)	AUC 2119	21	2					
Spring—gland	AUC 1158	22	1					
Bearing—top	AUC 3230	23	1					
Washer—top bearing (copper)	AUC 2122	24	1					
Needle—jet								
Rich (EB)	AUD 1149	25	1	★	★			
Standard (GG)	AUD 1211	25	1	★	★			
Weak (MOW)	AUD 1266	25	1	★	★			
Lever—jet	AUC 4045	26	1					
Spring—jet lever return	AUC 4667	27	1	★	★			
Link—jet lever	AUC 4719	28	1					
Pin Link to body	AUC 2381	29	1					
Link to lever	AUC 5009	30	1					
Lever to jet	AUC 2381	31	1					
Split	CPS 0204	32	2					Part No. change; was AUC 2109
Pivot—jet lever to stirrup	AUC 5058	33	1					
Screw—pivot pin	AUC 5047	34	1					
Washer—Starlock	AUC 5004	35	1					
Spindle—throttle	AUC 8404	36	1					
Lever—throttle stop	AUC 2197	37	1					
Screw—adjusting—lever	AUC 3464	38	1					
Spring—screw	AUC 3465	39	1					
Pin—taper—lever	AUC 2106	40	1					
Disc—throttle	AUC 2103	41	1					
Screw—disc	AUC 1858	42	2					
Chamber—float	AUC 8403	43	1					
Bolt—chamber to body	AUC 1135	44	1					
Washer—dished—bolt	AUC 1137	45	1					Not available; use AUC 1387
Washer—dished—bolt	AUC 1387	45	1				(E) 9C/U/H101 to ▼	
Grommet (rubber)	AUC 1334	46	2					Not available; use AUC 1534
Grommet (rubber)	AUC 1534	46	2	★	★			
Pillar—banjo	AUC 1387	47	1					
Washer Plain—pillar	AUC 1384	48	1					
Inner (steel)	AUC 1389	49	1				(E) 9C/U/H ▼ on	
Outer (steel)	AUC 1388	50	1					
Grommet (rubber)	AUC 1534	51	2	★	★			
Locknut—pillar	AJD 8206 Z	52	1					
Float	AUC 1223	53	1	★	★			
Lid—float chamber	AUC 8208	54	1					
Washer—lid	AUC 1412	55	1	★	★			
Needle and seat	AUC 8170	56	1				(E) 9C/U/H101 to 15304	Not available; use AUD 9096
Needle and seat	AUC 8091	57	1				(E) 9C/U/H15305 on	
Needle and seat	AUD 9096	57A	1	★	★			
Lever—hinged	AUC 1981	58	1					
Pin—hinge—lever	AUC 1152	59	1					
Nut—cap—lid	AUC 1168	60	1				(E) 9C/U/H101 to 1550	
Nut—cap—lid	AUC 1867	61	1				(E) 9C/U/H1551 on	
Cover—lid	AUC 1245	62	1				(E) 9C/U/H101 to 1550	
Washer (aluminium)	AUC 1557	63	1					
Pipe—air vent and overflow	AUC 8485	64	1				(E) 9C/U/H101 to ▼	
Pipe—air vent and overflow	AUC 3200	65	1				(E) 9C/U/H ▼ on	
Washer (fibre)	AUC 1928	66	1	★	★			

▼ Change point not available

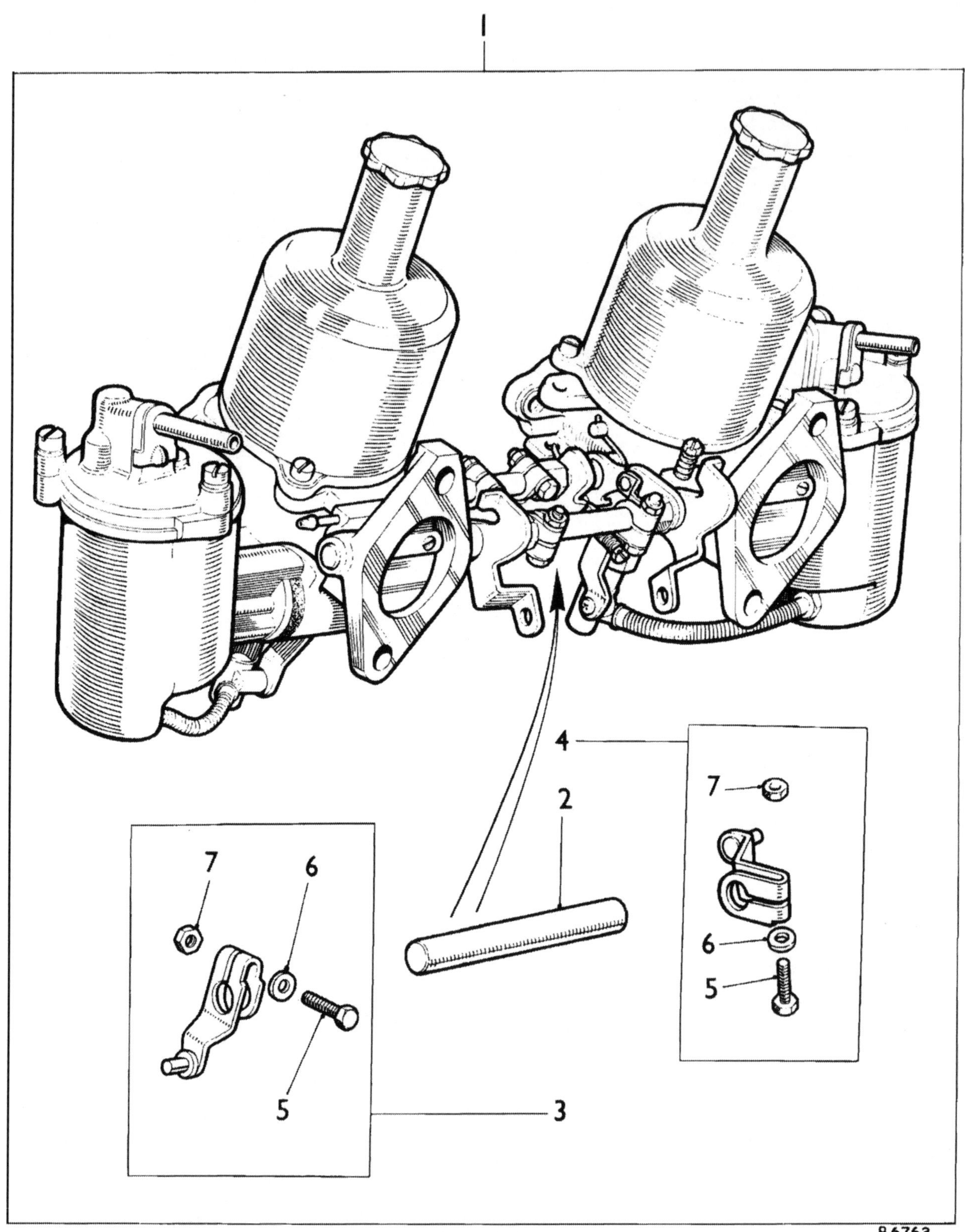

TYPE HS2

	DESCRIPTION	Part No.	Illus. No.	Quantity	Stock recoms. DIST. Exp.	UK	D	Change Point	REMARKS

CARBURETTERS—TYPE HS2

TWIN INSTALLATION	Page	Plate
AUC 990	SH 6-SH 8	H 5-H 7

Type HS2

TWIN INSTALLATION

DESCRIPTION	Part No.	Illus. No.	Quantity	Exp.	UK	D	Change Point	REMARKS
Carburetter installation	AUC 990	1	1 pr	★	★			
Rod—jet connecting	AUC 1457	2	1					
Lever and pin assembly—front	AUE 86	3	2					
Lever and pin assembly—rear	AUE 87	4	2					
Bolt—lever	AJD 1042	5	4					Part No. change; was AUC 2694
Washer—plain	AUC 8896	6	4					
Nut—bolt	AJD 8012 Z	7	4					

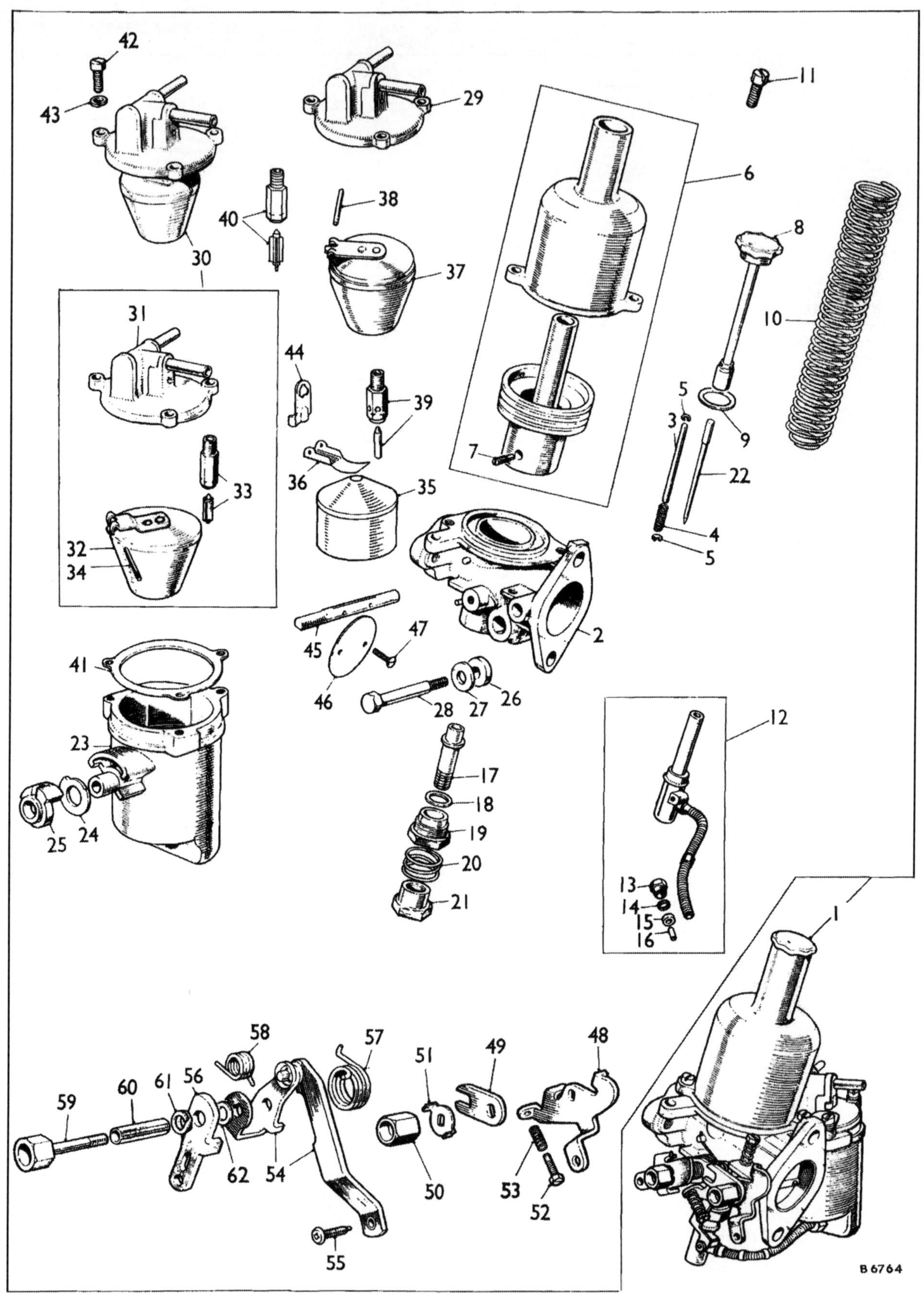
1
2
3
4
5
5
5
6
7
8
9
10
11
12
13
14
15
16
17
18
19
20
21
22
23
24
25
26
27
28
29
30
31
32
33
34
35
36
37
38
39
40
41
42
43
44
45
46
47
48
49
50
51
52
53
54
55
56
57
58
59
60
61
62
B 6764

TYPE HS2

DESCRIPTION	Part No.	Illus. No.	Quantity	Stock recoms. DIST. Exp.	UK	D	Change Point	REMARKS
Type HS2—*continued*								
Twin Installation—*continued*								
Carburetter assembly—front	AUC 9110	1	1					
Body	AUC 8700	2	1					
Pin—piston lifting	AUC 8464	3	1	★	★			
Spring—pin	AUC 1151	4	1	★	★			
Circlip—pin	AUC 1250	5	2					
Chamber and piston assembly	AUC 8044	6	1					Not available; use **AUD 9181**
Chamber and piston assembly	AUD 9181	6	1					
Screw—needle locking	AUC 2057	7	1					
Cap and damper	AUC 8114	8	1	★	★			
Washer (fibre)	AUC 4900	8	1	★	★			
Spring—piston—Blue	AUC 4587	10	1	★	★			
Screw—chamber to body	AUC 5156	11	2					
Jet	AUC 8780	12	1					Not available; use **AUD 9141**
Jet assembly	AUD 9141	12	1	★	★			
Nut	AUD 2129	13	1					
Washer	AUD 2193	14	1					
Gland	AUD 2194	15	1					
Ferrule	AUD 2195	16	1					
Bearing—jet	AUC 8460	17	1	★	★			
Washer—jet bearing (brass)	AUC 8478	18	1					
Screw—jet locking	AUC 2002	19	1					
Spring—jet locking	AUC 2114	20	1					
Screw—jet adjusting	AUC 8461	21	1					
Needle—jet								
Rich (V2)	AUD 1410	22	1	★	★			
Standard (V3)	AUD 1411	22	1	★	★			
Weak (GX)	AUD 1227	22	1	★	★			
Chamber—float	AUC 1310	23	1					
Washer—support	AUC 1329	24	1					
Grommet (rubber)	AUC 1367	25	1	★	★			
Washer (rubber)	AUC 1318	26	1					
Washer (steel)	AUC 1317	27	1					
Bolt—float chamber fixing	AUC 1378	28	1					
Lid—float chamber	AUC 8792	29	1					Not available; use **AUE 269**
Lid assembly—float chamber	AUE 269	30	1					
Lid	AUD 9255	31	1					
Float	AUD 9202	32	1	★	★			
Needle and seat	AUD 9096	33	1	★	★			
Pin—hinge	AUC 1152	34	1					
Float	AUC 8458	35	1					Not available; use **AUC 8667**
Lever—hinged	AUC 8475	36	1					(Not available; use **AUC 8667**)
Float	AUC 8667	37	1	★	★			
Pin—hinge	AUC 1152	38	1					
Needle and seat	AUC 8091	39	1					Not available; use **AUD 9096**
Needle and seat	AUD 9096	40	1	★	★			
Washer—lid	AUC 8459	41	1	★	★			
Screw—lid	AUC 2175	42	3					
Washer—spring	LWZ 303	43	3					Part No. change; was **AUC 2246**
Plate—baffle	AUC 1215	44	1					
Spindle—throttle	AUC 8469	45	1					
Disc—throttle	AUC 2169	46	1					
Screw—disc	AUC 1358	47	2					
Lever—throttle return	AUC 1145	48	1					
Lever—lost motion	AUC 1400	49	1					
Nut—lever	AUC 1424	50	1					
Washer—tab	AUC 1206	51	1					
Screw—throttle stop	AUC 8483	52	2					
Spring—screw	AUC 2451	53	2					
Lever and link—pick-up	AUD 9004	54	1					
Screw—link to jet	AUD 2104	55	1					
Lever—cam	AUC 8456	56	1					
Spring—pick-up lever	AUC 8462	57	1					
Spring—cam lever	AUC 8463	58	1					
Bolt—pivot	AUC 1426	59	1					
Tube—pivot bolt	AUC 8473	60	1					
Washer—spring	AUC 8474	61	1					
Washer—distance	AUC 5032	62	1					

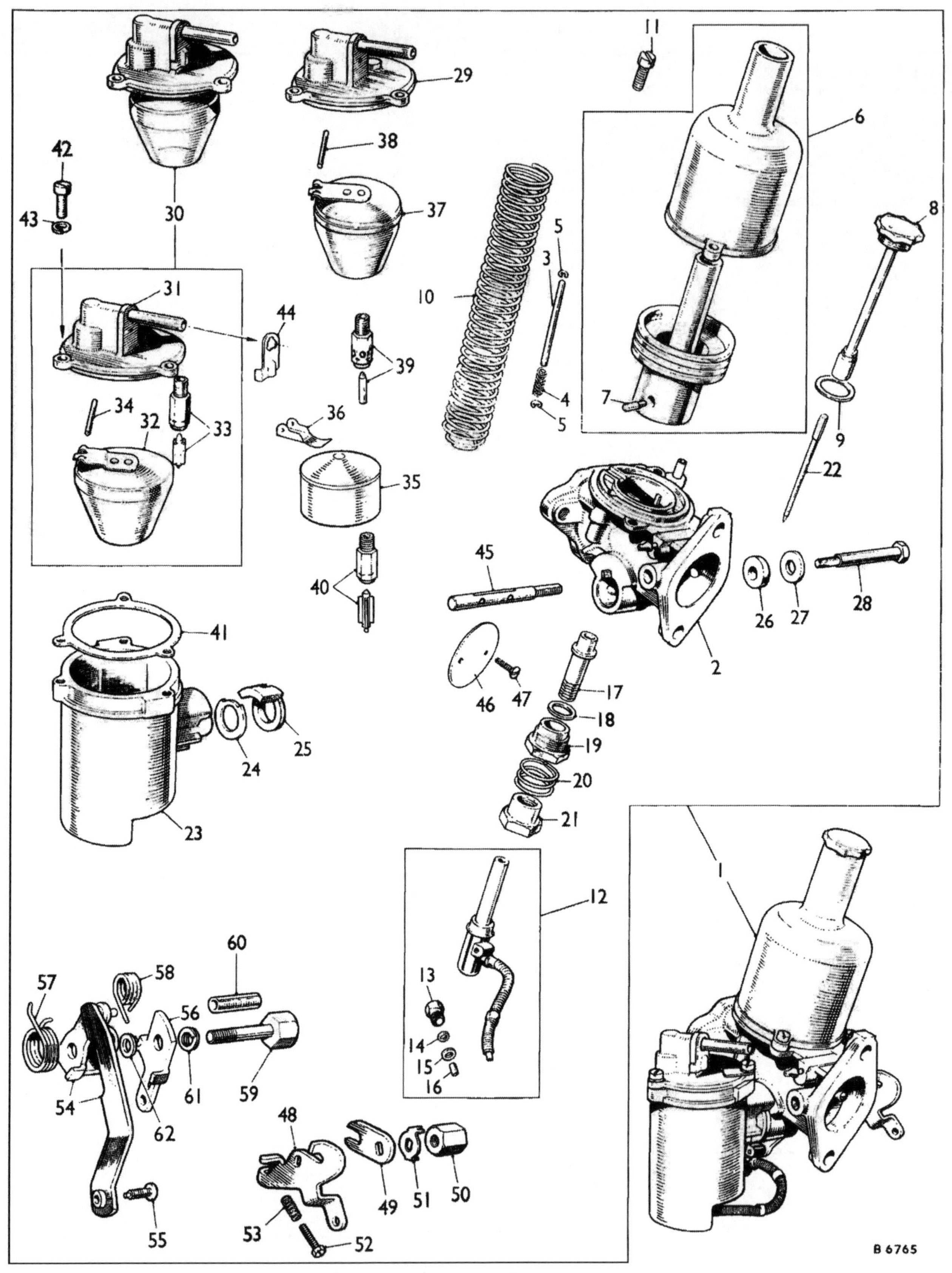
29
11
6
42
43
30
38
37
8
5
3
31
44
10
39
34
32
33
36
7
4
5
9
22
35
45
40
26
27
28
2
41
46
47
17
18
24
25
19
20
23
21
1
12
60
13
57
58
56
14
15
16
59
61
54
62
48
49
51
50
55
53
52
B 6765

TYPE HS2

Type HS2—*continued*
Twin Installation—*continued*

DESCRIPTION	Part No.	Illus. No.	Quantity	Stock recoms. DIST. Exp.	UK	D	Change Point	REMARKS
Carburetter assembly—rear	AUC 9111	1	1					
Body	AUC 8719	2	1					
Pin—piston lifting	AUC 8464	3	1	★	★			
Spring—pin	AUC 1151	4	1	★	★			
Circlip—pin	AUC 1250	5	2					
Chamber and piston assembly	AUC 8044	6	1					Not available; use AUD 9181
Chamber and piston assembly	AUD 9181	6	1					
Screw—needle locking	AUC 2057	7	1					
Cap and damper	AUC 8114	8	1	★	★			
Washer (fibre)	AUC 4900	9	1	★	★			
Spring—piston—Blue	AUC 4587	10	1	★	★			
Screw—chamber to body	AUC 5156	11	2					
Jet	AUC 8781	12	1					Not available; use AUD 9142
Jet assembly	AUD 9142	12	1	★	★			
Nut	AUD 2129	13	1					
Washer	AUD 2193	14	1					
Gland	AUD 2194	15	1					
Ferrule	AUD 2195	16	1					
Bearing—jet	AUC 8460	17	1	★	★			
Washer—jet bearing (brass)	AUC 8478	18	1					
Screw—jet locking	AUC 2002	19	1					
Spring—jet locking	AUC 2114	20	1					
Screw—jet adjusting	AUC 8461	21	1					
Needle—jet								
Rich (V2)	AUD 1410	22	1	★	★			
Standard (V3)	AUD 1411	22	1	★	★			
Weak (GX)	AUD 1227	22	1	★	★			
Chamber—float	AUC 1310	23	1					
Washer—support	AUC 1329	24	1					
Grommet (rubber)	AUC 1366	25	1	★	★			
Washer (rubber)	AUC 1318	26	1					
Washer (steel)	AUC 1317	27	1					
Bolt—float chamber fixing	AUC 1373	28	1					
Lid—float chamber	AUC 8371	29	1					Not available; use AUE 266
Lid assembly—float chamber	AUE 266	30	1					
Lid	AUD 9203	31	1					
Float	AUD 9202	32	1	★	★			
Needle and seat	AUD 9096	33	1	★	★			
Pin—hinge	AUC 1152	34	1					
Float	AUC 8458	35	1					Not available; use AUC 8667
Lever—hinged	AUC 8475	36	1					Not available; use AUC 8667
Float	AUC 8667	37	1	★	★			
Pin—hinge	AUC 1152	38	1					
Needle and seat	AUC 8091	39	1					Not available; use AUD 9096
Needle and seat	AUD 9096	40	1	★	★			
Washer—lid	AUC 8459	41	1	★	★			
Screw—lid	AUC 2175	42	3					
Washer—spring	LWZ 303	43	3					Part No. change; was AUC 2246
Plate—baffle	AUC 1215	44	1					
Spindle—throttle	AUC 8469	45	1					
Disc—throttle	AUC 2169	46	1					
Screw—disc	AUC 1358	47	2					
Lever—throttle return	AUD 2101	48	1					
Lever—lost motion	AUC 1400	49	1					
Nut—lever	AUC 1424	50	1					
Washer—tab	AUC 1206	51	1					
Screw—throttle stop	AUC 8483	52	2					
Spring—screw	AUC 2451	53	2					
Lever and link—pick-up	AUD 9005	54	1					
Screw—link to jet	AUD 2104	55	1					
Lever—cam	AUC 1371	56	1					
Spring—pick-up lever	AUC 1375	57	1					
Spring—cam lever	AUC 1520	58	1					
Bolt—pivot	AUC 1426	59	1					
Tube—pivot bolt	AUC 8473	60	1					
Washer—spring	AUC 8474	61	1					
Washer—distance	AUC 5032	62	1					

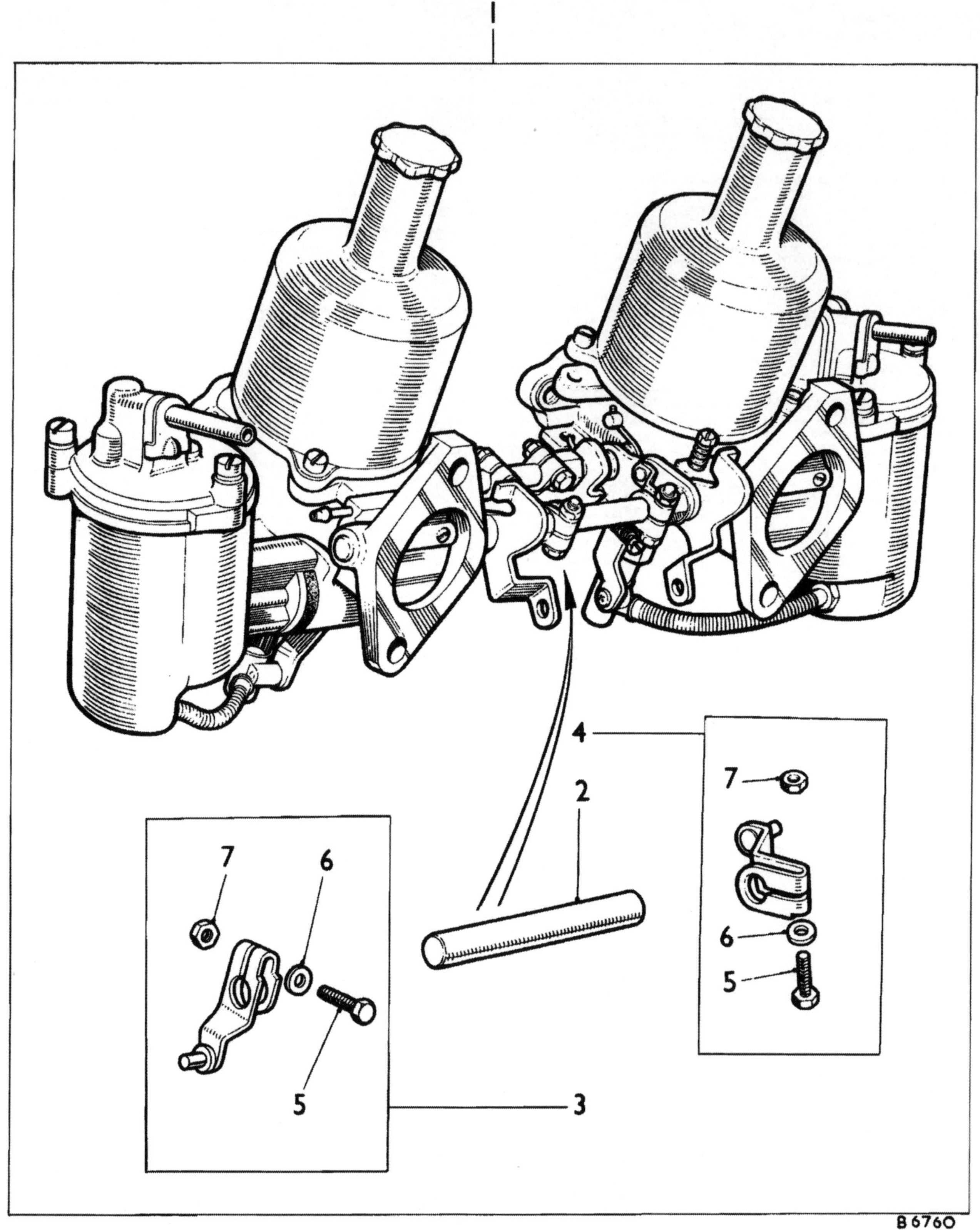

TYPE HS2

CARBURETTERS—TYPE HS2

TWIN INSTALLATION

	Page	Plate
AUD 73	SH 14–SH 16	H 11–H 13

DESCRIPTION	Part No.	Illus. No.	Quantity	Stock recoms. DIST. Exp.	UK	D	Change Point	REMARKS
Type HS2 **Twin Installation**								
Carburetter installation	AUD 73	1	1 pr				(E) 10CC/H101 to 517	Not available; use AUD 136
Carburetter installation	AUD 136	1	1 pr	★	★		(E) 10CC/H518 on	
Rod—jet connecting	AUC 1457	2	1					
Lever and pin assembly—front	AUE 86	3	2					
Lever and pin assembly—rear	AUE 87	4	2					
Bolt—lever	AJD 1042	5	4					Part No. change; was AUC 2694
Washer—plain	AUC 8396	6	4					
Nut—bolt	AJD 8012 Z	7	4					

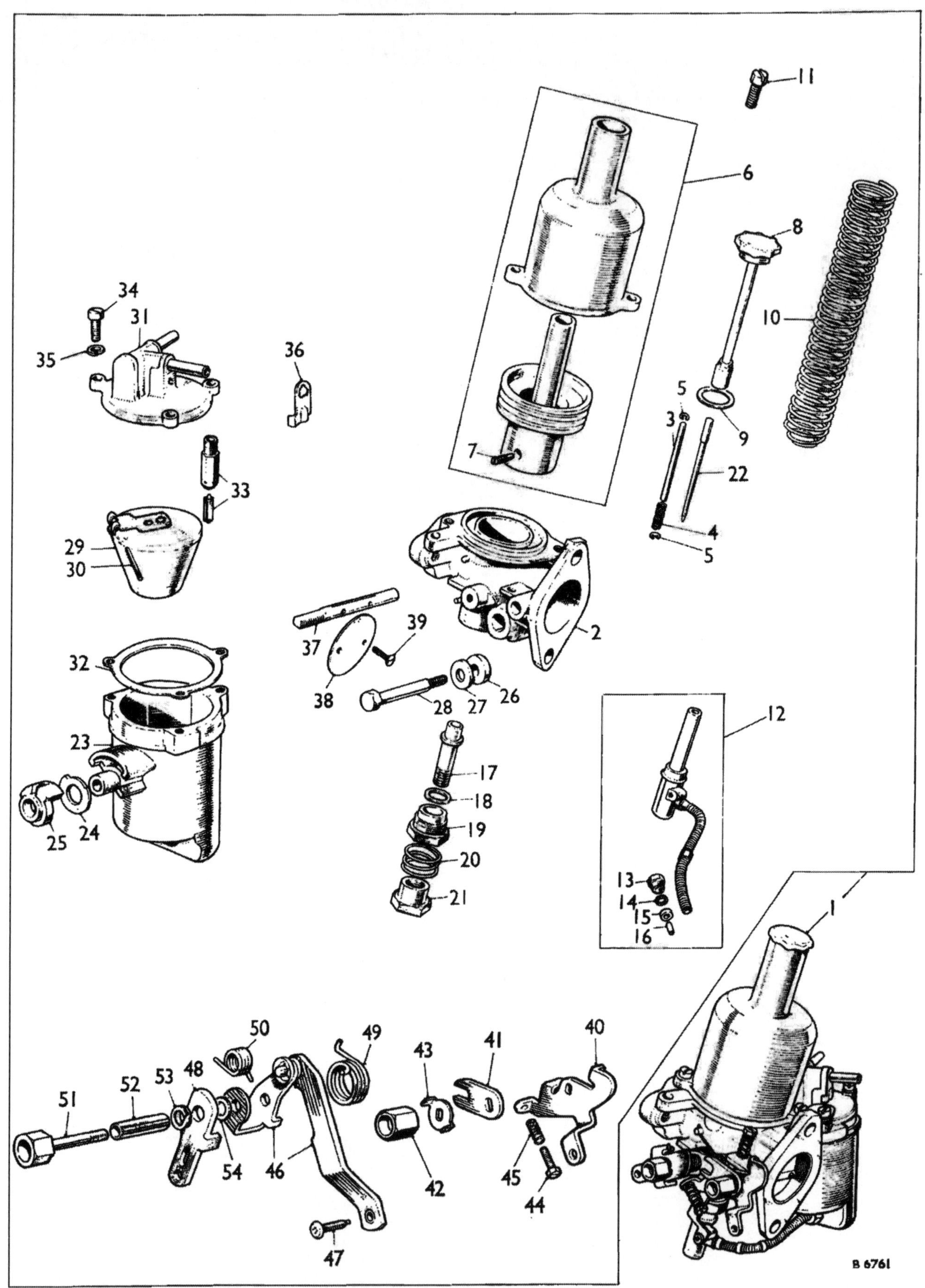

1
2
3
4
5
6
7
8
9
10
11
12
13
14
15
16
17
18
19
20
21
22
23
24
25
26
27
28
29
30
31
32
33
34
35
36
37
38
39
40
41
42
43
44
45
46
47
48
49
50
51
52
53
54
B 6761

TYPE HS2

Type HS2—*continued*
Twin Installation—*continued*

DESCRIPTION	Part No.	Illus. No.	Quantity	Stock recoms. DIST. Exp.	UK	D	Change Point	REMARKS
Carburetter assembly—front	AUC 9202	1	1				(E) 10CC/H101 to 517	
Carburetter assembly—front	AUC 9268	1	1				(E) 10CC/H518 on	
Body	AUC 8700	2	1					
Pin—piston lifting	AUC 8464	3	1	★	★			
Spring—pin	AUC 1151	4	1	★	★			
Circlip—pin	AUC 1250	5	2					
Chamber and piston assembly	AUD 9181	6	1					
Screw—needle locking	AUC 2057	7	1					
Cap and damper	AUC 8114	8	1	★	★			
Washer (fibre)	AUC 4900	9	1	★	★			
Spring—piston—Blue	AUC 4587	10	1	★	★			
Screw—chamber to body	AUC 5156	11	2					
Jet assembly	AUD 9141	12	1	★	★			
Nut	AUD 2129	13	1					
Washer	AUD 2193	14	1					
Gland	AUD 2194	15	1					
Ferrule	AUD 2195	16	1					
Bearing—jet	AUC 8460	17	1	★	★			
Washer—jet bearing (brass)	AUC 8478	18	1					
Screw—jet locking	AUC 2002	19	1					
Spring—jet locking	AUC 2114	20	1					
Screw—jet adjusting	AUC 8461	21	1					
Needle—jet								
Rich (M)	AUD 1261	22	1	★	★		(E) 10CC/H101 to 517	
Standard (GY)	AUD 1468	22	1	★	★		(E) 10CC/H101 to 517	
Weak (GG)	AUD 1211	22	1	★	★		(E) 10CC/H101 to 517	
Rich (H6)	AUD 1242	22	1	★	★		(E) 10CC/H518 on	
Standard (AN)	AUD 1478	22	1	★	★		(E) 10CC/H518 on	
Weak (GG)	AUD 1211	22	1	★	★		(E) 10CC/H518 on	
Chamber—float	AUC 1310	23	1					
Washer—support	AUC 1829	24	1					
Grommet (rubber)	AUC 1367	25	1	★	★		(E) 10CC/H101 to 517	
Grommet (rubber)	AUD 2677	25	1	★	★		(E) 10CC/H518 on	
Washer (rubber)	AUC 1318	26	1					
Washer—plain	AUC 1817	27	1					
Bolt—float chamber to body	AUC 1373	28	1					
Float	AUD 9202	29	1	★	★			
Pin—hinge	AUC 1152	30	1					
Lid—float chamber	AUD 9255	31	1					
Washer—lid	AUC 8459	32	1	★	★			
Needle and seat	AUD 9096	33	1	★	★			
Screw—lid	AUC 2175	34	3					
Washer—spring	LWZ 303	35	3					
Plate—baffle	AUC 1215	36	1					
Spindle—throttle	AUC 8469	37	1					
Disc—throttle	AUC 2169	38	1					
Screw—disc	AUC 1358	39	2					
Lever—throttle return	AUC 1145	40	1					
Lever—lost motion	AUC 1400	41	1					
Nut—lever	AUC 1424	42	1					
Washer—tab	AUC 1206	43	1					
Screw—throttle stop	AUC 8483	44	2					
Spring—screw	AUC 2451	45	2					
Lever and link—pick-up	AUD 9004	46	1					
Screw—link to jet	AUD 2104	47	1					
Lever—cam	AUC 8456	48	1					
Spring—pick-up lever	AUC 8462	49	1					
Spring—cam lever	AUC 8463	50	1					
Bolt—pivot	AUC 1426	51	1					
Tube—pivot bolt	AUC 8473	52	1					
Washer—spring	AUC 8474	53	1					
Washer—distance	AUC 5032	54	1					

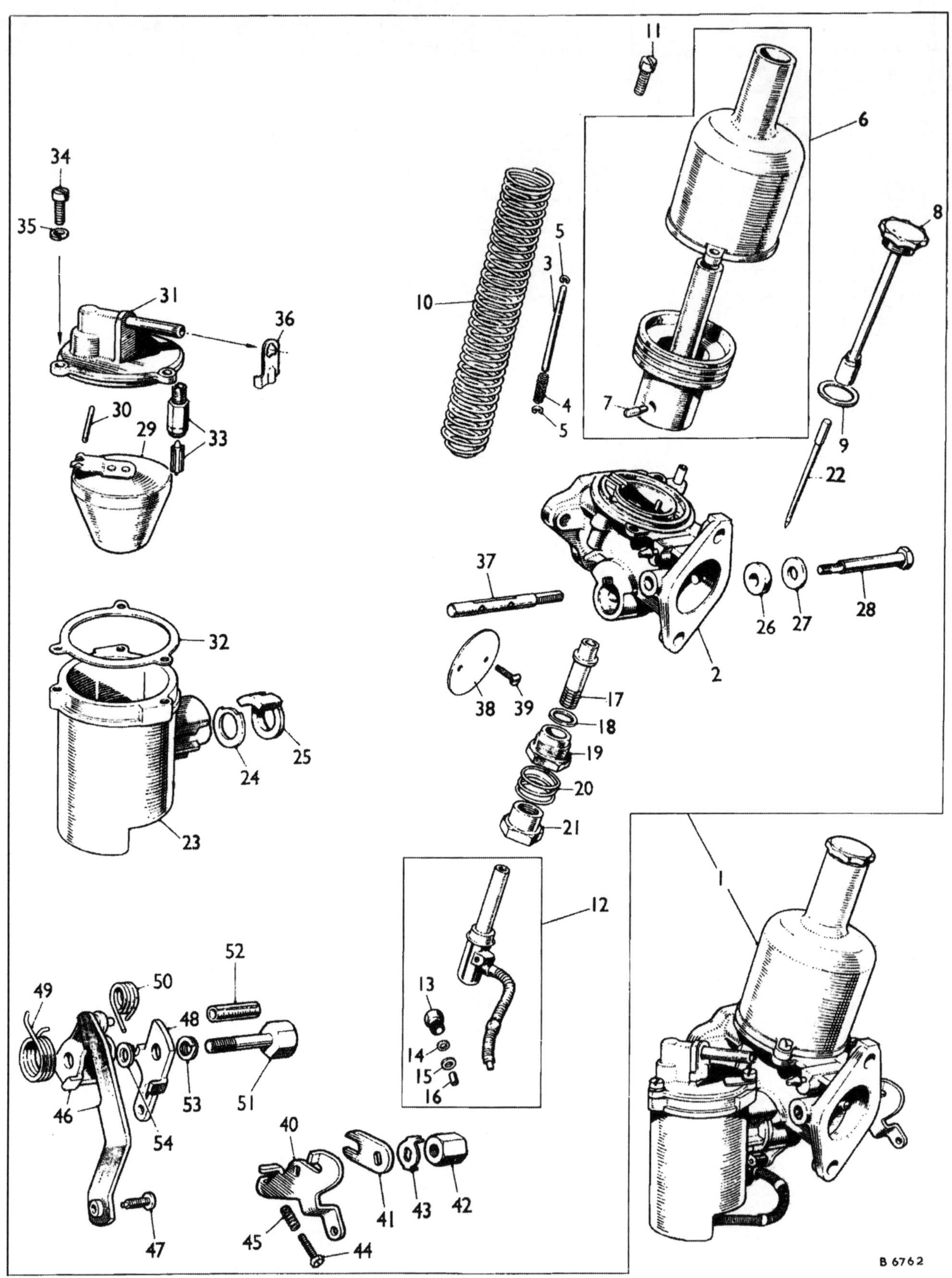
11
6
34
35
8
5
3
31
10
36
4
7
5
9
30
29
33
22
37
26
27
28
32
2
38
39
17
18
19
24
25
20
21
23
12
1
52
13
49
50
48
14
15
16
46
53
51
54
40
41
43
42
47
45
44
B 6762

TYPE HS2

Type HS2—*continued*
Twin Installation—*continued*

DESCRIPTION	Part No.	Illus. No.	Quantity	Stock recoms. DIST. Exp.	UK	D	Change Point	REMARKS
Carburetter assembly—rear	AUC 9203	1	1				(E) 10CC/H101 to 517	
Carburetter assembly—rear	AUC 9269	1	1				(E) 10CC/H518 on	
Body	AUC 8713	2	1					
Pin—piston lifting	AUC 8464	3	1	★	★			
Spring—pin	AUC 1151	4	1	★	★			
Circlip—pin	AUC 1250	5	2					
Chamber and piston assembly	AUD 9181	6	1					
Screw—needle locking	AUC 2057	7	1					
Cap and damper	AUC 8114	8	1	★	★			
Washer (fibre)	AUC 4900	9	1	★	★			
Spring—piston—Blue	AUC 4587	10	1	★	★			
Screw—chamber to body	AUC 5156	11	2					
Jet assembly	AUD 9142	12	1	★	★			
Nut	AUD 2129	13	1					
Washer	AUD 2193	14	1					
Gland	AUD 2194	15	1					
Ferrule	AUD 2195	16	1					
Bearing—jet	AUC 8460	17	1	★	★			
Washer—jet bearing (brass)	AUC 8478	18	1					
Screw—jet locking	AUC 2002	19	1					
Spring—jet locking	AUC 2114	20	1					
Screw—jet adjusting	AUC 8461	21	1					
Needle—jet								
Rich (M)	AUD 1261	22	1	★	★			
Standard (GY)	AUD 1468	22	1	★	★		(E) 10CC/H101 to 517	
Weak (GG)	AUD 1211	22	1	★	★			
Rich (H6)	AUD 1242	22	1	★	★			
Standard (AN)	AUD 1478	22	1	★	★		(E) 10CC/H518 on	
Weak (GG)	AUD 1211	22	1	★	★			
Chamber—float	AUC 1310	23	1					
Washer—support	AUC 1329	24	1					
Grommet (rubber)	AUC 1366	25	1	★	★		(E) 10CC/H101 to 517	
Grommet (rubber)	AUD 2676	25	1	★	★		(E) 10CC/H518 on	
Washer (rubber)	AUC 1318	26	1					
Washer—plain	AUC 1317	27	1					
Bolt—float chamber to body	AUC 1373	28	1					
Float	AUD 9202	29	1	★	★			
Pin—hinge	AUC 1152	30	1					
Lid—float chamber	AUC 9203	31	1					
Washer—lid	AUC 8459	32	1	★	★			
Needle and seat	AUD 9096	33	1	★	★			
Screw—lid	AUC 2175	34	3					
Washer—spring	LWZ 303	35	3					
Plate—baffle	AUC 1215	36	1					
Spindle—throttle	AUC 8469	37	1					
Disc—throttle	AUC 2169	38	1					
Screw—disc	AUC 1358	39	2					
Lever—throttle return	AUD 2101	40	1					
Lever—lost motion	AUC 1400	41	1					
Nut—lever	AUC 1424	42	1					
Washer—tab	AUC 1206	43	1					
Screw—throttle stop	AUC 8483	44	2					
Spring—screw	AUC 2451	45	2					
Lever and link—pick-up	AUD 9005	46	1					
Screw—link to jet	AUD 2104	47	1					
Lever—cam	AUC 1371	48	1					
Spring—pick-up lever	AUC 1375	49	1					
Spring—cam lever	AUC 1520	50	1					
Bolt—pivot	AUC 1426	51	1					
Tube—pivot bolt	AUC 8473	52	1					
Washer—spring	AUC 8474	53	1					
Washer—distance	AUC 5032	54	1					

Distributed by Brooklands Books Ltd., PO Box 146, Cobham, Surrey KT11 1LG, England Phone: 01932 865051
E-mail: sales@brooklands-books.com www.brooklandsbooks.com

Extract from Part No. AKD 5036

AUSTIN-HEALEY SPRITE
MK. 1 and MK. 2
MG MIDGET MK. 1
BODY
SERVICE PARTS LIST
AKD 3567

CONTENTS

	Section	Page
Key to Body Exterior and Main Trim Colour		314
Alphabetical Index		319
Part Number Index		320
Body Shell	BA	325
Bonnet and Control Details	BB	338
Wings	BC	344
Boot Lid and Fittings	BD	346
Doors and Fittings	BF	350
Side Curtains and Sidescreens	BG	352
Windscreen, Windscreen Washer and Mirrors	BH	358
Radiator Grille	BJ	366
Bumpers and Number-Plates	BK	368
Hood, Tonneau Cover and Hard Top	BL	374
Fascia Details	BM	382
Trimming Details	BN	384
Seats and Fittings	BO	417
Heating and Ventilating Equipment	BP	427
Paints	BQ	434

British Leyland Motor Corporation Limited
BMC Service division
COWLEY · OXFORD · ENGLAND

Telephone - - - - - - - - - - - Oxford 78941
Telegrams - - - - - - - - - BMCSERV. Telex. Oxford
Telex - - - - - - - - - - BMCSERV. Oxford 83145/6/7
Cables - - - - - - - - - BMCSERV. Telex. Oxford. England
Codes - - - - - Bentley's, Bentley's Second Phrase, A.B.C. (5th and 6th Editions), Western Union and Private

Key to Body Exterior and Main Trim Colour Combinations, from Start of Vehicle Production

The BMC colour code numbers quoted in the following text relate to the paint colour samples in the 'BMC Service Paint Scheme,' publication ref. AKD 1482.

In the case of two-tone body exterior colours the colour below the break line is quoted first.

In the case of two-tone body exterior colours where a principal colour appears above and below the central band of another colour, this is suitably indicated.

MODEL CODE

H-AN5—Sprite (H-AN5)
H-AN6 } —Sprite (Mark II)
H-AN7 }
G-AN1 } —Midget (Mark I)
G-AN2 }

Body Exterior and BMC Paint Code	Model	Seats	Seat Piping	Liners	Hood Tonneau Cover Hard Top	Door Seals	Carpet/Mats
WHITEHALL (NEVADA) BEIGE (BG.4)	H-AN5	Cherry Red	White	Cherry Red	A. } B. } Black or White C. Ivory White	Cherry Red	Cherry Red
BLACK (BK.1)	H-AN6	"	Black	"	A. Grey B. Red C. Grey or Old English White	"	D. Red/Black Fleck E. Cherry Red
		Red	"	Red	"	Red	"
	H-AN7	"	Grey	"	A. } B. } Black C. Grey or Old English White	"	Red
		Hazelnut	"	Hazelnut	A. } B. } Hazelnut C. Grey or Old English White	Hazelnut	Hazelnut
	G-AN1	Red	Black	Red	A. Grey B. Red C. Grey or Old English White	Red	Black/Red Fleck
		"	Grey	"	A. } B. } Black C. Grey or Old English White	"	Red
	G-AN2	Hazelnut	"	Hazelnut	A. } B. } Hazelnut C. Grey or Old English White	Hazelnut	Hazelnut

A. Hood B. Tonneau Cover C. Hard Top D. Carpets E. Mats

Key to Body Exterior and Main Trim Colour Combinations, from Start of Vehicle Production—*continued*

Body Exterior and BMC Paint Code	Model	Seats	Seat Piping	Liners	Hood Tonneau Cover Hard Top	Door Seals	Carpet/Mats
CLIPPER BLUE (BU.14)	G-AN1	Blue	Blue	Blue	A. } Blue B. } C. Blue or Old English White	Blue	Blue/ Black Fleck
ICE BLUE (BU.18)		"	"	"	"	"	"
	G-AN2	"	Grey	"	"	"	Blue
IRIS BLUE (BU.12)	H-AN5	"	Light Blue	"	A. } Black or B. } White C. Ivory White	"	"
	H-AN6	"	Blue	"	A. } Blue B. } C. Blue or Old English White	"	D. Blue/ Black Fleck E. Blue
	H-AN7	"	Grey	"	A. } Blue B. } C. Blue or Old English White	"	Blue
SPEEDWELL BLUE (BU.1)	H-AN5	"	Light Blue	"	A. } Black B. } C. Ivory White	"	"
	H-AN6	"	Blue	"	A. } Blue B. } C. Blue or Old English White	"	D. Blue/ Black Fleck E. Blue
ALMOND GREEN (GN.37)		Green	Green	Green	A. } Black B. } C. Old English White	Green	D. Black/ White Fleck E. Black
	G-AN1	"	"	"	"	"	Black/ White Fleck
BRITISH RACING GREEN (GN.25 OR GN.29)	H-AN7 G-AN2	Black	Grey	Black	"	Black	Black
DARK GREEN (GN.12)	H-AN5	Green	Green	Green	A. } Black B. } C. Ivory White	Green	Green
LEAF GREEN (GN.15)		"	"	"	A. } Black or B. } White C. Ivory White	"	"

A. Hood B. Tonneau Cover C. Hard Top D. Carpets E. Mats

Key to Body Exterior and Main Trim Colour Combinations, from Start of Vehicle Production—*continued*

Body Exterior and BMC Paint Code	Model	Seats	Seat Piping	Liners	Hood Tonneau Cover Hard Top	Door Seals	Carpet/Mats
DOVE GREY (GR.26)	G-AN1	Red	White	Red	A. Grey B. Red C. Grey or Old English White	Red	Red/White Fleck
	H-AN7 G-AN2	"	Grey	"	"	"	Red
FARINA GREY (GR.11)	G-AN1	"	White	"	"	"	Red/White Fleck
CHERRY RED (RD.4)	H-AN5	Cherry Red	"	Cherry Red	A. } Black or B. } White C. Ivory White	Cherry Red	Cherry Red
DEEP PINK (RD.18)	H-AN6	Black	"	Black	A. } Black B. } C. Grey or Old English White	Black	D. Black/White Fleck E. Black
SIGNAL RED (RD.2)	H-AN6	"	Red	"	A. } Black B. } C. Red or Old English White	"	D. Black/Red Fleck E. Black
		Cherry Red	Black	Cherry Red	A. Black B. Red C. Red or Old English White	Cherry Red	D. Red/Black Fleck E. Cherry Red
		Red	"	Red	"	Red	"
	H-AN7	"	Grey	"	A. } Red B. } C. Red or Old English White	"	Red
		Black	"	Black	"	Black	Black
TARTAN RED (RD.9)	G-AN1	Red	Black	"	A. Red B. Black C. Red or Old English White	"	Red/Black Fleck
		Black	Red	Red	A. } Red B. } C. Red or Old English White	Red	Black/Red Fleck

A. Hood   B. Tonneau Cover   C. Hard Top   D. Carpets   E. Mats

Key to Body Exterior and Main Trim Colour Combinations, from Start of Vehicle Production—*continued*

Body Exterior and BMC Paint Code	Model	Seats	Seat Piping	Liners	Hood Tonneau Cover Hard Top	Door Seals	Carpet/Mats
TARTAN RED (RD.9)	G-AN2	Red	Grey	Red	A. B. } Red C. Red or Old English White	Red	Red
		Black	"	Black	"	Black	Black
OLD ENGLISH WHITE (WT.3)	H-AN5	Cherry Red	White	Cherry Red	A. B. } Black or White C. Ivory White	Cherry Red	Cherry Red
		Black	"	Black	"	Black	Black
	H-AN6	"	"	"	A. Grey B. Black C. Red, Grey, Blue, or Old English White	"	D. Black/ White Fleck E. Black
		Cherry Red	"	Cherry Red	A. Grey B. Red C. Red, Grey, Blue, or Old English White	Cherry Red	D. Red/ Black Fleck E. Cherry Red
		Red	"	Red	"	Red	"
	G-AN1	Black	"	Black	A. Grey B. Black C. Grey or Old English White	Black	Black/ White Fleck
		Red	"	Red	A. Grey B. Red C. Grey or Old English White	Red	Red/White Fleck
	H-AN7 G-AN2	Hazelnut	Grey	Hazelnut	A. B. } Hazelnut C. Old English White	Hazelnut	Hazelnut
		Red	"	Red	A. Grey B. Red C. Old English White	Red	Red
		Black	"	Black	A. B. } Black C. Old English White	Black	Black

A. Hood B. Tonneau Cover C. Hard Top D. Carpets E. Mats

Key to Body Exterior and Main Trim Colour Combinations, from Start of Vehicle Production—*continued*

Body Exterior and BMC Paint Code	Model	Seats	Seat Piping	Liners	Hood Tonneau Cover Hard Top	Door Seals	Carpet/Mats
FIESTA YELLOW (YL.11)	H-AN7	Black	Grey	Black	A. B. Black C. Old English White	Black	Black
HIGHWAY YELLOW (YL.9)		"	White	"	A. B. Black C. Grey or Old English White	"	D. Black/White Fleck E. Black
PRIMROSE (YL.3)	H-AN5	"	Yellow	"	A. B. Black C. Ivory White	"	Black

A. Hood B. Tonneau Cover C. Hard Top D. Carpets E. Mats

Alphabetical Index

A

Arm—wing mirror .. .. BH 5

B

Badge—bonnet top .. BB 2, BB 4
Badge—'M.G.'—boot lid .. BD 2
Badge—'M.G.'—fascia panel .. BM 2
Badge—'M.G.'—radiator grille BJ 2
Bag—hood cover stowage .. BL 2
Bag—hood frame stowage .. BL 2
Bag—tonneau cover stowage .. BL 4
Blower—heater .. .. BP 3
Body shell .. .. BA 2–BA 7
Bonnet .. .. .. BB 2, BB 4
Boot lid .. .. BD 2
Bracket—bonnet lock striker .. BB 3
Bracket—over-rider .. BK 2, BK 4
Bracket—side curtain .. .. BG 2
Bulk material .. .. BN 5, BN 9, BN 13, BN 18
Bumpers .. .. BK 2, BK 3, BK 4

C

Carpets .. .. .. BN 9, BN 13, BN 17, BN 18
Case—side curtain .. BG 2, BG 3
Catch—bonnet—safety .. .. BB 3
Channel—windscreen .. .. BH 2
Control—push-pull—fresh-air unit .. .. BP 4
Control—windscreen washer BH 3, BH 4
Cover—hood .. .. BL 2
Cover—seat cushion .. BO 2, BO 3, BO 4, BO 5
Cover—seat squab .. BO 2, BO 4
Cover—tonneau .. .. .. BL 3
Curtain—side .. .. .. BG 2
Cushion—rear compartment .. BO 6
Cushion—seat .. .. BO 2–BO 6

D

Door—heater outlet .. .. BP 3
Doors .. .. BF 2

E

Elbow—demister .. .. BP 3

F

Fascia panel .. .. BM 2
Finisher—radiator grille surround BJ 2
Flash—'Midget' .. .. .. BD 2
Flash—'Sprite' .. .. .. BA 4
Frame—hood .. .. .. BL 2
Frame—seat base .. .. BO 5
Fresh-air unit .. .. .. BP 4
Front end assembly .. .. BA 6

G

Glass—mirror .. .. .. BH 5
Glass—windscreen .. .. BH 2
Grille—radiator .. .. BJ 2

H

Handle—bonnet .. .. BB 3
Handle—boot lid .. .. BD 2
Handle—grab .. .. .. BM 2
Hard top .. .. .. BL 5, BL 6
Heater .. .. BP 2
Hinge—bonnet .. .. BB 2, BB 4
Hinge—boot lid .. .. .. BD 2
Hinge—door .. .. .. BF 2
Holder—licence .. .. .. BH 2
Hood .. .. BL 2
Hose—heater and fresh-air unit BP 2, BP 3, BP 4

J

Jet—windscreen washer BH 3, BH 4

K

Key—boot lid .. .. .. BD 2
Knob—fresh-air unit control .. BP 4
Knob—heater switch .. .. BP 2
Knob—windscreen washer control BH 3, BH 4

L

Lid—boot .. .. .. BD 2
Licence holder .. .. .. BH 2
Lighter—cigar .. .. .. BM 2
Liner—door pocket .. BN 3, BN 8, BN 11, BN 16
Liner—trim .. .. BN 2–BN 18
Lock—bonnet .. .. .. BB 3
Lock—boot lid .. .. .. BD 2
Lock—door .. .. .. BF 2
Luggage grid .. .. BA 4, BD 3

M

Mats—floor .. BN 4, BN 9, BN 13
Mirror—interior .. .. .. BH 5
Mirror—wing .. .. .. BH 5
Motif—'Midget'—boot lid .. BD 2
Motif—'Sprite' .. .. .. BD 2
Moulding—bonnet centre .. BB 4
Mouldings—trim .. BN 2, BN 6, BN 14

N

Nozzle—demister .. .. BP 3
Number-plates .. BK 2, BK 3, BK 4

O

Over-rider .. BK 2, BK 3, BK 4

P

Paint—touching-up .. .. BQ 2
Panel—fascia .. .. .. BM 2
Panels—body .. .. BA 2–BA 6
Pipe—heater .. .. .. BP 2
Plate—fascia blanking .. .. BM 2
Plate—inlet flange .. BP 3, BP 4
Plate—number .. BK 2, BK 3, BK 4
Platform heater .. .. BA 3, BA 6
Plugs—blanking .. BA 4, BA 7
Pocket—door .. .. BN 3, BN 8, BN 11, BN 16

R

Rail—tonneau cover support .. BL 4
Rod—bonnet prop .. .. BB 4
Rod—boot lid prop .. .. BD 3
Rubber—bonnet sealing .. BB 2
Rubber—windscreen glazing and sealing .. .. BH 2
Runners—seats .. .. .. BO 5

S

Seal—door .. .. BN 3, BN 8, BN 12, BN 16
Seal—base—heater and fresh-air BP 2, BP 4
Seats and fittings .. BO 2–BO 6
Shell—body .. .. BA 2–BA 5
Side curtains .. .. .. BG 2
Sidescreen—sliding .. BG 3, BG 4
'Sprite' flash .. .. .. BA 4
Squab—seat .. .. BO 2–BO 6
Stay—bonnet .. .. .. BB 3
Strap—door check .. BN 3, BN 8, BN 12, BN 16
Striker—door lock .. .. BF 2
Strut—bonnet .. .. .. BB 2
Support—number-plates BK 2, BK 3, BK 4
Switch—heater .. .. .. BP 2

T

Tap—water control—heater .. BP 2
Tonneau cover .. .. .. BL 3
Towing eye—front .. .. BK 3
Trim roll—cockpit rear centre BN 14
Trim roll—fascia .. .. BN 14
Trimming .. .. .. BN 2–BN 18

U

Underframe .. .. BA 3, BA 6

V

Ventilating equipment .. BP 2–BP 4

W

Washer—windscreen .. BH 3, BH 4
Wheel arch .. .. BA 2, BA 3, BA 5, BA 6
Windscreen .. .. .. BH 2
Wing—front .. .. .. BC 2
Wing—rear .. .. .. BC 2

Part Number Index

The following is a complete index of parts in this List, giving the page reference of each part number

Part Number	Page
2A 5465	BA 3
2A 5509	BA 3
2A 5509	BA 6
2A 5524	BA 3
2A 5524	BA 6
2A 5527	BA 3
2A 5528	BA 3
2A 5533	BA 3
2A 5533	BA 6
2A 5557	BA 3
2A 5558	BA 3
2A 5612	BA 3
14A 81	BF 2
14A 82	BF 2
14A 84	BB 2
14A 89	BA 2
14A 90	BA 2
14A 366	BB 4
14A 716	BF 2
14A 733	BB 2
14A 764	BN 3
14A 764	BN 8
14A 764	BN 12
14A 764	BN 16
14A 1162	BP 3
14A 3411	BK 2
14A 3823	BH 2
14A 4497	BM 2
14A 4497	BO 2
14A 4497	BO 4
14A 4593	BA 3
14A 4594	BA 3
14A 4606	BA 2
14A 4606	BB 2
14A 4611	BA 2
14A 4612	BA 2
14A 4635	BA 3
14A 4635	BA 6
14A 4636	BA 3
14A 4636	BA 6
14A 4656	BM 2
14A 4657	BM 2
14A 4659	BK 2
14A 4673	BF 2
14A 4675	BF 2
14A 4676	BF 2
14A 4677	BF 2
14A 4684	BB 2
14A 4684	BB 4
14A 4691	BB 3
14A 4705	BB 3
14A 4706	BM 2
14A 4707	BB 3
14A 4708	BB 3
14A 4709	BB 3
14A 4712	BB 3
14A 4714	BB 3
14A 4715	BJ 2
14A 4718	BH 2
14A 4719	BH 2
14A 4720	BH 2
14A 4721	BH 2
14A 4722	BH 2
14A 4723	BH 2
14A 4724	BH 2
14A 4725	BH 2
14A 4726	BH 2
14A 4727	BH 2
14A 4728	BH 2
14A 4729	BH 2
14A 4730	BH 2
14A 4733	BB 2
14A 4734	BK 2
14A 4734	BK 4
14A 4738	BK 2
14A 4739	BK 2
14A 4744	BM 2
14A 4754	BL 2
14A 4762	BP 3
14A 4763	BP 3
14A 4763	BP 4
14A 4766	BP 3
14A 4769	BA 2
14A 4770	BA 2
14A 4771	BA 2
14A 4772	BA 2
14A 4773	BB 2
14A 4774	BB 2
14A 4775	BB 2
14A 4776	BB 2
14A 4778	BO 5
14A 4787	BO 2
14A 4787	BO 3
14A 4790	BA 4
14A 4790	BA 7
14A 4791	BA 4
14A 4791	BA 7
14A 4805	BH 2
14A 4806	BL 2
14A 4820	BN 2
14A 4820	BN 6
14A 4821	BN 2
14A 4822	BN 2
14A 4823	BN 2
14A 4824	BH 2
14A 4859	BA 4
14A 4860	BO 5
14A 4874	BB 2
14A 4879	BL 2
14A 4891	BB 3
14A 4892	BB 3
14A 4898	BB 2
14A 5472	BH 2
14A 5473	BH 5
14A 5507	BG 2
14A 5513	BG 2
14A 5519	BO 5
14A 5520	BO 5
14A 5521	BG 2
14A 5530	BH 3
14A 5531	BH 3
14A 5523	BH 3
14A 5542	BB 2
14A 5542	BB 4
14A 5706	BH 2
14A 5772	BP 4
14A 6536	BL 2
14A 6537	BL 2
14A 6537	BL 3
14A 6538	BL 2
14A 6538	BL 3
14A 6745	BN 8
14A 6745	BN 12
14A 6745	BN 16
14A 7074	BB 4
14A 8078	BA 7
14A 8196	BH 5
14A 8225	BH 5
14A 8226	BH 5
AAA 743	BN 18
AAA 836	BP 2
AAA 1524	BD 3
AAA 1645	BK 3
AAA 2064	BL 2
AAA 2398	BB 4
ACA 5172	BP 2
ACA 5173	BP 2
ACA 5455	BP 2
ACA 5456	BP 2
ACC 5811	BK 2
ACH 9287	BK 2
ACH 9287	BK 3
ACH 9287	BK 4
ACH 9373	BA 7
ADA 833	BO 2
ADA 833	BO 3
ADA 833	BO 4
ADA 833	BO 5
ADA 1874	BN 15
ADA 2493	BA 7
ADA 2765	BN 5
ADA 2889	BN 4
ADA 2889	BN 5
ADB 509	BM 2
ADB 2582	BO 2
ADB 2582	BF 2
ADB 4811	BG 2
ADB 4811	BN 5
ADB 4811	BN 9
ADB 4811	BN 13
ADB 4811	BN 19
ADE 539	BN 18
ADG 474	BK 2
ADG 474	BK 3
ADH 573	BL 6
ADH 2475	BD 2
ADH 2476	BD 2
ADH 2477	BD 2
ADH 4492	BD 2
AFH 1684	BF 2
AHA 5030	BO 2
AHA 5030	BO 3
AHA 5032	BO 2
AHA 5032	BO 3
AHA 5033	BO 2
AHA 5034	BO 2
AHA 5034	BO 3
AHA 5035	BO 2
AHA 5035	BO 3
AHA 5037	BO 2
AHA 5037	BO 3
AHA 5038	BO 2
AHA 5039	BO 2
AHA 5039	BO 3
AHA 5040	BO 2
AHA 5042	BO 2
AHA 5043	BO 2
AHA 5044	BO 2
AHA 5045	BO 2
AHA 5047	BO 2
AHA 5048	BO 2
AHA 5049	BO 2
AHA 5050	BN 3
AHA 5050	BN 8
AHA 5052	BN 3
AHA 5052	BN 8
AHA 5053	BN 3
AHA 5053	BN 8
AHA 5054	BN 3
AHA 5054	BN 8
AHA 5054	BN 11
AHA 5055	BN 3
AHA 5055	BN 8
AHA 5057	BN 3
AHA 5057	BN 8
AHA 5058	BN 3
AHA 5058	BN 8
AHA 5059	BN 3
AHA 5059	BN 8
AHA 5059	BN 11
AHA 5060	BN 2
AHA 5060	BN 6
AHA 5062	BN 2
AHA 5062	BN 6
AHA 5063	BN 2
AHA 5063	BN 6
AHA 5064	BN 2
AHA 5064	BN 6
AHA 5064	BN 10
AHA 5065	BN 2
AHA 5065	BN 6
AHA 5067	BN 2
AHA 5067	BN 6
AHA 5068	BN 2
AHA 5068	BN 6
AHA 5069	BN 2
AHA 5069	BN 6
AHA 5069	BN 10
AHA 5070	BN 2
AHA 5072	BN 2
AHA 5073	BN 2
AHA 5074	BN 2
AHA 5075	BN 2
AHA 5077	BN 2
AHA 5078	BN 2
AHA 5079	BN 2
AHA 5080	BN 4
AHA 5082	BN 4
AHA 5083	BN 4
AHA 5084	BN 4
AHA 5085	BN 4
AHA 5087	BN 4
AHA 5088	BN 4
AHA 5089	BN 4
AHA 5089	BO 4
AHA 5090	BN 2
AHA 5090	BN 6
AHA 5092	BN 2
AHA 5092	BN 6
AHA 5093	BN 2
AHA 5093	BN 6
AHA 5094	BN 2
AHA 5094	BN 6
AHA 5094	BN 10
AHA 5095	BN 3
AHA 5095	BN 8
AHA 5097	BN 3
AHA 5097	BN 8
AHA 5098	BN 3
AHA 5098	BN 8
AHA 5099	BN 3
AHA 5099	BN 8
AHA 5099	BN 12
AHA 5100	BN 2
AHA 5100	BN 7
AHA 5102	BN 2
AHA 5102	BN 7
AHA 5103	BN 2
AHA 5103	BN 7
AHA 5104	BN 2
AHA 5104	BN 7
AHA 5104	BN 11
AHA 5105	BN 2
AHA 5105	BN 7
AHA 5107	BN 2
AHA 5107	BN 7
AHA 5108	BN 2
AHA 5108	BN 7
AHA 5109	BN 2
AHA 5109	BN 7
AHA 5109	BN 11
AHA 5110	BN 4
AHA 5111	BN 4
AHA 5112	BN 4
AHA 5113	BN 4
AHA 5114	BN 5
AHA 5115	BN 5
AHA 5116	BN 5
AHA 5117	BN 5
AHA 5118	BN 3
AHA 5118	BN 8
AHA 5119	BN 3
AHA 5119	BN 8
AHA 5119	BN 12
AHA 5120	BA 4
AHA 5120	BN 3
AHA 5120	BN 8
AHA 5120	BN 12
AHA 5121	BN 3
AHA 5122	BN 3
AHA 5123	BN 3
AHA 5124	BN 3
AHA 5125	BN 3
AHA 5125	BO 4
AHA 5216	BN 3
AHA 5126	BO 4
AHA 5127	BN 3
AHA 5127	BO 4
AHA 5128	BN 3
AHA 5128	BO 4
AHA 5129	BN 3
AHA 5130	BN 4
AHA 5130	BN 9
AHA 5131	BN 4
AHA 5131	BN 9
AHA 5132	BN 4
AHA 5132	BN 9
AHA 5133	BN 4
AHA 5134	BN 4
AHA 5134	BN 9
AHA 5135	BN 4
AHA 5135	BN 9
AHA 5136	BN 4
AHA 5136	BN 9
AHA 5137	BN 4
AHA 5138	BN 4
AHA 5138	BN 9
AHA 5139	BN 4
AHA 5139	BN 9
AHA 5140	BN 4
AHA 5140	BN 9
AHA 5141	BN 4
AHA 5145	BA 2
AHA 5147	BA 2
AHA 5148	BA 2
AHA 5149	BA 2
AHA 5150	BB 3
AHA 5151	BB 3
AHA 5155	BB 2
AHA 5162	BB 2
AHA 5163	BB 2
AHA 5164	BB 2
AHA 5165	BB 2
AHA 5173	BA 3
AHA 5174	BA 3
AHA 5175	BA 3
AHA 5176	BA 3
AHA 5176	BA 6
AHA 5177	BA 3
AHA 5177	BA 6
AHA 5179	BA 2
AHA 5182	BA 2
AHA 5183	BA 2
AHA 5184	BA 2
AHA 5184	BA 5
AHA 5185	BA 2
AHA 5185	BA 5
AHA 5201	BN 2
AHA 5201	BN 6
AHA 5202	BN 2
AHA 5202	BN 6
AHA 5203	BN 2
AHA 5203	BN 6
AHA 5204	BN 2
AHA 5204	BN 6
AHA 5204	BN 10
AHA 5205	BN 2
AHA 5205	BN 6
AHA 5206	BN 2
AHA 5206	BN 6
AHA 5207	BN 2
AHA 5207	BN 6
AHA 5208	BN 2

Part Number Index—*continued*

Part Number	Page	Part Number	Page	Part Number	Page	Part Number	Page	Part Number	Page
AHA 5208	BN 6	AHA 5356	BN 5	AHA 5512	BJ 2	AHA 5798	BG 3	AHA 5973	BN 13
AHA 5208	BN 10	AHA 5371	BN 4	AHA 5513	BJ 2	AHA 5799	BG 2	AHA 5991	BN 7
AHA 5210	BA 4	AHA 5372	BN 4	AHA 5514	BJ 2	AHA 5799	BG 3	AHA 5992	BN 7
AHA 5211	BK 2	AHA 5373	BN 4	AHA 5515	BJ 2	AHA 5800	BG 3	AHA 5998	BL 3
AHA 5211	BK 3	AHA 5374	BN 4	AHA 5517	BB 4	AHA 5801	BG 3	AHA 5999	BL 3
AHA 5211	BK 4	AHA 5375	BN 4	AHA 5518	BB 4	AHA 5802	BG 3	AHA 6000	BL 3
AHA 5212	BP 2	AHA 5376	BN 4	AHA 5519	BB 4	AHA 5803	BG 3	AHA 6008	BO 6
AHA 5213	BP 2	AHA 5377	BN 4	AHA 5521	BK 3	AHA 5804	BK 4	AHA 6009	BO 6
AHA 5214	BP 2	AHA 5378	BN 4	AHA 5522	BK 3	AHA 5807	BD 2	AHA 6010	BO 6
AHA 5215	BP 2	AHA 5379	BN 4	AHA 5533	BK 3	AHA 5808	BD 3	AHA 6011	BL 4
AHA 5216	BG 2	AHA 5380	BN 4	AHA 5534	BK 3	AHA 5810	BD 2	AHA 6012	BL 4
AHA 5216	BG 3	AHA 5381	BN 4	AHA 5541	BA 5	AHA 5811	BD 3	AHA 6033	BN 13
AHA 5216	BG 4	AHA 5382	BN 4	AHA 5543	BB 4	AHA 5812	BN 6	AHA 6043	BN 13
AHA 5217	BL 2	AHA 5383	BN 5	AHA 5545	BC 2	AHA 5812	BN 10	AHA 6044	BN 13
AHA 5219	BO 5	AHA 5384	BN 5	AHA 5546	BC 2	AHA 5813	BN 6	AHA 6045	BN 13
AHA 5220	BH 3	AHA 5385	BN 5	AHA 5549	BA 6	AHA 5813	BN 10	AHA 6046	BN 13
AHA 5223	BO 5	AHA 5386	BN 5	AHA 5552	BA 3	AHA 5814	BN 6	AHA 6047	BN 13
AHA 5225	BB 2	AHA 5390	BA 3	AHA 5552	BA 6	AHA 5814	BN 10	AHA 6048	BN 13
AHA 5232	BB 3	AHA 5393	BB 2	AHA 5553	BA 3	AHA 5817	BC 2	AHA 6049	BN 13
AHA 5233	BB 3	AHA 5394	BB 2	AHA 5553	BA 6	AHA 5817	BF 2	AHA 6050	BN 13
AHA 5234	BB 3	AHA 5395	BB 2	AHA 5554	BA 6	AHA 5818	BC 2	AHA 6051	BN 13
AHA 5240	BN 4	AHA 5396	BB 2	AHA 5555	BA 3	AHA 5819	BF 2	AHA 6052	BN 13
AHA 5240	BN 9	AHA 5397	BB 2	AHA 5555	BA 6	AHA 5820	BM 2	AHA 6053	BN 13
AHA 5241	BN 4	AHA 5398	BB 2	AHA 5556	BA 6	AHA 5821	BM 2	AHA 6054	BN 13
AHA 5241	BN 9	AHA 5399	BB 2	AHA 5617	BB 4	AHA 5822	BC 2	AHA 6055	BN 13
AHA 5242	BN 4	AHA 5400	BB 2	AHA 5618	BB 4	AHA 5823	BF 2	AHA 6056	BN 13
AHA 5242	BN 9	AHA 5412	BN 3	AHA 5619	BC 2	AHA 5824	BF 2	AHA 6057	BN 13
AHA 5243	BN 4	AHA 5412	BN 8	AHA 5620	BA 6	AHA 5825	BC 2	AHA 6058	BN 13
AHA 5244	BN 4	AHA 5412	BN 11	AHA 5622	BA 6	AHA 5837	BA 5	AHA 6059	BN 13
AHA 5244	BN 9	AHA 5413	BN 3	AHA 5624	BA 6	AHA 5838	BA 5	AHA 6060	BN 13
AHA 5245	BN 4	AHA 5413	BN 8	AHA 5626	BA 6	AHA 5882	BM 2	AHA 6061	BN 13
AHA 5245	BN 9	AHA 5413	BN 11	AHA 5642	BA 6	AHA 5884	BL 2	AHA 6062	BN 13
AHA 5246	BN 4	AHA 5413	BN 16	AHA 5653	BB 4	AHA 5888	BL 4	AHA 6063	BN 13
AHA 5246	BN 9	AHA 5414	BG 2	AHA 5654	BB 4	AHA 5654	BG 2	AHA 6067	BO 4
AHA 5247	BN 4	AHA 5415	BG 2	AHA 5657	BL 3	AHA 5894	BG 3	AHA 6068	BO 4
AHA 5248	BN 4	AHA 5416	BG 2	AHA 5657	BL 4	AHA 5895	BG 2	AHA 6069	BO 4
AHA 5249	BN 4	AHA 5417	BG 2	AHA 5658	BL 3	AHA 5895	BG 3	AHA 6070	BO 4
AHA 5250	BN 4	AHA 5418	BG 2	AHA 5664	BJ 2	AHA 5896	BG 2	AHA 6071	BO 4
AHA 5251	BN 4	AHA 5419	BG 2	AHA 5673	BK 4	AHA 5896	BG 3	AHA 6080	BO 3
AHA 5255	BH 2	AHA 5420	BG 2	AHA 5674	BB 4	AHA 5897	BG 2	AHA 6081	BO 3
AHA 5256	BL 3	AHA 5420	BG 3	AHA 5675	BK 4	AHA 5897	BG 3	AHA 6082	BO 3
AHA 5257	BL 3	AHA 5420	BG 4	AHA 5677	BK 4	AHA 5899	BL 2	AHA 6083	BO 3
AHA 5259	BN 4	AHA 5421	BG 2	AHA 5678	BK 4	AHA 5900	BL 2	AHA 6084	BO 3
AHA 5259	BN 9	AHA 5421	BG 3	AHA 5679	BK 4	AHA 5901	BL 2	AHA 6132	BL 3
AHA 5260	BN 4	AHA 5421	BG 4	AHA 5683	BD 2	AHA 5902	BL 2	AHA 6133	BL 3
AHA 5260	BN 9	AHA 5422	BG 2	AHA 5685	BK 4	AHA 5903	BN 7	AHA 6134	BL 3
AHA 5261	BN 4	AHA 5423	BG 2	AHA 5686	BK 3	AHA 5903	BN 11	AHA 6137	BO 3
AHA 5261	BN 9	AHA 5424	BG 2	AHA 5686	BK 4	AHA 5904	BN 7	AHA 6138	BO 3
AHA 5262	BN 4	AHA 5426	BG 2	AHA 5687	BK 4	AHA 5904	BN 11	AHA 6140	BO 2
AHA 5263	BG 2	AHA 5427	BG 2	AHA 5693	BK 4	AHA 5905	BN 7	AHA 6141	BO 2
AHA 5263	BG 3	AHA 5428	BG 2	AHA 5695	BK 3	AHA 5905	BN 11	AHA 6142	BN 9
AHA 5264	BG 2	AHA 5429	BG 2	AHA 5696	BK 3	AHA 5906	BN 7	AHA 6142	BN 13
AHA 5265	BG 2	AHA 5430	BG 2	AHA 5698	BL 2	AHA 5906	BN 11	AHA 6143	BN 9
AHA 5266	BG 2	AHA 5437	BA 4	AHA 5699	BD 2	AHA 5907	BN 7	AHA 6143	BN 13
AHA 5367	BG 2	AHA 5437	BA 7	AHA 5700	BB 4	AHA 5908	BN 7	AHA 6144	BN 9
AHA 5268	BN 2	AHA 5442	BB 2	AHA 5701	BB 4	AHA 5934	BN 9	AHA 6144	BN 13
AHA 5268	BN 6	AHA 5455	BF 2	AHA 5702	BB 4	AHA 5955	BN 8	AHA 6145	BN 9
AHA 5268	BN 10	AHA 5456	BF 2	AHA 5708	BD 2	AHA 5955	BN 11	AHA 6145	BN 13
AHA 5269	BN 2	AHA 5459	BO 2	AHA 5709	BD 2	AHA 5956	BN 8	AHA 6146	BN 13
AHA 5269	BN 6	AHA 5459	BO 3	AHA 5725	BA 5	AHA 5956	BN 11	AHA 6150	BG 3
AHA 5269	BN 10	AHA 5460	BO 2	AHA 5726	BA 5	AHA 5957	BN 8	AHA 6151	BG 3
AHA 5283	BA 2	AHA 5460	BO 3	AHA 5729	BA 5	AHA 5957	BN 11	AHA 6152	BG 3
AHA 5283	BA 5	AHA 5461	BO 2	AHA 5730	BA 5	AHA 5958	BN 8	AHA 6153	BG 3
AHA 5284	BA 2	AHA 5462	BO 2	AHA 5731	BA 5	AHA 5958	BN 11	AHA 6154	BG 3
AHA 5284	BA 5	AHA 5465	BA 3	AHA 5732	BA 5	AHA 5959	BN 8	AHA 6155	BG 3
AHA 5291	BA 2	AHA 5465	BA 6	AHA 5733	BA 5	AHA 5959	BN 11	AHA 6156	BG 3
AHA 5292	BA 2	AHA 5466	BA 3	AHA 5749	BA 5	AHA 5960	BN 8	AHA 6157	BG 3
AHA 5299	BA 3	AHA 5466	BA 6	AHA 5750	BA 5	AHA 5960	BN 11	AHA 6158	BG 3
AHA 5300	BA 3	AHA 5467	BA 4	AHA 5753	BA 5	AHA 5961	BN 8	AHA 6159	BG 3
AHA 5314	BH 2	AHA 5472	BB 3	AHA 5754	BA 5	AHA 5961	BN 12	AHA 6160	BG 3
AHA 5315	BH 2	AHA 5479	BL 2	AHA 5755	BA 5	AHA 5962	BN 8	AHA 6161	BG 3
AHA 5316	BH 2	AHA 5480	BG 2	AHA 5756	BA 5	AHA 5962	BN 12	AHA 6162	BG 3
AHA 5317	BH 2	AHA 5481	BG 2	AHA 5757	BA 5	AHA 5963	BN 8	AHA 6163	BN 10
AHA 5318	BH 2	AHA 5482	BL 3	AHA 5765	BK 4	AHA 5963	BN 12	AHA 6164	BN 10
AHA 5319	BH 12	AHA 5483	BL 3	AHA 5768	BL 2	AHA 5964	BL 2	AHA 6165	BN 10
AHA 5320	BH 2	AHA 5485	BL 5	AHA 5769	BL 2	AHA 5965	BL 2	AHA 6177	BO 6
AHA 5321	BH 2	AHA 5486	BH 2	AHA 5791	BK 4	AHA 5968	BN 9	AHA 6178	BO 6
AHA 5322	BH 2	AHA 5494	BL 5	AHA 5792	BL 2	AHA 5968	BN 13	AHA 6179	BN 13
AHA 5323	BL 2	AHA 5495	BL 5	AHA 5794	BG 3	AHA 5969	BN 9	AHA 6180	BN 13
AHA 5324	BL 2	AHA 5498	BL 5	AHA 5795	BG 3	AHA 5969	BN 13	AHA 6181	BN 13
AHA 5329	BB 3	AHA 5499	BO 5	AHA 5796	BG 3	AHA 5970	BN 9	AHA 6182	BN 13
AHA 5329	BF 2	AHA 5500	BO 5	AHA 5797	BG 3	AHA 5970	BN 13	AHA 6183	BN 13
AHA 5355	BN 5	AHA 5501	BH 3	AHA 5798	BG 2	AHA 5973	BN 9	AHA 6184	BN 13

Part Number Index—*continued*

Part Number	Page	Part Number	Page	Part Number	Page	Part Number	Page	Part Number	Page
AHA 6185	BN 13	AHA 6327	BO 2	AHA 6627	BN 17	AHA 6847	BN 15	AJD 8012 Z	BH 2
AHA 6186	BN 13	AHA 6328	BO 2	AHA 6628	BN 17	AHA 6848	BN 7	AJD 8012 Z	BL 3
AHA 6187	BN 13	AHA 6330	BO 6	AHA 6641	BN 17	AHA 6848	BN 11	AJD 8012 Z	BL 4
AHA 6188	BN 13	AHA 6332	BL 6	AHA 6642	BN 17	AHA 6848	BN 15		
AHA 6189	BN 13	AHA 6333	BL 6	AHA 6643	BN 17	AHA 6849	BN 7	AKE 3012	BN 7
AHA 6190	BN 13	AHA 6336	BL 5	AHA 6644	BN 17	AHA 6849	BN 11	AKE 3013	BN 7
AHA 6191	BN 13	AHA 6336	BL 6	AHA 6645	BN 17	AHA 6849	BN 15	AKE 3014	BN 7
AHA 6192	BN 13	AHA 6352	BC 2	AHA 6646	BN 17	AHA 6850	BN 15	AKE 3016	BN 7
AHA 6193	BL 5	AHA 6353	BB 4	AHA 6647	BN 17	AHA 6851	BN 15	AKE 3017	BN 7
AHA 6200	BN 7	AHA 6354	BL 5	AHA 6648	BN 17	AHA 6852	BN 7	AKE 3018	BN 7
AHA 6200	BN 11	AHA 6354	BL 6	AHA 6649	BN 17	AHA 6852	BN 11	AKE 3020	BN 7
AHA 6201	BN 7	AHA 6355	BL 5	AHA 6650	BN 17	AHA 6852	BN 15	AKE 3021	BN 7
AHA 6201	BN 11	AHA 6355	BL 6	AHA 6651	BN 17	AHA 6853	BN 16	AKE 3022	BN 7
AHA 6204	BG 2	AHA 6357	BD 2	AHA 6652	BN 17	AHA 6854	BN 16	AKE 3024	BN 6
AHA 6204	BG 3	AHA 6379	BN 9	AHA 6653	BN 17	AHA 6855	BN 16	AKE 3024	BN 10
AHA 6204	BG 4	AHA 6379	BN 13	AHA 6654	BN 17	AHA 6856	BN 16	AKE 3025	BN 6
AHA 6205	BA 6	AHA 6380	BN 9	AHA 6655	BN 17	AHA 6861	BN 16	AKE 3025	BN 10
AHA 6206	BA 6	AHA 6380	BN 13	AHA 6656	BN 17	AHA 6862	BN 16	AKE 3026	BN 6
AHA 6207	BD 3	AHA 6386	BO 3	AHA 6660	BO 5	AHA 6863	BN 16	AKE 3026	BN 10
AHA 6213	BD 3	AHA 6387	BO 3	AHA 6678	BN 14	AHA 6864	BN 16	AKE 3026	BN 11
AHA 6216	BA 3	AHA 6388	BO 2	AHA 6679	BN 14	AHA 6881	BN 16	AKE 3027	BN 6
AHA 6216	BA 6	AHA 6388	BO 3	AHA 6680	BN 14	AHA 6882	BN 16	AKE 3027	BN 10
AHA 6217	BA 3	AHA 6399	BD 3	AHA 6681	BN 14	AHA 6883	BN 16	AKE 3028	BN 6
AHA 6217	BA 6	AHA 6417	BN 14	AHA 6682	BN 14	AHA 6884	BN 16	AKE 3028	BN 10
AHA 6220	BL 4	AHA 6419	BG 4	AHA 6683	BN 14	AHA 6886	BO 6	AKE 3029	BN 6
AHA 6221	BL 4	AHA 6429	BP 3	AHA 6684	BN 14	AHA 6887	BO 6	AKE 3029	BN 10
AHA 6223	BA 6	AHA 6450	BH 4	AHA 6685	BN 14	AHA 6888	BO 6	AKE 3030	BN 6
AHA 6226	BO 3	AHA 6458	BL 5	AHA 6712	BL 2	AHA 6889	BO 6	AKE 3030	BN 10
AHA 6227	BO 3	AHA 6459	BL 5	AHA 6715	BL 4	AHA 6906	BN 18	AKE 3031	BN 6
AHA 6228	BO 3	AHA 6460	BL 5	AHA 6716	BN 14	AHA 6917	BO 4	AKE 3031	BN 10
AHA 6229	BO 2	AHA 6461	BL 5	AHA 6717	BN 14	AHA 6918	BO 4	AKE 3032	BN 6
AHA 6230	BO 2	AHA 6462	BL 5	AHA 6718	BN 14	AHA 6919	BO 5	AKE 3032	BN 10
AHA 6231	BO 2	AHA 6467	BL 5	AHA 6719	BN 14	AHA 6920	BO 5	AKE 3033	BN 6
AHA 6236	BL 5	AHA 6468	BL 5	AHA 6724	BN 14	AHA 6922	BO 4	AKE 3033	BN 10
AHA 6236	BL 6	AHA 6470	BL 5	AHA 6725	BN 14	AHA 6923	BO 4	AKE 3034	BN 6
AHA 6237	BL 5	AHA 6471	BL 5	AHA 6726	BN 14	AHA 6924	BO 4	AKE 3034	BN 10
AHA 6237	BL 6	AHA 6473	BL 5	AHA 6727	BN 14	AHA 6925	BO 4	AKE 3035	BN 6
AHA 6238	BL 5	AHA 6474	BL 5	AHA 6732	BN 14	AHA 6932	BH 5	AKE 3035	BN 10
AHA 6238	BL 6	AHA 6487	BN 14	AHA 6733	BN 14	AHA 6933	BN 14	AKE 3036	BN 6
AHA 6239	BL 5	AHA 6488	BN 14	AHA 6734	BN 14	AHA 6979	BN 16	AKE 3036	BN 10
AHA 6239	BL 6	AHA 6490	BN 14	AHA 6735	BN 14	AHA 6981	BG 4	AKE 3037	BN 6
AHA 6240	BL 5	AHA 6491	BN 14	AHA 6740	BN 15	AHA 7003	BG 4	AKE 3037	BN 10
AHA 6240	BL 6	AHA 6497	BG 4	AHA 6741	BN 15	AHA 7004	BG 4	AKE 3038	BN 6
AHA 6241	BL 5	AHA 6498	BK 3	AHA 6742	BN 15	AHA 7044	BO 4	AKE 3038	BN 10
AHA 6241	BL 6	AHA 6499	BN 14	AHA 6743	BN 15	AHA 7045	BO 4	AKE 3039	BN 7
AHA 6242	BL 5	AHA 6500	BN 14	AHA 6748	BN 15	AHA 7046	BO 5	AKE 3039	BN 11
AHA 6242	BL 6	AHA 6501	BG 4	AHA 6749	BN 15	AHA 7047	BO 5	AKE 3040	BN 7
AHA 6244	BL 6	AHA 6502	BG 4	AHA 6750	BN 15	AHA 7391	BL 5	AKE 3040	BN 11
AHA 6245	BL 6	AHA 6503	BG 4	AHA 6751	BN 15	AHA 7391	BL 6	AKE 3041	BN 7
AHA 6246	BL 6	AHA 6504	BG 4	AHA 6756	BN 15	AHA 7393	BC 2	AKE 3041	BN 11
AHA 6249	BL 5	AHA 6505	BG 4	AHA 6757	BN 15	AHA 8098	BJ 2	AKE 3042	BN 7
AHA 6249	BL 6	AHA 6506	BG 4	AHA 6758	BN 15	AHA 8323	BP 2	AKE 3042	BN 11
AHA 6250	BL 5	AHA 6509	BG 4	AHA 6759	BN 15	AHA 8387	BA 6	AKE 3043	BN 7
AHA 6250	BL 6	AHA 6510	BG 4	AHA 6764	BN 15			AKE 3043	BN 11
AHA 6251	BL 5	AHA 6521	BG 4	AHA 6765	BN 15	AHH 5258	BM 2	AKE 3044	BN 7
AHA 6251	BL 6	AHA 6513	BG 4	AHA 6766	BN 15	AHH 5261	BD 2	AKE 3044	BN 11
AHA 6252	BD 3	AHA 6515	BG 4	AHA 6767	BN 15	AHH 5460	BB 3	AKE 3045	BN 7
AHA 6257	BB 4	AHA 6516	BG 4	AHA 6772	BN 15	AHH 5460	BB 4	AKE 3045	BN 11
AHA 6258	BO 3	AHA 6517	BG 4	AHA 6773	BN 15	AHH 5479	BK 2	AKE 3046	BN 7
AHA 6259	BL 6	AHA 6518	BG 4	AHA 6774	BN 15	AHH 5479	BK 3	AKE 3046	BN 11
AHA 6273	BO 6	AHA 6520	BN 14	AHA 6775	BN 15	AHH 5479	BK 4	AKE 3047	BN 7
AHA 6274	BO 6	AHA 6521	BN 14	AHA 6780	BN 15	AHH 5593	BP 2	AKE 3047	BN 11
AHA 6275	BO 6	AHA 6522	BN 14	AHA 6781	BN 15	AHH 5593	BP 4	AKE 3048	BN 7
AHA 6276	BO 6	AHA 6523	BN 14	AHA 6782	BN 15	AHH 5712	BK 2	AKE 3048	BN 11
AHA 6277	BO 6	AHA 6535	BN 14	AHA 6783	BN 15	AHH 5712	BK 3	AKE 3049	BN 7
AHA 6282	BO 6	AHA 6536	BN 14	AHA 6784	BN 15	AHH 5712	BK 4	AKE 3049	BN 11
AHA 6283	BO 6	AHA 6537	BN 14	AHA 6785	BN 15	AHH 5714	BP 3	AKE 3050	BN 7
AHA 6284	BO 6	AHA 6538	BN 14	AHA 6786	BN 15	AHH 5714	BP 4	AKE 3050	BN 11
AHA 6296	BA 7	AHA 6571	BN 15	AHA 6787	BN 15	AHH 5759	BM 2	AKE 3051	BN 7
AHA 6297	BG 3	AHA 6601	BN 17	AHA 6829	BN 15	AHH 6360	BN 14	AKE 3051	BN 11
AHA 6298	BG 3	AHA 6602	BN 17	AHA 6830	BN 15	AHH 6417	BN 14	AKE 3052	BN 7
AHA 6301	BL 6	AHA 6603	BN 17	AHA 6831	BN 15	AHH 7010	BM 2	AKE 3052	BN 11
AHA 6302	BL 6	AHA 6604	BN 17	AHA 6832	BN 15			AKE 3053	BN 7
AHA 6303	BL 6	AHA 6605	BN 17	AHA 6837	BN 15	AJA 5111	BB 4	AKE 3053	BN 11
AHA 6304	BO 3	AHA 6606	BN 17	AHA 6838	BN 15	AJA 5112	BD 2	AKE 3058	BO 4
AHA 6314	BD 2	AHA 6607	BN 17	AHA 6839	BN 15	AJA 5114	BA 5	AKE 3059	BO 4
AHA 6315	BD 2	AHA 6608	BN 17	AHA 6840	BN 15	AJA 5115	BA 5	AKE 3060	BO 4
AHA 6318	BL 6	AHA 6617	BN 17	AHA 6845	BN 7	AJA 6115	BA 5	AKE 3061	BO 4
AHA 6319	BL 6	AHA 6618	BN 17	AHA 6845	BN 11	AJA 5117	BB 4	AKE 3062	BO 4
AHA 6319	BO 6	AHA 6619	BN 17	AHA 6845	BN 15			AKE 3064	BO 4
AHA 6323	BL 6	AHA 6620	BN 17	AHA 6846	BN 7			AKE 3065	BO 4
AHA 6325	BO 3	AHA 6625	BN 17	AHA 6846	BN 11	AJD 7722	BD 3	AKE 3066	BO 4
AHA 6326	BO 3	AHA 6626	BN 17	AHA 6846	BN 15	AJD 7731	BB 3	AKE 3067	BO 4

Part Number Index—*continued*

Part Number	Page
AKE 3068	BO 4
AKE 3069	BO 4
AKE 3070	BO 2
AKE 3071	BO 2
AKE 3072	BO 3
AKE 3073	BO 3
AKE 3182	BO 4
AKE 3242	BO 4
AKE 3285	BO 3
AKE 3286	BO 3
AKE 3287	BO 3
AKE 3288	BO 3
AKE 3289	BO 3
AKE 3290	BO 2
AKE 3291	BO 2
AKE 3292	BO 2
AKE 3293	BO 2
AKE 3294	BO 2
AKE 4407	BO 4
AKE 4408	BO 4
AKE 4730	BN 7
AKE 4730	BN 11
AKE 4731	BN 7
AKE 4731	BN 11
AKE 4732	BO 6
AKE 4733	BO 6
AKE 4734	BN 7
AKE 4734	BN 11
AKE 4735	BN 7
AKE 4735	BN 11
AKE 4736	BN 7
AKE 4736	BN 11
AKE 4737	BO 3
AKE 4738	BO 4
AKE 4739	BO 4
AKE 4740	BO 4
AKE 4741	BN 10
AKE 5125	BO 4
AKE 5126	BO 4
AKE 5127	BO 4
AKE 5128	BO 4
AKE 5129	BO 5
AKE 5130	BO 5
AKE 5131	BO 5
AKE 5132	BO 5
AKE 5204	BO 5
AKE 5205	BO 5
AKE 5206	BO 5
AKE 5207	BO 5
ALA 1716	BB 2
ALA 2466	BD 2
ALA 3647	BC 2
ALA 3647	BF 2
ALH 2573	BD 2
ARA 113	BJ 2
ARA 226	BJ 2
ARA 249	BJ 2
ARA 1198	BJ 2
ARA 1205	BJ 2
ARA 1206	BJ 2
ARA 1207	BJ 2
ARA 1208	BJ 2
ARA 1209	BJ 2
ARA 1210	BJ 2
ARA 1211	BJ 2
ARA 1212	BJ 2
ARA 1215	BJ 2
ARA 1216	BJ 2
ARA 1218	BJ 2
ARA 1259	BJ 2
ARA 2070	BJ 2
ARH 596	BJ 2
AWZ 105	BB 3
4B 6821	BG 2
4B 8646	BB 4
4B 9713	BP 2

Part Number	Page
4B 9713	BP 4
11B 5721	BK 3
11B 5721	BK 4
14B 720	BB 4
14B 1729	BM 2
14B 1730	BL 2
14B 1917	BP 3
14B 1917	BP 4
14B 2685	BA 7
14B 2685	BK 4
14B 5862	BH 5
14B 7889	BG 2
14B 7889	BG 3
14B 7889	BG 4
24B 540	BL 5
24B 540	BL 6
BCA 4590	BC 2
BHA 4066	BH 5
BHA 4082	BC 2
BHA 4082	BD 2
BHA 4082	BJ 2
BHA 4205	BP 2
BHA 4207	BP 4
BHA 4219	BN 7
BHA 4219	BN 11
BHA 4245	BP 2
BHA 4246	BP 4
BHA 4251	BA 7
BHA 4361	BH 4
BHA 4426	BJ 2
BHA 4536	BA 4
BHA 4536	BA 7
BMK 924	BP 3
BNK 1500	BP 3
CFP 625	BA 7
CMC 0308	BN 10
CMZ 0203	BH 2
CMZ 0204	BG 2
CMZ 0308	BN 2
CMZ 0308	BN 6
CMZ 0308	BN 10
CMZ 0410	BF 2
CMZ 0410	BO 5
CNZ 102	BB 4
CNZ 102	BD 3
CNZ 102	BM 2
CRS 0206	BB 3
CRS 0410	BO 5
CTZ 604	BN 5
CTZ 604	BN 9
CTZ 604	BN 13
CTZ 604	BN 17
5D 4199	BN 18
5D 4230	BN 18
DMP 0721	BC 2
DMP 0721	BF 2
DMP 0819	BJ 2
DMP 0829	BJ 2
DMP 0835	BN 3
DMP 0835	BN 8
DMP 0835	BN 11
8F 2408	BL 2
8F 2409	BL 2
FNZ 103	BA 6
FNZ 103	BB 2
FNZ 103	BB 3

Part Number	Page
FNZ 103	BB 4
FNZ 103	BC 2
FNZ 103	BF 2
FNZ 103	BH 4
FNZ 103	BJ 2
FNZ 103	BK 2
FNZ 103	BL 2
FNZ 103	BL 5
FNZ 103	BN 2
FNZ 103	BN 6
FNZ 103	BN 10
FNZ 103	BN 14
FNZ 103	BP 3
FNZ 103	BP 4
FNZ 104	BB 3
FNZ 104	BC 2
FNZ 104	BH 4
FNZ 104	BJ 2
FNZ 104	BK 2
FNZ 104	BK 3
FNZ 104	BK 4
FNZ 104	BM 2
FNZ 104	BO 5
FNZ 104	BP 3
FNZ 104	BP 4
FNZ 105	BB 2
FNZ 105	BD 2
FNZ 105	BK 4
FNZ 105	BH 2
FNZ 106	BK 2
FNZ 106	BK 3
FNZ 106	BK 4
FNZ 108	BK 3
FNZ 205	BB 4
FNZ 206	BB 4
FRS 0408	BO 5
FWP 106	BL 5
FWP 106	BL 6
FWP 106	BN 2
FWP 106	BN 3
FWP 106	BN 5
FWP 106	BN 6
FWP 106	BN 7
FWP 106	BN 8
FWP 106	BN 10
FWP 106	BN 11
FWP 106	BN 12
FWP 106	BN 16
FWP 108	BN 3
FWP 108	BN 8
FWP 108	BN 11
FWP 110	BN 2
FWP 110	BN 6
FWP 110	BN 10
FWP 606	BN 16
FWP 906	BN 14
FWP 906	BN 15
FWP 908	BN 16
FWZ 106	BN 11
1G 9872	BK 2
4G 870	BO 5
4G 877	BO 5
4G 878	BO 5
4G 1588	BB 4
4G 1851	BA 4
4G 1851	BA 7
4G 2494	BB 4
4G 2541	BA 4
4G 2541	BA 7
4G 3035	BB 4
4G 3676	BB 4
4G 4920	BA 4
4G 4920	BA 7
4G 6957	BA 4
4G 6957	BA 7
4G 8621	BB 4
4G 9763	BA 4
4G 9763	BA 7

Part Number	Page
8G 531	BP 2
8G 9044	BP 2
8G 9110	BL 3
8G 9111	BL 3
8G 9112	BL 3
8G 9113	BL 3
8G 9114	BL 3
8G 9115	BL 3
8G 9176	BL 3
8G 9177	BL 3
14G 800	BP 3
14G 800	BP 4
14G 2444	BB 4
14G 3499	BP 3
14G 5716	BN 3
14G 5716	BN 8
14G 5716	BN 12
14G 5716	BN 16
14G 6451	BP 2
14G 6451	BP 4
14G 8736	BN 4
14G 8736	BN 5
14G 8736	BN 9
14G 8736	BN 13
14G 8736	BN 17
18G 8445	BH 2
24G 1052	BB 4
24G 1482	BP 2
24G 1482	BP 4
28G 102	BA 3
28G 103	BA 3
28G 104	BA 3
28G 105	BA 3
28G 106	BA 3
28G 118	BA 6
28G 119	BA 3
28G 119	BA 6
28G 120	BA 3
28G 120	BA 6
28G 121	BA 3
28G 121	BA 6
28G 122	BA 3
28G 122	BA 6
28G 123	BA 3
28G 124	BA 2
88G 221	BP 2
2H 3466	BP 2
2H 5133	BG 2
2H 5134	BG 2
2H 6136	BN 17
2H 8198	BA 4
2H 8198	BA 7
2H 8445	BN 4
2H 8445	BN 5
2H 8445	BN 9
2H 8445	BN 13
2H 8445	BN 17
3H 2615	BB 4
7H 9785	BH 3
7H 9866	BG 2
13H 51	BP 3
13H 53	BP 3
13H 54	BP 2
13H 55	BP 2
13H 56	BP 4
13H 57	BP 4
13H 58	BP 3
13H 58	BP 4
13H 59	BP 3
13H 206	BH 3
13H 231	BH 3
13H 231	BH 4
13H 4014	BN 3
13H 4014	BN 8

Part Number	Page
13H 4014	BN 12
13H 4014	BN 16
17H 577	BH 3
17H 578	BH 3
17H 579	BH 3
17H 819	BP 3
17H 823	BP 2
17H 823	BP 4
17H 824	BP 2
17H 824	BP 4
17H 825	BP 2
17H 825	BP 4
17H 1453	BP 3
17H 1455	BP 3
17H 1574	BP 3
17H 1590	BP 2
17H 1591	BP 2
17H 1592	BP 2
17H 1593	BP 2
17H 1594	BP 2
17H 1595	BP 2
17H 1596	BP 2
17H 1597	BP 3
17H 1601	BP 2
17H 1601	BP 4
17H 1602	BP 2
17H 1603	BP 2
17H 1603	BP 4
17H 1604	BP 4
17H 1605	BP 4
17H 1607	BP 4
17H 1608	BP 4
17H 1609	BP 4
17H 2670	BH 4
17H 2672	BH 4
17H 6836	BP 3
17H 8108	BP 3
17H 8146	BH 5
17H 8147	BH 5
17H 8148	BH 5
17H 9996	BH 3
17H 9997	BH 3
27H 168	BP 3
27H 602	BP 2
27H 1198	BP 4
27H 2114	BL 5
27H 2115	BG 4
27H 2116	BN 16
27H 9598	BL 5
27H 9607	BK 2
27H 9608	BK 2
27H 9609	BK 2
27H 9610	BK 2
27H 9611	BK 2
27H 9612	BK 2
27H 9613	BK 2
27H 9623	BH 3
27H 9623	BH 4
27H 9625	BH 3
27H 9625	BH 4
27H 9626	BH 3
27H 9654	BH 3
27H 9655	BH 3
27H 9655	BH 4
27H 9657	BH 3
27H 9657	BH 4
27H 9662	BH 3
27H 9781	BH 5
27H 9782	BH 5
27H 9863	BH 5
37H 537	BP 2
37H 2506	BF 2
37H 9708	BH 3
37H 9708	BH 4
37H 9715	BH 3
37H 9719	BH 2
37H 9729	BH 3
37H 9729	BH 4
37H 9730	BH 3
37H 9763	BH 3

Part Number Index—*continued*

Part Number	Page
37H 9797	BL 2
37H 9798	BH 3
37H 9799	BL 5
37H 9800	BL 5
37H 9801	BL 5
37H 9803	BL 5
37H 9871	BK 3
37H 9871	BK 2
37H 9915	BH 5
37H 9917	BH 5
37H 9946	BH 5
37H 9947	BH 5
37H 9951	BN 3
37H 9951	BN 8
37H 9952	BN 3
37H 9952	BN 8
37H 9952	BN 12
37H 9952	BN 16
37H 9953	BN 3
37H 9953	BN 8
37H 9953	BN 12
37H 9953	BN 16
37H 9954	BN 3
37H 9954	BN 12
37H 9967	BH 5
37H 9968	BH 5
37H 9970	BH 5
37H 9971	BH 5
37H 9972	BH 5
37H 9973	BH 5
37H 9974	BH 5
37H 9984	BN 8
37H 9984	BN 12
37H 9984	BN 16
47H 9510	BH 5
47H 9579	BH 5
47H 9601	BL 5
97H 717	BL 3
97H 2679	BH 4
HBZ 0524	BB 2
HBZ 0524	BB 4
HBZ 0532	BL 5
HBZ 0611	BK 3
HBZ 0611	BK 4
HBZ 0612	BK 2
HCS 168	BP 3
HCS 168	BP 4
HCS 368	BP 3
HCS 368	BP 4
HCS 0507	BP 2
HNS 0408	BB 3
HPS 0507	BL 5
HPS 0507	BL 6
HZS 0405	BB 2
HZS 0405	BB 3
HZS 0405	BB 4
HZS 0405	BC 2
HZS 0405	BD 2
HZS 0405	BK 3
HZS 0405	BM 2
HZS 0405	BO 5
HZS 0406	BA 6
HZS 0406	BO 5
HZS 0406	BP 2
HZS 0408	BH 4
HZS 0409	BO 5
HZS 0504	BK 2
HZS 0505	BD 2
HZS 0506	BH 5
HZS 0506	BK 2
HZS 0506	BK 4
HZS 0507	BK 2
HZS 0507	BK 4
HZS 0507	BP 2
HZS 0606	BK 3
HZS 0608	BK 3
HZS 0608	BK 4
2K 4936	BL 2
2K 4936	BL 3
2K 4936	BL 4
2K 9030	BB 3
2K 9679	BK 2
4K 9670	BL 2
4K 9671	BL 2
6K 9833	BB 3
11K 5564	BL 2
24K 2085	BP 3
53K 1016	BB 4
53K 1016	BP 2
53K 1016	BP 4
53K 1420	BD 2
53K 3423	BB 2
53K 3427	BB 2
53K 3427	BL 5
53K 3427	BL 6
54K 3021	BL 6
KMP 0835	BN 15
1AL 102	BN 5
1AL 102	BN 9
1AL 108	BN 9
1AL 108	BN 13
1AL 113	BN 5
1AL 113	BN 18
1AL 252	BN 5
1AL 252	BN 9
1AL 258	BN 18
1AL 276	BN 9
1AL 276	BN 13
1AL 351	BN 5
1AL 351	BN 9
1AL 351	BN 13
1AL 556	BN 9
1AL 556	BN 13
1AL 558	BN 18
1AL 566	BN 5
1AL 566	BN 9
1AL 608	BN 18
1KL 1113	BN 9
1KL 1258	BN 18
1KL 1553	BN 18
1KL 1558	BN 18
1KL 1608	BN 18
LFP 116	BL 4
LFP 116	BO 6
LFS 100	BL 2
LFS 100	BL 3
LFS 107	BL 2
LFS 107	BL 3
LNZ 105	BB 2
LNZ 105	BB 4
LNZ 205	BB 2
LNZ 205	BD 3
LWN 403	BF 2
LWN 406	BH 3
LWN 406	BH 4
LWZ 202	BB 4
LWZ 202	BD 3
LWZ 202	BM 2
LWZ 203	BA 6
LWZ 203	BB 2
LWZ 203	BB 3
LWZ 203	BB 4
LWZ 203	BC 2
LWZ 203	BD 2
LWZ 203	BF 2
LWZ 203	BG 2
LWZ 203	BG 3
LWZ 203	BG 4
LWZ 203	BH 4
LWZ 203	BJ 2
LWZ 203	BK 2
LWZ 203	BL 2
LWZ 203	BL 4
LWZ 203	BL 5
LWZ 203	BN 2
LWZ 203	BN 6
LWZ 203	BN 10
LWZ 203	BN 14
LWZ 203	BP 3
LWZ 203	BP 4
LWZ 204	BA 4
LWZ 204	BA 6
LWZ 204	BA 7
LWZ 204	BB 2
LWZ 204	BB 3
LWZ 204	BB 4
LWZ 204	BC 2
LWZ 204	BD 2
LWZ 204	BH 4
LWZ 204	BJ 2
LWZ 204	BK 2
LWZ 204	BK 3
LWZ 204	BK 4
LWZ 204	BL 5
LWZ 204	BL 6
LWZ 204	BM 2
LWZ 204	BO 5
LWZ 204	BP 2
LWZ 204	BP 4
LWZ 205	BA 7
LWZ 205	BD 2
LWZ 205	BH 2
LWZ 205	BK 2
LWZ 205	BK 4
LWZ 205	BL 5
LWZ 205	BL 6
LWZ 206	BB 4
LWZ 206	BK 2
LWZ 206	BK 3
LWZ 206	BK 4
LWZ 208	BK 3
LWZ 305	BB 3
LWZ 306	BK 2
LWZ 404	BF 2
LWZ 503	BN 2
LWZ 503	BN 6
LWZ 503	BN 10
LWZ 503	BN 14
LWZ 504	BF 2
PCR 0307	BB 4
PCR 0407	BH 4
PCR 0409	BH 4
PCR 0709	BN 3
PCR 0709	BN 8
PCR 0709	BN 12
PCR 0809	BP 2
PFS 103	BD 2
PFS 104	BA 4
PFS 303	BJ 2
PJZ 602	BP 2
PJZ 804	BJ 2
PMN 0408	BF 2
PMP 0516	BD 3
PMZ 204	BA 5
PMZ 0208	BM 2
PMZ 0210	BD 3
PMZ 0305	BL 2
PMZ 0306	BA 6
PMZ 0306	BB 3
PMZ 0306	BB 4
PMZ 0306	BH 4
PMZ 0306	BK 2
PMZ 0308	BB 3
PMZ 0308	BB 4
PMZ 0308	BD 2
PMZ 0308	BF 2
PMZ 0310	BP 3
PMZ 0310	BP 4
PMZ 0312	BL 5
PMZ 0314	BG 2
PMZ 0314	BG 3
PMZ 0314	BG 4
PMZ 0328	BB 2
PMZ 0407	BP 3
PMZ 0408	BA 4
PMZ 0408	BA 7
PMZ 0408	BB 3
PMZ 0408	BJ 2
PMZ 0408	BP 2
PMZ 0408	BP 3
PMZ 0408	BP 4
PMZ 0410	BJ 2
PMZ 0410	BK 2
PMZ 0410	BK 3
PMZ 0410	BM 2
PMZ 0412	BK 2
PMZ 0412	BK 4
PTP 603	BP 3
PTZ 603	BD 3
PTZ 603	BN 16
PTZ 603	BP 3
PTZ 605	BB 2
PTZ 804	BL 2
PTZ 805	BL 2
PTZ 806	BO 6
PWP 105	BL 5
PWP 105	BL 6
PWZ 102	BB 2
PWZ 103	BB 3
PWZ 103	BB 4
PWZ 103	BD 2
PWZ 103	BG 2
PWZ 103	BG 3
PWZ 103	BG 4
PWZ 103	BL 5
PWZ 103	BN 10
PWZ 103	BN 14
PWZ 103	BP 3
PWZ 103	BP 4
PWZ 104	BA 4
PWZ 104	BA 6
PWZ 104	BB 2
PWZ 104	BB 3
PWZ 104	BB 4
PWZ 104	BC 2
PWZ 104	BD 3
PWZ 104	BJ 2
PWZ 104	BM 2
PWZ 104	BO 5
PWZ 104	BP 2
PWZ 104	BP 4
PWZ 105	BA 7
PWZ 105	BB 3
PWZ 105	BB 4
PWZ 105	BD 3
PWZ 105	BK 2
PWZ 105	BK 4
PWZ 106	BK 2
PWZ 106	BK 3
PWZ 106	BK 4
PWZ 203	BB 2
PWZ 208	BK 2
PWZ 203	BL 2
PWZ 203	BN 2
PWZ 203	BN 3
PWZ 203	BN 6
PWZ 203	BN 8
PWZ 203	BN 10
PWZ 203	BN 12
PWZ 203	BN 14
PWZ 203	BN 16
PWZ 204	BA 4
PWZ 204	BA 7
PWZ 204	BM 2
PWZ 205	BH 2
PWZ 205	BH 5
PWZ 205	BO 5
PWZ 206	BL 5
PWZ 208	BK 3
PZZ 606	BJ 2
RFN 103	BB 4
RFN 204	BJ 2
RFN 206	BA 4
RFN 206	BA 7
RFN 210	BA 4
RFN 210	BA 7
RFN 216	BA 7
RFN 218	BA 4
RFN 220	BA 7
RFN 266	BA 5
RFR 207	BA 7
RMP 0308	BH 5
RMP 2312	BN 16
RMZ 0307	BH 2
RMZ 0308	BH 2
RMZ 0310	BN 2
RMZ 0310	BN 3
RMZ 0310	BN 6
RMZ 0310	BN 8
RMZ 0310	BN 10
RMZ 0310	BN 12
RMZ 0312	BG 3
RMZ 0312	BN 2
RMZ 0312	BN 6
RMZ 0312	BN 8
RMZ 0312	BN 10
RMZ 0312	BN 12
RMZ 0316	BN 2
RMZ 0316	BN 6
RMZ 0316	BN 10
RTP 403	BL 5
RTP 403	BL 6
RTP 603	BO 6
RTP 604	BL 4
RTP 2604	BN 14
RTP 2604	BN 15
RTP 2606	BN 15
RTP 2606	BN 16
RTZ 604	BN 2
RTZ 604	BN 5
RTZ 604	BN 6
RTZ 604	BN 7
RTZ 604	BN 10
RTZ 604	BN 11
RTZ 606	BN 2
RTZ 606	BN 3
RTZ 606	BN 7
RTZ 606	BN 8
RTZ 606	BN 11
RTZ 606	BN 12
RTZ 606	BN 16
RTZ 608	BN 7
RTZ 608	BN 11
TFP 1006	BL 2
TFS 106	BL 2
TFS 106	BL 3
7699	BN 3
7699	BN 8
7699	BN 11
7700	BN 2
7700	BN 3
7700	BN 5
7700	BN 6
7700	BN 7
7700	BN 8
7700	BN 10
7700	BN 11
7700	BN 12

BODY SHELL

SPRITE H-AN5

	Page	Plate
BODY SHELL	BA 2	A 1
PANEL ASSEMBLY—BODY REAR	BA 2	A 1
UNDERFRAME	BA 3	A 2
WINGS—REAR	BA 2	A 1

SPRITE MK. II AND MIDGET MK. I

BODY SHELL	BA 5	A 4
FRONT END	BA 6	A 5
PANEL ASSEMBLY—BODY REAR	BA 5	A 4
SHIELD—MUD	BA 6	A 5
UNDERFRAME	BA 6	A 5
WINGS—REAR	BA 5	A 4

† Revised Information.

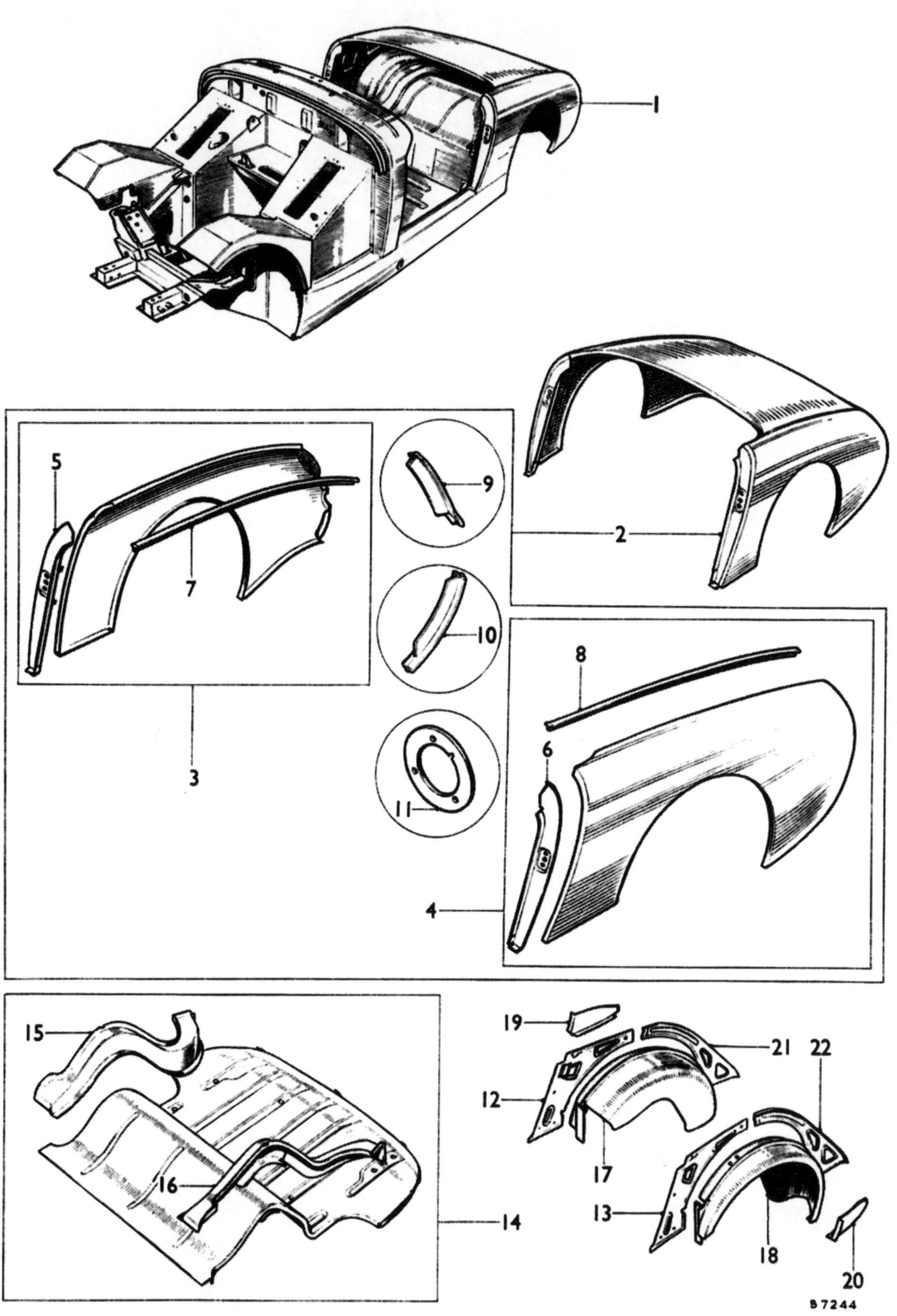
1
2
3
4
5
6
7
8
9
10
11
12
13
14
15
16
17
18
19
20
21
22
B7244

DESCRIPTION	Part No.	Illus. No.	Quantity	Change Point	REMARKS
BODY SHELL					
(SPRITE H-AN5)					
Body shell and underframe assembly—primed (less doors and bonnet)	AHA 5145	1	1		Not available; use 28G 124
Body shell and underframe assembly—primed (less doors and bonnet)	28G 124	1	1		When supplying AHA 5145 or 28G 124 prior to (C) H-AN5-4333 supply also exhaust pipe AHA 5360, 1 off bracket AHA 5361, 2 off clip AHA 5221, 4 off bolt HBZ 0626, 2 off shock absorber link AHA 5446, 1 off bracket AHA 5305, 1 off bracket AHA 5306, 2 off bolt HBZ 0630, 2 off bolt HBZ 0612, 4 off nut LNZ 106, 4 off washer PWZ 106, 4 off washer LWZ 306, and wheel arch and heelboard liners (see page BN 4 for details). When supplying AHA 5145 or 28G 124 prior to (C) H-AN5-5477 supply also exhaust pipe AHA 5360, 1 off bracket AHA 5361, 2 off clip AHA 5221, and 4 off bolt HBZ 0626
Panel assembly—body rear	AHA 5179	2	1		
Wing assembly—rear—RH	AHA 5182	3	1		
Wing assembly—rear—LH	AHA 5183	4	1		
'B' post—RH	AHA 5184	5	1		
'B' post—LH	AHA 5185	6	1		
Moulding—rear wing to panel—top—RH	14A 4769	7	1		
Moulding—rear wing to panel—top—LH	14A 4770	8	1		
Moulding—rear wing to panel—intermediate	14A 4771	9	2		
Moulding—lower—rear	14A 4772	10	2		
Filler—lamp	14A 4606	11	2		
Reinforcement—'B' post to wheel arch RH	14A 89	12	1		
Reinforcement—'B' post to wheel arch—LH	14A 90	13	1		
Panel assembly—luggage floor	AHA 5147	14	1		
Reinforcement—wheel arch to luggage floor—RH	AHA 5283	15	1		
Reinforcement—wheel arch to luggage floor—LH	AHA 5284	16	1		
Panel					
Wheel arch—rear—RH	AHA 5148	17	1		
Wheel arch—rear—LH	AHA 5149	18	1		
Luggage floor to wing—RH	14A 4611	19	1		
Luggage floor to wing—LH	14A 4612	20	1		
Gusset—wheel arch to luggage floor—rear—RH	AHA 5291	21	1		
Gusset—wheel arch to luggage floor—rear—LH	AHA 5292	22	1		

† Revised Information.

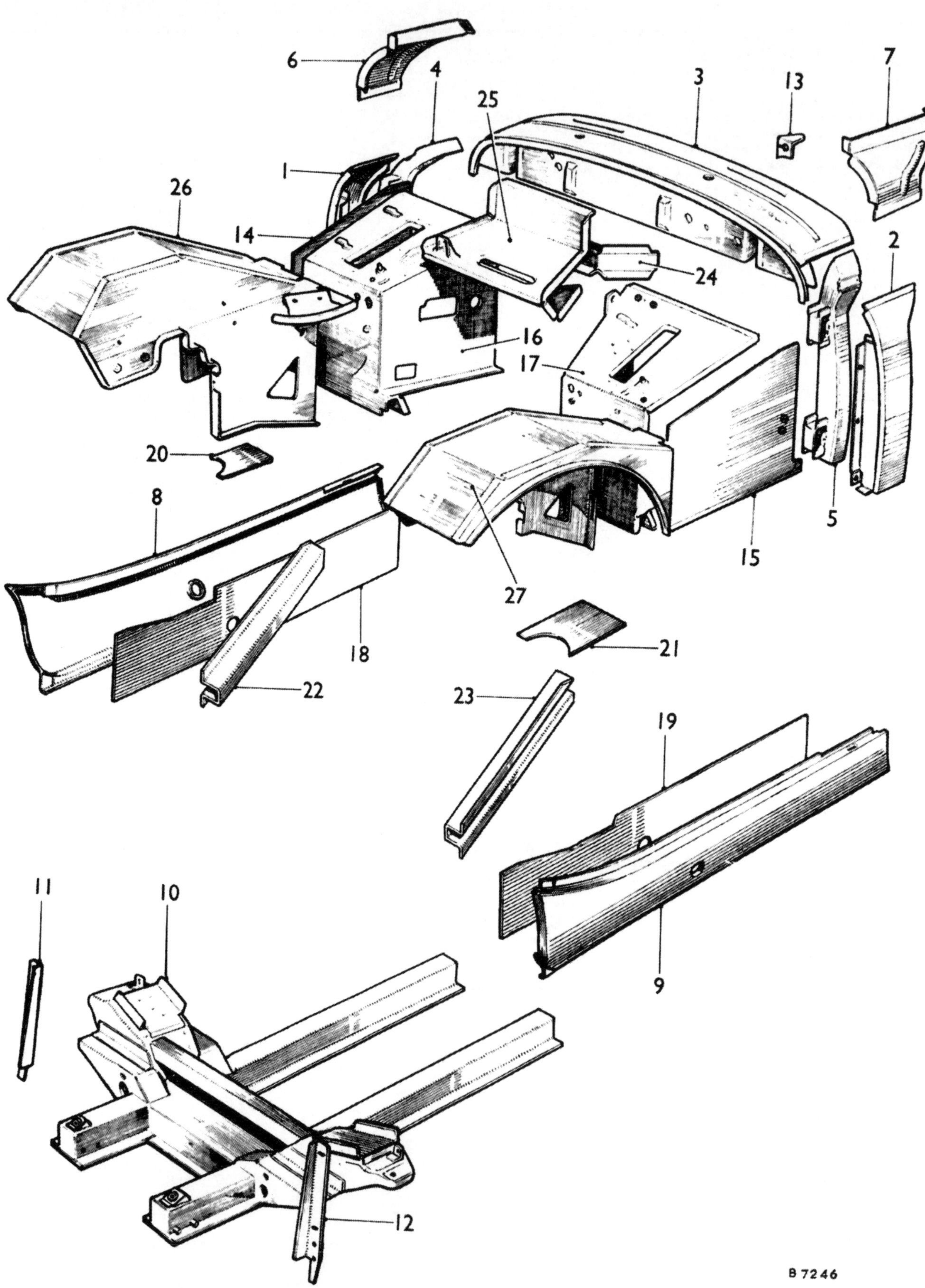
6
4
25
3
13
7
1
26
14
24
2
16
17
20
8
5
27
15
18
21
22
23
19
11
10
9
12
B 7246

DESCRIPTION	Part No.	Illus. No.	Quantity	Change Point	REMARKS
Body Shell—*continued*					
(Sprite H-AN5)—*continued*					
Panel					
Shroud—side—RH	AHA 5174	1	1		
Shroud—side—LH	AHA 5175	2	1		W.S.E. use AHA 5555
Shroud—side—LH	AHA 5555	2	1		
Shroud and dash top	AHA 5173	3	1		W.S.E. use 28G 123
Shroud and dash top	28G 123	3	1		
'A' post—RH	AHA 5176	4	1		
'A' post—LH	AHA 5177	5	1		
Extension—'A' post to scuttle—RH	14A 4635	6	1		
Extension—'A' post to scuttle—LH	14A 4636	7	1		
Sill—outer—RH	14A 4593	8	1		W.S.E. use AHA 5552
Sill—outer—RH	AHA 5552	8	1		
Sill—outer—LH	14A 4594	9	1		W.S.E. use AHA 5553
Sill—outer—LH	AHA 5553	9	1		
Underframe assembly	NSP		1		
Front suspension and main beam	28G 102	10	1		
Bracket					
Radiator mounting—RH	2A 5612	11	1		
Radiator mounting—LH	2A 5465	12	1	(C) H-AN5-501 to 6489	W.S.E. use AHA 5390
Radiator mounting—LH	AHA 5390	12	1	(C) H-AN5-6490 on	
Hand brake abutment	2A 5509	13	1		
Panel—foot-well					
Outer—RH	2A 5527	14	1		
Outer—LH	2A 5528	15	1		
Front and inner—RH	28G 103	16	1		W.S.E. use 28G 121
Front and inner—LH	28G 104	17	1		W.S.E. use 28G 122
Front and inner—RH	28G 121	16	1		
Front and inner—LH	28G 122	17	1		
Plate					
Sill side—RH	AHA 5299	18	1		W.S.E. use AHA 6216
Sill side—RH	AHA 6216	18	1		
Sill side—LH	AMA 5300	19	1		W.S.E. use AHA 6217
Sill side—LH	AHA 6217	19	1		
Splash—RH	AHA 5465	20	1	(C) H-AN5-5477 on, (plus 5137, 5287, and 5288)	
Splash—LH	AHA 5466	21	1	(C) H-AN5-5477 on, (plus 5137, 5287, and 5288)	
Strut—front suspension—RH	2A 5558	22	1	(C) H-AN5-501 to 5476 (less 5137, 5287, and 5288)	
Strut—front suspension—LH	2A 5557	23	1	(C) H-AN5-501 to 5476 (less 5137, 5287, and 5288)	
Support—heater platform	2A 5524	24	1		
Platform—heater	2A 5533	25	1		
Wheel arch—front					
Right-hand	†28G 105	26			W.S.E. use 28G 119
Right-hand	†28G 119	26			
Left-hand	†28G 106	27			W.S.E. use 28G 120
Left-hand	†28G 120	27			

† Revised Information.

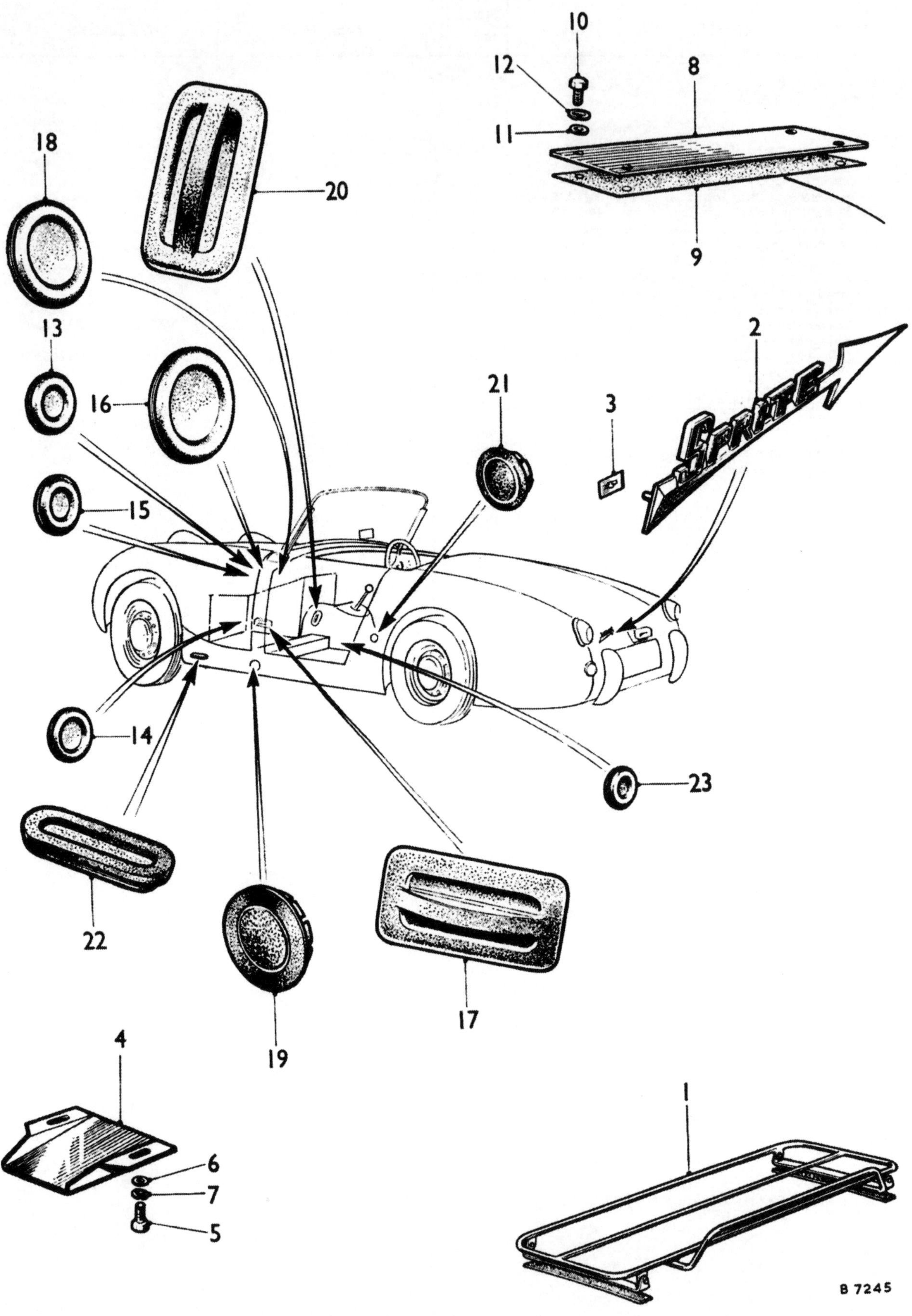
10
12
8
11
18
20
9
2
13
21
3
16
15
14
23
22
17
19
4
6
7
5
1
B 7245

DESCRIPTION	Part No.	Illus. No.	Quantity	Change Point	REMARKS
Body Shell—*continued*					
(Sprite H-AN5)—*continued*					
Kit—luggage grid	AHA 5467	1	1	(C) H-AN5-4685 on (plus 4333 to 4470, 4472 to 4621, 4623 to 4679, and 4681 to 4683)	
Flash—'Sprite'	14A 4859	2	1		
Push-on-fix	PFS 104	3	2		
Plate—cover—engine undershield—RH	AHA 5210	4	1	(C) H-AN5-501 to 5476 (less 5137, 5287, and 5288)	
Screw	PMZ 0408	5	2	(C) H-AN5-501 to 5476 (less 5137, 5287, and 5288)	
Washer—plain	PWZ 104	6	2	(C) H-AN5-501 to 5476 (less 5137, 5287, and 5288)	
Washer—spring	LWZ 204	7	2	(C) H-AN5-501 to 5476 (less 5137, 5287, and 5288)	
Plate—blanking—mounting platform hole	14A 4790	8	1		Required when heater or fresh-air unit is not fitted
Seal—plate	14A 4791	9	1		Required when heater or fresh-air unit is not fitted
Screw	PMZ 0408	10	4		Required when heater or fresh-air unit is not fitted
Washer—plain	PWZ 204	11	4		Required when heater or fresh-air unit is not fitted
Washer—spring	LWZ 204	12	4		Required when heater or fresh-air unit is not fitted
Plug—blanking					
Dash	RFN 210	13	1		Required when tachometer is not fitted
Dash	4G 2541	14	1		To be pierced when heater is fitted
Foot-well top panel—LH	RFN 210	15	1		
Demister elbow hole	4G 9763	16	2		Required when heater is not fitted
Toebox side—RH	4G 4920	17	1		
Steering column hole	RFN 218	18	1	(C) H-AN5-501 to 7432	
Steering column hole	†AHA 5437	18	1	(C) H-AN5-7433 on	W.S.E. use BHA 4536
Steering column hole	†BHA 4536	18	1	(C) H-AN5-7433 on	
Sill outer panel	2H 8198	19	2		
Gearbox filler hole	4G 4920	20	1		
Propeller shaft oiling hole	4G 1851	21	1		
Slinging hole in floor	4G 6957	22	2		
Hole in rear cross-member panel	RFN 206	23	2	(C) H-AN5-5321 on	
Sealer—Prestik—½" × $\frac{1}{16}$" (12·7 mm × 1·6 mm)	NSP		A/R		Was ADE 1596
Sealer—Prestik—⅛" (3·2 mm) dia	NSP		A/R		Was ADE 1600
Seal-a-Strip—⅛" (3·2 mm) dia	NSP		A/R		Was ADE 1584

† Revised Information.

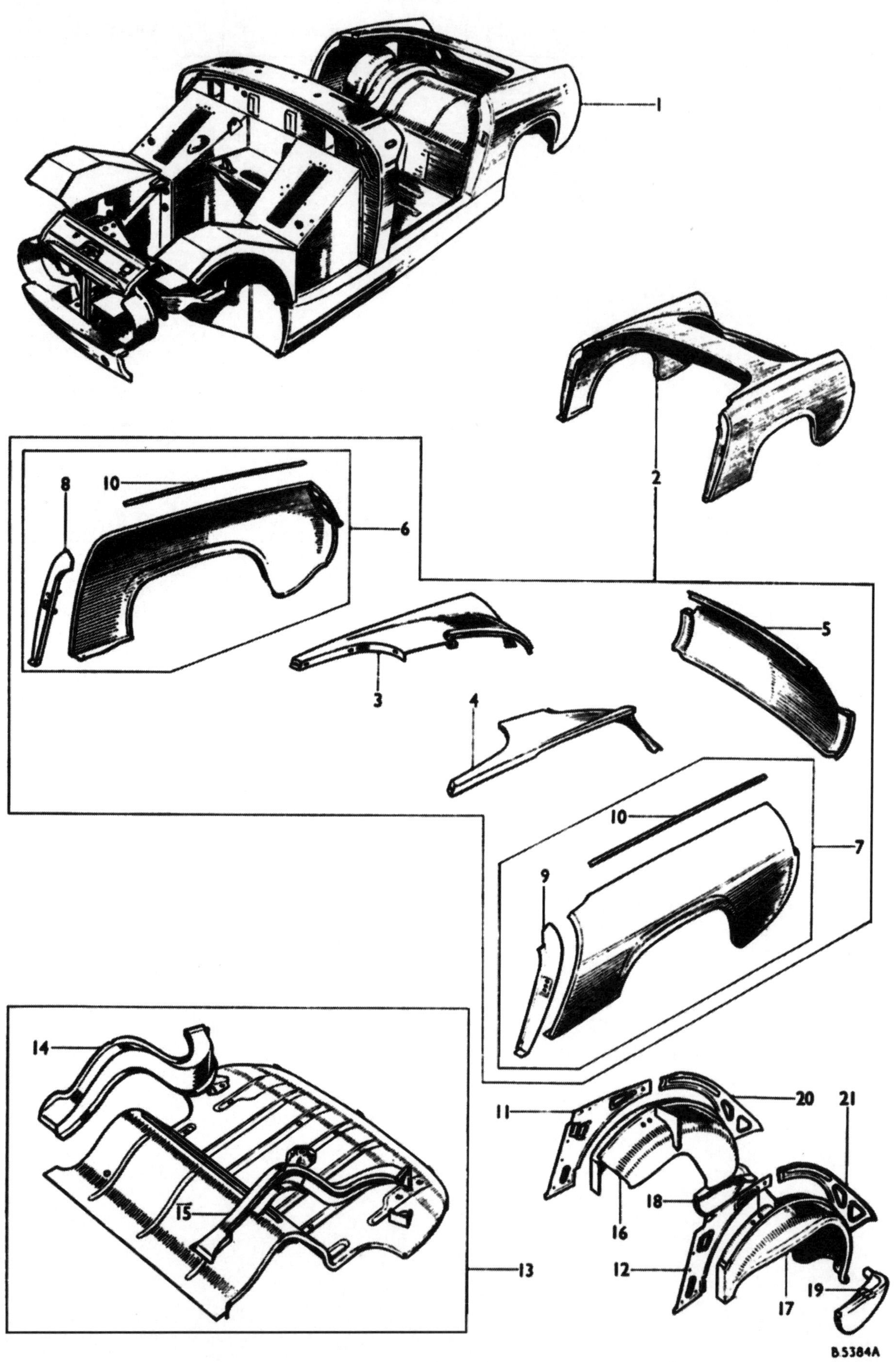
1
2
3
4
5
6
7
8
9
10
10
11
12
13
14
15
16
17
18
19
20
21
B5384A

DESCRIPTION	Part No.	Illus. No.	Quantity	Change Point	REMARKS
Body Shell—*continued*					
(SPRITE MK. II AND MIDGET)					
Body shell and underframe assembly—primed (less boot lid, bonnet top, doors, and front wings)	AHA 5541	1	1		
Panel assembly—body rear	AHA 5749	2	1		Not available; use AJA 5114
Panel assembly—body rear	AJA 5114	2	1		
Panel					
Wing inner—RH	AHA 5756	3	1		
Wing inner—LH	AHA 5757	4	1		
Body rear—lower	AHA 5750	5	1		
Wing assembly—rear					
Right-hand	AHA 5753	6	1		Not available; use AJA 5115
Right-hand	AJA 5115	6	1		
Left-hand	AHA 5754	7	1		Not available; use AJA 5116
Left-hand	AJA 5116	7	1		
'B' post—RH	AHA 5184	8	1		
'B' post—LH	AHA 5185	9	1		
Moulding—rear wing to panel	AHA 5755	10	2		
Reinforcement—'B' post to wheel arch—RH	AHA 5725	11	1		
Reinforcement—'B' post to wheel arch—LH	AHA 5726	12	1		
Panel assembly—luggage floor	AHA 5733	13	1		
Reinforcement—wheel arch to luggage floor—RH	AHA 5283	14	1		
Reinforcement—wheel arch to luggage floor—LH	AHA 5284	15	1		
Panel					
Wheel arch—rear—RH	AHA 5731	16	1		
Wheel arch—rear—LH	AHA 5732	17	1		
Extension—luggage floor rear—RH	AHA 5837	18	1		
Extension—luggage floor rear—LH	AHA 5838	19	1		
Gusset—wheel arch to luggage floor—rear—RH	AHA 5729	20	1		
Gusset—wheel arch to luggage floor—rear—LH	AHA 5730	21	1		

† Revised Information.

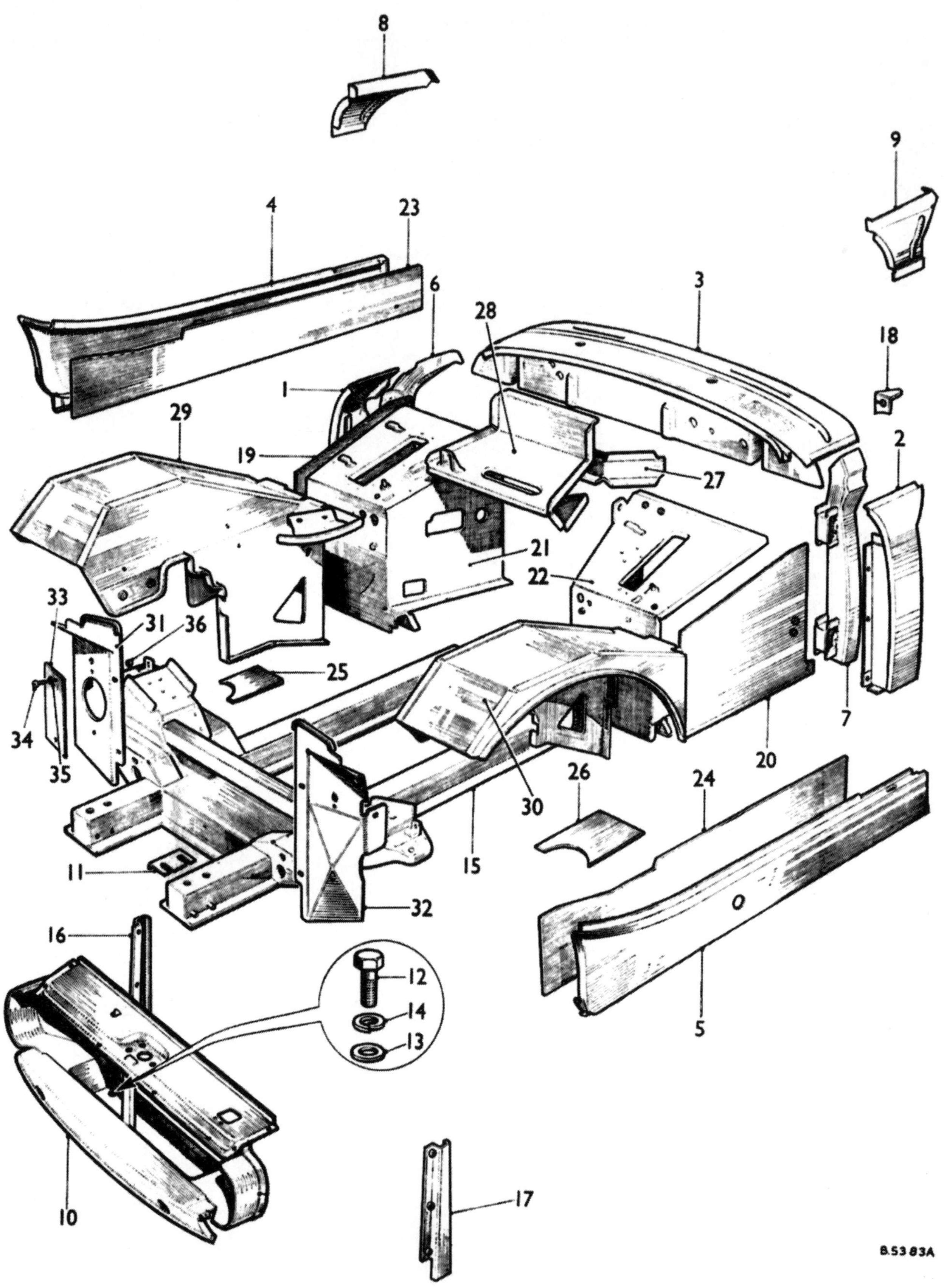
8
9
4
23
6
3
28
1
18
29
2
19
27
21
22
33
31
36
25
34
35
7
20
26
24
30
15
11
32
16
12
14
13
5
10
17
B.5383A

Body Shell—*continued*
(Sprite Mk. II and Midget)—*continued*

DESCRIPTION	Part No.	Illus. No.	Quantity	Change Point	REMARKS
Panel					
Shroud—side—RH	AHA 5554	1	1		
Shroud—side—LH	AHA 5555	2	1		
Shroud and dash top	AHA 5556	3	1		
Sill—outer—RH	AHA 5552	4	1		
Sill—outer—LH	AHA 5553	5	1		
'A' post—RH	AHA 5176	6	1		
'A' post—LH	AHA 5177	7	1		
Extension—'A' post to scuttle—RH	14A 4635	8	1		
Extension—'A' post to scuttle—LH	14A 4636	9	1		
Front end	AHA 5549	10	1		
Shim—front end to underframe	AHA 5642	11	A/R		Maximum of 4 used
Screw	HZS 0406	12	10		
Washer—plain	PWZ 104	13	10		
Washer—spring	LWZ 204	14	10		
Underframe assembly	NSP		1		
Front suspension and main beam	28G 118	15	1		
Bracket					
Radiator mounting—RH	AHA 5624	16	1		
Radiator mounting—LH	AHA 5626	17	1		
Hand brake abutment	2A 5509	18	1		
Panel—foot-well					
Outer—RH	AHA 5620	19	1		
Outer—LH	AHA 5622	20	1		
Front and inner—RH	28G 121	21	1		
Front and inner—LH	28G 122	22	1		
Plate					
Sill side—RH	AHA 6216	23	1		
Sill side—LH	AHA 6217	24	1		
Splash—RH	AHA 5465	25	1		
Splash—LH	AHA 5466	26	1		
Support—heater platform	2A 5524	27	1		
Platform—heater	2A 5533	28	1		
Wheel arch—front—RH	28G 119	29	1		
Wheel arch—front—LH	28G 120	30	1		
Shield—mud					
Right-hand	†AHA 6205	31	1		W.S.E. use AHA 8387
Right-hand	†AHA 8387	31	1		
Left-hand	†AHA 6206	32	1		
Plate—blanking—mudshield	AHA 6223	33	1		Not required when heater is fitted
Screw	PMZ 0306	34	2		
Washer—spring	LWZ 203	35	2		
Nut	FNZ 103	36	2		

† Revised Information.

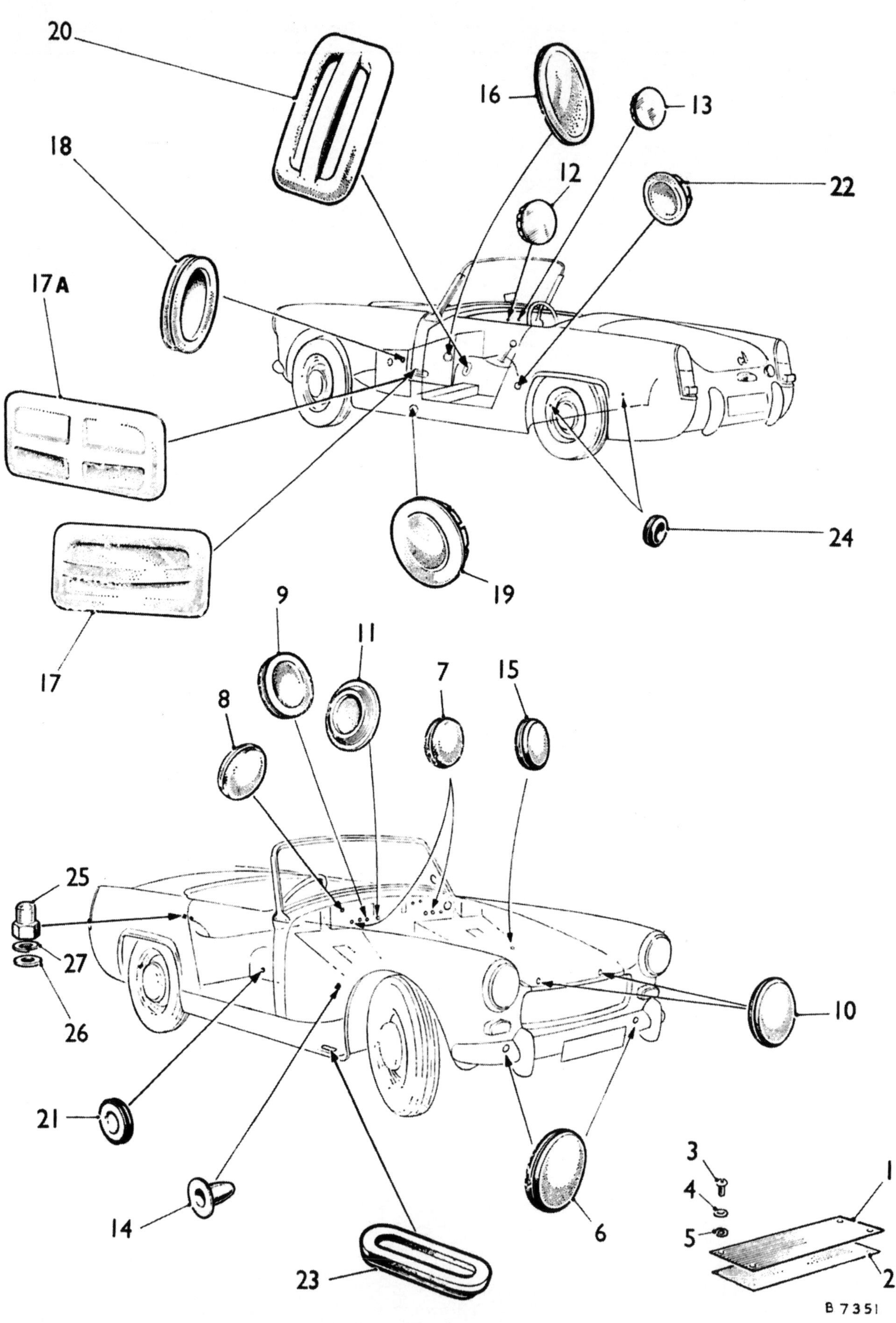
20
16
13
18
12
22
17A
24
19
17
9
11
7
15
8
25
27
10
26
21
3
1
4
5
14
6
2
23
B 7351

DESCRIPTION	Part No.	Illus. No.	Quantity	Change Point	REMARKS
Body Shell—*continued* (Sprite Mk. II and Midget)—*continued*					
Plate—blanking—mounting platform hole	14A 4790	1	1		Required when heater or fresh-air unit is not fitted
Seal—plate	14A 4791	2	1		Required when heater or fresh-air unit is not fitted
Screw	PMZ 0408	3	4		Required when heater or fresh-air unit is not fitted
Washer—plain	PWZ 204	4	4		Required when heater or fresh-air unit is not fitted
Washer—spring	LWZ 204	5	4		Required when heater or fresh-air unit is not fitted
Plug—blanking					
Bumper mounting bracket hole in front end — **Sprite Mk. II**	RFN 220	6	2		Required when front bumper is not fitted
Dash — **Sprite Mk. II**	RFN 210	7	1		Required when tachometer is not fitted
Dash **RHD**	RFN 210	8	1		To be pierced when fresh-air unit is fitted
Dash	4G 2541	9	1		To be pierced when heater is fitted
Mudshield	RFN 216	10	2		
Tachometer cable hole	CFP 625	11	1	(C) H-AN7-24732 on (C) G-AN2-16184 on	
Ignition switch hole	BHA 4251	12	1		Use ACH 9373 for this application — For use when steering lock is fitted
Ignition switch hole	ACH 9373	12	1		Part No. change; was BHA 4416 — For use when steering lock is fitted
Starter control hole	14A 8078	13	1		Part No. change; was BHA 4275 — For use when steering lock is fitted
Foot-well side panel	ADA 2493	14	2		
Foot-well top panel—LH	RFN 210	15	1		
Demister elbow hole	4G 9763	16	2		Required when heater is not fitted
Toebox side—RH	4G 4920	17	1	(C) H-AN6-101 to 11969 (C) G-AN1-101 to 6643	
Toebox side—RH	AHA 6296	17A	1	(C) H-AN6-11970 to 24731 (C) H-AN7-24732 on (C) G-AN1-6644 to 16183 (C) G-AN2-16184 on	
Steering column hole	†AHA 5437	18	1		W.S.E. use BHA 4536
Steering column hole	†BHA 4536	18	1		
Sill outer panel	2H 8198	19	2		
Gearbox filler hole	4G 4920	20	1		
Safety strap hole in tunnel	RFR 207	21	2		
Propeller shaft oiling hole	4G 1851	22	1		
Slinging hole in floor	4G 6957	23	2		
Hole in rear cross-member panel	RFN 206	24	2		
Nut—dome—safety strap weld bolt on rear wheel arch	14B 2685	25	4		
Washer—plain	PWZ 105	26	4		
Washer—spring	LWZ 205	27	4		

† Revised Information.

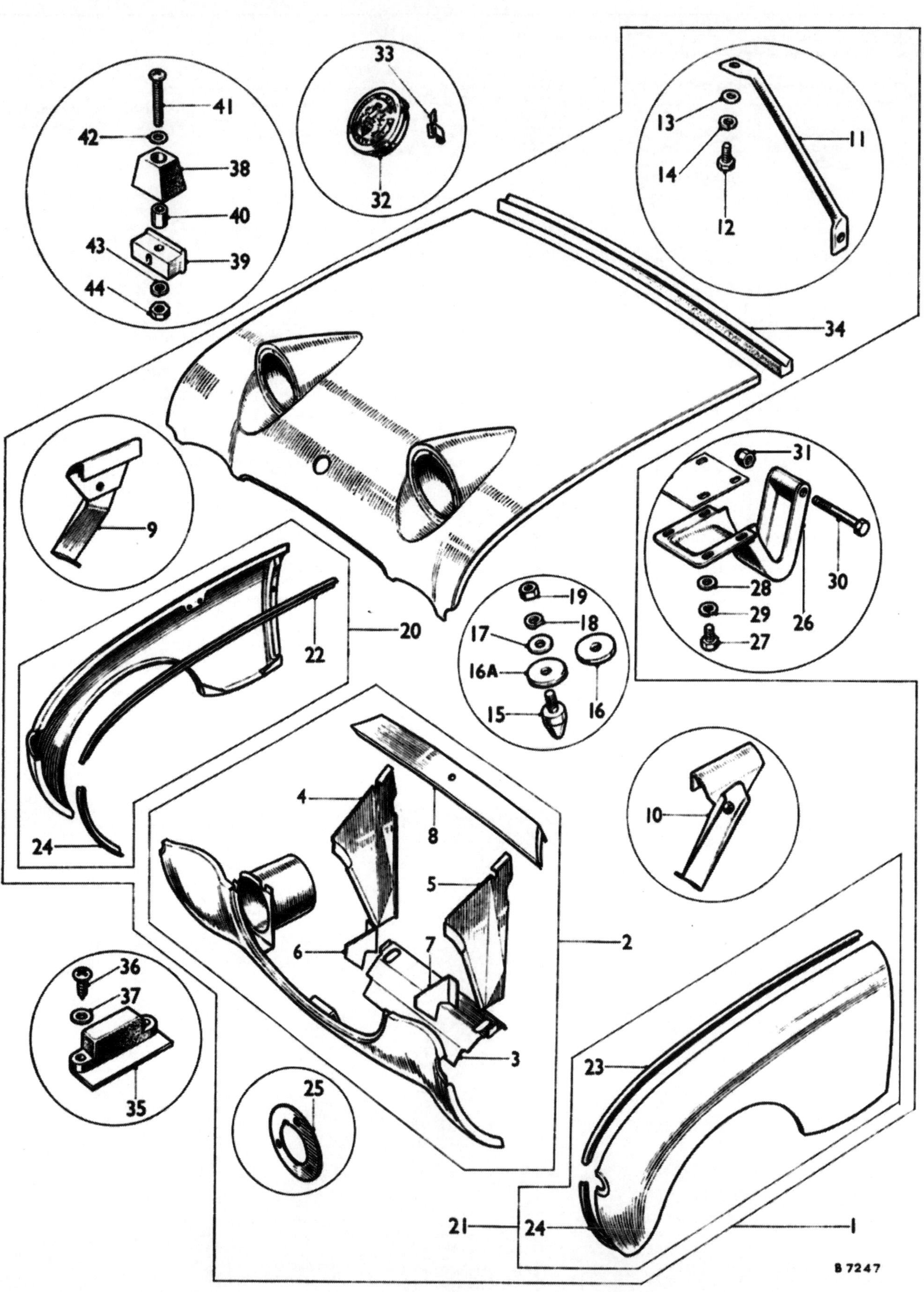
33
41
42
38
40
43
39
44
32
13
11
14
12
34
9
31
30
28
29
26
27
19
18
17
16A
16
15
20
22
24
4
8
5
6
7
2
3
10
36
37
35
25
23
21
24
1
B 7247

BONNET AND WING DETAILS

SPRITE H-AN5

	Page	Plate
BADGE—BONNET	BB 2	B 1
BONNET TOP	BB 2	B 1
CATCH—SAFETY	BB 3	B 2
HANDLE—BONNET RELEASE	BB 3	B 2
HINGE—BONNET	BB 2	B 1
MOULDING—WING	BB 2	B 1
STAY—TELESCOPIC	BB 3	B 2
WING—FRONT	BB 2	B 1

BONNET AND WING DETAILS (SPRITE H-AN5)

DESCRIPTION	Part No.	Illus. No.	Quantity	Change Point	REMARKS
Bonnet assembly	14A 84	1	1		
Panel—bonnet front—bottom	†8G 9044	2	1	(C) H-AN5-501 to 4694	W.S.E. use AHA 5155
Panel—bonnet front—bottom	AHA 5155	2A	1	(C) H-AN5-4695 on	
Panel—air intake					
Lower	AHA 5393	3	1		For vehicles prior to (C) H-AN5-4695 see Austin Service Journal A/55
Side—RH	AHA 5394	4	1		
Side—LH	AHA 5395	5	1		
Front—RH	AHA 5396	6	1		
Front—LH	AHA 5397	7	1		
Channel—support	AHA 5398	8	1		
Bracket—bonnet stay—RH	AHA 5164	9	1		
Bracket—bonnet stay—LH	AHA 5165	10	1		
Strut—bonnet	14A 4776	11	2		
Screw	HZS 0405	12	4		
Washer—plain	PWZ 104	13	4		
Washer—spring	LWZ 204	14	4		
Peg—bonnet locating	14A 4733	15	2		
Washer					
Large—plain	53K 3423	16	2	(C) H-AN5-501 to 9190	
(Rubber)	AHA 5442	16A	2	(C) H-AN5-9191 on	
Small—plain	53K 3427	17	2		
Spring	LWZ 305	18	2		
Nut	FNZ 105	19	2		
Wing assembly—front—RH	AHA 5162	20	1		
Wing assembly—front—LH	AHA 5163	21	1		
Moulding					
Top—RH	14A 4773	22	1		
Top—LH	14A 4774	23	1		
Lower	14A 4775	24	2		
Filler—lamp	14A 4606	25	2		
Hinge—bonnet	14A 4684	26	2		
Packing—hinge	NSP		2		Was 14A 4687
Screw	HZS 0405	27	8		
Washer—plain	PWZ 104	28	8		
Washer—spring	LWZ 204	29	8		
Bolt	HBZ 0524	30	2		
Locknut	LNZ 205	31	2		Use LNZ 105 for this application
Locknut	LNZ 105	31	2		
Badge—bonnet	14A 4898	32	1		
Clip—badge to bonnet	14A 5542	33	3		
Seal—bonnet rear	AHA 5225	34	1		
Buffer—bonnet	14A 4874	35	4		
Screw	PTZ 605	36	8		
Washer—plain	PWZ 102	37	8		
Buffer—bonnet	ALA 1716	38	2	(C) H-AN5-6068 on	
Block—packing	AHA 5400	39	2		
Tube—distance	AHA 5399	40	2		
Screw	PMZ 0328	41	2		
Washer—plain	PWZ 203	42	2		
Washer—spring	LWZ 203	43	2		
Nut	FNZ 103	44	2		

† Revised Information.

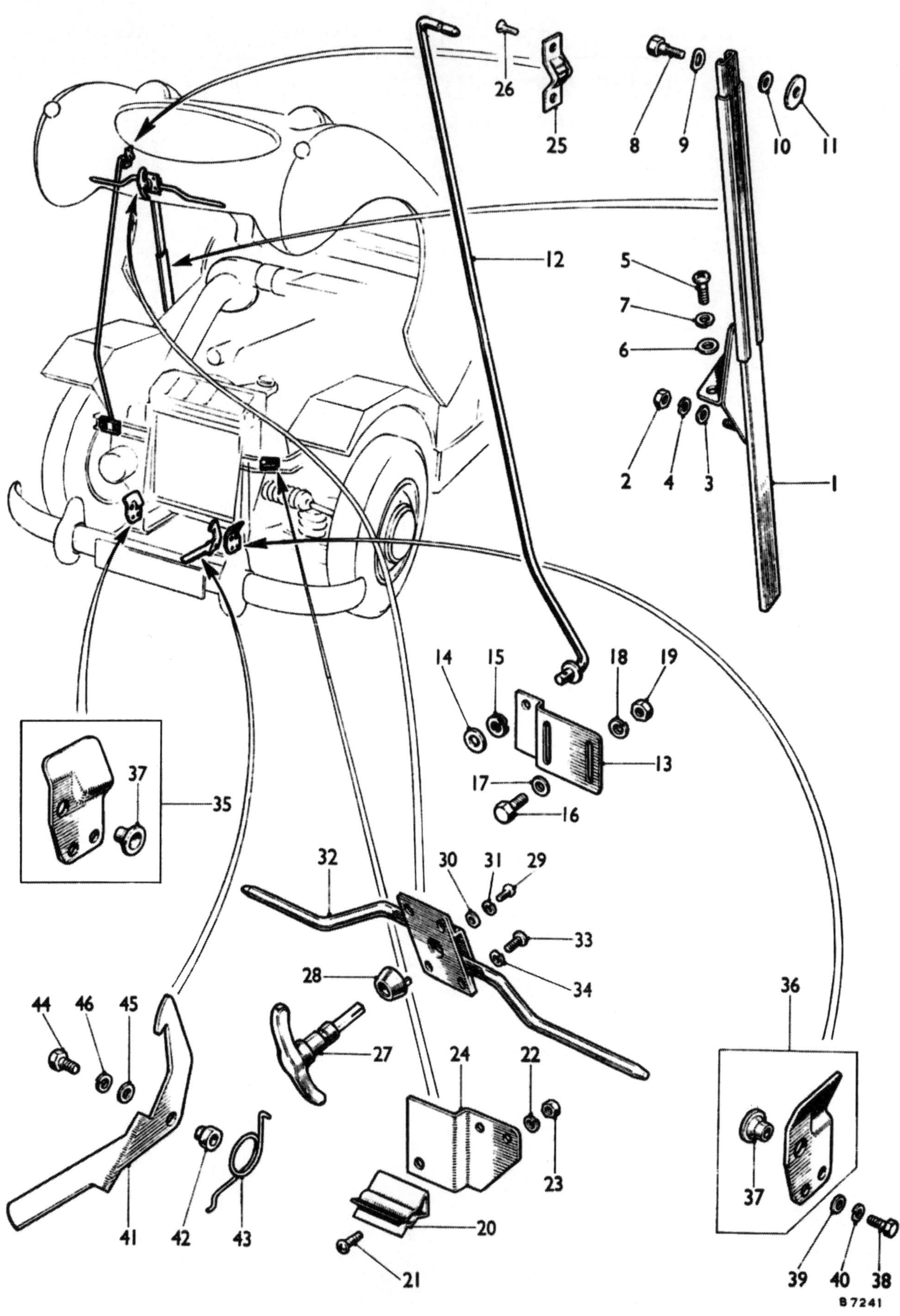
26
25
8
9
10
11
12
5
7
6
2
4
3
1
14
15
18
19
13
17
16
37
35
32
30
31
29
33
34
28
36
44
46
45
27
24
22
23
37
41
42
43
20
21
39
40
38
B 7241

DESCRIPTION	Part No.	Illus. No.	Quantity	Change Point	REMARKS
Bonnet and Wing Details (Sprite H-AN5)—*continued*					
Stay—telescopic—bonnet	14A 4691	1	2		
Nut	FNZ 103	2	2		
Washer—plain	PWZ 103	3	2		
Washer—spring	LWZ 203	4	2		
Screw	PMZ 0408	5	4		
Washer—plain	PWZ 104	6	4		
Washer—spring	LWZ 204	7	4		
Bolt—stay to bonnet	14A 4705	8	2		
Washer					
Anti-rattle	AWZ 105	9	2		
Plain—small	PWZ 105	10	2		
Plain—large	2K 9030	11	2		
Stay—auxiliary—bonnet	AHA 5232	12	1		
Bracket—pivot—stay	AHA 5234	13	1		
Washer—plain	PWZ 105	14	1		
Washer—spring	AJD 7731	15	1		
Screw	HZS 0405	16	1		
Washer—plain	PWZ 104	17	1		
Washer—spring	LWZ 204	18	1		
Nut	FNZ 104	19	1		
Clip—stay	AHH 5460	20	1		
Screw	PMZ 0306	21	2		
Washer—spring	LWZ 203	22	2		
Nut	FNZ 103	23	2		
Bracket—clip	AHA 5233	24	1		
Clip—spring	BNK 1500	25	1		
Rivet	CRS 0206	26	2		
Handle—bonnet release	14A 4891	27	1		
Escutcheon—handle	14A 4892	28	1		
Screw	6K 9833	29	1		
Washer—plain	PWZ 103	30	1		
Washer—spring	LWZ 203	31	1		
Lock—bonnet	14A 4712	32	1		
Screw	PMZ 0308	33	4		
Washer—spring	LWZ 203	34	4		
Bracket assembly—lock striker—RH	AHA 5150	35	1		
Bracket assembly—lock striker—LH	AHA 5151	36	1		
Bush	14A 4714	37	2		
Screw	HNS 0405	38	4		
Washer—plain	AHA 5329	39	4		
Washer—spring	LWZ 204	40	4		
Catch—safety—bonnet	14A 4707	41	1		
Bush—catch	14A 4708	42	1		
Spring—catch	14A 4709	43	1	(C) H-AN5-501 to 16150	Use AHA 5472 for all service replacements
Spring—catch	AHA 5472	23	1	(C) H-AN5-16151 on	
Screw	HNS 0408	44	1		
Washer—plain	AHA 5329	45	1		
Washer—spring	LWZ 204	46	1		

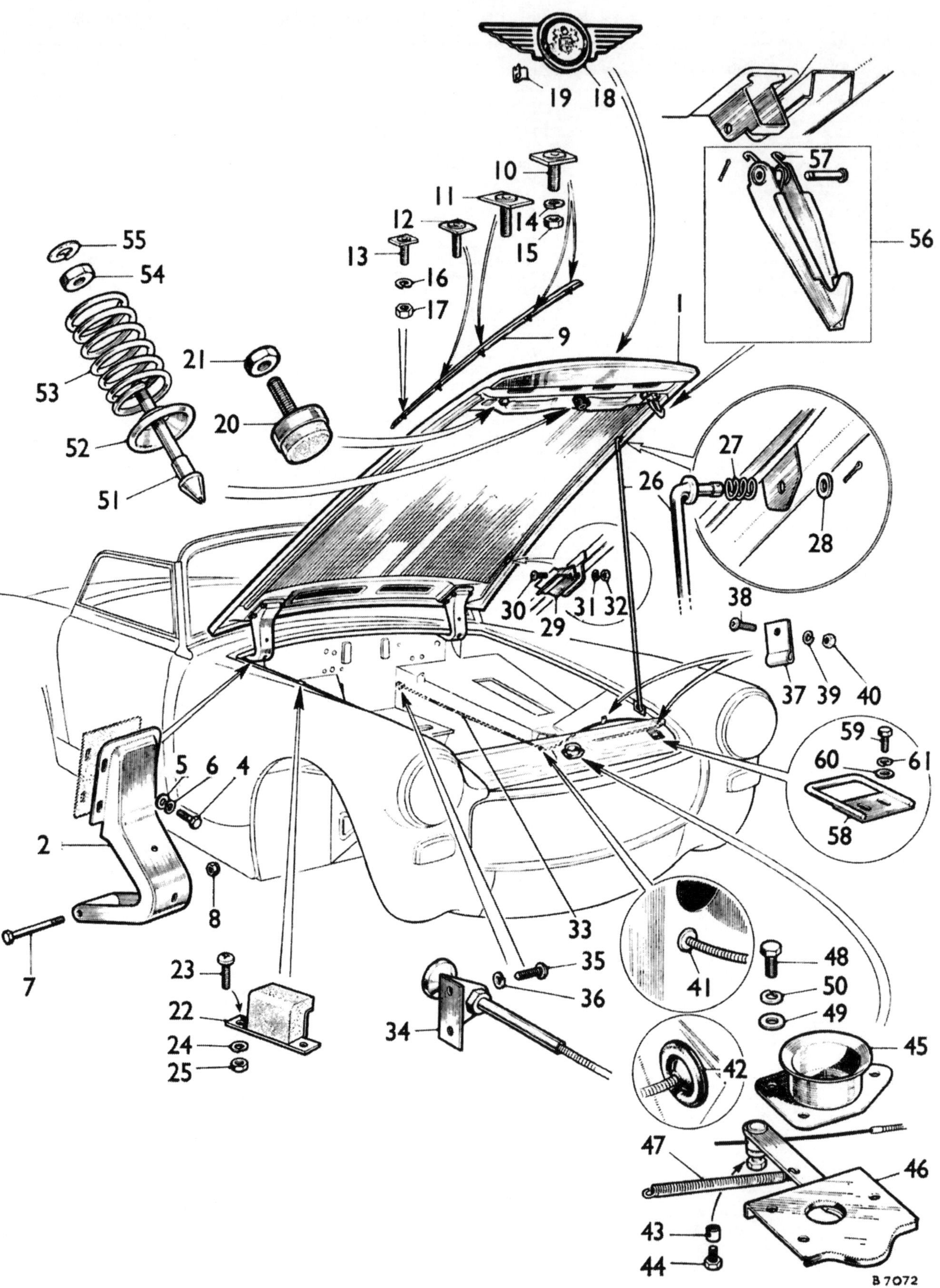
1
2
4
5
6
7
8
9
10
11
12
13
14
15
16
17
18
19
20
21
22
23
24
25
26
27
28
29
30
31
32
33
34
35
36
37
38
39
40
41
42
43
44
45
46
47
48
49
50
51
52
53
54
55
56
57
58
59
60
61
B 7072

BONNET DETAILS

SPRITE MK. II AND MIDGET MK. I

	Page	Plate
BADGE—BONNET	BB 4	B 3
BONNET TOP	BB 4	B 3
CATCH—SAFETY	BB 4	B 3
HINGE—BONNET	BB 4	B 3
MOULDING—BONNET CENTRE MIDGET MK. I	BB 4	B 3

BONNET DETAILS (SPRITE Mk. II AND MIDGET)

DESCRIPTION	Part No.	Illus. No.	Quantity	Change Point	REMARKS
Bonnet	AJA 5111	1	1		Not available; use AJA 5117
Bonnet	AJA 5117	1	1		
Hinge—bonnet	14A 4684	2	2		
Packing—bonnet hinge	NSP		2		Was 14A 4687
Screw	HZS 0405	4	8		
Washer—plain	PWZ 104	5	8		
Washer—spring	LWZ 204	6	8		
Bolt	HBZ 0524	7	2		
Nut	LNZ 105	8	2		
Moulding—bonnet centre (Midget)	14A 7074	9	1		
Plate—stud—moulding Front (Midget)	AHA 5700	10	2		
No. 3 (Midget)	AHA 5701	11	1		
No. 4 (Midget)	AHA 6257	12	1	(C) G-AN1-1508 to 16183 (C) G-AN2-16184 on	
Rear (Midget)	AHA 5702	13	1		
Washer — spring — stud plate — front and No. 3 (Midget)	LWZ 203	14	3		
Nut (Midget)	FNZ 103	15	3		
Washer — spring — stud plate — No. 4 and rear (Midget)	LWZ 202	16	1/2		Quantities increased at (C) G-AN1-1508
Nut (Midget)	CNZ 102	17	1/2		
Badge—bonnet top (Sprite Mk. II)	AHA 5518	18	1		
Clip—badge to bonnet (Sprite Mk. II)	14A 5542	19	4		
Buffer—bonnet	AHA 5654	20	2		
Locknut	FNZ 205	21	2		
Buffer—side	AHA 5674	22	2		
Screw	PMZ 0306	23	4		
Washer—spring	LWZ 203	24	4		
Nut	FNZ 103	25	4		
Rod—prop	AHA 5519	26	1		
Spring—prop rod to bonnet	AAA 2398	27	1		Part No. change; was 139282
Washer—plain	PWZ 105	28	1		
Clip—prop rod	AHH 5460	29	1		
Screw	PMZ 0306	30	2		
Washer—spring	LWZ 203	31	2		
Nut	FNZ 103	32	2		
Cable—bonnet release	AHA 5653	33	1		
Bracket cable	AHA 5517	34	1		
Screw	PMZ 0306	35	2		
Washer—spring	LWZ 203	36	2		
Clip—cable	PCR 0307	37	2		
Screw	PMZ 0308	38	2		
Washer—spring	LWZ 203	39	2		
Nut	FNZ 103	40	2		
Grommet—cable through foot-well	RFN 103	41	1		
Grommet—cable through mudshield	8H 2615	42	1		
Clamp—cable to lock	4G 8621	43	1	(C) H-AN6-101 to 16650 (C) G-AN1-101 to 10741	
Screw—clamp	14B 720	44	1		
Clamp—cable to lock	24G 1052	43	1	(C) H-AN6-16651 to 24731 (C) H-AN7-24732 on (C) G-AN1-10742 to 16183 (C) G-AN2-16184 on	
Screw—clamp	53K 1016	44	1		
Cup—lock locating	AHA 5543	45	1		
Plate—catch	4G 3035	46	1		
Spring—catch plate return	4G 2494	47	1		
Screw	HZS 0405	48	3		
Washer—plain	PWZ 104	49	3		
Washer—spring	LWZ 204	50	3		
Pin—bonnet lock	14G 2444	51	1		
Thimble—bonnet lock	4G 3676	52	1		
Spring—bonnet lock	4G 1588	53	1		
Locknut	FNZ 206	54	1		
Washer—spring	LWZ 206	55	1		
Catch assembly—safety	14A 366	56	1		
Spring	4B 8646	57	1		
Bracket—safety-catch	AHA 5617	58	1		
Screw—bracket	AHA 5618	59	2		Not available; use AHA 6353
Screw—bracket	AHA 6353	59	2		
Washer—plain	PWZ 103	60	2		
Washer—spring	LWZ 203	61	2		

† Revised Information.

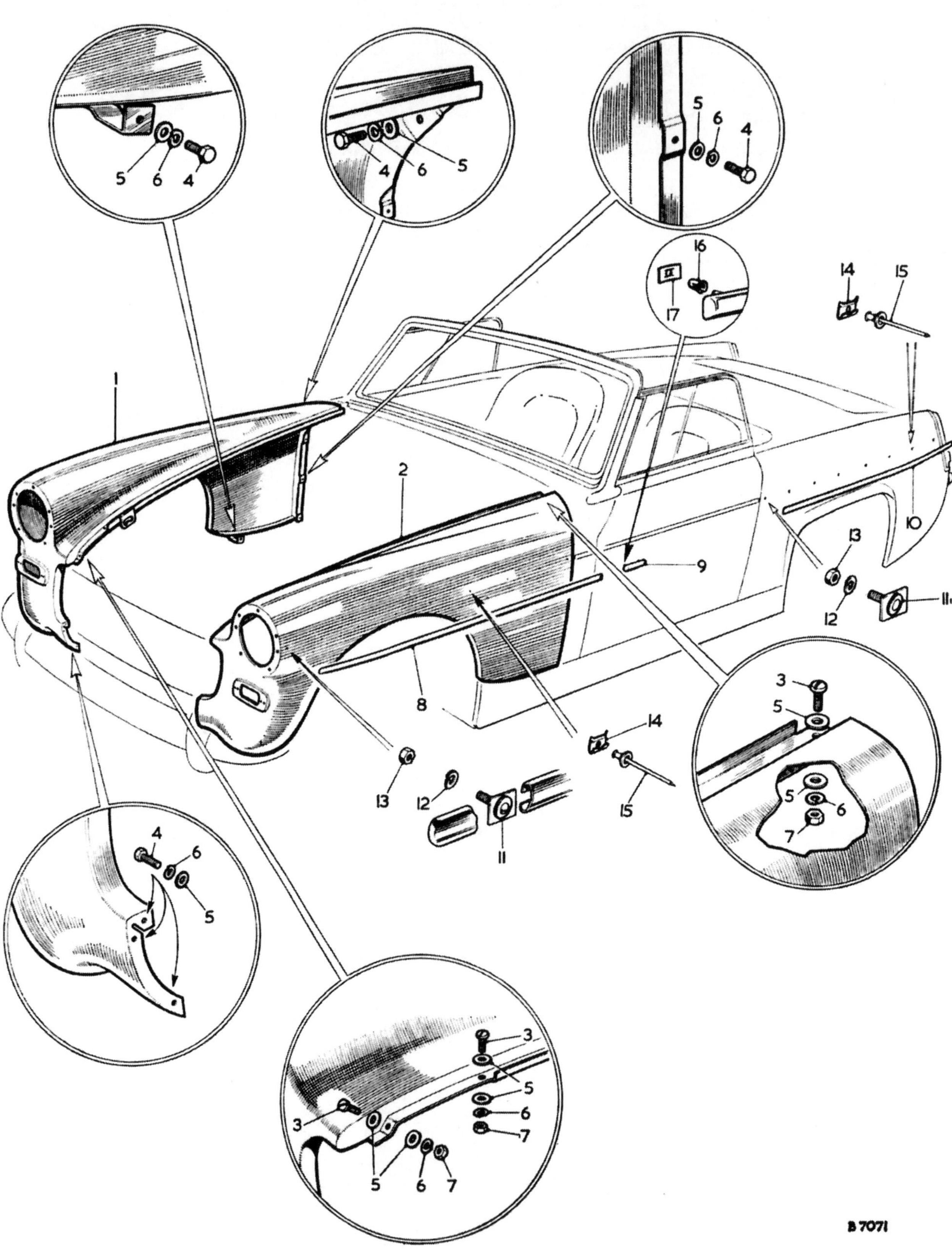
5
6
4
4
6
5
5
6
4
16
17
14
15
1
2
9
10
13
12
11
8
13
12
11
14
15
3
5
5
6
7
4
6
5
3
3
5
5
6
7
5
6
7
B 7071

	DESCRIPTION	Part No.	Illus. No.	Quantity	Change Point	REMARKS

WING DETAILS

		Page	Plate
MOULDING—FRONT WING	MIDGET MK. I	BC 2	C 1
MOULDING—REAR WING	MIDGET MK. I	BC 2	C 1
WINGS—FRONT ...		BC 2	C 1
WINGS—REAR ...		BC 2	C 1

WING DETAILS

(SPRITE H-AN5)

DESCRIPTION	Part No.	Illus. No.	Quantity	Change Point	REMARKS
Wing					
Front—RH					Included parts of bonnet assembly; see page BB 2
Front—LH					Included parts of bonnet assembly; see page BB 2
Rear—RH					Included parts of body shell; see page BA 2
Rear—LH					Included parts of body shell; see page BA 2

(SPRITE Mk. II AND MIDGET)

DESCRIPTION	Part No.	Illus. No.	Quantity	Change Point	REMARKS
Wing					
Front—RH	†AHA 5545	1	1		W.S.E. use AHA 7393
Front—RH	†AHA 7393	1	1		
Front—LH	AHA 5546	2	1		
Rear—RH					Included parts of body shell; see page BA 5
Rear—LH					Included parts of body shell; see page BA 5
Screw—front wing					
Round head	AHA 5619	3	6		W.S.E. use AHA 6352
Round head	AHA 6352	3	6		
Hexagon head	HZS 0405	4	16		
Washer—plain	PWZ 104	5	28		
Washer—spring	LWZ 204	6	22		
Nut	FNZ 104	7	6		
Moulding					
Front wing (Midget)	AHA 5825	8	2		
Shroud side panel (Midget)	AHA 5822	9	2		
Rear wing (Midget)	AHA 5818	10	2		
Plate—stud—wing moulding (Midget)	AHA 5817	11	4		
Washer—spring (Midget)	LWZ 203	12	4		
Nut (Midget)	FNZ 103	13	4		
Clip—wing moulding (Midget)	ALA 3647	14	30		
Rivet—clip (Midget)	ADB 2582	15	30	(C) G-AN1-101 to 266	Use DMP 0721 for this application
Rivet—clip (Midget)	DMP 0721	15	30	(C) G-AN1-267 to 16183 (C) G-AN2-16184 on	
Clip—speed—shroud side panel moulding (Midget)	BCA 4590	16	2		
Push-on-fix—shroud side panel moulding (Midget)	BHA 4082	17	2		

† Revised Information.

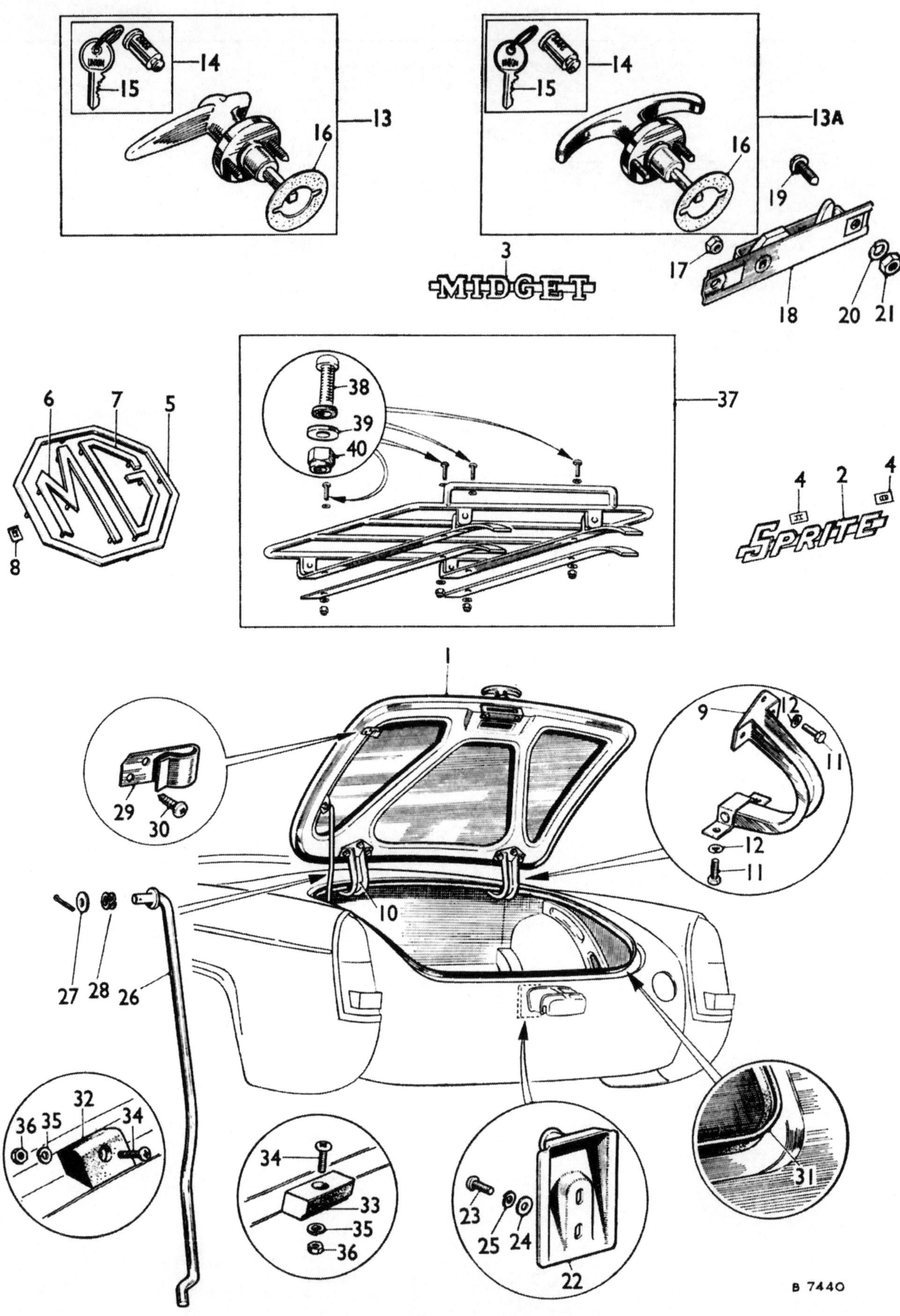
14
15
13
16
14
15
13A
16
19
3
MIDGET
17
18
20
21
6
7
5
8
38
39
40
37
4
2
4
SPRITE
1
9
12
11
29
30
12
11
10
27
28
26
32
36
35
34
34
33
35
36
23
25
24
22
31
B 7440

BOOT LID AND FITTINGS

	Page	Plate
GRID—LUGGAGE	BD 3	D 1
HANDLE—BOOT LID	BD 2	D 1
HINGE—BOOT LID	BD 2	D 1
LID—BOOT	BD 2	D 1
LOCK—BOOT LID	BD 2	D 1
MOTIF—BOOT LID	BD 2	D 1
RUBBER—SEALING—BOOT LID	BD 3	D 1

BOOT LID AND FITTINGS

(SPRITE MK. II AND MIDGET)

DESCRIPTION	Part No.	Illus. No.	Quantity	Change Point	REMARKS
Lid—boot	AJA 5112	1	1		
Motif—'Sprite'	AHA 5699	2	1		
Motif—'Midget'	AHA 5683	3	1		
Push-on fix—motif to boot lid	BHA 4082	4	2		
Surround—letters 'M.G.' (Midget)	ADH 2477	5	1	(C) G–AN1–101 to 7701	
Surround—letters 'M.G.' (Midget)	AHH 5261	5	1	(C) G–AN1–7702 to 16153 (C) G–AN2–16154 on	
Letter 'M' (Midget)	ADH 2475	6	1		
Letter 'C' (Midget)	ADH 2476	7	1		
Nut—Spire—surround and letters (Midget)	PFS 108	8	18		
Hinge—boot lid					
Right-hand	AHA 5708	9	1	(C) H–AN6–101 to 3547 (C) G–AN1–101 to 1208	Not available; use AHA 6314
Left-hand	AHA 5709	10	1		Not available; use AHA 6315
Right-hand	AHA 6314	9	1	(C) H–AN6–3548 to 24731 (C) H–AN7–24732 on (C) G–AN1–1209 to 16183 (C) G–AN2–16184 on	
Left-hand	AHA 6315	10	1		
Screw—hinge	HZS 0405	11	10		
Washer—spring	LWZ 204	12	10		
Handle assembly—locking	ALH 2573	13	1	(C) H–AN6–101 to 8691 (C) G–AN1–101 to 4581	
	AHA 6357	13A	1	(C) H–AN6–8692 to 24731 (C) H–AN7–24732 on (C) G–AN1–4582 to 16183 (C) G–AN2–16184 on	
West Germany	ALH 2573	13	1	(C) H–AN6–101 to 5395 (C) G–AN1–101 to 2591	Use AHA 6357 for this application
West Germany	AHA 6357	13A	1	(C) H–AN6–5396 to 24731 (C) H–AN7–24732 on (C) G–AN1–2592 to 16183 (C) G–AN2–16184 on	
Lock—barrel	ADH 4492	14	1		
Key	ANK 4646	15	2		
Washer—handle seating	ALA 2466	16	1		
Locknut—handle to boot lid	53K 1420	17	2		
Lock	AHA 5807	18	1		
Screw	HZS 0505	19	2		
Washer—spring	LWZ 305	20	2		
Nut	FNZ 105	21	2		
Plate—striker	AHH 5810	22	1		
Screw	PMZ 0308	23	2		
Washer—plain	PWZ 103	24	2		
Washer—spring	LWZ 203	25	2		

† Revised Information.

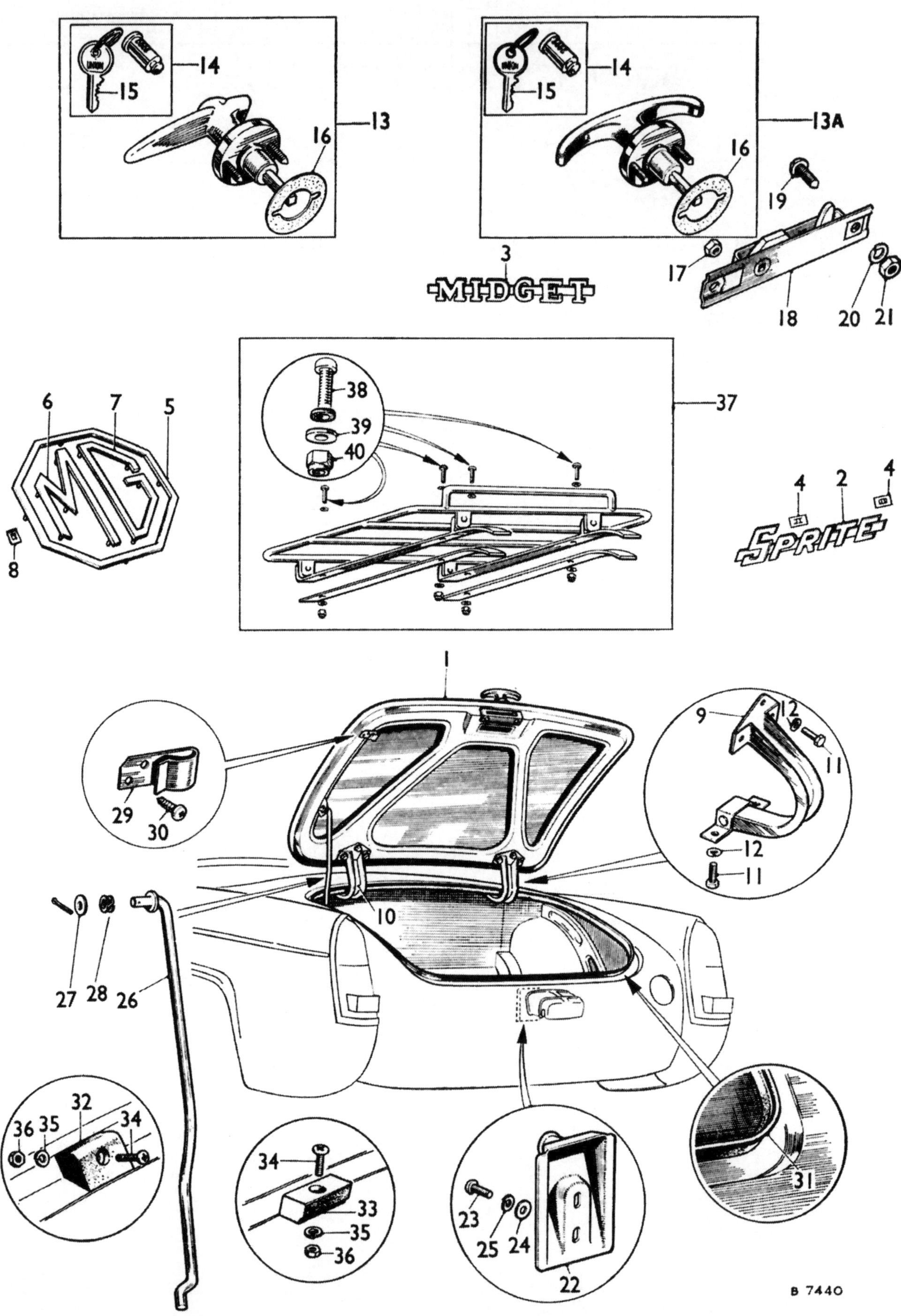
14
15
13
16
14
15
13A
16
19
3
MIDGET
17
18
20
21
6
7
5
8
38
39
40
37
4
2
4
SPRITE
1
9
12
11
29
30
12
11
10
27
28
26
32
36
35
34
34
33
35
36
23
25
24
22
31
B 7440

DESCRIPTION	Part No.	Illus. No.	Quantity	Change Point	REMARKS
Boot Lid and Fittings—*continued* **(Sprite Mk. II and Midget)**—*continued*					
Rod—prop	AHA 5811	26	1		
Washer—plain	PWZ 104	27	2		
Washer—spring	AJD 7722	28	1		
Cup—prop rod	AAA 1524	29	1		Part No. change; was 128978
Screw	PTZ 608	30	2		
Rubber—sealing—boot lid	AHA 5808	31	1	(C) H-AN6-101 to 17686 (C) G-AN1-101 to 11889	Not available; use AHA 6399
	AHA 6399	31	1	(C) H-AN6-17687 to 24731 (C) H-AN7-24732 on (C) G-AN1-11890 to 16183 (C) G-AN2-16184 on	
Switzerland	AHA 6399	31	1	(C) H-AN6-12717 to 24731 (C) H-AN7-24732 on (C) G-AN1-8991 to 16183 (C) G-AN2-16184 on	
Buffer—boot lid—front	AHA 6213	32	2	(C) H-AN6-8157 to 24731 (C) H-AN7-24732 on (C) G-AN1-4103 to 16183 (C) G-AN12-16184 on	
Buffer—boot lid—rear	AHA 6207	33	2		
Screw	PMZ 0210	34	4		
Washer—spring	LWZ 202	35	4		
Nut	CNZ 102	36	4		
Kit—luggage grid	AHA 6252	37	1		Optional extra. When supplying AHA 6252 prior to (C) H-AN6-3548 and (C) G-AN1-1209 supply also 1 off AHA 6314 and 1 off hinge AHA 6315. When supplying AHA 6252 prior to (C) H-AN6-8157 and (C) G-AN1-4103 supply also 2 off AHA 6213 and 2 off buffer AHA 6207
Screw	PMP 0516	38	4		
Washer—plain	PWZ 105	39	4		
Locknut	LNZ 205	40	4		

† Revised Information.

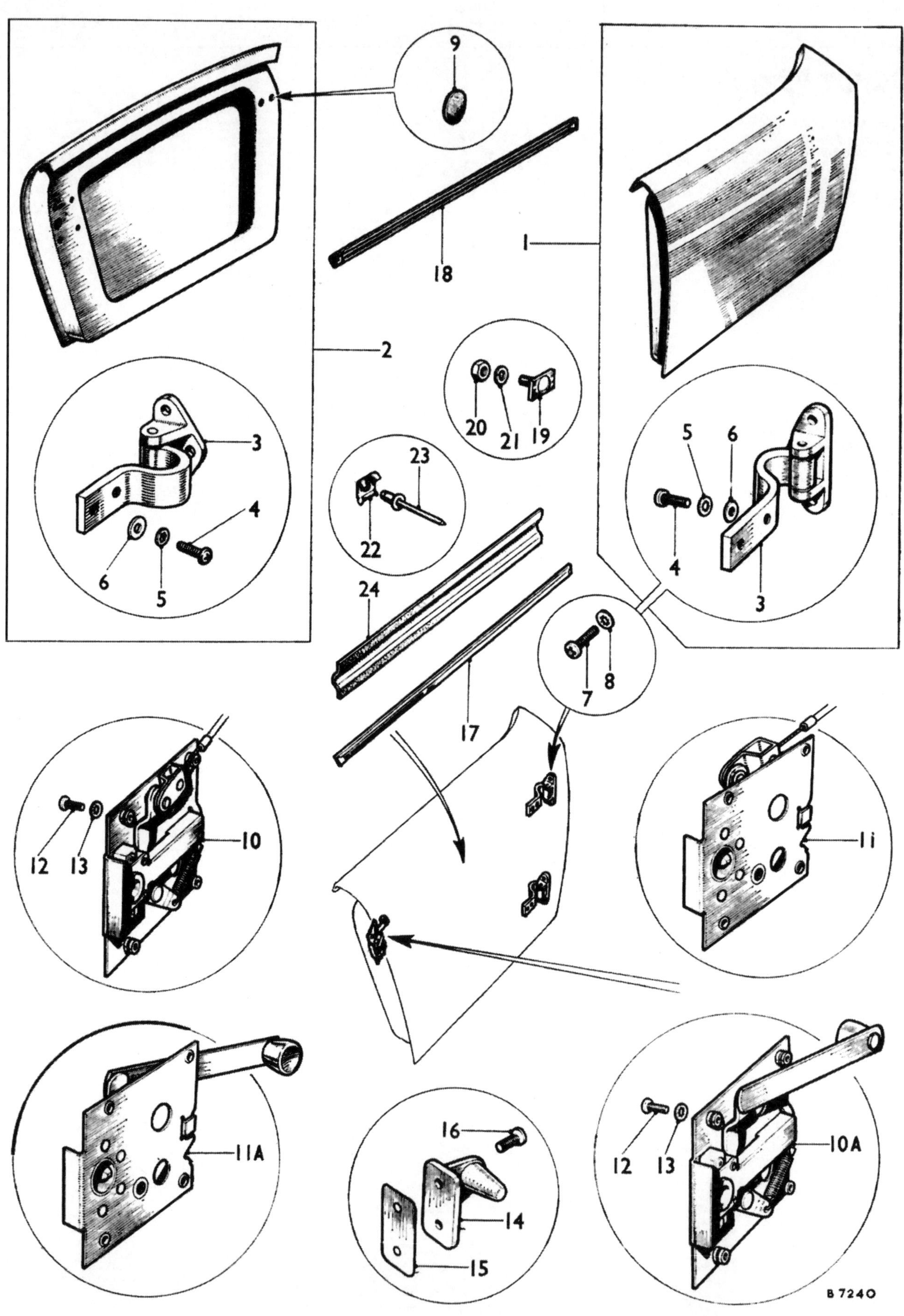
9
18
1
2
3
5
6
4
6
5
3
4
20
21
19
23
22
24
17
7
8
12
13
10
11
11A
16
14
15
12
13
10A
B 7240

DESCRIPTION	Part No.	Illus. No.	Quantity	Change Point	REMARKS

DOORS AND FITTINGS

	Page	Plate
DOORS	BF 2	F 1
HINGE—DOOR	BF 2	F 1
LOCKS—DOOR	BF 2	F 1
MOULDING—DOOR	BF 2	F 1

DOORS AND FITTINGS

DESCRIPTION	Part No.	Illus. No.	Quantity	Change Point	REMARKS
Door assembly—RH	14A 81	1	1		When supplying 14A 81 and 14A 82 prior to (C) H-AN5-1606 supply also 2 off screw AHA 5263
Door assembly—LH	14A 82	2	1		
Hinge	14A 4677	3	4		
Screw	PMN 0408	4	8		
Washer—shakeproof	LWZ 504	5	8		
Washer—plain	AHA 5329	6	8		
Screw	PMN 0408	7	12		
Washer—shakeproof	LWZ 404	8	12		
Plug—hinge holes (rubber)	14A 716	9	8	(C) H-AN5-501 to 50116 (C) H-AN6-101 to 24731 (C) G-AN1-101 to 16183	
Lock					
Right-hand	14A 4675	10	1	(C) H-AN5-501 to 10343	
Left-hand	14A 4676	11	1		
Right-hand	AHA 5455	10A	1	(C) H-AN5-10344 to 50116 (C) H-AN6-101 to 24731 (C) H-AN7-24732 on (C) G-AN1-101 to 16183 (C) G-AN2-16184 on	
Left-hand	AHA 5456	11A	1		
Screw	PMZ 0308	12	8		
Washer—shakeproof	LWN 403	13	8		Part No. change; was 2K 8609 and LWN 603
Striker—lock	AFH 1684	14	2		Part No. change; was 14A 4672
Packing—striker	14A 4673	15	2		
Screw	CMZ 0410	16	4		
Moulding—door—RH (Midget)	AHA 5823	17	1		
Moulding—door—LH (Midget)	AHA 5824	18	1		
Plate—stud—moulding (Midget)	AHA 5817	19	2		
Nut (Midget)	FNZ 103	20	2		
Washer—spring (Midget)	LWZ 203	21	2		
Clip—moulding (Midget)	ALA 3647	22	10		
Rivet—clip (Midget)	ADB 2582	23	10	(C) G-AN1-101 to 266	Use DMP 0721 for this application
Rivet—clip (Midget)	DMP 0721	23	10	(C) G-AN1-267 to 16183 (C) G-AN2-16184 on	
Cover—clip (Midget)	AHA 5819	24	2		
Tape—sealing—4½" (11·43 cm) wide	†37H 2506		A/R		Supplied in 50′ (15·24 m) rolls

† Revised Information.

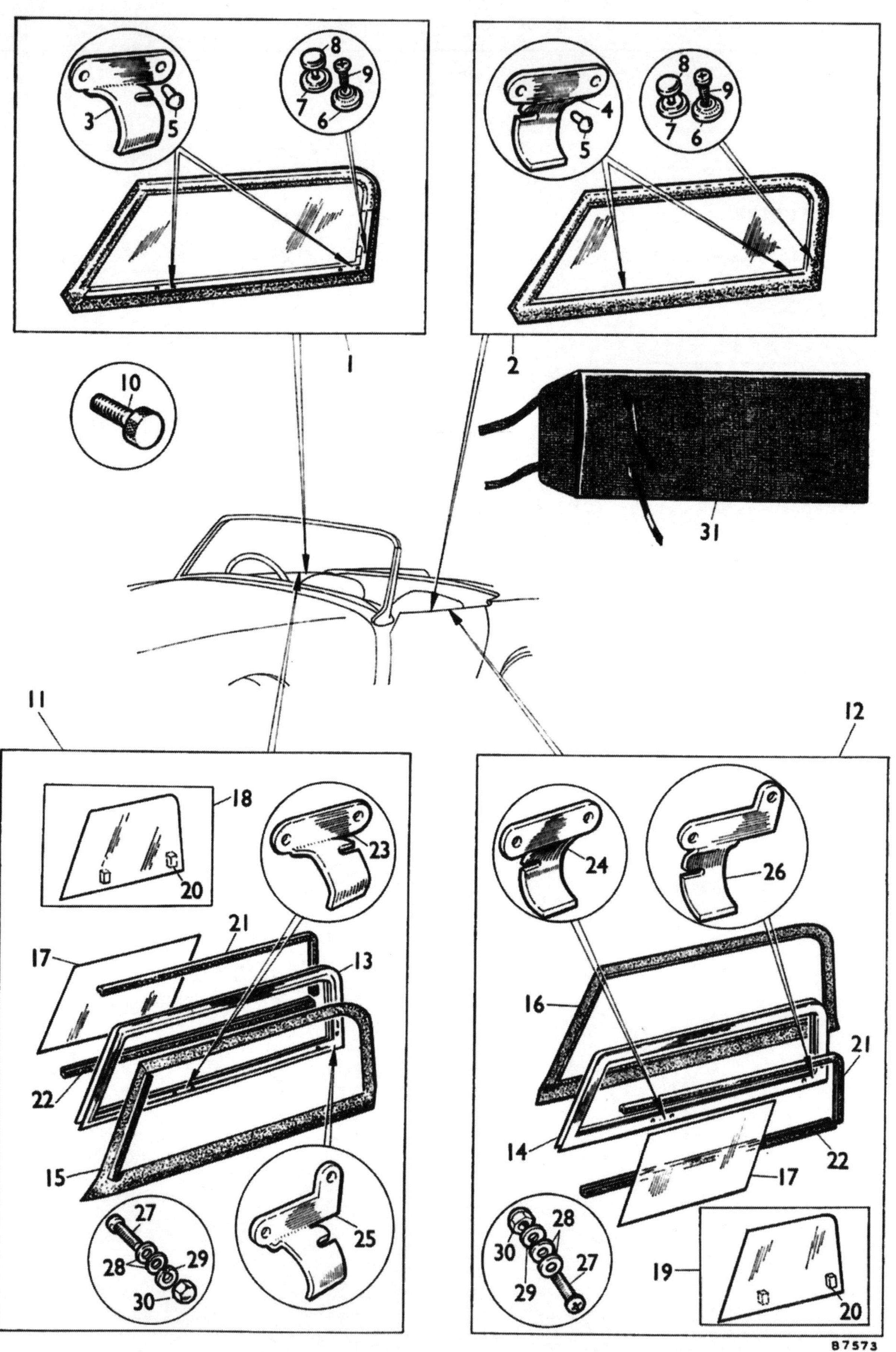
1
2
3
4
5
6
7
8
9
10
11
12
13
14
15
16
17
18
19
20
21
22
23
24
25
26
27
28
29
30
31
B7573

SIDE CURTAINS AND SIDESCREENS

	Page	Plate
CASE—STOWAGE	BG 2-BG 4	G 1-G 3
CURTAIN ASSEMBLY—SIDE	BG 2	G 1
SIDESCREEN ASSEMBLY—SLIDING	BG 2-BG 4	G 1-G 3

SIDE CURTAINS AND SIDESCREENS

DESCRIPTION		Part No.	Illus. No.	Quantity	Change Point	REMARKS
Curtain assembly—side						
Black RH		14A 5507	1	1	(C) H-AN5-501 to 1606	
Black LH		14A 5518	2	1		
RH		AHA 5264	1	1	(C) H-AN5-1607 to 50116	
LH		AHA 5265	2	1		
White RH		AHA 5480	1	1	(C) H-AN5-13548 to 50116	
White LH		AHA 5481	2	1		
Bracket—curtain to door—RH		AHA 5266	3	2		
Bracket—curtain to door—LH	**Sprite**	AHA 5267	4	2		
Rivet	**H-AN5**	CRS 0206	5	8		
Stud		2H 5138	6	2	(C) H-AN5-501 to 50116	Not available; use ADB 4811
Stud		ADB 4811	6	2		
Socket		2H 5134	7	2		Not available; use 7H 9866
Socket		7H 9866	7	2		
Button		4B 6821	8	2		
Screw—stud		CMZ 0204	9	2		
Screw—bracket to door		14A 5521	10	4	(C) H-AN5-101 to 1605	
Screw—bracket to door		AHA 5263	10	4	(C) H-AN5-1606 to 50116	
Sidescreen assembly—sliding—RH		AHA 5414	11	1		Optional extra for Sprite H-AN5
Sidescreen assembly—sliding—LH		AHA 5415	12	1		
Frame—RH		AHA 5416	13	1		
Frame—LH		AHA 5417	14	1		
Rubber—sealing						
Right-hand		AHA 5418	15	1		Not available; use AHA 5798
Right-hand		AHA 5798	15	1		
Left-hand		AHA 5419	16	1		Not available; use AHA 5799
Left-hand		AHA 5799	16	1		
Window—fixed		AHA 5422	17	2		
Window—sliding—RH		AHA 5423	18	1	(C) H-AN5-501 to 50116	
Window—sliding—LH		AHA 5424	19	1	(C) H-AN6-101 to 24731	
Pull—finger		AHA 6204	20	4		
Slide—upper (felt)		AHA 5420	21	2		
Slide—lower (felt)	**Sprite**	AHA 5421	22	2		
Bracket—securing	**H-AN5**					
Front—RH	**and Sprite**	AHA 5426	23	1		Not available; use AHA 5894
Front—RH	**Mk. II**	AHA 5894	23	1		
Front—LH		AHA 5427	24	1		Not available; use AHA 5895
Front—LH		AHA 5895	24	1		
Rear—RH		AHA 5428	25	1		Not available; use AHA 5896
Rear—RH		AHA 5896	25	1		
Rear—LH		AHA 5429	26			Not available; use AHA 5897
Rear—LH		AHA 5897	26	1		
Screw		PMZ 0314	27	8		
Washer—plain		PWZ 103	28	16		
Washer—spring		LWZ 203	29	8		
Nut—dome		AHA 5430	30	8		Not available; use 14B 7889
Nut—dome		14B 7889	30	8		
Screw—bracket to door		14A 5521	10	4	(C) H-AN5-101 to 1605	
Screw—bracket to door		AHA 5263	10	4	(C) H-AN5-1606 to 50116 (C) H-AN6-101 to 24731	
Case—stowage—side curtain and sidescreen		AHA 5216	31	1		

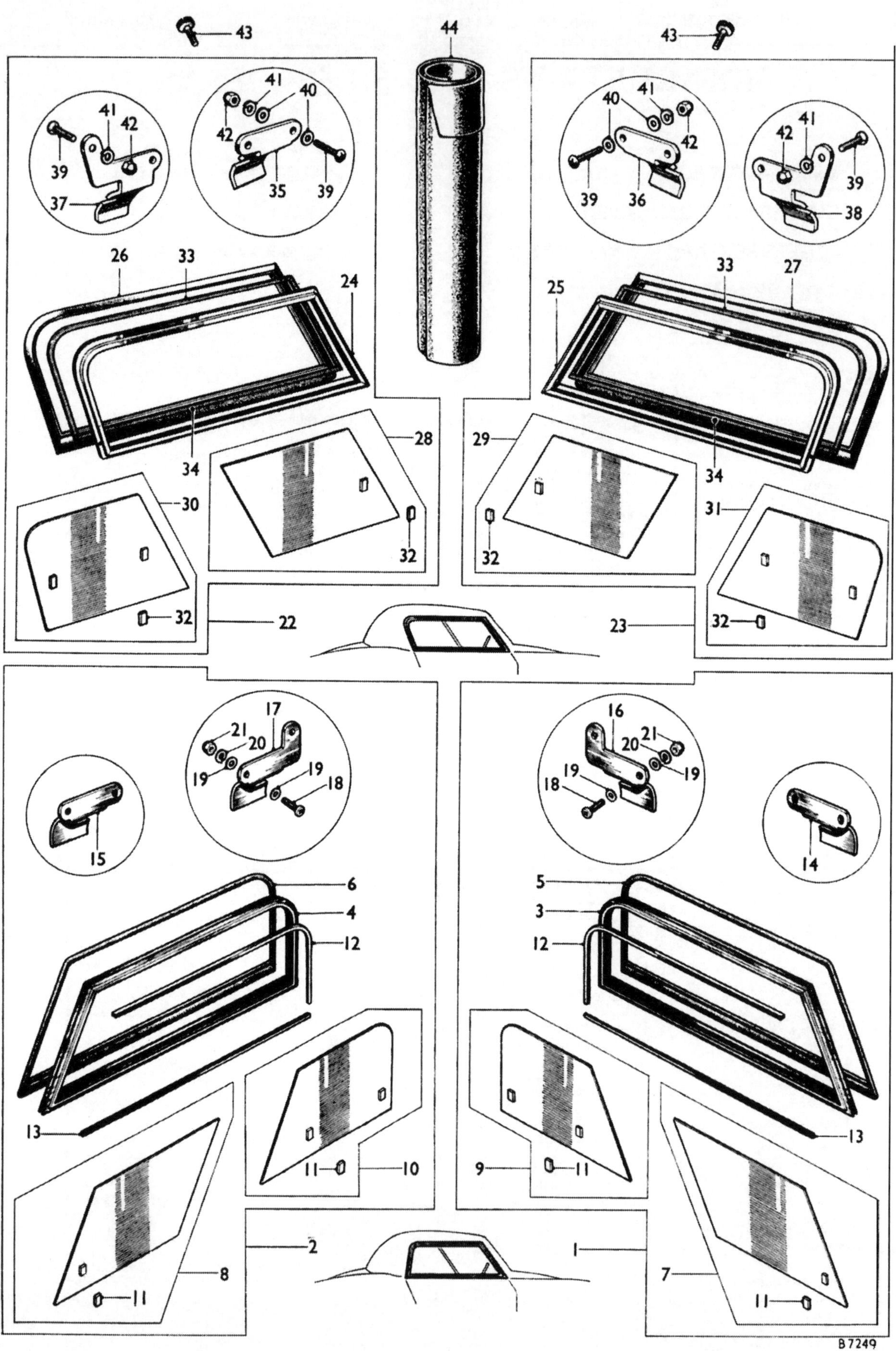
43
44
43
41
42
39
37
41
40
42
35
39
40
41
42
39
36
41
42
39
38
26
33
24
25
33
27
28
29
34
34
30
32
32
31
32
22
23
32
17
21
20
19
19
18
16
21
20
19
19
18
15
14
6
4
12
5
3
12
13
13
11
10
9
11
2
1
8
11
7
11
B 7249

DESCRIPTION	Part No.	Illus. No.	Quantity	Change Point	REMARKS
Side Curtains and Sidescreens—*continued*					
Sidescreen assembly—sliding—RH	AHA 5794	1	1		
Sidescreen assembly—sliding—LH	AHA 5795	2	1		
Frame—RH	AHA 5796	3	1		
Frame—LH	AHA 5797	4	1		
Rubber—sealing—RH	AHA 5798	5	1		
Rubber—sealing—LH	AHA 5799	6	1		
Window—sliding					
Front—RH	AHA 5800	7	1		
Front—LH	AHA 5801	8	1		
Rear—RH	AHA 5802	9	1		
Rear—LH	AHA 5803	10	1		
Pull—finger	AHA 6204	11	6		
Slide—upper (felt)	AHA 5420	12	4		
Slide—lower (felt)	AHA 5421	13	4		
Bracket—securing					
Front—RH	AHA 5894	14	1		
Front—LH	AHA 5895	15	1		
Rear—RH	AHA 5896	16	1		
Rear—LH	AHA 5897	17	1		
Screw	PMZ 0314	18	8		
Washer—plain	PWZ 103	19	16		
Washer—spring	LWZ 203	20	8		
Nut—dome	14B 7889	21	8		
Sidescreen assembly—sliding—RH **Midget**	AHA 6150	22	1	(C) G-AN1-101 to 16183	Optional extra for use with hard tops AHA 6301, AHA 6302, AHA 6303, and AHA 6323 only; see page BL 6
Sidescreen assembly—sliding—LH	AHA 6151	23	1		
Frame—RH	AHA 6152	24	1		
Frame—LH	AHA 6153	25	1		
Rubber—sealing—RH	AHA 6154	26	1		
Rubber—sealing—LH	AHA 6155	27	1		
Window—sliding					
Front—RH	AHA 6156	28	1		
Front—LH	AHA 6157	29	1		
Rear—RH	AHA 6158	30	1		
Rear—LH	AHA 6159	31	1		
Pull—finger	AHA 6204	32	6		
Slide—upper (felt)	AHA 6162	33	4		
Slide—lower (felt)	AHA 5421	34	4		
Bracket—securing					
Front—RH	AHA 6297	35	1		
Front—LH	AHA 6298	36	1		
Rear—RH	AHA 6160	37	1		
Rear—LH	AHA 6161	38	1		
Screw	PMZ 0314	39	6		
Screw	RMZ 0312	39	2		
Washer—plain	PWZ 103	40	12		
Washer—spring	LWZ 203	41	8		
Nut—dome	14B 7889	42	8		
Screw—bracket to door	AHA 5263	43	4		
Case—stowage—sidescreen	AHA 5216	44	1		

† Revised Information.

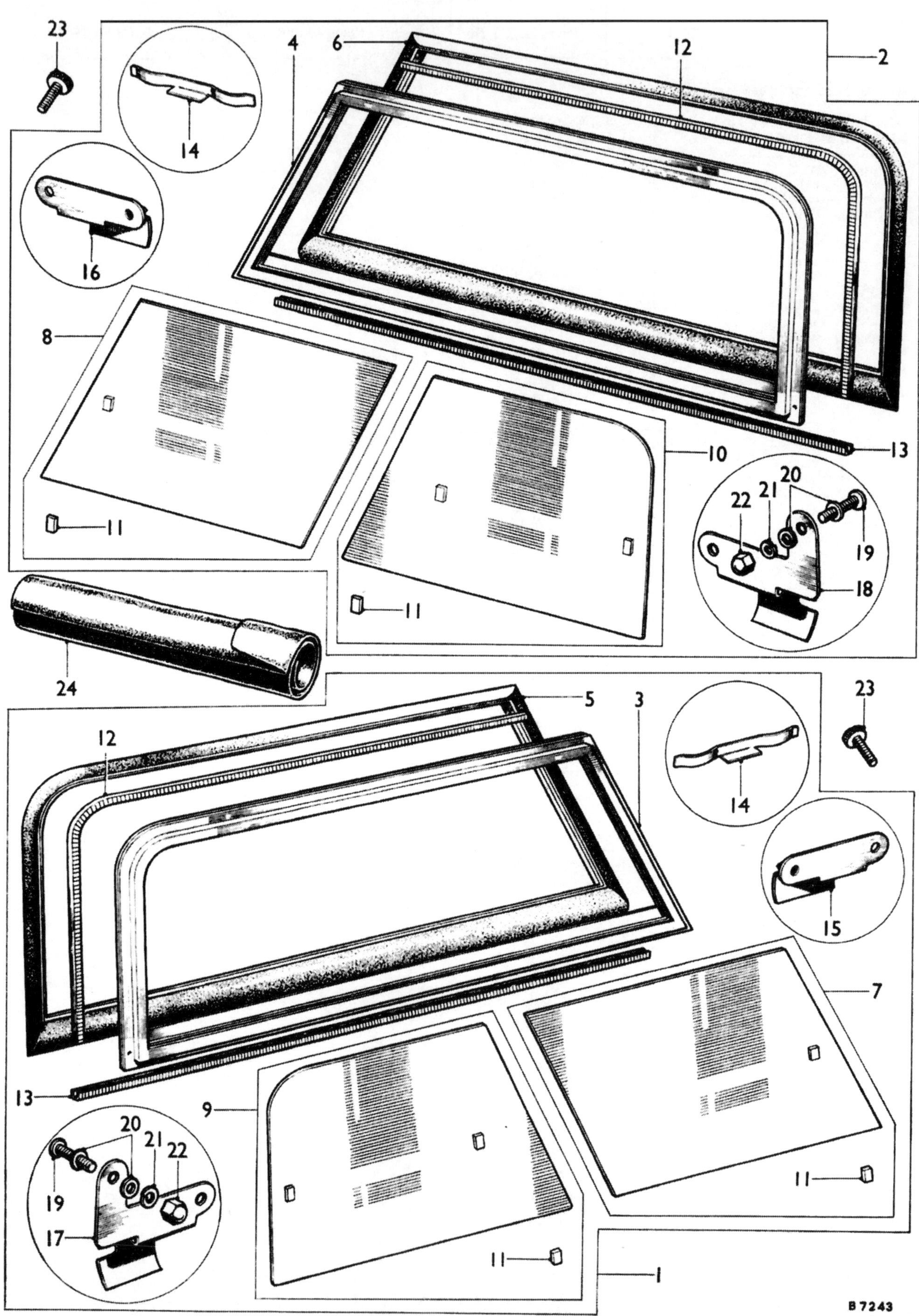
23
4
6
12
2
14
16
8
10
13
11
20
21
22
19
18
11
24
5
3
23
12
14
15
7
13
9
20
21
22
19
17
11
11
1
B 7243

DESCRIPTION	Part No.	Illus. No.	Quantity	Change Point	REMARKS
***Side Curtains and Sidescreens**—continued*					
Sidescreen assembly—sliding—RH	AHA 6501	1	1		
Sidescreen assembly—sliding—LH	AHA 6502	2	1		
Frame—RH	AHA 6503	3	1		
Frame—LH	AHA 6504	4	1		
Rubber—sealing—RH	AHA 6505	5	1	(C) H-AN7-24732 on	
Rubber—sealing—LH	AHA 6506	6	1	(C) G-AN2-16184 on	
Window—sliding					
Front—RH	AHA 6509	7	1		
Front—LH	AHA 6510	8	1		
Rear—RH	AHA 6512	9	1		
Rear—LH	AHA 6513	10	1		
Pull—finger	AHA 6204	11	6		
Slide (felt)					
Upper	AHA 5420	12	4	(C) H-AN7-24732 to 31010	
Lower	**Sprite** AHA 5421	13	4	(C) G-AN2-16184 to 20207	
Upper	**Mk. II** AHA 7003	12	4	(C) H-AN7-31011 on	W.S.E. use 27H 2115
Lower	**and** AHA 7004	13	4	(C) G-AN2-20208 on	W.S.E. use 27H 2115
Slide (felt)	**Midget** 27H 2115		A/R		
Upper—36" (97 cm)		12	4		
Lower—28" (71 cm)		13	4		
Spring—compression—slide	AHA 6981	14	4	(C) H-AN7-31011 on (C) G-AN2-20208 on	
Bracket—securing					
Front—RH	AHA 6515	15	1		
Front—LH	AHA 6516	16	1		
Rear—RH	AHA 6517	17	1		
Rear—LH	AHA 6518	18	1	(C) H-AN7-24732 on	
Screw—bracket to frame	†AHA 6419	19	8	(C) G-AN2-16184 on	W.S.E. use PMZ 0314
Screw—bracket to frame	PMZ 0314	19	8		
Washer—plain	PWZ 103	20	16		
Washer—spring	LWZ 203	21	8		
Nut—dome	14B 7889	22	8		
Screw—bracket to door	AHA 6497	23	4		
Case—stowage—sidescreen	AHA 5216	24	1		

† Revised Information.

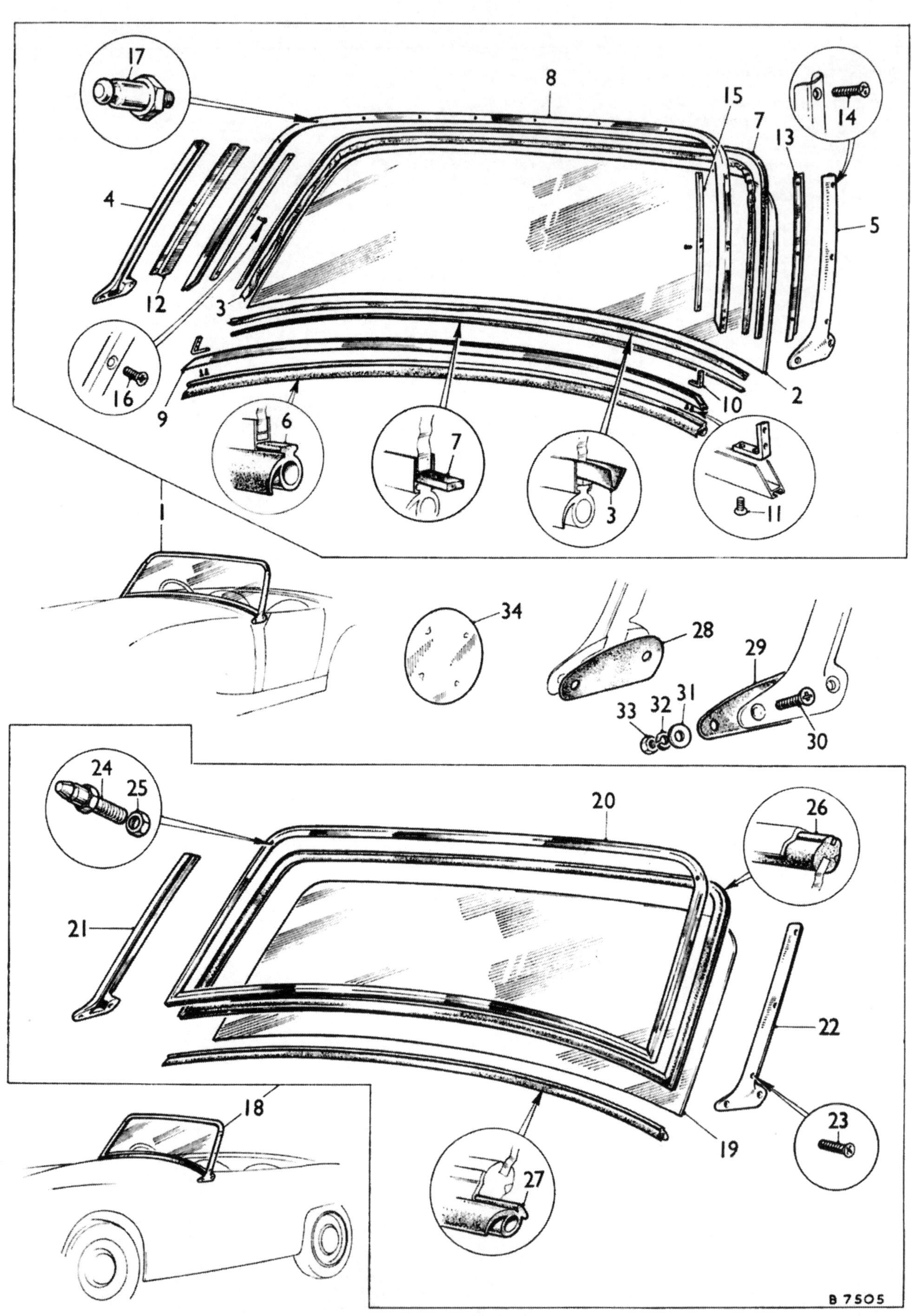
1
2
3
4
5
6
7
8
9
10
11
12
13
14
15
16
17
18
19
20
21
22
23
24
25
26
27
28
29
30
31
32
33
34
B 7505

WINDSCREEN, WINDSCREEN WASHER, AND MIRRORS

	Page	Plate
MIRROR—INTERIOR	BH 5	H 3
MIRROR—WING	BH 5	H 3
WINDSCREEN	BH 2	H 1
WINDSCREEN WASHER	BH 3	H 2

WINDSCREEN, WINDSCREEN WASHER, AND MIRRORS

DESCRIPTION	Part No.	Illus. No.	Quantity	Change Point	REMARKS
WINDSCREEN					
Windscreen assembly—toughened	14A 4824	1	1		W.S.E. use components
Windscreen assembly—laminated	14A 4718	1	1		Optional extra. W.S.E. use components
Glass—toughened	14A 4805	2	1		
Glass—laminated	14A 4719	2	1		Optional extra
Rubber—glazing	14A 4728	3			
Pillar—RH	14A 4723	4	1		
Pillar—LH	14A 4724	5	1		
Seal—windscreen to body	14A 4729	6	1		
Rubber—packing	14A 4727	7	1		
Channel—top	14A 4720	8	1	(C) H-AN5-501 to 5476	
Channel—bottom	14A 4721	9	1	(less 5187, 5287 and 5288)	
Bracket—corner angle	14A 4722	10	2		
Screw	CMZ 0203	11	8		
Angle—side curtain—RH	14A 4725	12	1		
Angle—side curtain—LH	14A 4726	13	1		
Screw	RMZ 0307	14	2		
Screw	RMZ 0308	14	4		
Plate—tapped—pillar	14A 5472	15	2		
Screw—plate	CMZ 0203	16	2		
Fastener—hood to windscreen	AHA 5255	17	9		
Windscreen assembly—					
Toughened	†AHA 5314	18	1		
Laminated	†AHA 5315	18	1		W.S.E. use 18G 8445
Laminated	†18G 8445	18	1		
Glass—toughened	AHA 5316	19	1	(C) H-AN5-5477 to 50116	
Glass—laminated	$AHA 5317	19	1	(plus 5187, 5287, and 5288)	
Frame—windscreen	AHA 5318	20	1	(C) H-AN6-101 to 24731	
Pillar—RH	AHA 5319	21	1	(C) H-AN7-24782 on	
Pillar—LH	AHA 5320	22	1	(C) G-AN1-101 to 16183	
Screw	RMZ 0308	23	6	(C) G-AN2-16184 on	
Fastener—hood to windscreen	87H 9719	24	2		
Nut	AJD 8012 Z	25	2		
Rubber—sealing	AHA 5321	26	1		
Seal—windscreen to body	AHA 5322	27	1		
Pad—pillar foot—RH (rubber)	14A 4730	28	1	(C) H-AN5-501 to 50116	
Pad—pillar foot—LH (rubber)	14A 5706	29	1		
Screw—foot to scuttle	AHA 5486	30	4		
Washer—plain	PNZ 205	31	2		
Washer—spring	LWZ 205	32	2		
Nut	FNZ 105	33	2		
Holder—licence	14A 3828	34	1		

$ This item is subject to safety regulations.

† Revised Information.

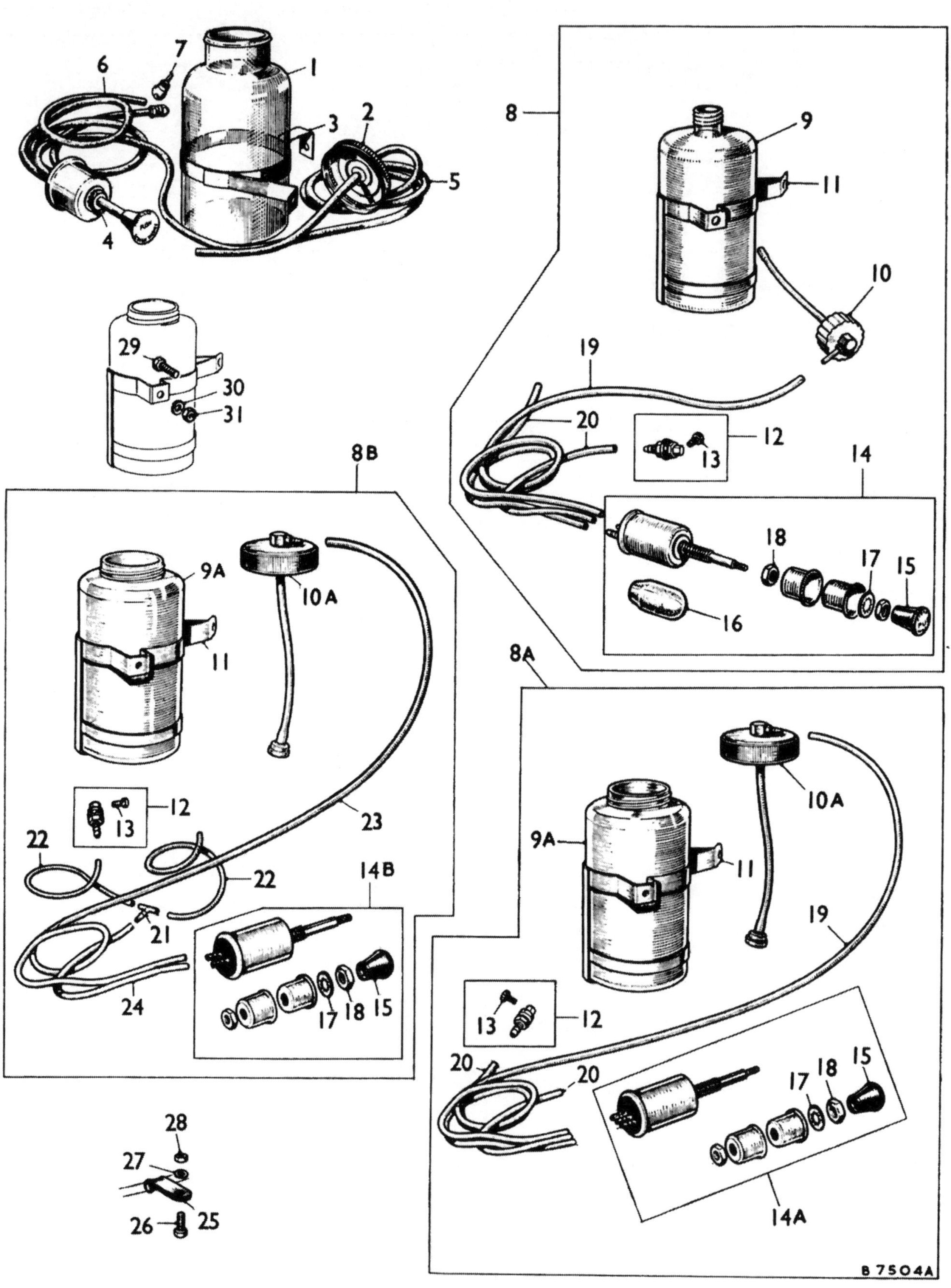
1
2
3
4
5
6
7
8
9
10
11
12
13
14
15
16
17
18
19
20
29
30
31
8B
9A
10A
11
12
13
22
23
22
21
24
14B
17
18
15
8A
10A
9A
11
19
12
13
20
20
17
18
15
14A
28
27
26
25
B 7504A

Windscreen, Windscreen Washer, and Mirrors—*continued*

DESCRIPTION	Part No.	Illus. No.	Quantity	Change Point	REMARKS
WINDSCREEN WASHER					
Kit—windscreen washer (Trafalgar type)	NSP		1		Single jet mounting
Container	17H 579	1	1		W.S.E. use 37H 9798
Container	37H 9798	1	1		
Cap and tube	27H 9662	2	1		
Bracket—container	14A 5530	3	1		
Control	17H 577	4	1		W.S.E. use 13H 206
Control	13H 206			(C) H-AN5-501 to 50116	
Tubing—⅜" (9·5 mm) OD	17H 9997		A/R		Supplied in multiples of feet
Control to container—25" (64 cm) long	14A 5531	5	1		W.S.E. use 17H 9997
Tubing—¼" (6·4 mm) OD	17H 9996		A/R		Supplied in multiples of feet
Control to jet—18" (46 cm) long	14A 5532	6	1		W.S.E. use 17H 9996
Jet	17H 578	7	1		
Kit—windscreen washer (Tudor type)	**Sprite** AHA 5220	8	1		W.S.E use AHA 5501
Container	**H-AN5** 37H 9763	9	1		W.S.E. use 37H 9729 with 37H 9715
Cap	7H 9785	10	1		
Bracket—container	27H 9657	11	1		
Mounting assembly—jet	13H 231	12	2		Part No. change; was 27H 9622
Jet	27H 9623	13	2		
Control assembly	27H 9654	14	1	(C) H-AN5-501 to 26723	W.S.E. use 37H 9730
Knob	27H 9625	15	1		
Bulb (rubber)	27H 9626	16	1		
Washer—shakeproof	LWN 406	17	1		Part No. change; was 7H 9782
Nut	27H 9655	18	2		
Tubing	37H 9708		A/R		Supplied in multiples of feet
Control to container—63" (160 cm) long		19	1		
Control to jet—13" (33 cm) long		20	2		
Kit—windscreen washer	†AHA 5501	8A	1		W.S.E. use AHA 6450
Container	37H 9729	9A	1		
Cap	37H 9715	10A	1		
Bracket—container	27H 9657	11	1		
Mounting assembly—jet	13H 231	12	2	(C) H-AN5-26724 to 50116	Part No. change; was 27H 9622
Jet	27H 9623	13	2	(C) H-AN6-101 to 20104	
Control assembly	†37H 9730	14A	1	(C) G-AN1-101 to 13448	
Knob	27H 9625	15	1		
Washer—shakeproof	LWN 406	17	1		
Nut	27H 9655	18	2		
Tubing	37H 9708		A/R		Supplied in multiples of feet
Control to container—63" (160 cm) long		19	1		
Control to jet—13" (33 cm) long		20	2		

† Revised Information.

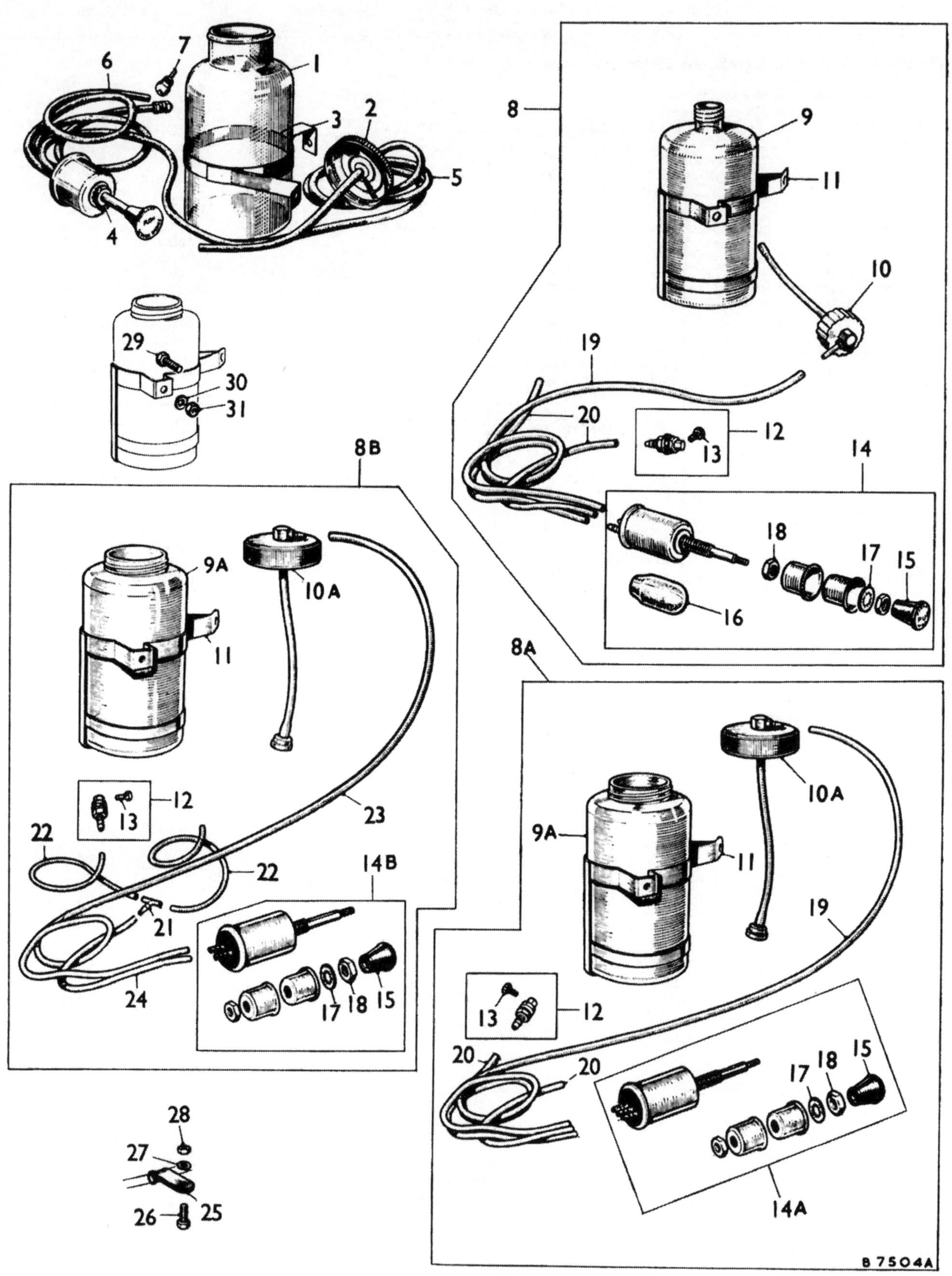
1
2
3
4
5
6
7
8
9
10
11
12
13
14
15
16
17
18
19
20
29
30
31
8B
9A
10A
11
12
13
23
22
22
21
24
14B
17
18
15
8A
10A
9A
11
19
12
13
20
20
17
18
15
14A
28
27
25
26
B 7504A

Windscreen, Windscreen Washer, and Mirrors—*continued*
Windscreen Washer—*continued*

DESCRIPTION		Part No.	Illus. No.	Quantity	Change Point	REMARKS
Kit—windscreen washer		†AHA 6450	8B	1		
Container		37H 9729	9A	1		
Cap		17H 2670	10A	1		
Bracket—container		27H 9657	11	4		
Mounting assembly—jet		13H 231	12	2		Part No. change; was 27H 9622
Jet		27H 9623	13	2		
Control assembly	**Sprite**	†17H 2672	14B	1	(C) H-AN6-20105 to 24731	
Knob	**Mk. II**	27H 9625	15	1	(C) H-AN7-24732 on	
Washer—shakeproof	**and**	LWN 406	17	1	(C) G-AN1-13449 to 16183	
Nut	**Midget**	27H 9655	18	2	(C) G-AN2-16184 on	
Connection—3-way		BHA 4361	21			
Tubing—$\frac{3}{16}$" (4·8 mm) OD		37H 9708		A/R		Supplied in multiples of feet
3-way connection to jet —6" (16 cm) long			22	2		
Tubing—$\frac{1}{4}$" (6·4 mm) OD		97H 2679		A/R		Supplied in multiples of feet
Control to container—55" (140 cm) long			23	1		
Control to 3-way connection—6" (16 cm) long			24	1		
Clip		PCR 0409	25	1		
Clip		PCR 0407	25	2		
Screw		PMZ 0806	26	2		
Washer—spring		LWZ 203	27	2		
Nut		FNZ 103	28	2		
Screw		HZS 0408	29	1		
Screw		HZS 0404	29	1		
Washer—spring		LWZ 204	30	1		
Nut		FNZ 104	31	2		

† Revised Information.

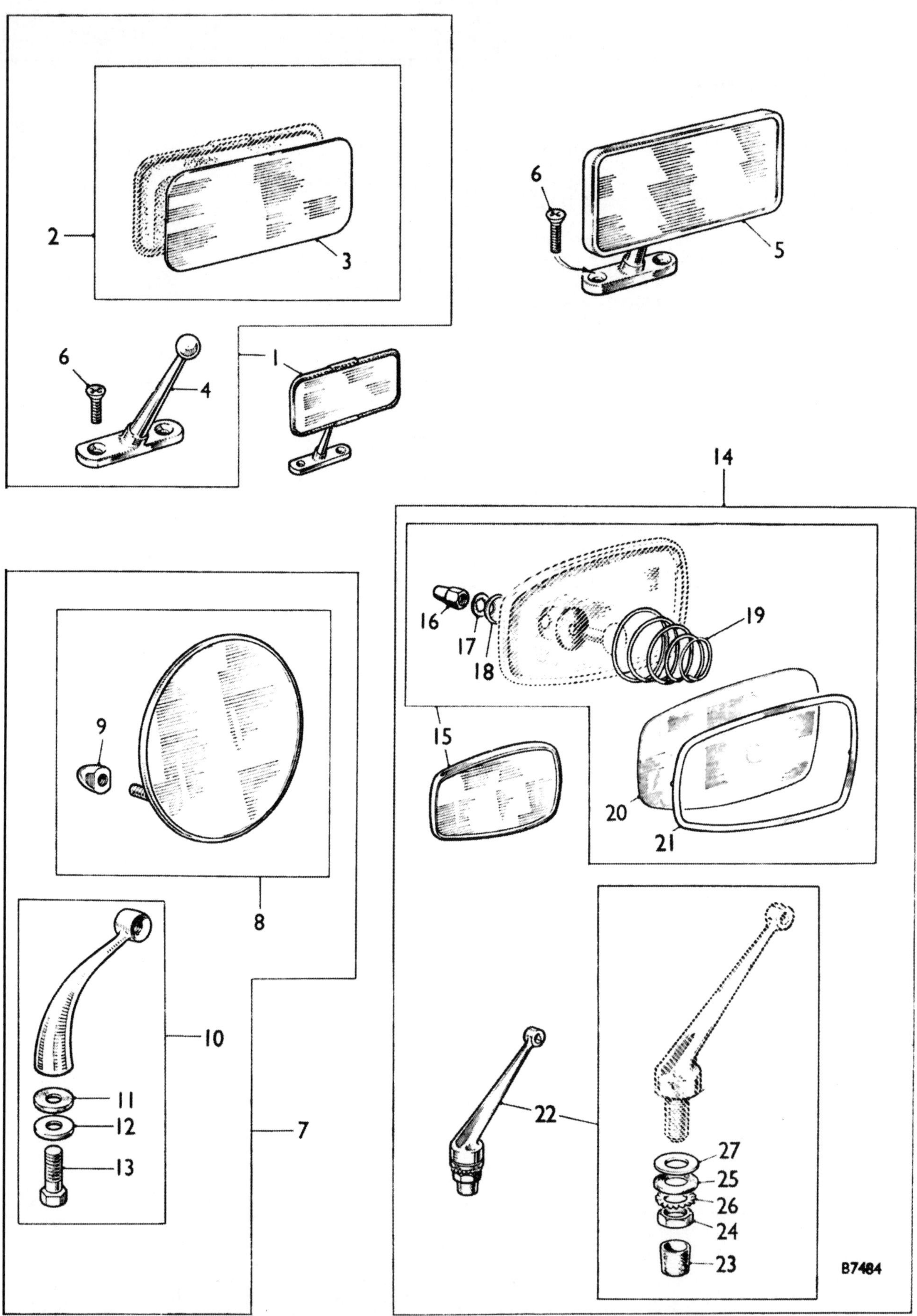
1
2
3
4
5
6
6
7
8
9
10
11
12
13
14
15
16
17
18
19
20
21
22
23
24
25
26
27
B7484

DESCRIPTION	Part No.	Illus. No.	Quantity	Change Point	REMARKS
Windscreen, Windscreen Washer, and Mirrors—*continued*					
MIRRORS					
Mirror—interior	14A 5473	1	1		W.S.E. use AHA 6932
Head assembly	47H 9579	2	1		
Glass	27H 9782	2	1		
Bracket—mounting	†27H 9781	4	1		Correction; was 27H 9721
Mirror—interior	AHA 6932	5	1	(C) H–AN7–28148 on (C) G–AN2–18476 on	
Screw—mirror to body	RMP 0308	6	2		
Mirror—wing	BHA 4066	7	2		W.S.E. use 14B 5862
Mirror assembly—wing	14B 5862	7	2		W.S.E. use component parts
Head assembly	14A 8196	8	2		Part No. change; was 37H 9914
Nut—dome	14A 8226	9	2		Part No. change; was 37H 9786
Stem assembly	37H 9915	10	2		
Washer					
(Rubber)	37H 9917	11	2		W.S.E. use 14A 8225
(Rubber)	14A 8225	11	2		
(Steel)	PWZ 205	12	2		Part No. change; was 37H 9916 — Optional extra
Screw	HZS 0506	13	2		Part No. change; was 37H 9788
Mirror—wing—boomerang	27H 9863	14	2		
Head assembly	37H 9947	15	2		
Nut—dome	37H 9967	16	2		
Washer—shakeproof	37H 9968	17	2		
Collar	47H 9510	18	2		
Spring	17H 8148	19	2		
Glass	17H 8146	20	2		
Ring—glass retaining (plastic)	17H 8147	21	2		
Arm assembly	37H 9946	22	2		
Ferrule (rubber)	37H 9974	23	2		
Nut	37H 9970	24	2		
Washer					
(Rubber)	37H 9971	25	2		
Shakeproof	37H 9972	26	2		
Plain	37H 9973	27	2		

† Revised Information.

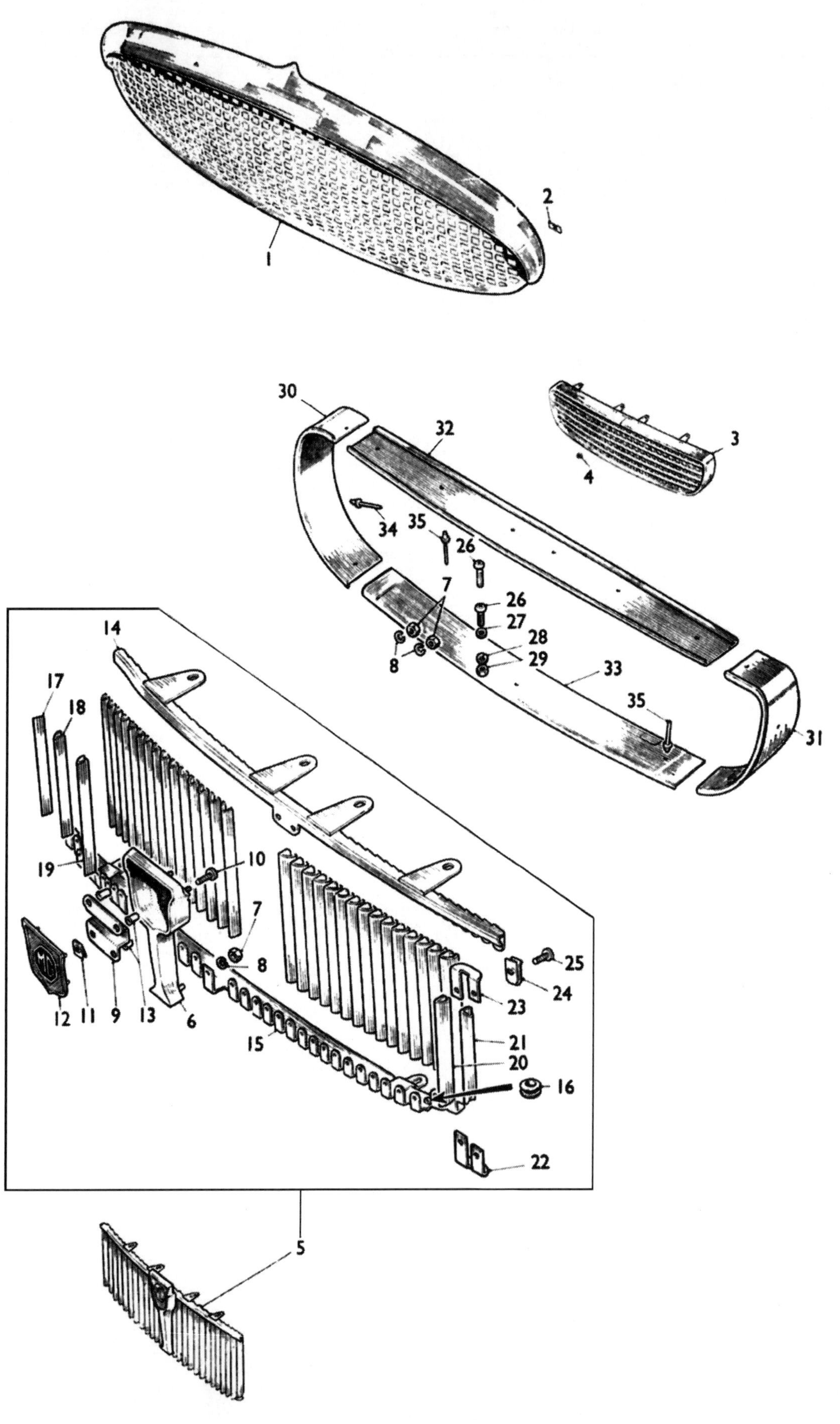
2
1
30
32
3
4
34
35
26
7
26
27
28
8
29
33
35
31
14
17
18
19
10
7
8
25
24
23
12
11
9
13
6
15
21
20
16
22
5

RADIATOR GRILLE

		Page	Plate
FINISHER—GRILLE SURROUND	... ...	BJ 2	J 1
GRILLE—RADIATOR	... ...	BJ 2	J 1

RADIATOR GRILLE

DESCRIPTION		Part No.	Illus. No.	Quantity	Change Point	REMARKS
Grille—radiator	**Sprite**	14A 4715	1	1		
Push-on-fix	**H-AN5**	BHA 4082	2	18		
Grille—radiator	**Sprite**	†AHA 5664	3	1		W.S.E. use AHA 8098
Grille—radiator	**Mk. II**	†AHA 8098	3	1		
Grommet—grille—lower		RFN 204	4	4		
Grille assembly—radiator		†ARA 113	5	1		W.S.E. use ARA 226
		†ARA 226	5	1		W.S.E. use ARA 249
		†ARA 249	5	1		
Centre bar		ARA 1212	6	1		
Nut—centre bar		FNZ 103	7	3		
Washer—spring		LWZ 203	8	3		
Bracket—badge mounting		ARA 1218	9	1		
Screw		PJZ 804	10	1		
Nut—spring		PFS 308	11	1		
Badge		ARA 1211	12	1		
Fix—blind—badge		BHA 4426	13	4		Part No. change; was ARA 1288
Bar—grille	**Midget**					
Upper		†ARA 1198	14	1		W.S.E. use ARA 2070
Upper		†ARA 2070	14	1		
Lower		†ARA 1205	15	1		
Grommet—lower bar		ARA 1259	16	4		
Slat						
Short—RH—No. 1		ARA 1208	17	1		
Long—RH—No. 2		ARA 1215	18	1		
Nos. 3 to 24 inclusive		ARA 1210	19	32		
Long—LH—No. 35		ARA 1216	20	1		
Short—LH—No. 36		ARA 1209	21	1		
Link—slat—RH		ARA 1206	22	2		
Link—slat—LH		ARA 1207	23	2		
Clip—slat		ARH 596	24	76		
Screw—clip		PZZ 606	25	76		Part No. change; was ARG 642
Screw—short		PMZ 0408	26	4		
Screw—long		PMZ 0410	26	2		
Washer—plain		PWZ 104	27	6		
Washer—spring		LWZ 204	28	6		
Nut	**Sprite**	FNZ 104	29	6		
Finisher—grille surround	**Mk. II**					
Right-hand	**and**	AHA 5512	30	1		
Left-hand	**Midget**	AHA 5518	31	1		
Upper		AHA 5514	32	1		
Lower		AHA 5515	33	1		
Rivet—side finisher		DMP 0829	34	6		Part No. change; was 6K 9788
Rivet—upper and lower finisher		DMP 0819	35	10		Part No. change; was ADB 2582

† Revised Information.

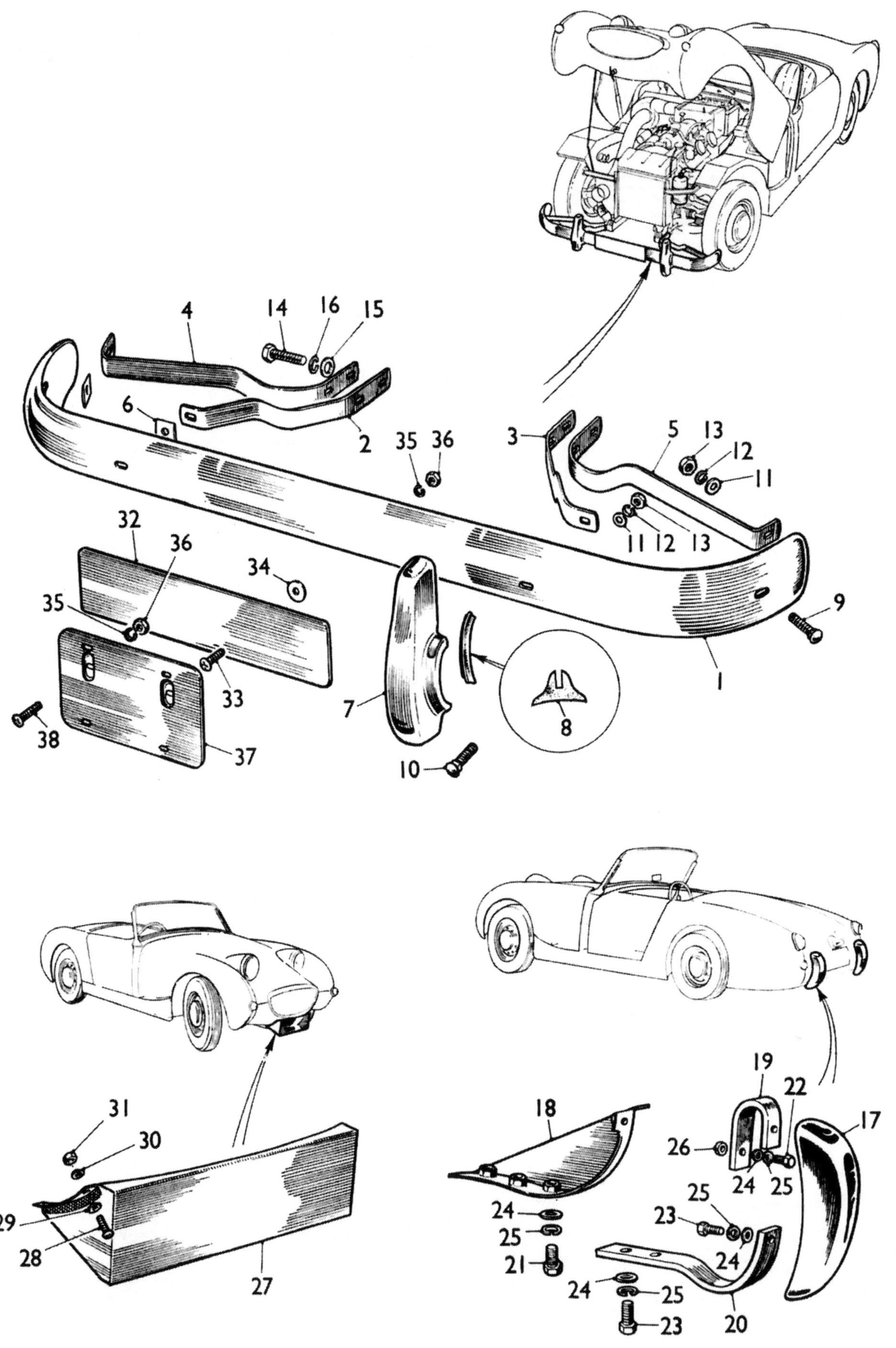

1
2
3
4
5
6
7
8
9
10
11
12
13
14
15
16
17
18
19
20
21
22
23
24
25
26
27
28
29
30
31
32
33
34
35
36
37
38

BUMPERS AND NUMBER-PLATES

	Page	Plate
BUMPER—FRONT	BK 2, BK 3	K 1, K 2
BUMPER—REAR	BK 4	K 3
NUMBER-PLATE—FRONT	BK 2, BK 3	K 1, K 2
NUMBER-PLATE—REAR	BK 4	K 3
OVER-RIDER—FRONT	BK 2, BK 3	K 1, K 2
OVER-RIDER—REAR	BK 4	K 3

BUMPERS AND NUMBER-PLATES

(SPRITE H-AN5)

DESCRIPTION	Part No.	Illus. No.	Quantity	Change Point	REMARKS
Bumper assembly—front	NSP		1		Optional extra
Bar—bumper	27H 9607	1	1		
Bar—mounting					
Inner—RH	27H 9608	2	1		
Inner—LH	27H 9609	3	1		
Outer—RH	27H 9610	4	1		
Outer—LH	27H 9611	5	1		
Plate—packing	ACC 5811	6	4		
Over-rider	27H 9612	7	2		
Moulding—over-rider	†37H 9871		A/R		Supplied in multiples of feet
5″ (13 cm)	†27H 9613	8	4		W.S.E. use 37H 9871
Bolt					
Bumper bar to mounting bar	1G 9872	9	2		Part No. change; was 7H 9740
Over-rider and bumper bar to mounting bar	†AHH 5479	10	2		Part No. change; was 185373. W.S.E. use ACH 9287
Over-rider and bumper bar to mounting bar	ACH 9287	10	2		
Washer—plain	PWZ 106	11	4		
Washer—spring	LWZ 306	12	4		
Nut	FNZ 106	13	4		
Bolt	HBZ 0612	14	4		
Washer—plain	PWZ 106	15	4		
Washer—spring	LWZ 206	16	4		
Over-rider—rear	14A 4734	17	2		
Bracket—over-rider					
Inner	14A 8411	18	2		
Upper	14A 4738	19	2		
Lower	14A 4739	20	2		
Screw					
Inner bracket	HZS 0504	21	7		
Upper bracket	HZS 0507	22	2		
Lower bracket and over-rider	HZS 0506	23	8		
Washer					
Plain	PWZ 105	24	12		
Spring	LWZ 205	25	12		
Upper bracket to body (rubber)	2K 9679	26	2		
Number-plate—front	14A 4659	27	1		Required when bumper is not fitted
Screw	PMZ 0306	28	4		Required when bumper is not fitted
Washer—plain	PWZ 203	29	4		Required when bumper is not fitted
Washer—spring	LWZ 203	30	4		Required when bumper is not fitted
Nut	FNZ 103	31	4		Required when bumper is not fitted
Number-plate—front (**Except N. America**)	ADG 474	32	1		For use when bumper is fitted
Screw (**Except N. America**)	PMZ 0412	33	2		For use when bumper is fitted
Washer—packing (**Except N. America**)	AHH 5712	34	6		For use when bumper is fitted
Washer—spring (**Except N. America**)	LWZ 204	35	2		For use when bumper is fitted
Nut (**Except N. America**)	FNZ 104	36	2		For use when bumper is fitted
Support—number-plate (**N. America**)	AHA 5211	37	1		For use when bumper is fitted
Screw (**N. America**)	PMZ 0410	38	2		For use when bumper is fitted
Washer—spring (**N. America**)	LWZ 204	35	2		For use when bumper is fitted
Nut (**N. America**)	FNZ 104	36	2		For use when bumper is fitted

† Revised Information.

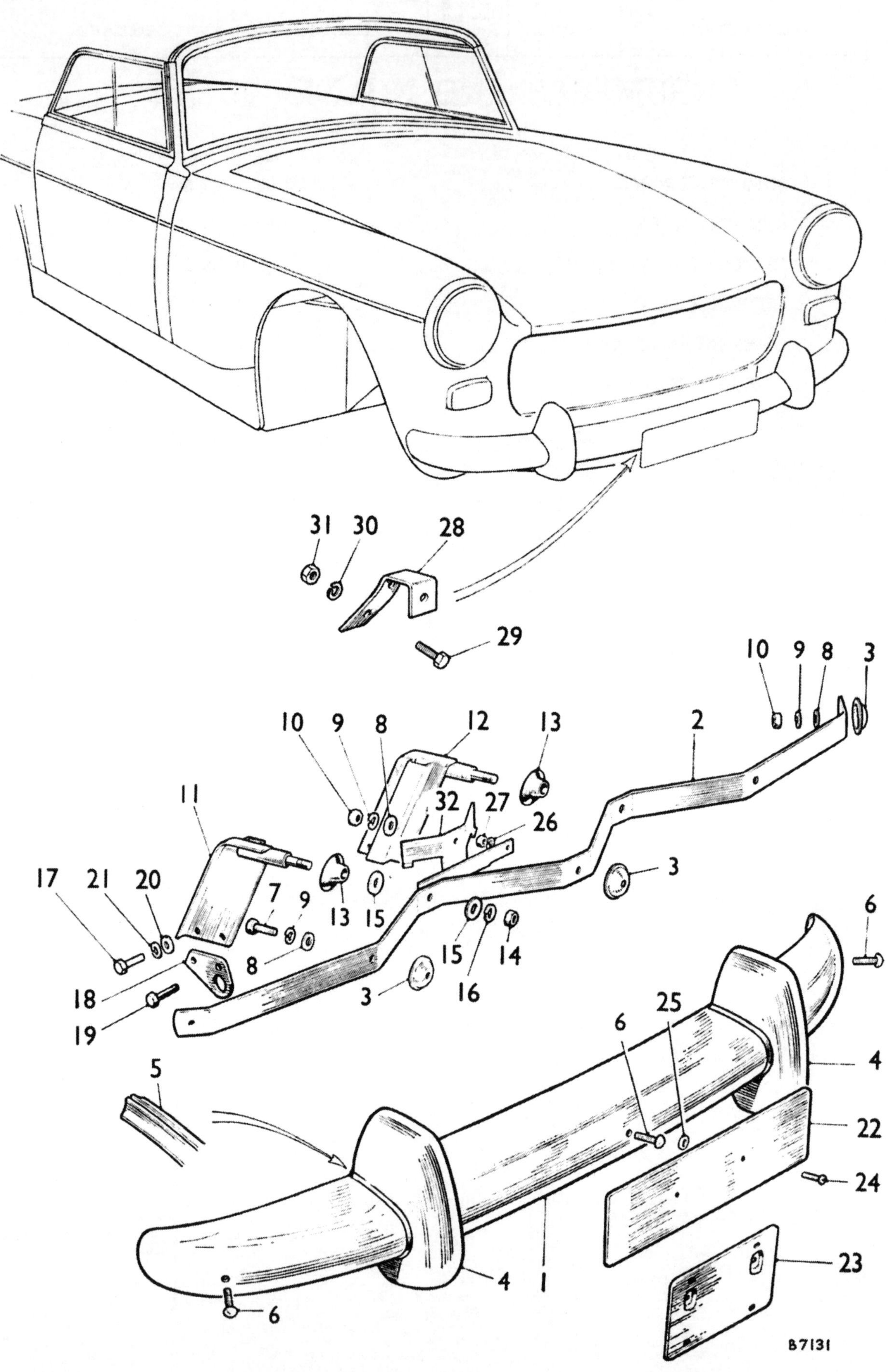
31
30
28
29
10
9
8
3
10
9
8
12
13
2
11
32
27
26
17
21
20
7
9
13
15
3
6
8
15
14
18
3
16
19
6
25
5
4
22
24
4
1
23
6
B7131

DESCRIPTION	Part No.	Illus. No.	Quantity	Change Point	REMARKS
Bumpers and Number-plates—*continued*					
(SPRITE Mk. II AND MIDGET)					
Bumper assembly—front	NSP		1		
Bar—bumper	AHA 5695	1	1		
Bar—mounting	AHA 5696	2	1		
Washer—cup—packing	11B 5721	3	5		
Over-rider	AHA 5686	4	2		
Moulding—over-rider	†37H 9871		A/R		Supplied in multiples of feet. Correction; was 37H 9271
Bolt 5″ (13 cm)		5	4		
Bolt Bumper bar to mounting bar	AHH 5479	6	5/3		W.S.E. use ACH 9287; Quantity reduced when over-riders are fitted
Bolt Bumper bar to mounting bar	ACH 9287	6	5/3		Quantity reduced when over-riders are fitted
Bolt Over-rider and bumper bar to mounting bar	HBZ 0611	7	2		
Washer—plain	PWZ 106	8	5		
Washer—spring	LWZ 206	9	5		
Nut	FNZ 106	10	5/3		Quantity reduced when over-riders are fitted
Bracket—bumper mounting—RH	AHA 5521	11	1		
Bracket—bumper mounting—LH	AHA 5522	12	1		
Grommet—bracket (rubber)	AAA 1645	13	2		Part No. change; was 130383
Nut	FNZ 108	14	2		
Washer—plain	PWZ 208	15	2		
Washer—spring	LWZ 208	16	2		
Screw	HZS 0606	17	4		Required when towing eye is not fitted
Eye—towing—front **Canada**	AHA 6498	18	2	(C) H-AN6-24125 to 24731 (C) H-AN7-24732 on (C) G-AN1-15850 to 16183 (C) G-AN2-16184 on	
Screw **Canada**	HZS 0608	19	4	(C) H-AN6-24125 to 24731 (C) H-AN7-24732 on (C) G-AN1-15850 to 16183 (C) G-AN2-16184 on	
Washer—plain	PWZ 106	20	4		
Washer—spring	LWZ 206	21	4		
Number-plate—front **Except N. America**	ADG 474	22	1		
Support—number-plate **N. America**	AHA 5211	23	1		
Screw	PMZ 0410	24	2		
Washer—packing	AHH 5712	25	2		
Washer—spring	LWZ 204	26	2		
Nut	FNZ 104	27	2		
Bracket—mounting—number-plate and support **Sprite Mk. II**	AHA 5534	28	2		Required when bumper is not fitted
Screw **Sprite Mk. II**	HZS 0405	29	4		Required when bumper is not fitted
Washer—spring **Sprite Mk. II**	LWZ 204	30	4		Required when bumper is not fitted
Nut **Sprite Mk. II**	FNZ 104	31	4		Required when bumper is not fitted
Bracket—mounting—number-plate and support	AHA 5533	32	1		For use when bumper is fitted

† Revised Information.

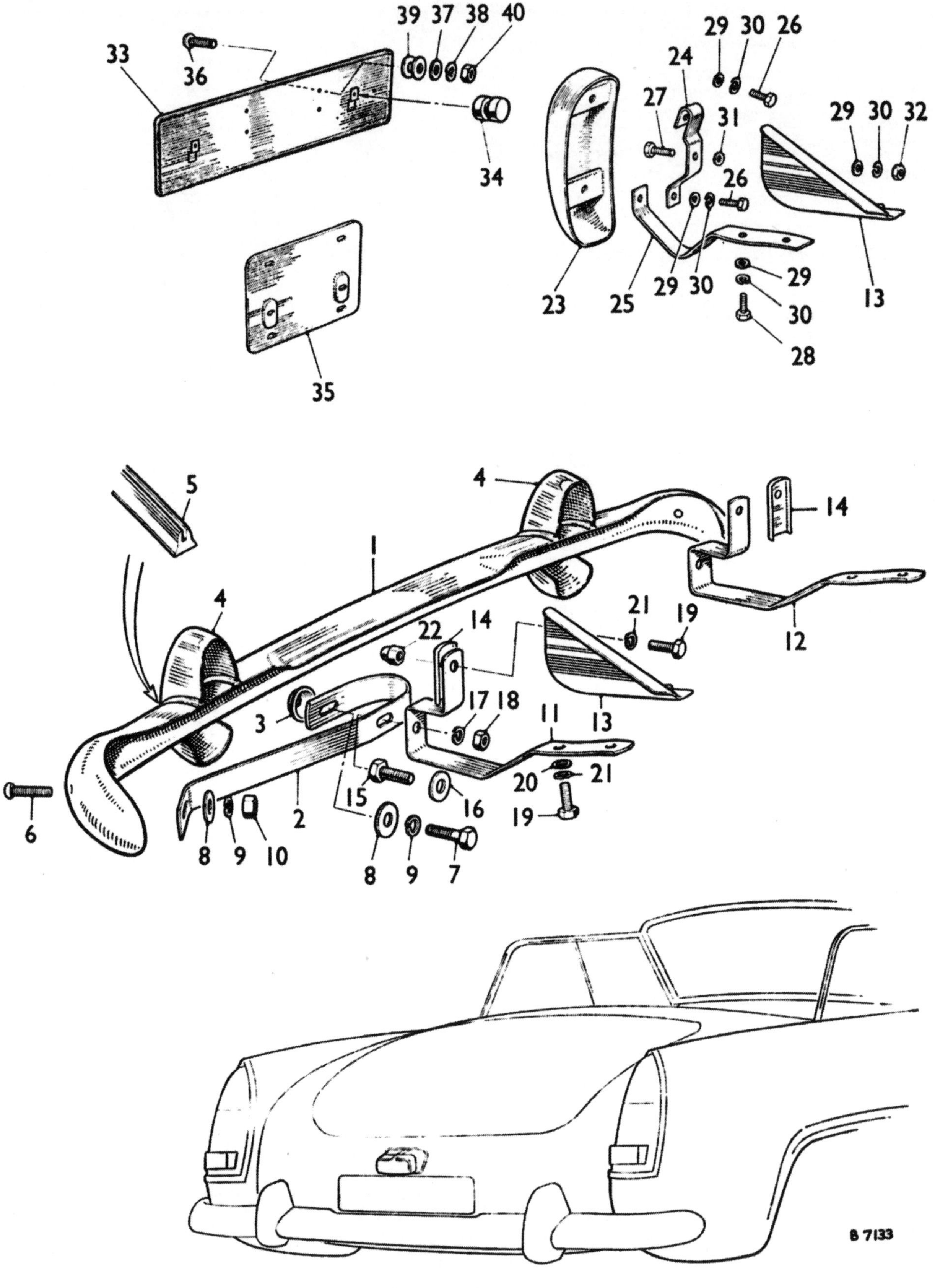
39 37 38 40
29 30 26
33
36
24
27
31
29 30 32
34
26
29 30
29
30
13
23
25
28
35
4
5
14
1
4
21
19
22
14
12
13
17 18
11
3
20
21
6
15
16
19
2
8 9 10
8 9 7
B 7133

Bumpers and Number-plates—*continued*
(Sprite Mk. II and Midget)—*continued*

DESCRIPTION	Part No.	Illus. No.	Quantity	Change Point	REMARKS
Bumper assembly—rear	NSP		1		
Bar—bumper	AHA 5673	1	1		
Bar—mounting	AHA 5675	2	2		
Washer—cup—packing	11B 5721	3	4		
Over-rider	AHA 5686	4	2		For use when bumper is fitted
Moulding—over-rider	37H 9871		A/R		Supplied in multiples of feet
5" (13 cm)		5	4		
Bolt					
Bumper bar to mounting bar	AHH 5479	6	4/2		Not available; use ACH 9287 — Quantity reduced when over-riders are fitted
Bumper bar to mounting bar	ACH 9287	6	4/2		
Over-rider and bumper bar to mounting bar	HBZ 0611	7	2		
Washer—plain	PWZ 106	8	4		
Washer—spring	LWZ 206	9	4		
Nut	FNZ 106	10	4/2		Quantity reduced when over-riders are fitted
Bracket					
Bumper support—RH	AHA 5677	11	1		
Bumper support—LH	AHA 5678	12	1		
Mounting—bumper or over-rider	AHA 5765	13	2		
Finisher—support bracket	AHA 5679	14	2		
Screw	HZS 0608	15	2		
Washer—plain	PWZ 106	16	2		
Washer—spring	LWZ 206	17	2		
Nut	FNZ 106	18	2		
Screw	HZS 0506	19	8		
Washer—plain	PWZ 105	20	6		
Washer—spring	LWZ 205	21	8		
Nut—dome	14B 2685	22	2		
Over-rider—rear	14A 4734	23	2		
Bracket—over-rider—upper	AHA 5685	24	2		
Bracket—over-rider—lower	AHA 5687	25	2		
Screw					
Bracket to over-rider	HZS 0506	26	4		
Upper bracket **Sprite Mk. II**	HZS 0507	27	2		
Lower bracket and mounting bracket	HZS 0506	28	6		Not required when bumper is fitted
Washer					
Plain	PWZ 105	29	12		
Spring	LWZ 205	30	12		
Upper bracket to body (fibre)	AHA 5693	31	2		
Nut	FNZ 105	32	2		
Number-plate—rear **Except N. America**	AHA 5791	33	1		
Buffer—number-plate	AHA 5804	34	2		
Support—number-plate **N. America**	AHA 5211	35	1		
Screw	PMZ 0412	36	4		
Washer					
Plain	PWZ 104	37	4		
Spring	LWZ 204	38	4		
Packing	AHH 5712	39	6		
Nut	FNZ 104	40	4		

† Revised Information.

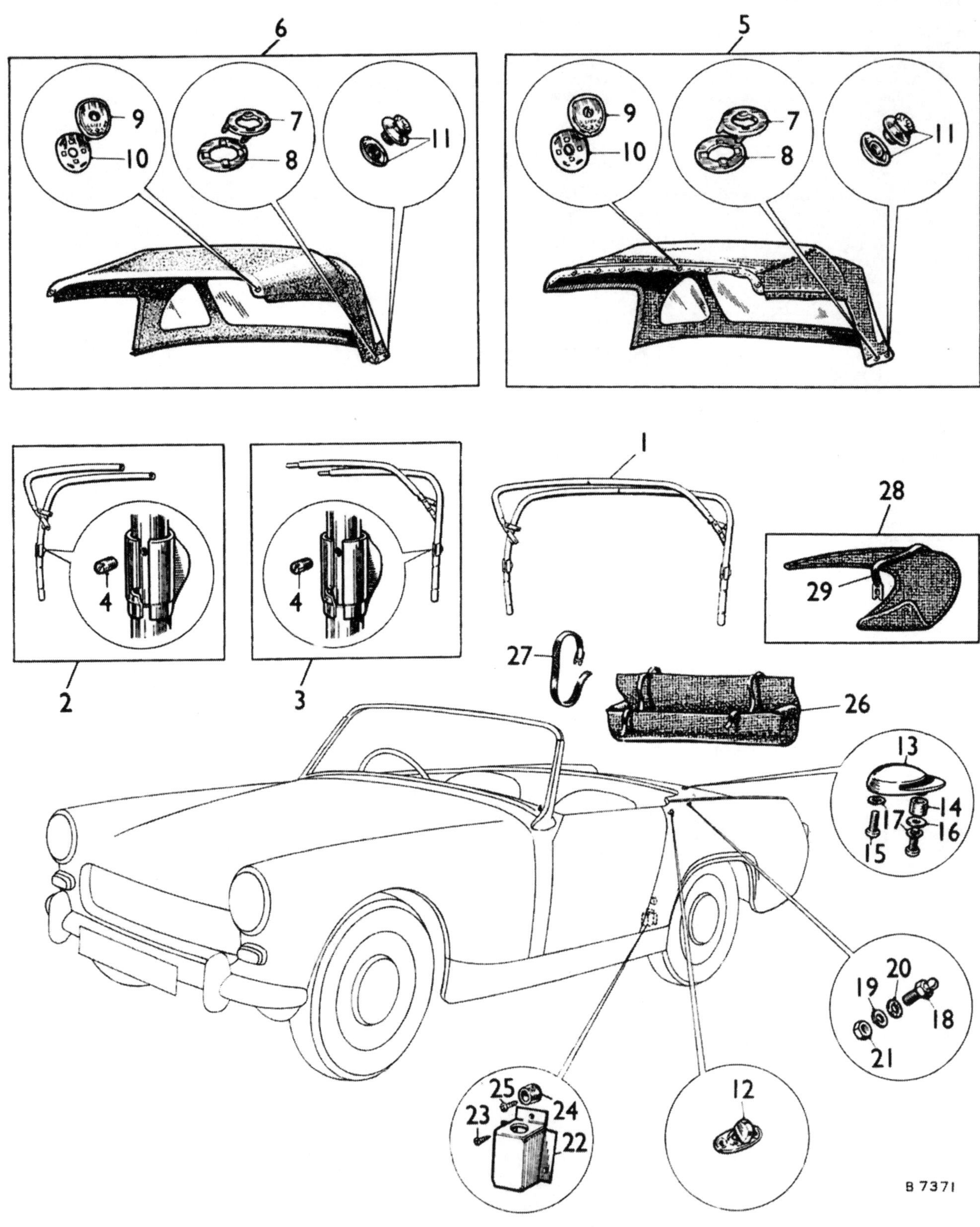
6
5
9
10
7
8
11
1
2
3
4
28
29
27
26
13
14
17
16
15
20
19
18
21
25
24
23
22
12
B 7371

HOOD, TONNEAU COVER AND HARD TOP

	Page	*Plate*
BAG — STOWAGE — HOOD FRAME AND HOOD COVER	BL 2	L 1
BAG—STOWAGE—TONNEAU COVER	BL 4	L 2
COVER—HOOD	BL 2	L 1
COVER—TONNEAU	BL 3	L 2
FRAME—HOOD	BL 2	L 1
HARD TOP	BL 5, BL 6	L 3, L 4
RAILS—TONNEAU COVER SUPPORT	BL 4	L 2

HOOD, TONNEAU COVER, AND HARD TOP

HOOD

DESCRIPTION	Part No.	Illus. No.	Quantity	Change Point	REMARKS
Frame—hood	14A 4754	1	1	(C) H-AN5-501 to 5476 (less 5137, 5287, and 5288)	Not available; use AHA 5324
Frame—hood	AHA 5324	1	1	(C) H-AN5-5477 to 50116 (plus 5137, 5287, and 5288)	Not available; use AHA 5768 and AHA 5769
Frame assembly—hood—RH	AHA 5768	2	1	(C) H-AN6-101 to 24731	
Frame assembly—hood—LH	AHA 5769	3	1	(C) H-AN7-24732 on	
Peg—release catch	37H 9797	4	2	(C) G-AN1-101 to 16183	
				(C) G-AN2-16184 on	
Cover assembly—hood					
Black (**Sprite H-AN5**)	14A 4806	5	1	(C) H-AN5-501 to 5476 (less 5137, 5287, and 5288)	
Black (**Sprite H-AN5**)	AHA 5823	6	1	(C) H-AN5-5477 to 50116	
White (**Sprite H-AN5**)	AHA 5479	6	1	(plus 5137, 5287, and 5288)	
Black (**Sprite Mk. II**)	AHA 5792	6	1	(C) H-AN6-101 to 24731	Not available; use AHA 5902
Blue (**Sprite Mk. II**)	AHA 5964	6	1	(C) H-AN7-24732 on	
Grey (**Sprite Mk. II**)	AHA 5965	6	1		Not available; use AHA 5901
Red (**Sprite Mk. II**)	AHA 5899	6	1	(C) H-AN7-24732 on	
Hazelnut (**Sprite Mk. II**)	AHA 6712	6	1		
Red (**Midget**)	AHA 5899	6	1	(C) G-AN1-101 to 16183	
Blue (**Midget**)	AHA 5900	6	1	(C) G-AN2-16184 on	
Grey (**Midget**)	AHA 5901	6	1		
Black (**Midget**)	AHA 5902	6	1	(C) G-AN2-16184 on	
Hazelnut (**Midget**)	AHA 6712	6	1		
Eyelet	8F 2408	7	2		Not available; use 14A 6537
Eyelet	14A 6537	7	2		
Washer—eyelet	8F 2409	8	2		Not available; use 14A 6538
Washer—eyelet	14A 6538	8	2		
Fastener (Lift-the-dot)	4K 9671	9	A/R		Not available; use LFS 107
Fastener (Lift-the-dot)	LFS 107	9	A/R		
Plate—fastener	4K 9670	10	A/R		Not available; use LFS 100
Plate—fastener	LFS 100	10	A/R		
Fastener	TFS 106	11	4		Part No. change; was 14B 2465
Button—turn	14A 6536	12	2		Part No. change; was 8F 2480
Retainer—cover	14B 1730	13	2		
Collar—distance—retainer	11K 5564	14	2		
Screw	PMZ 0305	15	4		
Washer—plain	PWZ 203	16	2		
Washer—spring	LWZ 203	17	4		
Peg—fastener	TFP 1006	18	4		Part No. change; was 14B 2464
Washer—spring	LWZ 203	19	4		
Washer (leather)	2K 4936	20	4		
Nut	FNZ 103	21	4		
Bracket—stowage—hood tubes	14A 4879	22	2		
Screw	PTZ 804	23	6	(C) H-AN5-501 to 50116	
Buffer	2H 5905	24	2		
Screw	PTZ 805	25	2		
Bag—stowage—cover	AHA 5884	26	1	(C) H-AN6-101 to 24731	
Strap—bag to bulkhead	AHA 5217	27	2	(C) H-AN7-24732 on	
Bag—stowage—frame	AHA 5698	28	1	(C) G-AN1-101 to 16183	
Strap	AAA 2064	29	1	(C) G-AN2-16184 on	Not available; use AAA 4258
Strap	AAA 4258	29	1		

† Revised Information.

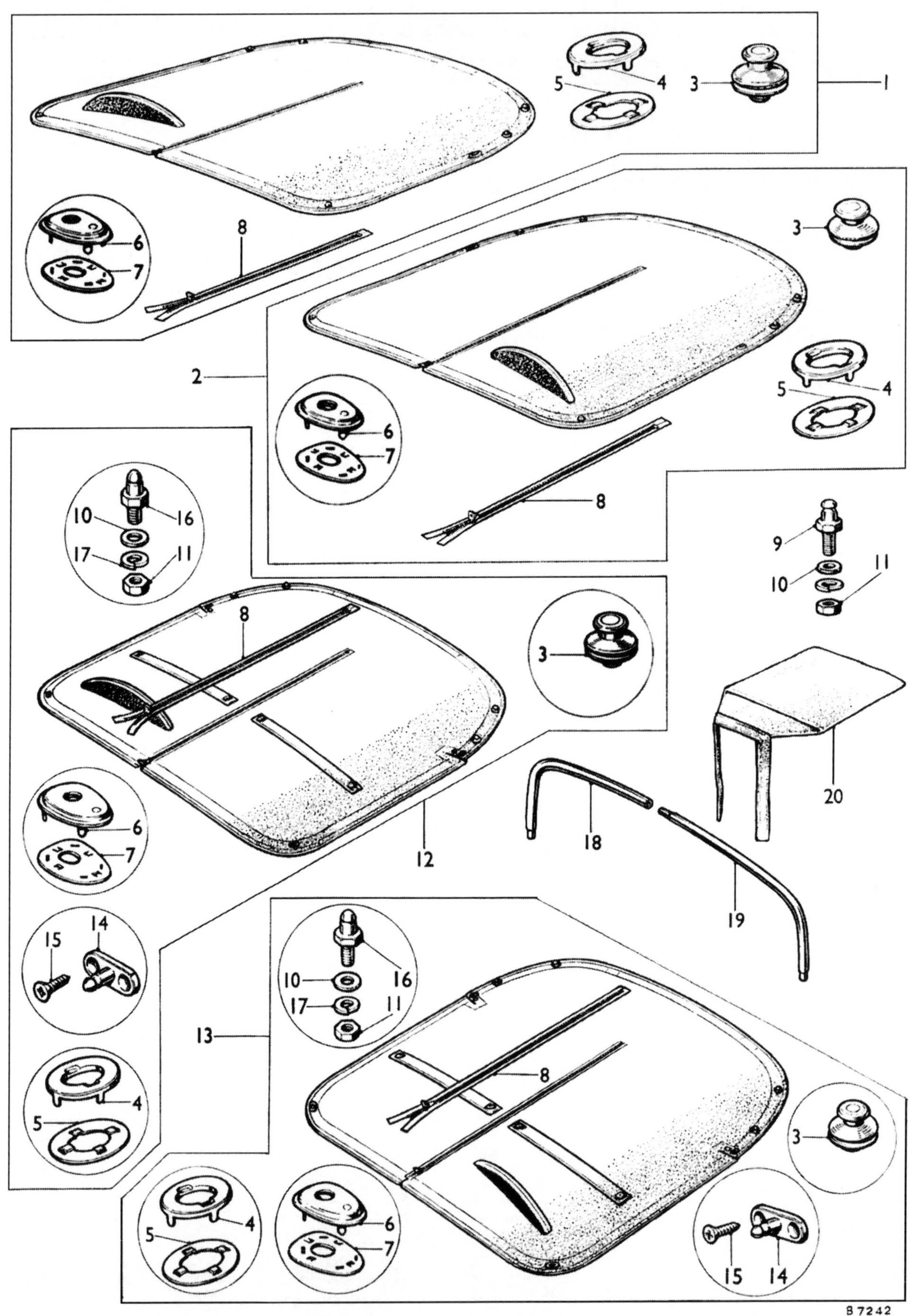
1
2
3
4
5
6
7
8
9
10
11
12
13
14
15
16
17
18
19
20
B 7242

Hood, Tonneau Cover, and Hard Top—*continued*

TONNEAU COVER (OPTIONAL EXTRA)

DESCRIPTION		Part No.	Illus. No.	Quantity	Change Point	REMARKS
Cover assembly—tonneau						
Black RHD		AHA 5256	1	1	(C) H-AN5-501 to 50116	
Black LHD		AHA 5257	2	1		
White RHD		AHA 5482	1	1	(C) H-AN5-13548 to 50116	
White LHD		AHA 5483	2	1		
Fastener		TFS 106	3	4		Part No. change; was 14B 2465
Eyelet		14A 6537	4	2		Part No. change; was 97H 498
Washer—eyelet	**Sprite H-AN5**	14A 6538	5	2		Part No. change; was 97H 497
Fastener (Lift-the-dot)		LFS 107	6	3		Part No. change; was 7H 9961 and 2H 5008
Plate—fastener		LFS 100	7	3		Part No. change; was 2H 5004
Fastener—zip—Black		AHA 5657	8	1		
Fastener—zip—White		AHA 5658	8	1	(C) H-AN5-13543 to 50116	
Peg—fastener		97H 717	9	3		
Washer (leather)		2K 4936	10	3		
Nut		AJD 8012 Z	11	3		
Cover assembly—tonneau						
Red RHD		AHA 5999	12	1	(C) H-AN6-101 to 1523	Not available; use 8G 9110
Red LHD		AHA 6133	13	1		Not available; use 8G 9113
Red RHD		8G 9110	12	1	(C) H-AN6-1524 to 24731	
Red LHD		8G 9113	13	1	(C) H-AN7-24732 on	
Blue RHD	**Sprite Mk. II**	AHA 6000	12	1	(C) H-AN6-101 to 3947	Not available; use 8G 9111
Blue LHD		AHA 6134	13	1		Not available; use 8G 9114
Blue RHD		8G 9111	12	1	(C) H-AN6-3948 to 24731	
Blue LHD		8G 9114	13	1	(C) H-AN7-24732 on	
Black RHD		AHA 5998	12	1		Not available; use 8G 9112
Black LHD		AHA 6132	13	1		Not available; use 8G 9115
Hazelnut RHD		8G 9176	12	1	(C) H-AN7-24732 on	
Hazelnut LHD		8G 9177	13	1		
Black RHD		8G 9112	12	1		Part No. change; was AHA 5952
Black LHD		8G 9115	13	1		Part No. change; was AHA 6128
Blue RHD		8G 9111	12	1		Part No. change; was AHA 5953
Blue LHD	**Midget**	8G 9114	13	1		Part No. change; was AHA 6129
Red RHD		8G 9110	12	1		Part No. change; was AHA 5954
Red LHD		8G 9113	13	1		Part No. change; was AHA 6130
Hazelnut RHD		8G 9176	12	1	(C) G-AN2-16184 on	
Hazelnut LHD		8G 9177	13	1		
Fastener		TFS 106	3	4		Part No. change; was 14B 2465
Eyelet		14A 6537	4	2		
Washer—eyelet		14A 6538	5	2		
Fastener (Lift-the-dot)		LFS 107	6	7		Part No. change; was 2H 5008
Plate—fastener		LFS 100	7	7		Part No. change; was 2H 5004
Fastener—zip						
Black		AHA 5657	8	1		
Blue		AHA 6221	8	1		
Red		AHA 6220	8	1		
Hazelnut		AHA 6715	8	1	(C) H-AN7-24732 on (C) G-AN2-16184 on	
Peg—fastener		LFP 116	14	4		Part No. change; was 97H 499
Screw		RTP 604	15	8		
Peg—fastener		LFP 1006	16	8		Part No. change; was 17H 9510
Washer (leather)		2K 4936	10	3		
Washer—spring		LWZ 208	17	3		
Nut		AJD 8012 Z	11	3		
Rail—support—tonneau cover—RH	**Sprite Mk. II and Midget**	AHA 6011	18	1		
Rail—support—tonneau cover—LH		AHA 6012	19	1		
Bag—stowage		AHA 5888	20	1		

† Revised Information.

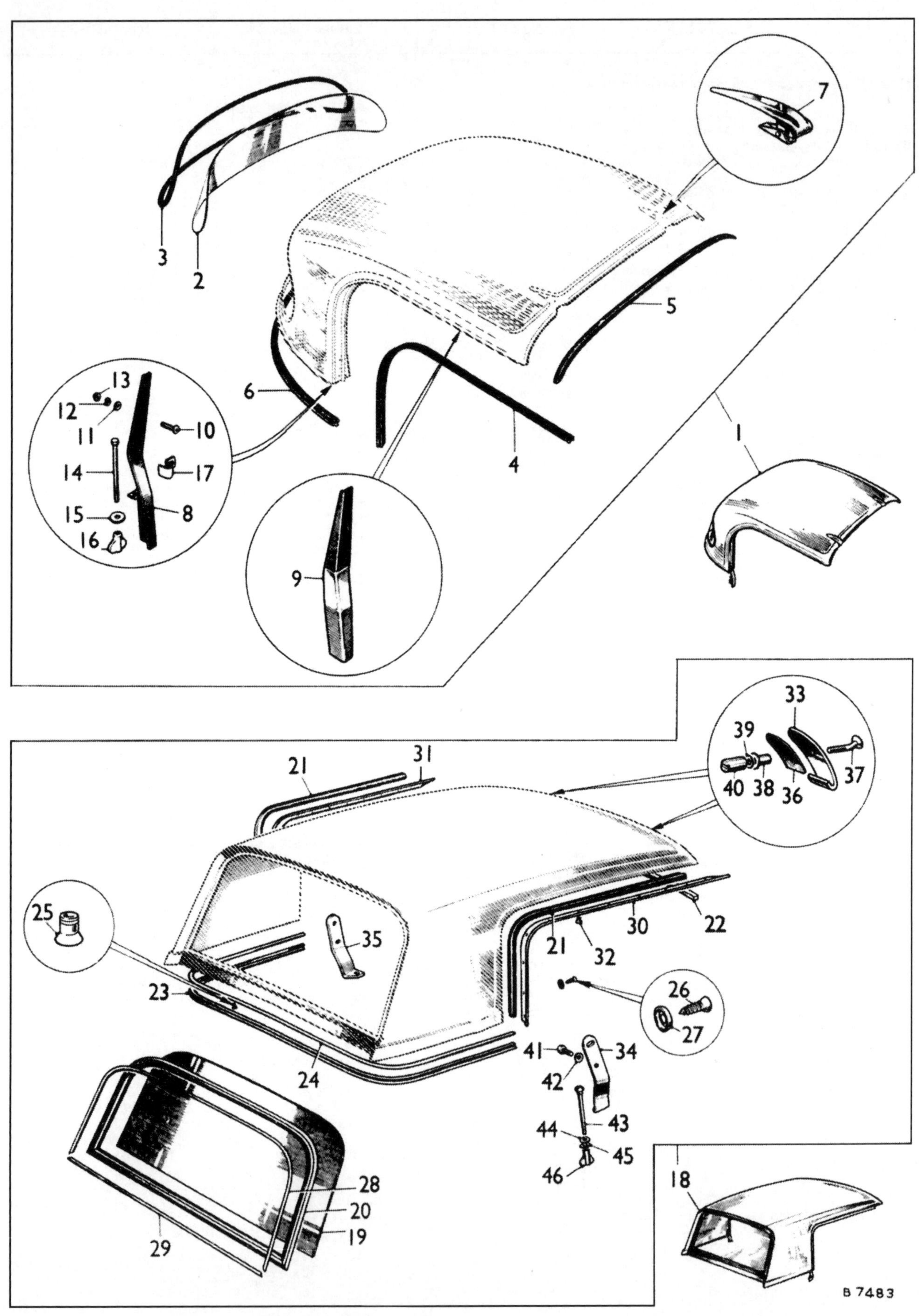
1
2
3
4
5
6
7
8
9
10
11
12
13
14
15
16
17
18
19
20
21
21
22
23
24
25
26
27
28
29
30
31
32
33
34
35
36
37
38
39
40
41
42
43
44
45
46
B 7483

DESCRIPTION	Part No.	Illus. No.	Quantity	Change Point	REMARKS
Hood, Tonneau Cover, and Hard Top—*continued*					
HARD TOP (OPTIONAL EXTRA)					
Hard top assembly—Ivory White Sprite H-AN5	AHA 5485	1	1	(C) H-AN5-5477 to 50116 (plus 5137, 5287, and 5288)	
Hard top assembly—Old English White Sprite Mk. II	AHA 6193	1	1		W.S.E. use AHA 6462
Back-light	37H 9803	2	1		
Rubber—sealing					
Back-light	37H 9800	3	1		
Cant rail	27H 9598	4	2		
Header rail	37H 9801	5	1		
Hard top to body	47H 9601	6	1		
Clamp—toggle	37H 9799	7	2		
Bracket—securing—RH	AHA 5494	8	1		
Bracket—securing—LH	AHA 5495	9	1		
Screw	PMZ 0312	10	8		
Washer—plain	PWZ 103	11	8		
Washer—spring	LWZ 203	12	8		
Nut	FNZ 103	13	8		
Bolt	HBZ 0532	14	2		
Washer—plain	PWZ 206	15	2		
Nut—wing	24B 540	16	2		
Clip—cant rail sealing rubber	AHA 5498	17	2		
Hard top assembly					
Primed	†AHA 6458	18	1		
Red	†AHA 6459	18	1		W.S.E. use AHA 6458
Blue	†AHA 6460	18	1		W.S.E. use AHA 6458
Grey	†AHA 6461	18	1		W.S.E. use AHA 6458
Old English White	†AHA 6462	18	1		W.S.E. use AHA 6458
Back-light	AHA 6242	19	1		
Rubber—sealing					
Back-light	AHA 6336	20	1		
Sidescreen	AHA 6239	21	2		
Hard top to windscreen	AHA 6250	22	1		
Hard top to body	†AHA 6240	23	1		W.S.E. use AHA 7391
Hard top to body	†AHA 7391	23	1		
Retainer—sealing rubber—hard top to body	AHA 6241	24	1		
Rivet—retainer	AHA 6355	25	12		
Screw	RTP 403	26	4		
Washer—cup	FWP 106	27	4		
Finisher—back-light rubber	**Sprite** 27H 2114		A/R		Supplied in multiples of feet
Upper—62″ (158 cm)	**Mk. II** AHA 6473	28	1		W.S.E. use 27H 2114
Lower—44″ (112 cm)	**and** AHA 6474	29	1		W.S.E. use 27H 2114
Moulding—drip—RH	**Midget** AHA 6467	30	1		
Moulding—drip—LH	AHA 6468	31	1		
Rivet—moulding	AHA 6355	32	24		
Clamp					
Front	AHA 6236	33	2		
Side—RH	AHA 6470	34	1		
Side—LH	AHA 6471	35	1		
Washer—seating—front clamp	AHA 6251	36	2		
Bolt—front clamp	AHA 6354	37	2		
Bush	AHA 6237	38	2		
Washer—spring	LWZ 204	39	2		
Nut	AHA 6238	40	2		
Screw	HPS 0507	41	4		
Washer—plain	PWP 105	42	4		
Bolt—side clamp to body	AHA 6249	43	2		
Washer—plain	53K 3427	44	2		
Washer—spring	LWZ 205	45	2		
Nut—wing	24B 540	46	2		

† Revised Information.

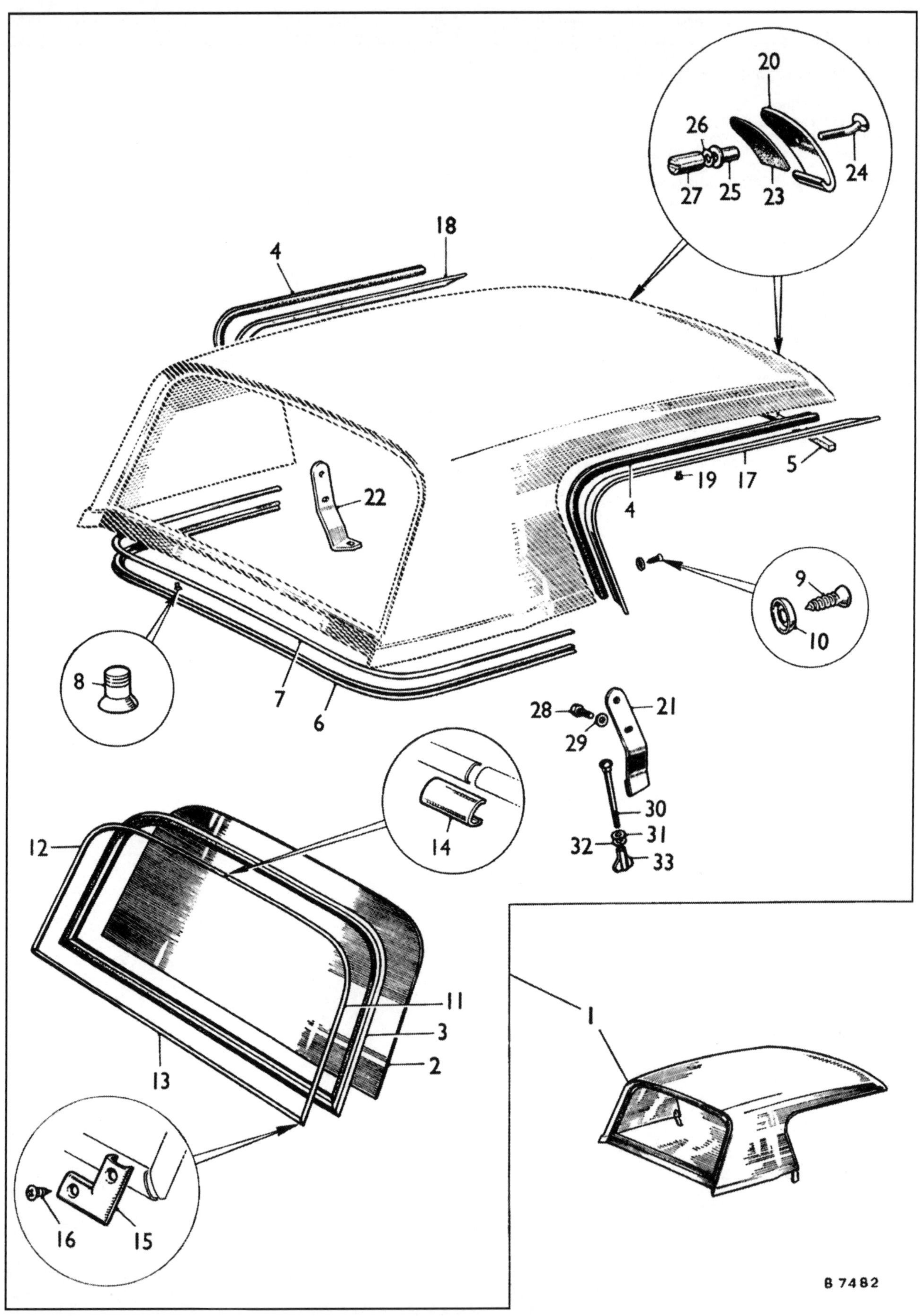
1
2
3
4
5
6
7
8
9
10
11
12
13
14
15
16
17
18
19
20
21
22
23
24
25
26
27
28
29
30
31
32
33
B 7482

Hood, Tonneau Cover, and Hard Top—*continued*
Hard Top (Optional Extra)—*continued*

DESCRIPTION	Part No.	Illus. No.	Quantity	Change Point	REMARKS
Hard top assembly					
Red	†AHA 6301	1	1		W.S.E. use AHA 6459
Blue	AHA 6302	1	1		W.S.E. use AHA 6460
Grey	AHA 6303	1	1		W.S.E. use AHA 6461
Old English White	AHA 6323	1	1		W.S.E. use AHA 6462
Back-light	AHA 6242	2	1		
Rubber—sealing					
Back-light	AHA 6336	3	1		
Sidescreen	AHA 6239	4	1		
Hard top to windscreen	AHA 6250	5	1		
Hard top to body	†AHA 6240	6	1		W.S.E. use AHA 7391
Hard top to body	†AHA 7391	6	1		
Retainer—sealing rubber—hard top to body	AHA 6241	7	1		
Rivet—retainer	AHA 6355	8	1		Use with optional extra sidescreens AHA 6150 RH and AHA 6151 LH (see page BG 3)
Screw	RTP 403	9	4		
Washer—cup	FWP 106	10	4		
Finisher—back-light rubber					
Upper—RH	**Midget** AHA 6244	11	1	(C) G–AN1–101 to 16183	
Upper—LH	AHA 6245	12	1		
Lower	AHA 6259	13	1		
Capping—finisher—centre	ADH 578	14	1		
Capping—finisher—corner	AHA 6246	15	2		
Screw	54K 3021	16	4		
Moulding—drip—RH	AHA 6318	17	1		
Moulding—drip—LH	AHA 6319	18	1		
Rivet—moulding	AHA 6355	19	24		
Clamp					
Front	AHA 6236	20	2		
Side—RH	AHA 6332	21	1		
Side—LH	AHA 6333	22	1		
Washer—seating—front clamp	AHA 6251	23	2		
Bolt—front clamp	AHA 6354	24	2		
Bush	AHA 6237	25	2		
Washer—spring	LWZ 204	26	2		
Nut	AHA 6238	27	2		
Screw	HPZ 0507	28	4		
Washer—plain	PWP 105	29	4		
Bolt—side clamp to body	AHA 6249	30	2		
Washer—plain	53K 8427	31	2		
Washer—spring	LWZ 205	32	2		
Nut—wing	24B 540	33	2		

† Revised Information.

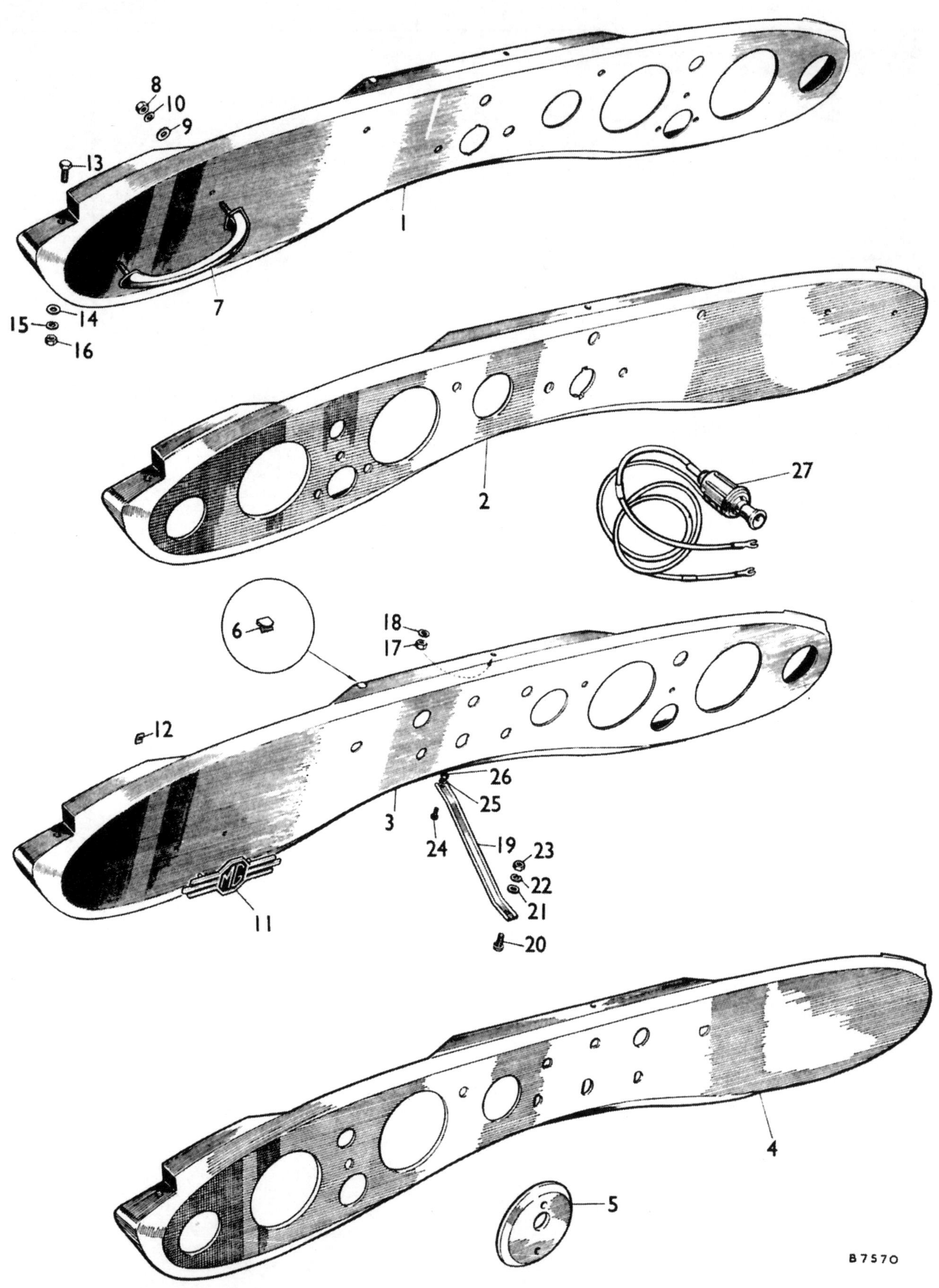
8
10
9
13
1
7
14
15
16
2
27
6
18
17
12
26
25
3
24
19
23
22
21
11
20
4
5
B7570

DESCRIPTION	Part No.	Illus. No.	Quantity	Change Point	REMARKS

FASCIA DETAILS

	Page	Plate
CIGAR-LIGHTER	BM 2	M 1
MOTIF—FASCIA PANEL	BM 2	M 1
PANELS—FASCIA AND INSTRUMENT	BM 2	M 1

FASCIA DETAILS

DESCRIPTION	Part No.	Illus. No.	Quantity	Change Point	REMARKS
Panel—fascia **RHD** **Sprite H-AN5**	14A 4656	1	1		
LHD **Sprite H-AN5**	14A 4657	2	1		
RHD **Sprite Mk. II and Midget**	AHA 5820	3	1		
LHD **Sprite Mk. II and Midget**	AHA 5821	4	1		
Plate—blanking **Sprite H-AN5**	14A 4744	5	1		Not required when tachometer is fitted
Plate—blanking **Sprite Mk. II**	AHA 5882	5	1		Not required when tachometer is fitted
Clip—trim	14A 4497	6	A/R		
Handle—grab **Sprite H-AN5 and Sprite Mk. II**	14B 1729	7	1		
Nut **Sprite H-AN5 and Sprite Mk. II**	FNZ 104	8	2		
Washer—plain **Sprite H-AN5 and Sprite Mk. II**	PWZ 204	9	2		
Washer—spring **Sprite H-AN5 and Sprite Mk. II**	LWZ 204	10	2		
Motif—'M.G.' **Midget**	AHH 5258	11	1		
Nut—Spire—motif to panel **Midget**	ADB 509	12	2		
Screw	HZS 0405	13	2		
Washer—plain	PWZ 104	14	2		
Washer—spring	LWZ 204	15	2		
Nut	FNZ 104	16	2		
Nut	FNZ 104	17	1		
Washer—spring	LWZ 204	18	1		
Stay—panel	14A 4706	19	2		
Screw	PMZ 0410	20	2		
Washer—plain	PWZ 104	21	2		
Washer—spring	LWZ 204	22	2		
Nut	FNZ 104	23	2		
Screw	PMZ 0208	24	2		
Washer—spring	LWZ 202	25	2		
Nut	CNZ 102	26	2		
Cigar-lighter	AHH 5759	27	1		Not available; use AHH 7010 — Optional extra
Cigar-lighter	AHH 7010	27	1		Optional extra

† Revised Information.

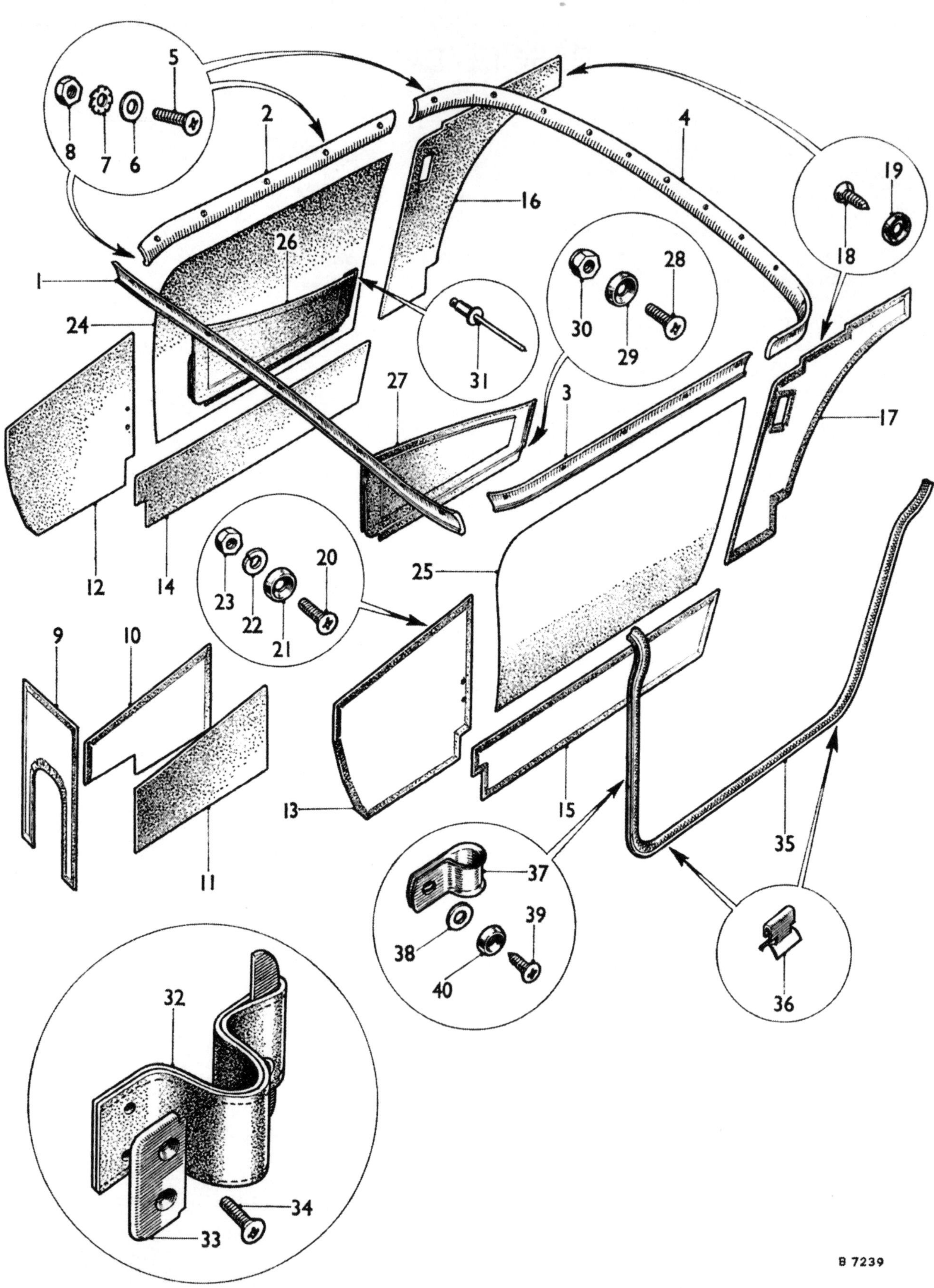
1
2
3
4
5
6
7
8
9
10
11
12
13
14
15
16
17
18
19
20
21
22
23
24
25
26
27
28
29
30
31
32
33
34
35
36
37
38
39
40
B 7239

TRIMMING DETAILS

SPRITE H-AN5

	Page	Plate
BULK MATERIALS	BN 5	—
LINERS—TRIM	BN 2-BN 5	N 1, N 2
MATS	BN 4	N 2
MOULDINGS	BN 2	N 1
SEAL—DOOR	BN 3	N 1

TRIMMING DETAILS (SPRITE H-AN5)

DESCRIPTION	Part No.	Illus. No.	Quantity	Change Point	REMARKS
Moulding					
Scuttle top	14A 4820	1	1		
Door top—RH	14A 4821	2	1	(C) H-AN5-501 to 1605	
Door top—LH	14A 4822	3	1	(C) H-AN5-501 to 1605	
Door top—RH	AHA 5268	2	1	(C) H-AN5-1606 on	
Door top—LH	AHA 5269	3	1	(C) H-AN5-1606 on	
Cockpit rear	14A 4823	4	1		
Screw—moulding					
Scuttle, door and cockpit rear	RMZ 0310	5	22		
Scuttle and cockpit rear	RMZ 0312	5	4/2		Quantity reduced at (C) H-AN5-7256
Scuttle	RMZ 0316	5	2	(C) H-AN5-7256 on	
Washer—plain	PWZ 203	6	2	(C) H-AN5-7256 on	
Washer—shakeproof	LWZ 503	7	26		Part No. change; was 58K 8464 and LWZ 703
Nut	FNZ 103	8	26		
Liner—engine front					
Red	AHA 5090	9	1		
Blue	AHA 5092	9	1		
Black	AHA 5093	9	1		
Green	AHA 5094	9	1		
Liner—engine side					
Red RH	AHA 5201	10	1		
Red LH	AHA 5205	11	1		
Blue RH	AHA 5202	10	1		
Blue LH	AHA 5206	11	1		
Black RH	AHA 5203	10	1		
Black LH	AHA 5207	11	1		
Green RH	AHA 5204	10	1		
Green LH	AHA 5208	11	1		
Liner—scuttle					
Red RH	AHA 5060	12	1		
Red LH	AHA 5065	13	1		
Blue RH	AHA 5062	12	1		
Blue LH	AHA 5067	13	1		
Black RH	AHA 5063	12	1		
Black LH	AHA 5068	13	1		
Green RH	AHA 5064	12	1		
Green LH	AHA 5069	13	1		
Liner—sill					
Red RH	AHA 5100	14	1		
Red LH	AHA 5105	15	1		
Blue RH	AHA 5102	14	1		
Blue LH	AHA 5107	15	1		
Black RH	AHA 5103	14	1		
Black LH	AHA 5108	15	1		
Green RH	AHA 5104	14	1		
Green LH	AHA 5109	15	1		
Liner—rear quarter					
Red RH	AHA 5070	16	1		
Red LH	AHA 5075	17	1		
Blue RH	AHA 5072	16	1		
Blue LH	AHA 5077	17	1		
Black RH	AHA 5073	16	1		
Black LH	AHA 5078	17	1		
Green RH	AHA 5074	16	1		
Green LH	AHA 5079	17	1		
Screw—short	RTZ 604	18	A/R		
Screw—long	RTZ 606	18	A/R		
Washer—cup	7700	19	A/R		Not available; use FWP 106
Washer—cup	FWP 106	19	A/R		
Screw—liner to 'A' post	CMZ 0308	20	2		
Washer—cup	FWP 110	21	2		Part No. change; was 7698
Washer—spring	LWZ 203	22	2		
Nut	FNZ 103	23	2		

† Revised Information.

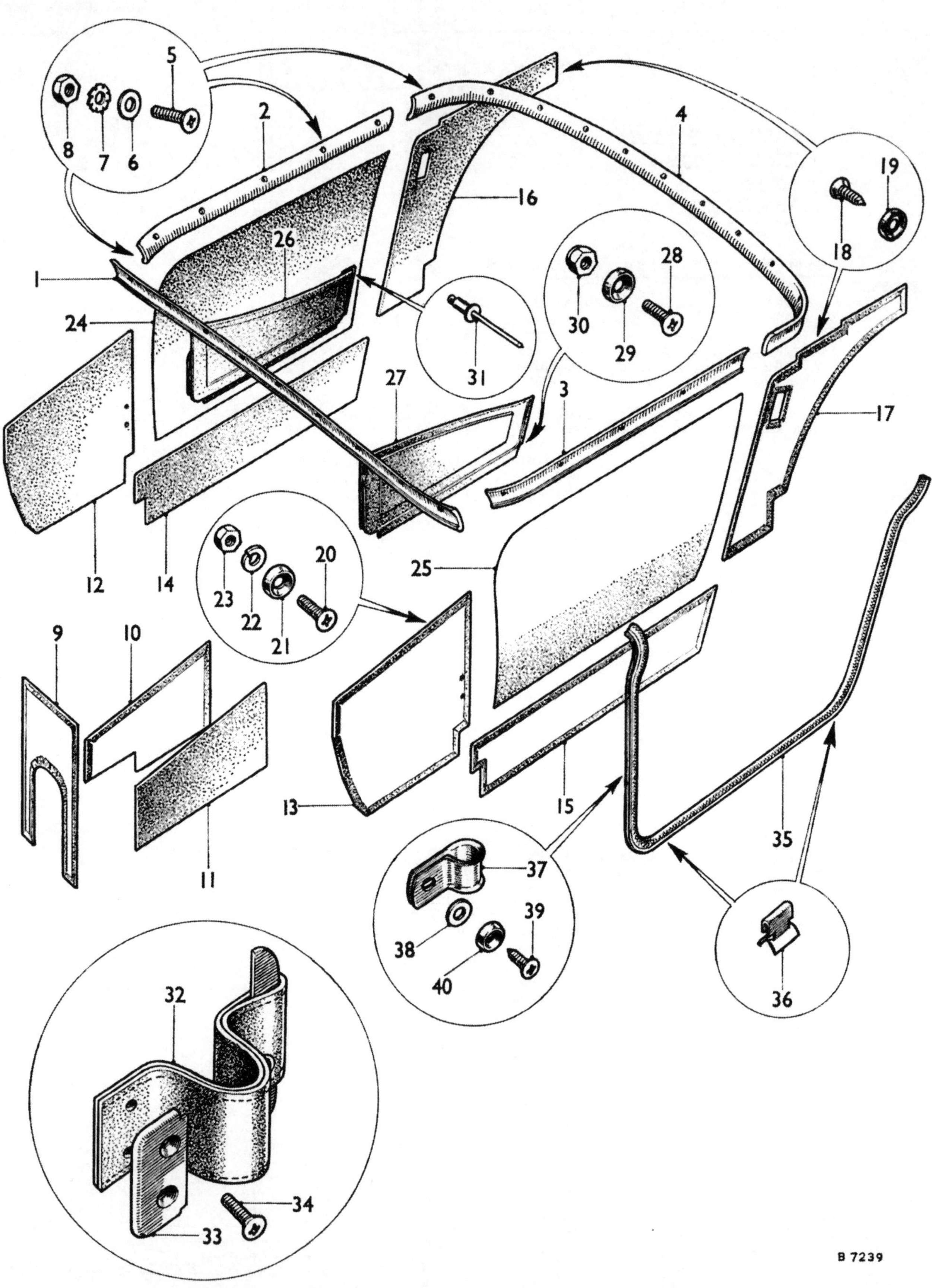
1
2
3
4
5
6
7
8
9
10
11
12
13
14
15
16
17
18
19
20
21
22
23
24
25
26
27
28
29
30
31
32
33
34
35
36
37
38
39
40
B 7239

DESCRIPTION	Part No.	Illus. No.	Quantity	Change Point	REMARKS
Trimming Details—*continued*					
(Sprite H-AN5)—*continued*					
Liner—door inner					
Red RH	AHA 5122	24	1		
Red LH	AHA 5126	25	1		
Blue RH	AHA 5123	24	1		
Blue LH	AHA 5127	25	1		
Black RH	AHA 5124	24	1		
Black LH	AHA 5128	25	1		
Green RH	AHA 5125	24	1		
Green LH	AHA 5129	25	1		
Liner—door pocket					
Red RH	AHA 5050	26	1		
Red LH	AHA 5055	27	1		
Blue RH	AHA 5052	26	1		
Blue LH	AHA 5057	27	1		
Black RH	AHA 5053	26	1		
Black LH	AHA 5058	27	1		
Green RH	AHA 5054	26	1		
Green LH	AHA 5059	27	1		
Screw—liner to door	AHA 5412	28	4	(C) H-AN5-6652 on	
Washer—cup	†7699	29	4	(C) H-AN5-6652 on	W.S.E. use FWP 108
Washer—cup	FWP 108	29	4	(C) H-AN5-6652 on	
Nut	AHA 5418	30	4	(C) H-AN5-6652 on	
Rivet	DMP 0835	31	4		Part No. change; was 6K 9789
Strap—door check					
Red	AHA 5095	32	2		
Blue	AHA 5097	32	2		
Black	AHA 5098	32	2		
Green	AHA 5099	32	2		
Retainer—strap	14A 764	33	2		
Screw	RMZ 0310	34	4		
Seal—door—67" (171 cm)					
Red	†AHA 5118	35	2		W.S.E. use 37H 9951
Blue	†AHA 5119	35	2		W.S.E. use 37H 9952
Black	†AHA 5120	35	2		W.S.E. use 37H 9953
Green	†AHA 5121	35	2		W.S.E. use 37H 9954
Red	37H 9951	35	A/R		Supplied in multiples of yards
Blue	37H 9952	35	A/R		Supplied in multiples of yards
Black	37H 9953	35	A/R		Supplied in multiples of yards
Green	37H 9954	35	A/R		Supplied in multiples of yards
Clip—seal	†14G 5716	36	64		W.S.E. use 13H 4014
	†13H 4014	36	64		
	†PCR 0709	37	2		
Screw	RTZ 606	39	2		
Washer—cup	†7700	40	2		W.S.E. use FWP 106
Washer—cup	FWP 106	40	2		

† Revised Information.

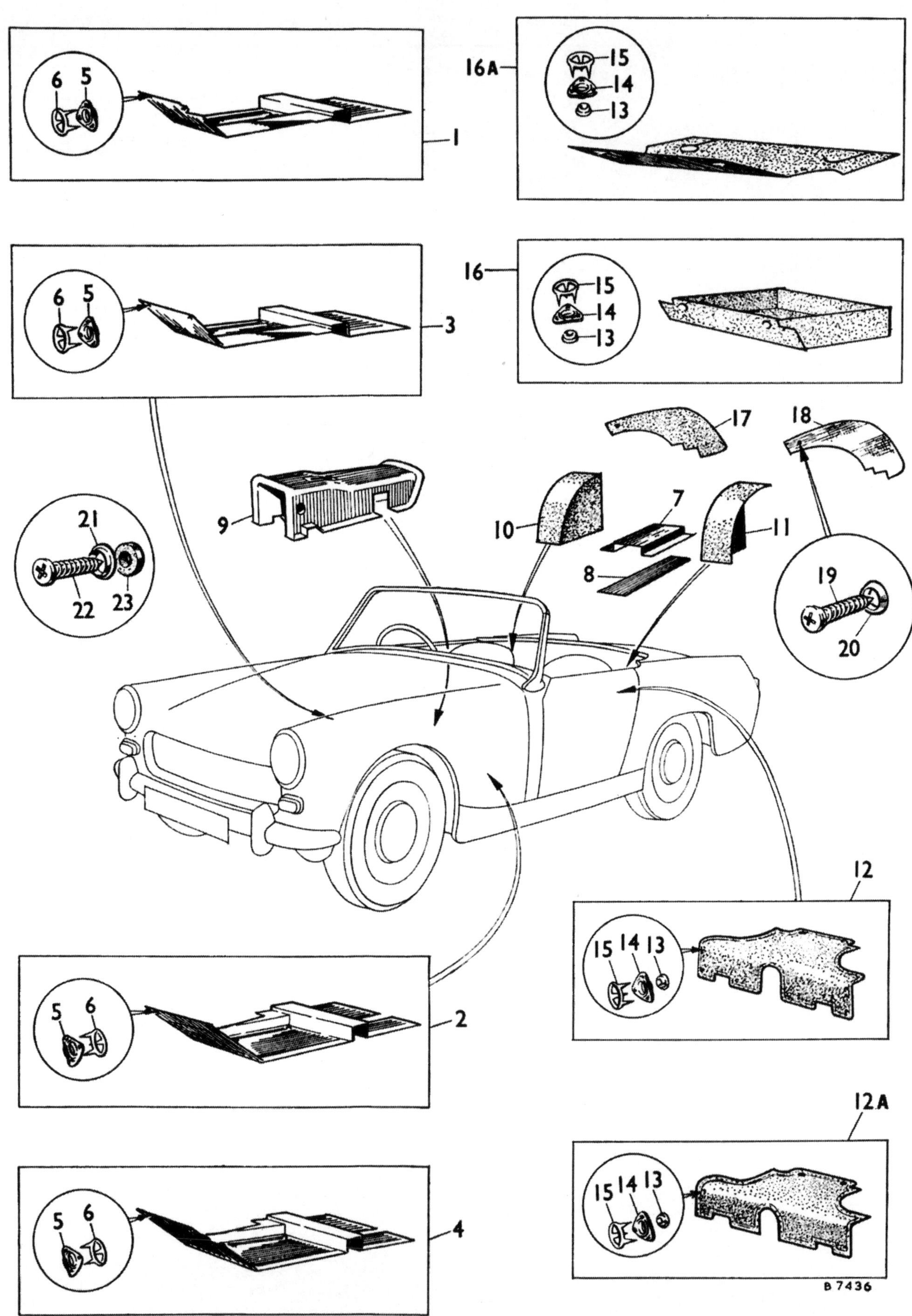
16A
15
14
13
6
5
1
16
3
17
18
9
7
10
11
21
8
22
23
19
20
12
2
4
12A
B 7436

Trimming Details—*continued*
(Sprite H-AN5)—*continued*

DESCRIPTION	Part No.	Illus. No.	Quantity	Change Point	REMARKS
Mat assembly—front **RHD**					
Red RH	AHA 5130	1	1		
Red LH	AHA 5134	2	1		
Blue RH	AHA 5131	1	1		
Blue LH	AHA 5135	2	1		
Black RH	AHA 5132	1	1		
Black LH	AHA 5136	2	1		
Green RH	AHA 5133	1	1		
Green LH	AHA 5137	2	1		
Mat assembly—front **LHD**					
Red RH	AHA 5240	3	1		
Red LH	AHA 5244	4	1		
Blue RH	AHA 5241	3	1		
Blue LH	AHA 5245	4	1		
Black RH	AHA 5242	3	1		
Black LH	AHA 5246	4	1		
Green RH	AHA 5243	3	1		
Green LH	AHA 5247	4	1		
Socket—fastener	2H 8445	5	14		
Ring—socket	14G 8736	6	14		
Mat—longitudinal member					
Red	AHA 5248	7	2	(C) H-AN5-501 to 21546	
Blue	AHA 5249	7	2	(C) H-AN5-501 to 26185	
Black	AHA 5250	7	2	(C) H-AN5-501 to 26464	
Green	AHA 5251	7	2	(C) H-AN5-501 to 37492	
Mat—side					
Red	AHA 5259	8	2		
Blue	AHA 5260	8	2		
Black	AHA 5261	8	2		
Green	AHA 5262	8	2		
Mat—gearbox and tunnel					
Red	AHA 5138	9	1		
Blue	AHA 5139	9	1		
Black	AHA 5140	9	1		
Green	AHA 5141	9	1		
Liner—wheel arch					
Red RH	AHA 5080	10		(C) H-AN5-501 to 4684 (less 4333 to 4470, 4472 to 4621, 4623 to 4679, and 4681 to 4683)	
Red LH	AHA 5085	11			
Blue RH	AHA 5082	10			
Blue LH	AHA 5087	11			
Black RH	AHA 5083	10			
Black LH	AHA 5088	11			
Green RH	AHA 5084	10			
Green LH	AHA 5089	11			
Red RH	AHA 5371	10		(C) H-AN5-4685 on (plus 4333 to 4470, 4472 to 4621, 4623 to 4679, and 4681 to 4683)	
Red LH	AHA 5375	11			
Blue RH	AHA 5372	10			
Blue LH	AHA 5376	11			
Black RH	AHA 5373	10			
Black LH	AHA 5377	11			
Green RH	AHA 5374	10			
Green LH	AHA 5378	11			
Liner assembly—heelboard					
Red	AHA 5110	12	1	(C) H-AN5-501 to 4684 (less 4333 to 4470, 4472 to 4621, 4623 to 4679, and 4681 to 4683)	
Blue	AHA 5111	12	1		
Black	AHA 5112	12	1		
Green	AHA 5113	12	1		
Red	AHA 5379	12A	1	(C) H-AN5-4685 on (plus 4333 to 4470, 4472 to 4621, 4623 to 4679, and 4681 to 4683)	
Blue	AHA 5380	12A	1		
Black	AHA 5381	12A	1		
Green	AHA 5382	12A	1		
Fastener	ADA 2889	13	A/R		Not available; use 2H 8445 together with 14G 8736
Socket—fastener	2H 8445	14	A/R		
Ring—socket	14G 8736	15	A/R		

† Revised Information.

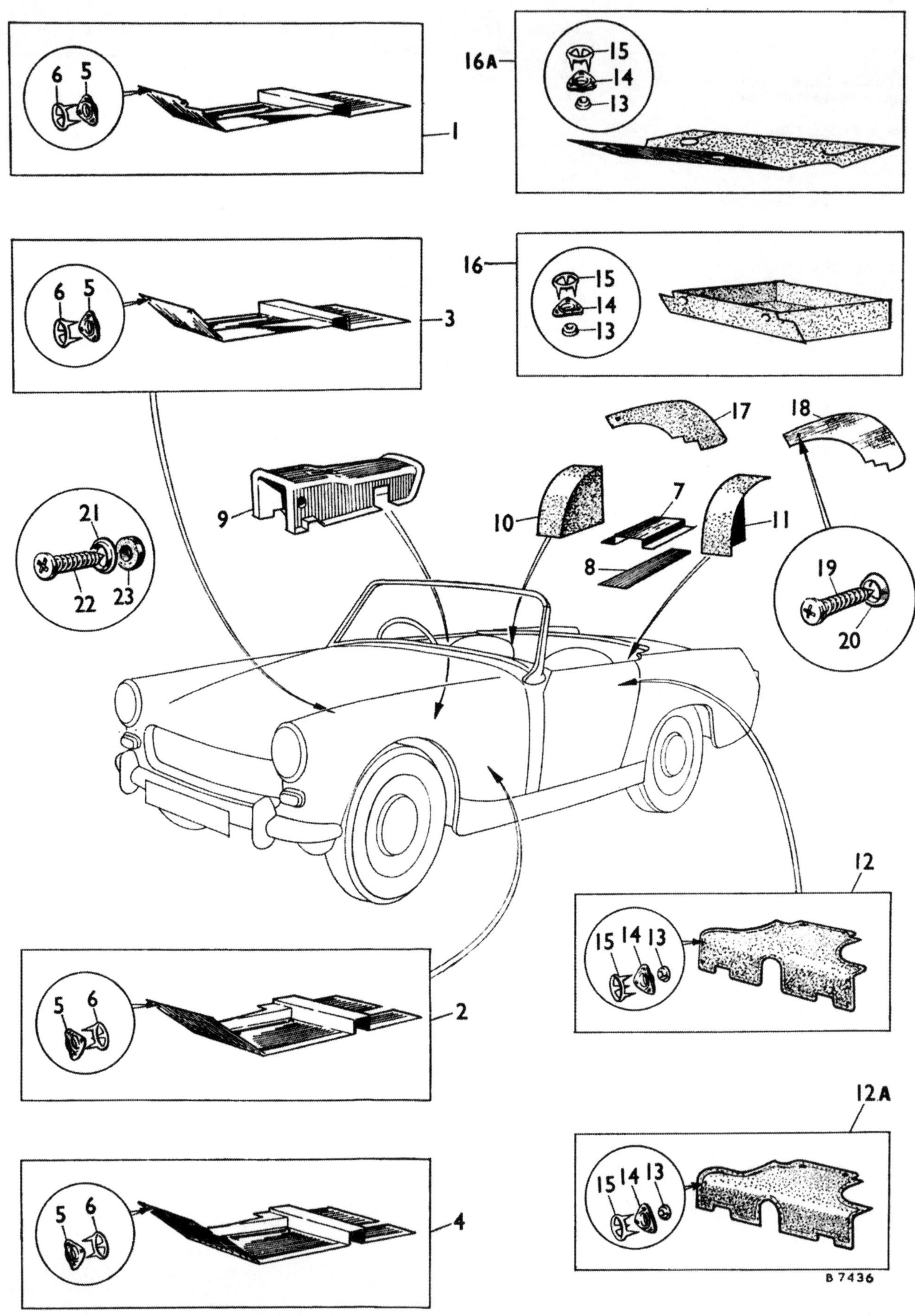
6
5
1
16A
15
14
13
6
5
3
16
15
14
13
17
18
9
10
7
11
21
8
19
22
23
20
12
15
14
13
5
6
2
12A
15
14
13
5
6
4
B 7436

DESCRIPTION	Part No.	Illus. No.	Quantity	Change Point	REMARKS
Trimming Details—*continued*					
(Sprite H-AN5)—*continued*					
Liner assembly—boot floor					
Red	AHA 5114	16	1	(C) H-AN5-501 to 4684 (less 4338 to 4470, 4472 to 4621, 4623 to 4679, and 4681 to 4683)	
Blue	AHA 5115	16	1		
Black	AHA 5116	16	1		
Green	AHA 5117	16	1		
Red	AHA 5383	16A	1	(C) H-AN5-4685 on (plus 4338 to 4470, 4472 to 4621, 4623 to 4679, and 4681 to 4683)	
Blue	AHA 5384	16A	1		
Black	AHA 5385	16A	1		
Green	AHA 5386	16A	1		
Fastener	ADA 2889	13	A/R		W.S.E. use 2H 8445 together with 14G 8736
Socket—fastener	2H 8445	14	A/R		
Ring—socket	14G 8736	15	A/R		
Liner—boot side—Grey—RH	AHA 5355	17	1	(C) H-AN5-4685 on (plus 4338 to 4470, 4472 to 4621, 4623 to 4679, and 4681 to 4683)	
Liner—boot side—Grey—LH	AHA 5356	18	1		
Screw	RTZ 604	19	2		
Washer—cup	7700	20	2		W.S.E. use FWP 106
Washer—cup	FWP 106	20	2		
Stud—socket	ADB 4811	21	A/R		
Screw	CTZ 604	22	A/R		
Washer (fibre)	ADA 3765	23	A/R		
BULK MATERIAL					
Leathercloth—50″ (127 cm) wide					
Red	1AL 566		A/R		Part No. change; was AHA 5005 — Supplied in multiples of yards
Blue	†1AL 252		A/R		Part No. change; was AHA 5006. W.S.E. use 1AL 113
Blue	†1AL 113		A/R		
Black	1AL 102		A/R		Part No. change; was AHA 5007
Green	1AL 351		A/R		Part No. change; was AHA 5008

† Revised Information.

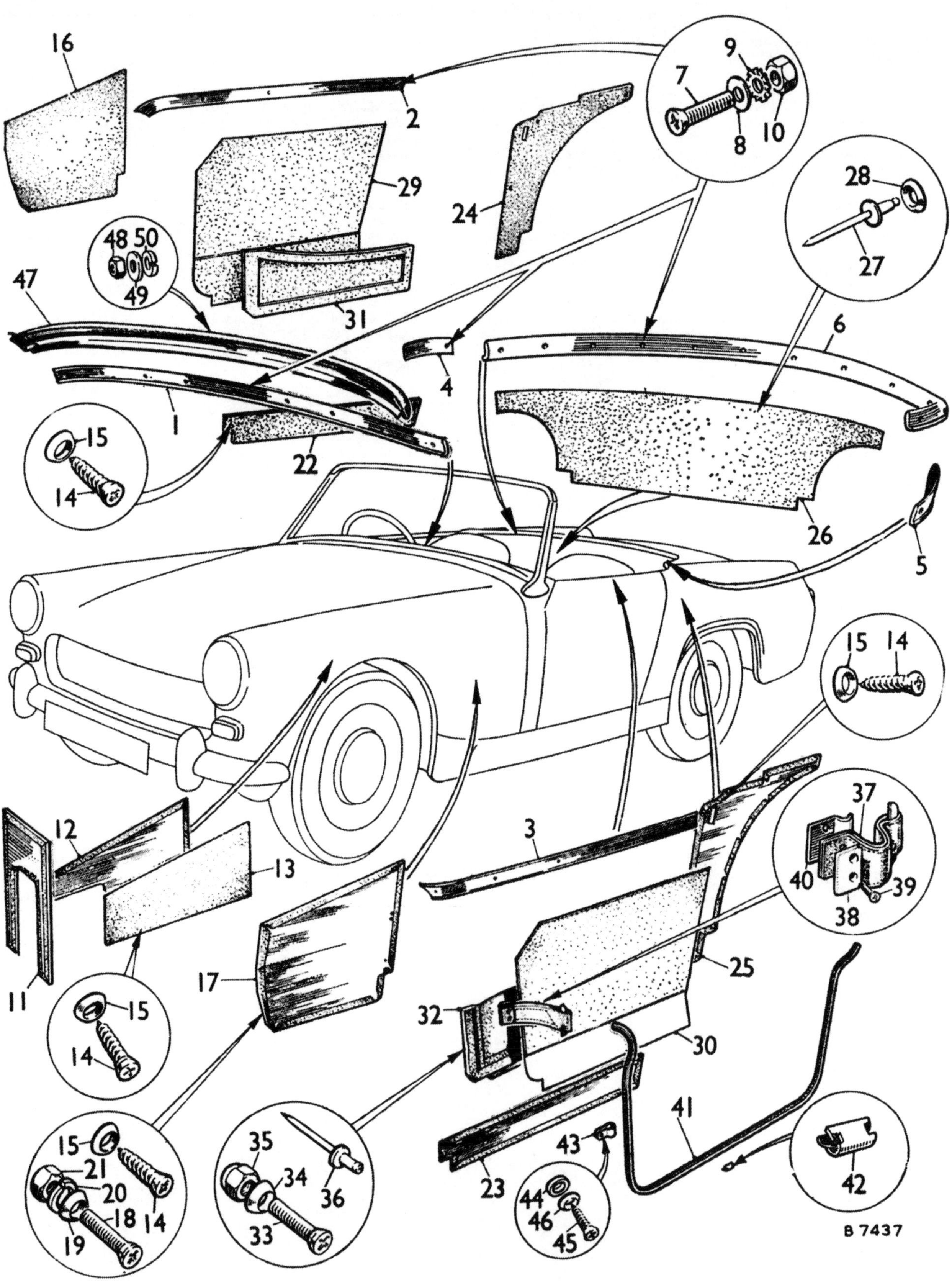
16
2
9
7
8
10
29
24
28
27
48 50
49
47
31
6
4
1
15
14
22
26
5
15 14
12
13
3
37
40
39
38
11
17
15
14
25
32
30
41
43
42
15
21
20
18
14
19
35
34
36
33
23
44
46
45
B 7437

TRIMMING DETAILS

SPRITE MK. II AND MIDGET MK. I

	Page	Plate
BULK MATERIALS	BN 9, BN 13, BN 18	—
CARPETS	BN 9, BN 13, BN 17, BN 18	N 4, N 5, N 7
LINERS—TRIM	BN 6–BN 16	N 3, N 4, N 6
MATS	BN 9, BN 13	N 2
MOULDINGS	BN 6, BN 10, BN 14	N 3–N 5
SEAL—DOOR	BN 8, BN 12, BN 16	N 3, N 4, N 6

Trimming Details—*continued*

(SPRITE MK. II AND MIDGET)

DESCRIPTION		Part No.	Illus. No.	Quantity	Change Point	REMARKS
Moulding						
Scuttle top		14A 4820	1	1		
Door top—RH		AHA 5268	2	1		
Door top—LH		AHA 5269	3	1		
Cockpit rear—RH		AHA 5812	4	1		
Cockpit rear—LH		AHA 5813	5	1		
Cockpit rear—centre		AHA 5814	6	1		
Screw—moulding					(C) H-AN6-101 to 24731	
Scuttle and door		RMZ 0310	7	13		
Scuttle and cockpit rear		RMZ 0312	7	15		
Cockpit rear—RH and LH		RMZ 0316	7	2		
Washer—plain		PWZ 203	8	15		
Washer—shakeproof		LWZ 503	9	30		
Nut		FNZ 103	10	30		
Liner—engine front						
Red		AHA 5090	11	1	See (1) foot of page	
Red		AKE 3025	11	1	See (2) foot of page	
Blue		AHA 5092	11	1	(C) H-AN6-101 to 6284	
Blue		AKE 3026	11	1	(C) H-AN6-6285 to 24731	
Black		AHA 5093	11	1	(C) H-AN6-101 to 6722	
Black		AKE 3024	11	1	(C) H-AN6-6723 to 24731	
Green		AHA 5094	11	1	(C) H-AN6-101 to 24731	
Liner—engine side						
Red RH		AHA 5201	12	1	See (1) foot of page	
Red LH		AHA 5205	13	1		
Red RH		AKE 3028	12	1	See (2) foot of page	
Red LH		AKE 3031	13	1		
Blue RH		AHA 5202	12	1	(C) H-AN6-101 to 6284	
Blue LH		AHA 5206	13	1		
Blue RH		AKE 3029	12	1	(C) H-AN6-6285 to 24731	
Blue LH		AKE 3032	13	1		
Black RH	**Sprite**	AHA 5203	12	1	(C) H-AN6-101 to 6722	
Black LH	**Mk. II**	AHA 5207	13	1		
Black RH		AKE 3027	12	1	(C) H-AN6-6723 to 24731	
Black LH		AKE 3030	13	1		
Green RH		AHA 5204	12	1		
Green LH		AHA 5208	13	1		
Screw		RTZ 604	14	6	(C) H-AN6-101 to 24731	
Washer—cup		7700	15	6		Not available; use FWP 106
Washer—cup		FWP 106	15	6		

CHANGE POINTS

(1) (C) H-AN6-101 to 15218 (less 14842 to 14965, and 14980 to 15211)

(2) (C) H-AN6-15219 to 24731 (plus 14842 to 14965, and 14980 to 15211)

† Revised Information.

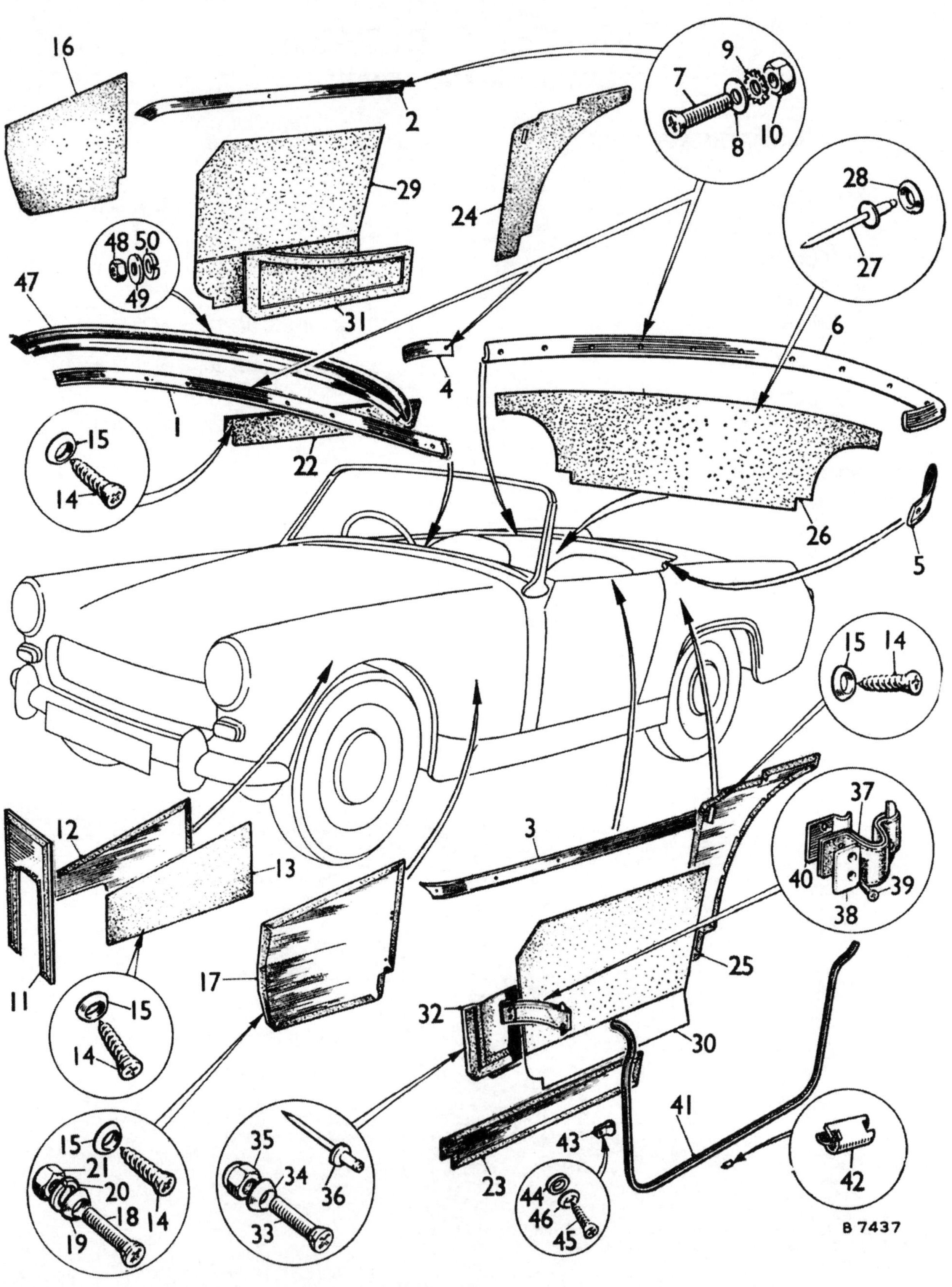
16
2
9
7
8
10
29
24
28
27
48 50
49
47
31
6
4
15
1
14
22
26
5
15 14
12
3
37
13
40
39
38
11
17
25
32
30
41
35
15
21
34
20
36
43
18 14
33
23
44
46
45
42
19
B 7437

DESCRIPTION	Part No.	Illus. No.	Quantity	Change Point	REMARKS
Trimming Details—*continued*					
(Sprite Mk. II and Midget)—*continued*					
Liner—scuttle					
Red RH	AHA 5060	16	1	See (1) foot of page	
Red LH	AHA 5065	17	1		
Red RH	AKE 3034	16	1	See (2) foot of page	
Red LH	AKE 3037	17	1		
Blue RH	AHA 5062	16	1	(C) H-AN6-101 to 6284	
Blue LH	AHA 5067	17	1		
Blue RH	AKE 3035	16	1	(C) H-AN6-6285 to 24731	
Blue LH	AKE 3038	17	1		
Black RH	AHA 5063	16	1	(C) H-AN6-101 to 6722	
Black LH	AHA 5068	17	1		
Black RH	AKE 3033	16	1	(C) H-AN6-6723 to 24731	
Black LH	AKE 3036	17	1		
Green RH	AHA 5064	16	1		
Green LH	AHA 5069	17	1		
Screw	RTZ 604	14	4		
Washer—cup	7700	15	4		Not available; use FWP 106
Washer—cup	FWP 106	15	4	(C) H-AN6-101 to 24731	
Screw	CMZ 0308	18	2		
Washer—cup	FWP 110	19	2		Part No. change; was 7698
Washer—spring	LWZ 203	20	2		
Nut	FNZ 103	21	2		
Liner—sill					
Red RH	AHA 5100	22	1	See (1) foot of page	
Red LH	AHA 5105	23	1		
Red RH	AKE 3046	22	1	See (2) foot of page	
Red LH	AKE 3049	23	1		
Blue RH	AHA 5102	22	1	(C) H-AN6-101 to 6284	
Blue LH	AHA 5107	23	1		
Blue RH	AKE 3047	22	1	(C) H-AN6-6285 to 24731	
Blue LH	AKE 3050	23	1		
Black RH	AHA 5103	22	1	(C) H-AN6-101 to 6722	
Black LH	AHA 5108	23	1		
Black RH	AKE 3045	22	1	(C) H-AN6-6723 to 24731	
Black LH	AKE 3048	23	1		
Green RH	AHA 5104	22	1		
Green LH	AHA 5109	23	1		
Screw—short	RTZ 604	14	8	(C) H-AN6-101 to 24731	
Screw—long	RTZ 606	14	2		
Washer—cup	7700	15	10		Not available; use FWP 106
Washer—cup	FWP 106	15	10		
Liner—rear quarter					
Red RH	AKE 3016	24	1	See (1) foot of page	
Red LH	AKE 3020	25	1		
Red RH	AKE 3040	24	1	See (2) foot of page	
Red LH	AKE 3043	25	1		
Blue RH	AKE 3017	24	1	(C) H-AN6-101 to 6284	
Blue LH	AKE 3021	25	1		
Blue RH	AKE 3041	24	1	(C) H-AN6-6285 to 24731	
Blue LH	AKE 3044	25	1		
Black RH	AKE 3018	24	1	(C) H-AN6-101 to 6722	
Black LH	AKE 3022	25	1		
Black RH	**Sprite** AKE 3039	24	1	(C) H-AN6-6723 to 24731	
Black LH	**Mk. II** AKE 3042	25	1		
Green RH	AKE 4734	24	1		
Green LH	AKE 4735	25	1		
Screw—short	RTZ 604	14	8		
Screw—long	RTZ 608	14	4	(C) H-AN6-101 to 24731	
Washer—cup	†7700	15	12		W.S.E. use FWP 106
Washer—cup	FWP 106	15	12		
Liner—rear bulkhead					
Red	AKE 3012	26	1	See (1) foot of page	
Red	AKE 3052	26	1	See (2) foot of page	
Blue	AKE 3013	26	1	(C) H-AN6-101 to 6284	
Blue	AKE 3053	26	1	(C) H-AN6-6285 to 24731	
Black	AKE 3014	26	1	(C) H-AN6-101 to 6722	
Black	AKE 3051	26	1	(C) H-AN6-6723 to 24731	
Green	AKE 4736	26	1		
Rivet—liner	BHA 4219	27	10	(C) H-AN6-101 to 24731	
Washer—cup	FWZ 106	28	10		

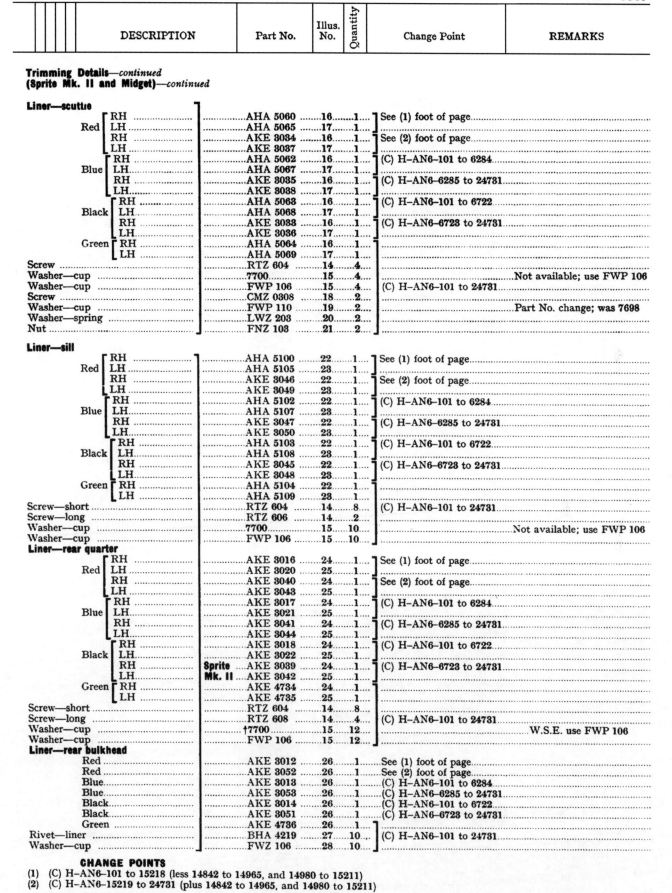

CHANGE POINTS

(1) (C) H-AN6-101 to 15218 (less 14842 to 14965, and 14980 to 15211)
(2) (C) H-AN6-15219 to 24731 (plus 14842 to 14965, and 14980 to 15211)

† Revised Information.

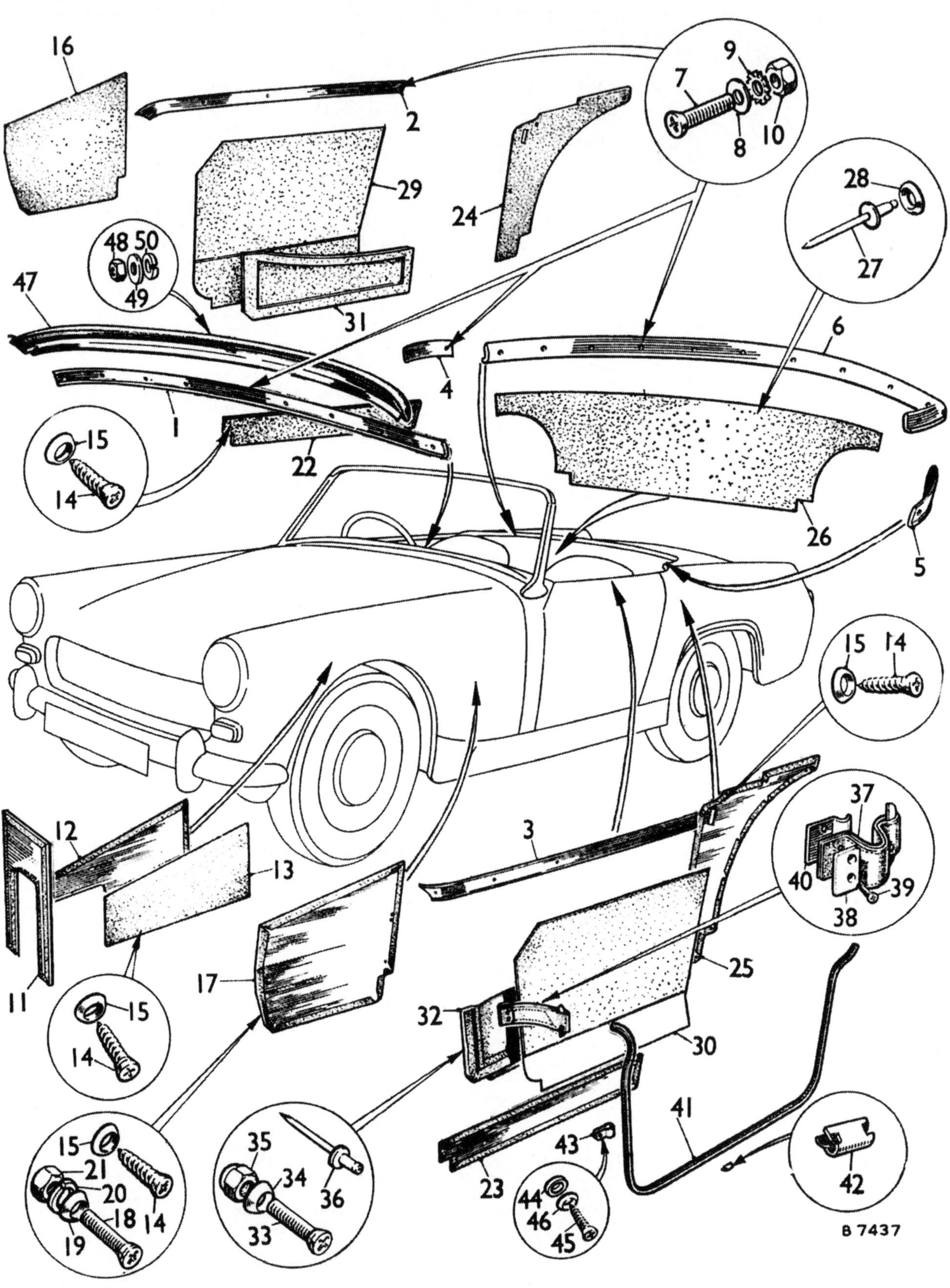
16
2
9
7
8
10
29
24
28
27
48 50
49
47
31
6
4
1
15
14
22
26
5
15 14
37
12
3
40
39
38
13
25
17
11
15
14
32
30
41
15
21
20
18
14
19
35
34
36
33
43
23
44
46
45
42
B 7437

Trimming Details—*continued*
(Sprite Mk. II and Midget)—*continued*

DESCRIPTION	Part No.	Illus. No.	Quantity	Change Point	REMARKS
Liner—door inner					
Red RH	AHA 5991	29	1	See (1) foot of page	
Red LH	AHA 5992	30	1		
Red RH	†AHA 5905	29	1		W.S.E. use AHA 6845
Red RH	AHA 6845	29	1	See (2) foot of page	
Red LH	†AHA 5906	30	1		W.S.E. use AHA 6849
Red LH	AHA 6849	30	1		
Blue RH	AHA 5907	29	1	(C) H-AN6-101 to 6284	
Blue LH	AHA 5908	30	1		
Blue RH	†AHA 6200	29	1		W.S.E. use AHA 6848
Blue RH	AHA 6848	29	1	(C) H-AN6-6285 to 24731	
Blue LH	†AHA 6201	30	1		W.S.E. use AHA 6852
Blue LH	AHA 6852	30	1		
Black RH	†AHA 5903	29	1		W.S.E. use AHA 6846
Black RH	†AHA 6846	29	1		
Black LH	AHA 5904	30	1	(C) H-AN6-101 to 24731	
Green RH	AKE 4730	29	1		
Green LH	AKE 4731	30	1		
Liner—door pocket					
Red RH	AHA 5050	31	1	See (1) foot of page	
Red LH	AHA 5055	32	1		
Red RH	AHA 5955	31	1	See (2) foot of page	
Red LH	AHA 5958	32	1		
Blue RH	AHA 5052	31	1	(C) H-AN6-101 to 6284	
Blue LH	AHA 5057	32	1		
Blue RH	AHA 5957	31	1	(C) H-AN6-6285 to 24731	
Blue LH	AHA 5960	32	1		
Black RH	AHA 5053	31	1	(C) H-AN6-101 to 6722	
Black LH	AHA 5058	32	1		
Black RH	AHA 5956	31	1	(C) H-AN6-6723 to 24731	
Black LH	AHA 5959	32	1		
Green RH	AHA 5054	31	1		
Green LH	AHA 5059	32	1		
Screw—liner to door	AHA 5412	33	4		
Washer—cup	†7699	34	4	(C) H-AN6-101 to 24731	W.S.E. use FWP 108
Washer—cup	FWP 108	34	4		
Nut	AHA 5413	35	4		
Rivet	DMP 0835	36	4		Part No. change; was 6K 9789
Strap—door check					
Red	AHA 5095	37	2	See (1) foot of page	
Red	AHA 5962	37	2	See (2) foot of page	
Blue	**Sprite** AHA 5097	37	2	(C) H-AN6-101 to 6284	
Blue	**Mk. II** AHA 5963	37	2	(C) H-AN6-6285 to 24731	
Black	AHA 5098	37	2	(C) H-AN6-101 to 6722	
Black	AHA 5961	37	2	(C) H-AN6-6723 to 24731	
Green	AHA 5099	37	2	(C) H-AN6-101 to 24731	
Retainer—strap	14A 764	38	2		
Screw	RMZ 0310	39	4	(C) H-AN6-101 to 23842	
Bracket—strap	14A 6745	40	2	(C) H-AN6-23843 to 24731	
Screw	RMZ 0312	39	4		
Seal—door—67" (171 cm)					
Red	†AHA 5118	41	2	See (1) foot of page	W.S.E. use 37H 9951
Blue	†AHA 5119	41	2	(C) H-AN6-101 to 24731	W.S.E. use 37H 9952
Black	†AHA 5120	41	2		W.S.E. use 37H 9953
Red	37H 9951	41	A/R	See (1) foot of page	Supplied in multiples of yards
Red	37H 9984	41	A/R	See (2) foot of page	
Blue	37H 9952	41	A/R		
Black	37H 9953	41	A/R		
Green	37H 9954	41	A/R		
Clip—seal	†14G 5716				W.S.E. 13H 4014
	†13H 4014			(C) H-AN6-101 to 24731	
	†PCR 0709				
Washer—plain	PWZ 203	44	2		
Screw	RTZ 606	45	2		
Washer—cup	†7700	46	2		W.S.E. use FWP 106
Washer—cup	FWP 106	46	2		

CHANGE POINTS

(1) (C) H-AN6-101 to 15218 (less 14842 to 14965, and 14980 to 15211)
(2) (C) H-AN6-15219 to 24731 (plus 14842 to 14965, and 14980 to 15211)

† Revised Information.

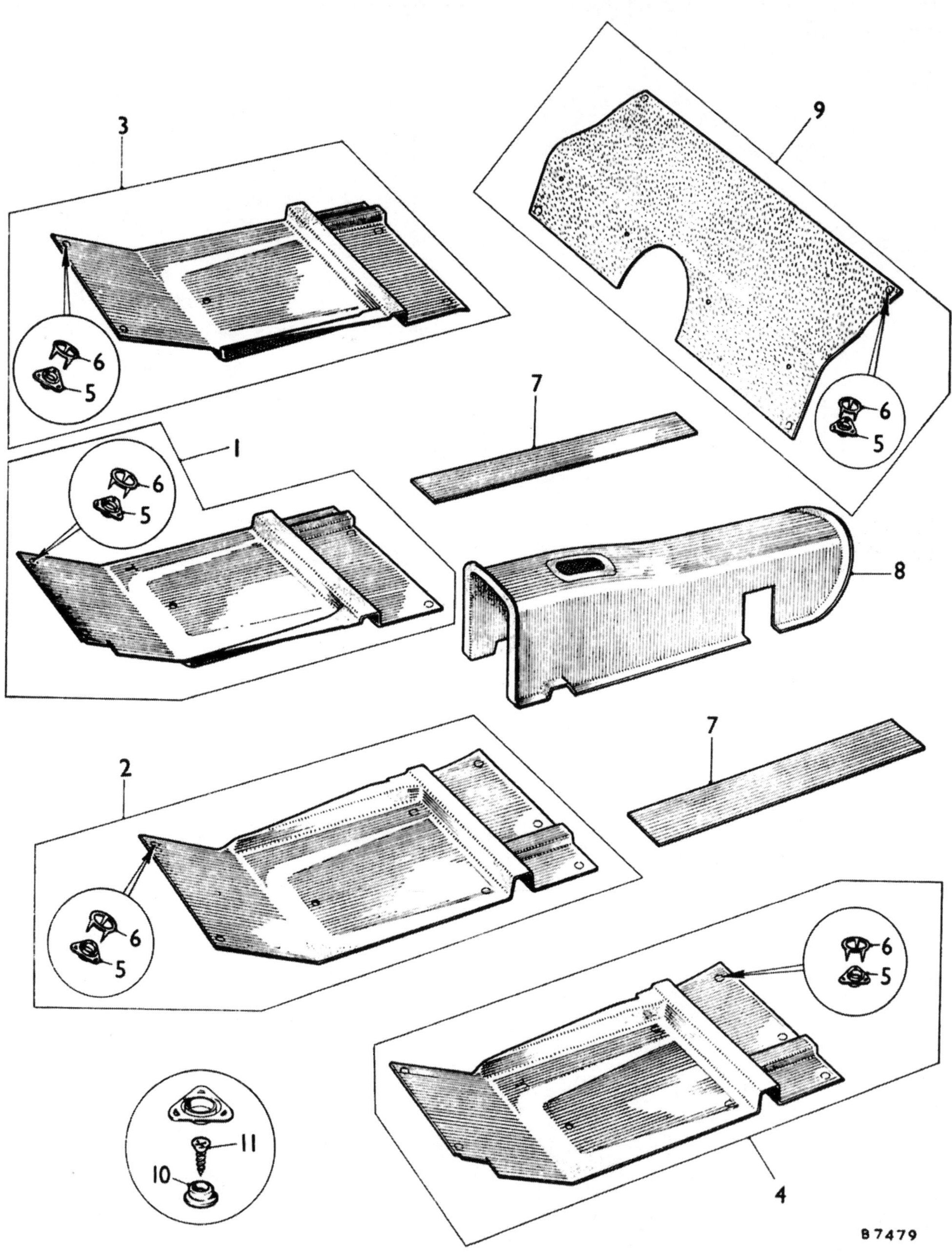
3
9
6
5
7
1
6
5
6
5
8
2
7
6
5
6
5
11
10
4
B7479

DESCRIPTION	Part No.	Illus. No.	Quantity	Change Point	REMARKS
Trimming Details—*continued*					
(Sprite Mk. II and Midget)—*continued*					
Mat assembly—front **RHD**					
Red RH	AHA 5130	1	1		
Red LH	AHA 5134	2	1		
Blue RH	AHA 5131	1	1		
Blue LH	AHA 5135	2	1		
Black RH	AHA 5132	1	1		
Black LH	AHA 5136	2	1		
Mat assembly—front **LHD**					
Red RH	AHA 5240	3	1		
Red LH	AHA 5244	4	1		
Blue RH	AHA 5241	3	1		
Blue LH	AHA 5245	4	1		
Black RH	AHA 5242	3	1	(C) H-AN6-101 to 24731	
Black LH	AHA 5246	4	1		
Socket—fastener	2H 8445	5	14		
Ring—socket	**Sprite Mk. II** 14G 8736	6	14		
Mat—side					
Red	AHA 5259	7	2		
Blue	AHA 5260	7	2		
Black	AHA 5261	7	2		
Mat—gearbox and tunnel					
Red	AHA 5138	8	1		
Blue	AHA 5139	8	1		
Black	AHA 5140	8	1		
Carpet assembly—rear centre					
Black/Red Fleck	AHA 5968	9	1	(C) H-AN6-101 to 16471	
Red/Black Fleck	AHA 5969	9	1		
Red/Black Fleck	AHA 6380	9	1	(C) H-AN6-16472 to 24731	
Blue/Black Fleck	AHA 5970	9	1		
Black/White Fleck	AHA 5973	9	1		
Socket—fastener	2H 8445	5	7	(C) H-AN6-101 to 24731	
Ring—socket	14G 8736	6	7		
Stud—socket	ADB 4811	10	21		
Screw	CTZ 604	11	21		
BULK MATERIAL					
Leathercloth—50″ (127 cm) wide					
Red	1AL 566		A/R	(C) H-AN6-101 to 15218 (less 14842 to 14965, and 14980 to 15211)	Part No. change; was AHA 5005
Red	1AL 556		A/R	(C) H-AN6-15218 to 24731 (plus 14842 to 14965, and 14980 to 15211)	Part No. change; was AHA 5934
Blue	1AL 252		A/R	(C) H-AN6-101 to 6284	Part No. change; was AHA 5006
Blue	1AL 276		A/R	(C) H-AN6-6285 to 24731	Part No. change; was AHA 5936
Black	**Sprite Mk. II** †1AL 102		A/R	(C) H-AN6-101 to 6722	W.S.E. use 1KL 1118. Part No. change; was AHA 5007
Black	†1KL 1118		A/R		
Black	1AL 108		A/R	(C) H-AN6-6723 to 24731	Part No. change; was AHA 5935
Green	1AL 351		A/R	(C) H-AN6-101 to 24731	Part No. change; was AHA 5008
Carpet—40″ (102 cm) wide					
Black/Red Fleck	AHA 6143		A/R	(C) H-AN6-101 to 16471	
Red/Black Fleck	AHA 6142		A/R		
Red/Black Fleck	AHA 6379		A/R	(C) H-AN6-16472 to 24731	
Blue/Black Fleck	AHA 6144		A/R	(C) H-AN6-101 to 24731	
Black/White Fleck	AHA 6145		A/R		

Bulk material: Supplied in multiples of yards

† Revised Information.

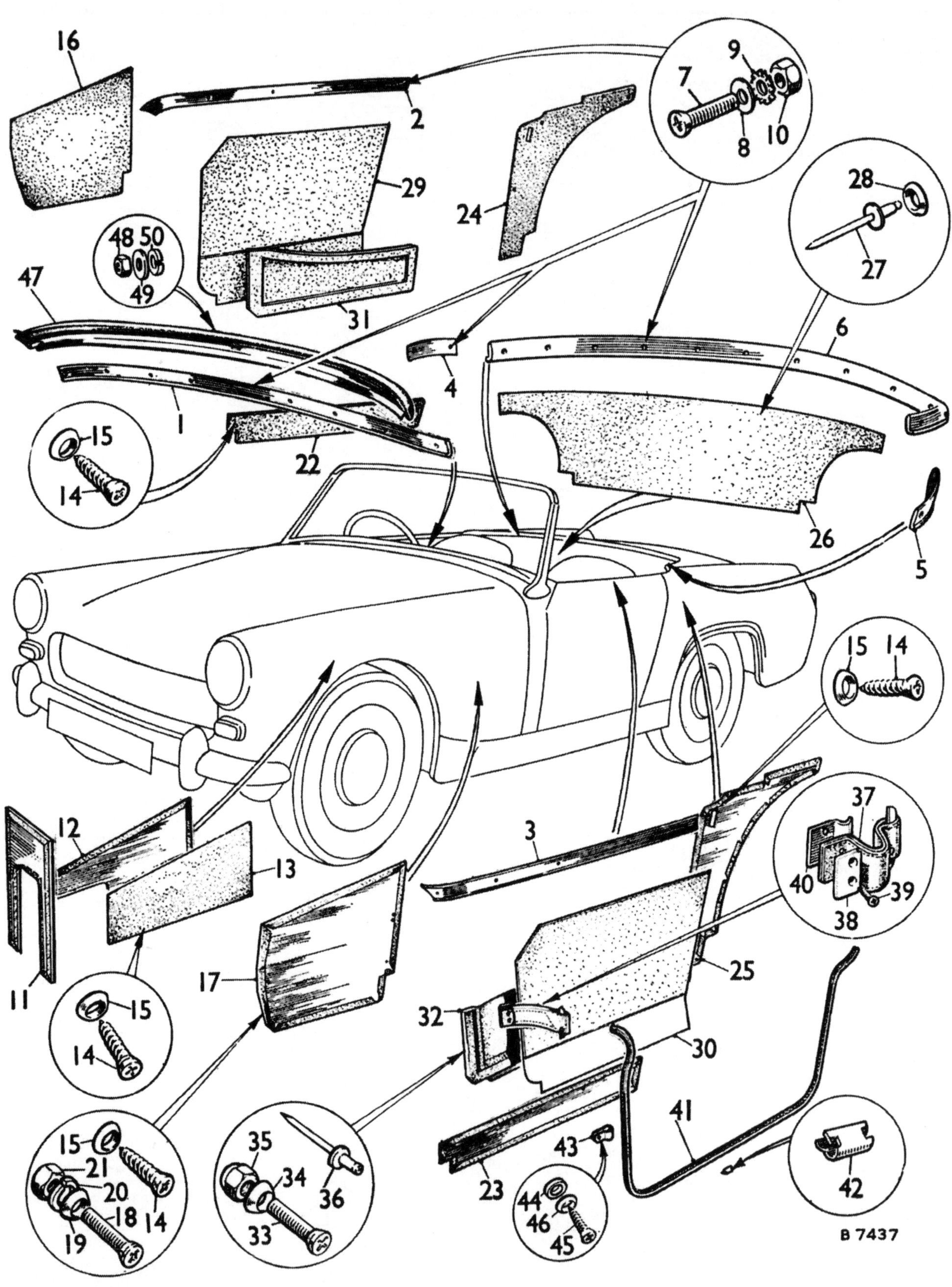
16
2
9
7
8
10
29
24
28
27
48 50
49
47
31
6
4
1
15
14
22
26
5
15 14
12
3
37
13
40
39
38
11
17
25
32
15
14
30
41
15
21
20
18
19
14
35
34
36
33
43
23
44
46
45
42
B 7437

DESCRIPTION		Part No.	Illus. No.	Quantity	Change Point	REMARKS
Trimming Details—*continued* **(Sprite Mk. II and Midget)**—*continued*						
Roll—trim—scuttle top						
Red		AHA 6164	47	1		
Blue		AHA 6165	47	1		
Black		AHA 6163	47	1		
Green		AKE 4741	47	1		
Nut		FNZ 103	48	9		
Washer—plain		PWZ 103	49	9		
Washer—spring		LWZ 203	50	9		
Moulding						
Door top—RH		AHA 5268	2	1		
Door top—LH		AHA 5269	3	1		
Cockpit rear—RH		AHA 5812	4	1		
Cockpit rear—LH		AHA 5813	5	1		
Cockpit rear—centre		AHA 5814	6	1		
Screw—moulding						
Door		RMZ 0310	7	6		
Cockpit rear—RH and LH		RMZ 0316	7	2		
Cockpit rear		RMZ 0312	7	13		
Washer—plain		PWZ 203	8	15		
Washer—shakeproof		LWZ 503	9	21		
Nut		FNZ 103	10	21		
Liner—engine front						
Red		AKE 3025	11	1		
Blue		AKE 3026	11	1		
Black		AKE 3024	11	1		
Green		AHA 5094	11	1		
Liner—engine side	**Midget**				(C) G–AN1–101 to 16183	
Red RH		AKE 3028	12	1		
Red LH		AKE 3031	13	1		
Blue RH		AKE 3029	12	1		
Blue LH		AKE 3032	13	1		
Black RH		AKE 3027	12	1		
Black LH		AKE 3030	13	1		
Green RH		AHA 5204	12	1		
Green LH		AHA 5208	13	1		
Screw—liner		RTZ 604	14	6		
Washer—cup		7700	15	6		Not available; use FWP 106
Washer—cup		FWP 106	15	6		
Liner—scuttle						
Red RH		AKE 3034	16	1		
Red LH		AKE 3037	17	1		
Blue RH		AKE 3035	16	1		
Blue LH		AKE 3038	17	1		
Black RH		AKE 3033	16	1		
Black LH		AKE 3036	17	1		
Green RH		AHA 5064	16	1		
Green LH		AHA 5069	17	1		
Screw—liner		RTZ 604	14	4		
Washer—cup		7700	15	4		Not available; use FWP 106
Washer—cup		FWP 106	15	4		
Screw—liner		CMZ 0308	18	2		
Washer—cup		FWP 110	19	2		Part No. change; was 7698
Washer—spring		LWZ 203	20	2		
Nut		FNZ 103	21	2		

† Revised Information.

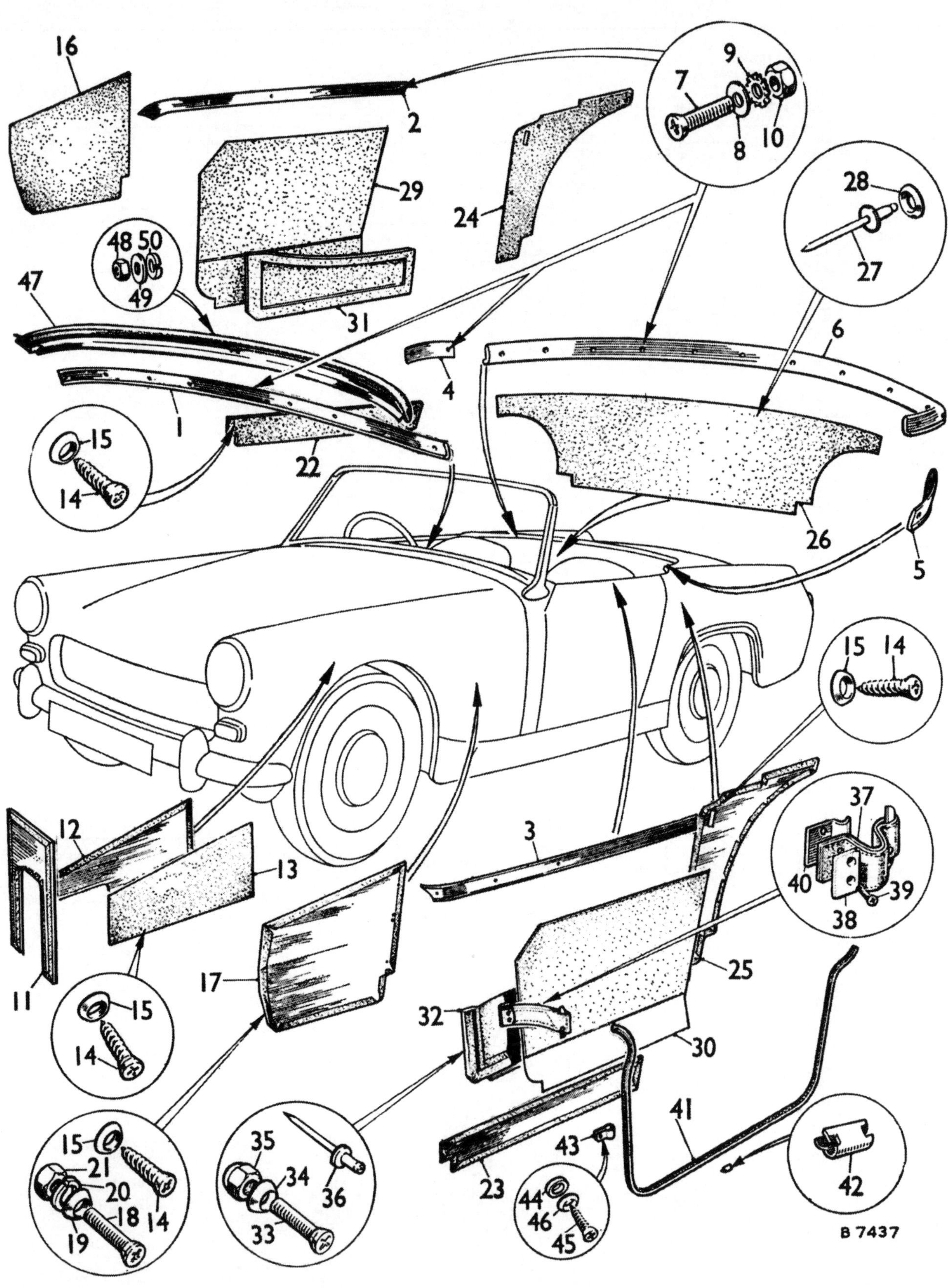
16
2
9
7
8
10
29
24
28
27
48 50
49
47
31
6
4
1
15
14
22
26
5
15 14
12
3
37
13
40
39
38
25
11
17
15
14
32
30
41
15
21
20
18
14
19
35
34
36
33
43
23
44
46
45
42
B 7437

DESCRIPTION	Part No.	Illus. No.	Quantity	Change Point	REMARKS
Trimming Details—*continued*					
(Sprite Mk. II and Midget)—*continued*					
Liner—sill					
Red RH	AKE 3046	22	1		
Red LH	AKE 3049	23	1		
Blue RH	AKE 3047	22	1		
Blue LH	AKE 3050	23	1		
Black RH	AKE 3045	22	1		
Black LH	AKE 3048	23	1		
Green RH	AHA 5104	22	1		
Green LH	AHA 5109	23	1		
Screw—short	RTZ 604	14	8		
Screw—long	RTZ 606	14	2		
Washer—cup	†7700	15	10		W.S.E. use FWP 106
Washer—cup	FWP 106	15	10		
Liner—rear quarter					
Red RH	AKE 3040	24	1		
Red LH	AKE 3043	25	1		
Blue RH	AKE 3041	24	1		
Blue LH	AKE 3044	25	1		
Black RH	AKE 3039	24	1		
Black LH	AKE 3042	25	1		
Green RH	AKE 4734	24	1		
Green LH	AKE 4735	25	1		
Screw—short	RTZ 604	14	8		
Screw—long	RTZ 608	14	4		
Washer—cup	†7700	15	12		W.S.E. use FWP 106
Washer—cup	FWP 106	15	12		
Liner—rear bulkhead					
Red	AKE 3052	26	1		
Blue	AKE 3053	26	1		
Black	AKE 3051	26	1		
Green	AKE 4736	26	1		
Rivet—liner	**Midget** BHA 4219	27	10	(C) G–AN1–101 to 16183	
Washer—cup	FWZ 106	28	10		
Liner—door inner					
Red RH	†AHA 5905	29	1		W.S.E. use AHA 6845
Red RH	AHA 6845	29	1		
Red LH	†AHA 5906	30	1		W.S.E. use AHA 6849
Red LH	AHA 6849	30	1		
Blue RH	†AHA 6200	29	1		W.S.E. use AHA 6848
Blue RH	AHA 6848	29	1		
Blue LH	†AHA 6201	30	1		W.S.E. use AHA 6852
Blue LH	AHA 6852	30	1		
Black RH	AHA 5903	29	1		
Black LH	AHA 5904	30	1		
Green RH	AKE 4730	29	1		
Green LH	AKE 4731	30	1		
Red RH	AHA 5955	31	1		
Red LH	AHA 5958	32	1		
Blue RH	AHA 5957	31	1		
Blue LH	AHA 5960	32	1		
Black RH	†AHA 5956	31	1		W.S.E. use AHA 6846
Black RH	†AHA 6846	31	1		
Black LH	AHA 5959	32	1		
Green RH	AHA 5054	31	1		
Green LH	AHA 5059	32	1		
Screw—liner to door	AHA 7699 2	33	4		
Washer—cup	7699	34	4		W.S.E. use FWP 108
Washer—cup	FWP 108	34	4		
Nut	AHA 5413	35	4		
Rivet	DNP 0835	36	4		Part No. change; was 6K 9789

† Revised Information.

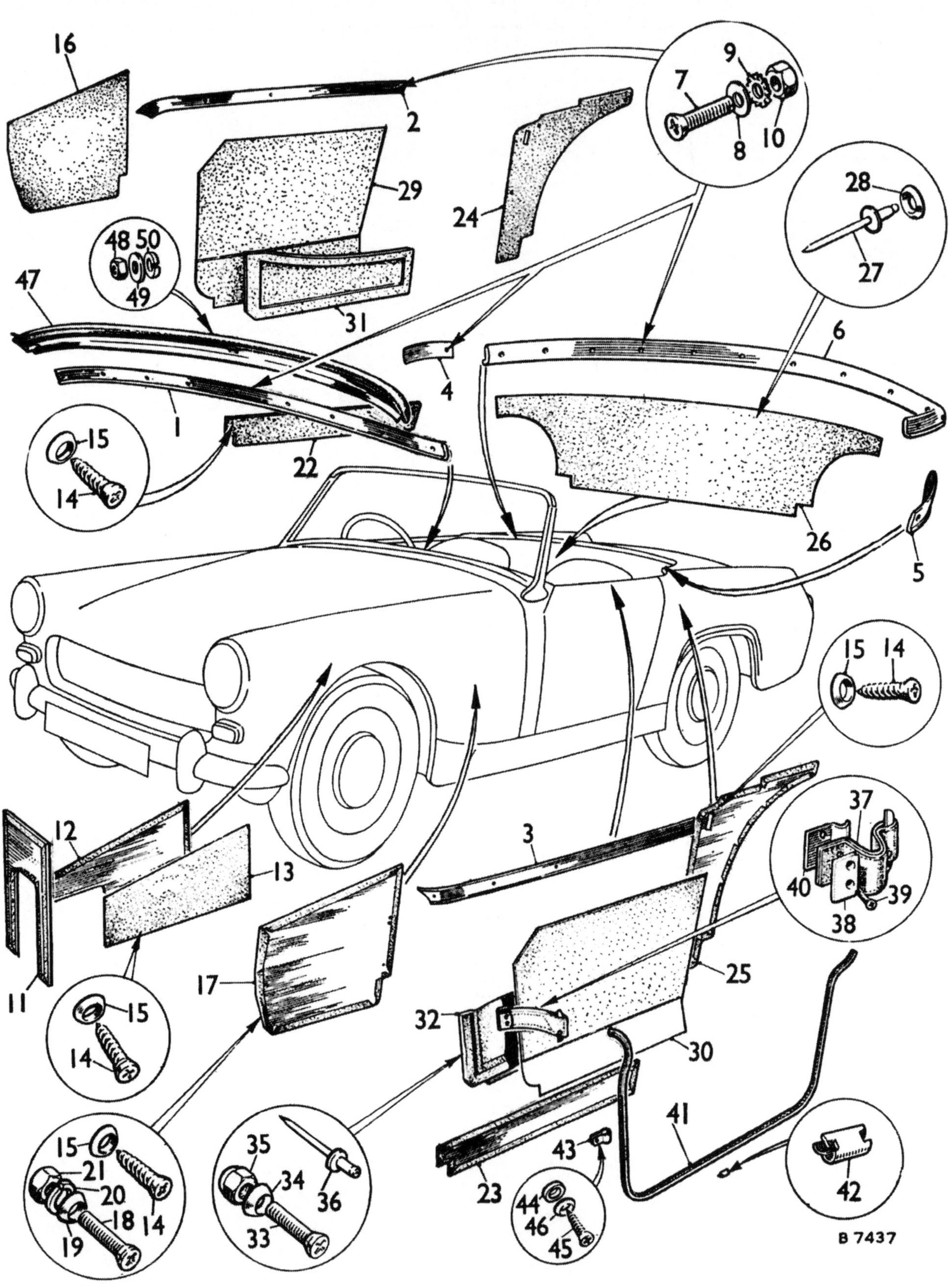
16
2
9
7
8
10
29
24
28
27
48 50
49
47
31
6
4
1
15
14
22
26
5
15 14
12
3
37
13
40
39
38
11
17
25
15
14
32
30
41
15
21
20
18
19
14
35
34
36
33
43
23
44
46
45
42
B 7437

DESCRIPTION		Part No.	Illus. No.	Quantity	Change Point	REMARKS
Trimming Details—*continued* **(Sprite Mk. II and Midget)**—*continued*						
Strap—door check						
Red		AHA 5962	37	2	(C) G-AN1-101 to 16183	
Blue		AHA 5963	37	2		
Black		AHA 5961	37	2		
Green		AHA 5099	37	2		
Retainer—strap		14A 764	38	2		
Screw		RMZ 0310	39	4	(C) G-AN1-101 to 15308	
Bracket—strap		14A 6745	40	2	(C) G-AN1-15309 to 16183	
Screw		RMZ 0312	39	4		
Seal—door—67" (171 cm)						
Blue		†AHA 5119	41	2		W.S.E. use 37H 9952
Black	**Midget**	†AHA 5120	41	2		W.S.E. use 37H 9953
Red		37H 9984	41	A/R	(C) G-AN1-101 to 16183	Supplied in multiples of yards
Blue		37H 9952	41	A/R		
Black		37H 9953	41	A/R		
Green		37H 9954	41	A/R		
Clip—seal		†14G 5716	42	64		W.S.E. use 13H 4014
		†13H 4014	42	64		
		†PCR 0709	43	2		
Clip—seal		14G 5716	42	64		
Clip—seal		PCR 0709	43	2		
Washer—plain		PWZ 203	44	2		
Screw		RTZ 606	45	2		
Washer—cup		†7700	46	2		W.S.E. use FWP 106
Washer—cup		FWP 106	46	2		

† Revised Information.

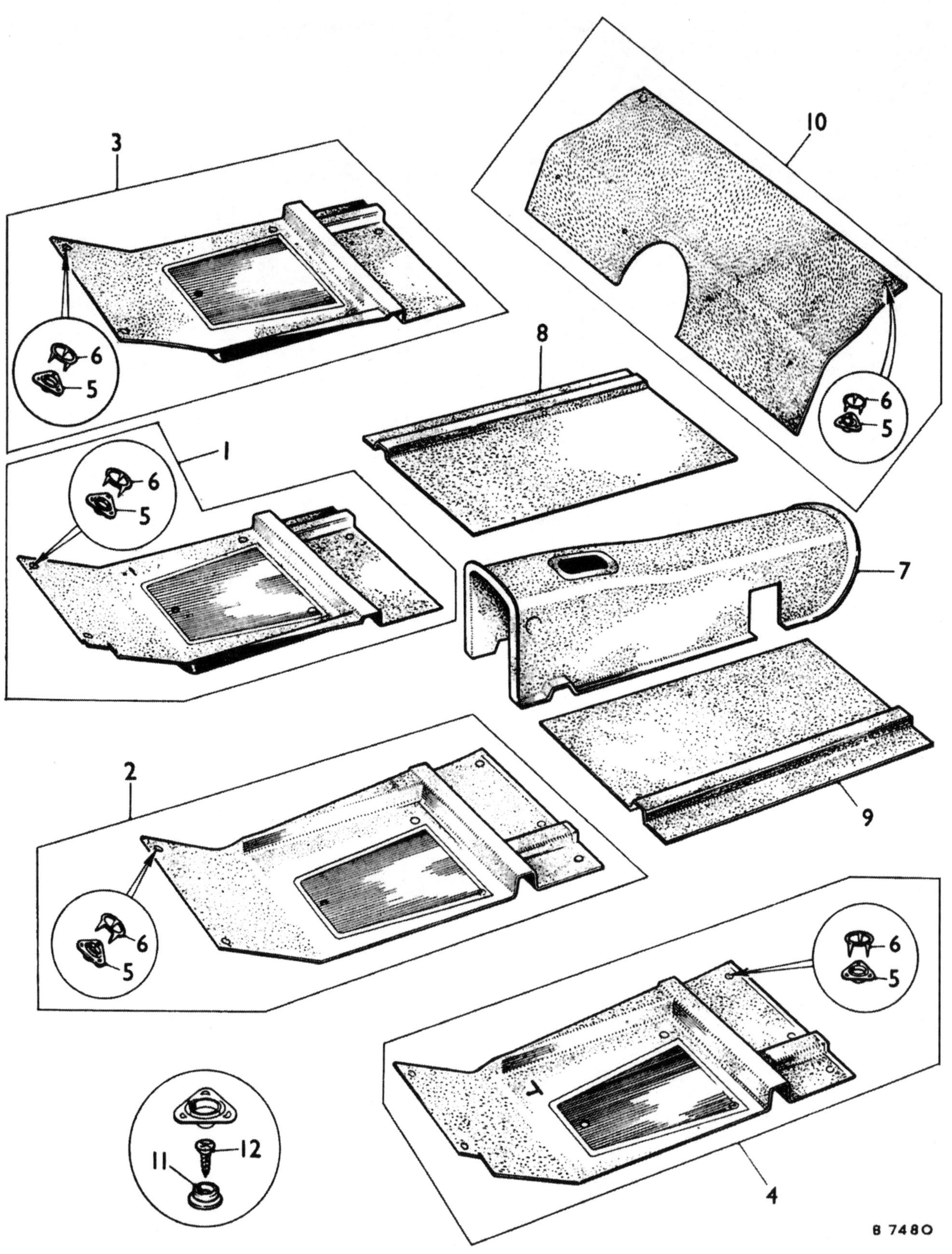
3
10
6
5
8
1
6
5
7
2
9
6
5
6
5
12
11
4
B 7480

Trimming Details—*continued*
(Sprite Mk. II and Midget)—*continued*

DESCRIPTION	Part No.	Illus. No.	Quantity	Change Point	REMARKS
Mat assembly—front .... **RHD**					
Black/ Red Fleck RH	AHA 6044	1	1		
Black/ Red Fleck LH	AHA 6047	2	1		
Black/ White Fleck RH	AHA 6179	1	1		
Black/ White Fleck LH	AHA 6181	2	1		
Red/ Black Fleck RH	AHA 6043	1	1		
Red/ Black Fleck LH	AHA 6046	2	1		
Red/ White Fleck RH	AHA 6180	1	1		
Red/ White Fleck LH	AHA 6182	2	1		
Blue/ Black Fleck RH	AHA 6045	1	1		
Blue/ Black Fleck LH	AHA 6048	2	1		
Mat assembly—front .... **LHD**					
Black/ Red Fleck RH	AHA 6050	3	1		
Black/ Red Fleck LH	AHA 6053	4	1		
Black/ White Fleck RH	AHA 6183	3	1		
Black/ White Fleck LH	AHA 6185	4	1		
Red/ Black Fleck RH	AHA 6049	3	1		
Red/ Black Fleck LH	AHA 6052	4	1		
Red/ White Fleck RH	AHA 6184	3	1		
Red/ White Fleck LH	AHA 6186	4	1	(C) G–AN1–101 to 16188	
Blue/ Black Fleck RH	AHA 6051	3	1		
Blue/ Black Fleck LH	AHA 6054	4	1		
Socket—fastener	2H 8445	5	14		
Ring—socket	14G 8736	6	14		
Mat—geargox and tunnel					
Black/Red Fleck	**Midget** AHA 6056	7	1		
Black/White Fleck	AHA 6187	7	1		
Red/Black Fleck	AHA 6055	7	1		
Red/White Fleck	AHA 6188	7	1		
Blue/Black Fleck	AHA 6057	7	1		
Mat—rear					
Black/ Red Fleck RH	AHA 6059	8	1		
Black/ Red Fleck LH	AHA 6062	9	1		
Black/ White Fleck RH	AHA 6189	8	1		
Black/ White Fleck LH	AHA 6191	9	1		
Red/ Black Fleck RH	AHA 6058	8	1		
Red/ Black Fleck LH	AHA 6061	9	1		
Red/ White Fleck RH	AHA 6190	8	1		
Red/ White Fleck LH	AHA 6192	9	1		
Blue/ Black Fleck RH	AHA 6060	8	1		
Blue/ Black Fleck LH	AHA 6063	9	1		
Carpet assembly—rear centre					
Black/Red Fleck	AHA 5968	10	1	(C) G–AN1–101 to 10741	
Red/Black Fleck	AHA 5969	10	1		
Red/Black Fleck	AHA 6380	10	1	(C) G–AN1–10742 to 16188	
Black/White Fleck	AHA 5973	10	1		
Red/White Fleck	AHA 6038	10	1		
Blue/Black Fleck	AHA 5970	10	1		
Socket—fastener	2H 8445	5	7	(C) G–AN1–101 to 16188	
Ring—socket	14G 8736	6	7		
Stud—socket	ADB 4811	11	21		
Screw	CTZ 604	12	21		

BULK MATERIAL

DESCRIPTION	Part No.	Illus. No.	Quantity	Change Point	REMARKS
Leathercloth—50″ (127 cm) wide					
Red	1AL 556		A/R		Part No. change; was AHA 5984
Blue	1AL 276		A/R		Part No. change; was AHA 5986
Black	1AL 108		A/R	(C) G–AN1–101 to 16188	Part No. change; was AHA 5985
Green	**Midget** 1AL 351		A/R		Part No. change; was AHA 5008
Carpet—40″ (102 cm) wide					Supplied in multiples of yards
Black/Red Fleck	AHA 6143		A/R	(C) G–AN1–101 to 10741	
Red/Black Fleck	AHA 6142		A/R		
Red/Black Fleck	AHA 6379		A/R	(C) G–AN1–10742 to 16188	
Black/White Fleck	AHA 6145		A/R		
Red/White Fleck	AHA 6146		A/R	(C) G–AN1–101 to 16188	
Blue/Black Fleck	AHA 6144		A/R		

† Revised Information.

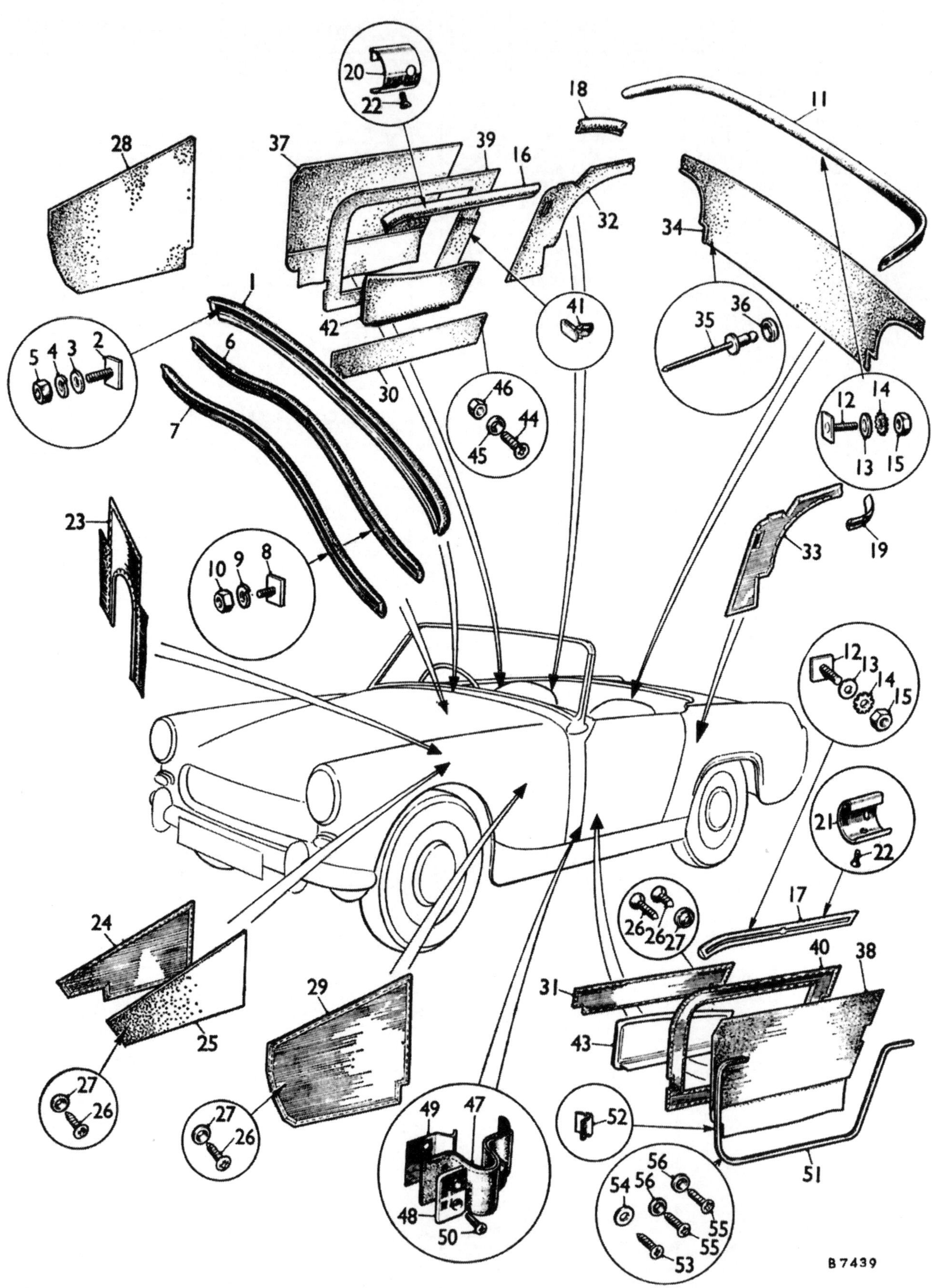
B 7439

DESCRIPTION	Part No.	Illus. No.	Quantity	Change Point	REMARKS
Trimming Details—*continued*					
(Sprite Mk. II and Midget)—*continued*					
Roll—trim—fascia—upper					
Red	AHA 6585	1	1		
Black	AHA 6586	1	1		
Blue	AHA 6587	1	1		
Hazelnut	AHA 6588	1	1		
Plate—stud—trim roll	AHH 6417	2	9		
Washer—plain	PWZ 103	3	9		
Washer—spring	LWZ 203	4	9		
Nut	FNZ 103	5	9		
Roll—trim—fascia—lower					
Red (RHD)	AHA 6678	6	1		
Black (RHD)	AHA 6679	6	1		
Blue (RHD)	AHA 6680	6	1		
Hazelnut (RHD)	AHA 6681	6	1		
Red (LHD)	AHA 6682	7	1		
Black (LHD)	AHA 6683	7	1		
Blue (LHD)	AHA 6684	7	1		
Hazelnut (LHD)	AHA 6685	7	1		
Plate—stud—trim roll	AHH 6360	8	7		
Washer—spring	LWZ 203	9	7		
Nut	FNZ 103	10	7		
Roll—trim—cockpit rear—centre					
Red	AHA 6520	11	1		
Black	AHA 6521	11	1		
Blue	AHA 6522	11	1		
Hazelnut	AHA 6523	11	1		
Plate—stud—trim roll	AHH 6417	12	11		
Washer—plain	PWZ 203	13	11	(C) H-AN7-24782 on	
Washer—shakeproof	LWZ 503	14	11	(C) G-AN2-16184 on	
Nut	FNZ 103	15	11		
Moulding					
Door top—RH	AHA 6490	16	1		
Door top—LH	AHA 6491	17	1		
Cockpit rear—RH	AHA 6487	18	1		
Cockpit rear—LH	AHA 6488	19	1		
Capping—door top moulding—RH	AHA 6499	20	2		
Capping—door top moulding—LH	AHA 6500	21	2		
Screw—capping	AHA 6933	22	4		
Plate—stud—moulding	AHA 6417	12	10		
Washer—plain	PWZ 203	13	4		
Washer—shakeproof	LWZ 503	14	10		
Nut	FNZ 103	15	10		
Liner—engine front					
Red	AHA 6716	23	1		
Black	AHA 6717	23	1		
Blue	AHA 6719	23	1		
Hazelnut	AHA 6718	23	1		
Liner—engine side					
Red RH	AHA 6724	24	1		
Red LH	AHA 6732	25	1		
Black RH	AHA 6725	24	1		
Black LH	AHA 6733	25	1		
Blue RH	AHA 6727	24	1		
Blue LH	AHA 6735	25	1		
Hazelnut RH	AHA 6726	24	1		
Hazelnut LH	AHA 6734	25	1		
Screw	RTP 2604	26	6		
Washer—cup	FWP 906	27	6		

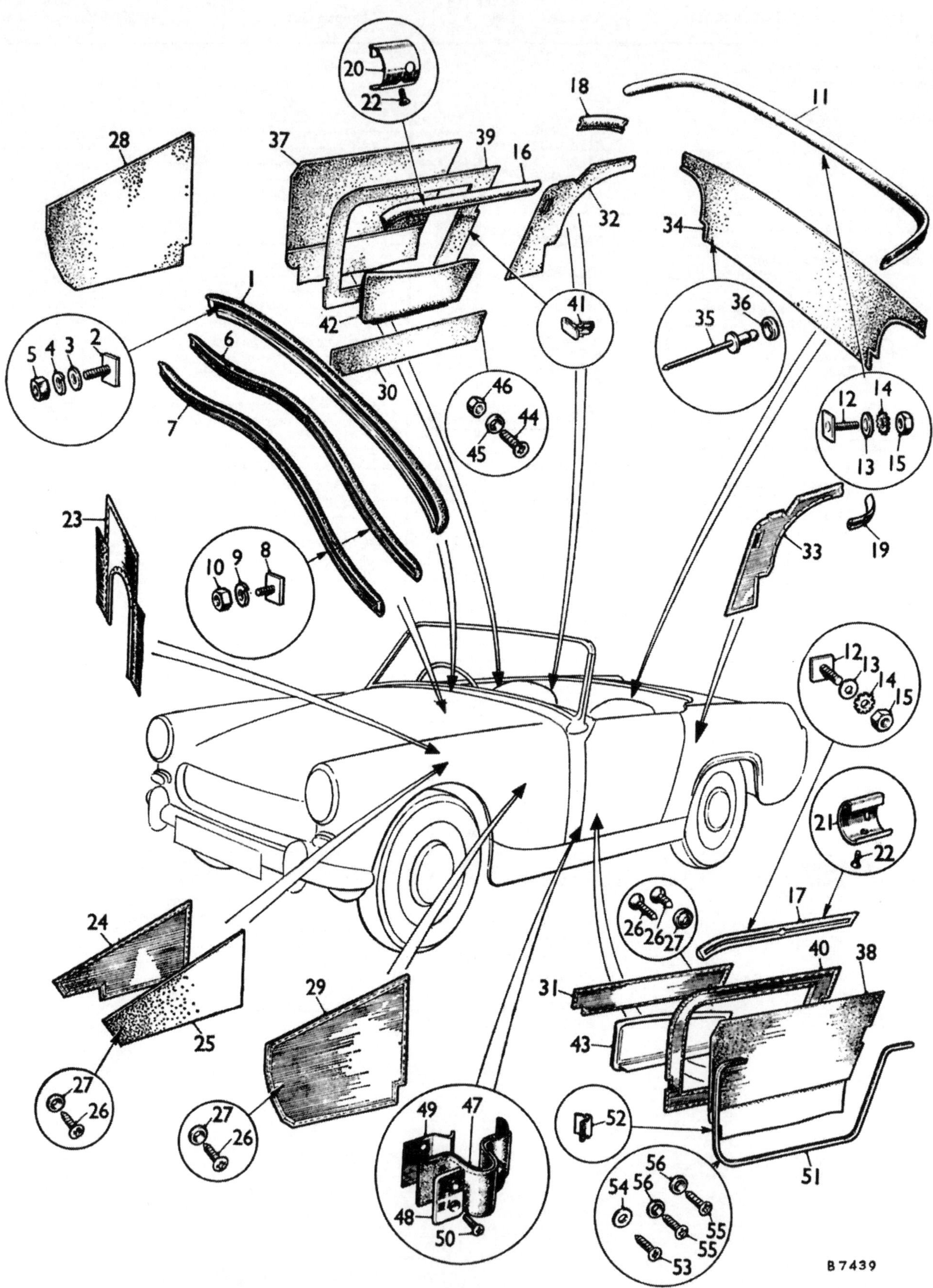
B 7439

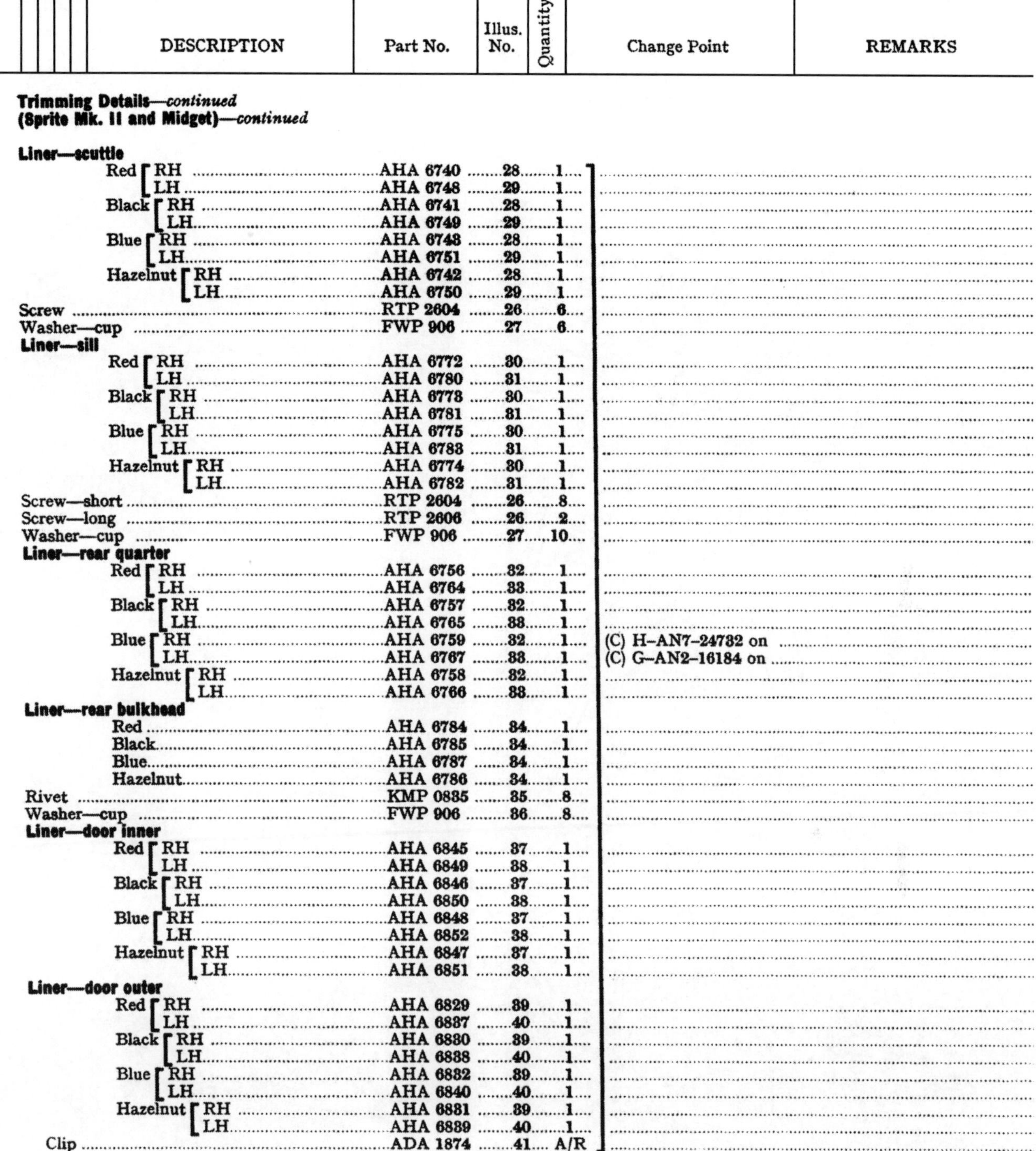

DESCRIPTION	Part No.	Illus. No.	Quantity	Change Point	REMARKS
Trimming Details—*continued* **(Sprite Mk. II and Midget)**—*continued*					
Liner—scuttle					
Red RH	AHA 6740	28	1		
Red LH	AHA 6748	29	1		
Black RH	AHA 6741	28	1		
Black LH	AHA 6749	29	1		
Blue RH	AHA 6743	28	1		
Blue LH	AHA 6751	29	1		
Hazelnut RH	AHA 6742	28	1		
Hazelnut LH	AHA 6750	29	1		
Screw	RTP 2604	26	6		
Washer—cup	FWP 906	27	6		
Liner—sill					
Red RH	AHA 6772	30	1		
Red LH	AHA 6780	31	1		
Black RH	AHA 6773	30	1		
Black LH	AHA 6781	31	1		
Blue RH	AHA 6775	30	1		
Blue LH	AHA 6783	31	1		
Hazelnut RH	AHA 6774	30	1		
Hazelnut LH	AHA 6782	31	1		
Screw—short	RTP 2604	26	8		
Screw—long	RTP 2606	26	2		
Washer—cup	FWP 906	27	10		
Liner—rear quarter					
Red RH	AHA 6756	32	1		
Red LH	AHA 6764	33	1		
Black RH	AHA 6757	32	1		
Black LH	AHA 6765	33	1		
Blue RH	AHA 6759	32	1	(C) H-AN7-24782 on	
Blue LH	AHA 6767	33	1	(C) G-AN2-16184 on	
Hazelnut RH	AHA 6758	32	1		
Hazelnut LH	AHA 6766	33	1		
Liner—rear bulkhead					
Red	AHA 6784	34	1		
Black	AHA 6785	34	1		
Blue	AHA 6787	34	1		
Hazelnut	AHA 6786	34	1		
Rivet	KMP 0835	35	8		
Washer—cup	FWP 906	36	8		
Liner—door inner					
Red RH	AHA 6845	37	1		
Red LH	AHA 6849	38	1		
Black RH	AHA 6846	37	1		
Black LH	AHA 6850	38	1		
Blue RH	AHA 6848	37	1		
Blue LH	AHA 6852	38	1		
Hazelnut RH	AHA 6847	37	1		
Hazelnut LH	AHA 6851	38	1		
Liner—door outer					
Red RH	AHA 6829	39	1		
Red LH	AHA 6837	40	1		
Black RH	AHA 6830	39	1		
Black LH	AHA 6838	40	1		
Blue RH	AHA 6832	39	1		
Blue LH	AHA 6840	40	1		
Hazelnut RH	AHA 6831	39	1		
Hazelnut LH	AHA 6839	40	1		
Clip	ADA 1874	41	A/R		

† Revised Information.

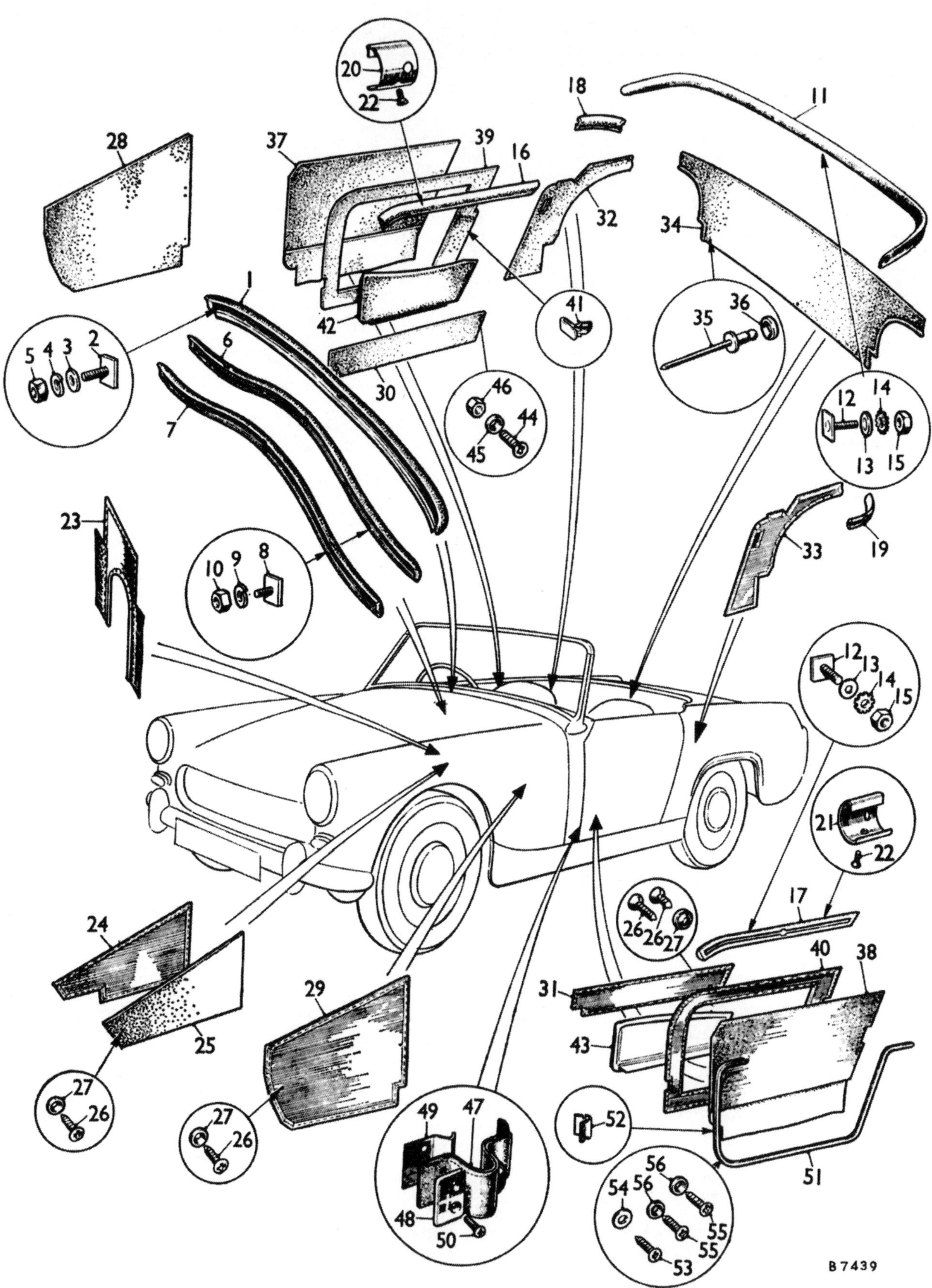
1
2
3
4
5
6
7
8
9
10
11
12
13
14
15
16
17
18
19
20
21
22
23
24
25
26
27
28
29
30
31
32
33
34
35
36
37
38
39
40
41
42
43
44
45
46
47
48
49
50
51
52
53
54
55
56
B 7439

DESCRIPTION	Part No.	Illus. No.	Quantity	Change Point	REMARKS
Trimming Details—*continued*					
(Sprite Mk. II and Midget)—*continued*					
Liner—door pocket					
Red RH	AHA 6853	42	1		
Red LH	AHA 6861	43	1		
Black RH	AHA 6854	42	1		
Black LH	AHA 6862	43	1		
Blue RH	AHA 6856	42	1		
Blue LH	AHA 6864	43	1		
Hazelnut RH	AHA 6855	42	1		
Hazelnut LH	AHA 6863	43	1		
Screw—liner to door	AHA 6979	44	4		
Washer—cup	FWP 908	45	4		
Nut	AHA 5413	46	4		
Strap—door check				(C) H-AN7-24732 on	
Red	AHA 6881	47	2	(C) G-AN2-16184 on	
Black	AHA 6882	47	2		
Blue	AHA 6884	47	2		
Hazelnut	AHA 6883	47	2		
Retainer—strap	14A 764	48	2		
Bracket—strap	14A 6745	49	2		
Screw	RMP 2312	50	4		
Seal—door—67" (171 cm)					
Red	37H 9984	51	A/R		Supplied in multiples of yards
Black	37H 9953	51	A/R		Supplied in multiples of yards
Blue	37H 9952	51	A/R		Supplied in multiples of yards
Hazelnut	27H 2116	51	A/R		Supplied in multiples of yards
Clip—seal	†14G 5716	52	64		W.S.E. use 13H 4014
Clip—seal	†13H 4014	52	64		
Screw	PTZ 603	53	2	(C) H-AN7-24732 to ▼	
Washer—plain	PWZ 203	54	2	(C) G-AN2-16184 to ▼	
Screw	RTZ 606	55	2		
Washer—cup	FWP 106	56	2		
Screw	RTP 2606	55	4	(C) H-AN7- ▼ on	
Washer—cup	FWP 606	56	4	(C) G-AN8- ▼ on	

▼ Change point not available

† Revised Information.

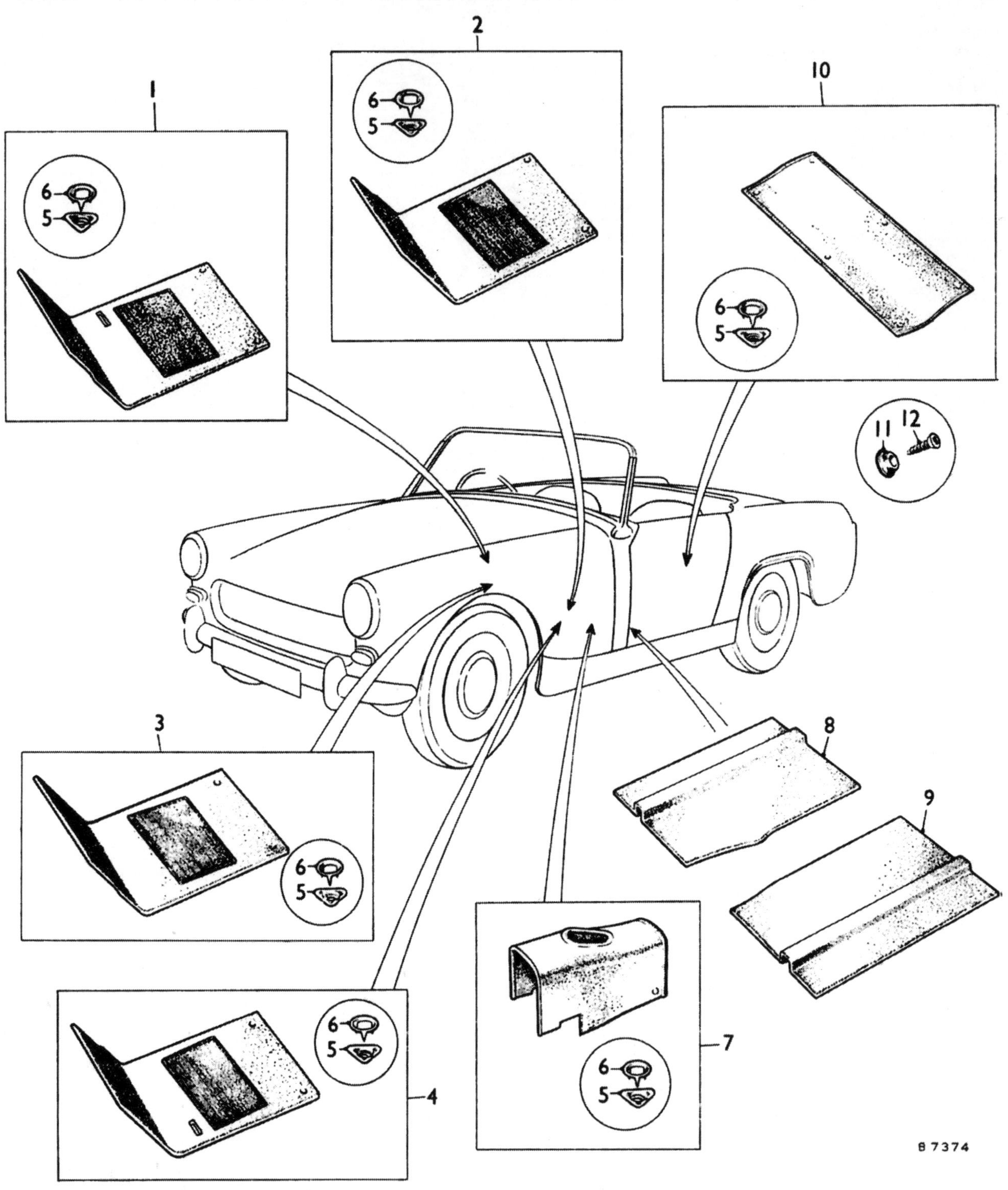
1
2
10
6
5
11
12
3
8
9
4
7
B 7374

DESCRIPTION	Part No.	Illus. No.	Quantity	Change Point	REMARKS
Trimming Details—*continued* **(Sprite Mk. II and Midget)**—*continued*					
Carpet assembly—front **RHD**					
Cardinal Red RH	AHA 6641	1	1		
LH	AHA 6645	2	1		
Black RH	AHA 6642	1	1		
LH	AHA 6646	2	1		
Hazelnut RH	AHA 6643	1	1		
LH	AHA 6647	2	1		
Blue RH	AHA 6644	1	1		
LH	AHA 6648	2	1		
Carpet assembly—front **LHD**					
Cardinal Red RH	AHA 6649	3	1		
LH	AHA 6653	4	1		
Black RH	AHA 6650	3	1		
LH	AHA 6654	4	1		
Hazelnut RH	AHA 6651	3	1		
LH	AHA 6655	4	1		
Blue RH	AHA 6652	3	1		
LH	AHA 6656	4	1		
Socket—fastener	2H 8445	5	8		
Ring—socket	†2H 6136	6	8		W.S.E. use 14G 8736
Ring—socket	†14G 8736	6	6		
Carpet assembly—tunnel—front					
Cardinal Red	AHA 6617	7	1	(C) H-AN7-24732 on	
Black	AHA 6618	7	1	(C) G-AN2-16184 on	
Hazelnut	AHA 6619	7	1		
Blue	AHA 6620	7	1		
Socket—fastener	2H 8445	5	4		
Ring—socket	†2H 6136	6	4		W.S.E. use 14G 8736
Ring—socket	†14G 8736	6	6		
Carpet—rear					
Cardinal Red RH	AHA 6601	8	1		
LH	AHA 6605	9	1		
Black RH	AHA 6602	8	1		
LH	AHA 6606	9	1		
Hazelnut RH	AHA 6603	8	1		W.S.E. use bulk material
LH	AHA 6607	9	1		
Blue RH	AHA 6604	8	1		
LH	AHA 6608	9	1		
Carpet assembly—rear centre					
Cardinal Red	AHA 6625	10	1		
Black	AHA 6626	10	1		
Hazelnut	AHA 6627	10	1		
Blue	AHA 6628	10	1		
Socket—fastener	2H 8445	5	6		
Ring—socket	†2H 6136	6	6		W.S.E. use 14G 8736
Ring—socket	†14G 8736	6	6		
Stud—socket	ADB 4811	11	18		
Screw	CTZ 604	12	18		

† Revised Information.

DESCRIPTION	Part No.	Illus. No.	Quantity	Change Point	REMARKS
Trimming Details—*continued*					
(Sprite Mk. II and Midget)—*continued*					
BULK MATERIAL					
Leathercloth—2-way stretch—50″ (127 cm) wide					
Red	1KL 1558		A/R		Part No. change; was AHA 6890
Black	1KL 1113		A/R		Part No. change; was AHA 6891
Blue	1KL 1258		A/R		Part No. change; was AHA 6893
Hazelnut	1KL 1608		A/R		Part No. change; was AHA 6892
Leathercloth—50″ (127 cm) wide					
Red	1AL 558		A/R		Part No. change; was AHA 6894
Black	1AL 113		A/R	(C) H-AN7-24732 on (C) G-AN2-16184 on	Part No. change; was AHA 6895
Blue	1AL 258		A/R		Part No. change; was AHA 6897
Hazelnut	1AL 608		A/R		Part No. change; was AHA 6896
Carpet—40″ (102 cm) wide					
Cardinal Red	5D 4199		A/R		Part No. change; was AHA 6903
Black	ADE 589		A/R		Part No. change; was AHA 6904
Hazelnut	5D 4230		A/R		Part No. change; was AHA 6905
Blue	AHA 6906		A/R		
Underfelt—mat	†AAA 743		A/R		

Supplied in multiples of yards (applies to all items above)

SEATS AND FITTINGS

	Page	Plate
CUSHION ASSEMBLY	BO 2-BO 5	O 1
CUSHION—REAR COMPARTMENT	BO 6	O 2
RUNNERS—SEAT	BO 5	O 1
SQUAB ASSEMBLY	BO 2-BO 4	O 1

† Revised Information.

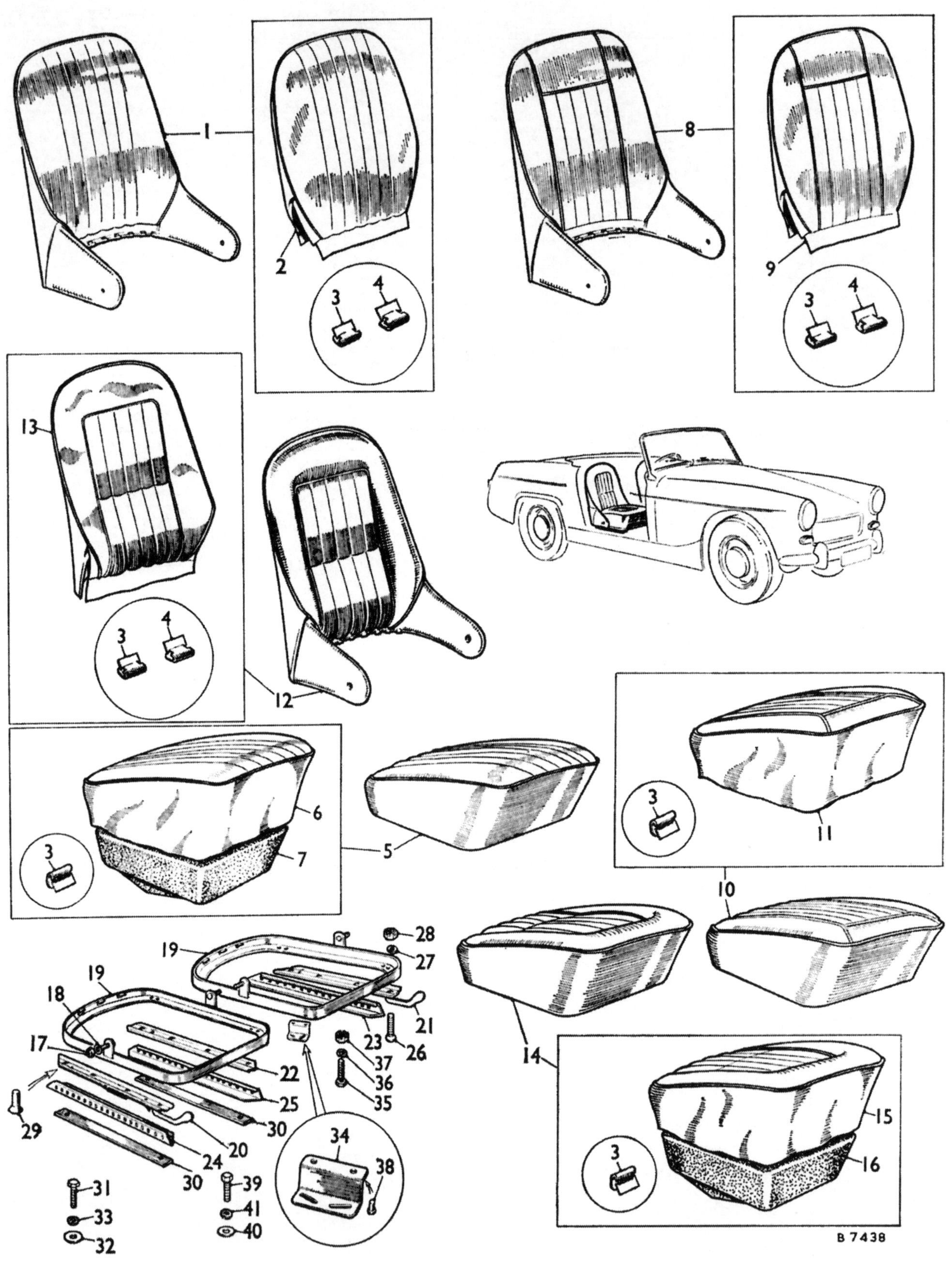
1
2
3
4
8
9
13
12
6
7
5
11
10
14
15
16
19
18
17
29
28
27
21
26
23
37
36
35
22
25
30
20
24
31
33
32
39
41
40
34
38
B 7438

SEATS AND FITTINGS

DESCRIPTION		Part No.	Illus. No.	Quantity	Change Point	REMARKS
Squab assembly						
Red with White piping		AHA 5040	1	2		
Blue with Blue piping		AHA 5042	1	2		
Black with Yellow piping		AHA 5043	1	2	(C) H-AN5-501 to 9604	
Black with White piping		AHA 5461	1	2	(C) H-AN5-9605 on	
Green with Green piping		AHA 5044	1	2		
Cover—squab						
Red with White piping		AHA 5045	2	2		
Blue with Blue piping		AHA 5047	2	2		
Black with Yellow piping		AHA 5048	2	2	(C) H-AN5-501 to 9604	
Black with White piping		AHA 5462	2	2	(C) H-AN5-9605 on	
Green with Green piping		AHA 5049	2	2		
Clip—trim		ADA 833	8	12		
Clip—trim		14A 4497	4	20		
Cushion assembly	**Sprite**					
Red with White piping	**H-AN5**	AHA 5030	5	2		
Blue with Blue piping		AHA 5032	5	2		
Black with Yellow piping		AHA 5033	5	2	(C) H-AN5-501 to 9604	
Black with White piping		AHA 5459	5	2	(C) H-AN5-9605 on	
Green with Green piping		AHA 5034	5	2		
Cover—cushion						
Red with White piping		AHA 5035	6	2		
Blue with Blue piping		AHA 5037	6	2		
Black with Yellow piping		AHA 5038	6	2	(C) H-AN5-501 to 9604	
Black with White piping		AHA 5460	6	2	(C) H-AN5-9605 on	
Green with Green piping		AHA 5039	6	2		
Pad—cushion		14A 4787	7	2		Not available; use AHA 6388
Pad—cushion		AHA 6388	7	2		
Clip—trim		ADA 833	8	44		
Squab assembly						
Red with White piping		AHA 5040	1	2	See (1) foot of page	
Red with Black piping		AHA 6140	1	2		
Red with White piping		AHA 6229	1	2	See (2) foot of page	
Red with Black piping		AHA 6231	1	2		
Blue with Blue piping		AHA 5042	1	2	(C) H-AN6-101 to 6284	
Blue with Blue piping		AHA 6230	1	2	(C) H-AN6-6285 to 24731	
Black with Red piping		AHA 6141	1	2	(C) H-AN6-101 to 6722	
Black with White piping		AHA 5461	1	2		
Black with Red piping		AHA 6327	1	2	(C) H-AN6-6723 to 24731	Correction; was AHA 6237
Black with White piping		AHA 6328	1	2		
Green with Green piping		AHA 5044	1	2	(C) H-AN6-101 to 24731	
Cover—squab	**Sprite**					
Red with White piping	**Mk. II**	AHA 5045	2	2	See (1) foot of page	
Red with Black piping		AKE 3070	2	2		
Red with White piping		AKE 3290	2	2	See (2) foot of page	
Red with Black piping		AKE 3293	2	2		
Blue with Blue piping		AHA 5047	2	2	(C) H-AN6-101 to 6284	
Blue with Blue piping		AKE 3291	2	2	(C) H-AN6-6285 to 24731	
Black with Red piping		AKE 3071	2	2	(C) H-AN6-101 to 6722	
Black with White piping		AHA 5462	2	2		
Black with Red piping		AKE 3294	2	2	(C) H-AN6-6723 to 24731	
Black with White piping		AKE 3292	2	2		
Green with Green piping		AHA 5049	2	2		
Clip—trim		ADA 833	8	12	(C) H-AN6-101 to 24731	
Clip—trim		14A 4497	4	20		

CHANGE POINTS

(1) (C) H-AN6-101 to 15218 (less 14842 to 14965, and 14980 to 15211)
(2) (C) H-AN6-15219 to 24731 (plus 14842 to 14965, and 14980 to 15211)

† Revised Information.

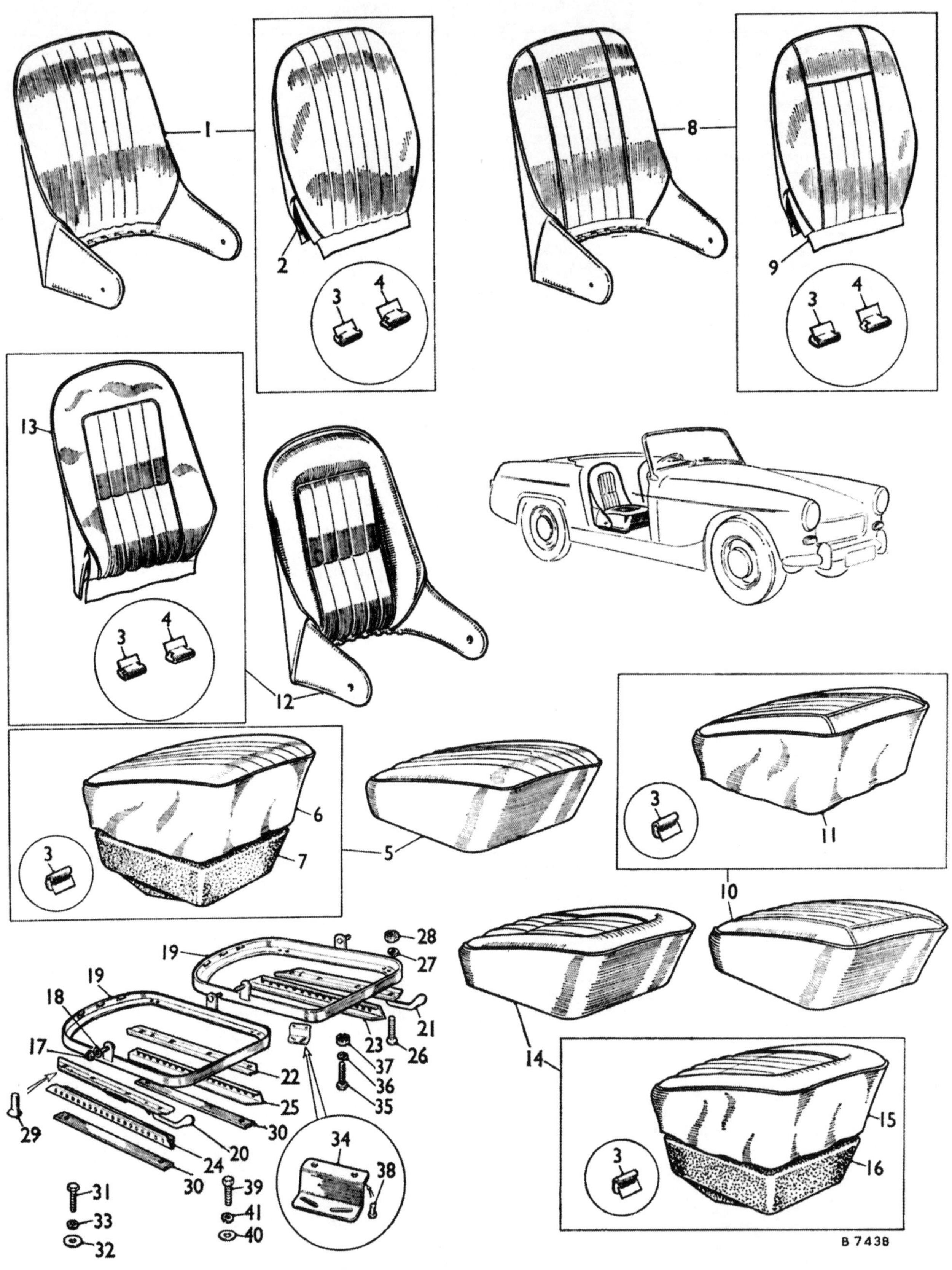
1
2
3
4
8
9
3
4
13
3
4
12
6
7
3
5
3
11
10
28
19
27
19
18
21
23
26
17
22
37
36
25
35
29
30
20
34
38
24
30
39
31
41
33
40
32
14
15
3
16
B 7438

DESCRIPTION		Part No.	Illus. No.	Quantity	Change Point	REMARKS
Seats and Fittings—*continued*						
Cushion assembly						
Red with White piping		AHA 5030	5	2	See (1) foot of page	
Red with Black piping		AHA 6137	5	2		
Red with White piping		AHA 6226	5	2	See (2) foot of page	
Red with Black piping		AHA 6228	5	2		
Blue with Blue piping		AHA 5032	5	2	(C) H-AN6-101 to 6284	
Blue with Blue piping		AHA 6227	5	2	(C) H-AN6-6285 to 24731	
Black with Red piping		AHA 6138	5	2	(C) H-AN6-101 to 6722	
Black with White piping		AHA 5459	5	2		
Black with Red piping		AHA 6325	5	2	(C) H-AN6-6723 to 24731	Correction; was AHA 6235
Black with White piping		AHA 6326	5	2		
Green with Green piping		AHA 5034	5	2	(C) H-AN6-101 to 24731	
Cover—cushion						
Red with White piping	**Sprite**	AHA 5035	6	2	See (1) foot of page	
Red with Black piping	**Mk. II**	AKE 3072	6	2		
Red with White piping		AKE 3285	6	2	See (2) foot of page	
Red with Black piping		AKE 3288	6	2		
Blue with Blue piping		AHA 5037	6	2	(C) H-AN6-101 to 6284	
Blue with Blue piping		AKE 3286	6	2	(C) H-AN6-6285 to 24731	
Black with Red piping		AKE 3073	6	2	(C) H-AN6-101 to 6722	
Black with White piping		AHA 5460	6	2		
Black with Red piping		AKE 3289	6	2	(C) H-AN6-6723 to 24731	
Black with White piping		AKE 3287	6	2		
Green with Green piping		AHA 5039	6	2	(C) H-AN6-101 to 24731	
Pad—cushion		14A 4787	7	2	(C) H-AN6-101 to 15556	Not available; use AHA 6388
Pad—cushion		AHA 6388	7	2	(C) H-AN6-15557 to 24731	
Clip—trim		ADA 833	3	44	(C) H-AN6-101 to 24731	
Squab assembly						
Black with Red piping and Black/Red Fleck carpet		AHA 6081	8	2	(C) G-AN1-101 to 10741	
Black with Red piping and Red/Black Fleck carpet		AHA 6387	8	2	(C) G-AN1-10742 to 16183	
Black with White piping and Black/White Fleck carpet		AHA 6084	8	2	(C) G-AN1-101 to 16183	
Red with Black piping and Red/Black Fleck carpet		AHA 6080	8	2	(C) G-AN1-101 to 10741	
Red with Black piping and Black/Red Fleck carpet		AHA 6258	8	2		
Red with Black piping and Red/Black Fleck carpet	**Midget**	AHA 6386	8	2	(C) G-AN1-10742 to 16183	
Red with White piping and Red/Black Fleck carpet		AHA 6083	8	2	(C) G-AN1-101 to 16183	
Red with White piping and Red/White Fleck carpet		AHA 6304	8	2		
Blue with Blue piping and Blue/Black Fleck carpet		AHA 6082	8	2		
Green with Green piping and Black/White Fleck carpet		AKE 4737	8	2		

CHANGE POINTS

(1) (C) H-AN6-101 to 15218 (less 14842 to 14965, and 14980 to 15211)
(2) (C) H-AN6-15219 to 24731 (plus 14842 to 14965, and 14980 to 15211)

† Revised Information.

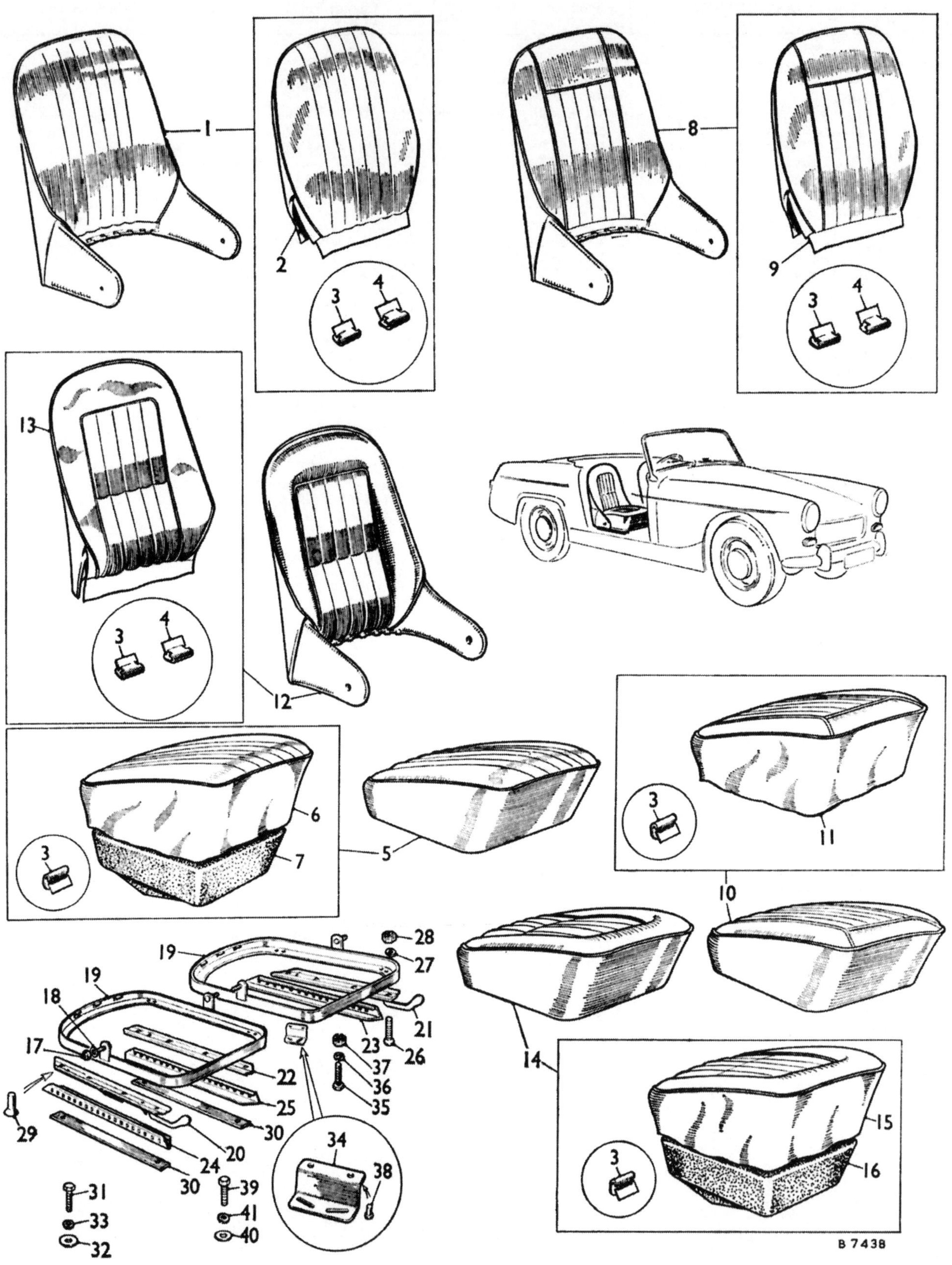
1
2
3
4
8
9
3
4
13
3
4
12
6
7
3
5
3
11
10
19
28
27
19
18
21
17
23
26
22
37
36
25
35
29
30
20
34
38
24
30
31
39
33
41
32
40
14
15
3
16
B 7438

DESCRIPTION		Part No.	Illus. No.	Quantity	Change Point	REMARKS
Seats and Fittings—*continued*						
Cover—squab						
Black with Red piping and Black/Red Fleck carpet	Midget	AKE 3065	9	2	(C) G-AN1-101 to 10741	
Black with Red piping and Red/Black Fleck carpet		AKE 4408	9	2	(C) G-AN1-10742 to 16183	
Black with White piping and Black/White Fleck carpet		AKE 3068	9	2	(C) G-AN1-101 to 16183	
Red with Black piping and Red/Black Fleck carpet		AKE 3064	9	2	(C) G-AN1-101 to 10741	
Red with Black piping and Black/Red Fleck carpet		AKE 3182	9	2		
Red with Black piping and Red/Black Fleck carpet		AKE 4407	9	2	(C) G-AN1-10742 to 16183	
Red with White piping and Red/Black Fleck carpet		AKE 3067	9	2	(C) G-AN1-101 to 16183	
Red with White piping and Red/White Fleck carpet		AKE 3242	9	2		
Blue with Blue piping and Blue/Black Fleck carpet		AKE 3066	9	2		
Green with Green piping and Black/White Fleck carpet		AKE 4738	9	2		
Clip—trim		ADA 833	8	12		
Clip—trim		14A 4497	4	20		
Cushion assembly						
Black with Red piping		AHA 6068	10	2		
Black with White piping		AHA 6071	10	2		
Red with Black piping		AHA 6067	10	2		
Red with White piping		AHA 6070	10	2		
Blue with Blue piping		AHA 6069	10	2		
Green with Green piping		AKE 4739	10	2		
Cover—cushion						
Black with Red piping		AKE 3059	11	2		
Black with White piping		AKE 3062	11	2		
Red with Black piping		AKE 3058	11	2		
Red with White piping		AKE 3061	11	2		
Blue with Blue piping		AKE 3060	11	2		
Green with Green piping		AKE 4740	11	2		
Clip—trim		ADA 833	8	44		
Squab assembly	Sprite Mk. II and Midget				(C) H-AN7-24732 on (C) G-AN2-16184 on	
Red		AHA 6922	12	2		
Black		AHA 6923	12	2		
Blue		AHA 6925	12	2		
Hazelnut		AHA 6924	12	2		
Cover—squab						
Red		AKE 5125	13	2		
Black		AKE 5126	13	2		
Blue		AKE 5127	13	2		
Hazelnut		AKE 5128	13	2		
Clip—trim		ADA 833	8	12		
Clip—trim		14A 4497	4	20		
Cushion assembly						
Red		AHA 6917	14	2	(C) H-AN7-24732 to 32094 (C) G-AN2-16184 to 21090	
Red		AHA 7044	14	2	(C) H-AN7-32095 on (C) G-AN2-21091 on	
Black		AHA 6918	14	2	(C) H-AN7-24732 to 32075 (C) G-AN2—16184 to 21040	
Black		AHA 7045	14	2	(C) H-AN7-32076 on (C) G-AN2-21041 on	

† Revised Information.

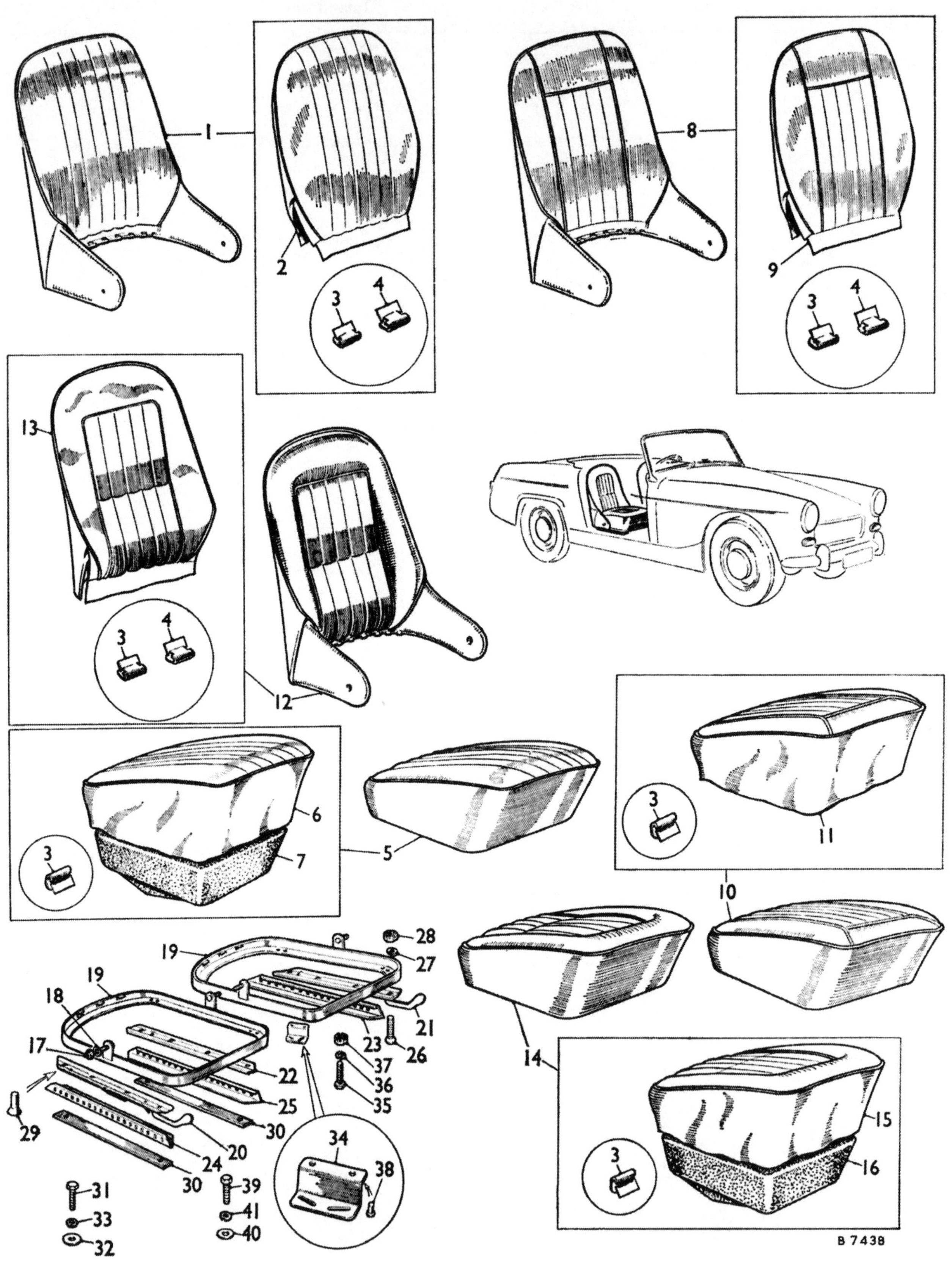
1
2
3
4
8
9
3
4
13
3
4
12
6
7
5
3
3
11
10
19
19
18
17
28
27
21
23
26
37
36
35
22
25
30
20
24
29
34
38
30
31
33
32
39
41
40
14
15
3
16
B 7438

DESCRIPTION	Part No.	Illus. No.	Quantity	Change Point	REMARKS
Seats and Fittings—*continued*					
Cushion assembly					
Blue	AHA 6920	14	2	(C) H-AN7-24732 to 32147 (C) G-AN2-16184 to 20885	
Blue	AHA 7047	14	2	(C) H-AN7-32148 on (C) G-AN2-20886 on	
Hazelnut	AHA 6919	14	2	(C) H-AN7-24732 to 31700 (C) G-AN2-16184 to 20940	
Hazelnut	AHA 7046	14	2	(C) H-AN7-31701 on (C) G-AN2-20941 on	
Cover—cushion					
Red	AKE 5129	15	2	(C) H-AN7-24732 to 32094 (C) G-AN2-16184 to 21090	
Red	**Sprite Mk. II and Midget** AKE 5204	15	2	(C) H-AN7-32095 on (C) G-AN2-21091 on	
Black	AKE 5130	15	2	(C) H-AN7-24732 to 32075 (C) G-AN2-16184 to 21040	
Black	AKE 5205	15	2	(C) H-AN7-32076 on (C) G-AN2-21041 on	
Blue	AKE 5131	15	2	(C) H-AN7-24732 to 32147 (C) G-AN2-16184 to 20885	
Blue	AKE 5206	15	2	(C) H-AN7-32148 on (C) G-AN2-20886 on	
Hazelnut	AKE 5132	15	2	(C) H-AN7-24732 to 31700 (C) G-AN2-16184 to 20940	
Hazelnut	AKE 5207	15	2	(C) H-AN7-31701 on (C) G-AN2-20941 on	
Pad—cushion	AHA 6660	16	2	(C) H-AN7-24732 on (C) G-AN2-16184 on	
Clip—trim	ADA 833	8	44		
Nut—squab to pivot bracket	AHA 5219	17	4		
Washer—plain	PWZ 205	18	8		
Frame—seat base	14A 4778	19	2		
Runner—seat					
Top—RH (with catch)	†14A 5519	20	1		Correction; was AHA 5519
Top—LH (with catch)	†14A 5520	21	1		Correction; was AHA 5520
Top (less catch)	4G 877	22	1/2		Quantity increased at (C) H-AN6-101 and (C) G-AN1-101
Bottom	4G 878	23	2	(C) H-AN5-501 to 26138	
Bottom—RH	AHA 5499	24	1	(C) H-AN5-26139 to 50116 (C) H-AN6-101 to 24731 (C) H-AN7-24732 on (C) G-AN1-101 to 16183 (C) G-AN2-16184 on	
Bottom—LH	AHA 5500	25	1		
Screw	CMZ 0410	26	4		
Washer—spring	LWZ 204	27	4	(C) H-AN5-501 to 31902	
Nut	FNZ 104	28	4		
Rivet	CRS 0410	29	4/8	(C) H-AN5-31903 to 50116 (C) H-AN6-101 to 24731 (C) H-AN7-24732 on (C) G-AN1-101 to 16183 (C) G-AN2-16184 on	Quantities increased at (C) H-AN6-101 and (C) G-AN1-101
Packing—bottom runner	AHA 5223	30	2/4		
Screw	HZS 0409	31	4/8		
Washer—plain	PWZ 104	32	4/8		
Washer—spring	LWZ 204	33	4/8		
Bracket—support—seat	14A 4860	34	4	(C) H-AN5-501 to 50116 (C) H-AN6-101 to 24731	
Screw	HZS 0405	35	8		
Washer—spring	LWZ 204	36	8	(C) H-AN5-501 to 31902	
Nut	FNZ 104	37	8		
Rivet	FRS 0408	38	8	(C) H-AN5-31903 to 50116 (C) H-AN6-101 to 24731	
Screw	HZS 0406	39	4	(C) H-AN5-501 to 50116 (C) H-AN6-101 to 24731	
Washer—plain	PWZ 104	40	4		
Washer—spring	LWZ 204	41	4		

† Revised Information.

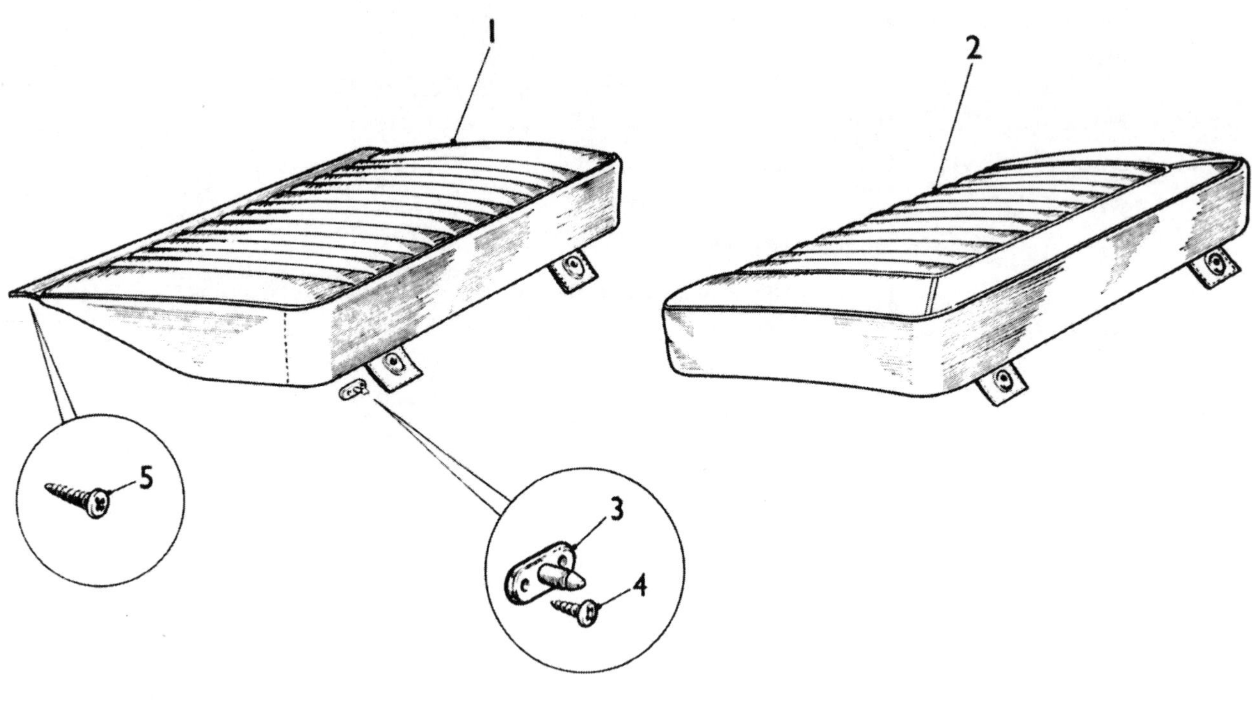
1
2
5
3
4

B 7372

DESCRIPTION		Part No.	Illus. No.	Quantity	Change Point	REMARKS
Seats and Fittings—*continued*						
Cushion—rear compartment						
Red with White piping	Sprite Mk. II	AHA 6273	1	1	(C) H-AN6-101 to 15218 (less 14842 to 14965, and 14980 to 15211)	
Red with Black piping	Sprite Mk. II	AHA 6276	1	1		
Red with White piping	Sprite Mk. II	AHA 6282	1	1	(C) H-AN6-15219 to 24731 (plus 14842 to 14965, and 14980 to 15211)	
Red with Black piping	Sprite Mk. II	AHA 6284	1	1		
Blue with Blue piping	Sprite Mk. II	AHA 6274	1	1	(C) H-AN6-101 to 6284	
Blue with Blue piping	Sprite Mk. II	AHA 6283	1	1	(C) H-AN6-6285 to 24731	
Black with Red piping	Sprite Mk. II	AHA 6277	1	1	(C) H-AN6-101 to 6722	
Black with White piping	Sprite Mk. II	AHA 6275	1	1		
Black with Red piping	Sprite Mk. II	AHA 6329	1	1	(C) H-AN6-6723 to 24731	
Black with White piping	Sprite Mk. II	AHA 6330	1	1		
Green with Green piping	Sprite Mk. II	AKE 4732	1	1	(C) H-AN6-101 to 24731	Optional extra
Black with Red piping	Midget	AHA 6009	2	1	(C) G-AN1-101 to 16183	
Black with White piping	Midget	AHA 6178	2	1		
Red with Black piping	Midget	AHA 6008	2	1		
Red with White piping	Midget	AHA 6177	2	1		
Blue with Blue piping	Midget	AHA 6010	2	1		
Green with Green piping	Midget	AKE 4733	2	1		
Red	Sprite Mk. II and Midget	AHA 6886	2	1	(C) H-AN7-24782 on (C) G-AN2-16184 on	
Black	Sprite Mk. II and Midget	AHA 6887	2	1		
Blue	Sprite Mk. II and Midget	AHA 6889	2	1		
Hazelnut	Sprite Mk. II and Midget	AHA 6888	2	1		
Peg—fastener—cushion	Sprite Mk. II and Midget	LFP 116	3	2		
Screw	Sprite Mk. II and Midget	RTP 603	4	4		
Screw	Sprite Mk. II and Midget	PTZ 806	5	4		

HEATING AND VENTILATING EQUIPMENT

	Page	Plate
BLOWER—HEATER	BP 3	P 2
CONTROL—FRESH-AIR UNIT	BP 4	P 3
FRESH-AIR UNIT	BP 4	P 3
HEATER UNIT	BP 2	P 1
HOSE—FRESH-AIR	BP 3	P 2
HOSES—HEATER	BP 3	P 2
NOZZLE—DEMISTER	BP 3	P 2
PIPE—WATER—HEATER	BP 2	P 1
SWITCH—HEATER	BP 2	P 1
TAP—WATER CONTROL	BP 2	P 1

† Revised Information.

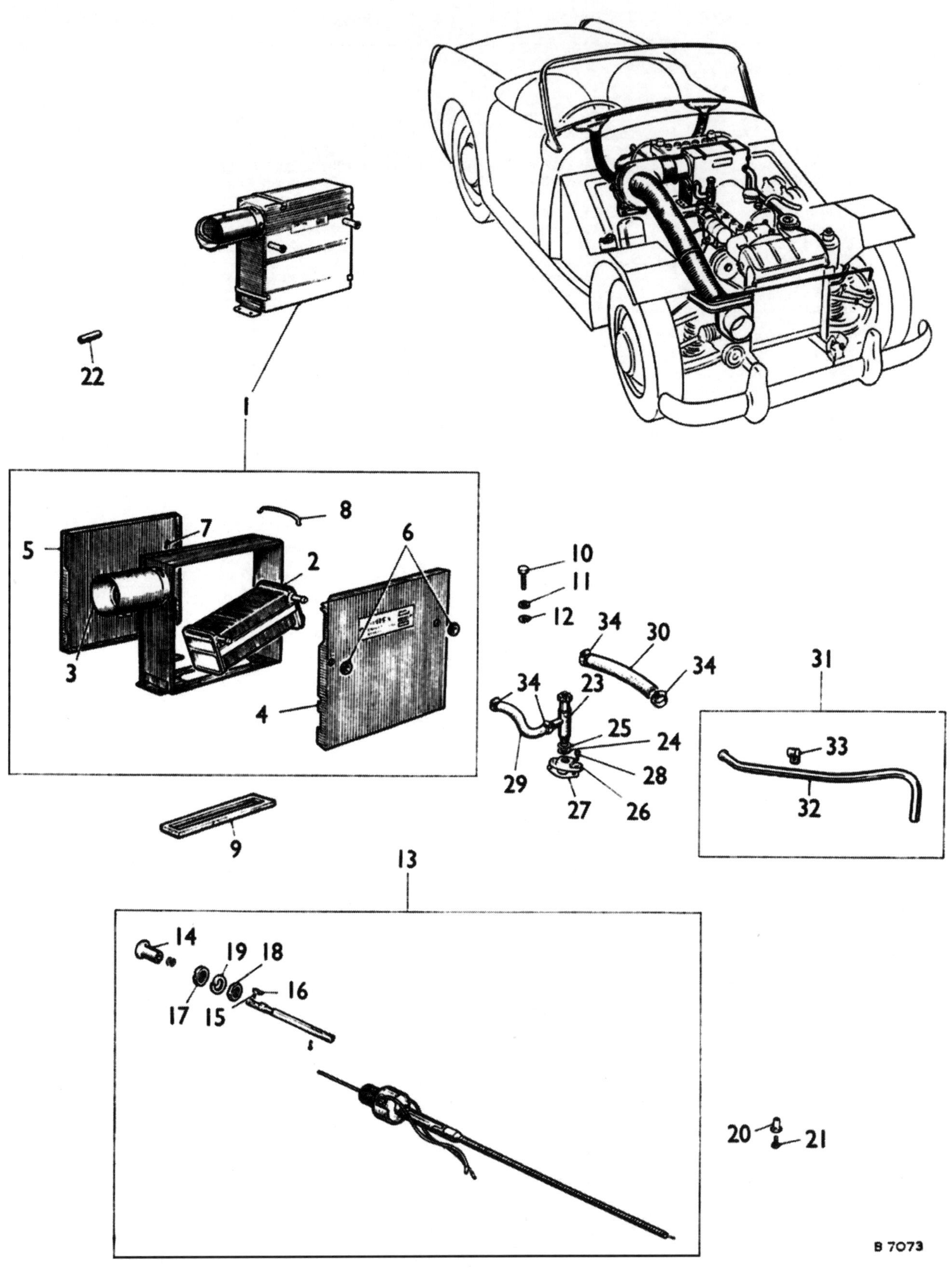
1
2
3
4
5
6
7
8
9
10
11
12
13
14
15
16
17
18
19
20
21
22
23
24
25
26
27
28
29
30
31
32
33
34
B 7073

HEATING AND VENTILATING EQUIPMENT

HEATER (OPTIONAL EXTRA)

DESCRIPTION	Part No.	Illus. No.	Quantity	Change Point	REMARKS
Kit—heater	NSP		1		For accessory kit see the 'Approved Accessories Salesman's Guide'
Unit assembly—heater	13H 54	1	1		
Radiator and seals	17H 1590	2	1		
Tube—inlet	17H 1592	3	1		
Plate—front	17H 1594	4	1		
Plate—rear	17H 1596	5	1		
Grommet	17H 1591	6	2		
Screw	†17H 1593	7	3		W.S.E. use PJZ 602
Screw	PJZ 602	7	3		
Clip	17H 1595	8	10		
Seal—unit base	4B 9718	9	1		
Screw	PMZ 0408	10	4		
Washer—plain	PWZ 104	11	4		
Washer—spring	LWZ 204	12	4		
Switch assembly—heater	†13H 55	13	1	(C) H-AN5-501 to 50116	W.S.E. use BHA 4205
RHD	BHA 4205	13	1	See (1) foot of page	
LHD	BHA 4245	13	1	See (1) foot of page	
Knob	17H 1602	14	1		
Pin—knob	17H 1603	15	1		
Clip—knob	17H 1601	16	1		
Locknut—round	17H 823	17	1		
Locknut—hexagon	17H 824	18	1		
Washer—spring	17H 825	19	1		
Trunnion—control cable	14G 6451	20	1	(C) H-AN5-501 to 50116	Part No. change; was AHH 5439
Screw—trunnion	AHH 5593	21	1	(C) H-AN5-501 to 50116	
Trunnion—control cable	24G 1482	20	1	See (1) foot of page	
Screw—trunnion	53K 1016	21	1	See (1) foot of page	
Connector—snap—switch to blower	2H 3406	22	1		Part No. change; was 17H 1634
Tap—water control	†ACA 5455	23	1		W.S.E. use AHA 8323. Part No. change; was 17H 1631
Tap—water control	†AHA 8323	23	1		
Washer—tap	AAA 836	24	1		
Shim—control tap adjustment—·028″ (·70 mm)	ACA 5172	25	A/R		
Shim—control tap adjustment—·014″ (·35 mm)	ACA 5173	25	A/R		
Adaptor—tap	ACA 5456	26	1		
Washer—joint—adaptor to cylinder head	88G 221	27	1		Part No. change; was 2A 179 and 12A 32
Screw	HZS 0406	28	2		
Hose—tap to heater inlet	AHA 5213	29	1		
Hose—water	37H 537		A/R		Supplied in multiples of feet
Heater outlet to pipe—9″ (23 cm) long	†AHA 5212	30	1		W.S.E. use 37H 537
Pipe assembly—water	†AHA 5214	31	1		W.S.E. use components
Pipe	AHA 5215	32	1		
Clip	PCR 0809	33	2		
Hose—pipe to radiator hose	NSP		1		For service replacements use hose—radiator to pump 2A 2084
Cutter—hose	NSP		1		For service replacements use hose—radiator to pump 2A 2084
Connector—hose	NSP		1		For service replacements use hose—radiator to pump 2A 2084
Clip—hose	†8G 531	34	6		W.S.E. use HCS 0507
Clip—hose	HCS 0507	34	6		

CHANGE POINTS

(1) (C) H-AN6-101 to 24731, (C) H-AN7-24732 on, (C) G-AN1-101 to 16183, (C) G-AN2-16184 on

† Revised Information.

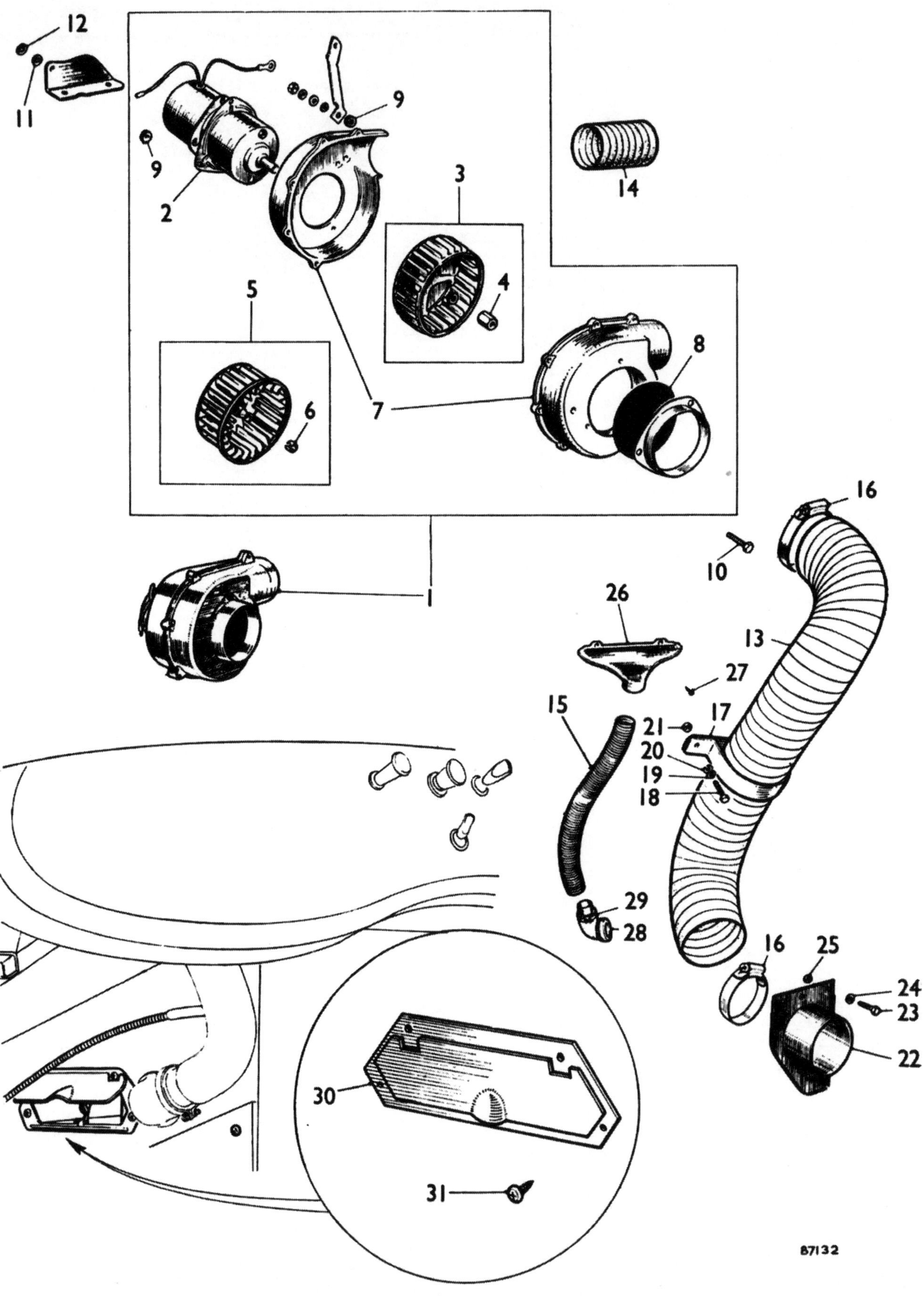
12
11
9
9
2
3
14
4
5
8
6
7
16
10
1
26
13
27
15
21
17
20
19
18
29
28
16
25
24
23
22
30
31
87132

DESCRIPTION	Part No.	Illus. No.	Quantity	Change Point	REMARKS
Heating and Ventilating Equipment—*continued*					
Heater (Optional Extra)—*continued*					
Blower assembly	13H 51	1	1		
Motor	17H 1455	2	1		
Rotor (metal)	17H 1574	3	1		Part No. change; was 17H 1598. Alternative to 17H 8108
Nut—collet	27H 602	4	1		
Rotor (plastic)	17H 8108	5	1		Alternative to 17H 1574
Ring—compression	17H 6836	6	1		
Casing	17H 819	7	1		
Mesh—intake	17H 1597	8	1		
Grommet	24K 2085	9	3		Part No. change; was 17H 1292
Screw	PMZ 0408	10	3		
Washer—plain	PWZ 104	11	3		
Washer—spring	LWZ 204	12	3		
Hose					
Inlet flange plate to blower	13H 53	13	1	(C) H–AN5–501 to 50116	
Inlet flange plate to blower	13H 58	13	1	See (1) foot of page	
Blower to heater	14A 4762	14	1	(C) H–AN5–501 to 50116	Not available; use AHA 6429
Blower to heater	AHA 6429	14	1	See (1) foot of page	
Demister	14A 4766	15	2		
Clip					
Hose	14G 800	16	2		Not available; use HCS 168
Hose	HCS 168	16	2		Not available; use HCS 368
Hose	HCS 368	16	2		
Hose to wheel arch	14B 1917	17	1	(C) H–AN5–501 to 6135	Not available; use AHH 5714
Hose to wheel arch	AHH 5714	17	1	(C) H–AN5–6136 to 50116 (C) H–AN6–101 to 24731 (C) H–AN7–24732 on (C) G–AN1–101 to 16183 (C) G–AN2–16184 on	
Screw	PMZ 0310	18	1		
Washer—plain	PWZ 103	19	1		
Washer—spring	LWZ 203	20	1		
Nut	FNZ 103	21	1		
Plate—inlet flange	14A 4768	22	1	(C) H–AN5–501 to 50116	
Screw	PMZ 0408	23	1	(C) H–AN5–501 to 50116	
Washer—plain	PWZ 104	24	1	(C) H–AN5–501 to 50116	
Nut	FNZ 104	25	1	(C) H–AN5–501 to 50116	
Nozzle—demister	14A 1162	26	2		
Screw	PTP 603	27	4		
Elbow—demister	14G 3499	28	2		
Clip	27H 168	29	2		Not available; use BMK 924
Clip	BMK 924	29	2		
Door—heater or fresh-air outlet	13H 59	30	2		Standard fitment
Screw	PTZ 603	31	8		Standard fitment

CHANGE POINTS

(1) (C) H–AN6–101 to 24731, (C) H–AN7–24732 on, (C) G–AN1–101 to 16183, (C) G–AN2–16184 on

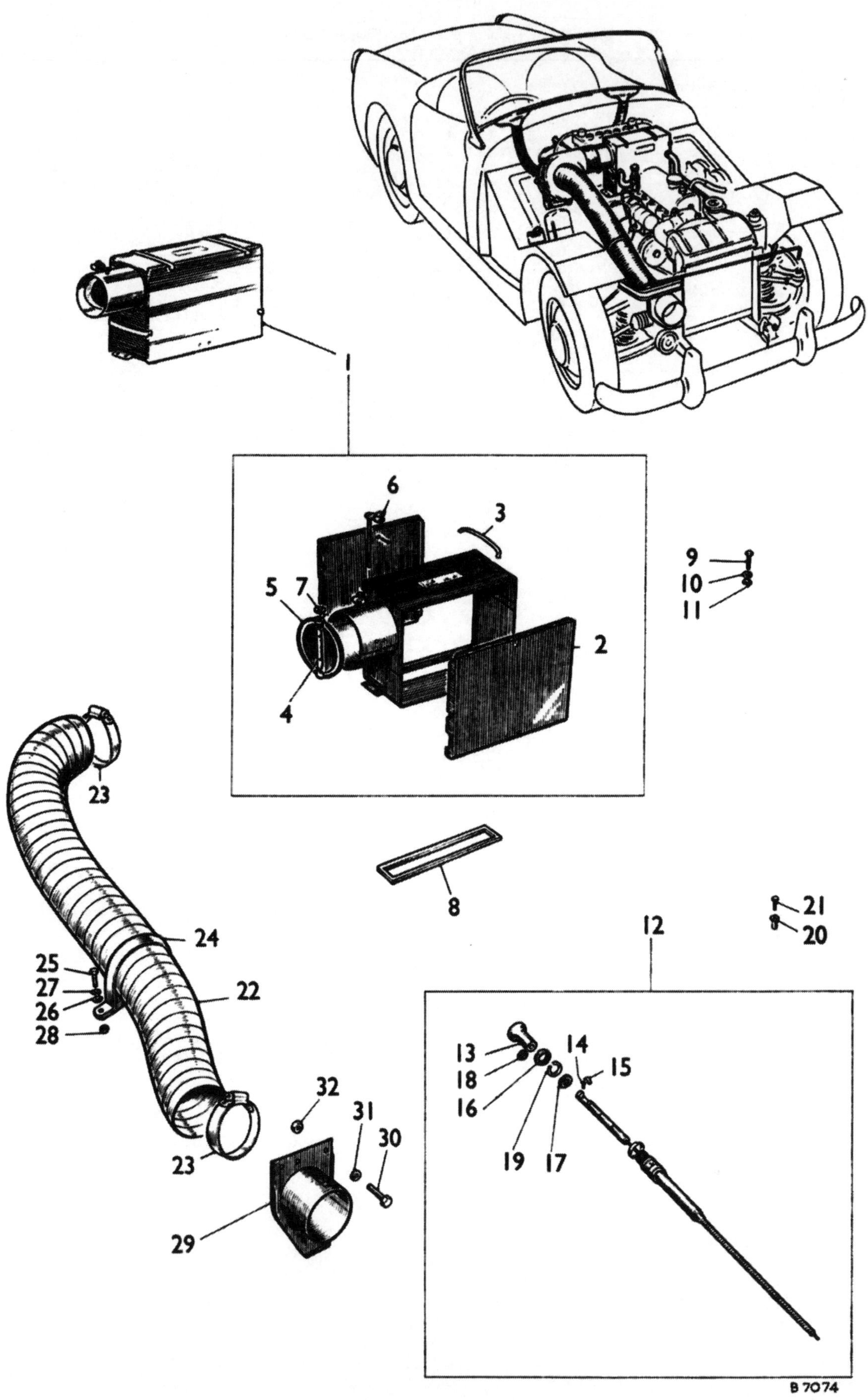
1
2
3
4
5
6
7
8
9
10
11
12
13
14
15
16
17
18
19
20
21
22
23
23
24
25
26
27
28
29
30
31
32
B 7074

DESCRIPTION	Part No.	Illus. No.	Quantity	Change Point	REMARKS
Heating and Ventilating Equipment—*continued*					
FRESH-AIR UNIT (OPTIONAL EXTRA)					
Kit—fresh-air unit	NSP		1		For accessory kit see the 'Approved Accessories Salesman's Guide'
Unit assembly—fresh-air	13H 56	1	1		
Cover—side	17H 1604	2	1		
Clip	17H 1605	3	4		
Flap—valve	†NSP	4	1		Was 17H 1606
Seal—flap	17H 1607	5	1		
Arm and spindle—flap operating	17H 1609	6	1		
Washer	17H 1608	7	2		
Seal—unit base	4B 9718	8	1		
Screw	PMZ 0409	9	4		
Washer—plain	PWZ 104	10	4		
Washer—spring	LWZ 204	11	4		
Control assembly—push-pull	13H 57	12	1	(C) H-AN5-501 to 50116	
RHD	13H 57	12	1	See (1) foot of page	
LHD	BHA 4246	12	1	See (1) foot of page	
Knob	14A 5772	13	1		Part No. change; was 17H 1612
Pin—knob	17H 1603	14	1		
Clip—knob	17H 1601	15	1		
Locknut—round	17H 823	16	1		
Locknut—hexagon	17H 824	17	1		
Washer (rubber)	27H 1198	18	1		
Washer—spring	17H 1825	19	1		
Trunnion—control cable	14G 6451	20	1	(C) H-AN5-501 to 50116	
Screw—trunnion	AHH 5593	21	1	(C) H-AN5-501 to 50116	
Trunnion—control cable	24G 1482	20	1	See (1) foot of page	
Screw—trunnion	53K 1016	21	1	See (1) foot of page	
Hose—inlet flange plate to unit	13H 58	22	1	(C) H-AN5-501 to 50116	
Hose—inlet flange plate to unit	BHA 4207	22	1	See (1) foot of page	
Clip					
Hose	†14G 800	23	2		W.S.E. use HCS 168
Hose	†HCS 168	23	2		W.S.E. use HCS 368
Hose	HCS 368	23	2		
Hose to wheel arch	†14B 1917	24	1	(C) H-AN5-501 to 6135	W.S.E. use AHH 5714
Hose to wheel arch	AHH 5714	24	1	(C) H-AN5-6136 to 50116 (C) H-AN6-101 to 24731 (C) H-AN7-24732 on (C) G-AN1-101 to 16183 (C) G-AN2-16184 on	
Screw	PMZ 0310	25	1		
Washer—plain	PWZ 103	26	1		
Washer—spring	LWZ 203	27	1		
Nut	FNZ 103	28	1		
Plate—inlet flange	14A 4763	29	1	(C) H-AN5-501 to 50116	
Screw	PMZ 0408	30	1	(C) H-AN5-501 to 50116	
Washer—plain	PWZ 104	31	1	(C) H-AN5-501 to 50116	
Nut	FNZ 104	32	1	(C) H-AN5-501 to 50116	
Door—fresh-air outlet					For details see page BP 3
Screw					For details see page BP 3

CHANGE POINTS

(1) (C) H-AN6-101 to 24731, (C) H-AN7-24732 on, (C) G-AN1-101 to 16183, (C) G-AN2-16184 on

† Revised Information.

PAINTS

PAINTS

DESCRIPTION	Part No.	Illus. No.	Quantity	Change Point	REMARKS
Aluminium (Code AL.1)					For Part Nos., container sizes, primers, undercoats, and thinners, etc., refer to 'BMC Service Paint Scheme' book
Whitehall Nevada Beige (Code BG.4) Sprite H-AN5					
Black (Code BK.1) Sprite Mk. II and Midget					
Speedwell Blue (Code BU.1) Sprite H-AN5 and Sprite Mk. II					
Iris Blue (Code BU.12) Sprite H-AN5 and Sprite Mk. II					
Clipper Blue (Code BU.14) Midget					
Ice Blue (Code BU.18) Midget					
Dark Green (Code GN.12) Sprite H-AN5					
Leaf Green (Code GN.15) Sprite H-AN5					
British Racing Green (Code GN.25) Sprite Mk. II and Midget					
British Racing Green—Dark (Code GN.29) Sprite Mk. II and Midget					
Almond Green (Code GN.37) Sprite Mk. II and Midget					
Farina Grey (Code GR.11) Midget					
Dove Grey (Code GR.26) Sprite Mk. II and Midget					
Signal Red (Code RD.2) Sprite Mk. II					
Cherry Red (Code RD.4) Sprite H-AN5					
Tartan Red (Code RD.9) Midget					
Deep Pink (Code RD.18) Sprite Mk. II					
Old English White (Code WT.8)					
Primrose (Code YL.8) Sprite H-AN5					
Highway Yellow (Code YL.9) Sprite Mk. II					
Fiesta Yellow (Code YL.11) Sprite Mk. II					

Distributed by Brooklands Books Ltd., PO Box 146, Cobham, Surrey KT11 1LG, England Phone: 01932 865051
E-mail: sales@brooklands-books.com www.brooklandsbooks.com

Part No. AKD 3567

Distributed by Brooklands Books Ltd., PO Box 146, Cobham,
Surrey KT11 1LG, England Phone: 01932 865051
E-mail: sales@brooklands-books.com www.brooklandsbooks.com

Part No. AKD 3566, AKD 3567 and Extract from Part No. AKD 5036

ISBN: 9781783180509 MGS1PC 2347/3T5

OFFICIAL TECHNICAL BOOKS

Brooklands Technical Books has been formed to supply owners, restorers and professional repairers with official factory literature.

Model	Original Part No.	ISBN
Workshop Manuals		
Austin-Healey 100 BN1 & BN2	97H997D	9780907073925
Austin-Healey 100/6 & 3000 (100/6 - BN4, BN6, 3000 MK. 1, 2, 3 - BN7, BT7, BJ7 & BJ8)	AKD1179	9780948207471
Austin-Healey Sprite Mk. 1 Frogeye	AKD4884	9781855201262
Austin-Healey Sprite Mk. 2, Mk. 3 & Mk. 4 and MG Midget Mk. 1, Mk. 2 & Mk. 3	AKD4021	9781855202818
Parts Catalogues / Service Parts Lists		
Austin-Healey 100 BN1 & BN2	050 Edition 3	9781783180363
Austin-Healey 100/6 BN4	AKD1423	9781783180493
Austin-Healey 100/6 BN6	AKD855 Ed.2	9781783180486
Austin-Healey 3000 Mk. 1 and Mk. 2 (BN7 & BT7) Mk. 1 BN7 & BT7 Car no. 101 to 13750, Mk. 2 BN7 Car no. 13751 to 18888, Mk. 2 BT7 Car no. 13751 to 19853	AKD1151 Ed.5	9781783180370
Austin-Healey 3000 Mk. 2 and Mk. 3 (BJ7 & BJ8) BJ7 Mk. 2 Car no. 17551 to 25314 and BJ8 Mk. 3 Car no. 25315 to 43026	AKD 3523 & AKD 3524	9781783180387
Austin-Healey Sprite Mk. 1 & Mk. 2 and MG Midget Mk. 1	AKD 3566 & AKD 3567	9781783180509
Austin-Healey Sprite Mk. 3 & Mk. 4 and MG Midget Mk. 2 & Mk. 3 (Mechanical & Body Edition 1969)	AKD 3513 & AKD 3514	9781783180554
Austin-Healey Sprite Mk. 3 & Mk. 4 and MG Midget Mk. 2 & Mk. 3 (Feb 1977 Edition)	AKM 0036	9780948207419
Handbooks		
Austin-Healey 100	97H996E	9781869826352
Austin-Healey 100/6	97H996H	9781870642903
Austin-Healey 3000 Mk 1 & 2	AKD3915A	9781869826369
Austin-Healey 3000 Mk 3	AKD4094B	9781869826376
Austin-Healey Sprite Mk 1 'Frogeye'	97H1583A	9780948207945
Also Available		
Austin-Healey 100/6 & 3000 Mk. 1, 2 & 3 Owners Workshop Manual		9781783180455
Austin-Healey Sprite Mk. 1, 2, 3 & 4 MG Midget 1, 2, 3 & 1500 1958-1980 Owners Workshop Manual Glovebox Edition		9781855201255
Austin-Healey Sprite Mk. 1, 2, 3 & 4 MG Midget 1, 2, 3 & 1500 1958-1980 Owners Workshop Manual		9781783180332
Carburetters		
SU Carburetters Tuning Tips & Techniques		9781855202559
Restoration Guide		
Restoring Sprite & Midgets		9781855205987
Road Test Series		
Austin-Healey 100 & 100/6 Gold Portfolio 1952-1959		9781855200487
Austin-Healey 3000 Road Test Portfolio		9791783180394
Austin-Healey Frogeye Sprite Road Test Portfolio 1958-1961		9781783180530
Austin-Healey Sprite Gold Portfolio 1958-1971		9781855203716

From Austin-Healey specialists, Amazon and all good motoring bookshops.

Brooklands Books Ltd., P.O. Box 146, Cobham, Surrey, KT11 1LG, England, UK

www.brooklandsbooks.com

Printed in Great Britain
by Amazon

49481193R00242